NEW PERSPECTIVES ON

Adobe® Photoshop® CS5

COMPREHENSIVE

NEW PERSPECTIVES ON

Adobe® Photoshop® CS5

COMPREHENSIVE

Jane Hosie-Bounar
Mitch Geller
Kelly Hart

COURSE TECHNOLOGY
CENGAGE Learning™

Australia • Brazil • Japan • Korea • Mexico • Singapore • Spain • United Kingdom • United States

COURSE TECHNOLOGY
CENGAGE Learning™

New Perspectives on Adobe Photoshop CS5, Comprehensive

Vice President, Publisher: Nicole Jones Pinard

Executive Editor: Marie L. Lee

Associate Acquisitions Editor: Amanda Lyons

Senior Product Manager: Kathy Finnegan

Product Manager: Leigh Hefferon

Associate Product Manager: Julia Leroux-Lindsey

Editorial Assistant: Jacqueline Lacaire

Director of Marketing: Elisa G. Roberts

Senior Marketing Manager: Ryan DeGrote

Developmental Editor: Mary Pat Shaffer

Senior Content Project Manager: Jill Braiewa

Composition: GEX Publishing Services

Art Director: Marissa Falco

Text Designer: Althea Chen

Cover Designer: Roycroft Design

Cover Art: © Image Source/Getty Images

Copyeditor: Karen Annett

Proofreader: Vicki Zimmer

Indexer: Alexandra Nickerson

For product information and technology assistance, contact us at
Cengage Learning Customer & Sales Support, 1-800-354-9706
For permission to use material from this text or product, submit all requests online at www.cengage.com/permissions
Further permissions questions can be emailed to
permissionrequest@cengage.com

Some of the product names and company names used in this book have been used for identification purposes only and may be trademarks or registered trademarks of their respective manufacturers and sellers.

Adobe® and Photoshop® are either registered trademarks or trademarks of Adobe Systems Incorporated in the United States and/or other countries. THIS PRODUCT IS NOT ENDORSED OR SPONSORED BY ADOBE SYSTEMS INCORPORATED, PUBLISHER OF ADOBE® PHOTOSHOP®.

Disclaimer: Any fictional data related to persons or companies or URLs used throughout this book is intended for instructional purposes only. At the time this book was printed, any such data was fictional and not belonging to any real persons or companies.

Library of Congress Control Number: 2011925423

ISBN-13: 978-0-538-75794-2

ISBN-10: 0-538-75794-9

Course Technology
20 Channel Center Street
Boston, MA 02210
USA

Cengage Learning is a leading provider of customized learning solutions with office locations around the globe, including Singapore, the United Kingdom, Australia, Mexico, Brazil, and Japan. Locate your local office at:
international.cengage.com/global

Cengage Learning products are represented in Canada by Nelson Education, Ltd.

To learn more about Course Technology, visit **www.cengage.com/course technology**

To learn more about Cengage Learning, visit **www.cengage.com**

Purchase any of our products at your local college store or at our preferred online store **www.cengagebrain.com**

Printed in the United States of America
1 2 3 4 5 6 7 17 16 15 14 13 12 11

Preface

The New Perspectives Series' critical-thinking, problem-solving approach is the ideal way to prepare students to transcend point-and-click skills and take advantage of all that Adobe Photoshop CS5 has to offer.

In developing the New Perspectives Series, our goal was to create books that give students the software concepts and practical skills they need to succeed beyond the classroom. We've updated our proven case-based pedagogy with more practical content to make learning skills more meaningful to students.

With the New Perspectives Series, students understand *why* they are learning *what* they are learning, and are fully prepared to apply their skills to real-life situations.

About This Book

This book provides complete coverage of the new Adobe Photoshop CS5 software, and includes the following:

- Hands-on instruction of essential digital editing concepts, such as file formats, color modes, raster versus vector graphics, and the new CS5 features such as Content-Aware Fill
- Coverage of important skills including drawing and using work paths; and filling text and objects with images, gradients, and patterns using selections and clipping masks
- Highlights of Adobe Photoshop innovations such as adjustment layers, layer comps and styles, painting and drawing tools, non-destructive editing techniques, filters, and masks
- Instruction on correcting, adjusting, and retouching photographic images and working with Camera Raw images and the Camera Raw plug-in

New for this edition!

- Each session begins with a Visual Overview, a new two-page spread that includes colorful, enlarged screenshots with numerous callouts and key term definitions, giving students a comprehensive preview of the topics covered in the session, as well as a handy study guide.
- New ProSkills boxes provide guidance for how to use the software in real-world, professional situations, and related ProSkills exercises integrate the technology skills students learn with one or more of the following soft skills: decision making, problem solving, teamwork, verbal communication, and written communication.
- Important steps are now highlighted in yellow with attached margin notes to help students pay close attention to completing the steps correctly and avoid time-consuming rework.

System Requirements

This book assumes a typical installation of Adobe Photoshop CS5 and Microsoft Windows 7 Ultimate using an Aero theme. You will need a graphics card that supports OpenGL 2.0. The browser used for any steps that require a browser is Internet Explorer 8.

www.cengage.com/ct/newperspectives

v

The New Perspectives Approach

"The clear step-by-step instructions, real-world data files, and helpful figures make New Perspectives texts excellent for courses taught in the classroom, the hybrid/blended format, or entirely online."
—Sylvia Amito'elau
Coastline Community College

Context

Each tutorial begins with a problem presented in a "real-world" case that is meaningful to students. The case sets the scene to help students understand what they will do in the tutorial.

Hands-on Approach

Each tutorial is divided into manageable sessions that combine reading and hands-on, step-by-step work. Colorful screenshots help guide students through the steps. **Trouble?** tips anticipate common mistakes or problems to help students stay on track and continue with the tutorial.

VISUAL OVERVIEW

Visual Overviews

New for this edition! Each session begins with a Visual Overview, a new two-page spread that includes colorful, enlarged screenshots with numerous callouts and key term definitions, giving students a comprehensive preview of the topics covered in the session, as well as a handy study guide.

PROSKILLS

ProSkills Boxes and Exercises

New for this edition! ProSkills boxes provide guidance for how to use the software in real-world, professional situations, and related ProSkills exercises integrate the technology skills students learn with one or more of the following soft skills: decision making, problem solving, teamwork, verbal communication, and written communication.

KEY STEP

Key Steps

New for this edition! Important steps are highlighted in yellow with attached margin notes to help students pay close attention to completing the steps correctly and avoid time-consuming rework.

INSIGHT

InSight Boxes

InSight boxes offer expert advice and best practices to help students achieve a deeper understanding of the concepts behind the software features and skills.

TIP

Margin Tips

Margin Tips provide helpful hints and shortcuts for more efficient use of the software. The Tips appear in the margin at key points throughout each tutorial, giving students extra information when and where they need it.

REVIEW
APPLY

Assessment

Retention is a key component to learning. At the end of each session, a series of Quick Check questions helps students test their understanding of the material before moving on. Engaging end-of-tutorial Review Assignments and Case Problems have always been a hallmark feature of the New Perspectives Series. Colorful bars and brief descriptions accompany the exercises, making it easy to understand both the goal and level of challenge a particular assignment holds.

REFERENCE
TASK REFERENCE
GLOSSARY/INDEX

Reference

Within each tutorial, Reference boxes appear before a set of steps to provide a succinct summary and preview of how to perform a task. In addition, a complete Task Reference at the back of the book provides quick access to information on how to carry out common tasks. Finally, each book includes a combination Glossary/Index to promote easy reference of material.

www.cengage.com/ct/newperspectives

Our Complete System of Instruction

Coverage To Meet Your Needs

Whether you're looking for just a small amount of coverage or enough to fill a semester-long class, we can provide you with a textbook that meets your needs.

- Brief books typically cover the essential skills in just 2 to 4 tutorials.
- Introductory books build and expand on those skills and contain an average of 5 to 8 tutorials.
- Comprehensive books are great for a full-semester class, and contain 9 to 12+ tutorials.

So if the book you're holding does not provide the right amount of coverage for you, there's probably another offering available. Go to our Web site or contact your Course Technology sales representative to find out what else we offer.

CourseCasts – Learning on the Go. Always available…always relevant.

Want to keep up with the latest technology trends relevant to you? Visit our site to find a library of podcasts, CourseCasts, featuring a "CourseCast of the Week," and download them to your mp3 player at http://coursecasts.course.com.

Our fast-paced world is driven by technology. You know because you're an active participant—always on the go, always keeping up with technological trends, and always learning new ways to embrace technology to power your life.

Ken Baldauf, host of CourseCasts, is a faculty member of the Florida State University Computer Science Department where he is responsible for teaching technology classes to thousands of FSU students each year. Ken is an expert in the latest technology trends; he gathers and sorts through the most pertinent news and information for CourseCasts so your students can spend their time enjoying technology, rather than trying to figure it out. Open or close your lecture with a discussion based on the latest CourseCast.

Visit us at http://coursecasts.course.com to learn on the go!

Instructor Resources

We offer more than just a book. We have all the tools you need to enhance your lectures, check students' work, and generate exams in a new, easier-to-use and completely revised package. This book's Instructor's Manual, ExamView testbank, PowerPoint presentations, data files, solution files, figure files, and a sample syllabus are all available on a single CD-ROM or for downloading at login.cengage.com.

Content for Online Learning

Course Technology has partnered with the leading distance learning solution providers and class-management platforms today. To access this material, visit www.cengage.com/webtutor and search for your title. Instructor resources include the following: additional case projects, sample syllabi, PowerPoint presentations, and more. For students to access this material, they must have purchased a WebTutor PIN-code specific to this title and your campus platform. The resources for students might include (based on instructor preferences): topic reviews, review questions, practice tests, and more. For additional information, please contact your sales representative.

www.cengage.com/ct/newperspectives

SAM: Skills Assessment Manager

SAM is designed to help bring students from the classroom to the real world. It allows students to train and test on important computer skills in an active, hands-on environment.

SAM's easy-to-use system includes powerful interactive exams, training, and projects on the most commonly used Microsoft Office applications. SAM simulates the Office application environment, allowing students to demonstrate their knowledge and think through the skills by performing real-world tasks, such as bolding text or setting up slide transitions. Add in live-in-the-application projects, and students are on their way to truly learning and applying skills to business-centric documents.

Designed to be used with the New Perspectives Series, SAM includes handy page references, so students can print helpful study guides that match the New Perspectives textbooks used in class. For instructors, SAM also includes robust scheduling and reporting features.

Acknowledgments

Getting this first edition to press has been a daunting task, made much less daunting with the help of many, many people. I'd like to thank the following reviewers, who looked at these chapters early on and provided invaluable feedback to help make the book the best it can be. Their experience teaching Photoshop in the classroom and their insights into what works and what doesn't were very helpful: Jason Travers, Lehigh University; Dennise Wilson-Kuhn, Lake Land College; Linda Ciccarelli Morosko, Stark State College; and Gabe Oakley, University of Northwestern Ohio.

I'd also like to thank everyone on the New Perspectives Team, especially Kathy Finnegan, who encouraged me to write the book in the first place, Marie Lee and Brandi Shailer, who got me up and running, and Leigh Hefferon, who managed all the moving parts with patience and expertise. Special thanks go to Mary Pat Shaffer, my editor extraordinaire, whose insights and contributions improved each chapter at every twist and turn of the development process. I'd also like to thank Jill Braiewa, Senior Content Product Manager for her flexibility with the schedule, Marisa Taylor at GEX for managing the production schedule, and the talented Manuscript Quality Assurance team, Susan Whalen, Ashlee Welz Smith, Susan Pedicini, Teresa Storch, and John Freitas. Finally, I'd like to thank my family, Khaled, Maya, and Anya who patiently supported me as I worked through dinners, weekends, and yes, vacations.
– Jane Hosie-Bounar

We want to thank Mark Chapman for his unique assistance in tracking Adobe developments and changes, the staff and management of Meshnet.com, and the staff of the Sid Richardson Museum and Store (www.sidrichardsonmuseum.org/store) for their support and generosity in allowing us to use images from their catalog and collection.

I would like to thank Edyie and Joe Geller, Pam, Gregg, and the rest of the family for their love and support…you guys rock! He would also like to thank John Knecht, John Orentlicher, and Don Little.
– Mitch Geller

I would like to thank Mary O'Brien for much needed C8H10N4O2 infusions and linguistic reality checks, Robin Romer for always answering the phone, along with the rest of the Nu-Design.com team, Tika and Matt, for their support.
– Kelly Hart

BRIEF CONTENTS

PHOTOSHOP   Level I Tutorials

Level II Tutorials

TABLE OF CONTENTS

Credits

The images and artwork distributed in this book are for use in completing the tutorial assignments only. All copyrights are retained by the original artists. Images may not be distributed or used outside of the parameters of tutorial assignment completion.

Tutorial 1:

Visual Overview 1.1 and Visual Overview 1.2: dcnature.com, Creative Commons License, Copyright Joe Milmoe

Beach, beach fire, airplane window, boardwalk and flower photos: Courtesy of A. Bounar

Porcelain berry photo: dcnature.com, Creative Commons License, Copyright Andrew Evans

Rainbow over Meridian Hill Park: dcnature.com, Creative Commons License, Copyright Chadwick Cipiti

Thunderstorm: dcnature.com, Creative Commons License, Copyright Brian Gratwicke

Landscape photo: morguefile.com

Tutorial 2:

Cabin in snow: Creative Commons License, Copyright Steve Carlton

Construction photos: Copyright Alex Snyder, www.alexsnyder.com

House under construction and "key color" house: Courtesy of C. H. Gorman

Rusted Wrench: Creative Commons License, Copyright Hernan Vargas

All other images in this tutorial are royalty-free and the property of morguefile.com

Tutorial 3:

Construction site: Courtesy of C. H. Gorman

Clouds: Courtesy of A. Bounar

All other images in this tutorial are royalty-free and the property of morguefile.com

Tutorial 4:

Sneakers: Courtesy of A. Bounar

All other images in this tutorial are royalty-free and the property of morguefile.com

Tutorial 5:

All images in this tutorial are royalty-free and the property of morguefile.com

Tutorial 6:

All images in this tutorial are royalty-free and the property of morguefile.com

Tutorial 7:

Sports & Leisure: © Getty Images/PhotoObjects.net/Thinkstock Photos

Man suspended from rope in forest, Islas del Rosario, Colombia: © Getty Images/Brand X Pictures /Thinkstock Photos

Woman in climbing gear in tree branches: ©Jupiterimages/Getty Images/Thinkstock Photos

Man going through zipline: © Sean Murphy/Digital Vision/Thinkstock Photos

Mid-adult woman smiling, portrait, close-up: © David De Lossy/Photodisc/Thinkstock Photos

Portrait of couple: © Jupiterimages/Comstock/Getty Images /Thinkstock Photos

Hiking, Nature, Pathway: © Ryan McVay/Getty Images/Lifesize/Thinkstock Photos

Portrait of a young man sitting on a rock: © George Doyle/Stockbyte/Thinkstock Photos

Woman making preserves: © Jupiter images/Brand X Pictures/Getty Images/Thinkstock Photos

Jazz musicians: © Jupiterimages/ Photos.com/Getty Images/Thinkstock Photos

Preserves: © Zedcor Wholly Owned/PhotoObjects.net/Getty Images/Thinkstock Photos

Group of people sitting at counter in sushi bar: © Andrea Chu/Digital vision/Thinkstock Photos

Businessman on cell phone in posh restaurant: ©Comstock Images/Thinkstock Photos

Teenage boy posing: © Jupiterimages/Comstock/Getty Images/Thinkstock Photos

Man by graffiti: © Brand X Pictures/Thinkstock Photos

Teens standing by graffiti: © BananaStock/Thinkstock Photos

Abstract design: © Ablestock.com/Getty Images/Thinkstock Photos

Getting Started with Adobe Photoshop CS5

Introducing Graphics and Photoshop CS5

PHOTOSHOP

OBJECTIVES

Session 1.1
- Learn the role of Photoshop in professional production
- Define raster versus vector graphics
- Start and exit Photoshop, and explore the workspace
- Examine Photoshop Help
- Open, rename, and close files
- Navigate and arrange file windows

Session 1.2
- Set Photoshop Preferences
- Work with the Photoshop interface, tools, and tool presets
- Work with panels and use the panel menu
- Choose a preset workspace
- Display and use rulers, grid, and guides
- Add content to the canvas

Case | *Mirabeau Media*

Mirabeau Media is a consulting firm in Burlington, Vermont that was founded in 2006 by Sarah Alward, a 2006 college graduate with a double major in journalism and graphic design. Sarah spent two years working for a local news organization, but decided her interests really lay in using her skills to help clients promote their products and companies through brochures, print ads, and Web-based media.

Sarah's firm uses Adobe Photoshop along with the other applications in the Adobe Creative Suite to create logos, flyers, brochures, catalogs, and online advertising for various clients in the Burlington area. You have recently been hired by Sarah to help in all aspects of the company, from design to production. Sarah knows you haven't used Photoshop, but based on your interview, she has decided that you are a quick learner with a lot to offer.

STARTING DATA FILES

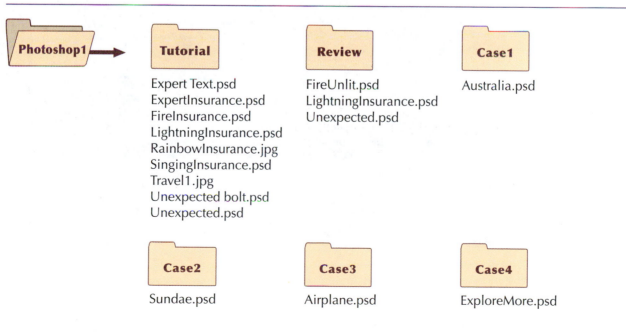

Photoshop1 →

Tutorial
Expert Text.psd
ExpertInsurance.psd
FireInsurance.psd
LightningInsurance.psd
RainbowInsurance.jpg
SingingInsurance.psd
Travel1.jpg
Unexpected bolt.psd
Unexpected.psd

Review
FireUnlit.psd
LightningInsurance.psd
Unexpected.psd

Case1
Australia.psd

Case2
Sundae.psd

Case3
Airplane.psd

Case4
ExploreMore.psd

SESSION 1.1 VISUAL OVERVIEW

The **Document window** is where Photoshop displays the images you open or create.

The **options bar** displays the settings for the currently selected tool.

The **Tools panel** includes tools for zooming, panning, selecting, and working with colors and bitmap and vector objects.

The **status bar** displays information about the current file, such as magnification, size, and resolution.

PHOTOSHOP PROGRAM WINDOW

The **workspace switcher** lets you change the workspace or save a custom workspace.

CS Live takes you to the Web, where you can share and critique work with other users.

The **Application bar** includes commands for managing files, panels, and windows, as well as controls for file management, window display, and workspace selection.

Panels consist of groups of related tools.

Introducing Graphics and Photoshop CS5

Nearly 20 years ago, Photoshop 1.0 was released exclusively for the Macintosh operating system. It has since become an industry standard for both Mac and PC image editing, and is widely used by graphics professionals, news organizations, educational institutions, nonprofit organizations, and nearly everyone with a product to sell or an idea to present. Over the years, the product's name has even morphed from a noun to a verb, and most industries now routinely *photoshop* images to sell products, market ideas, and educate consumers.

How Graphics Are Used to Enhance Communications

Think for a moment about how images are used everyday, everywhere, in print and in Web media. You might use an image to add interest to a printed page by illustrating a story or by showing a product. You might also use an image to teach the mechanics of something—for example, an image of someone kneading bread dough in a cookbook or changing an oil filter in a video for auto mechanics. Images are an important part of how we communicate—and they always have been, from cave drawings to digital photography. This fact explains a great deal about the appeal of Photoshop. Using Photoshop, you can remove the flaws in an image, refine its color and contrast, and modify it in a variety of other ways. You can also compose something completely new by combining digital photographs, text, and other artwork—all in Photoshop.

The Role of Photoshop in Professional Production

Since its inception, Photoshop has grown from a relatively straightforward digital image-editing program to a multifaceted, powerful tool used in many industries, from professional photography to Web design to advertising, and just about any aspect of modern communication. A **digital image** is a photograph or drawing in electronic form—in other words, a digital image can be displayed on a computer monitor or the LCD screen of a camera or mobile device. An **image-editing program** is software that lets you manipulate a digital image and then save it with the changes you have made. Many enhancements and adjustments can be achieved with the click of a mouse. Figure 1-1 shows three versions of a photograph enhanced merely by adding an adjustment (top right) and applying a filter (bottom right). Furthermore, Photoshop lets you save images in different file formats—using different color settings and different resolutions depending on whether your output will be print or digital media.

Figure 1-1   **Image enhanced in Photoshop**

a simple adjustment or filter can dramatically alter a photograph

original photograph

Sarah's newest client is a small, local insurance company hoping to run an ad campaign that will help it go national. Sarah has asked you to learn the basics of digital photography and Photoshop so that you can help her mock up a series of proposed ads for the business.

Bitmap vs. Vector Graphics

Digital images consist of two types of graphics—bitmap and vector. A **bitmap** graphic (also called a **raster** graphic) consists of closely spaced rows of pixels, the smallest element in a digital image. Each **pixel** (short for "picture element") is a square that defines a color. Multiple pixels laid out in a rectangular grid give the illusion of continuity and smoothness in an image. In other words, the human eye cannot distinguish between pixels unless the image is enlarged so much or the quality is so poor that the individual pixels and the spaces between them are visible. See Figure 1-2.

Figure 1-2 Comparing pixels in an enlarged bitmap image

square pixels spaced closely together provide the illusion of continuity

pixels can be seen as squares or jagged edges in an image when it is enlarged

Resolution is the measure of pixels per inch (ppi), or the level of detail in an image. The default resolution for a Web image is 72 ppi, which is also the default resolution in Photoshop. The resolution for a printed photo is higher and depends on your output device. You calculate resolution by multiplying the number of pixels running across an image (horizontal pixels) by the number of pixels running down an image (vertical pixels). Because the resolution is usually measured in millions of pixels, we use the term **megapixel** (mega means millions) when we talk about resolution. The higher the resolution (the more pixels per inch), the sharper the image appears.

A **vector** graphic is a collection of points, lines, curves, and shapes stored as a set of mathematical instructions. You can create vector graphics in a drawing program such as Adobe Illustrator, but you can also create them in Photoshop, which includes a number of vector tools in its Tools panel. The mathematical instructions in a vector graphic define the lines and curves that make up the graphic. They also define the object's position on the screen and its colors. Text is one example of a vector graphic. You can compose images in Photoshop that include both vector and bitmap graphics. Because of the way vector graphics are stored on a computer, you can resize them proportionally and maintain their quality. See Figure 1-3.

Figure 1-3   Enlarged bitmap loses quality but vector stays crisp

when enlarged, the vector image remains crisp, whereas the bitmap image becomes blurry

bitmap and vector images are both clear at the proper resolution

PROSKILLS

Decision Making: Knowing When Enough Is Enough

Photoshop is a fun program to work with, and using its features correctly and in moderation can lead to great success. However, because the image-editing possibilities are limitless, it is easy to get carried away. As a Photoshop user in the business world, it will be your responsibility to decide when an image is finished. For example, if you are providing artwork for a repair manual, your photographs should be clear representations of the device and its workings. Fancying up a repair manual with special effects photography would be counterproductive and a waste of your time. On the other hand, there are instances where altering a photograph or combining it with another actually makes it stronger. For example, a photograph might be in need of minor color or brightness adjustments to improve its appearance. An image for an advertisement might need to be altered drastically so that the product you are showcasing stands out. As you decide how to manipulate an image in Photoshop, you should keep at least three things in mind: the message, the client, and the intended audience. Careful decision making will produce positive results.

Now that you have a better sense of what kinds of files you can work with in Photoshop, Sarah suggests that you start Photoshop and explore the workspace.

TIP

You can restore Photoshop's defaults by pressing and holding the Ctrl+Alt+Shift keys while starting the application.

Starting Photoshop and Touring the Photoshop Workspace

When you start Photoshop CS5 for the first time, it opens with the default workspace displayed. In subsequent sessions, restarting Photoshop will display the workspace and settings that were in effect when you exited your last session. The **workspace** includes every element of the Photoshop program window, including the Document window, panels, and other elements that you'll explore in this tutorial.

TIP

Depending on your resolution, some elements may have a different appearance in your Photoshop window.

To start Photoshop and view the Photoshop program window:

1. Click the **Start** button ⊕ on the taskbar, click **All Programs**, and then click **Adobe Photoshop CS5** while pressing and holding the **Ctrl+Alt+Shift** keys. When you are prompted to delete the Adobe Photoshop settings, click **Yes**. The Photoshop program window opens and displays the default workspace, which is called Essentials. The largest area of the workspace, the Document window, is empty.

   Trouble? If you see an Adobe Creative Suite name, such as Adobe Design Premium CS5, listed before Adobe Photoshop CS5 on the All Programs menu, click the suite name and then click Adobe Photoshop CS5.

   Trouble? If you can't find Adobe Photoshop CS5 on the All Programs menu, navigate to the Adobe folder in the Program Files folder on your hard drive, and then double-click Adobe Photoshop CS5.

   Trouble? If a User Account Control dialog box appears asking if you want to allow Photoshop to make changes to your computer, click No. Then, restart Photoshop, making sure to press and hold the **Ctrl+Alt+Shift** keys immediately *after* clicking Adobe Photoshop CS5 so you are prompted to delete the Photoshop settings file.

   Trouble? If the Adobe Product Activation dialog box opens, click the appropriate option button, click Continue, enter the information requested, and then click the Register button. If you do not know your serial number or need additional assistance, ask your instructor or technical support person for help.

2. If necessary, click the **Maximize** button 回 on the title bar to maximize the Photoshop program window. See Figure 1-4.

Figure 1-4 **Photoshop program window**

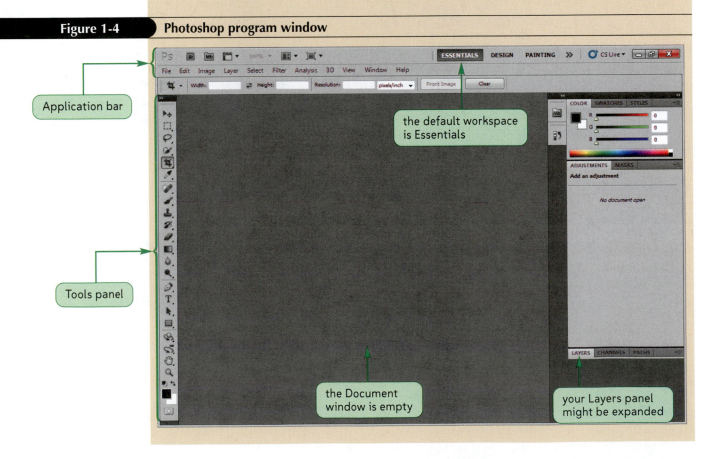

Application bar

the default workspace is Essentials

Tools panel

the Document window is empty

your Layers panel might be expanded

Opening a File

You open a file in Photoshop using the File command on the Application bar. Sarah has given you two Photoshop files that you can open to begin exploring Photoshop.

To open the file and tour the Photoshop workspace:

1. On the Application bar, click **File**, and then click **Open**. The Open dialog box opens.

2. Navigate to the Photoshop1\Tutorial folder included with your Data Files, click **LightningInsurance.psd** in the file list, and then click the **Open** button. The LightningInsurance document opens in the Document window.

   Trouble? If you can't find the Photoshop1\Tutorial folder, ask your instructor or technical support person for help.

   So that you can see how Photoshop handles multiple open files at a time, you'll also open a second file.

3. On the Application bar, click **File**, and then click **Open**. The Open dialog box opens.

   Because the last file you opened was in the Photoshop1\Tutorial folder, the Open dialog box opens to the Photoshop1\Tutorial folder by default.

4. Double-click **ExpertInsurance.psd**. The ExpertInsurance file opens on a new tab, but you can still see the LightningInsurance file's tab behind the current tab. See Figure 1-5.

Figure 1-5   **Most recently opened file is visible**

options bar

tabs show filenames

Document window

status bar

panels collapsed to icons

panels

collapsed panel

You opened two files so that you could see how the Photoshop tools and panels are laid out around the images on which you will be working. Now you'll tour the Photoshop workspace so that you understand the function of its different elements.

Touring the Photoshop Workspace

The main components of the Photoshop workspace are the Application bar, the Tools panel, the options bar, the Document window, and any panels displayed in the currently selected workspace. In the Essentials workspace, the default panels are Color, Swatches, Styles, Adjustments, Masks, Layers, Channels, and Paths. The Mini Bridge and History panels also appear, but they are collapsed. You'll explore all of these panels in later sessions as you work toward becoming a Photoshop expert.

Application Bar

The left side of the Application bar displays a list of 11 commands that open drop-down menus, similar to the menus you find in other applications. Above the menu are controls for opening **Adobe Bridge** and **Mini Bridge**, the file management tools in many Adobe products; as well as controls for displaying **extras**, such as guides, grids, and rulers; and controls for changing the zoom level, changing the way files are displayed in the Document window; and various other tools that control how you view the workspace, its panels, and its contents. The workspace switcher on the far right of the Application bar lets you change the workspace or save the current workspace as a custom workspace. The CS Live button takes you to the Adobe Web site, where you can share your work and have it critiqued by colleagues or clients. Figure 1-6 describes the icons found on the Application bar.

Figure 1-6   **Application bar**

Icon	Tool	Use To
Br	Bridge	Launch Bridge, the file management software used in many Creative Suite applications
Mb	Mini Bridge	Launch Mini Bridge, a scaled down version of Bridge
▾	View Extras	Display guides, grids, and rulers
100% ▾	Zoom Level	Select a custom or preset zoom level
▾	Arrange Documents	Choose from different configurations for arranging open documents
▾	Screen Mode	Choose a standard or full screen viewing mode
≫	Workspace switcher	Change, reset, save, and delete workspaces
◯	CS Live	Access the CS Live site where you and your colleagues can share and review each other's work

Tools Panel

The Tools panel contains tools for creating vector images such as geometric shapes, selecting portions of a document, adding text, adding brushstrokes, and modifying pixels in bitmap images. Related tools are grouped on the panel. You can display the Tools panel as a single column (the default) or in two columns. When you point to a tool on the Tools panel, Photoshop displays a **tool tip**, which includes the name of the tool plus any shortcut key for selecting the tool. For example, the shortcut key for selecting the Zoom Tool is Z.

The Tools panel also includes hidden tools. In fact, any tool with a small triangle displayed in the lower right corner has other tools hidden beneath it. To display a list of hidden tools, point to the top level tool in the Toolbar, and then press and hold the left mouse button. Click the tool you want to make active.

Options Bar

The options bar includes the controls, or options, for the current tool. For example, if you select the Horizontal Type Tool from the Tools panel, Photoshop displays options for text orientation, font, style, and size.

Document Window

The Document window displays the current file. When you have multiple files open, the Document window displays each filename on a tab along the top of the window by default. Clicking a tab displays the document named on the tab. You can also change Document window settings to display open files tiled in a grid or side by side vertically or horizontally. As soon as you open a file in the Document window, the status bar appears in the bottom left corner of the window. By default, the status bar displays the current zoom percentage as well as the document size. You can change what is displayed on the status bar by clicking the arrow to the right of the document size, and then clicking the information you want to display (for example, the document dimensions or the name of the currently selected tool).

Panels

Panels consist of groups of related tools. For example, the Swatches panel displays samples of colors available in the current color mode, and stores the most frequently used colors. You can change the set of swatches displayed on the panel, or add your own swatches to an existing set. The Adjustments panel lets you modify your images by changing different settings, such as brightness and contrast, or by changing a photograph from color to black and white. You'll explore panels and how to arrange them in Session 1.2.

Sarah suggests that you make use of Photoshop's Help system to help you master the features of Photoshop. You decide to spend time exploring Help now so that you can use it efficiently in the future.

Getting Help in Photoshop

Photoshop includes two versions of Help. One is stored in a PDF file on your hard drive. To open the PDF file, you need to install Adobe Reader, free software available from Adobe at *www.adobe.com*. The other version of Help is available online. You can update the PDF that is stored on your hard drive whenever you are online, or you can choose to use the online Help exclusively to ensure that you are getting the most up-to-date information. See Figure 1-7.

Figure 1-7   Adobe Community Help

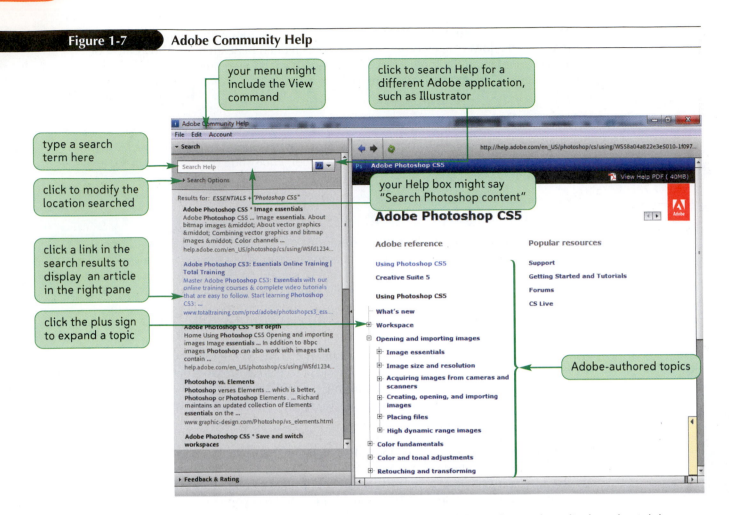

When you open Adobe Help, the right pane of the Help window displays the Adobe-authored version of Help. You can explore Adobe-authored Help by clicking the links in the right pane to open Adobe articles on a variety of topics. The left pane of the Help window allows you to search for specific information by typing a term in the Search Help box. You can use the Search Options to search Local Help or the online version of Help, called Adobe Community Help, which displays links to articles, videos, tutorials, and blogs related to your search term. Adobe Community Help lets you get tips and information from professional photographers and designers willing to share their insights. Some of the topics are written by Adobe and Adobe partners, but others are not. When you click on a link in the left pane, the Help article is displayed in the right pane.

You'll explore Help to find more about workspaces in Photoshop.

To get help in Photoshop:

1. On the Application bar, click **Help**, and then click **Photoshop Help**. The Adobe Community Help window opens.

2. In the list of topics in the right pane, click the **plus sign (+)** to the left of Workspace. The Workspace menu expands to list the subtopics available.

3. Click the **plus sign (+)** to the left of Workspace basics. The menu expands again to display additional subtopics.

4. Click **Manage windows and panels**. Photoshop Help opens a new page showing a list of subtopics, followed by detailed information about each subtopic. The list of subtopics includes links that take you directly to the topic without having to scroll the page.

5. Click **Rearrange, dock, or float document windows**. Photoshop takes you to the location on the page showing detailed information about working with Document windows. See Figure 1-8.

Figure 1-8   **Help topic**

Notice that some of the information presented is about other products in the Adobe Creative Suite. Once you know how to manage the elements in Photoshop, you will recognize many of the same elements in other Adobe products, such as Illustrator or InDesign.

Sarah wants to make sure you understand how to work efficiently in Photoshop, and wants you to find information in Help about panels. You can find this information using the Search feature in Help.

To search Help in Photoshop:

1. In the Search Help box in the left pane of the Help window, type **swatches panel** and then press the Enter key.

   Trouble? If your Search box says "Search Photoshop content" you can still complete these steps.

2. In the left pane, click the first topic in the list of search results. The contents of the Help article are displayed in the right panel. See Figure 1-9.

| Figure 1-9 | Searching Help |

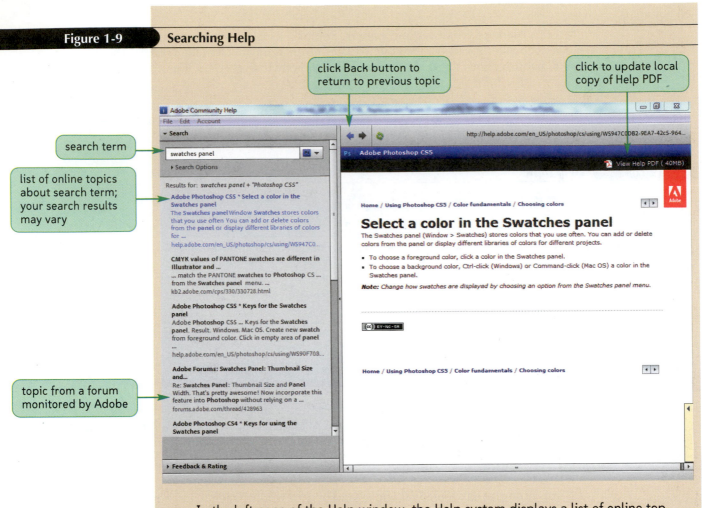

In the left pane of the Help window, the Help system displays a list of online topics about the Swatches panel. It also displays a topic about selecting a color in the Swatches panel that comes directly from Adobe's Help PDF.

3. Click the **Back** button at the top of the right pane to return to the previous topic.

4. Click the **Close** button ⬛ on the Adobe Community Help window title bar to close the Help system. The Help system closes, and the Photoshop program window is now displayed.

INSIGHT

Understanding How to Use External Help

You have seen that you can use the Help system to search the Web for information on using Adobe Photoshop. Keep in mind that when you do this, the information you find has not necessarily been approved by Adobe (even though it appears in the Search results) and, therefore, might not be as accurate as the information within the Help system itself. For the most reliable help, go to a site like *forums.adobe.com*, which is monitored by Adobe, or to *adobe.com* itself.

Now that you have a sense of how to find information about any tool you need to use in Photoshop, you'll practice working with multiple files.

Working with Multiple Files

Photoshop is not only an image-editing program; it also lets you combine elements to create a completely new photo composition. When you do this kind of complex work, you will most likely need to have multiple files open at one time. The way you open, save, and close Photoshop files is similar to the way you perform file handling in other applications, so many of the commands might be familiar to you.

REFERENCE

Opening Multiple Files at Once

- On the Application bar, click File, and then click Open, or press the Ctrl+O keys.
- To open contiguous files (files next to each other), click the first filename, press and hold down the Shift key, click the last filename, and then release the Shift key.
- To open noncontiguous files, click the first filename, press and hold down the Ctrl key, and then click any other file in the list.
- Click Open, or press the Enter key.

Sarah has given you a number of photographs and photo compositions that she wants you to review so that you can better understand the power of Photoshop.

To open multiple files:

Be sure to press the Ctrl key and not the Shift key. If you press Shift, all the files in between will be selected as well.

1. On the Application bar, click **File**, and then click **Open**. The Open dialog box opens. You can select multiple files and apply the Open command to all of them at once.

2. Navigate to the Photoshop1\Tutorial folder included with your Data Files, if necessary, click **FireInsurance.psd**, press and hold down the **Ctrl** key, scroll down the file list, if necessary, and then click **Unexpected.psd**.

3. Click **Open**. Photoshop opens both files at once, each in its own Document window. See Figure 1-10.

Figure 1-10 Multiple open files

filenames of open
files are displayed
in tabbed
Document windows

the last file you
selected is visible

The last file you selected, Unexpected, is visible. The first file you selected, FireInsurance, is behind it, as are the two files you opened previously, ExpertInsurance and LightningInsurance.

Sarah explains that because you will often modify files in Photoshop, it is best to preserve the original file so that you can reuse it or backtrack if you make and then save unwanted changes. She asks you to save the Unexpected file with a new name.

Saving a File with a New Name

When you save files in Photoshop, you have many different options. You can save a file with the same name by overwriting the original file. You can save a file with a new name in the same file format (for example, JPG). You can also save a file with a new name in a new format. No matter which option you choose, it is best to save your work often in Photoshop so that you don't lose your changes should something unexpected occur.

To save a file with a new name:

TIP
You can also press the Shift+Ctrl+S keys to open the Save As dialog box.

1. Make sure the **Unexpected** tab is selected in the workspace, click **File** on the Application bar, and then click **Save As**. The Save As dialog box opens. You can save the file in a different format, or as a copy of the original file. You'll explore a number of these save options in later tutorials, but for now, you'll save the file with a new name.

   Trouble? If the Photoshop Format Options dialog box opens, click the **OK** button to accept the default options.

2. Type **newUnexpected** in the File name box. You don't need to type the PSD file extension, because Photoshop automatically adds the extension of the selected file type.

3. Click **Save**. Photoshop saves the file with a new name. To confirm that the original file is still intact, you can open the Open dialog box.

4. Press the **Ctrl+O** keys, navigate to the Photoshop1/Tutorial folder and then scroll to the bottom of the Open dialog box, if necessary. The Ctrl+O keys are a shortcut for the File, Open command. Notice that the new file, newUnexpected, and the original file, Unexpected, both appear in the file list in the Tutorial folder. Any changes that you make to the newly saved file will not affect the original.

5. Click **Cancel** to close the Open dialog box.

Now that you've practiced opening and saving files, Sarah explains that you need to learn how to best arrange the Document windows and navigate through open files so that you can work efficiently in Photoshop.

Navigating and Arranging File Windows

Photoshop provides many different ways to navigate through and arrange the files with which you are working. You can navigate by clicking the Document window tabs, or you can use predefined key combinations. You can also use a menu to select a file and switch to it.

Navigating Open File Windows and Changing Tab Order

You can move from one open file to another by clicking the Document window tabs. Photoshop also provides two key combinations for navigating open files. Pressing the Ctrl+Tab keys cycles through the open files in the order in which they were opened. Pressing the Ctrl+Shift+Tab keys cycles through the open files in reverse.

To navigate the open file windows:

1. Click the **LightningInsurance** Document window tab. Photoshop displays the LightningInsurance photograph.

2. Click the **ExpertInsurance** Document window tab.

3. Press the **Ctrl+Tab** keys. Photoshop displays the FireInsurance file. Release both keys.

4. Press the **Ctrl+Shift** keys, and then press the **Tab** key two times. Photoshop cycles through the files in reverse order.

5. On the Application bar, click **File**, click **Open Recent**, and then click **Unexpected.psd**. Because you have more files open in the Document window than Photoshop has room for which to display tabs, there is now a new window element, a double arrow pointing to the right on the right side of the tab area.

6. Click the **double arrow** 🔽. Photoshop displays a list of all open files. The active file has a check mark next to the filename. See Figure 1-11.

Trouble? Your view might vary depending on the size of your monitor and your monitor resolution. Such differences shouldn't cause problems as you complete these steps. However, if you don't see the double arrow 🔽, read but don't perform Step 6.

Figure 1-11 | Open file list displayed

the workspace window does not have room to completely display all of the open tabs

clicking the double arrows displays a list of open files

You can display an image by clicking its name on the list.

7. Click **LightningInsurance**, which is the file whose tab you cannot see. Photoshop displays the LightningInsurance image.

You might want to change the order of tabs so that you can navigate more easily between related files. You can change the order by dragging the tabs with the mouse.

To change tab order:

1. Point to the **LightningInsurance** tab, press and hold the left mouse button, and then drag to the right along the tab bar until the LightningInsurance tab appears to the right of the FireInsurance tab. See Figure 1-12.

Figure 1-12 | Moving a tab

move the LightningInsurance tab here

2. Release the mouse button.

Dragging a tab changes its position, but it does not change the order in which you can use shortcut keys to cycle through files. They will always cycle from first opened to last opened when you press the Ctrl+Tab key combination.

Arranging File Windows

You can arrange file windows so that multiple files appear in the Document window at one time. The file arrangement can be predetermined by the commands on the Arrange Documents menu, or you can display images in floating Document windows and drag them around the workspace.

Next, you'll explore how to work with floating Document windows, and then you'll arrange the windows in one of the arrangement choices provided by Photoshop.

To float the Document window:

1. Point to the **ExpertInsurance** tab, press and hold down the mouse button, drag the tab down to the middle of the workspace, and release the mouse button. The Document window "detaches" from the other tabs and appears in its own free-floating Document window. See Figure 1-13.

Figure 1-13 **Free-floating Document window**

other tabs are still anchored in position

free-floating window includes Minimize, Maximize, and Close buttons

image appears in a free-floating window

Expert, Inc.
Because Mother Nature
doesn't always have your back

2. Click the **Minimize** button 🔲 in the floating Document window title bar. The ExpertInsurance window seems to disappear from the Photoshop program window.

3. Point to the Photoshop program icon 🔲 on the Windows 7 taskbar, and you will see that the ExpertInsurance file is still there, but minimized. Click the thumbnail. The ExpertInsurance Document window is restored to its floating size.

4. Click the **Maximize** button 🔲 for the ExpertInsurance file. The file is maximized in its own window and covers the Photoshop window.

5. Click the **Restore** button 🔲. The file floats in its own Document window.

6. Point to the title bar, press and hold the mouse button, and then drag the Document window up to the tabs until a translucent blue bar is visible. The ExpertInsurance Document window is now one of the tabbed windows.

Photoshop also provides a variety of predefined arrangements for your open documents. You can find the different choices on the Arrange Documents menu.

To arrange the documents using the Arrange Documents menu:

1. On the Application bar, click the **Arrange Documents** button 🔲▾. Photoshop displays a gallery of icons, each representing a window arrangement, as well as a series of commands for displaying your files in the Document window. The gallery changes based on the number of open files. The default arrangement is Consolidate All, which is the arrangement you have been working in.

2. Click **Tile All in Grid** 🔲. Photoshop arranges the Document window so that all open files are visible. Notice that Photoshop does not change the zoom levels for any of the images. It merely fits the file in a smaller window so that less of each image is visible.

3. On the Application bar, click the **Arrange Documents** button 🔲▾, and then click the **2 Up** button 🔲. Photoshop arranges the topmost file and the next file in the tab order into two windows in the Document window. You can view the other open files by clicking the double arrow to display the file list. See Figure 1-14.

Figure 1-14   **2 Up arrangement**

click to display window arrangement options

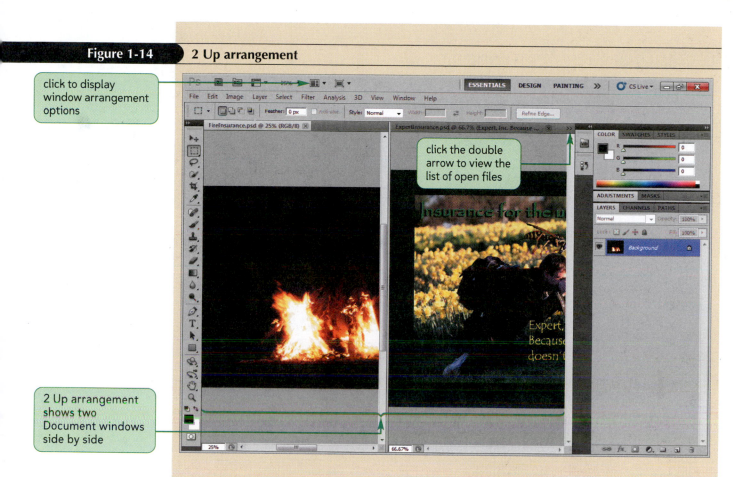

click the double arrow to view the list of open files

2 Up arrangement shows two Document windows side by side

4. On the Application bar, click the **Arrange Documents** button ▦▾, and then click **Float All in Windows**. Photoshop stacks all of the files in free-floating Document windows. To navigate these windows, you click their title bars.

5. Click the **LightningInsurance** title bar. The LightningInsurance Document window moves to the front. See Figure 1-15.

Figure 1-15 | **Stacked floating windows**

click a window title bar to display the file

your arrangement might look different

Although you can no longer see the title bars of the other files, and there is no double-headed arrow displayed, you can still access these files using the Window menu.

▶ **6.** On the Application bar, click **Window**, and then click **ExpertInsurance**. The ExpertInsurance window is now on top.

▶ **7.** On the Application bar, click the **Arrange Documents** button, and then click the **Consolidate All** button to return to tabbed windows.

Now that you have spent time exploring the Photoshop workspace and have learned some of the basics of working with files and file windows, Sarah suggests you close all the files you have opened.

Closing Files

After you finish working on a file, you should close it. This saves system resources on your computer.

To close all the open files:

▶ **1.** On the Application bar, click **File**, and then click **Close**. The top file closes.

Trouble? If you are prompted to save the file, you might have inadvertently changed the file while you were exploring the workspace. Click No to close the file without saving it.

▶ **2.** Click the **Close** button ☒ on the current Document window tab. The file closes.

▶ **3.** On the Application bar, click **File**, and then click **Close All** to close the rest of the open files. The Photoshop window is now empty. You can open additional files, or you can exit Photoshop.

Exiting Photoshop

If you are no longer working in Photoshop, you should exit the application. This saves system resources as you work in other programs. You can also exit Photoshop without first closing the files. When you do, Photoshop asks you if you want to save any modified files before they are closed.

To exit Photoshop:

▶ **1.** On the Application bar, click **File**, and then click **Exit**. Photoshop closes.

In this session, you learned how to start Photoshop and view the program window. You also learned how to open and close files, how to find the information you need in Help, how to arrange windows, and how to exit Photoshop.

Now that you know the basics of working with files and Document windows, Sarah asks you to spend time learning about some additional features of Photoshop. In the next session, you will explore preference settings, panels, grids, and guides.

REVIEW

Session 1.1 Quick Check

1. Photoshop is a(n) _____ program.
2. Explain how a bitmap graphic is different from a vector graphic.
3. The smallest unit in a bitmap graphic is called a(n) _____.
4. What is the name of the default workspace in Photoshop?
5. The _____ panel on the left side of the program window lets you create and modify vector graphics and modify the pixels in bitmap graphics in your Photoshop file.
6. True or False. You can only have one Photoshop file open at a time.
7. The _____ _____ button on the Application bar lets you tile open documents within the Document window.

SESSION 1.2 VISUAL OVERVIEW

Use vector tools to add a drawing to your image.

Guides are lines that you draw in a Document window to aid in aligning and moving objects in a document, or drawing objects with specific dimensions or alignments.

Use the Move pointer to place objects.

Dragging a title bar in a stack will move all of the panels in the stack together.

Use the Shape Tools to draw vector objects.

A **stack**, a collection of panels or panel groups joined top to bottom, can improve workflow.

Select a layer before working with it.

GRIDS, GUIDES, AND PANELS

The **ruler** displays the measurement of your document in pixels, inches, centimeters, or other units.

Panels can be collapsed to icons.

A **dock** displays a group of complementary panels or panel groups one on top of the other using tabs.

The **grid** divides your document into squares that you can also use for guidance as you draw, move, and place objects in a document.

Panel groups organize related panels.

Viewing and Changing Photoshop Preferences

Once you have some experience working with Photoshop, you will find that you develop certain preferences for how the program window is set up. Photoshop lets you customize those preferences and save them for different tasks.

Now that you understand how to arrange and manipulate the display of files in the Document window, Sarah suggests you learn about Photoshop Preferences.

REFERENCE

Setting Photoshop Preferences

- On the Application bar, click Edit, point to Preferences, click General, and then click Next until you reach the panel you want to work with.
- Set preferences on the panel, and click the OK button to close the panel and save the preferences, or click the Next button or the Prev button to display the next or previous Preferences panel.

or

- On the Application bar, click Edit, point to Preferences, and then click the name of the panel you want to work with.
- Set preferences on the panel, and click the OK button to close the panel and save the preferences, or click the Next button or the Prev button to display the next or previous Preferences panel.

Photoshop gives you plenty of options for customizing its tools, performance, file handling, and interface. Many of those options are covered in later tutorials, but it's important to know that they exist and where to access them so that you can use them as your expertise in Photoshop grows.

Sarah suggests that you begin to explore the preferences in Photoshop by changing one of the Preference settings.

To set Photoshop Preferences:

1. Start Photoshop. Navigate to the Photoshop1\Tutorial folder, and open the file **SingingInsurance.psd**.

2. On the Application bar, click **Edit**, point to **Preferences**, and then click **General**. All of the preferences are available in different panels of the Preferences dialog box. See Figure 1-16.

Figure 1-16   **Preferences dialog box**

Preferences

General	Color Picker: Adobe	OK
Interface	HUD Color Picker: Hue Strip	Cancel
File Handling	Image Interpolation: Bicubic (best for smooth gradients)	Prev
Performance		Next
Cursors	Options	
Transparency & Gamut		
Units & Rulers		
Guides, Grid & Slices		
Plug-Ins		
Type		
3D		

use Interface preferences to change the way Photoshop looks

click to display different Preferences settings

Options
- ☐ Auto-Update Open Documents
- ☐ Beep When Done
- ☑ Dynamic Color Sliders
- ☑ Export Clipboard
- ☑ Use Shift Key for Tool Switch
- ☑ Resize Image During Place
- ☑ Animated Zoom
- ☐ Zoom Resizes Windows
- ☐ Zoom with Scroll Wheel
- ☐ Zoom Clicked Point to Center
- ☑ Enable Flick Panning
- ☑ Place or Drag Raster Images as Smart Objects

click to move to next set of Preferences

☐ History Log

Save Log Items To: ◉ Metadata
　　　　　　　　　　 ○ Text File   Choose...
　　　　　　　　　　 ○ Both

Edit Log Items: Sessions Only ▾

Reset All Warning Dialogs

You change panels by clicking panel names in the left panel of the dialog box, or by clicking the Next button or the Prev button in the right panel.

3. Click **Interface** in the left panel of the dialog box. The Interface settings let you change the way Photoshop looks. You will change the color of the standard screen, which is the area that appears around a file.

4. Click the **Standard Screen Mode** arrow in the General section, click **Black**, and then click the **OK** button. The area around the document in the Document window is now black. See Figure 1-17.

Figure 1-17   **Changing an Interface setting**

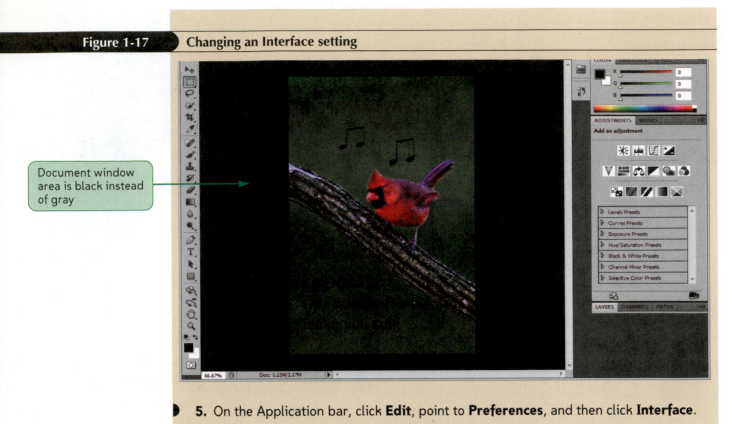

Document window area is black instead of gray

5. On the Application bar, click **Edit**, point to **Preferences**, and then click **Interface**.

6. Click the **Standard Screen Mode** arrow in the General section, click **Gray**, and then click the **OK** button. The area around the file in the Document window is now gray, the default setting.

Restoring Default Photoshop Preferences

If you make changes to Photoshop Preferences but later decide you want to restore the defaults, you do not have to go back to the individual Preferences panels and undo each change individually. Instead, you can simply exit Photoshop and restart it while pressing and holding the Ctrl+Alt+Shift keys. When you are prompted to delete the Adobe Photoshop Settings File, click Yes. When Photoshop opens, the default preferences will be restored.

Working with Panels

You have seen how you can arrange Document windows in different ways. You can also rearrange the panels in the workspace, or open panels that don't appear by default in a particular workspace. Furthermore, you can increase your work area by hiding and collapsing panels, or floating panels and then dragging them out of the way. See Figure 1-18.

Figure 1-18   **Panel groups and docks**

Each panel in Photoshop is a collection of related tools and settings. Beyond that, groups of panels are often collected in docks. For example, in the Essentials workspace, the Layers, Channels, and Paths panels are displayed in a group by default because those panels are often used together. In turn, they are docked with two other panel groups: Adjustments and Masks; and Color, Swatches, and Styles. The default Essentials workspace includes three panel docks plus the Tools panel. The Essentials workspace also includes two collapsed panels, History and Mini Bridge. You move from one docked panel to another by clicking the tabs.

Panels can also be displayed in stacks. The panels in a stack share a title bar, and you can drag the title bar to move the stack anywhere in the Photoshop window. See Figure 1-19.

Figure 1-19 Panel stack

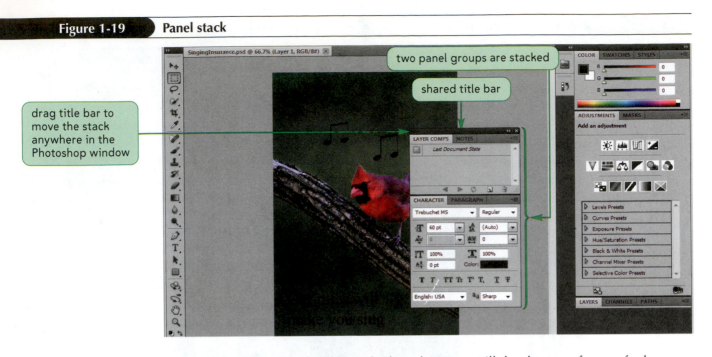

As you become more familiar with Photoshop, you will develop a preference for how you want your panels displayed, depending on what you are working on.

The way you work with Document window tabs is similar to the way you work with tabs in open panels: You click them to move from one panel to the next in a group.

Now that you have a general idea of how a Photoshop workspace is set up, Sarah wants you to practice rearranging its interface and working with some of its tools.

To choose a tab in an open panel:

1. Open **Unexpected.psd** from the Photoshop1\Tutorial folder. The file opens on top of SingingInsurance in the Essentials workspace. The workspace includes three panel groups, two collapsed panels, and the Tools panel. The top group includes the Color, Swatches, and Styles panels.

2. Click the **Swatches** tab in the top panel group. The Swatches panel displays a set of frequently used colors.

3. On the bottom panel group, click the **Layers** tab, if necessary, to expand it. The Layers panel for the Unexpected file displays a single layer called Background.

4. Click the **workspace switcher** icon ⟫, and then click **Reset Essentials**. The Essentials workspace returns to its default settings.

Displaying and Closing a Panel

You do not always have to work with the default panels provided in a workspace. You can open and close panels at will. To access any of the panels not displayed in the current workspace, click Window on the Application bar to display a list of available panels, including panels for working with color, text, and brushes.

Sarah wants you to explore some of the panels that are not open by default in the Essentials workspace so that you can learn how to open and close panels as you need them.

TIP

You can also open the Brush window by pressing the F5 shortcut key.

To display and close panels:

1. On the Application bar, click **Window**. The Window menu includes commands for arranging the windows and changing the workspace. It also includes a list of panels ranging from 3D to Tool Presets. See Figure 1-20.

Figure 1-20   Window menu

checkmark indicates panel is displayed in the workspace

click a panel name to open it

list of available panels

Any panel name with a checkmark is currently open in the workspace. To open a panel that isn't visible in the workspace, click its name.

2. Click **Brush**. The Brush panel opens. See Figure 1-21.

Figure 1-21 **Brush panel**

Clone Source is docked with Brush panel

Brush Presets is docked with Brush panel

Brush Presets icon

Brush panel

Brush panel icon

Clone Source icon

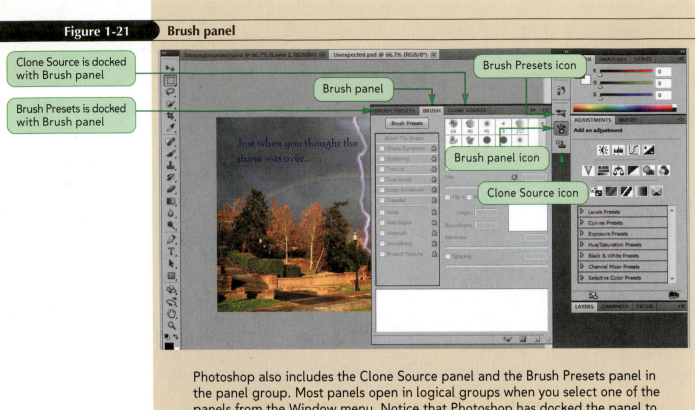

Photoshop also includes the Clone Source panel and the Brush Presets panel in the panel group. Most panels open in logical groups when you select one of the panels from the Window menu. Notice that Photoshop has docked the panel to the left of the Adjustments panel in the panels area of the workspace, and that a Brush panel icon appears to the right of the Brush panel. Above that icon is the Brush Presets icon, and below is the Clone Source icon.

▶ **3.** On the Application bar, click **Window**, and then click **Character**. The Brush panel is collapsed, and the Character panel opens in a dock, with the Paragraph panel behind it. A collapsed version of the panel group also appears to the left of the default panels. See Figure 1-22.

Figure 1-22 **Character panel**

Character panel appears expanded, but also docked, and with collapsed panel icons to the right

Character panel icon

Paragraph panel icon

▶ **4.** On the title bar for the Character panel, click the **panel options** button, and then click **Close** to close the panel. The Character panel closes, but the Paragraph panel with which it was docked remains open.

5. On the title bar for the Color panel, click the **panel options** button, and then click **Close Tab Group**. The Color panel group closes. See Figure 1-23.

Figure 1-23   **Closing a panel group**

You can also use the Window menu to close a panel.

6. On the Application bar, click **Window**, and then click **Tools** to deselect the panel and remove the check mark. The Tools panel closes, and the Document window fills the space on the left side of the window.

7. Click the **workspace switcher** button, and then click **Reset Essentials** to reset the workspace. All of the default panels reopen.

Sarah suggests that you experiment with minimizing, hiding, and redisplaying panels before you tackle a project.

Minimizing, Hiding, and Redisplaying Panels

As you work in Photoshop, you'll often find that you want more of the workspace area to display your file, and that you don't need all of the panels that might be displayed in the current workspace all of the time. To save real estate on your screen, you can minimize open panels or even hide them temporarily. This flexibility streamlines your work in Photoshop, and lets you work the way that suits you best.

To minimize, hide, and redisplay panels:

1. On the right side of the title bar for the docked panels, click the **Collapse to Icons** button. The panels collapse and the Document window expands to fill the space. See Figure 1-24.

Figure 1-24 | **Collapsed panel groups**

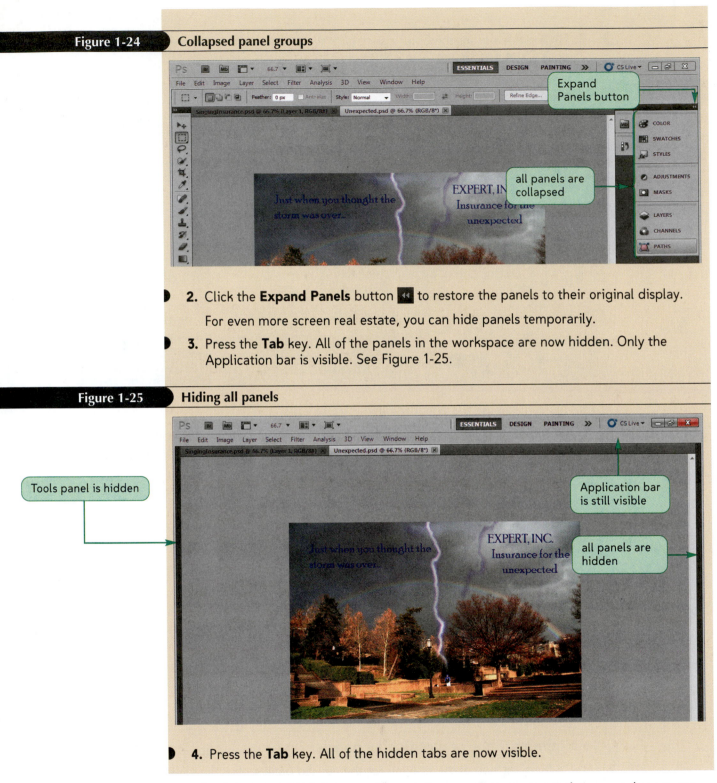

2. Click the **Expand Panels** button ◄◄ to restore the panels to their original display.

   For even more screen real estate, you can hide panels temporarily.

3. Press the **Tab** key. All of the panels in the workspace are now hidden. Only the Application bar is visible. See Figure 1-25.

Figure 1-25 | **Hiding all panels**

4. Press the **Tab** key. All of the hidden tabs are now visible.

Sarah has explained that you will sometimes want to group panels in ways that are not provided by Photoshop. She says that you should experiment with docking.

Moving and Stacking Panels

Because everyone has different work habits and difference preferences, Photoshop provides even more ways to manipulate panels. For example, you can create custom groups of panels by docking them. You can also stack them.

To move the panels:

1. On the Application bar, click **Window**, and then click **Brush** to open the Brush panel group.

2. Point to the **panel bar** to the right of the Clone Source tab.

3. Press and hold the mouse button, and then drag the panel group to the left, into the Document window. A "ghost" version of the panel appears, indicating where it will be placed when you release the mouse button. See Figure 1-26.

Figure 1-26   Moving a panel group

ghosted image indicates new location

blue border indicates original location

4. Release the mouse button. The panel is now floating in the middle of the Document window. Notice that the panel now has its own title bar that includes a Collapse to Icons button and a Close button.

Stacking Panels

Stacks of panel groups let you move multiple panels and panel groups around the work-space as a single unit. Next, you'll experiment with stacking panels so that you can move groups of panels together around the Photoshop window as you work.

To stack panels:

1. Point to the right of the word PATHS in the bottom panel group, click the **panel bar**, and drag the **Layers, Channels, and Paths** panel group to the left and under the Brushes panel group until you see a blue line between the two panel docks. See Figure 1-27.

Figure 1-27   **Stacking panels**

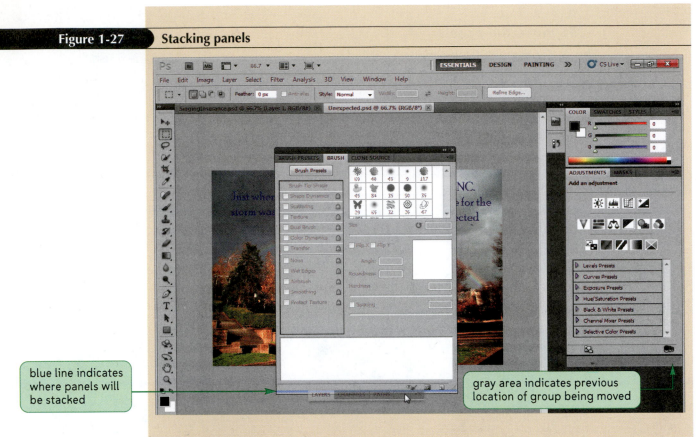

blue line indicates where panels will be stacked

gray area indicates previous location of group being moved

2. Release the mouse button. The panels are now stacked.

3. Point to the stacked panels title bar, press the left mouse button, and drag the stack up and to the right. The entire stack moves as you drag.

Preset Workspaces

The Photoshop workspace is customizable so you can change the way it appears based on your preferences. As you become more comfortable in Photoshop, you might find that you prefer one layout to another, depending on the task at hand. So far, you have been working in and modifying the default Essentials workspace. However, Photoshop also comes with a number of other predefined workspaces that you will explore throughout this book. For example, the Painting workspace opens the Swatches, Brush, and Brush Presets panels, which give you many different options for brush shape, color, and texture. The Design workspace displays the Character and Paragraph panels to give you multiple text formatting options when you add text to a file. Unless otherwise noted, the figures in this book show the workspace in the default Essentials layout. See Figure 1-28 for a description of all the available workspace layouts.

Figure 1-28   Workspace layouts

Workspace Layout	Description
Essentials	Displays the most frequently used panels for accomplishing basic tasks in Photoshop, such as navigating a document, manipulating layers and channels, working with paths, and setting colors
Design	Displays panels for working with type, including Character and Paragraph panels that let you make quick formatting changes to text
Painting	Displays panels for working with painting features, such as brushes, brush presets, and colors
Photography	Displays advanced panels for making fine adjustments to photographs, including modifying color balance, hue, and saturation; applying filters; and mixing color channels
3D	Displays panels for working with imported 3D objects and converting 2D layers to 3D objects; 3D features are only available in Photoshop Extended
Motion	Displays panels that let you create motion effects and animate 3D objects
New in CS5	Displays the new CS5 panels, as well as panels with new features, and highlights new commands on the menu

Photoshop comes with seven preset workspaces. You can switch workspaces at any point in an editing session, and then switch back, depending on your current task. You use the workspace switcher to change workspace. You can also click Window on the menu, click Workspace, and then click a workspace on the shortcut menu.

Sarah explains that depending on what your focus will be in an editing session, you might find you need to work in a different workspace. She suggests that you explore some of the other available workspaces.

To choose a preset workspace:

1. On the Application bar, click **Design**, which appears next to Essentials. Panels specific to working extensively with text appear. See Figure 1-29.

Figure 1-29   Design workspace

Design workspace is selected

the Design workspace includes panels for working with text

2. Click the **workspace switcher** ⟩⟩, and then click **Painting**. The workspace changes again to include tools and settings that are most helpful for working with the various brush and pencil tools on the Tools panel. Notice that in addition to the Brush Presets panel, which is docked by itself, the Brush panel appears collapsed to the left of the Swatches panel.

3. Click the **Brush Tool** 🖌 on the Tools panel. The Brushes Presets panel display changes to show active settings appropriate for the Brush Tool.

You have explored a number of the workspaces Photoshop provides by default, but now you'll explore the other workspace options you might need in your work for Mirabeau Media.

INSIGHT

Saving, Redisplaying, and Deleting a Custom Workspace

In Photoshop, you can save **custom workspaces** to display the panels and tools you need for specific tasks, such as working on a photograph for a brochure or designing a poster. To create a custom workspace, make the changes you want—for example, by opening additional panels, closing panels you don't want, and rearranging the docks or stacks to your liking. When you have designed the workspace you want, click the workspace switcher and then click New Workspace. Type a name for the new workspace, and then click Save. The next time you click the workspace switcher, your new workspace will be displayed in the workspace list. By using custom workspaces, you can improve your workflow and become more efficient.

Using the Rulers, Grid, and Guides

Photoshop provides a number of tools for keeping track of the measurements of your document, as well as guiding you as you make selections or add and position objects. For example, you might use the rulers to help you crop an image so that it is the exact dimensions you need. If you are adding an object such as text or a vector drawing to an image, you can first draw guides so that you can place the object exactly at their intersection. You can also display the grid to help you quickly align multiple objects added to an image.

Sarah has suggested that you experiment with the grid, guides, and rulers as you continue to use other tools in Photoshop.

Showing and Hiding the Rulers

You can display rulers so that you can keep track of the measurements of elements in your Document window, whether or not the window is zoomed. Sarah has provided you with a photograph of a field that she intends to use in one of her print ads for a travel agency.

To show and hide the rulers:

1. Close all open files, display the Essentials workspace and then reset it. Open **Travel1** from the Photoshop1/Tutorial folder included with your Data Files.

2. On the Application bar, click **View**, and then click **Fit on Screen**. The image fills the available area on the screen.

3. On the Application bar, click **View**, and then click **Rulers**. Two rulers appear around the Document window, one along the top, and one along the left side. See Figure 1-30.

TIP

You can also press the Ctrl+R keys to display and hide the rulers.

Figure 1-30	Displaying rulers

horizontal ruler

zero points on rulers are at left and top edge of image

tree is just under 4 inches tall

vertical ruler

By default, the rulers' zero points are at the upper-left corner of the document. Using the vertical ruler, notice that the tree, from top to bottom, is slightly less than 4 inches tall.

4. On the Application bar, click the **Arrange Documents** button , and then click **Actual Pixels**.

5. Drag the horizontal scroll bar and the vertical scroll bar until the large tree is centered in the Document window. See Figure 1-31.

Figure 1-31   **Actual pixels display size (100%)**

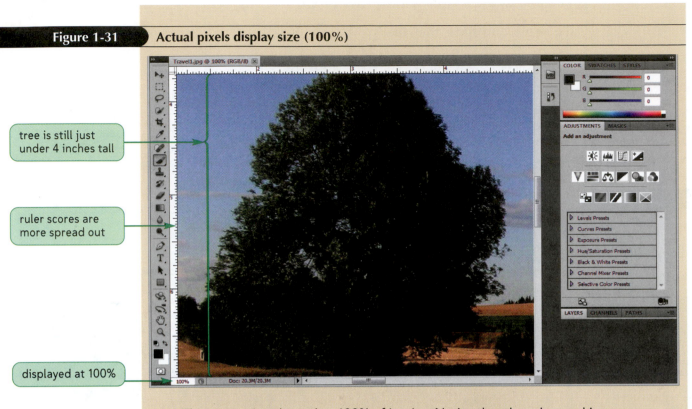

tree is still just under 4 inches tall

ruler scores are more spread out

displayed at 100%

The picture is enlarged to 100% of its size. Notice that the ruler markings are more spread out, and that the tree is still a little less than 4 inches tall.

6. Move the mouse pointer around the Document window. Notice that dotted lines along both rulers indicate the position of the mouse pointer as you move it. This feature is helpful in determining the exact point at which you begin making a selection or drawing a vector object.

7. Close **Travel1** without saving the file. When you close the file, the rulers disappear. Since they were displayed when the Travel1 file was open, the next time you open that file, they will be redisplayed.

You can change the **origin** of the rulers (where the number 0 appears) by pointing to the intersection of the rulers until a crosshair pointer appears, and then dragging diagonally down and to the right. The crosshairs indicate the new intersection of the rulers, and 0 appears at the spot where you release the mouse button. To reset the ruler, double-click the intersection of the rulers.

You can also work with the grid to help you align objects in a document, which you'll do next.

Showing and Hiding the Grid

The grid helps you align multiple objects, or arrange them exactly where you want them in your document. It can also help you make an exact selection. You show and hide the grid using commands on the View menu.

To show and hide the grid:

1. Open **Expert Text.psd** from the Photoshop1\Tutorial folder, click **View** on the menu, click **Fit on Screen**, and make sure the rulers are displayed.

Trouble? If you get a message about missing fonts, click the OK button and let Photoshop make a substitution.

2. On the Application bar, click **View**, point to **Show**, and then click **Grid**. Photoshop displays a pattern of equally spaced horizontal and vertical lines. These lines can be especially useful if you want to align two or more objects exactly.

   Photoshop uses the Layers panel to store different elements in a composition on layers that can be edited and manipulated separately. You'll select a layer on the Layers panel to move it.

3. On the Layers panel, click the **Layers** tab if necessary to expand the Layers panel, and then click the **Expert Insurance** layer to select it. You must always select a layer before you can work with it in Photoshop.

TIP

You can also press V to select the Move Tool.

4. Click the **Move Tool** on the Tools panel, if necessary, and then move the mouse pointer over the document. The move pointer appears.

5. Point to the **Expert Insurance text**, press and hold down the mouse button, and then drag the text to the left so that the *E* is aligned with the second vertical gridline.

6. On the Layers panel, click the **always a bright idea** layer to select it. The Move Tool is still active.

7. Point to the **always a bright idea** text, press and hold down the mouse button, and then drag the text to the right and up so that the *a* is aligned with the second vertical gridline (and also aligned with the *E* in Expert) and so that it sits on the gridline at 6½ inches on the vertical ruler. See Figure 1-32.

Figure 1-32   **Aligning objects on a grid**

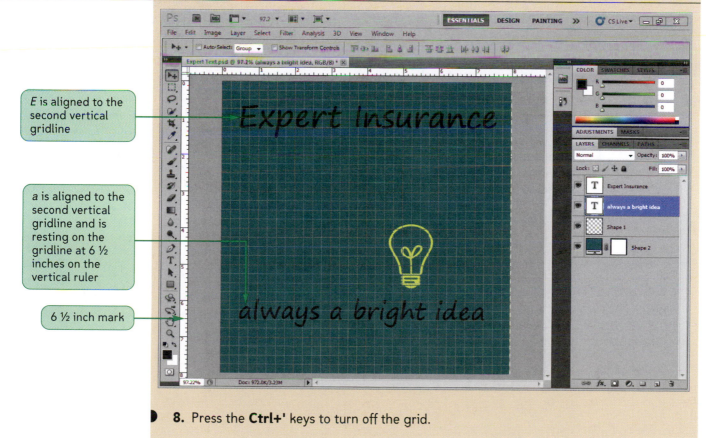

E is aligned to the second vertical gridline

a is aligned to the second vertical gridline and is resting on the gridline at 6 ½ inches on the vertical ruler

6 ½ inch mark

8. Press the **Ctrl+'** keys to turn off the grid.

INSIGHT

Snapping to the Grid and Guides

Photoshop includes a **Snap To** feature that lets you easily align objects with gridlines or guides. Snap To "magnetizes" the lines so that when you drag a selection or shape, or move an object, the object aligns to the closest gridlines or guides. This is a useful feature for placing objects, but it can be annoying if you are trying to draw, for example, a diagonal line. With Snap To turned on, the diagonal line looks more like a staircase than a line, as it follows the layout of the grid. You can turn Snap To on and off by clicking View on the Application bar, clicking Snap To, and then clicking the choice you want to turn on or off.

Turning on Guide Display and Adding Guides

Guides act in a similar manner to the grid; however, unlike grids, you can customize the location of guides and place them exactly where you want them. There are two ways to place guides in your document. You can use the View command on the Application bar, or you can drag guides from the rulers.

You'll experiment with guides as you continue to improve your Photoshop skills.

To turn on guide display and add guides:

1. Make sure that the rulers are visible. On the Application bar, click **View**, click **New Guide**, click the **Vertical** option button, if necessary, type **4** in the Position box, and then click the **OK** button. A vertical guide appears at 4 inches on the horizontal ruler and runs from the top of the Document window to the bottom.

   You can also add a guide by dragging from the ruler. To add a vertical guide, you drag from the vertical ruler. To add a horizontal guide, you drag from the horizontal ruler.

2. Point to the **horizontal ruler**, press and hold down the mouse button, and then drag down to the **4-inch mark** on the vertical ruler.

   Trouble? If the "always a bright idea" text moves when you drag, the Move Tool is still active, and you are not pointing to the ruler. Make sure the arrow pointer ▸⊕ appears before you drag.

3. Release the mouse button. Photoshop adds a horizontal guide to the Document window.

4. Click the **Shape 1** layer to select it in the Layers panel.

5. Drag the **light bulb** in the document so that it is centered at the intersection of the vertical and horizontal guides. See Figure 1-33.

Figure 1-33   **Using guides to position an object**

use the intersection of the guides to position the light bulb

Shape 1 layer is selected

6. Save the file as **Expert Text1.psd** in the Photoshop1\Tutorial folder included with your Data Files, and then close the file.

Using Tools on the Tools Panel

You might have noticed while you were working with panels earlier in this tutorial that there is one panel, the Tools panel, that appears on the left side of the window, whereas all of the other panels appear on the right by default. Because Photoshop provides so many tools on its Tools panel, some of the tools are grouped to improve your work flow. The triangle on the lower-right corner of a tool on the Tools panel indicates that there are additional tools, called a **tool group**, hidden beneath the tool you see on the panel. You display the hidden tools either by right-clicking the top tool (the tool that is displayed on the panel), or by pointing to the tool and pressing and holding the left mouse button until a shortcut menu of additional tool names appears.

Sarah explains that much of your work will involve fine-tuning images and that this kind of work might require you to zoom in and pan an image. You can find the tools for this kind of work on the Tools panel.

Selecting and Using Tools

You select a tool on the Tools panel by clicking it with the mouse. Some tools also have shortcut keys assigned. For example, earlier in this tutorial, you saw that pressing V activates the Move Tool. When you select a tool, the mouse pointer changes to reflect the selection.

To select and use a tool:

1. Open **Unexpected bolt.psd** from the Photoshop1\Tutorial folder included with your Data Files, and turn off the ruler display if necessary. Notice on the status bar that the photograph is displayed in the Document window at a low zoom percentage, depending on your monitor.

2. Click the **Zoom** Tool 🔍 on the Tools panel, and then move the mouse pointer over the photograph. The mouse pointer changes to a Zoom In pointer ⊕, a magnifying glass with a plus sign.

3. Click the center of the photograph. The photograph is enlarged in the window and centered at the place you clicked.

4. On the status bar in the lower left corner of the document window, click in the **zoom percentage** box, double-click the current zoom percentage to select it, type **300**, and then press the **Enter** key. The image zooms in again. Because the zoom percentage is so high, the image looks blurry, or pixelated.

5. Click the **Hand** Tool 🖐 on the Tools panel. The Hand Tool lets you drag a file within the Document window to display different areas.

6. Point to the center of the **lightning bolt**, and then drag the image all the way to the right until the lightning is no longer visible.

7. Click the **Zoom** Tool 🔍, press and hold the **Alt** key, and point to the center of the Document window. The Zoom In icon ⊕ changes to the Zoom Out icon ⊖ when you press the Alt key.

8. Click the **center** of the document. The image zooms out.

9. Press the **Ctrl+1** keys. The image zooms to 100%.

TIP

You can also press Z to activate the Zoom Tool.

TIP

You can also press H to select the Hand Tool.

INSIGHT

Changing the Zoom Level

When you work to modify individual pixels in an image—for example, to change their color—the zoom feature will be an important tool for your work. The maximum zoom percentage for an image is 3200%. You will rarely need to zoom in this much, but if you are doing extremely precise work—for example, pixel-by-pixel corrections on an image—the ability to zoom in this much is an advantage. You might also find that you need to zoom way out (decrease the zoom percentage) on a very large image in order to see the whole effect. The minimum zoom percentage is .36%, which you'll probably never use. However, it is often helpful to have this much flexibility in zooming in and zooming out on an image.

Using the Options Bar to Change Tool Settings

Many tools on the Tools panel let you modify the default options using the options bar, which appears beneath the Application bar in the Photoshop window. The options bar changes depending on which tool is selected in the Tools panel. Using the options bar, you can define custom settings for the tool.

Now that you're comfortable with the Photoshop environment, Sarah asks you to modify certain elements on the canvas. She would like you to start by erasing the faint lightning bolt near the Expert text in the Unexpected bolt image.

To use the options bar:

1. On the Layers panel, click **Layer 1** to select it, and then click the **Eraser** Tool on the Tools panel. The options bar displays the default settings for the Eraser Tool or the settings in effect the last time the tool was used.

2. On the left side of the options bar, right-click the **Eraser** icon , and then click **Reset Tool**. This command ensures that the default settings are in effect.

3. On the options bar, click the **Brush setting** arrow (to the right of the number 13) to open the Brush Preset picker. See Figure 1-34.

Figure 1-34   Eraser Tool settings and Brush Preset picker

Eraser Tool settings on options bar

click to display the Brush Preset picker

the Brush Size box

Eraser Tool

You can change the diameter of the brush by dragging the Size slider, by typing in the Size box, or by selecting one of the **brush presets**, which are commonly used Photoshop brush sizes. Presets are discussed later in this tutorial.

Trouble? If the Brush setting arrow isn't available, confirm that the mode is set to Brush and not Pencil or some other setting. To change the mode, click the Mode arrow, and then click Brush.

4. Type **100** in the Size box.

5. Click the **Brush Preset picker** button again to close the Brush Preset picker. You are now ready to use the Eraser Tool.

6. Position the **Eraser Tool** pointer over the bottom of the faint lightning bolt, and then click. The lightning disappears where you clicked.

7. Drag the **Eraser Tool** pointer over the lightning image until it has disappeared entirely. If you miss any parts of the lightning bolt, you can drag over the area again. The faint lightning bolt has been removed from the image. See Figure 1-35.

Figure 1-35	Using the Eraser Tool

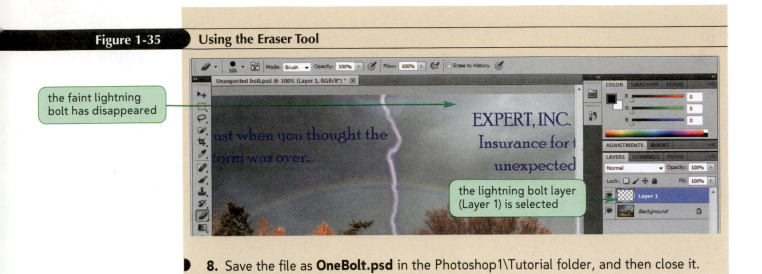

the faint lightning bolt has disappeared

the lightning bolt layer (Layer 1) is selected

8. Save the file as **OneBolt.psd** in the Photoshop1\Tutorial folder, and then close it.

Adding Content to the Canvas and Using Tool Presets

You can use the drawing tools on the Tools panel to add content to the canvas. **Tool presets** are custom settings for tools like text, brushes, gradients, shapes, or swatches that you can save and use again and again. You might want specific text—for example, a company name—to always appear in the same font and font color, no matter what document you are working in. You can set these options on the options bar for the Horizontal Type Tool and then save the settings as a preset. When you need the settings again, you can open the preset after you select the tool. Photoshop also comes with its own presets. For example, when you used the Eraser Tool earlier, you saw that it had Brush size presets associated with it.

Sarah wants you to work with custom shapes and add them to the canvas. She gives you an image of a rainbow and asks you to add a vector lightning bolt to the image for an insurance company campaign she's working on. To draw a lightning bolt, you can use the Custom Shape Tool, which is hidden under the Rectangle Tool on the Tools panel.

To add content to the canvas:

1. Open **RainbowInsurance.jpg** from the Photoshop1\Tutorial folder included with your Data Files.

2. Point to the **Rectangle** Tool 🔲 on the Tools panel and then press and hold down the left mouse button. Photoshop displays a list of hidden tools.

3. Click the **Custom Shape** Tool 🎨, and then reset the tool. The options bar displays the default settings for the Custom Shape tool.

4. On the options bar, click the **Custom Shape picker** button ▾ to open the Custom Shape picker. See Figure 1-36.

Figure 1-36   **Custom Shape picker**

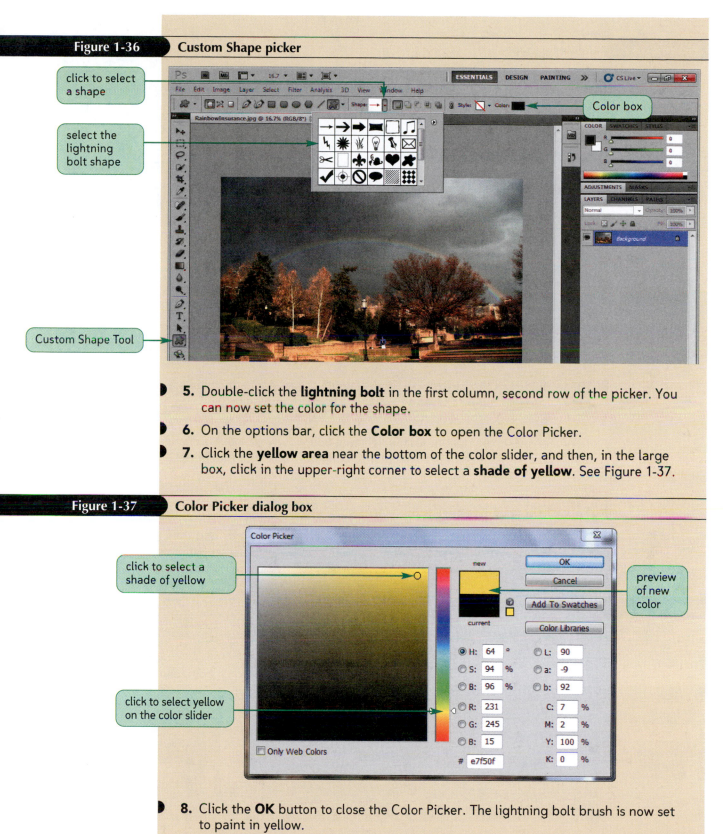

click to select a shape

select the lightning bolt shape

Color box

Custom Shape Tool

5. Double-click the **lightning bolt** in the first column, second row of the picker. You can now set the color for the shape.

6. On the options bar, click the **Color box** to open the Color Picker.

7. Click the **yellow area** near the bottom of the color slider, and then, in the large box, click in the upper-right corner to select a **shade of yellow**. See Figure 1-37.

Figure 1-37   **Color Picker dialog box**

click to select a shade of yellow

preview of new color

click to select yellow on the color slider

8. Click the **OK** button to close the Color Picker. The lightning bolt brush is now set to paint in yellow.

9. Drag from slightly to the left of the top center of the photograph down to the top of the person in the image, and then release the mouse button. You added a custom shape to the file. See Figure 1-38.

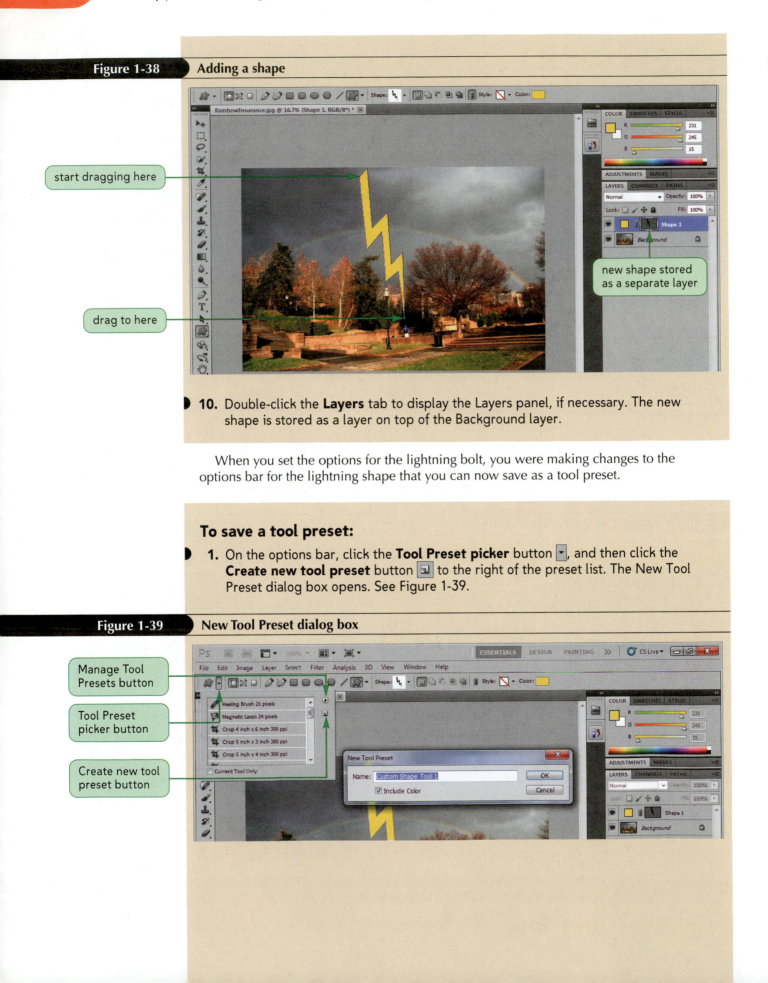

Figure 1-38 Adding a shape

start dragging here

drag to here

new shape stored as a separate layer

10. Double-click the **Layers** tab to display the Layers panel, if necessary. The new shape is stored as a layer on top of the Background layer.

When you set the options for the lightning bolt, you were making changes to the options bar for the lightning shape that you can now save as a tool preset.

To save a tool preset:

1. On the options bar, click the **Tool Preset picker** button , and then click the **Create new tool preset** button to the right of the preset list. The New Tool Preset dialog box opens. See Figure 1-39.

Figure 1-39 New Tool Preset dialog box

Manage Tool Presets button

Tool Preset picker button

Create new tool preset button

2. Type **bolt preset** in the Name box, click the **Include Color** check box to select it, if necessary, and then click the **OK** button. The preset is added to the Tool Preset picker list. See Figure 1-40.

Figure 1-40   Tool preset added to Tool Preset picker list

new tool preset

The next time you choose the Custom Shape Tool, the options will be set to a yellow lightning bolt by default.

3. Click the **Tool Preset picker** button again to close the list.

You might use a custom tool preset frequently on a particular project, but then find that you no longer need it once the project is finished. In that case, you can easily delete the custom tool preset from the Tool Preset picker list.

To delete a tool preset:

1. On the options bar, click the **Tool Preset picker** button .

2. Click the **bolt preset** on the list, click the **Manage Tool Presets** button to the right of the preset list, and then click **Delete Tool Preset**.

3. Save the file as **Rainbow.psd** in the Photoshop1\Tutorial folder, and then close it.

4. Exit Photoshop.

In this session, you learned how to set Photoshop Preferences and then to restore the default preferences. You also worked with different elements of the Photoshop interface, including panels, workspaces, and tools. You learned how to display and use the rulers, grid, and guides; how to customize and save a workspace; and how to define and use tool presets. You also added content to the canvas.

PROSKILLS

Decision Making: Understanding Permissions

If you don't have a photograph that's appropriate for the job you need to accomplish, the Web provides a limitless supply—or does it? Just because an image is easy to download from the Web, does that mean that it is free to use in any way you want? Think about it. If you are writing a paper for a class, it is easy to find online sources, but can you copy paragraphs wholesale and not give credit to the original author?

As you acquire images, keep in mind that similar copyright issues apply to photographs (as well as video, music, and sound files). You should always operate under the assumption that every image on the Web is protected by copyright. Therefore, before you use someone else's work, find out if you need to obtain permission for its use, give credit or **attribution**, or pay a fee. You might be required to pay a **royalty** each time you use an image. Images that are **royalty-free** may still require payment, but usually it's a one-time fee. Some photographers assign a flexible copyright license that allows others to use their work. This might seem like an easy agreement to follow, but even a color correction would constitute an alteration, and would be copyright infringement if the photographer did not grant the right to modify the photograph. Some government images, and older works that are no longer protected by copyright law are in the **public domain**, and can be used however you want.

As you search for images to use in your work, you need to keep all of these issues in mind and make sure to read any licensing agreements or conditions posted by the owner of the photograph before you download an image. Two of the best resources for finding images you might be able to use are *morguefile.com* and Creative Commons at *www.creativecommons.org*.

By taking the time to understand copyright law and any pertinent licensing agreements, you can make the right decisions about the images you use in your projects.

REVIEW

Session 1.2 Quick Check

1. The Preferences command can be found on the _____ menu.
2. A _____ displays a group of panels one on top of the other using tabs.
3. A _____ is a collection of panels or panel groups joined top to bottom and sharing a title bar.
4. You can modify a predefined workspace in Photoshop and save it as a _____ workspace.
5. The _____ divides your document into squares that you can also use for guidance as you draw, move, and place objects in a document.
6. _____ are lines that you can add to the Document window to aid in aligning and moving objects.
7. True or False. Any image that you can easily download from the Web is free to use in any manner.

Review Assignments

Data Files needed for the Review Assignments: FireUnlit.psd, LightningInsurance.psd, Unexpected.psd

Sarah has given you some of the files that she plans to use in the Expert Insurance campaign so that you can use them to familiarize yourself with the Photoshop interface, toolbars, and commands. She would also like you to create an image using a photograph of a campfire that she can use to present to her client as an idea for a new ad. Complete the following steps:

1. Start Photoshop while pressing the Ctrl+Alt+Shift keys. When you are prompted to delete the Adobe Photoshop Settings File, click Yes.
2. Open the **FireUnlit.psd**, **LightningInsurance.psd**, and **Unexpected.psd** files located in the Photoshop1\Review folder provided with your Data Files.
3. Save Unexpected as **RevUnexpected.psd** and FireUnlit as **FireLit.psd** in the Photoshop1\Review folder.
4. Switch to a 2 Up view of the files, and then switch back to the Consolidate All view to view a single file in the Document window.
5. Open the original files, **Unexpected.psd** and **FireUnlit.psd**, so that you have five files open in the Document window.
6. Switch to the FireLit file.
7. Rearrange the tabs so that both Unexpected files are next to each other and both Fire files are next to each other. Press the Alt+Print Screen keys to capture an image of the current Photoshop window; then open WordPad, which is available on the Accessories menu of the All Programs menu in Windows 7; and press the Ctrl+V keys to paste the image into a new file. Save the WordPad file as **PSTabs.rtf** in the Photoshop1\Review folder provided with your Data Files.
8. Display FireUnlit in a maximized, free-floating Document window.
9. Stack the Color, Swatches, and Styles panel group on top of the Layers panel group on the left side of the Document window. Press the Alt+Print Screen keys to capture an image of the current Photoshop window, switch to WordPad, and then press the Ctrl+V keys to paste the image into the PSTabs file you created in Step 6.
10. Consolidate all of the documents in the Document window with the FireLit file on top, and then switch to the Photography workspace.
11. Change the Guides, Grid, & Slices preferences so that the Grid color is Medium Blue, and then display the grid.
12. Reset the workspace to the default Essentials workspace.
13. Display the rulers; and then, in the FireLit file, add a horizontal guide at 4 ½ inches on the vertical ruler; add a vertical guide at 6 inches on the horizontal ruler. Use the Custom Shape Tool to add a shape that looks like fire on top of the wood. (*Hint*: Use the Grass 2 custom shape, which is in the second row, third column of the Custom Shape picker, and assign it an orange color to look like fire.)
14. With the Shape 1 layer selected, use the Move Tool to center the drawing at the intersection of the horizontal and vertical guides, and then press Enter. Press the Alt+Print Screen keys to capture an image of the current Photoshop window, switch to WordPad, and press the Ctrl+V keys to paste the image into the PSTabs file you created in Step 6.
15. Save your work in the **PSTabs.rtf** file, and then close WordPad.
16. Save your work in the **FireLit.psd** file, and then exit Photoshop.
17. Submit the results of the preceding steps to your instructor either in printed or electronic form, as requested.

Use your skills to create a magazine ad for an investment firm.

APPLY

Case Problem 1

Data File needed for this Case Problem: Australia.psd

Safe Harbour Securities Maria Velasco, the marketing manager at Safe Harbour Securities, wants to place an ad for the company in a travel magazine. She asks you to create a mock-up for a magazine ad that would appeal to readers of a travel magazine. Complete the following steps:

1. Start Photoshop while pressing the Ctrl+Alt+Shift keys. When you are prompted to delete the Adobe Photoshop Settings File, click Yes.
2. Open the **Australia.psd** file located in the Photoshop1\Case1 folder provided with your Data Files, and then save the file as **SafeHarbour.psd** in the same folder.
3. Display the image at 100% magnification, and show the rulers.
4. Add guides at 2 ½ inches on the horizontal ruler and at 5 ½ inches on the vertical ruler.
5. Use the Custom Shape Tool to draw a light blue heart so that it is centered at the intersection of the horizontal and vertical guides.
6. Select the text layer, and move the **Safe Harbour Securities** text to the right of the heart so that the top line of text is resting on the horizontal guide.
7. Add guides at 8 ½ inches on the horizontal ruler and 1 inch on the vertical ruler.
8. Use the Custom Shape Tool to add a yellow flower shape in the upper right corner of the image, at the intersection of the two guides you just added.
9. Turn off the display of the guides to see what your ad will look like in final form.
10. Turn on the grid, and then turn the guides back on.
11. Save your work, and then exit Photoshop.
12. Submit the results of the preceding steps to your instructor, either in printed or electronic form, as requested.

Use Help to learn about and use tools to modify a photograph for a restaurant.

CHALLENGE

Case Problem 2

Data File needed for this Case Problem: Sundae.psd

Yaya's Restaurant Yaya Krishna, the owner of Yaya's Restaurant, wants to modify a photograph of an ice cream sundae so that she can place it on a different background for an upcoming ad. She asks you to help her make the necessary changes. Yaya thinks the Magic Eraser Tool will do what she wants, but she suggests that you research the tool in Help before using it. Complete the following steps:

1. Start Photoshop while pressing the Ctrl+Alt+Shift keys. When you are prompted to delete the Adobe Photoshop Settings File, click Yes.
2. Open the **Sundae.psd** file, located in the Photoshop1\Case 2 folder provided with your Data Files. Save the file as **Yayas.psd** in the same folder.

⊕ **EXPLORE** 3. Search Community Help for the Magic Eraser Tool. Read the information provided by Adobe. (*Hint*: The topic should be called "Change similar pixels with the Magic Eraser Tool.")

⊕ **EXPLORE** 4. Use the Magic Eraser Tool to erase the black around the Sundae layer. Experiment with Tolerance levels to make sure you erase the black, but not the dark areas of the sundae dish and sauce. (*Hint*: If you make a mistake, press the Ctrl+Z keys to undo your last action.)

5. Display the rulers and add guides at 6 inches on the horizontal ruler and 5 inches on the vertical ruler.

6. Select the Shape 2 layer, and move the crown so that it's centered on the image.

EXPLORE

7. Select the Show Transform Controls check box on the Move Tool options bar. Expand the crown by dragging a corner control until the crown is large enough to cover the sundae, and then center it again. When the crown is centered, press the Enter key to accept the size and position change.

EXPLORE

8. Click the Paint Bucket Tool on the Tools panel. (*Hint:* The Paint Bucket Tool is hidden beneath the Gradient Tool on the Tools panel.) Press X to switch the foreground and background colors so that the foreground color is white. On the Layer 0 layer, click the black band surrounding the text with the Paint Bucket Tool pointer to change the black band to white.

9. On the Sundae layer, use the Paint Bucket Tool to change the area surrounding the sundae to white.

10. Save your work, and then exit Photoshop.

11. Submit the results of the preceding steps to your instructor, either in printed or electronic form, as requested.

Using Figure 1-41 as a guide, enhance a photograph for a placement agency.

CREATE

Case Problem 3

Data File needed for this Case Problem: Airplane.psd

Career Centers Fiona Friedman runs a careers placement agency and wants to create a new brochure to promote her company. She asks you to modify a photograph that includes the company's trademark phrase so she can use the new image as the cover for the brochure. Figure 1-41 shows the final result.

Figure 1-41 **Career Centers image**

Complete the following steps:

1. Start Photoshop while pressing the Ctrl+Alt+Shift keys. When you are prompted to delete the Adobe Photoshop Settings File, click Yes.
2. Open the **Airplane.psd** file, located in the Photoshop1\Case3 folder provided with your Data Files, and then save the file as **Careers.psd** in the same folder. Make sure that you are using the Essentials workspace.
3. Zoom the image to fit on the screen.
4. Show the rulers, and add guides to the Document window, as shown in Figure 1-41.
5. Select the Background layer, and then add the blue shape shown in the figure.
6. Save the shape settings as a preset named **Bubble**.
7. Drag the **Where do you want to go?** text so that it is centered in the blue shape. Use the guides to position the text as shown in the figure.
8. Reset all of the tools. (*Hint*: On the options bar, right-click the Move Tool icon, and click Reset All Tools.)
9. Drag the **Career Centers** text to position it as shown in the figure.
10. Select the Horizontal Type Tool on the Tools panel, reset the tool, click in the upper left side of the image, and then type your name. Drag your name so that it is centered at the 1-inch mark on the horizontal ruler and the half inch mark on the vertical ruler.
11. Delete the Bubble tool preset.
12. Save your work, and then exit Photoshop.
13. Submit the results of the preceding steps to your instructor, either in printed or electronic form, as requested.

Using Figure 1-42 as a guide, enhance a photograph for a travel agency.

CREATE

Case Problem 4

Data File needed for this Case Problem: ExploreMore.psd

Explore More Travel   Hamid Brahim has hired you to help him with a new advertising campaign for his travel agency. He asks you to add text and drawings to a photograph that he has already "posterized," or adjusted to look like a painting rather than a photograph. Figure 1-42 shows the final result.

Figure 1-42   Explore More Travel image

Complete the following steps:

1. Start Photoshop while pressing the Ctrl+Alt+Shift keys. When you are prompted to delete the Adobe Photoshop Settings File, click Yes.
2. Open the **ExploreMore.psd** file located in the Photoshop1\Case 1 folder provided with your Data Files, and save the file as **Footprints.psd** in the same folder.
3. Zoom the image so that it fills the document window.
4. Change Preferences so that the color of guides is Light Red.
5. Add guides to the Document window, as shown in Figure 1-42.
6. Draw a yellow starburst at the position indicated by the guides in the figure.
7. Draw three footprints at the positions indicated in the figure.

8. Zoom the image to 300%, and then pan until the starburst is at the center of the screen.

9. Press the Alt+Print Screen keys to capture an image of the current Photoshop window, then open WordPad and press Ctrl+V to paste the image into a new file. Save the file as **Starburst.rtf** in the Photoshop1\Review folder provided with your Data Files. Close WordPad.

10. Change the zoom to 95%.

11. Save your work, and close the file.

12. Submit the results of the preceding steps to your instructor either in printed or electronic form, as requested.

ENDING DATA FILES

Photoshop1 → **Tutorial**

Expert Text1.psd
newUnexpected.psd
OneBolt.psd
Rainbow.psd

Review

FireLit.psd
PSTabs.rtf
RevUnexpected.psd

Case1

SafeHarbour.psd

Case2

Yayas.psd

Case3

Careers.psd

Case4

Footprints.psd
Starburst.rtf

OBJECTIVES

Session 2.1
- Learn about file formats and their uses
- Change file type, file size, and resolution
- Examine Bridge and Mini Bridge
- Understand and change color modes
- Create new files using document presets and custom settings
- Place an image in a new file

Session 2.2
- Make image adjustments
- Change canvas size
- Zoom and pan an image
- Rotate and flip an image

Working with Image Files

Working with File Sizes, Color Modes, and Image Adjustments

Case | *GreenHouse Construction*

GreenHouse Construction is an environmental construction firm in Fort Myers, Florida, founded in 1992 by C.J. Kohl. The company designs "green" homes and buildings, so its building plans usually include features such as photovoltaic (solar) panels, automatic dimming fluorescent lights, double-paned windows, rooftop gardens, and plenty of natural lighting.

In the past, C.J. has created his own promotional materials. However, he feels he needs help updating the materials to broaden his client base. He wants you to work with him on campaigns for both Web and print advertising. As you do, you'll explore various file sizes and color modes, and determine which resolutions are best for which media. You'll also place images in files, make adjustments to images, and modify canvas and image size.

STARTING DATA FILES

Tutorial

GreenDream.psd
GreenHouseConstruction.tif
GreenHouseText.psd
GreenHouseText2.psd
HeatCosts.psd
HeatCosts2.psd
Hi_Res.jpg
LeaderboardText.psd
Sun.psd
WireCutter.jpg
Wrench.jpg

Review

GreenHouseText.psd
Hammer.psd

Case1

ConcertHall.jpg

Case2

Eye.tif
EyeMask.psd

Case3

Mash.jpg
RockNRoll.psd

Case4

Cakes.jpg
FinnText.psd
FinnText2.psd

SESSION 2.1 VISUAL OVERVIEW

A JPEG is one type of **file format**, which determines how the information (or data) in your file is organized when it is stored on a storage device, such as a camera's memory card, a hard drive, or a flash drive.

When you save a JPEG file, you can specify the Quality setting, which determines the file size. The lower the Quality setting, the more Photoshop will **compress** the image, which reduces the file size.

You can select an option for how the file will load in a Web browser.

Photoshop previews the file size based on the JPEG settings you specify.

The Image Size dialog box provides options for changing the image size, resolution, and interpolation method, among other things.

When you change the resolution of an image, Photoshop **resamples** the image, which changes the number of pixels in the image.

The **interpolation method** determines how Photoshop will add or subtract pixels when you resample an image.

FILE FORMAT AND SIZE OPTIONS

Set the dimensions, resolution, color mode, and bit depth of a new file manually or use a preset.

Select a document preset to create a new file.

Use the New dialog box to set basic file specifications when creating a new document in Photoshop.

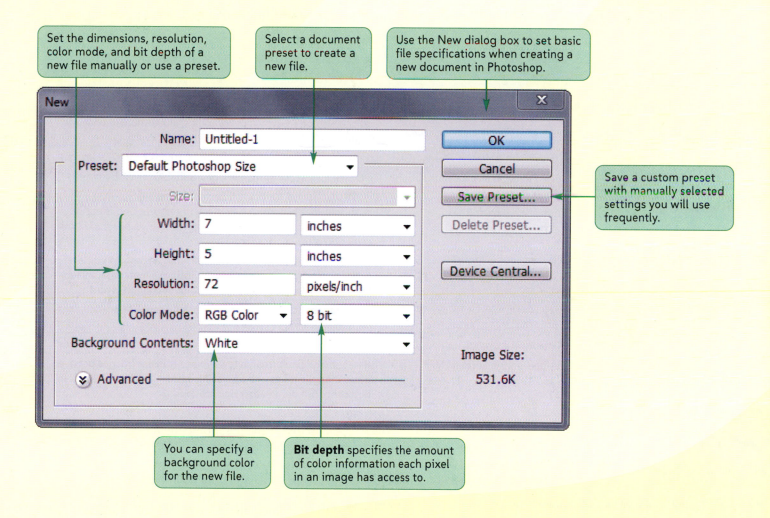

Save a custom preset with manually selected settings you will use frequently.

You can specify a background color for the new file.

Bit depth specifies the amount of color information each pixel in an image has access to.

Understanding File Formats and Their Uses

You can open and save images in well over a dozen file formats in Photoshop. In an image-editing program like Photoshop, the file format, or file type, also determines how much space an image takes up in memory, how it handles color, and how it is printed as output.

Although files with different formats might look the same in the Photoshop Document window, certain characteristics of each format can affect things like upload time on the Web, the print quality of a finished piece, and even the Photoshop features you can use to manipulate the file. The number of file formats might seem overwhelming at first, but as you continue to work with Photoshop, you'll find that choosing the right file format will eventually be second nature. Figure 2-1 summarizes some commonly used file formats.

Figure 2-1   **File formats**

Format	Details
Bitmap (BMP)	Bitmap image file format for Windows; does not support CMYK color
Encapsulated PostScript (EPS)	File format that supports both vector and bitmap graphics; can be used for high-quality printouts on a PostScript printer; and can also be read by most graphics, illustration, and layout programs
Graphics Interchange Format (GIF)	Lossless file format for bitmap images; suitable for Web images
Joint Photographic Experts Group (JPEG or JPG)	Lossy file format for bitmap images; suitable for Web images; and supports CMYK, RGB, and Grayscale
Photoshop format (PSD)	File format that supports all Photoshop features and is easily imported by other Creative Suite applications; can include both vector and bitmap graphics
Photoshop Raw (RAW)	File format that allows you to transfer images between different applications and operating systems; includes metadata, including camera type and exposure, but cannot contain layers
Portable Document Format (PDF)	File format that can display images in different applications and operating systems
Portable Network Graphics (PNG)	Lossless file format for bitmap images; suitable for Web images
Tagged Image Format (TIFF, TIF)	Bitmap image file format; allows you to transfer images between different applications and operating systems; supports layers in Photoshop, but not in other applications

Each file format has its own advantages and disadvantages. Some file formats support only vector graphics, whereas others support only bitmap graphics. **PSD**, the default Photoshop format, stands for Photoshop document. The PSD format can store both vector and bitmap data and stores multiple image components and enhancements on separate elements called **layers** so that you can make changes to one part of a composition while leaving the other parts intact. **GIF** (Graphics Interchange Format), **PNG** (Portable Network Graphics), and **JPEG** (Joint Photographic Experts Group, sometimes written as JPG) formats are **flat formats** consisting of single layers. These file types are best for the Web because they tend to have smaller file sizes, so they upload more quickly. Other file types, such as **TIFF** (Tagged Image File Format) and **EPS** (Encapsulated Postscript), contain a great deal of data and are used to output high-quality print pieces.

Some file formats are **proprietary**, meaning that they can only be edited in the program in which they were created. For example, the PSD file extension is a proprietary extension that indicates that the file is **native** to, or created in, Photoshop. PSD files can be easily manipulated in other Adobe products like Adobe Illustrator, Adobe Flash, and Adobe Fireworks, but many drawing, Web design, and image-editing programs do not support the PSD file format. If you need to use a file you have created in Photoshop in a program that doesn't support PSD files, you must save it in a compatible format so that you can open and manipulate it in the other application. When you convert a file to another format, you might lose some features—for example, Photoshop layers—that are supported in the original file. However, you also gain some benefits, such as the ability to use a file in many different applications. You can save an image in different formats for use in different media, such as in a four-color printed piece, on a Web page, or in a newspaper advertisement.

Changing File Type, File Size, and Resolution

In Photoshop, you have the flexibility to change the properties of a file not only by changing its file type, but also by changing its file size and its resolution. There are a number of ways to do this, including compressing a file and resampling a file. As you learn the nuances of the different file types in Photoshop, you'll be able to achieve the results you want for each project by using the appropriate file type, size, and resolution.

Optimizing an Image

When you edit or enhance images in Photoshop, each layer of editing you add can increase the size of a file by many megabytes. Larger file sizes are a necessity if you want to print high-quality images. To achieve the most accurate colors and the sharpest printout, you need the layers of detail and color data stored with an image. However, on the Web, large image file sizes can result in painfully slow download times for the end user, as well as file storage challenges. Because of this, images on Web sites are often compressed to allow for quicker download times. Finding the right balance between image quality and file size is called **optimization**.

Three image file formats commonly used on the Web are GIF, JPEG, and PNG. These formats all use compression to optimize images and reduce the size of image files. The JPEG format uses **lossy compression** to reduce file size by throwing out, or "losing" some of the original data in an image. For example, it reduces the number of colors in an image and uses a process called **dithering** to replace the discarded colors with colors from the new, smaller color palette. A file format that uses lossy compression is called a **lossy file format**. The GIF file format is a **lossless file format**; it uses **lossless** compression, which means it doesn't discard data when it compresses the file. Instead, it stores data more efficiently—for example, by mapping all colors to a color table instead of storing each pixel's color information with the pixel itself.

It's wise to make edits to an image file while working in a high-resolution, non-lossy format. Doing so gives you more editing options. Then, when the image is finished, you can optimize the image by saving it in a file format, such as JPEG, that is better suited to Web use. When you save a file as a JPEG, the JPEG Options dialog box opens, as shown in Figure 2-2.

Figure 2-2 JPEG Options dialog box

In the JPEG Options dialog box, you can select the **matte**, which is the color that will appear in the background of an image as it downloads while a user is trying to view it on the Web. You can also specify the quality of the image. The lower the quality, the smaller the file size and the faster the download time; however, you should always confirm that you haven't compromised the image quality on your Web site for the sake of a smaller file size. The JPEG Options dialog box offers three format options, including Baseline ("Standard"), which saves the file in a format most browsers can read. Baseline Optimized optimizes the color and results in a smaller than standard file size; however, not all browsers support optimized images. The Progressive format option results in an image that will initially be displayed with little detail, and then increase in detail as the file loads. In other words, it will appear as the ghost of an image, and then be filled in as the file loads. With the Progressive format option, you can specify three, four, or five **scans**, or stages, that the viewer will see before the image has finished loading. If you select the Preview check box, Photoshop calculates the approximate size of the file based on the selections you have made and displays it beneath the check box.

C.J. has an image that he'd like to use on the company's Web site. He asks you to save the file in a format that is suitable for Web use. You'll save the file as a JPEG and then use the JPEG Options dialog box to see the effect that compression has on file size.

TIP

Always keep a copy of the original, unedited image file so that it is available for other projects.

To save the file in a lossy file format:

1. Start Photoshop while pressing the **Ctrl+Alt+Shift** keys. When you are prompted to delete the Adobe Photoshop Settings File, click **Yes**. On the Application bar, right-click **Essentials**, click **Reset Essentials** to reset the default Essentials workspace layout. On the options bar, right-click the **Rectangular Marquee Tool** icon , and then click **Reset All Tools**. When you are asked if you want to reset all tools to the default settings, click the **OK** button.

2. On the Application bar, click **File**, and then click **Open** to display the Open dialog box.

3. Navigate to the Photoshop2\Tutorial folder included with your Data Files, click the **View Menu** button in the Open dialog box, and then click **Details** to select it, if necessary.

4. Click **GreenHouseConstruction.tif**. Scroll to the right, if necessary, to see the Size column. Notice that this file is large, over 19 megabytes.

   Trouble? If the Size column does not appear in the Open dialog box, right-click any column header and then click Size on the shortcut menu to add the Size column to the dialog box.

5. Click **Open**. The GreenHouseConstruction.tif file opens in the Photoshop Document window.

   Trouble? If you get a message about missing fonts, click the OK button, and let Photoshop make the substitution.

6. Click the **Layers panel** tab, if necessary, to expand the Layers panel. The TIFF file has many layers, including a text layer with special effects and a shape layer. You'll learn more about layers in Tutorial 3. Preserving these layers in a TIFF file lets you modify them at a later point.

7. On the Application bar, click **File**, and then click **Save As**. The Save As dialog box opens with the Layers check box selected, indicating that the file includes layers.

8. Click the **Format** arrow, and then click **JPEG (*.JPG, *.JPEG, *.JPE)** in the list of available image file formats. The filename changes to GreenHouseContruction.jpg. See Figure 2-3.

| Figure 2-3 | Save As dialog box |

.jpg extension is added when you select the JPEG format

Photoshop will save the file as a copy and keep the original open

Layers check box is no longer available, and Photoshop displays a warning icon

When you select JPEG, the Layers check box is cleared and is no longer available; at the bottom of the dialog box, next to an exclamation point, Photoshop indicates that the file must be saved as a copy. When Photoshop saves the file, it will save it with the same name plus a .jpg extension in the current folder, but it will keep the original TIFF file open. To see the saved file, you'll need to open it in Photoshop.

9. Navigate to the Photoshop2\Tutorial folder included with your Data Files, if necessary, and click **Save**. The JPEG Options dialog box opens, as shown in Figure 2-4.

Figure 2-4 JPEG Options dialog box

click the Quality arrow to change the setting to Medium

select the Baseline Optimized option

preview the file size here; your file size may vary slightly

If you save the file with the default JPEG settings, the file size is reduced to around 471 kilobytes, as shown under the Preview check box in the JPEG Options dialog box. This is a fraction of the original TIFF file size. Next, you'll see what effect changing the Quality and Format Options has on file size.

10. Click the **Quality** arrow, click **Medium**, and then, under Format Options, click **Baseline Optimized**. Photoshop previews the file size at around 298 kilobytes.

Trouble? If you can't see the file size in the JPEG Options dialog box, click the Preview check box to select it and show the file size.

The new file size is only about 60 percent as large as the file size that results from using the default settings in the JPEG Options dialog box. It is also only 2 percent of the original 19 MB file size. This difference should give you a very clear idea of how important optimization can be when you prepare images for the Web.

11. Click the **OK** button. Photoshop saves a copy of the file in JPEG format. The original version of the file, in TIFF format, remains open. To view the JPEG version, you need to open the new file.

Next, you'll open the file so that you can show C.J. that in spite of the huge difference in file size, the images look very similar on screen.

To compare the two GreenHouseConstruction files:

1. On the Application bar, click **File**, and then click **Open**. Notice that the file size of the JPEG file is even smaller than it was in the preview, and is listed at around 284 KB. This is because when Photoshop saves the file to disk, it compresses it even more. When you open it, it will expand slightly in memory for better display, and return to about 298 KB. Your file sizes may vary.

2. Double-click the **GreenHouseConstruction.jpg** file to open it. Notice on the Layers panel that this file consists of a single layer labeled *Background*.

Trouble? If you can't see the Layers panel, click the Layers panel tab to expand the panel.

3. On the Application bar, click the **Arrange Documents** button 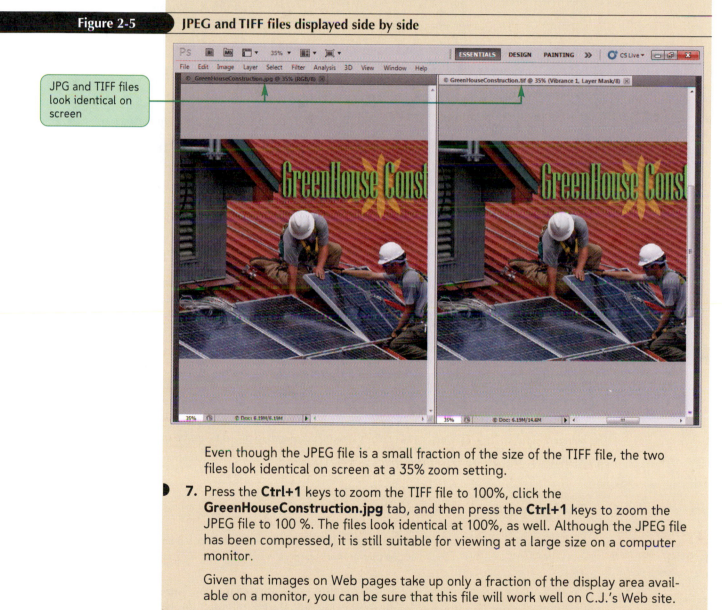, and then click the vertical **2 Up** button.

4. Press the **Tab** key to hide all panels so that the images appear larger.

5. On the status bar of the GreenHouseConstruction.jpg window, type **35** in the zoom percentage box, and then press the **Enter** key to zoom GreenHouseConstruction.jpg to 35%.

6. On the status bar of the GreenHouseConstruction.tif window, type **35** in the zoom percentage box, and then press the **Enter** key to zoom GreenHouseConstruction.tif to 35%. See Figure 2-5.

Figure 2-5   **JPEG and TIFF files displayed side by side**

JPG and TIFF files look identical on screen

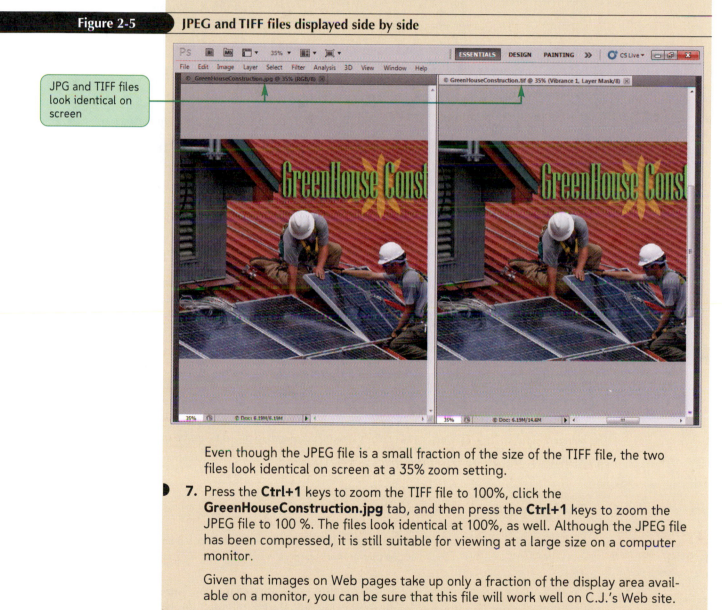

Even though the JPEG file is a small fraction of the size of the TIFF file, the two files look identical on screen at a 35% zoom setting.

7. Press the **Ctrl+1** keys to zoom the TIFF file to 100%, click the **GreenHouseConstruction.jpg** tab, and then press the **Ctrl+1** keys to zoom the JPEG file to 100 %. The files look identical at 100%, as well. Although the JPEG file has been compressed, it is still suitable for viewing at a large size on a computer monitor.

Given that images on Web pages take up only a fraction of the display area available on a monitor, you can be sure that this file will work well on C.J.'s Web site.

8. Close GreenHouseConstruction.tif. Leave the GreenHouseConstruction.jpg file open, and press the **Tab** key to redisplay the panels.

Changing Image Resolution

Because different projects require files with different resolutions, Photoshop gives you the option of changing the resolution of a file. To change resolution, you open the Image Size dialog box and type in a new value. See Figure 2-6.

| Figure 2-6 | Image Size dialog box |

- pixel dimensions
- document size
- change resolution here
- select Resample Image to change the number of pixels in the image
- select Scale Styles so any applied styles still fit when the image resolution or size changes
- select Constrain Proportions to ensure that the height changes proportionally when you change the width and vice versa

Remember that resolution is defined as pixels per inch, so when you change resolution, you are changing the number of pixels per inch. Photoshop uses a process called resampling to achieve the new resolution. You can resample an image in two different directions, depending on whether you want to decrease or increase the resolution. If you **upsample** an image, Photoshop adds pixels to the image so that there are more pixels per inch. It does this using a mathematical algorithm that uses interpolation to calculate what each added pixel should look like based on the surrounding pixels. The different interpolation methods are outlined in Figure 2-7.

| Figure 2-7 | Interpolation methods |

Method	Details
Nearest Neighbor	Makes exact copies of pixels when upsampling; can result in jagged edges
Bilinear	Averages the color values of surrounding pixels to create new pixels
Bicubic	The default interpolation method; uses complex calculations to determine values for new pixels; higher quality than Nearest Neighbor or Bilinear; best choice for most images
Bicubic Smoother	Uses more complex calculations to calculate values for new pixels; higher quality than Nearest Neighbor, Bilinear, or Bicubic
Bicubic Sharper	Sharpens an image using a calculation similar to Bicubic Smoother; can result in edges that are too sharp

TIP

Although you can upsample a low-resolution digital image to increase the dimensions of a photo, you'll achieve higher quality results if you simply start with a high-resolution image.

Upsampling can't improve the quality of a blurry image because the interpolation algorithm can only use the information already contained in the file. If the existing pixels display an imperfect image, the upsampled image will be imperfect as well. If you **downsample** an image by decreasing the resolution, Photoshop throws out pixels to keep the document the same physical dimensions—for example, 6 × 4 inches.

What do you think might happen to the size of a file if you decrease the number of pixels per inch by downsampling? Rather than thinking in terms of pixels, think of a high-resolution photograph as a bucket of pebbles—with dozens of evenly spaced pebbles completely covering the bottom of the bucket. Now consider what happens to the weight of the bucket when you take some pebbles out so that the remaining pebbles are still evenly spaced, but no longer touching—the bucket will be lighter. When you downsample, you are decreasing the resolution (you have fewer pixels per inch), which results in a "lighter" file.

PPI vs. DPI

Note that *ppi*, or pixels per inch, is different from the *dpi* (dots per inch) setting used to describe printer resolution. On a printer, one pixel can be created by multiple dots, depending on the resolution of your printer. In other words, there is not a one-to-one correspondence between ppi and dpi. A resolution of 300 ppi is excellent for a high-quality print piece, but 300 dpi could result in a grainy-looking printout if an image includes many different color gradations. An image with a resolution of 300 pixels per inch printed on a high-resolution printer might very well have 1200, or even 2880, dots per inch. It is a good idea to make sure everyone involved in a project is using these terms correctly so the final output quality meets the project's requirements.

You can also decrease the resolution of an image without resampling to increase the physical dimensions of your image. For example, you can change the resolution of a 4 × 6-inch photograph from 300 ppi to 150 ppi. If you deselect Resample Image in the Image Size dialog box, Photoshop will achieve the new resolution by spreading out the pixels over a larger area. Cutting the resolution in half will result in an image that is twice the dimensions of the original—or, using this example, 8 × 12 inches. This decrease in resolution will *not* result in a smaller file size because the image will still have the same number of pixels. If we return to the bucket analogy, you'll be carrying around a bucket with the same number of pebbles in it, but the bucket itself will be twice the size of the original, and the pebbles will be more spread out. Depending on your needs, this method might produce an acceptable image. However, if you plan to use the image in a printed piece, remember that spreading out pixels can result in poorer image quality.

Changing Image Resolution Using Resampling
- On the Application bar, click Image, and then click Image Size.
- Confirm that the Resample Image check box is selected.
- Type a new value in the Resolution box.
- Click the OK button to change the resolution.
- Save the file with a new filename.

You'll experiment with different resolution settings so that you are familiar with the different options available for the various advertising media C.J. plans to use.

To change the resolution of the GreenHouseConstructon.jpg image using resampling:

1. Make sure that the GreenHouseConstruction.jpg file is open in Photoshop at 100% magnification.

2. On the Application bar, click **Image**, and then click **Image Size**. The Image Size dialog box opens. It displays the Pixel Dimensions of the image (1800 pixels wide × 1202 pixels high). It also displays the Document Size, which is the size at which the image is currently set to print. At present, the document size is about 6 × 4 inches.

3. Click the **Resample Image** check box to select it, if necessary. Highlight **300** in the Resolution box to select it, and then type **150**. Leave the default interpolation method, Bicubic (best for smooth gradients), unchanged. See Figure 2-8.

Figure 2-8	Changing the resolution

Pixel Dimensions have changed after resampling

press the Alt key to make this the Reset button

new resolution

Trouble? If you make a mistake while working in the Image Size dialog box, hold down the Alt key and then click the Reset button in the dialog box to return to the original settings.

When the Resample Image option is selected, Photoshop throws out pixels to reach the lower resolution (fewer pixels per inch). The pixel dimensions are now 900 × 601, or exactly half the pixel dimensions of the 300 ppi image.

4. Click the **OK** button, and then press the **Ctrl+0** keys to fit the image on the screen.

Trouble? If the Open dialog box appears, you pressed the letter O instead of the number zero. Click the Cancel button to close the dialog box and press the Ctrl+0 keys.

Be sure to save the file with the new name so you still have a copy of the original high resolution file, which you'll need for later steps.

5. Save the file as **GreenHouseConstruction 150ppi.jpg** in the Photoshop2\Tutorial folder included with your Data Files, and then click the **OK** button to accept the settings in the JPEG Options dialog box.

A resolution of 150 ppi will be appropriate for a newspaper ad or for a 4 × 6-inch photograph printed on your home printer. You can also resave the file at a lower resolution appropriate for Web graphics.

6. On the Application bar, click **Image**, and then click **Image Size**.

7. Highlight **150** in the Resolution box to select it, and then type **72**. The pixel dimensions are now 432 × 289, or a little less than half the pixel dimensions of the 150 ppi image. This resolution will be sufficient for displaying the construction image on the Web.

8. Click the **OK** button, and then save the file as **GreenHouseConstruction 72ppi.jpg** in the Photoshop2\Tutorial folder using the current JPEG settings.

9. Close GreenHouseConstruction 72ppi.jpg.

PROSKILLS

Decision Making: What Is the Best Resolution for Your Needs?

You already know that the resolution you need for an image is determined by how you plan to use the image, but which resolutions are best for which needs? If you are going to display the image on the Web, a relatively low resolution of 72 ppi is the standard. If your image will appear in black and white in a newspaper, 150 ppi is acceptable. If you are going to print an image on your color printer and want it to look good enough to frame, the resolution should be about 240 ppi or above. Finally, if your image will appear in a magazine or professional journal, 300 ppi is your safest bet. At a lower resolution, you risk having your image look grainy. A resolution higher than 300 ppi adds many megabytes to the file size, but not much in terms of quality.

These guidelines can help you make decisions about which images you'll use for a project, but you also need to decide in advance whether you'll manipulate resolution in Photoshop, or whether you'll start with a file that already fits the bill. There are many factors that will go into making this decision, including time constraints (you are on a deadline), client needs (you are required to use the images provided), and budget (the client cannot afford to send a photographer into the field to shoot a new image or cannot afford to purchase a different image). Familiarizing yourself with all of your options ahead of time will ensure that you make the best decision to meet the needs of any given project.

Managing Multiple Image Files with Adobe Bridge and Mini Bridge

After you have worked with Photoshop for a while, you are bound to have dozens or even hundreds of different image files on your computer, but how do you organize them? Photoshop ships with a file management application called Adobe Bridge that simplifies storing, finding, sorting, and filtering your images. You work with Bridge outside of Photoshop, and you can use it in much the same way you use Windows Explorer to navigate folders on your computer. See Figure 2-9.

Figure 2-9 Adobe Bridge

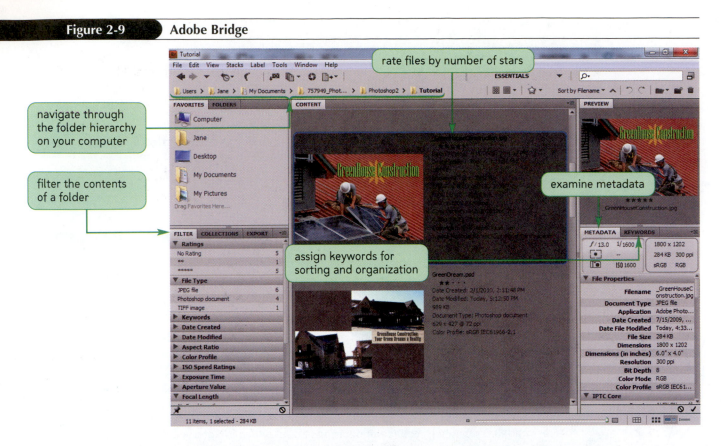

Bridge also has powerful tools that let you use metadata and keywords to categorize your images. In general terms, **metadata** is data about data—for example, information describing how data is formatted, or how it was collected. In Bridge, metadata information could include details about the camera that a photographer used to shoot a photograph, the lighting conditions, copyright information, the date a file was created, the date a file was modified, file dimensions, resolution, color mode, and bit depth, among other things. You can use the tools in Bridge to categorize your images with **keywords**, or words that describe your photographs in some way. For example, you might assign the keyword *People* to all photographs of people. You can also rate your photographs using a system of stars. A five-star image is better than a two-star image. You can then use this information to filter a folder containing photographs. A **filter** hides all files except those specified by the filter. So, you could filter by keyword so that only photos assigned the keyword *People* are listed, or you could filter by rating to display only the five-star photographs. You can also sort your images by rating, by filename, by file type, or by a number of other sort options. Bridge is fully integrated with Photoshop, so it is easy to switch between the two applications.

Photoshop also includes a stripped-down version of Bridge called Mini Bridge that opens directly in Photoshop. Adobe Mini Bridge is the "pocket-sized" version of Adobe Bridge. It has some, but not all, of the features of Bridge. For example, you can't assign a rating to a file in Mini Bridge, but you can view ratings, navigate folders, and search for and preview images without leaving the Photoshop workspace. You can also preview a file in Full Screen mode before you open it in Photoshop or see a slide show of all of the files in a folder before opening them.

TIP

You can also click the Mini Bridge panel icon to the right of the Document window to expand Mini Bridge.

To use Mini Bridge:

1. On the Application bar, click the Launch Mini Bridge button [Mb]. Mini Bridge opens on the right side of the Document window.

2. Under Welcome to Mini Bridge, click the Browse Files button. Mini Bridge opens a Navigation pod and a Content pod. See Figure 2-10.

Figure 2-10 **Adobe Mini Bridge**

The **Navigation pod** displays a list of choices for areas to search, including folders you have recently opened. It also displays the folder path of the currently highlighted folder, for example, Photoshop2\Tutorial. The **Content pod** lists the files in the current folder. It also shows the star rating assigned to images, and has options for filtering and sorting the images in the current folder.

3. In the Navigation pod, click **Favorites**. Mini Bridge displays a list of favorites on the right side of the Navigation pod, including Computer, Desktop, My Documents, and My Pictures. If you have specified any Favorites in Windows, it displays those folders as well.

4. In the Favorites list, click **My Pictures**. Mini Bridge displays the contents of the My Pictures library.

5. In the Navigation pod, click **Recent Files**, and then click **Photoshop** in the right pane. In the Content pod, scroll down if necessary, and then double-click **GreenHouseConstruction.jpg**. The GreenHouseConstruction.jpg file opens in the Document window.

6. Click the **Mini Bridge** panel icon [MB] to the right of the Document window. Mini Bridge collapses to an icon.

Now that you have a good understanding of file formats, resolution, and file size, and know how to find and sort files in Mini Bridge, C.J. asks you to spend some time learning about the different color modes available in Photoshop so that you'll be able to meet the needs of his advertising campaign on the Web, in four-color printed pieces, and in black-and-white newspapers.

INSIGHT

Adding User Information and Metadata in the File Info Dialog Box

In Photoshop, you have many options for viewing and adding metadata to a file. You have already seen that you can categorize and add metadata to files using Bridge. You can also open the File Info dialog box from the File menu and make changes there. You can use the tabs in the dialog box to add a description of your image, or to enter camera data, among other things. Whether you choose to use the File Info dialog box or Bridge, it is a good idea to enter as much information about a file as possible in case you need to reference it later.

Understanding Color Modes and Intensities

Color mode is an important setting that you must take into consideration when preparing an image in Photoshop. A **color mode** consists of a few **primary**, or starting, colors (for example, red, green, and blue) that you can combine in different intensities to create hundreds of thousands, or even millions, of other colors. Common color modes are RGB, CMYK, and Grayscale. To understand how many color choices you can end up with using different combinations of only a few colors, consider the RGB mode. The RGB color mode uses only three colors, red, green, and blue, but each of these colors can be assigned a value from 0 (for no color) to 255 (for maximum color intensity). In Photoshop, **intensity** simply refers to the value you have assigned to one of the primary colors. That means you have 256 choices (or intensities) for red (remember that 0 is a choice), 256 choices for green, and 256 choices for blue. That's $256 \times 256 \times 256$ color possibilities, or about 16.7 million choices. See Figure 2-11.

Figure 2-11   **Differing color intensities**

You can think of intensity in terms of paint. If you dip your brush in red paint and then paint on a canvas, you'll get one version of the red paint. However, if you first put a bit of blue paint on your brush, and then dip the brush in the red paint, you'll get a different red with a different intensity. Finally, if you first dip your brush in a bit of green and then dip it in the red paint, you get still another version of the color red. Now imagine that you mix that first deep color of red thoroughly with a deep blue, but no green. You'll get a color that is neither red, nor blue, nor green, but a combination of red and blue. Or perhaps you combine it with green, but not blue. You'll get a different color.

As you have seen, Photoshop lets you specify the intensity of colors using numbers. Each color mode uses a different numbering system, but the results are similar: You start with a few color settings, but you wind up with a seemingly unlimited palette of colors to choose from. Different media require different color modes, and although the orange color you see on screen and the orange color you see on a printed page might look identical, they are created in completely different ways, by combining different colors in different color modes.

Understanding the RGB Color Mode

By default, new files in Photoshop use the RGB color mode. The **RGB** (red, green, blue) color mode is an additive color mode. As you might expect, an **additive color mode** adds colors together to create a different color. See Figure 2-12.

Figure 2-12	RGB color mode

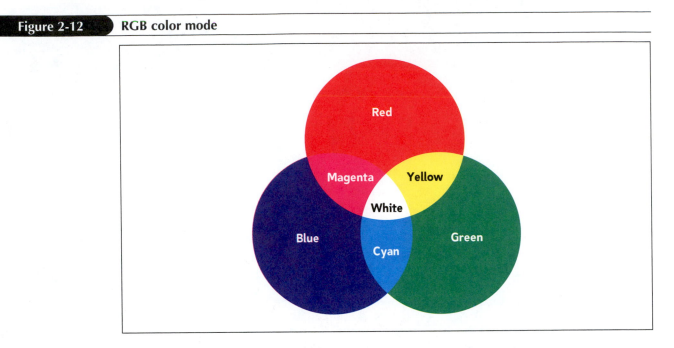

Combining the three primary colors in varying intensities results in the colors cyan, magenta, and yellow. For example, in Photoshop, a red setting of 142, a green setting of 61, and a blue setting of 151 results in an intense magenta. A red setting of 255, a green setting of 255, and a blue setting of 0 results in a yellow color, as shown in the color sliders in Figure 2-13.

Figure 2-13	Color values

You have seen that red, green, and blue additive colors can create cyan, magenta, and yellow, but where do the colors white and black come from? If you have ever taken a physics course, you know that white light contains all of the colors in the color spectrum, and that black is the absence of color. In fact, the RGB color mode follows the laws of physics; combining all three colors at their maximum intensities (255, 255, 255) results in white. Specifying a setting of 0 for all three colors (0, 0, 0) results in the color black.

Understanding the CMYK Color Mode

CMYK (cyan, magenta, yellow, key) is a color mode specifically meant for printed output. CMYK is a **subtractive color mode** because each color subtracts the light from the white page on which it's printed. Because printed output involves putting ink on white paper, the CMYK mode might make more sense to you than RGB. You don't need to have studied physics to understand CMYK. In fact, you learned all you need to know about this mode in kindergarten, where you discovered that mixing two paint colors together results in a third color, but mixing all paint colors together results in black. See Figure 2-14.

Figure 2-14 CMYK color mode

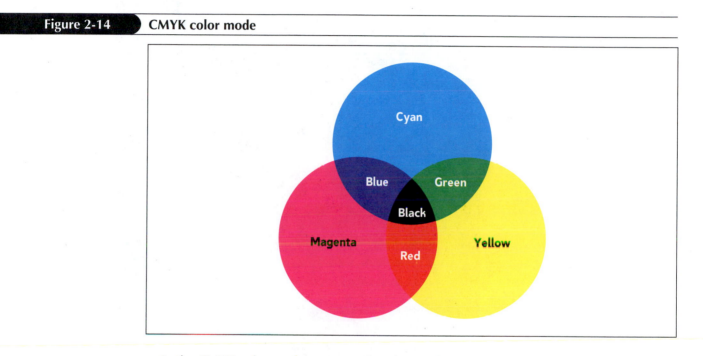

In the CMYK color mode, you specify color combinations in terms of percentages rather than intensity values, but CMYK still involves combining the primary colors of the mode, which in this case are cyan, magenta, yellow, and black.

You might wonder why the mode is called CMYK (for key) instead of CMYB (for black). In the CMYK color mode, *key* does refer to black, which is the color used on the key plate in the four-color printing process. The **key plate** is the plate in the printing process used to print the details in an image. To understand how printed output might look without the color black (and to understand why black is "key"), see Figure 2-15.

Figure 2-15 **Image with and without black, a "key" color**

black adds detail and contrast to shadows and light

absence of black makes the photo look washed out

The photograph on the top of the figure includes the key color (black). The photograph on the bottom shows the image as it would look without any black. You can see that the key color is essential to a crisp, clean image.

Because CMYK involves one more color than RGB, the file size of a CMYK image can be about 50 percent larger than its RGB counterpart, depending on optimization settings. Therefore, if you are only using a file for the Web, it's wise to use RGB.

Understanding Indexed Colors

The 8-bit Indexed color mode uses a palette of 256 colors, which might seem limited given the millions of colors available in other modes. However, for many applications, such as Web animations and Web pages, 256 colors is more than enough. The advantage of using an Indexed color mode rather than RGB is smaller file size. When you convert a file to Indexed color, Photoshop analyzes the colors in the image and then creates a **color lookup table** (or CLUT) of 256 colors. The CLUT can consist of any of the colors in the image you are converting. For example, if you are converting from RGB, Photoshop creates the CLUT using just 256 of the 16.7 million color choices. See Figure 2-16.

 Figure 2-16   **Color lookup table**

the CLUT includes only 256 of the 16.7 million colors available to the RGB image

If a color in the image matches a color stored in the table, Photoshop maps the pixel to that cell in the table. If a color has no matches in the table, Photoshop chooses the closest color from the table, or maps it to two or more indexed colors to simulate the color needed in the image. Switching an image to the Indexed color mode is another way to optimize an image. Furthermore, the Indexed color mode is supported by many different applications and, therefore, "travels" well from application to application. Your challenge is to ensure that the reduction of color choices doesn't result in a reduction in image quality.

Understanding the Grayscale Color Mode

When you convert an image from one of the color modes to Grayscale mode in Photoshop, Photoshop translates every intensity or shade of every color to a different shade, or **tone**, of gray. White is 0 percent, and black is 100 percent gray. See Figure 2-17.

Figure 2-17   Grayscale color percentages

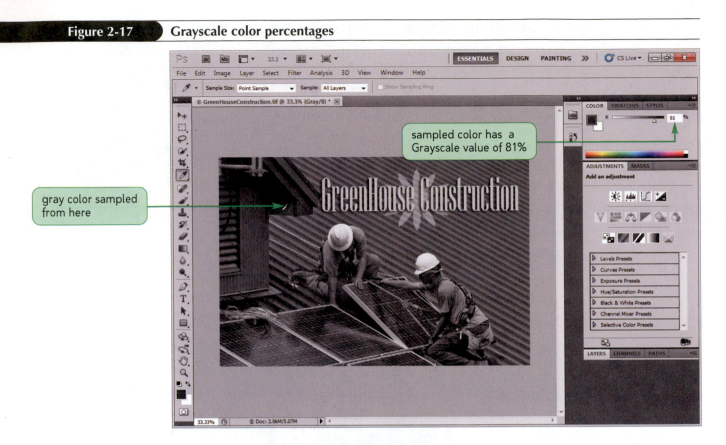

You can modify the tones of gray in an image converted to grayscale—in other words, make them lighter or darker, but you cannot get the original color back once you save the file and close it. Converting the color mode to grayscale is an example of **destructive editing**—all of the original color information is discarded when you save and close the file. Therefore, when you convert a file to grayscale, you should immediately save it with a new name, so that you do not overwrite your original color file with the grayscale file.

Understanding How Bit Depth Combined with Color Mode Affects File Size

Each pixel in an image represents a single color. When the eye views hundreds or thousands of pixels together, the colors blend together and appear to transition smoothly from one part of the image to the next. Images with higher bit depths result in more realistically colored images because they have more available colors for shading and variations. Figure 2-18 explains the relationship between bit depth and color mode.

| | Figure 2-18 | Bit depth and color mode |

Color Mode	Bit Depth	Number of Colors
Black and White	1	Each pixel in a black-and-white image has two possible values, black (0) or white (1), resulting in 2^1 possible colors—in other words, two.
Grayscale	8	The bit depth of a grayscale image in Photoshop is 8, which allows you to access 2^8, or 256 shades of gray.
RGB	8	An RGB image with a bit depth of 8 has a possible 16.7 million colors, 2^8 (or 256) choices of red, times 2^8 (or 256) choices of green, times 2^8 (or 256) choices of blue.
CMYK	8	A CMYK image with a bit depth of 8 has 256 times the number of colors available in an RGB image. In other words, it has over 4.2 billion possible colors (256 x 256 x 256 x 256).

Photoshop also supports 32-bit and 16-bit images, but not all of its features are available at these bit depths. Typically, you would use a 32-bit image, also called a **high dynamic range** or **HDR image**, in a computer graphics scene that requires great contrast between dark and light areas and great detail; you might also use 32-bit images in 3D imagery. HDR images are very large, and if you're using Photoshop for print pieces and Web ads, you are safe sticking with 8-bit imagery.

Changing Color Modes

You can change color mode based on your needs. For example, if you have a CMYK image that you would also like to use on the Web, you can switch from CMYK mode to RGB mode. To do so, you use the Mode command on the Image menu. If you switch from CMYK or RGB to the Indexed color mode, Photoshop will confirm that you want to flatten your image because Indexed color doesn't support layers. If you switch from any color mode to Grayscale, Photoshop will display a warning asking you to confirm that you want to discard the color information in the file.

C.J. wants you to save his GreenHouseConstruction.jpg image so that it is suitable for a newspaper ad. To do so, you'll convert it to Grayscale and decrease the resolution.

To change the color mode and decrease the resolution of the GreenHouseConstruction.jpg image:

1. Save GreenHouseConstruction.jpg as **BWGreenHouse.jpg** in the Photoshop2\ Tutorial folder included with your Data Files, using High quality and Baseline ("Standard") JPEG settings.

2. On the Application bar, click **Image**, click **Mode**, and then click **Grayscale**. Photoshop displays a dialog box prompting you to confirm that you want to discard color information. See Figure 2-19.

Figure 2-19 Discarding color information

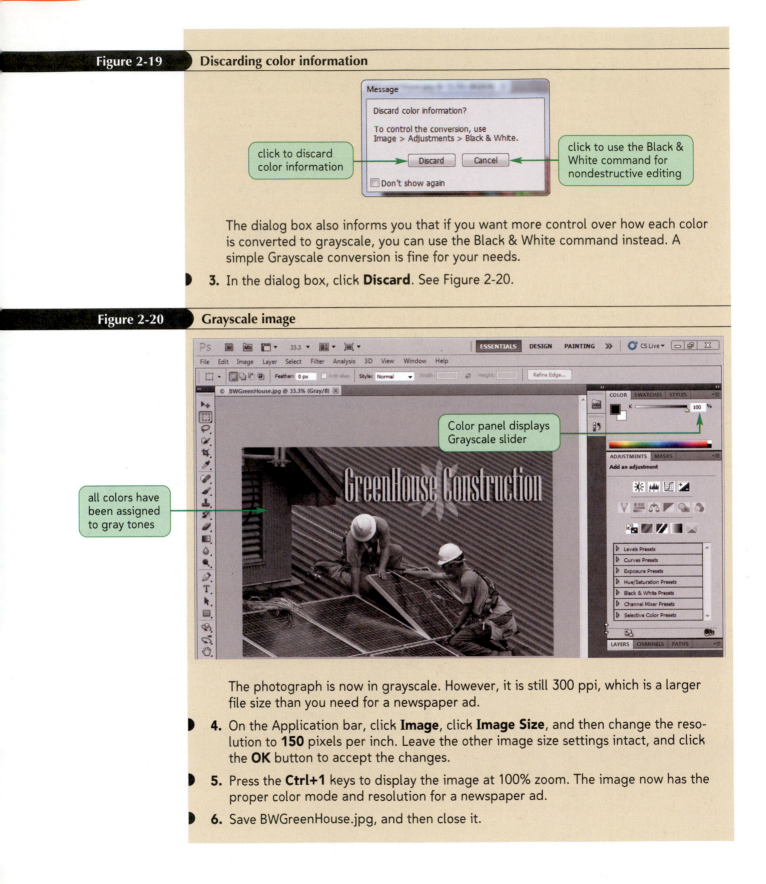

The dialog box also informs you that if you want more control over how each color is converted to grayscale, you can use the Black & White command instead. A simple Grayscale conversion is fine for your needs.

3. In the dialog box, click **Discard**. See Figure 2-20.

Figure 2-20 Grayscale image

The photograph is now in grayscale. However, it is still 300 ppi, which is a larger file size than you need for a newspaper ad.

4. On the Application bar, click **Image**, click **Image Size**, and then change the resolution to **150** pixels per inch. Leave the other image size settings intact, and click the **OK** button to accept the changes.

5. Press the **Ctrl+1** keys to display the image at 100% zoom. The image now has the proper color mode and resolution for a newspaper ad.

6. Save BWGreenHouse.jpg, and then close it.

C.J. wants you to experiment with creating a few new files of your own so you are more familiar with the options available in Photoshop, and so you can feel confident making choices based on project needs.

Creating a New File

So far, you have only opened existing files in Photoshop. However, it's easy to open a new blank file in Photoshop and create your own composition. Before you create a new file in Photoshop, you should decide on the document's size, resolution, and background color based on the needs of your project. You can always modify a file's specifications later, but it will save you time and effort to set them up properly in advance. See Figure 2-21.

Figure 2-21 | **Default settings for a new file**

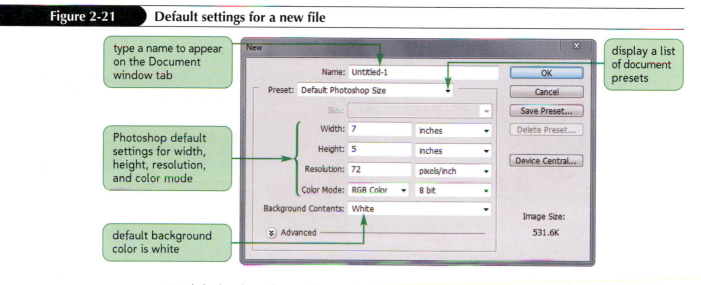

By default, Photoshop will create a new 7 × 5-inch file—using the RGB color mode, a bit depth of 8, and a white background. Once you have created the new file, you can add to it using the tools on the Tools panel, or you can copy an image from another file and paste it into the Document window. You can also place an image in the file.

Placing an Image in a New File

When you create a new file, you can think of yourself as an artist starting with a blank canvas. The **canvas** in Photoshop is the blank area in the middle of the Photoshop Document window, on which you can "paint" with bitmap images, vector graphics, and text. In Photoshop, you can use vector drawing tools to paint on the canvas, but you can also copy and paste bitmap images or vector objects, or place them on the canvas. When you **place** an image in Photoshop, you import a copy of the image file that is still linked to the original. If you open and then edit the original file—for example, if you adjust a dark image by increasing its brightness—that change is reflected in the placed image in your new document file as well. A placed object is an example of a Photoshop feature called a **Smart Object**, which gives you the flexibility to transform the placed object in some way—for example, you can **transform** a placed image by rotating it or distorting it by making it wider or taller—without affecting the original object. To place an image file in a Photoshop document, you use the Place command on the File menu.

Creating a New File Using a Preset

- On the Application bar, click File, and then click New. The New dialog box opens.
- In the Name box, type a name for the new file.
- Click the Preset arrow, and select the desired preset.
- Click the OK button to create the new file.

C.J. has asked you to create three new files, each based on a different design need. First, he wants you to create a variation of the company's logo for a Web-based campaign, using two separate files. You will not be making any changes to the placed images.

To create a new file and place an image:

1. On the Application bar, click **File**, and then click **New**. The New dialog box opens.

2. In the Name box, type **Logo1**. This is the name that will appear on the Document window tab.

3. Click the **Preset** arrow. Photoshop displays a list of available presets. See Figure 2-22.

Figure 2-22	Available new file presets

4. Click **Default Photoshop Size**, if necessary. The Default Photoshop Size preset creates a document that is 7 × 5 inches, with a resolution of 72 ppi.

5. Click the **OK** button. Photoshop creates the new file and displays the blank canvas at 100% zoom in the Document window.

6. On the Application bar, click **File**, and then click **Place**.

7. Navigate to the Photoshop2\Tutorial folder included with your Data Files, click **Sun.psd**, click **Place**, and then press the **Enter** key. The image is placed at the center of the new file. Next, you'll place text on top of this image.

8. On the Application bar, click **File**, and then click **Place**.

9. Navigate to the Photoshop2\Tutorial folder included with your Data Files, click **GreenHouseText.psd**, click **Place**, and then press the **Enter** key. See Figure 2-23.

Figure 2-23   Default new Photoshop file with placed images

You created a new file using the default Photoshop settings and placed two images in it. You'll save this file and present it to C.J. as a possible new logo for the company's Web site.

10. Save the file as **Logo1.psd** in the Photoshop2\Tutorial folder, and then close the file.

You can also create a new file using a Web preset, which will create a file with dimensions suitable for displaying in a Web browser. Photoshop includes Web presets for low-resolution monitors (640 pixels by 480 pixels), high-resolution monitors (1600 pixels by 1200 pixels), and many resolutions in between. It also includes file sizes appropriate for navigation bars and **leaderboards**, which are advertising banners that often appear at the top of a Web page.

C.J. wants you to create a leaderboard for the company logo. You'll create a new file with the proper dimensions and then place the logo on the canvas and resize it.

To create the file using the Leaderboard Web preset:

1. On the Application bar, click **File**, and then click **New**. The New dialog box opens.

2. In the Name box, type **Leaderboard**.

3. Click the **Preset** arrow, and then click **Web**.

4. Click the **Size** arrow, click **Leaderboard, 728 x 90**, and then click the **OK** button to create the new file.

5. On the Application bar, click **File**, and then click **Place**.

6. Navigate to the Photoshop2\Tutorial folder, included with your Data Files, click **LeaderboardText.psd**, click **Place**, and then press the **Enter** key. The text is now placed in the new file. See Figure 2-24.

Figure 2-24 | Leaderboard file with placed image

7. Save the file as **Leaderboard.psd** in the Photoshop2\Tutorial folder, and close the file.

Now C.J. can use this file as a banner on a Web site.

PROSKILLS

Decision Making: Using a Standard or a Nonstandard Size for a Photoshop Document

Photoshop gives you the flexibility to create documents using any dimensions. It provides presets for the Web or for printing photographs, but you might want to create a brochure with three panels, and there is no preset for that. You can easily create your own preset using any dimensions you want, but it is wise to first check with your commercial printer to see if they have a standard size for a three-panel brochure. If they do, you need to decide whether following your original vision is worth the extra expense you're sure to incur if you use a nonstandard size for your piece. By exploring the options available in Photoshop and conferring with your printer before you start a project, you can ensure that you will make a decision about the size of your final documents that results in a visually appealing marketing piece, while staying within your project budget.

C.J. frequently creates images that he then makes into posters for use at trade shows, so he asks you to create a document preset that you can use for trade show posters. You'll create and save a custom document preset for this project.

Creating a Custom Document Preset

You might find that the new document presets that come with Photoshop aren't exactly what you need for a particular project. You can specify custom options in the New dialog box and then save them as presets. Once you save a preset, it is listed along with all of the other presets in the New dialog box. If at any time you decide you will no longer use a particular custom preset, you can delete it.

REFERENCE

Saving a Custom Document Preset

- On the Application bar, click File, and then click New. The New dialog box opens.
- In the Name box, type a name for the new file.
- In the Width box, type a width for the canvas, and then specify the unit of measurement (such as pixels or inches).
- In the Height box, type a value for the height of the canvas.
- In the Resolution box, enter the resolution.
- Click the Save Preset button. The New Document Preset dialog box opens.
- Name the preset, and then select the necessary options in the New Document Preset dialog box.
- Click the OK button to save the custom preset.

To save a custom document preset for trade show posters:

1. On the Application bar, click **File**, and then click **New**. The New dialog box opens.

2. In the Name box, type **PosterPreset**.

3. Type **24** in the Width box, click the **Width** arrow, and then click **inches**, if necessary. Notice that the pixels arrow for Height also changes to inches.

4. In the Height box, type **36**.

5. In the Resolution box, type **300**.

6. Click the **Save Preset** button. The New Document Preset dialog box opens. See Figure 2-25.

Figure 2-25   Saving a new file preset

enter a name for the custom document preset

You can leave the default preset name, which is the dimensions of the new document, or you can type a new name.

▶ 7. In the Preset Name box, type **PosterPreset**, accept the default settings (all check boxes checked) so that every setting is saved with the preset, and then click the **OK** button.

▶ 8. In the New dialog box, click the **Preset** arrow.

The new preset name appears in the Preset list. It will be available for all your future Photoshop sessions unless you delete it.

▶ 9. Click **PosterPreset**, and then click the **OK** button. Photoshop opens the blank canvas with the custom dimensions and resolution you entered.

▶ 10. On the Application bar, click **File**, and then click **Place**.

▶ 11. Navigate to the Photoshop2\Tutorial folder included with your Data Files, click **Logo1.psd**, click **Place**, and then press the **Enter** key to place the logo. Use the Move Tool to center the logo at the top of the poster.

▶ 12. Save the file as **PosterPreset.psd** in the Photoshop2\Tutorial folder, and then close the file.

You have shown your preset to C.J., and he wants to change it substantially. Because you know that you'll never use this preset again, you decide to delete it to prevent a cluttered preset list.

REFERENCE

Deleting a Custom Document Preset

- On the Application bar, click File, and then click New.
- Click the Preset arrow, and then click the custom preset you want to delete.
- Click Delete Preset, and then click Yes in the dialog box to confirm that you want to delete the preset.
- Click the OK button.

To delete the custom preset:

▶ **1.** On the Application bar, click **File**, and then click **New**.

▶ **2.** In the New dialog box, click the **Preset** arrow, and then click **PosterPreset**, which is the preset you want to delete.

▶ **3.** Click **Delete Preset**. A dialog box opens asking you to confirm that you want to delete the preset.

▶ **4.** Click **Yes**. Photoshop deletes the PosterPreset custom preset.

▶ **5.** Click the **OK** button, close the open file without saving it, and then exit Photoshop.

REVIEW

Session 2.1 Quick Check

1. Name one advantage of the PSD file format.

2. The higher the resolution, the _____ the file size.

3. Finding the right balance between image quality and file size is called _____.

4. True or False. A JPEG version of an image is larger than a PSD version of the same image.

5. The default resolution for a Photoshop file is _____ ppi.

6. True or False. Resampling does not alter the number of pixels in the image.

7. _____ _____ specifies the amount of color information for each pixel in an image.

SESSION 2.2 VISUAL OVERVIEW

Open the Image menu to access the Image Rotation command.

Use the Rotate Canvas dialog box to specify an angle of rotation, and whether to rotate clockwise or counterclockwise.

You can rotate an image 180 degrees, or you can flip it vertically or horizontally.

Rotate an image using presets of 90 degrees clockwise and counterclockwise.

If you rotate an image by an **arbitrary angle**, which is an angle that you specify, Photoshop increases the dimensions of the canvas to compensate for the change.

ADJUST, VIEW, AND ROTATE IMAGES

The Brightness/Contrast adjustment lets you change the lighting and the contrast between dark and light in an image.

The **adjustments** feature in Photoshop lets you easily manipulate an image and preview an adjustment as you make it.

Clicking any of these adjustments adds an adjustment layer to your file. An **adjustment layer** changes your image in a nondestructive way.

The Posterize adjustment turns an image into a stylized painting that resembles a poster.

Many image adjustments include multiple presets for you to choose from.

You can expand presets for even more options.

In the Navigator panel, you can **pan** your image, which means to move the image within the Document window so that a different part of the image is visible.

The **view box** outlines the area of the image that is displayed in the Document window.

The Navigator panel can be collapsed to an icon.

Type the zoom percentage in zoom box or in the zoom box on the status bar.

Drag the Zoom slider to change the zoom setting.

ADJUSTMENTS MASKS

Add an adjustment

Levels Presets
Curves Presets
Exposure Presets
Hue/Saturation Presets
Black & White Presets
Blue Filter
Darker

NAVIGATOR HISTO INFO

296.12%

Making Image Adjustments

As you work with digital images, you'll often find that an image is *almost* what you're looking for, but not quite. For example, perhaps the colors are a bit off or the image is overexposed. Maybe you'd prefer more shadows, or more light, or even a red door on the house instead of a blue door. Using Photoshop's adjustments feature, you can easily modify an image by making changes to the color and tone, among other things. If you make an image adjustment using the Adjustment command on the Image menu, the adjustment is made directly on the selected layer. This kind of adjustment is called a **destructive image adjustment** because it actually changes the pixels in the image. Once you save a file with this kind of adjustment, you have permanently changed the file. Unless you save the adjusted file with a different name, there is no way to return to the original. If this makes you nervous, it should. However, Photoshop has a feature called nondestructive image editing that should put you at ease. **Nondestructive image adjustments** are stored as layers on top of the original image. They are applied to the image, but rather than altering the pixels in the image, they are overlaid on the image as separate layers. As a result, you can easily turn them on or off or even delete them without harming the image itself. This session gives you a brief introduction to the Adjustments panel. As with many of the features in Photoshop, the Adjustments panel offers countless possibilities for editing your images, including adjusting the brightness and contrast of an image using the Brightness/Contrast adjustment.

The Adjustments panel includes 15 icons, each offering different adjustment options. Some adjustments have additional presets listed in the bottom half of the panel. For example, the Levels preset (the second icon in the first row) includes the default settings, but also includes multiple levels presets that you can display by clicking the triangle to the left of the words Levels Preset in the list of presets in the bottom half of the panel.

C.J. is working on a campaign to persuade consumers to switch from gas and oil heat to solar and geothermal heat. He has started to compose an image meant to convince people that continuing with their current heating plans will cost them money and have a negative effect on the environment. He would like you to adjust the image so that it has more impact. You'll also experiment with brightness, contrast, and levels settings to see if those changes make the image stronger. You'll also experiment with a black-and-white preset to see how dramatic the change would be.

To add the Brightness/Contrast adjustment layer:

1. Start Photoshop while pressing the **Ctrl+Alt+Shift** keys, and click **Yes** to delete the Settings File when asked, then reset Photoshop to the default Essentials workspace layout, and reset all tools.

2. Navigate to the Photoshop2\Tutorial folder included with your Data Files, and open **HeatCosts.psd**.

   As you work with the Adjustments panel, it is helpful to see the changes on the Layers panel. To do so, you need to create some space in the Photoshop window.

3. On the Color panel, click the **panel options** button ![icon], and then click **Close Tab Group**. The Adjustments panel group moves up. The Layers panel group moves up as well.

4. Click the **Layers** and **Adjustments** panel tabs to expand the panels, if necessary.

5. Select the **Background** layer, if necessary. See Figure 2-26.

| Figure 2-26 | Adjustments panel icons and options |

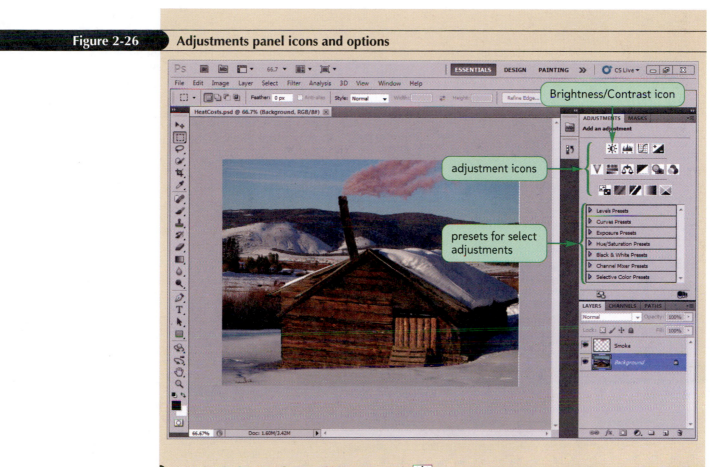

6. Click the **Brightness/Contrast** icon. See Figure 2-27.

| Figure 2-27 | Brightness/Contrast settings |

TIP

You can also work with adjustment layers using the New Adjustment Layer command on the Layer menu.

Photoshop adds an adjustment layer above the Background layer. An adjustment layer affects any layers beneath it on the Layers panel by default. If you have multiple layers beneath an adjustment layer but only want to affect the layer directly beneath the adjustment, you can **clip** it to that layer by clicking the Clip to layer icon at the bottom of the Adjustments panel.

Next, you'll use the slider to adjust the brightness of the image, and you'll type a new contrast value to see the effect of these changes.

7. Drag the **Brightness** slider to the left until the value reads **-45**.

8. Type **15** in the Contrast box.

   Notice that the color of the smoke hasn't changed because the Smoke layer is above the adjustment layer.

9. Click the **Smoke** layer to select it, and then, in the Adjustments panel, click the **Clip to layer** icon [icon] to direct Photoshop to clip the adjustment to the selected layer. The icon changes to [icon].

10. Click the **Expand** icon [icon] to the left of Hue/Saturation Presets, scroll the list, click **Strong Saturation**, and then on the Adjustments panel, drag the **Lightness** slider to the left until the box reads **-65**. See Figure 2-28.

Figure 2-28   **Hue/Saturation adjustment layer clipped to Smoke layer**

The Smoke layer is now much darker, but because the adjustment was clipped only to that layer, the rest of the image is unchanged.

Trouble? If the entire image changes, click the Clip to layer icon [icon] at the bottom of the panel.

11. Save the file as **AdjustHeatCosts.psd** in the Photoshop2\Tutorial folder.

You decide that the original brightness and contrast of the Background layer was fine, so you'll delete the Brightness/Contrast layer.

To delete the adjustment:

1. Drag the **Hue/Saturation** layer to the lower right of the Layers panel, until it is over the Delete Layer icon 🗑, then release the mouse button. See Figure 2-29.

Figure 2-29 | **Dragging the adjustment layer to delete it**

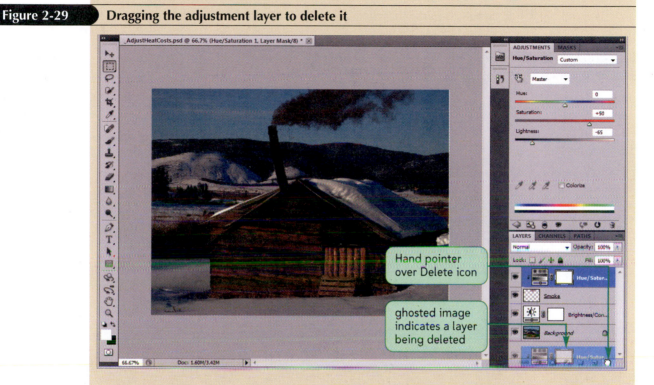

The Hue/Saturation layer is deleted and the smoke returns to its original color. However, this is not the layer you really want to delete, so you'll undo the deletion and select the Brightness/Contrast layer to delete it.

2. Press the **Ctrl+Z** keys to undo the deletion. The smoke is now the darker, adjusted color.

3. Select the **Brightness/Contrast** layer, and then press the **Delete** key to delete that layer. The Background layer reverts to its original brightness and contrast levels.

4. Save the file and close it.

You can also use adjustment layer presets as is, without any modifications, to get an entirely new effect with the click of a button. You'll use a black-and-white preset to see if it will convey the message of your image more powerfully.

To use the Black & White adjustment layer preset:

1. Navigate to the Photoshop2\Tutorial folder included with your Data Files, and open **HeatCosts2.psd** and then click the **Background** layer to select it, if necessary.

2. On the Adjustments panel, click the **Expand** icon ▶ to the left of Black & White Presets.

   Trouble? If you can't see Black & White Presets, scroll down the list.

3. Scroll the list, and click **High Contrast Red Filter** to apply the preset. See Figure 2-30.

Figure 2-30 | Black & White adjustment applied to the Background layer

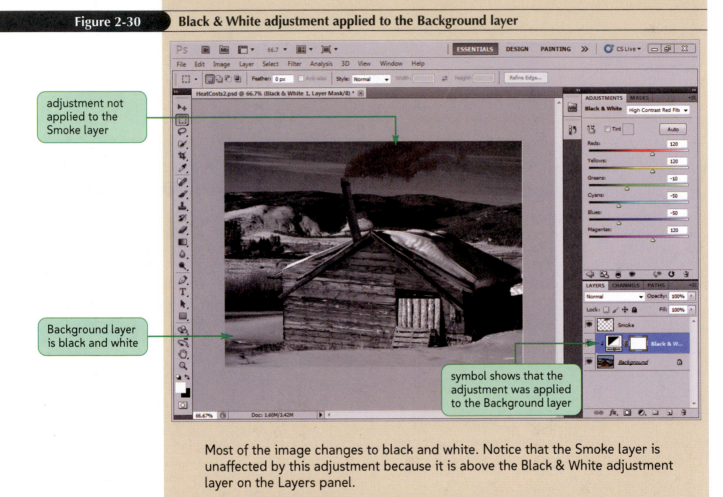

adjustment not applied to the Smoke layer

Background layer is black and white

symbol shows that the adjustment was applied to the Background layer

Most of the image changes to black and white. Notice that the Smoke layer is unaffected by this adjustment because it is above the Black & White adjustment layer on the Layers panel.

4. Save the file as **BWHeatCosts2.psd** in the Photoshop2\Tutorial folder, and then close the file.

Problem Solving: Acquiring an Image from a Scanner

You might have a project that requires you to acquire photographs taken before the days of digital imaging. In fact, what if the ideal photograph for your project was taken in 1959? How can you get that image into Photoshop and use it in your work? The fact is, you don't have to start with a digital file to end up with a digital file. You can use a scanner to scan a printed photograph either directly into Photoshop or you can scan it to a storage device on your computer and then open the file in Photoshop. (Keep in mind that you shouldn't scan a copyrighted photo without first obtaining permission.) If the scanner uses its own software to scan the image to your hard drive, make sure to specify the file format you want. If you have a scanner that includes a Photoshop plug-in, make sure to install the plug-in software. You can then import the file directly into Photoshop. If your scanner has a preview option, it's a good idea to preview the image before you scan it because previewing lets you adjust scanner settings and saves you time and effort.

Once you scan an image, you haven't necessarily finished with the file. You might find that the image needs adjusting to make it work in your project. With Photoshop's image-adjustment features, your problem is solved: Not only have you performed magic by digitizing an image that was made before the digital age, you have actually repurposed the image to suit your needs using Photoshop's image-editing features. In fact, being required to use an old photograph for a project isn't much of a problem at all. Scanning the photograph to digitize it, and then manipulating it with Photoshop, can bring any photograph, no matter how old, into the twenty-first century.

Working with the Canvas

You saw earlier in this tutorial that when you create a new file, you often start with a blank canvas. As you create your composition, you might find that you need more or less room on the canvas to finalize your work. To enlarge the canvas, you can use the Canvas Size command on the Image menu to open the Canvas Size dialog box.

In the Canvas Size dialog box, you specify the new dimensions for your canvas. If you select the Relative check box, you can specify the width and height dimensions you want to add to the canvas, rather than the final dimensions of the canvas. You can also select an anchor position for your image. The **anchor** determines whether the existing content on the canvas will remain in the center of the extended canvas, or whether it will be aligned with an edge or a corner of the canvas.

You have created a mock-up for a postcard campaign based on a sketch that C.J. provided, and you want to increase the canvas size so that you can add a border around the composition.

REFERENCE

Extending the Canvas

- With an image file open, on the Application bar, click Image, and then click Canvas Size. The Canvas Size dialog box opens.
- With the Relative check box deselected, specify the final Width and Height measurements for the canvas.
- Select an Anchor setting to determine where the existing image will appear on the larger canvas.
- Select a Canvas extension color, and click the OK button.

or

- With the Relative check box selected, specify the additional Width and Height measurements you want to add to the canvas size.
- Select an Anchor setting to determine where the existing image will appear on the larger canvas.
- Select a Canvas extension color, and click the OK button.

To extend the canvas:

1. Navigate to the Photoshop2\Tutorial folder included with your Data Files, and open **GreenDream.psd**. The file opens in the Photoshop window. The image consists of the area containing the photographs, the text, and the rectangles. The image size and the canvas size are identical.

2. On the Application bar, click **Image**, and then click **Canvas Size**. The Canvas Size dialog box opens showing the Current Size, which is a little less than 9 inches × 6 inches. See Figure 2-31.

| Figure 2-31 | Canvas Size dialog box |

current dimensions of canvas

new dimensions of canvas

Anchor grid; default is to anchor the image in the center

select the Relative check box to add width and/or height

select an extension color for the canvas

You want to add a half-inch border around the postcard image. To do so, you need to increase the canvas size one inch in height and one inch in width.

3. Click the **Relative** check box to select it. When the Relative check box is selected, you can specify the width and height you want to add to the canvas, rather than the final width and height. Notice that under New Size, the Width and Height settings are now both 0 because you haven't yet specified what dimensions you want to add.

4. In the Width box, type **1**, and then in the Height box, type **1**. This will make the canvas ½ inch larger on all four sides.

   If you wanted to anchor the image at the top, bottom, or side of the larger canvas, you could click one of the anchor buttons. Because you want to create a border of equal width around all four sides of the image, leave the anchor setting in the center. You also want the extension to be the background color, which is white, so you won't change that setting.

5. Click the **OK** button. The canvas increases in size with the image anchored in the middle of the canvas. See Figure 2-32.

Figure 2-32   **Extending the canvas**

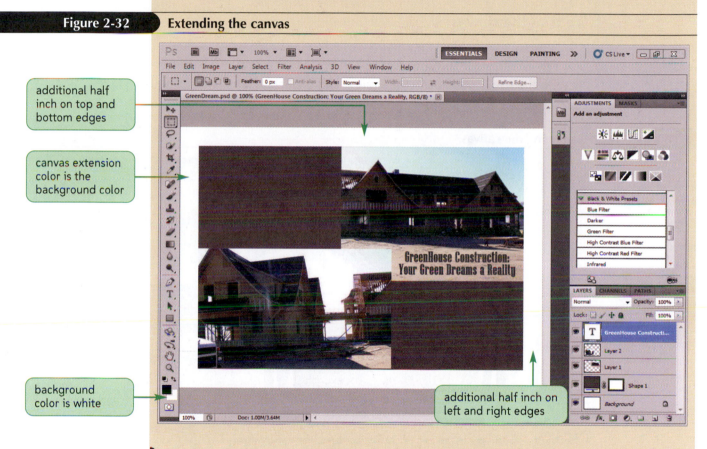

additional half inch on top and bottom edges

canvas extension color is the background color

background color is white

additional half inch on left and right edges

6. Save the file as **CanvasSize.psd** in the Photoshop2\Tutorial folder, and close the file.

You can also trim a canvas to make an image smaller. Choosing Trim from the Image menu opens the Trim dialog box, where you can specify the color on which you want to base the trim, as well as whether you want Photoshop to trim the top, bottom, left, or right of the image, or some combination of these choices.

C.J. has given you a second file for a solar panel advertising campaign that he would like you to trim so that there's no white space around the image.

Trimming the Canvas

- On the Application bar, click Image, and then click Trim.
- Click the option button for the pixel color on which to base the trim—Top Left Pixel Color, Bottom Right Pixel Color, or Transparent Pixels.
- Specify which areas to trim by selecting or deselecting check boxes in the Trim Away section.
- Click the OK button to trim the image.

To trim the canvas:

1. Navigate to the Photoshop2\Tutorial folder included with your Data Files, and open **WireCutter.jpg**, which is an image that has extra white space on all sides.

2. On the Application bar, click **Image**, and then click **Trim**. The Trim dialog box opens. See Figure 2-33.

Figure 2-33 Trimming the canvas

top left pixel color is white

trim will be based on selected value

select sides to trim

You can trim an image based on pixel colors. Photoshop will start the trim at the edges of the image based on either transparent pixels (if any), or the top left or bottom right pixel color. In this case, the top left and bottom right pixel colors are both white.

3. Click the **Top Left Pixel Color** option button to select it, if necessary. You can trim the top, left, bottom, or right part of the canvas, or any combination of those choices. For this image, you want to trim all sides of the image, so leave all four check boxes selected.

4. Click the **OK** button. Photoshop trims the canvas.

5. Save the file as **Trim.jpg** in the Photoshop2\Tutorial folder using the current JPEG settings, and then close the file.

INSIGHT

Trimming versus Cropping

When you trim an image, you are cutting out image data by removing pixels in the image based on the criterion you specify in the Trim dialog box. For example, you can specify that Photoshop should trim away transparent pixels, or trim away pixels the color of the corner pixels in the image. When you **crop** an image, you are also cutting out image data, but when you crop, you can control additional features. For example, you can specify the dimensions of the crop, or rotate the cropping marquee to straighten the image. You can also control whether or not you want to transform the perspective of an image. When you **transform perspective**, you remove the distortion produced by taking a photograph at an angle. For example, you have probably seen a photograph of a tall building shot directly in front of the building, looking up. The photograph makes the building appear wider at the bottom than at the top. The Crop Tool lets you correct this distortion and square the corners of the building so that it appears that the photograph was shot straight on, rather than at an angle. There will be times when you want this kind of detailed control over the image you're working with, and you'll choose to crop rather than trim.

Zooming and Panning an Image

As you spend more time working in Photoshop, you'll find that you use its zoom feature frequently. You can zoom in on an image to select, copy, or modify individual pixels. Zooming gives you the flexibility to fine-tune an image in ways not possible if you were always looking at a photograph displayed at its actual screen or print size. Panning lets you keep the image at a high magnification while quickly moving to the next area you want to modify.

Zooming an Image

There are many ways to zoom an image in or out in Photoshop, and a number of these are available on the Zoom Tool options bar. When the Zoom Tool is selected, the options bar changes to reflect available zoom settings, as shown in Figure 2-34.

Figure 2-34   Options on the Zoom Tool options bar

Option	Details
🔍	Indicates currently selected tool; click to open the Tool Preset picker.
🔍	Select to zoom in.
🔍	Select to zoom out.
Resize Windows to Fit	Resizes the window automatically when you zoom in or out.
Zoom All Windows	When you have multiple documents open, zooming one image zooms all the other images the same amount.
Scrubby Zoom	Only available with an Open GL video card; drag to the left to zoom out, or drag to the right to zoom in.
Actual Pixels	Shows the image at 100% magnification.
Fit Screen	Fits the image in the Document window.
Fill Screen	Fills the document window top to bottom. If the image is taller than it is wide, there will be space on either side of the image; if the image is wider than it is tall, the sides of the image will not show in this view.
Print Size	Displays the file in the size at which it will print.

TIP

You can also press the Ctrl++ keys to zoom in on the image and the Ctrl+- keys to zoom out.

To use the Zoom In pointer (a magnifying glass with a plus sign), position the pointer over the area on which you want to zoom in, and then click. How much the image is zoomed depends on your monitor size and the starting zoom percentage. For example, for an image displayed at a 25% zoom on a 19-inch monitor, clicking the Zoom In Pointer once increases the zoom percentage to 33.33%. (The zoom percentage is also called the magnification level.) Clicking it a second time increases the zoom to 50%. Additional clicks result in 66.67% and then 100 % zoom settings.

If you have a video card that supports OpenGL and if you have selected Animated Zoom in the General Preferences, you can zoom continuously in Photoshop rather than zooming in increments. When you zoom continuously, you achieve the same effect that you see when you use your digital camera's zoom feature to zoom in on a scene to get a close-up photograph. To zoom continuously in Photoshop when the Zoom Tool is active, point to the area of the image on which you want to zoom in, and then press and hold the mouse button until you zoom to the level you want. If you press and hold the Alt key while zooming, you can achieve a similar animated zoom effect while zooming out continuously.

Photoshop provides another useful way to examine an image close up. Dragging a zoom selection marquee simplifies the zooming process and is often more practical than clicking the image repeatedly when the Zoom Tool is active. To zoom in on a specific rectangular area of an image, activate the Zoom Tool and then position the Zoom In pointer over the area on which you want to focus and drag a box, called a **selection marquee**, around the area. Photoshop zooms the image so that the area inside the marquee is centered in and fills the Document window. If your computer is equipped with a video card that supports OpenGL, dragging the pointer will zoom continuously rather than draw a marquee.

You can also zoom an image using Zoom presets on the options bar, including Actual Pixels, Fit Screen, Fill Screen, and Print Size. They are available as buttons on the options bar when the Zoom tool is selected. Fit on Screen, Actual Pixels, and Print Size are also available on the View menu.

To zoom the image using presets:

1. Navigate to the Photoshop2\Tutorial folder included with your Data Files, and open **Hi_Res.jpg**, display the rulers, and change the zoom setting to 50%, if necessary.

2. Click the **Zoom Tool** 🔍 on the Tools panel to display the zoom options on the options bar.

3. On the options bar, click the **Actual Pixels** button to display the image at a 100% zoom setting. If you have a large monitor, the inches on the rulers might appear wider than the inches on a real ruler. Because this image has a resolution of 240 pixels per inch and is five inches wide, what you see on screen is 1200 pixels across the width of the Document window. (5 inches times 240 pixels per inch equals 1200 pixels.) If you have a smaller monitor, or if you haven't maximized the Photoshop window, the inches on the ruler might appear smaller than real inches.

4. Click the **Print Size** button on the options bar. The image is now displayed at a lower zoom setting. Again, the actual setting depends on the size of your monitor. Notice that the ruler measurements are closer together. When the zoom is set to Print Size, an inch on the ruler is a true inch.

5. Click the **Fit Screen** button on the options bar. Photoshop enlarges the image so that it is as large as possible but still fits on screen.

6. Click the **Fill Screen** button on the options bar. The image fills the Document window area.

Because zooming often hides parts of an image with which you might want to work, sometimes you need to pan an image to see an area that was previously hidden.

Panning an Image

When you are doing detail work on an image and have zoomed in to a high magnification level, there will often be large parts of the image that you can't see. To move from one part of the image to another, you could zoom out, find the area of the photo you want to work with, and then zoom in again. However, it is much simpler to pan the image so that you can see a different area of the image.

Panning an image is like looking at a photograph on your desk using a magnifying glass. You can only see a part of the image at the high magnification the magnifying glass provides. To see another area, you can either slide the photo across the desk, or move the magnifying glass to a different part of the photo. Either way, you are panning the image.

The Hand Tool on the Tools panel is one of the most convenient ways to pan an image. To use the Hand Tool, select it on the Tools panel, and then move your mouse pointer over the image. When you do, the pointer takes the shape of a hand. You can press the left mouse button and drag in the direction you want to pan the photo. As you drag, a different part of the image comes into view. If you drag to the right, the left part of the image comes into view. If you drag to the left, the right part of the image comes into view. Dragging up displays the bottom of the image, while dragging down displays the top.

C.J. is working on a new stationary letterhead, and thinks it would be interesting to use the grid of a solar panel as part of the company logo. You'll use the Hand tool to pan the image when it is zoomed in and then you'll select the solar panels and copy them to use in a new file.

TIP

You can temporarily turn off the panning feature by pressing the Ctrl key to change the pointer to the Zoom In pointer, or by pressing the Alt key to change it to the Zoom Out pointer.

To use the Hand tool to pan the Hi_Res.jpg image:

1. Press the **Ctrl++** keys to zoom to 200%.

2. Click the **Hand tool** 🖐 on the Tools panel.

   Trouble? If you can't see the Hand Tool, click the Rotate View Tool, hold down the mouse button until you see the tools list, and then click the Hand Tool.

3. Move the mouse pointer over the Document window. When it is over the Document window, the pointer changes to a hand 🖐.

4. Press the left mouse button and drag to the right until the coil of wires is completely visible.

5. Point to the coil of wires, press the mouse button, and drag up until the wires are no longer visible.

6. Click the **Rectangular Marquee Tool** ⬚ and drag a selection marquee over part of the solar panel, as shown in Figure 2-35.

Figure 2-35   Making a selection

select part of
the solar panel

7. Press the **Ctrl+C** keys to copy the selection.

8. Navigate to the Photoshop2\Tutorial folder, and open **GreenHouseText2.psd**. In the Layers panel, select **Background Layer**, and then press the **Ctrl+V** keys to paste the copied solar panels into the file.

9. Use the Move Tool to move the copied panels so that they are centered below the text.

10. Save the file as **SolarText.psd** in the Photoshop2\Tutorial folder, and then close the file.

The Navigator is another excellent tool for zooming and panning an image. It is especially useful because it displays a thumbnail of the entire image so that you can easily choose your next "destination," or the place on the image to where you want to pan. You access the Navigator from the Window menu.

You'll work with the Navigator to become more comfortable focusing on different areas of a complex image. You know this skill will come in handy when you do detailed pixel editing work for C.J. in the future.

To use the Navigator to pan and zoom the image:

1. Hi_Res.jpg should still be open at 200% in the Document window. On the Application bar, click **Select**, and then click **Deselect** to deselect the solar panel.

2. On the Application bar, click **Window**, and then click **Navigator**. The Navigator opens to the left of the Adjustments panel group. It is grouped with two other panels, History and Info. Notice that there is a thumbnail of the open photograph and a box, called the proxy preview area or view box, which outlines the portion of the image currently displayed in the Document window. The size of the view box changes based on the magnification. The lower the magnification, the larger the box because a larger part of the image is being displayed in the Document window.

3. Drag the **view box** in the Navigator up and to the right so that it encloses the man on the right. See Figure 2-36.

Figure 2-36   **Using the Navigator**

image is panned to man

view box encloses man

collapsed Navigator panel icon

Dragging the view box pans the image.

4. Press the **Ctrl++** keys to change the zoom percentage to 300%. Notice that the view box has gotten smaller in the Navigator because a smaller portion of the image appears in the Document window.

5. Click the Zoom Tool 🔍, if necessary, and then click the **Fit Screen** button on the options bar. The view box is as large as the document in the Document window because the entire image is visible.

6. Click the **Actual Pixels** button on the options bar. The view box appears smaller on the thumbnail because by zooming in, you are viewing a smaller part of the image. You can also use the settings in the Navigator to zoom your image.

7. Type **500** in the box on the lower-left side of the Navigator, and then press the **Enter** key. The image in the Document window zooms to a 500% magnification level. The view box on the thumbnail decreases substantially in size.

8. Drag the **Zoom** slider at the bottom of the Navigator all the way to the left, and then all the way to the right. The maximum zoom setting allowed by Photoshop is 3200%. Notice that the view box has nearly disappeared because you are focused on such a small part of the image.

9. Close the file without saving it, click the workspace switcher icon ⏩, and click **Reset Essentials**.

Rotating and Flipping an Image

TIP

If you want to rotate the view while you are working, but don't want to permanently rotate the photo and alter the pixels, you can use the Rotate View tool if you have an OpenGL video card.

There might be times when you have the perfect image for a project—with one small problem: The door of the house needs to be on the right, not the left, or the photographer took the photograph with the camera held sideways in order to fit the tall person in the photo. As a result, the orientation is wrong. Or maybe you have photographs of two different people that you want to put in a composition so that they are facing each other. Unfortunately, the man is facing to the left in his photograph and the boy is facing left as well. What can you do to fix this problem so the two people are facing each other? You can rotate or flip one of the images. It's important to note that rotating and flipping an image is a destructive form of editing: That is, it permanently alters the pixels in the photograph.

Photoshop provides a number of options for rotating and flipping images. You can access the rotation commands on the Image menu by clicking Image Rotation and then making a selection. Figure 2-37 shows the six options available for image rotation.

Figure 2-37	Image rotation options

Option	Details
180°	Flips the image so that it is upside down and facing in the opposite direction
90°CW and 90°CCW	Rotates the image 90 degrees clockwise and 90 degrees counterclockwise, respectively
Flip Canvas Horizontal	Flips the image around an imaginary vertical line drawn through the center of the image
Flip Canvas Vertical	Flips the image around an imaginary horizontal line drawn through the center of the image
Arbitrary	Lets you specify an angle of rotation for your image and whether you want to rotate the image clockwise or counterclockwise; when you rotate an image at an angle other than 90°, 180°, or 360°, Photoshop increases the size of the canvas to accommodate the image

C.J. wants you to experiment with rotating and flipping an image of a wrench so that you are prepared to manipulate other images as needed on future projects.

To rotate and flip the image of the wrench:

1. On the options bar, reset all tools. Navigate to the Photoshop2\Tutorial folder, and open **Wrench.jpg**, display the rulers, if necessary, and fit the image on the screen. A photograph of a wrench that is 12 inches wide and 9 inches high appears in the Document window.

2. On the Application bar, click **Image**, and then click **Image Rotation**. Photoshop displays the commands for rotating an image.

3. Click **90°CW**. See Figure 2-38. The photograph is now 9 inches wide by 12 inches high.

Figure 2-38 **Rotated image**

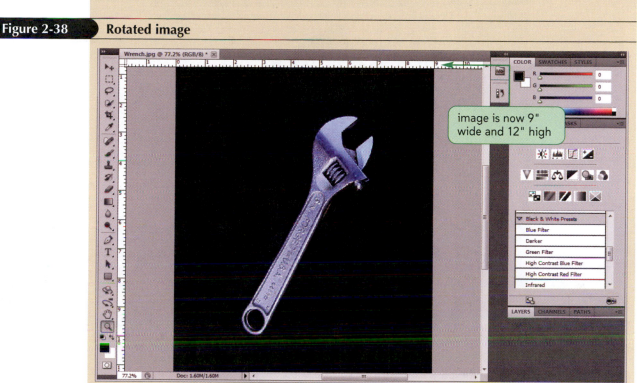

4. On the Application bar, click **Edit**, and then click **Undo Rotate Canvas**.

5. On the Application bar, click **Image**, click **Image Rotation**, and then click **Arbitrary**. The Rotate Canvas dialog box opens. You can specify the angle and direction (clockwise or counterclockwise) of the rotation.

6. Type **60** in the Angle box, select the **°CCW** option button to rotate the image 60 degrees counterclockwise, and then click the **OK** button. The image rotates 60 degrees counterclockwise, and Photoshop expands the dimensions of the canvas to accommodate the rotation.

7. On the Tools panel, click the **Zoom tool**, if necessary, and then click the **Fit Screen** button on the options bar. See Figure 2-39.

Figure 2-39 **Extended canvas accommodates rotation**

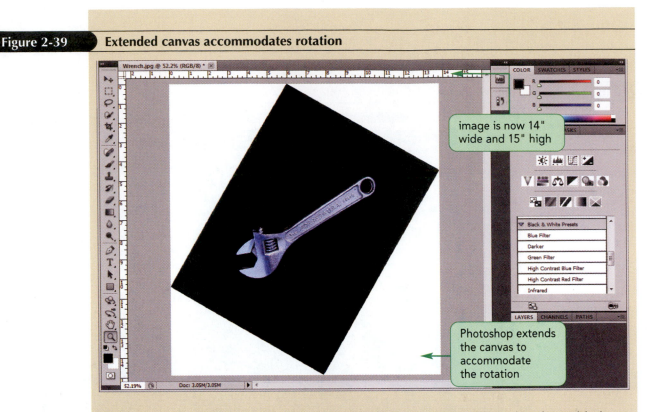

The canvas is now 14 inches wide and 15 inches high, and Photoshop has added to the canvas to accommodate the new angle of the image.

8. Save the file as **WrenchRotate.jpg** in the Photoshop2\Tutorial using the current JPEG settings, close the file, and then exit Photoshop.

In this session, you learned how to use the Adjustments panel to quickly make adjustments to an image. You also learned how to pan and zoom an image and how to rotate an image.

Session 2.2 Quick Check

REVIEW

1. An adjustment that changes the nature of the pixels in an image is called _____.
2. Nondestructive image edits are stored in _____.
3. Brightness/Contrast settings for an image can be found on the _____ panel.
4. When you drag an image within the Document window to see an area that was previously hidden, you are _____ the image.
5. True or False. The keyboard shortcut Ctrl+- increases the zoom magnification of an image.
6. The _____ panel provides a convenient way to zoom and pan an image.
7. The Image Rotation command can be found on the _____ menu.

Review Assignments

PRACTICE

Data Files needed for the Review Assignments: Hammer.psd, GreenHouseText.psd

C.J. wants you to continue exploring Photoshop on your own so that you become more comfortable working with and making adjustments to images. He suggests that you work with an image of a hammer that he is thinking of including on a postcard he plans to send to his customers. Complete the following steps:

1. Start Photoshop while pressing the Ctrl+Alt+Shift keys, and click Yes to delete the Settings File when asked, then reset Photoshop to the default Essentials workspace layout, and reset all tools.

2. Open **Hammer.psd**, located in the Photoshop2\Review folder provided with your Data Files.

3. Add a Brightness/Contrast adjustment layer to the image, and set the Brightness to -60 and the Contrast to 25.

4. Add a Hue/Saturation adjustment layer, and set the Hue to +95. Save the file as **HammerAdjust.psd** in the Photoshop2\Review folder.

5. Delete the Hue/Saturation layer.

6. Rotate the image 90° counterclockwise.

7. Increase the canvas size half an inch on every side, and set the Canvas extension color to black.

8. Save the file as **HammerExtend.psd** in the Photoshop2\Review folder.

9. Save the file again as **HammerExtend.jpg** in the Photoshop2\Review folder using Medium quality and 3 Progressive scans.

10. Open **HammerExtend.psd** and view both files in 2 Up vertical view. Zoom both files to 100% view, and then fit them on screen.

11. Close HammerExtend.jpg, and then change HammerExtend.psd to grayscale and flatten it. Save the file as **GrayHammer.psd**.

12. Zoom the image to 200 percent, and use the Navigator to center the end of the hammer in the Document window.

13. Pan to the HELPING HAND DROP FORGED text on the hammer, select the portion of the image that shows the text, and then copy it to the Clipboard.

14. Create a new file using the Clipboard preset and paste the portion of the image showing the text into the file. Save the new file as **HammerText.psd** and close it.

15. Place **GreenHouseText.psd** from the Photoshop4\Review folder in the upper-right corner of GrayHammer.psd, and resize it to fit in the gray area without overlapping the hammer.

16. Save GrayHammer.psd and exit Photoshop.

17. Submit the results of the preceding steps to your instructor either in printed or electronic form, as requested.

Use your skills
to modify a
photograph for a
presentation.

APPLY

Case Problem 1

Data Files needed for this Case Problem: ConcertHall.jpg

Sound Plan Engineering   Sound Plan Engineering is an organization of acoustic, audio, and noise control consultants in Santa Fe, New Mexico. The firm specializes in acoustic and audiovisual system design. The firm was founded by Manuel Ramirez in 2002 and has grown from 10 employees to 150 in less than a decade. You have been tasked with preparing variations on an image of the firm's most recent work to present at a meeting with board members. Complete the following steps:

1. Start Photoshop while pressing the Ctrl+Alt+Shift keys, and click Yes to delete the Settings File when asked, then reset Photoshop to the default Essentials workspace layout, and reset all tools.

2. Open **ConcertHall.jpg** located in the Photoshop2\Case1 folder provided with your Data Files, and fit the image on the screen.

3. Trim the image based on the top left pixel color. Do not trim away the bottom part of the image, as this is where text for the final piece will go.

4. Select the Zoom tool, and drag a zoom selection marquee from the bottom of the curtain above the piano to the floor, making its width about the width of the piano. (*Hint*: If your computer is equipped with a video card that supports OpenGL, dragging the pointer will zoom continuously rather than draw a marquee. Zoom so that you can see the area described in Step 4.)

5. Open the Navigator panel. Press the Alt+Print Screen keys to capture an image of the current Photoshop window, then open WordPad, which is available on the Accessories menu of the All Programs menu in Windows 7, and press the Ctrl+V keys to paste the image into a new file. Save the WordPad file as **Marquee.rtf** in the Photoshop2\Case1 folder provided with your Data Files.

6. Use the Navigator to pan to the seats in the audience on the lower-right side of the image. Press the Alt+Print Screen keys to capture an image of the current Photoshop window, switch to WordPad, create a new file, and press the Ctrl+V keys to paste the image into the new file. Save the WordPad file as **Navigator.rtf** in the Photoshop2\Case1 folder provided with your Data Files.

7. Collapse the Navigator panel. Fit the image on screen, and then apply the Black & White adjustment using the Blue Filter preset.

8. Save the file as **BWConcertHall.jpg** using maximum quality and the Baseline Optimized format option.

9. Delete the black-and-white adjustment layer.

10. Change the Brightness setting to -38 and the Contrast Setting to 10.

11. Save the file as a JPEG image named **ConcertHallAdjust** in the Photoshop2\Case1 folder, using the same JPEG options you used in Step 8.

12. Close ConcertHall.jpg without saving it, and exit Photoshop.

13. Submit the results of the preceding steps to your instructor either in printed or electronic form, as requested.

Use your skills to create an image for an online costume company.

APPLY

Case Problem 2

Data File needed for this Case Problem: EyeMask.psd, Eye.tif

FrightSite   Darron Murtha owns FrightSite, an online costume company specializing in exotic masks, based in Columbus, Ohio. Darron recently hired you to work in FrightSite's Marketing Department. Currently, you are working on a composition that will combine an ancient mask with a real eye, and you want to use Photoshop to achieve the creepy effect you're looking for. Complete the following steps:

1. Start Photoshop while pressing the Ctrl+Alt+Shift keys, and click Yes to delete the Settings File when asked, then reset Photoshop to the default Essentials workspace layout, and reset all tools.

2. Open **EyeMask.psd** located in the Photoshop2\Case2 folder provided with your Data Files.

3. Change the image size to 8 inches × 11inches, change the resolution to 72 ppi, select Scale Styles, constrain the proportions to ensure that the height and width change proportionally, and resample the image using Nearest Neighbor.

4. Zoom the image to 100%, and then change the canvas size to 8 inches × 9 inches, anchoring the image at the top center. (*Hint*: Allow clipping when prompted.)

EXPLORE

5. Place **Eye.tif** from the Photoshop2\Case2 folder on top of Layer 1, and resize and move the image so that it fits in the open eye socket. (*Hint*: Click the Show Transform Controls check box on the options bar when using the Move Tool, and press the Shift key when resizing to constrain proportions.)

EXPLORE

6. Deselect Show Transform Controls, if necessary, and adjust the eye until you get a creepy effect. (*Hint*: To adjust only the eye, make sure you clip the adjustment to the Eye layer. For a creepy effect, try adjusting the hue and saturation.) If you are unhappy with an adjustment, you can delete it from the Layers panel.

7. Adjust the text layer by changing its brightness to -125.

8. Place another copy of **Eye.tif** in the file and resize it and move it so that it fits between the two lines of text. (*Hint*: The Eye layer should appear at the top of the Layers panel.) Adjust the eye by changing its hue to -40 and its saturation to +100.

9. Switch the image to RGB mode, rasterize the image when prompted, and merge the layers.

10. Save the file as **Fright.jpg** in the Photoshop2\Case2 folder, using a background color matte, medium quality, and a Baseline ("Standard") for optimization.

11. Close the file, close EyeMask.psd without saving it, and exit Photoshop.

12. Submit the results of the preceding steps to your instructor either in printed or electronic form, as requested.

Use your skills to create different versions of a profile photo.

Case Problem 3

Data Files needed for this Case Problem: Mash.jpg, RockNRoll.psd

MashMatch Music   MashMatch Music is an online site for sharing original music and creating mashups with other musicians. You have joined the site as a solo musician, and want to post a profile photo showcasing your instrument. You plan to use the same composition for a newspaper and for a poster that you'll hang up around town. Complete the following steps:

1. Start Photoshop while pressing the Ctrl+Alt+Shift keys, and click Yes to delete the Settings File when asked, then reset Photoshop to the default Essentials workspace layout, and reset all tools.
2. Open **Mash.jpg** from the Photoshop2\Case3 folder provided with your Data Files.
3. Change the size of the image to 12 inches × 9 inches at 72 ppi. Resample the image when you resize, using the default settings.
4. Display the image at a magnification that's convenient to work with, then change the brightness of the image so that the hand stands out more against the guitar.
5. Extend the canvas to add two inches to the top only, and make the extension color gray.
6. Place the file **RockNRoll.psd** from the Photoshop2\Case3 folder in the file, and position the text so it is centered in the gray area.
7. Apply a posterize adjustment to the Background layer using the default settings.
8. Save the file as **Profile.jpg** in the Photoshop2\Case3 folder, using the default settings.
9. Delete the posterize adjustment layer.
10. Change the color mode to CMYK and rasterize the SmartObjects in the image when prompted. Do not flatten the image.
11. Save the file as **CMYKRock.jpg** in the Photoshop2\Case3 folder, using Low quality and an optimized baseline.
12. Change the color mode to Grayscale.
13. Change the brightness to -60 and the Contrast to 25.
14. Save the file as **GrayRock.jpg** in the Photoshop2\Case3 folder, using the default settings, close Mash.jpg without saving it, and exit Photoshop.
15. Submit the results of the preceding steps to your instructor either in printed or electronic form, as requested.

Use the skills you learned, plus some new skills, to modify a photograph and add text.

CHALLENGE

Case Problem 4

Data Files needed for this Case Problem: Cakes.jpg, FinnText.psd, FinnText2.psd

Finnegan's Cake   You are the sole proprietor of Finnegan's Cake, a neighborhood bakery in Northport, New York. You are just learning Photoshop, and want to use your new skills to modify an image for the cover of the menu. You'll create a color menu for in-house customers and a black-and-white menu for takeout. Complete the following steps:

1. Start Photoshop while pressing the Ctrl+Alt+Shift keys, and click Yes to delete the Settings File when asked, then reset Photoshop to the default Essentials workspace layout, and reset all tools.

2. Open **Cakes.jpg** located in the Photoshop2\Case4 folder provided with your Data Files.

3. Zoom in on the green triangle on the cake.

⊕ **EXPLORE**   4. Change the background color in Photoshop to the green from the cake. (*Hint*: Click the background square on the Color panel. When the Color Picker (Background Color) dialog box opens, click the green triangle on the cake using the Eyedropper pointer, and then click the OK button.)

5. Fit the image on screen. Extend the canvas by increasing the canvas by 4 inches in height, with no change in width. Leave the image anchored in the center, and use the Background color for the canvas extension.

6. Place **FinnText.psd** from the Photoshop2\Case4 folder at the top of the canvas.

⊕ **EXPLORE**   7. On the Tools panel, click the Eyedropper Tool and then click the off-white background around the cakes to sample its color and assign it as the background color.

8. Switch the background and foreground colors by pressing the X key, and then use the Rectangle Tool to draw an off-white rectangle over the green extension at the bottom of the image so that it is as wide as the image, and about three-quarters of an inch tall. Center it vertically in the green area.

9. Place **FinnText2.psd** from the Photoshop2\Case4 folder at the bottom of the canvas, on top of the off-white rectangle.

⊕ **EXPLORE**   10. Display the Styles panel, and apply the Double Yellow Strokes style to the text you just placed at the bottom of the canvas. (*Hint*: Double Yellow Strokes is in the second to last row on the Styles panel, and is the second button from the right. You may need to scroll to see the button.)

11. Convert the image to CMYK mode, and rasterize and flatten it.

12. Save the file as **Menu.tif** in the Photoshop2\Case4 folder, using the default TIFF settings.

13. Change the color mode to Grayscale.

14. Adjust the brightness to -40 and the contrast to 40.

15. Save the file as **GrayCakes.jpg** in the Photoshop2\Case4 folder, with the current JPEG settings.

16. Submit the results of the preceding steps to your instructor either in printed or electronic form, as requested.

ENDING DATA FILES

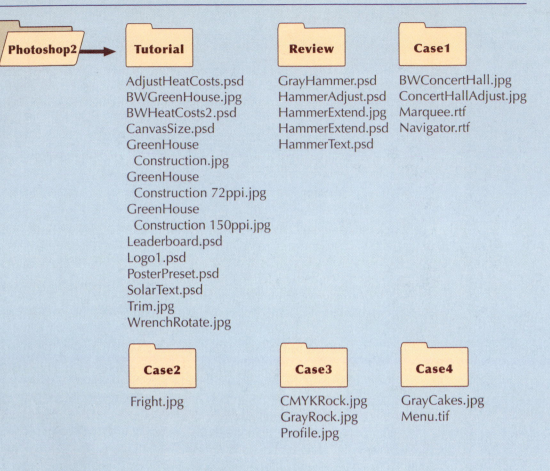

Photoshop2 → **Tutorial**

AdjustHeatCosts.psd
BWGreenHouse.jpg
BWHeatCosts2.psd
CanvasSize.psd
GreenHouse
  Construction.jpg
GreenHouse
  Construction 72ppi.jpg
GreenHouse
  Construction 150ppi.jpg
Leaderboard.psd
Logo1.psd
PosterPreset.psd
SolarText.psd
Trim.jpg
WrenchRotate.jpg

Review

GrayHammer.psd
HammerAdjust.psd
HammerExtend.jpg
HammerExtend.psd
HammerText.psd

Case1

BWConcertHall.jpg
ConcertHallAdjust.jpg
Marquee.rtf
Navigator.rtf

Case2

Fright.jpg

Case3

CMYKRock.jpg
GrayRock.jpg
Profile.jpg

Case4

GrayCakes.jpg
Menu.tif

PHOTOSHOP

Layering Content to Compose Images

Working with Layers in Compositions

OBJECTIVES

Session 3.1
- Select, add, duplicate, and delete layers
- Change layer properties and visibility
- Move, align, and distribute layers
- Hide and unhide layers
- Place, resize, and reposition an image on a layer

Session 3.2
- Lock and unlock layer content
- Work with layer comps
- Apply blending modes and adjust opacity
- Create layer groups
- Merge layers and flatten an image

Case | *Cooking the Books Publishing*

Cooking the Books Publishing is a small publishing house based in Madison, Wisconsin. The company was founded by Elena Genoa in 2008, and currently has 25 titles on its list. Upcoming titles include *The Fruit Fantastic: Recipes for the Adventurous Palate*, and *The New Old-Fashioned: 19th Century Recipes with a 21st Century Twist*. You are an assistant to Art Director Kaye Eastman. Because it's a small company, you and Kaye are tasked with creating all of the artwork for the publishing house, including illustrations and covers. Kaye has asked you to work on some cover and illustration ideas for the new titles. You'll use layers in Photoshop to develop a series of possible compositions to present to her at your next meeting.

STARTING DATA FILES

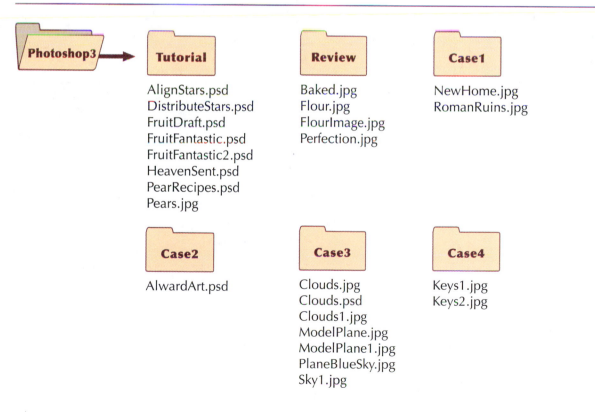

Photoshop3 →

Tutorial
AlignStars.psd
DistributeStars.psd
FruitDraft.psd
FruitFantastic.psd
FruitFantastic2.psd
HeavenSent.psd
PearRecipes.psd
Pears.jpg

Review
Baked.jpg
Flour.jpg
FlourImage.jpg
Perfection.jpg

Case1
NewHome.jpg
RomanRuins.jpg

Case2
AlwardArt.psd

Case3
Clouds.jpg
Clouds.psd
Clouds1.jpg
ModelPlane.jpg
ModelPlane1.jpg
PlaneBlueSky.jpg
Sky1.jpg

Case4
Keys1.jpg
Keys2.jpg

SESSION 3.1 VISUAL OVERVIEW

The Align icons on the options bar let you choose how to **align**, or line up, selected objects along their centers or edges.

Select the Show Transform Controls check box to see **transform controls**, the squares at each corner of a selection that let you change the shape and size of an object.

You can set the layer name and the layer color in the Layer Properties dialog box.

You can display **layer edges** to see where a layer begins and ends on the canvas.

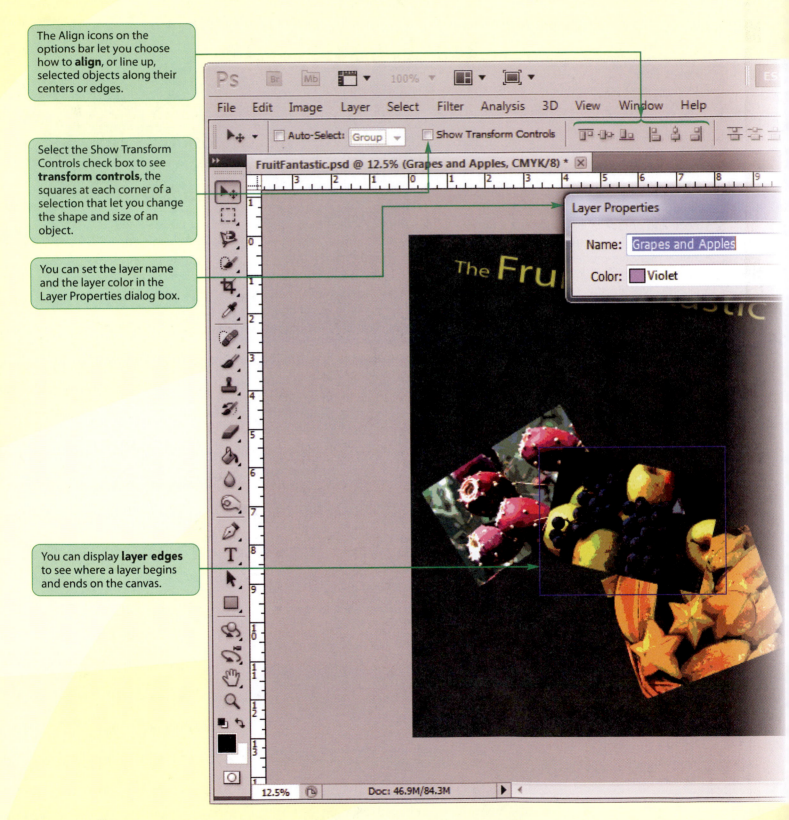

WORKING WITH MULTIPLE LAYERS

The Distribute icons on the options bar let you **distribute**, or spread out, selected objects evenly across or down the canvas.

Creating a **layer group** lets you organize related layers in a way that makes sense to you.

When there is no Eye icon next to a layer, the layer is **hidden**, or not visible on the canvas.

The currently selected layer is called the **active layer** and is highlighted on the Layers panel.

You can assign related layers the same layer color.

Click the Eye icon to hide a layer.

The Background layer is locked and is always at the bottom of the layer hierarchy.

Click the Create a new layer icon to add a new layer above the selected layer, or, if no layers are selected, at the top of the layers list on the Layers panel.

Understanding Layers

You have already witnessed the power of layers in Photoshop. In Tutorial 2, when you placed an image in a file, it appeared on its own layer. When you added an image adjustment, you were actually adding it as a layer on top of the layer to where it was clipped. An adjustment layer affects the way an image looks, but it does so in a nondestructive way because it does not alter the pixels in the image. It is like placing a sheet of clear plastic over the original image with the changes etched on it. Through this virtual layer of plastic, it appears as if the image has changed in some fundamental way. However, if you want to restore that image to its original appearance, all you have to do is delete or hide the layer containing the adjustment—as if you were removing the sheet of plastic containing your changes. See Figure 3-1.

Figure 3-1   **Nondestructive editing with an adjustment layer**

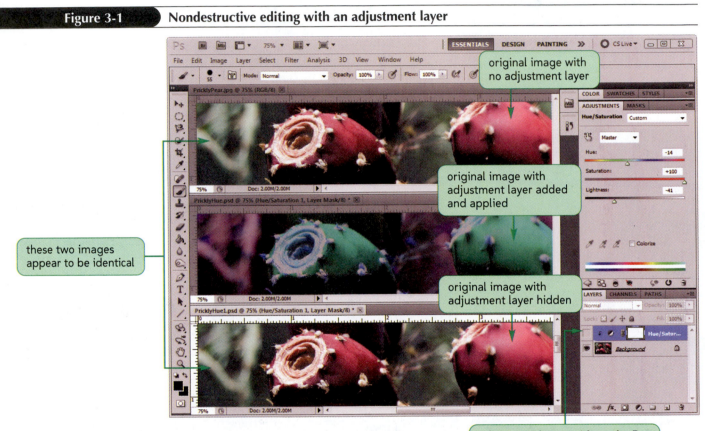

Figure 3-1 shows an image opened for the first time in Photoshop, then the same image with a Hue/Saturation adjustment layer applied, and a third version of the same image with the Hue/Saturation layer "turned off," or hidden. When the adjustment layer is visible, as shown in the image in the middle, it looks as if the underlying image itself has changed. However, when you hide the adjustment layer, you can see that the image pixels remain the same—with or without the adjustment layer.

If you do not make use of layers functionality in Photoshop, any changes you make to an image are permanent once you save the file. If you haven't saved a backup of the original file, there is no way to go back. With layers, however, you can experiment endlessly with a file by adding layer upon layer of changes, hiding layers, redisplaying layers, saving the file, working on it the next day and the next, and then deleting any layers you decide you don't want. Even with multiple changes, your original image remains intact—as long as you use layers to make those changes in a nondestructive way.

Understanding Layer Positioning

As a rule, if no layer is selected, any new layer that you add to a document appears at the top of the layers list on the Layers panel. If you select a layer first and then add a layer, the new layer appears directly above the selected layer. This is important to know because the order of layers on the Layers panel means a lot. The layer listed at the top of the Layers panel is the top layer in the document. See Figure 3-2.

Figure 3-2   **The importance of layer order**

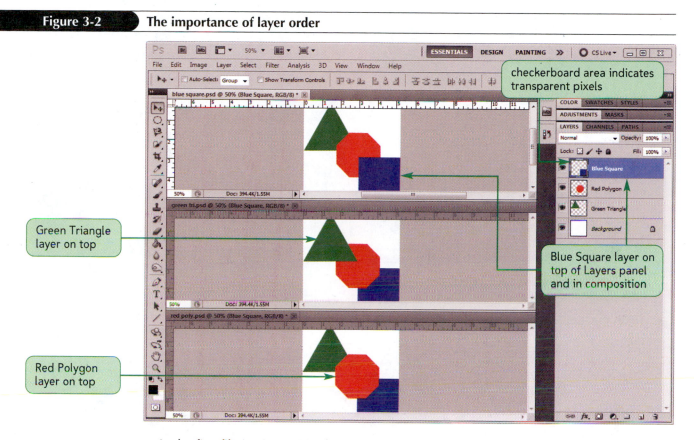

In the first file in Figure 3-2, the Blue Square layer is at the top of the list of layers, followed by the Red Polygon layer and then the Green Triangle layer. In the next file, the Green Triangle layer has been moved to the top of the list of layers, and appears on the top of the stacked objects in the document. In the third file, the Red Polygon layer is at the top of the Layers panel and appears on top in the document.

Notice that the thumbnail for each of these shapes on the Layers panel shows a checkerboard pattern around the shape. The checkerboard design in Photoshop indicates that the pixels in the checkerboard area are **transparent**, so you can see through them. Imagine that each of the shapes in Figure 3-2 has been painted on a rectangle of clear glass. Any area beneath the glass, except where the shape appears, is visible through the glass.

The position of adjustment layers on the Layers panel affects how the adjustments are applied to a file. An adjustment at the top of the Layers panel will affect all of the layers beneath it, unless it is clipped to a particular layer. When an adjustment is clipped to a layer on the Layers panel, it affects only that layer. See Figure 3-3.

Figure 3-3   An adjustment affecting one layer and an adjustment affecting all layers beneath it

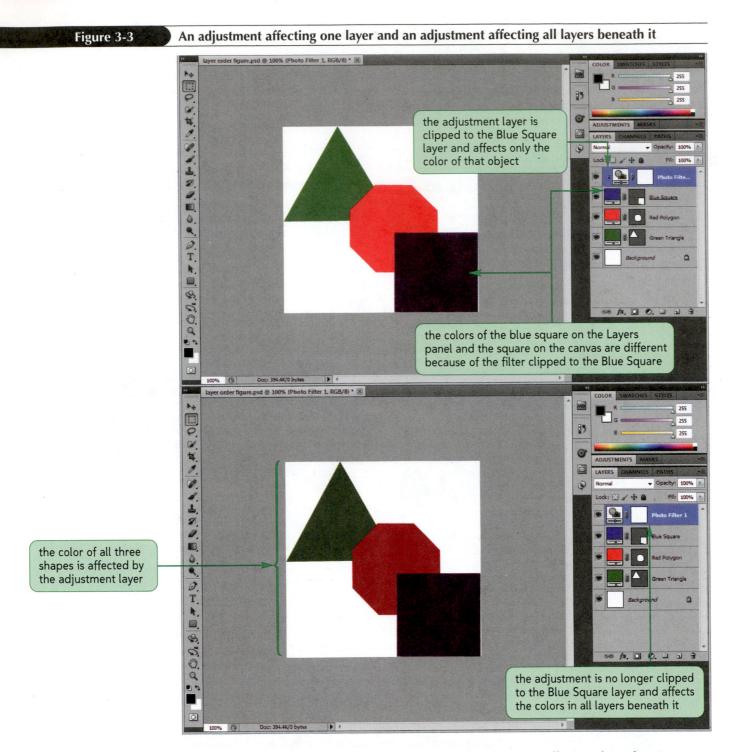

The Photo Filter adjustment used in Figure 3-3 has the same effect on the colors in an image that putting a colored filter over your camera lens would have: It changes the colors of the objects in the image. In the top image, the Photo Filter adjustment layer is clipped to the layer beneath it (the blue square). As a result, the color of the blue square in the image is different from the color of the blue square on the Layers panel. In the bottom image, the same Photo Filter adjustment layer affects *all* layers beneath it.

You'll find that most of the work you do in a complex document involves layers. You will frequently add, duplicate, select, name, and move layers. You'll group layers so their organization is logical, and you'll hide and redisplay them to compare their impact or effect. In this session, you'll learn many of the basic layer tasks you'll perform in Photoshop.

Selecting and Deselecting Layers

To work with any layer in a Photoshop file, you first need to select it so it becomes active. More than one layer can be active at a time, and a layer must be active if you want to work with it. It's a common mistake to start working on an image with a particular goal in mind only to realize that you are not actually working with the correct layer. See Figure 3-4.

| Figure 3-4 | Trying to copy pixels in an unselected layer |

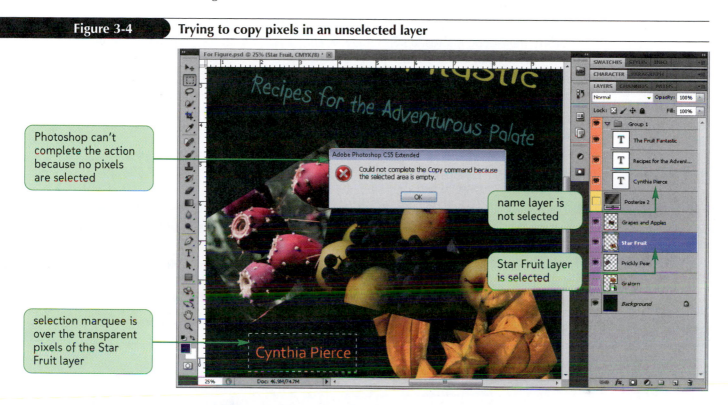

Photoshop can't complete the action because no pixels are selected

name layer is not selected

Star Fruit layer is selected

selection marquee is over the transparent pixels of the Star Fruit layer

In Figure 3-4, the selection marquee appears around the name on the book cover. It is logical to think that you could use the Copy command on the Edit menu to copy the selection to the Clipboard. However, although the selection marquee is over the name in the document, the Star Fruit layer is the selected layer. If you hid all the layers except the Star Fruit layer, you would see that the selected area consists of transparent pixels. In other words, there is nothing to copy. If you try to copy a selection that is empty, Photoshop displays the error message shown in the figure.

Selecting and Deselecting Single Layers

Often, you will want to select a single layer so you can make changes that affect that layer only. When you select certain layers in an image, a **bounding box** shows the borders of the layer; the transform controls are the squares on the sides and at each corner of the bounding box. Bounding boxes do not appear on **locked layers**, which are layers (such as the Background layer that appears by default at the bottom of the Layers panel) that you cannot move or resize. If you want to move or make changes to the locked Background layer, you can convert it to a regular layer by right-clicking the Background layer and selecting the Layer From Background option on its shortcut menu.

Kaye has created a couple of mock-ups for the new *Fruit Fantastic* cookbook, and she wants you to experiment with the layers in her composition to see if you can improve on her ideas. You'll start by selecting and deselecting layers in order to make changes on a single layer at a time.

To select and make changes to a single layer:

1. Start Photoshop while pressing the **Ctrl+Alt+Shift** keys. When you are prompted to delete the Adobe Photoshop Settings File, click **Yes**. On the Application bar, right-click **Essentials**, and then click **Reset Essentials** to reset the default workspace layout. Reset all tools, and then select the **Move Tool** ⊹ on the Tools panel.

2. Navigate to the Photoshop3\Tutorial folder included with your Data Files, and open **FruitFantastic.psd**. Close the **Color** panel group, minimize the **Adjustments** panel group, and then expand the **Layers** panel, if necessary.

   The Layers panel lists all of the layers in the file, including text layers, image layers, an adjustment layer, and the Background layer. You'll select The Fruit Fantastic layer so you can change its font.

3. On the Layers panel, click **The Fruit Fantastic** layer to select it. The text layer is selected on the panel and in the document, as indicated by the bounding box and the transform controls. See Figure 3-5.

   Trouble? If you can't see the bounding box and the transform controls, click the Show Transform Controls check box on the options bar to display them in the document.

Figure 3-5 **Text layer selected on the Layers panel and in the document**

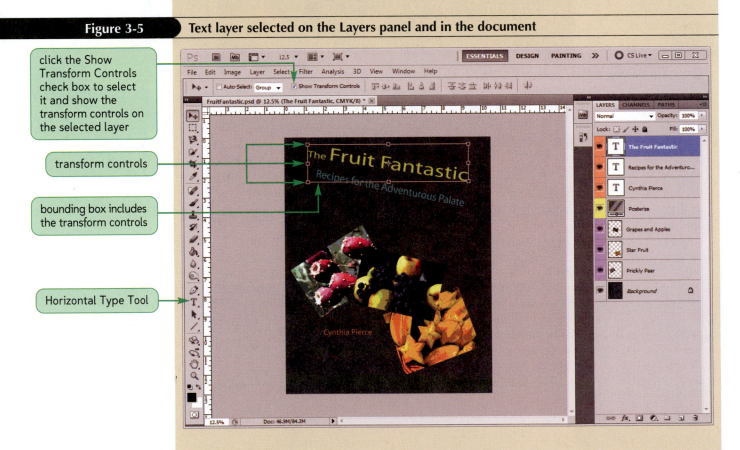

click the Show Transform Controls check box to select it and show the transform controls on the selected layer

transform controls

bounding box includes the transform controls

Horizontal Type Tool

4. On the Tools panel, click the **Horizontal Type Tool** T , and then on the options bar, click the **Font family** arrow `Times New Roman ▼` .

5. On the font list, click **Papyrus**. The title font changes to Papyrus.

   Trouble? If Papyrus does not appear on the font list, click a different font.

6. Select the **Move Tool** ⊹ , and then on the Layers panel, click the **Grapes and Apples** layer. The text layer is deselected, and the layer with the grapes and apples image is selected on the Layers panel and in the document.

7. Select the **Background** layer. The Background layer is selected on the Layers panel, but no bounding box appears in the document. This is because the Background layer is a locked layer and can't be moved (as indicated by the lock icon 🔒 that appears on the Layers panel).

8. Click the **Posterize** layer. The Posterize layer is selected on the Layers panel, but there is no selection in the document. This is because the Posterize layer is an adjustment layer. It affects the layers beneath it, but doesn't appear as an object in the composition.

9. On the Application bar, click **Select**, and then click **Deselect Layers**. Now there are no layers selected on the Layers panel.

TIP

You can also press and hold the Ctrl key and then click a layer to deselect it.

To work more efficiently, you can change many layers in a file at one time. To do so, you'll select multiple layers at once.

Selecting and Deselecting Multiple Layers

You will often find that you want to apply the same effect to multiple layers in a document. You could select the first layer, apply the effect, select the next layer, apply the effect, and so on. However, it's faster to select multiple layers at the same time and apply an effect to all of them at once. You can apply an adjustment to many layers at the same time by selecting all of the layers you want to work with to make them all active. For example, you might want to posterize all of the photographs in your composition using the same settings. When Photoshop **posterizes** an image, it removes the gradual changes in color and intensity that are typically found in a high-resolution photo and replaces them with abrupt changes in color and intensity, making the image look like a painting or a vector drawing, not a photograph. The three images shown in Figure 3-5 were selected together and then posterized all at once.

REFERENCE

Selecting Multiple Layers

- To select contiguous layers, on the Layers panel, click the first layer, press and hold the Shift key, and then click the last layer. To select noncontiguous layers, on the Layers panel, click the first layer, press and hold the Ctrl key, and then click each additional layer.

or

- To select all of the layers, on the Application bar, click Select, and then click All Layers.

You can also select similar layers using the Select menu. **Similar layers** are layers with common characteristics. For example, all adjustment layers on the Layers panel would be considered similar layers, as would all image layers and all text layers. Selecting similar layers lets you apply a single change to all similar layers at once.

If you select the Horizontal Type Tool to make changes to one or more text layers, the options for the Horizontal Type Tool appear on the options bar, indicating that Photoshop is in **text-edit mode**. In text-edit mode you can modify text on a layer by changing the font style and color, among other things.

Kaye asks you to see what the composition will look like if all of the text is the same color. You'll select all the text layers in the file at the same time to make the change.

To select similar layers:

1. On the Layers panel, select the **Cynthia Pierce** layer. You will use this text layer selection to select similar layers.

2. On the Application bar, click **Select**, and then click **Similar Layers**. All three of the text layers are selected, so you can modify all three layers at the same time.

3. Press the **T** key to activate the Horizontal Type Tool. When you do so, the Transform Controls are hidden, and the options for the Horizontal Type Tool appear on the options bar.

4. On the options bar, click the **Set the text color** icon ■. The Select text color dialog box opens.

5. In the dialog box, select a **yellow** color. See Figure 3-6.

Figure 3-6   **Using the Select text color dialog box**

6. Click the **OK** button. The yellow color is applied to the text on all three text layers at the same time. See Figure 3-7.

   Trouble? If a warning dialog box about missing fonts opens, click Continue to make the substitution.

Figure 3-7   **Similar layers with similar formatting applied**

all text layers are selected

all text layers are now yellow

7. On the Application bar, click **Select**, and then click **Deselect Layers**. No layers are selected on the Layers panel.

8. Save the file as **Fantastic2.psd** in the Photoshop3\Tutorial folder included with your Data Files, and leave it open in the Photoshop workspace.

PROSKILLS

Teamwork: Using CS Live to Reach a Consensus

Much of the work you do in any job is a collaborative effort. Whether you are making changes to a mock-up of a book cover, designing a Web page, developing an ad campaign, or writing a proposal, you'll most likely want input from other team members, and possibly from your client. The CS Live options available with Adobe Creative Suite give you the online tools you need to collaborate. CS Live includes five online services:

• Adobe BrowserLab lets Web site developers test their content on a variety of browsers.
• Adobe Story streamlines video production.
• SiteCatalyst NetAverages gives developers information about the latest trends on the Internet so they can optimize their Web development.
• Adobe CS Review lets you share your work with team members online and get feedback on projects; colleagues can see and respond to each other's comments so you can get a thorough review of your work.
• Adobe.com lets you set up Web conferences and share and collaborate in real time as you work on Photoshop or other Creative Suite files.

 As a Photoshop user, you're most likely to use the last two options when working with a team. These tools can also be useful if you just want feedback on individual projects from colleagues, peers, or managers. Capitalizing on the teamwork options provided with Photoshop will help you create your best work and achieve success not only on individual projects, but throughout your career.

Adding and Duplicating Layers

There are many ways to add a layer to a file. You can add an empty layer and then fill it with content. You can duplicate a selected layer so an exact copy of the layer appears on the Layers panel and in the composition. You can add a layer by drawing a vector object or by using the Type Tools on the Tools panel. You can cut or copy a selection on one layer—or even in another file—and paste it into your composition to add it as a new layer. You can use the options on the Adjustments panel to add an adjustment layer. You can add an **effects layer** by applying a style to a layer. You can also add a fill layer to fill the background of a composition with a color, pattern, or gradient.

Adding an Empty Layer

To add a layer before adding any content or making an adjustment, use the Create a new layer icon at the bottom of the Layers panel. You can then place a photograph, enter text, or draw a vector object in the new layer, and it will appear on the canvas on top of the Background layer.

Kaye has asked you to develop some additional options for the *Fruit Fantastic* book cover by starting with a plain background and adding some new layers.

To add an empty layer and add a shape to the new layer:

1. Open **FruitDraft.psd** from the Photoshop3\Tutorial folder provided with your Data Files.

2. At the bottom of the Layers panel, click the **Create a new layer** icon 🔲. Photoshop creates a new layer, named Layer 1, above the Background layer.

   Next, you'll add a shape to the empty layer.

3. On the Tools panel, click the **Rectangle Tool** 🔲. The options bar changes to display settings for the Rectangle Tool.

4. On the options bar, click the **Color** icon, and then, in the Color Picker dialog box, select a **blue** color and click the **OK** button.

5. On the canvas, draw a rectangle similar in size to the one shown in Figure 3-8.

Figure 3-8 | **Drawing a rectangle in an empty layer**

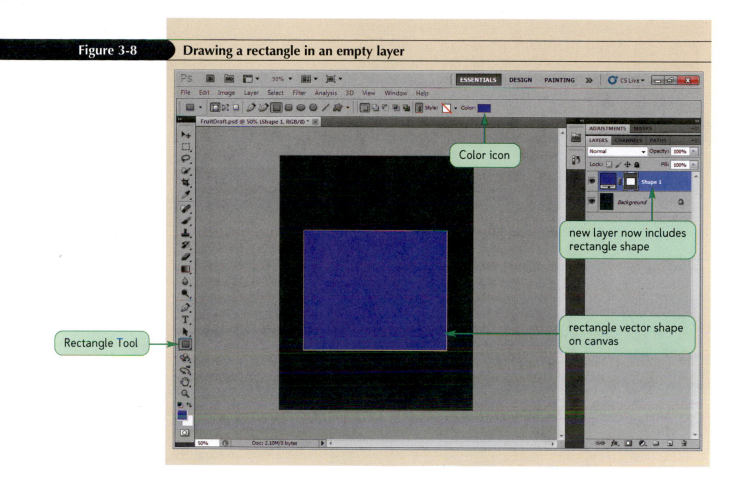

Rectangle Tool

Color icon

new layer now includes rectangle shape

rectangle vector shape on canvas

Adding a Vector Layer and an Adjustment Layer

When you use any of the vector drawing tools on the Tools panel when there are no layers selected, Photoshop places each vector object you draw on its own layer. When you modify the layer by adding an effect, Photoshop adds an effects layer indented underneath the layer you are modifying and adds an *fx* designation next to the layer name.

To add more interest to your cover design, you'll add another layer by drawing another shape in the file.

To add a vector layer and an effects layer:

1. On the Application bar, click **Select**, and then click **Deselect Layers**.

2. Using the Rectangle Tool, draw a rectangle inside the blue rectangle. Photoshop adds the rectangle to the document and places it on its own layer on the Layers panel. You'll change its color by changing the settings on the options bar.

3. On the options bar, click the **Color** icon, select a **purple** color, and then click the **OK** button.

4. On the Application bar, click **Window**, and then click **Styles** to redisplay the Color panel group with the Styles panel on top.

5. On the Styles panel, click the **Tie-Dyed Silk (Texture)** icon 🟧 to add a tie-dyed effect to the new layer. See Figure 3-9.

Trouble? If you don't see the Tie-Dyed Silk (Texture) icon 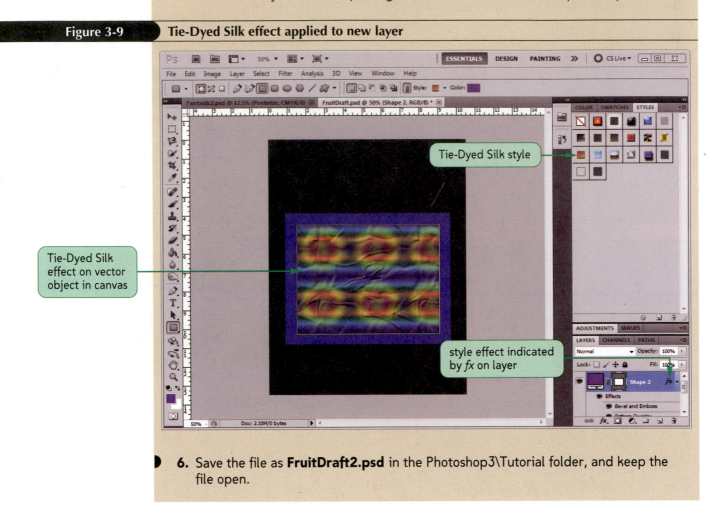 on the Styles panel, click the panel options button ▾☰, click Reset Styles, and then click the OK button to replace the current styles with the default styles. If prompted to save changes to the current styles before replacing them, click the No button. Repeat Step 5.

Figure 3-9   **Tie-Dyed Silk effect applied to new layer**

6. Save the file as **FruitDraft2.psd** in the Photoshop3\Tutorial folder, and keep the file open.

Creating a New Layer by Cutting or Copying and Pasting a Selection

You may find that you want to reuse part or all of an image, either in the current composition or in another composition. To do so, you can use one of the selection marquee tools to select the part of an image that you want to reuse, and then copy or cut the selection to the Windows Clipboard, which stores the selection in memory so you can paste it into the current file or another file. When you paste a selection, Photoshop puts the object on a new layer on the Layers panel. You can then use the Move Tool to position the object where you want it to appear on the canvas.

To continue creating your mock-up for the cookbook cover, you'll copy the grapes from the Fantastic2 file to the FruitDraft2 file and paste them on a new layer.

To create a layer by copying and pasting:

1. Click the **Fantastic2.psd** document tab to switch to that open file, and then zoom the file to 50% magnification.

2. On the Layers panel, select the **Grapes and Apples** layer.

3. On the Tools panel, click the **Rectangular Marquee Tool** [▭], and then drag a marquee around four of the grapes in the bunch of grapes on the right. See Figure 3-10.

Figure 3-10	Copying a rectangular marquee selection

click Copy on the Edit menu

Rectangular Marquee Tool selected

50% magnification

rectangular marquee around grapes

Grapes and Apples layer selected

50% magnification

4. On the Application bar, click **Edit**, and then click **Copy**.

5. Switch back to the **FruitDraft2.psd** file.

6. On the Application bar, click **Edit**, and then click **Paste**. Collapse the Styles panel so more of the Layers panel is visible. Photoshop pastes the selection in the file and on a new layer. Note that you selected and copied only the grapes, not the Posterize effect that was applied to them in the original file. See Figure 3-11.

Figure 3-11 | **Pasting a selection on the canvas**

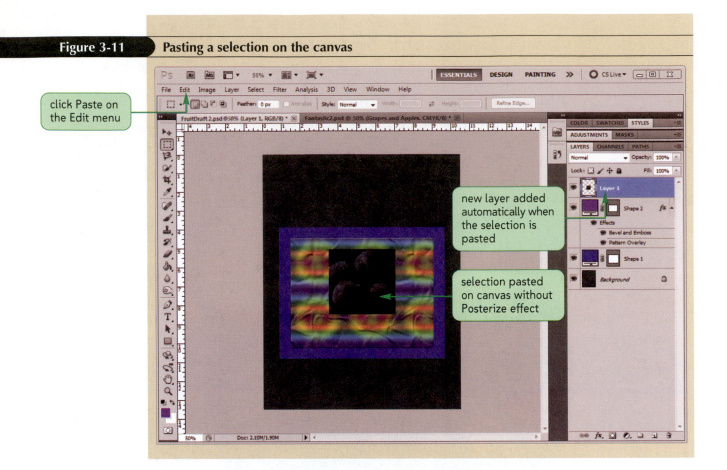

click Paste on the Edit menu

new layer added automatically when the selection is pasted

selection pasted on canvas without Posterize effect

Changing Layer Properties

When you are working in a file with many layers, it is helpful to name each layer in a way that makes it easy for you to remember its purpose. By default, Photoshop names generic layers by number: Layer 1, Layer 2, Layer 3, et cetera. When you create a text layer, Photoshop names it using the actual text you have typed, and places a text icon (the letter *T*) in the thumbnail. When you draw a shape, Photoshop names the shape layer Shape 1, Shape 2, Shape 3, et cetera. You can change the default name to make it more descriptive.

You can also change the color of a layer in the Layer Properties dialog box. Note that when you change the color of a layer, you are not changing the way the layer content looks on the canvas; rather, you are changing the color of the background of the Eye icon on the Layers panel. If you assign the same color to related layers, you provide yourself with an easy visual overview of the organization of your document. For example, in the Session 3.1 Visual Overview, all text layers have an orange color assigned to them, as does the group that contains the text layers; all digital images have been assigned a violet color; and all adjustment layers are yellow.

Kaye suggests that you organize your file by changing layer properties. You'll change the names and colors of the layers in your draft file so you can keep track of them more easily.

To change the name of a layer:

1. Press **V** to activate the Move Tool, if necessary.

2. On the Layers panel, click **Layer 1** to select it, if necessary. Point to *Layer 1* and double-click. The layer name appears highlighted in a box.

3. Type **Grapes** and then press the **Enter** key. Photoshop renames the layer.

4. On the Layers panel, click **Shape 1** to select it, right-click the layer, and then click **Layer Properties**.

5. In the Name box, type **Blue Rectangle**, and then click the **OK** button.

6. Change the name of the Shape 2 layer to **Tie Dye**, and then deselect all layers. See Figure 3-12.

| Figure 3-12 | Renaming layers |

The layers on the Layers panel now have names that help you identify them quickly. Next, you'll assign layer colors to the FruitDraft2.psd file to keep it organized.

To change the color of a layer:

1. Right-click the **Grapes** layer, and then click **Layer Properties**. In the Layer Properties dialog box, click the Color arrow, click **Violet**, and then click the **OK** button. Photoshop changes the color of the layer on the Layers panel to violet.

2. Change the color of the **Tie Dye** layer to **Orange**. Photoshop assigns the orange color to the Tie Dye layer and its associated effects layers.

3. Change the color of the **Blue Rectangle** layer to **Blue**. See Figure 3-13.

Figure 3-13   **Changing layer colors**

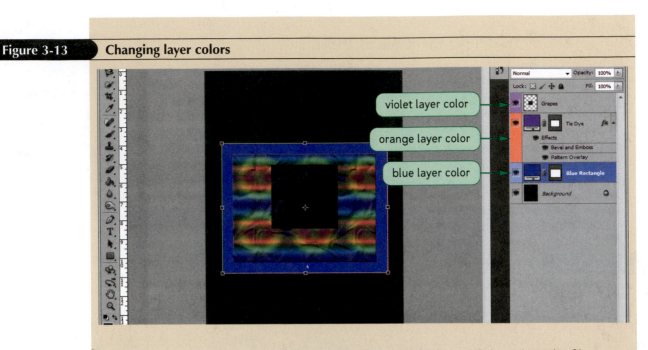

violet layer color

orange layer color

blue layer color

4. Save FruitDraft2.psd in the Photoshop3\Tutorial folder, and then close the file.

INSIGHT

Keeping the Layers Panel Manageable

If you add many layers to your composition, and apply many adjustments to those layers, the Layers panel might become unwieldy. You can organize your layers by grouping them and color-coding them, but it can be tempting to go overboard when you do. For example, if you have one each of many different kinds of layers (shapes, text, adjustment) you should ask yourself whether it's worth the time and effort to change the color properties or even the names of each layer. Each composition will dictate its own best practice, and as you continue to familiarize yourself with Photoshop, you'll develop the insight you need to be able to determine which tools you should make use of in each situation.

Displaying Layer Edges

It is often helpful to be able to see where a layer begins and ends on the canvas. For some layers, you can see a bounding box when you turn on the display of transform controls with the Move Tool selected. When you turn on the display of layer edges, however, each layer selected on the Layers panel is enclosed in a box in the Document window. To see the boundaries of all of the layers, select them all.

To display layer edges in the Fantastic2.psd file:

1. On the Application bar, click **Select**, and then click **Deselect** to turn off the selection marquee.

2. On the Application bar, click **Select**, and then click **Deselect Layers** to deselect all of the layers of the Fantasic2.psd file, if necessary.

To make it easier to see the layer edges, you can turn off the Show Transform Controls setting.

3. Press **V** to activate the Move Tool, if necessary, and then, on the options bar, click the **Show Transform Controls** check box to deselect it.

4. On the Application bar, click **View**, point to **Show**, and then click **Layer Edges**.

5. Zoom out so the document fits on the screen and then, on the Layers panel, click the **Prickly Pear** layer to select it.

   Edges appear as a blue box around the layer. You might have expected the edges to appear only around the picture of the prickly pears, but the transparent pixels in the layer are also counted within the image boundaries.

6. On the Layers panel, click **The Fruit Fantastic** layer. Edges appear around the text layer.

7. On the Application bar, click **Select**, and then click **All Layers** to select all of the layers in the document other than the Background layer. Photoshop displays the edges of all of the layers, except the Background layer. See Figure 3-14.

| Figure 3-14 | Showing layer edges |

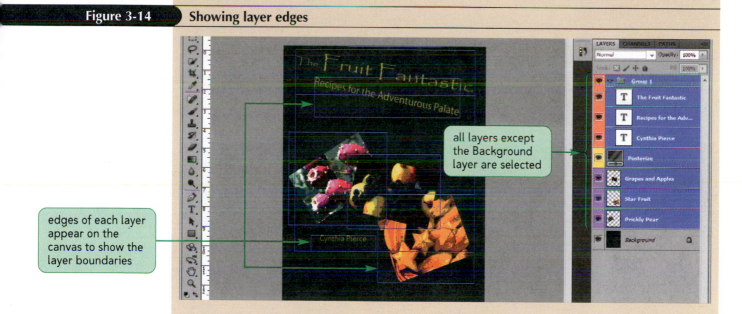

all layers except the Background layer are selected

edges of each layer appear on the canvas to show the layer boundaries

8. On the Application bar, click **View**, point to **Show**, and then click **Layer Edges** to turn off the display of layer edges.

Moving a Layer to Change Its Visibility

A layer's position on the Layers panel affects its appearance in the document. If it is near the bottom of the panel, it might be partially or completely hidden on the canvas by the layers above it. If a layer is at the top of the panel, it might obscure the layers underneath it.

Moving a Layer to Change Its Visibility

- On the Layers panel, select a layer.
- Drag the layer down or up on the Layers panel to change its visibility on the canvas.

or

- On the Application bar, click Layer, click Arrange, and then click Bring to Front, Bring Forward, Send Backward, or Send to Back to change the position of the layer on the Layers panel. You can also click Reverse to reverse the order of two or more selected layers.

Kaye suggests that you experiment with the position of the layers in the Fantastic2.psd file to see how changing their visibility affects the overall look of the composition.

To move a layer to change its visibility:

1. On the Layers panel, click the **Grapes and Apples** layer, and then drag it down until it is under the **Star Fruit** layer. As you drag, a ghosted image of the Grapes and Apples layer indicates its new position on the Layers panel.

2. Release the mouse button. The Grapes and Apples layer appears beneath the Star Fruit layer on the Layers panel, and the Star Fruit image obscures part of the Grapes and Apples image in the document. See Figure 3-15.

Figure 3-15 | Moving a layer on the Layers panel

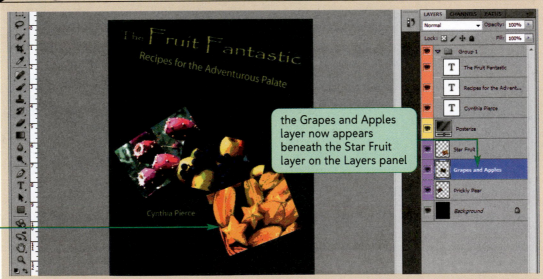

the Grapes and Apples layer now appears beneath the Star Fruit layer on the Layers panel

part of the Grapes and Apples layer is hidden by the Star Fruit layer

3. Click the **Background** layer and drag it to the top of the Layers panel. As you drag, the mouse pointer changes to the unavailable pointer ⃠, which indicates that the action you are trying to perform is not allowed. Because the Background layer is locked, you can't move it—unless you change it to a regular layer.

4. Release the mouse button. The Background layer remains at the bottom of the panel.

5. Drag the **Posterize** layer under the Grapes and Apples layer. See Figure 3-16.

| Figure 3-16 | Dragging an adjustment layer |

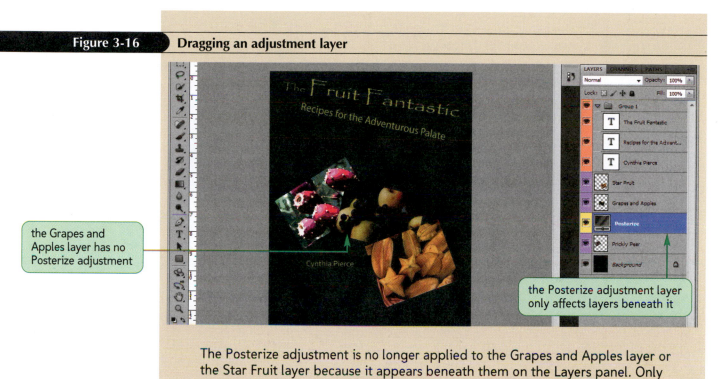

the Grapes and Apples layer has no Posterize adjustment

the Posterize adjustment layer only affects layers beneath it

The Posterize adjustment is no longer applied to the Grapes and Apples layer or the Star Fruit layer because it appears beneath them on the Layers panel. Only the Prickly Pear layer is posterized.

6. On the Application bar, click **Edit**, and then click **Undo Layer Order** to move the Posterize layer back to its original position.

Moving a Layer to Change Its Position on the Canvas

You can drag a layer to change its position on the canvas by selecting the layer on the Layers panel and using the Move Tool to drag the image, drawing, or text to where you want it to appear on the canvas. If a part of the layer ends up outside of the canvas area when you reposition it, that part will not show in the final composition and will be cropped when you finalize the image. You'll learn how to finalize an image later in this tutorial.

Kaye asks you to move some of the images on the canvas to see if you can improve the composition.

To move a layer to change its position on the canvas:

1. On the Layers panel, select the **Grapes and Apples** layer, point to the image of the grapes and apples on the canvas, press the mouse button, and drag the image up and to the right so it is partially off the canvas.

2. On the Layers panel, select the **Cynthia Pierce** text layer, point to the name on the canvas, and then drag it until it is under the subtitle. See Figure 3-17.

Figure 3-17   **Moving a layer on the canvas**

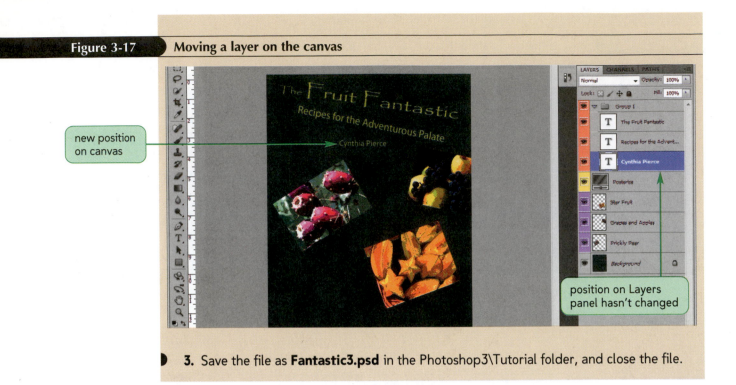

new position on canvas

position on Layers panel hasn't changed

3. Save the file as **Fantastic3.psd** in the Photoshop3\Tutorial folder, and close the file.

Aligning and Distributing Layers

In Tutorial 1, you used the grid and guides to help you align and place images and text in a document. Photoshop offers a number of additional tools to help you align and place objects. To align or distribute selected layers, you can use commands on the Layers menu or icons on the Move Tool options bar, shown in Figure 3-18.

Figure 3-18   **Alignment and distribution icons and commands**

Icon	Command
	Layer, Align, Top Edges
	Layer, Align, Vertical Centers
	Layer, Align, Bottom Edges
	Layer, Align, Left Edges
	Layer, Align, Horizontal Centers
	Layer, Align, Right Edges
	Layer, Distribute, Top Edges
	Layer, Distribute, Vertical Centers
	Layer, Distribute, Bottom Edges
	Layer, Distribute, Left Edges
	Layer, Distribute, Horizontal Centers
	Layer, Distribute, Right Edges

When you **align** layers, you can line them up along their top, bottom, left, or right edges, or you can align them based on their center points. When you **distribute** layers, you place them an equal distance apart along either an invisible horizontal or vertical axis.

Aligning Layers in a Composition

- Select the layers you want to align.
- On the Application bar, click Layer, point to Align, and then click an alignment option.

or

- Click one of the alignment icons on the options bar.

Kaye has given you a file of yellow star fruits on a green background. She'd like to create a logo to put next to any star fruit recipes in the book, but isn't sure how she wants to arrange the images. You'll experiment with aligning them to find the best arrangement.

To align the layers:

1. Open **AlignStars.psd** from the Photoshop3\Tutorial folder, and make sure that the Move Tool is selected in the Tools panel and that Show Transform Controls is selected on the options bar.

2. On the Layers panel, select **Small star fruit**, **Medium star fruit**, and **Large star fruit**.

3. On the Application bar, click **Layer**, point to **Align**, and then click **Top Edges**. The top three star fruits are now aligned along their top edges.

4. On the Layers panel, select **Small star fruit 2**, **Medium star fruit 2**, and **Large star fruit 2**.

5. On the options bar, click the **Align vertical centers** icon. The bottom three star fruits are now aligned along their vertical centers. See Figure 3-19.

> **TIP**
>
> You can also align the layers by clicking the Align top edges icon on the options bar.

Figure 3-19 **Using the alignment options**

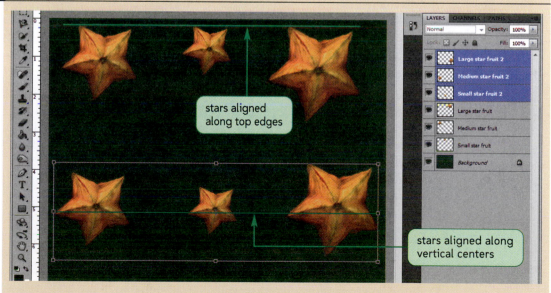

stars aligned along top edges

stars aligned along vertical centers

6. Save the file as **StarsAligned.psd** in the Photoshop3\Tutorial folder, and then close the file.

Distributing Layers in a Composition

- Select the layers you want to distribute. You must select at least three layers to distribute them.
- On the Application bar, click Layer, point to Distribute, and then click a distribute option.

or

- Click one of the distribute icons on the options bar.

Kaye has also given you a different star fruit file to see if you can come up with an idea for a logo using three of the same size fruits. You'll distribute them to see if the result is acceptable.

To distribute the star fruit layers:

1. Open **DistributeStars.psd** from the Photoshop3\Tutorial folder.

2. On the Layers panel, select **Small star fruit**, **Small star fruit 2**, and **Small star fruit 3**.

3. On the Application bar, click **Layer**, point to **Distribute**, and then click **Vertical Centers**. Photoshop distributes the stars so they are evenly spaced.

4. Save the file as **StarsDistributed.psd** in the Photoshop3\Tutorial folder, and then close the file.

Kaye has created another possible cover for *The Fruit Fantastic* book; this file contains even more layers and images in the composition. She wants you to decide whether the composition works with all of the different layers, or if some of the image layers should be deleted.

Deleting a Layer

One of the benefits of working with layers is that you can experiment with many different images, vector objects, and adjustments in the same composition, and then hide them, move them, and redisplay them to judge their effect. However, eventually you'll want your image to include only the layers that you want in the final composition. If you have added an adjustment, an image, or a vector object that you decide you no longer want to include, you can delete it from the Layers panel, which deletes it from the document.

To delete a layer:

1. Open **FruitFantastic2.psd** from the Phostoshop3\Tutorial folder. This file includes five images of fruit and three text layers.

2. Select the **Gratorn Fruit** layer, and then press the **Delete** key. Photoshop deletes the layer without prompting you for confirmation.

3. Select the **Quince** layer, and then click the **Delete layer** icon 🗑 at the bottom of the Layers panel. Photoshop prompts you to confirm the deletion.

4. Click the **Yes** button to confirm the deletion. Photoshop deletes the Quince layer.

Even without the deleted layers, Kaye feels that the composition is still too busy for a cover. She wants you to experiment with hiding different layers to see if you can get a better result.

Hiding and Redisplaying Layers

On the Layers panel, the Eye icon indicates that a layer is currently visible in the document. If you click the Eye icon in the left column of the Layers panel, the icon disappears, and the layer is hidden on the canvas. If you click in the column again, the Eye icon reappears and the layer is redisplayed in the Document window.

To hide and redisplay a layer:

1. On the Layers panel, click the **Eye** icon 👁 to the left of the Grapes and Apples layer. The Eye icon disappears and the layer no longer appears on the canvas.

2. Click the empty **Eye** icon box ☐. The Eye icon reappears and the photo of the grapes and apples reappears on the canvas.

You can hide all of the layers but one by pressing and holding the Alt key and then clicking the Eye icon for the layer you want to stay visible. Photoshop hides all layers but the one you click. If you press and hold the Alt key and click the icon again, Photoshop redisplays the hidden layers. This is very convenient if you want to focus only on a single layer—to make detailed pixel corrections, for example, or to make a careful selection.

Next, you'll hide all of the layers except the Prickly Pear layer.

To hide all but one layer and then redisplay all layers:

1. Select the **Prickly Pear** layer, press and hold the **Alt** key, and then click the **Prickly Pear Eye** icon 👁. All of the layers are hidden except the Prickly Pear layer. See Figure 3-20.

Figure 3-20   Hiding all but one layer

all but one layer hidden on canvas

only visible layer

2. Alt-click the empty **Eye** icon box ▢ on the left of the Prickly Pear thumbnail. The rest of the layers are redisplayed on the panel and in the document.

You can also drag down the Eye column on the Layers panel. As you drag, the Eye icon for each layer disappears and the layer is hidden. To redisplay all of the layers, you can drag back over the column and the Eye icons reappear.

To hide and redisplay layers by dragging:

1. Point to the **Group 1 Eye** icon 👁, press and hold the left mouse button, drag down the column to the Background layer, and then release the mouse button. All of the layers are hidden.

2. Point to the empty column to the left of the **Background thumbnail**, press and hold the left mouse button, drag up the column to the Group 1 layer, and then release the mouse button. All of the layers are redisplayed.

3. Save the file as **FruitFantastic3.psd** in the Photoshop3\Tutorial folder, and then close it.

Placing, Resizing, and Positioning an Image on a Layer

As you saw in Tutorial 2, you can place an image in a file to add it to your composition. When you place an image, Photoshop resizes the image to fit the canvas and places it on a new layer, positioned in the center of the canvas. The placed image is bounded by a box, and has diagonal lines running from corner to corner through a center point. You can use the options bar to change the placement and size of the image, as well as the angle at which it is rotated on the canvas. When you are satisfied with the placement of an image, you can click the Commit button on the options bar. See Figure 3-21.

Figure 3-21   **Placing an image**

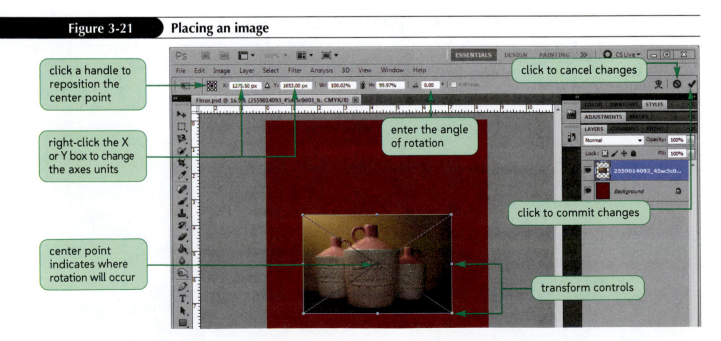

In Photoshop, the **center point** is the point at which a placed image will rotate if you change its angle on the canvas. By default, the center point is located in the exact center of the image, but you can change its location by clicking a handle on the Center Point icon on the options bar, or by dragging the center point to a new location.

Kaye wants you to set up a chapter opener page for the section on pear recipes. You'll place an image of a pear on the canvas, and then size and rotate it.

To place the image:

1. Open **PearRecipes.psd** from the Photoshop3\Tutorial folder.

2. On the Application bar, click **File**, and then click **Place**.

3. In the Place dialog box, select **Pears.jpg**, located in the Photoshop3\Tutorial folder, and then click **Place**. Photoshop places the image in the center of the canvas.

Right now, the image fills the whole canvas. See Figure 3-22.

> Do not press the Enter key after you place the file. Doing so will place the image in the file without giving you any options to transform it or modify its placement.

Figure 3-22	Options bar for placing an image

Maintain aspect ratio icon

Use relative positioning for reference point icon

default (0,0) reference point or point of origin

relative reference point becomes new (0,0) point

Commit button

Rotate box

You can resize a placed image using the width and height options on the options bar. To ensure that the image does not become distorted when you resize it, you need to maintain the aspect ratio. The **aspect ratio** is the relationship between the width and the height of an image. If the height is two times greater than the width, it will still be two times greater than the width if you maintain the aspect ratio when resizing the image.

TIP

You can also press the Shift key while dragging a transform control to maintain the aspect ratio when you resize.

To resize the placed image:

1. On the options bar, click the **Maintain aspect ratio** icon 🔒 to select it.

2. In the W box on the options bar, highlight the current value, type **50**, and then press the **Enter** key. You changed the width of the image to 50% of its original width, and because you chose to maintain the aspect ratio, the height of the image is also set to 50%.

To reposition a placed image, you can point inside the image with the mouse and drag the image to where you want it on the canvas. However, to place the image exactly, you can use the reference point on the canvas and the X, Y settings on the options bar.

The **reference point** is located at the (0,0) point on invisible X and Y axes and is the point from which Photoshop will measure any change in position. If you have worked with graphs, you know that the (0,0) point is also called the **origin.** By default, Photoshop places the reference point in the upper-left corner of the document, as you saw in Figure 3-22. (This is also where it places the 0 mark on the rulers.) However, if you select the Use relative positioning for reference point icon on the options bar, the center point of the placed file becomes the new reference point.

To allow room for text to be added to the bottom of the chapter opener, Kaye suggests that you move the image up one inch.

To reposition the placed image:

1. Click the **Use relative positioning for reference point** icon △ on the options bar to select it. The X and Y boxes on the options bar both change to zero values, indicating that the center point of the placed file is the new origin or reference point.

2. Right-click the **Y** box and then click **inches** on the shortcut menu to select it, if necessary.

3. In the Y box on the options bar, highlight the current value, type **-1**, and then press the **Enter** key. The image moves up one inch on the canvas.

Next, you'll rotate the placed image to see if that improves the effect.

Rotating a Placed Image

You can rotate a placed image around its center point in two ways. To rotate an image using the mouse, position the pointer outside of the image until it changes to a curved arrow, and then drag in the direction you want to rotate the image. This is called a **free transform** rotation. You can constrain a free transform rotation to 15-degree increments by pressing and holding the Shift key as you drag. You can also type a value for the rotation in the Rotation box on the options bar.

To rotate a placed image:

1. Place the mouse pointer outside of the image on the upper-right corner of the canvas until it turns to the rotate pointer ⤵.

2. Press and hold the **Shift** key and drag counterclockwise until the Rotate box on the options bar reads -30.00.

   You can also rotate the image by an exact amount by entering the degrees rotation in the Rotate box on the options bar.

3. In the Rotate box on the options bar, select the value and then type **45**. The image rotates 45 degrees clockwise from its original position.

4. On the options bar, click the **Commit** button ✔.

5. Save the file as **PearRecipes2.psd** in the Photoshop3\Tutorial folder, and then close the file and exit Photoshop.

You've spent a lot of time working with layers and should now have a good understanding of their benefits. You have also learned how nondestructive editing works in a Photoshop file. In the next session, you'll continue to work with and finalize the layers in the files that Kaye has given you, and you'll create some files of your own.

REVIEW

Session 3.1 Quick Check

1. When you change an image using an adjustment layer rather than modifying the pixels on the image layer, it is called _____ editing.

2. True or False. Adjustments on the Adjustments panel directly affect the image pixels.

3. A checkerboard display on the canvas or in a thumbnail in Photoshop is an indication of _____ pixels.

4. True or False. When an adjustment is clipped to the layer beneath it, it affects all of the layers in the composition.

5. In Photoshop, the selected layer is also called the _____ layer.

6. True or False. The Background layer is locked by default.

7. To move a layer on the canvas, you must first _____ it on the Layers panel.

8. True or False. When you distribute layers, you space them an equal distance apart.

SESSION 3.2 VISUAL OVERVIEW

You can select a layer comp to see it applied to the document.

On the Layer Comps panel, you can save multiple **layer comps**, which are snapshots of layer visibility, position, and appearance settings.

The lock icons include Lock transparent pixels, Lock image pixels, Lock position, and Lock all.

The area within the box but outside the image contains transparent pixels.

Transparent pixels are indicated by a checkerboard pattern on the thumbnail.

The lock icon indicates that all or part of the layer is locked.

BLENDING AND FINALIZING LAYERS

Each star fruit layer has a different blending mode applied; each mode is determined by a different mathematical **algorithm**, or formula.

Blending modes are listed on the Layers panel; **blending modes** determine how the colors in a layer **blend**, or interact, with the colors in the layers beneath that layer.

Use the Opacity settings on the Layers panel to create different effects when blending layers.

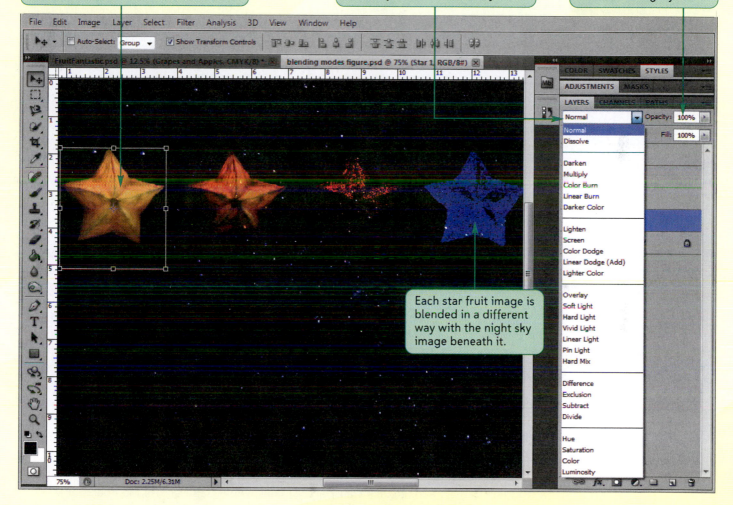

Each star fruit image is blended in a different way with the night sky image beneath it.

Locking and Unlocking Layer Content

After you have finished working with a layer, it is a good idea to lock it so you don't make any unintended changes to that layer. When locking a layer, you can choose among four options:

- You can lock the transparent pixels so nothing can be added in those areas.
- You can lock the image pixels so the image itself cannot be altered.
- You can lock an image in position so it cannot be moved or resized.
- You can lock the entire layer: transparent pixels, image pixels, and image position.

In order to lock a layer, you select it, and then click one of the lock icons at the top of the Layers panel. See Figure 3-23.

Figure 3-23   Locking layer content

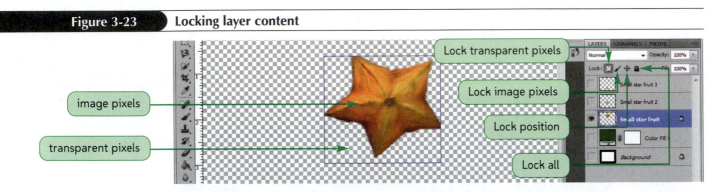

You'll practice locking image pixels and position so you're prepared to work with and manipulate multiple layers in any future compositions you create for Kaye.

To lock pixels and position:

1. Start Photoshop while pressing the **Ctrl+Alt+Shift** keys. When you are prompted to delete the Adobe Photoshop Settings File, click **Yes**. On the Application bar, right-click **Essentials**, click **Reset Essentials** to reset the default workspace layout and then collapse the Adjustments panel, if necessary.

2. Open **DistributeStars.psd** from the Photoshop3\Tutorial folder, and then, on the Layers panel, select the **Small star fruit** layer.

3. On the Application bar, click **View**, point to **Show**, and then click **Layer Edges** to turn on the display of layers.

4. Hide all of the other layers, and then on the Layers panel, click the **Lock transparent pixels** icon ⊠. The transparent pixels in the layer are locked, but the image pixels are not.

   To see what it means to lock transparent pixels, you'll paint across the image area on the canvas using the Brush Tool.

5. On the Tools panel, click the **Brush Tool** ✎, and then press **D** to reset the foreground and background colors to the default—black and white.

6. On the options bar, click the **Brush Preset picker** button ⬦, click the first preset—Soft Round, and then type **23** in the Size box.

7. Point to the lower-left corner of the star fruit image area, press and hold the left mouse button, and then drag to the upper-right corner of the image area. See Figure 3-24.

Figure 3-24   **Locking transparent pixels**

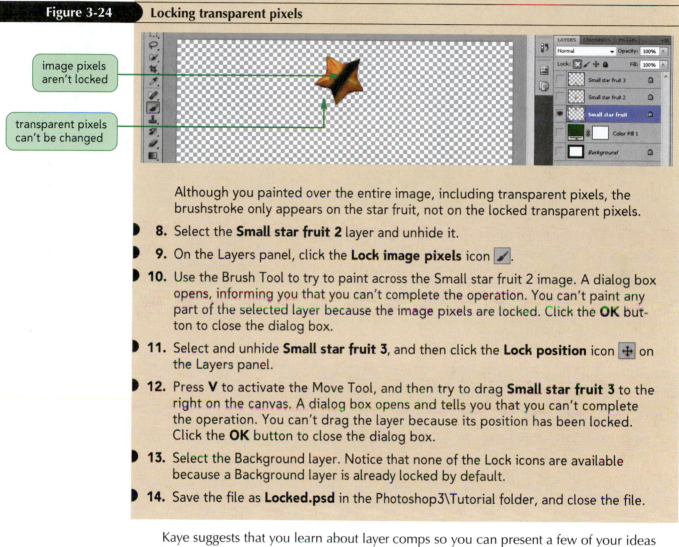

image pixels aren't locked

transparent pixels can't be changed

Although you painted over the entire image, including transparent pixels, the brushstroke only appears on the star fruit, not on the locked transparent pixels.

8. Select the **Small star fruit 2** layer and unhide it.

9. On the Layers panel, click the **Lock image pixels** icon.

10. Use the Brush Tool to try to paint across the Small star fruit 2 image. A dialog box opens, informing you that you can't complete the operation. You can't paint any part of the selected layer because the image pixels are locked. Click the **OK** button to close the dialog box.

11. Select and unhide **Small star fruit 3**, and then click the **Lock position** icon on the Layers panel.

12. Press **V** to activate the Move Tool, and then try to drag **Small star fruit 3** to the right on the canvas. A dialog box opens and tells you that you can't complete the operation. You can't drag the layer because its position has been locked. Click the **OK** button to close the dialog box.

13. Select the Background layer. Notice that none of the Lock icons are available because a Background layer is already locked by default.

14. Save the file as **Locked.psd** in the Photoshop3\Tutorial folder, and close the file.

Kaye suggests that you learn about layer comps so you can present a few of your ideas to her at your next meeting using a single file.

Working with Layer Comps

One of the greatest benefits of layers in Photoshop is that they give you the ability to store and experiment with many different versions of a composition in a single file using layer comps. A **comp** is a mock-up or sketch of what a final design will look like, and a layer comp is the electronic version of a graphic designer's comp. A Photoshop file can have multiple layer comps. You can use layer comps to present several ideas to a client before finalizing a file, or to save different versions of your layout so you can work on them and decide on a final version later. See Figure 3-25.

Figure 3-25 Working with layer comps

In the New Layer Comp dialog box, you can give the composition a descriptive name and select the elements you want Photoshop to consider when creating the comp, including Visibility, Position, and Appearance (also called Layer Style). You can also add a comment to help you remember details about the comp—for example, notes on why you think a particular layer comp might be a good choice for the final composition, questions you might have for the client about the composition, or information about related comps.

To create a layer comp:

1. Open **FruitFantastic.psd** from the Photoshop3\Tutorial folder, and then hide the Grapes and Apples layer.

2. On the Application bar, click **Window**, and then click **Layer Comps** to open the Layer Comps panel.

3. At the bottom of the Layer Comps panel, click the **Create New Layer Comp** icon. The New Layer Comp dialog box opens.

4. In the Name box of the New Layer Comp dialog box, type **Hidden Fruits**. In the Comment box, type **No apples**, and then click the **OK** button. The dialog box closes and Photoshop displays the new layer comp layout.

5. Redisplay the Grapes and Apples layer, and create a new layer comp called **All Visible**.

Next, you'll switch back to the Hidden Fruits layer comp to see if you prefer that layout for the book cover.

To apply a layer comp to a file:

1. On the Layer Comps panel, click in the column to the left of Hidden Fruits to display that layout. See Figure 3-26.

Figure 3-26   **Switching to a different layer comp**

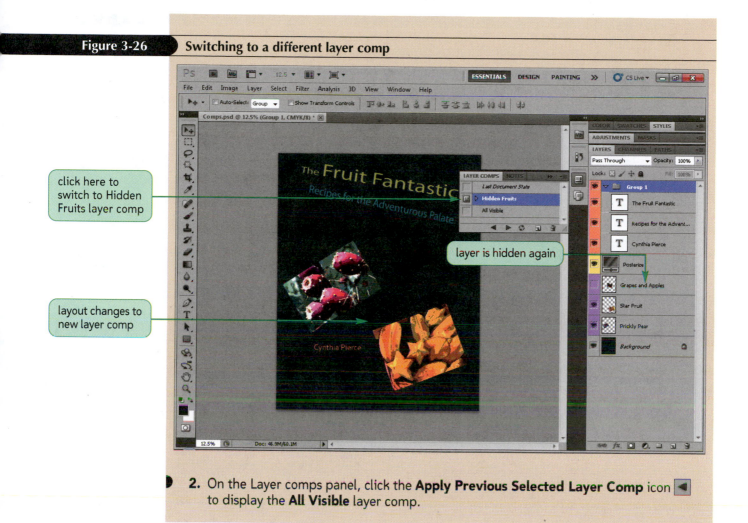

click here to switch to Hidden Fruits layer comp

layer is hidden again

layout changes to new layer comp

2. On the Layer comps panel, click the **Apply Previous Selected Layer Comp** icon ◀ to display the **All Visible** layer comp.

After Kaye reviews your work, she decides that the layout of the Hidden Fruits layer comp won't work for the cover, so you'll delete it from the file.

To delete a layer comp:

1. Click the **Hidden Fruits** layer comp to select it on the Layer Comps panel, and then click the **Delete Layer Comp** icon 🗑 at the bottom of the Layer Comps panel.

2. Close the Layer Comps panel group.

3. Save the file as **Comps.psd** in the Photoshop3\Tutorial folder, and then close the file.

Teamwork: Using Layer Comps to Collaborate

If you work on a creative team that collaborates, layer comps can be a great tool to help you generate a final version of a composition. For example, team members can use the Comment field in a layer comp to critique a particular layout and make suggestions for improving it. They can also add text layers to a composition that include critiques or suggestions, or draw arrows and other vector objects to point out areas of the composition they would like to see changed. You can view their feedback by saving a layer comp with the comment layers visible, and then hide the comments in a different layer comp. Alternatively, each team member can save a layer comp with his or her name in order to show the group their preferred layout, and the team can review the different options by selecting and then discussing each individual named layer comp.

Reviewing a single file using various layer comps keeps your work in a single location, and avoids any problems you might have with version control. Once the team has made its final decisions, you can delete any unnecessary layers and finalize the file. By using layer comps to collaborate with team members, you can create a final file that is the best it can be.

Now that you have spent some time working with Layer comps, Kaye would like you to try to improve some of your compositions by experimenting with blending modes and opacity.

Working with Blending Modes and Opacity

As you have seen, the order of layers on the Layers panel affects how each layer appears in your composition. You can also change how a layer appears by blending it with the layer or layers beneath it to achieve an interesting effect. Photoshop comes with numerous blending modes.

You can also apply different opacity settings to an image to achieve additional effects. A setting of 100% means that a layer is completely opaque and nothing will show through. The lower the setting, the more transparent the layer becomes. An Opacity setting of 0% means that a layer is completely transparent.

Applying Blending Modes

When you apply a blending mode to a layer, you are specifying that you want the colors in the layer with which you are working to interact in some way with all of the colors in the layers beneath it. When you work with blending modes, it helps to think of each different mode as a new experiment—such as in a chemistry class. Each mode blends the chemicals (or layer colors) of all of the layers together in a way that's unpredictable until you actually put them in the test tube and shake (apply the mode). If you make even the slightest change to one of the layers in the blend—for example, by modifying its color slightly, you have changed the chemicals in the test tube and will see a different result. See Figure 3-27.

Figure 3-27   Different blending modes applied to same object

The first star fruit in Figure 3-27 has the Normal blending mode, which is the default mode for any image you place on the canvas. With the Normal blending mode, the star fruit layer does not blend at all with the image of the night sky, which is on a layer beneath it; it simply covers the pixels in that image. The second star fruit has the Hard Light blending mode applied to it. The third has Color Dodge applied, and the fourth has Divide. All of these blending modes have dramatically different effects when applied to the same image.

To apply a blending mode to a layer, select the layer on the Layers panel. When you do, the blending mode options become available. You can click the blending mode arrow on the Layers panel, and then choose a blending mode. After you have applied one blending mode to a layer, you can press the Ctrl key and the down arrow key to apply the next blending mode on the list to that layer—without having to click the blending mode arrow. To go up the list, press the Ctrl key and the up arrow key. You will often find that you need to experiment with many different blending modes to find the one you want.

You'll apply different blending modes to the artwork you're preparing for the cookbook section on star fruits.

To apply a blending mode:

1. Open **HeavenSent.psd** from the Photoshop3\Tutorial folder.

2. Select the **Star 1** layer, and at the top of the Layers panel, click the **blending modes** arrow, and then click **Color Burn**.

   Color Burn darkens the base color and makes everything but the lightest color (the night stars) darker.

3. Select the **Star 2** layer, press and hold the **Ctrl** key, and then press the down arrow key until **Color Dodge** is selected. Color Dodge brightens the base color and decreases the dark/light contrast.

   Trouble? If you pass Color Dodge by mistake, press and hold the Ctrl key and press the up arrow key until you select it.

4. On the Layers panel, apply the **Linear Light** blending mode to the Star 3 layer, and then apply the **Divide** blending mode to the Star 4 layer. See Figure 3-28.

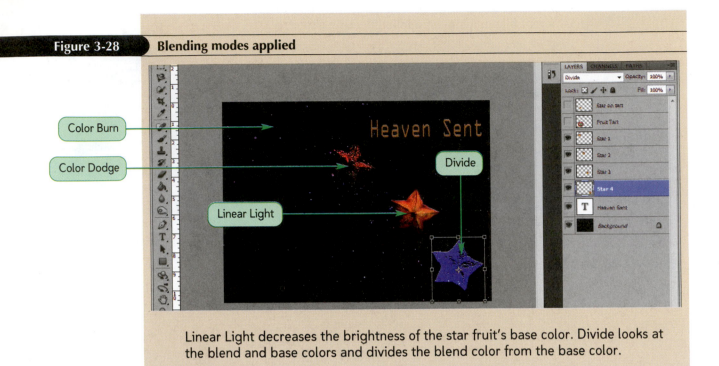

| Figure 3-28 | Blending modes applied |

Linear Light decreases the brightness of the star fruit's base color. Divide looks at the blend and base colors and divides the blend color from the base color.

Each blending mode produces a completely different effect. Next, you'll experiment with opacity settings on the Layers panel to see what other effects you can achieve when blending layers.

Changing Opacity

You can also use the Opacity setting on the Layers panel to blend layers. An Opacity setting of 100% means that the layer is completely opaque or solid, with no pixels from the layer beneath it showing through. As you decrease the opacity, the layer becomes more and more transparent, showing some of the pixels on the layer beneath it. You can change the opacity by dragging the opacity slider, by typing a percentage value, or by scrubbing over the word *Opacity* to change the setting. When you **scrub**, the mouse pointer changes to the scrub pointer. Scrubbing left decreases the setting, and scrubbing right increases the setting. In addition, if the Move Tool is selected on the Tools panel, you can press a number key to change the opacity. For example, pressing 2 changes the opacity to 20%, and pressing 5 changes the opacity to 50%.

Figure 3-29 shows a black-and-white image with no blending applied, and then the same image modified by unhiding the solid blue fill layer above the image layer and then blending it with the photograph by changing the opacity of the layer to give the photograph a blue tint.

Figure 3-29 | **Changing opacity for blending effect**

To change the opacity to blend an image:

1. In HeavenSent.psd, select and unhide the **Fruit Tart** layer, and then drag the scrub pointer 🖑 to the left until the Opacity setting at the top of the Layers panel is about **30%**.

2. Unhide and select the Star on tart layer, and then press **4** to change the Opacity setting to 40%.

INSIGHT

Combining Settings for a Unique Effect

You'll sometimes find that a blending mode is almost what you want as an effect, but not quite. To achieve the result you want, you can combine the blending mode with opacity settings. In addition, if an object has a shadow, you can change the Fill setting rather than the Opacity setting to maintain the intensity of the shadow, but reduce the opacity of the fill. In other words, with Photoshop layers, the possibilities for achieving different effects are almost limitless, and you should take the time to explore them.

Creating Layer Groups

Earlier in the tutorial, you learned how to organize layers by changing their order on the Layers panel, by giving each layer a meaningful name, and by changing the color of layers for a visual overview of layer organization. You can also group related layers into layer groups so you can easily change the style of multiple layers at the same time or show and hide a group as necessary as you work on your composition.

Grouping Layers

- Select the layers you want to group, and then, on the Application bar, click Layer, and then click Group Layers.

or

- Select the layers you want to group, and then press the Ctrl+G keys.

or

- Click the New layer group icon at the bottom of the Layers panel. Photoshop creates a new group layer. Drag the layers you want to add to the new group on top of the group layer.

You'll organize the layers by grouping them in the HeavenSent file so Kaye can easily understand how you laid out the composition. You'll also ungroup one of the groups.

To group and ungroup layers:

1. Select **Star 1**, **Star 2**, **Star 3**, and **Star 4**, and then on the Application bar, click **Layer**, and then click **Group Layers**. Photoshop moves all of the selected layers into a group called Group 1 and collapses the group.

2. Click the **triangle** to the left of the Group1 name to expand the group and view all of the layers.

3. Select the **Star on tart** and **Fruit Tart** layers, and then press the **Ctrl+G** keys.

4. Select **Group 2** if necessary, on the menu, click **Layer**, and then click **Ungroup Layers**. The Group 2 layers are no longer in a group.

Next, you will finalize your work in the HeavenSent file so it is ready to present to Kaye.

Finalizing Layers

After you have created many versions of a composition and shown different layer comps to a client, you will reach the point when you are ready to finalize your work. A file with multiple layers can take up many megabytes of storage space. However, you can do a number of things to reduce file size and ensure that your work can't be accidentally changed.

Merging Layers

You can merge an adjustment layer with an underlying content layer to permanently apply the adjustment to the image. You can also merge related layers to reduce file size. When you merge image layers, the pixels on the top layer replace the pixels on the layers beneath it. Reducing the number of pixels reduces file size. To merge selected layers, you can right-click the Layers panel and click Merge Layers on the shortcut menu, or you can select Merge Layers on the Layer menu. You can also use the Merge Visible Layers command to merge the visible layers on the Layers panel.

To merge selected layers and visible layers:

1. With the top two layers selected, on the Application bar, click **Layer**, and then click **Merge Layers**. The two layers are merged into one layer. The name of the top layer, Star on tart, is given to the merged layers.

2. Hide all of the layers except for **Heaven Sent** and **Background**, and select the **Background** layer if necessary.

3. On the Application bar, click **Layer**, and then click **Merge Visible**. The two layers are merged into a single Background layer. See Figure 3-30.

| Figure 3-30 | Merging visible layers |

hidden layers are not affected by merge

visible layers are merged into one locked Background layer

4. Unhide all of the layers.

Stamping Layers vs. Merging Layers

INSIGHT

When you stamp layers instead of merging them, Photoshop keeps the original layers intact and creates a new composite layer, called a **stamp**, with all of the selected or visible layers merged. To stamp selected layers, press the Ctrl+Alt+E keys. If you select a layer that is linked to other layers, pressing the Ctrl+Alt+E keys stamps the linked layers. You can also stamp visible layers by pressing Shift+Ctrl+Alt+E. You can use the stamp to sharpen or adjust the stamped part of the image as one layer, or you can copy the stamp to a different file so you have both a layered and a flattened version of the same file. Because you have merged the layers, the flattened version will have a smaller file size.

Flattening an Image

The final step you should take when finalizing any composition is to flatten it. If you think you might want to use the composition later and modify it, be sure to save a copy of the PSD file with all of its layers. Then flatten the image to reduce file size and make the image portable to other file formats, such as JPEG. When you flatten an image, Photoshop merges all visible layers and throws out any hidden layers. It also replaces transparent pixels with white pixels. Once you flatten and save an image, you cannot go back to the layered file, so it is essential that you are sure you have finished with the file before you take this last step.

As a final step before you show the HeavenSent file to Kaye, you'll flatten the composition so it has a manageable file size.

> ### To flatten an image:
>
> ▶ 1. On the Application bar, click **Layer**, and then click **Flatten Image**. All of the layers have been flattened into a single layer on the Layers panel.
>
> ▶ 2. Save the file as **FlatFile.psd** in the Photoshop3\Tutorial folder, and then close the file and exit Photoshop.

In this session, you learned how to work with layers. You selected, added, duplicated, and deleted layers and changed their properties and their visibility. You also moved, aligned, and distributed layers, and hid and unhid them. You learned how to lock layer content and how to work with layer comps and groups to improve your workflow. You also learned about blending modes and opacity settings, and you finalized a file by merging layers and flattening it.

REVIEW

Session 3.2 Quick Check

1. A version of layer visibility, position, and appearance settings is called a _____.

2. A _____ _____ works with the colors and opacity of one layer and combines it with the layer beneath it.

3. When you combine two or more layers into a single layer, you are _____ the layers.

4. True or False. You can undo a merge after you have saved the file.

5. You _____ a layer by merging selected or visible layers into a new layer and leaving the original layers intact.

6. To finalize a file so it consists of only one layer, you _____ it.

Practice the skills
you learned in
the tutorial using
the same case
scenario.

PRACTICE

Review Assignments

**Data Files needed for the Review Assignments: Flour.jpg, Baked.jpg, FlourImage.jpg,
Perfection.jpg**

Kaye wants you to work on the graphics for another cookbook, *Baked to Perfection*.
She supplies you with three images and asks you to place them in a file and modify it to
develop ideas for the cover. You'll work with layers and layer comps as well as blending modes and opacity settings to create a file to present to Kaye as a possible cover.
Complete the following steps:

1. Start Photoshop while pressing the Ctrl+Alt+Shift keys. When you are prompted to
   delete the Adobe Photoshop Settings File, click Yes. On the Application bar, right-
   click Essentials, and then click Reset Essentials to reset the default workspace layout.
2. Open **Flour.jpg** from the Photoshop3\Review folder included with your Data Files,
   and save it as **BakeBook.psd** in the same folder. Place **Baked.jpg** in the file, and then
   move the image down 2 inches using a relative reference point.
3. Place **FlourImage.jpg** from the Photoshop3\Review folder, in the BakeBook.psd
   file. Rotate it 45 degrees counterclockwise, set its Opacity to 80%, and position it
   2 inches lower than its original placement using a relative reference point.
4. Place the file called **Perfection.jpg** in the BakeBook.psd file, and then position it using
   the rulers so its center point is at 4¼ inches on the horizontal ruler, and 2 inches on
   the vertical ruler.
5. Apply the **Pin Light** blending mode to the Perfection layer.
6. Save the current layer comp as **Flour Comp** and enter the comment **Flour overlaid
   on muffins**.
7. Hide the FlourImage layer, and then enter **Colin Cameron** in horizontal 48 point
   black text in any font directly under the book title. Commit the text entry, and use
   the Move Tool to adjust its placement if necessary.
8. Select the Background layer, and then add another text layer in black 30 point text
   using the same font. Type **with Amanda Parker** centered at the bottom of the cover.
9. Arrange the layers so all of the placed layers are grouped together, and then put them
   in a layer group called **Placed**.
10. On the Layers panel, make both of the text layers green.
11. Hide the **with Amanda Parker** layer and then create a new layer comp called **No
    coauthor**.
12. Switch to the Flour Comp, and then apply the previous selected layer comp. Close
    the Layer Comps panel group.
13. Redisplay the **with Amanda Parker** layer, select all of the text layers, and then change
    the text color to brown (R=102, G=51, and B=51).
14. Apply the Exclusion blending mode to the Colin Cameron layer. Apply the Multiply
    blending mode to the Baked layer.
15. Ungroup the Placed group, and then merge all of the visible layers. Delete the
    FlourImage layer.
16. Save BakeBook.psd, close the file, and exit Photoshop.
17. Submit the results of the preceding steps to your instructor either in printed or elec-
    tronic form, as requested.

Use your skills to create an interesting visual effect for an ad.

APPLY

Case Problem 1

Data Files needed for this Case Problem: RomanRuins.jpg, NewHome.jpg

Norton & Company   Emma Gottfried, lead architect of Norton & Company, a high-end architectural design firm, wants to launch a campaign with a "ruins to riches" theme using photo compositions of new homes rising out of Roman ruins. She gives you two photographs to work with and asks you to create a comp to present at your next meeting with her. Complete the following steps:

1. Start Photoshop while pressing the Ctrl+Alt+Shift keys. When you are prompted to delete the Adobe Photoshop Settings File, click Yes. On the Application bar, right-click Essentials, and then click Reset Essentials to reset the default workspace layout.

2. Create a new file with a black background that is 14 inches wide and 12 inches high and save it as **NewRuins.psd** in the Photoshop3\Case1 folder provided with your Data Files. Use Figure 3-31 as a guide as you complete this exercise.

Figure 3-31   Riches from Ruins file and Layers panel

3. Place **RomanRuins.jpg** from the Photoshop3\Case1 folder in the NewRuins.psd file.

4. Place **NewHome.jpg** from the Photoshop3\Case1 folder as a layer above the RomanRuins image.

5. Change the Opacity of the NewHome layer to 60%.

6. Apply the Linear Light blending mode to the RomanRuins layer.

7. Create a text layer using a red Myriad Pro 60 point font, and type **Riches Rise from the Ruins**.

8. Duplicate the text layer you just created, move it slightly down, and then change its Opacity to 30%.

9. At the top of the canvas, add a 72-point red text layer, and type **norton & company** in any font; center the text layer above the image.

10. Rearrange the layers so the text layers appear together and the image layers appear together.

11. Put the image layers in a group called Image Layers.

12. On the Layers panel, change the color of all of the text layers to red.

13. Hide the Riches Rise from the Ruins copy layer, and then save the layer comp as **No Shadow**.

14. Redisplay the Riches Rise from the Ruins copy layer, and then save the layer comp as **All Layers**.

15. Save NewRuins.psd, close the file, and exit Photoshop.

16. Submit the results of the preceding steps to your instructor either in printed or electronic form, as requested.

Using Figure 3-32 as a guide, modify a composition by using what you know about layers and groups.

CREATE

Case Problem 2

Data Files needed for this Case Problem: AlwardArt.psd

Alward Art Museum   You have been working on a logo for Director Guy Blanc at the Alward Art Museum. You'd like to present the file to Guy and give clear information about its organization so he can modify it as he sees fit. The file has many layers and effects, and you need to organize it so it is more manageable. Complete the following steps:

1. Start Photoshop while pressing the Ctrl+Alt+Shift keys. When you are prompted to delete the Adobe Photoshop Settings File, click Yes. On the Application bar, right-click Essentials, and then click Reset Essentials to reset the default workspace layout.

2. Open **AlwardArt.psd** from the Photoshop3\Case2 folder provided with your Data Files, and using Figure 3-32 as a guide, name and group the layers.

Figure 3-32   Alward Art file and Layers panel

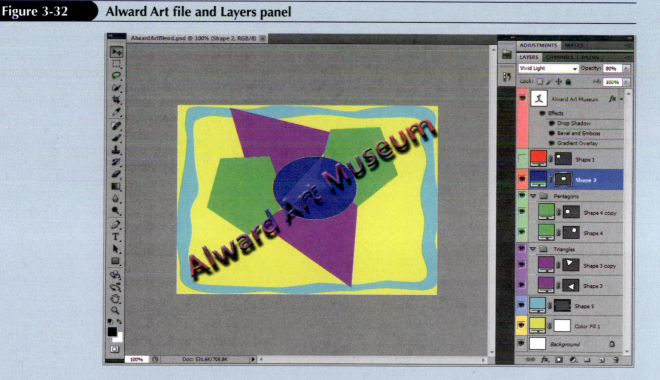

3. Move the layers so they appear in the order shown in the figure.

4. Hide layers as shown in the figure.

5. On the Layers panel, change the layer colors to match the figure.

6. Apply the blending mode and opacity shown on the Layer panel in the figure.

7. Save the file as **AlwardArtBlend.psd** in the Photoshop3\Case2 folder. Close the file, and exit Photoshop.

8. Submit the results of the preceding steps to your instructor either in printed or electronic form, as requested.

Create a unique composition by working with layers and effects.

CREATE

Case Problem 3

Data Files needed for this Case Problem: Clouds.jpg, Clouds.psd, Clouds1.jpg, ModelPlane.jpg, ModelPlane1.jpg, PlaneBlueSky.jpg, Sky1.jpg

Flight Plan, Inc. You are the owner of Flight Plan, Inc., a flight school in Dayton, Ohio. You will soon be meeting with an ad agency to present your ideas and launch a campaign that inspires people to learn how to fly. You'll use your Photoshop skills to combine images and work with blending modes, layers, and comps to present a couple of ideas to the agency so they will know what you want when they begin working on the campaign. Complete the following steps:

1. Start Photoshop while pressing the Ctrl+Alt+Shift keys. When you are prompted to delete the Adobe Photoshop Settings File, click Yes. On the Application bar, right-click Essentials, and then click Reset Essentials to reset the default workspace layout.

2. The Photoshop3\Case3 folder provided with your Data Files includes photographs of airplanes and clouds in the sky. You'll choose at least two airplanes and two cloud images and place them in a new file to create a unique composition with at least two layer comps, as shown in the two examples in Figure 3-33.

Figure 3-33 | **Layer comps for Flight Plan campaign**

3. Create a new file using the dimensions and background color of your choosing.

4. Create a new layer and place an image of an airplane from the Photoshop3\Case3 folder on the new layer.

5. Create a new layer and place an image of clouds from the Photoshop3\Case3 folder on the new layer.

6. Create at least one additional cloud layer and one additional airplane layer, using images from the Photoshop3\Case3 folder.

7. Apply blending modes and adjust the opacity of layers to achieve interesting effects.

8. Add at least two text layers and apply styles, colors, or blending modes to them. The text should include the company name and any catch phrase you think will work for the company. You can use different phrases for different layer comps.

9. Assign colors to layers to organize them, and create at least one logical group of layers on the Layers panel.

10. Lock at least two layers.
11. Hide and unhide layers to create at least two layer comps.
12. Save the file as **FlightPlan.psd** in the Photoshop3\Case3 folder.
13. Flatten the file and then save it as **FlightPlan.jpg** in the Photoshop3\Case3 folder. Close the open file, and exit Photoshop.
14. Submit the results of the preceding steps to your instructor either in printed or electronic form, as requested.

Extend your skills to create a Web ad for an employment agency.

CHALLENGE

Case Problem 4

Data Files needed for this Case Problem: Keys1.jpg, Keys2.jpg

TempIT   Sylvia Potter founded TempIT, an employment agency providing temporary clerical and administrative assistants to large corporations, five years ago in Denver, Colorado. You are Sylvia's administrative assistant but would like to take on more responsibility. You will use your Photoshop skills to create an interesting idea for a Web ad that you can present to Sylvia at the next staff meeting. Complete the following steps:

1. Start Photoshop while pressing the Ctrl+Alt+Shift keys. When you are prompted to delete the Adobe Photoshop Settings File, click Yes. On the Application bar, right-click Essentials, and then click Reset Essentials to reset the default workspace layout.
2. Create a new file of any size and background color and then extend the canvas using a second color for the extension. The extension should have room for three lines of text. Refer to Figure 3-34 for an example of a possible layer comp.

Figure 3-34   **A sample comp for TempIT**

3. Use Mini Bridge to preview the images of keyboards in the Photoshop3\Case 4 folder provided with your Data Files, and place one of the files in your composition.

4. Duplicate the layer containing the keyboard image, change the opacity setting, apply a blending mode, and rotate it on the canvas. Create additional duplicates, and rotate each duplicate a different amount to achieve the effect of a spinning keyboard.

5. Rearrange the layers so the original keyboard layer is on top on the Layers panel and is displayed at 100% opacity.

6. Place the second keyboard file on the canvas; size and move it so it appears in the background, behind the spinning keyboards you created.

7. Draw a rectangle of any color on top of the second keyboard on the Layers panel, and change its opacity so the keyboard shows through. Rearrange the layers if necessary.

8. Add text to the image on at least three layers. One layer should include the name of the company.

⊕ **EXPLORE**   9. Duplicate the three text layers all at once. (*Hint*: Select similar layers and then apply the Duplicate Layer command to all three layers at the same time. You will not be able to assign unique names until after the duplication.)

10. Hide the original text layers.

⊕ **EXPLORE**   11. Use the text style presets on the Styles panel to modify at least two of the duplicate layers. To display the presets, click the Styles panel options button, click Text Effects 2 or Text Effects, and then replace the current styles with the Text Effects styles.

12. Apply at least two text styles to the duplicate text.

⊕ **EXPLORE**   13. Use the Styles panel options menu to replace the Text styles with the default styles.

14. Give some of the layers more descriptive names, and group or color-code related layers.

15. Create and save at least two layer comps.

16. Save the file as **HelpIT.psd** in the Photoshop3\Case4 folder. Close the file, and exit Photoshop.

17. Submit the results of the preceding steps to your instructor either in printed or electronic form, as requested.

ENDING DATA FILES

Photoshop3 → Tutorial
Comps.psd
Fantastic2.psd
Fantastic3.psd
FlatFile.psd
FruitDraft2.psd
FruitFantastic3.psd
Locked.psd
PearRecipes2.psd
StarsAligned.psd
StarsDistributed.psd

Review
BakeBook.psd

Case1
NewRuins.psd

Case2
AlwardArtBlend.psd

Case3
FlightPlan.jpg
FlightPlan.psd

Case4
HelpIT.psd

Adding Content

Adding Content and Working with Color

Case | *ReCycle Bike Shop*

ReCycle Bike Shop is a used bicycle shop in Concord, Massachusetts, that also offers bicycle repair classes and mountain biking lessons. Founded in 2006 by Lee duBois, ReCycle has five employees who handle the front-of-store business, teach classes, and give mountain biking lessons. For years, Lee has been doing all of the promotion and bookkeeping; however, because the business has been growing, she has hired you to help her develop promotional materials for the shop, including posters to hang in surrounding towns, Web ads for the local Chamber of Commerce Web site, and mailers for customers who have done business with the shop in the past. She is also interested in developing a logo for the shop that can appear on a sign above the door and on all of the promotional pieces.

You'll use the color selection tools, the Paint Bucket Tool, and the drawing and painting tools in Photoshop for the projects Lee has in mind. You'll also add fill layers to an image and compose an image that places your proposed sign in a photograph of the shop so Lee can see what the finished product will look like.

STARTING DATA FILES

Photoshop4 → Tutorial

Tutorial	Review	Case1	Case2	Case3	Case4
BikeSign.psd	Accident.psd	CD.jpg	ArchiText.psd	Easel.jpg	(none)
BikeSign2.psd	TrafficCone.jpg	TekSell.jpg			
FillLayers.psd					
FourBikes.psd					
PoliceLine.psd					
RedBicycle.jpg					
Submerged.jpg					
Tricycle.jpg					
Upgrade.psd					

SESSION 4.1 VISUAL OVERVIEW

A **point sample** uses the color of a single pixel to set the color when you use the Eyedropper Tool.

Select the **foreground color** icon on the Color panel to specify the color Photoshop uses when you work with the drawing tools.

Drag the R, G, and B **color sliders** to fine-tune the color selected on the color ramp.

Select the **background color** icon on the Color panel to specify the color used to extend the canvas or to create a gradient.

You can use the Eyedropper Tool to **sample**, or copy the color of, pixels in an image so that you can apply them to another part of the image or to another image.

Click the color ramp on the Color panel to select a foreground or background color and then adjust the color using the color sliders.

The Paint Bucket Tool is hidden under the Gradient Tool on the Tools panel.

The pointer takes the shape of an eyedropper when you sample a color.

CONTROLLING CONTENT COLOR

The **color field** displays shades of a selected color.

The Color Picker displays the new color and compares it to the current color.

The triangle symbol indicates that the current color is **out of gamut**, or will not print properly.

The cube symbol indicates that the current color is not **Web-safe**; a Web-safe color is one that will be displayed properly in a Web browser.

You can select Only Web Colors to display a palette of colors that will always work on a Web site.

Clicking the **color ramp** in the Color Picker dialog box displays shades of the selected color in the color field.

A **hexadecimal color value** expresses a Web-safe color as a series of numbers and letters that can be used to specify color in the RGB color mode for an HTML file.

Color values specify the current foreground or background color and are based on the color mode.

Understanding the Effect of Color

In the advertising world, certain brands are consistently identified with particular colors. For example, think of your favorite soft drink. Is its label red? blue? green? If your favorite soft drink has a red label, what might happen if the label were suddenly changed to yellow or pink? Would the identity of the brand change for you in some fundamental way? As you work to create the most effective compositions—that is, compositions that successfully convey your intended message, or draw attention to a product you're trying to sell—you should spend some time considering the importance of color. Color can make or break a brand, can affect a viewer's mood, and can even help persuade someone to buy a product. See Figure 4-1.

Figure 4-1   The effect of color

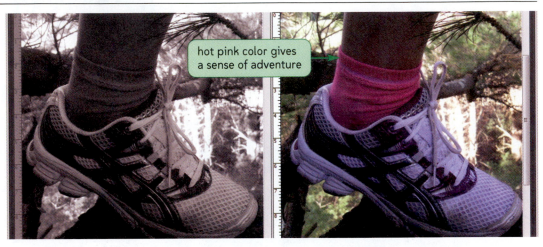

Figure 4-1 provides a simple example of using color to create interest. Imagine that you're trying to sell the running shoes shown in the images. Which photograph draws the most attention to the shoes? Obviously, the grayscale image does not express the excitement you'd want to convey to a potential buyer. Not only does the color image generate more interest in the product, but the hot pink socks convey a sense of adventure that, for example, pastel pink or forest green socks would not.

As you work with color, you might find it convenient to keep a color wheel nearby. A **color wheel** is a diagram used to the show the relationships between colors. See Figure 4-2.

Figure 4-2   Sample color wheel

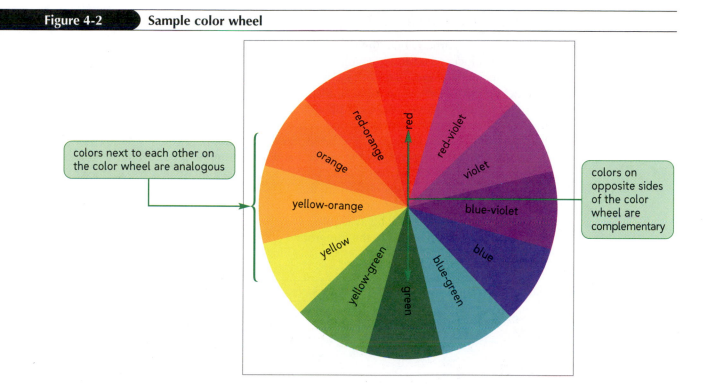

colors next to each other on the color wheel are analogous

colors on opposite sides of the color wheel are complementary

A color wheel can help you choose a **color scheme**, which is a combination of colors that work well together. Examples of color schemes include monochromatic, complementary, and analogous. A **monochromatic** color scheme uses different shades of a single color. A **complementary** color scheme includes colors that are on opposite sides of a color wheel. An **analogous** color scheme uses colors that are next to each other on a color wheel. Color schemes can also be described in terms of temperature. Certain colors, like red, orange, and yellow, convey a feeling of warmth, while others like blue and green are considered cool. **Neutral** colors are colors that aren't on a color wheel, such as browns and grays.

INSIGHT

The Psychology of Color

When working on a composition in Photoshop, you might find your choice of a color scheme dictated in part by the colors in a photograph you plan to use. However, you should also consider other factors, such as the message you want to convey, the emotions you want to elicit, or the audience you want to attract. There have been many studies about the psychology of color, and it can be helpful to have some understanding of color psychology. Knowing how colors affect people not only in your own culture, but also in other cultures, can help you convey a message or close a sale. For example, you might already know that wearing black makes you appear thinner, but did you know that it also gives you a look of authority or power? Red can elicit intense emotions, while blue and green can produce a calming effect. In certain cultures, green symbolizes paradise. Color is a very powerful tool, and the more you know about it, the more effectively you'll use it. Photoshop offers a variety of tools that allow you to experiment with color to achieve the effect you want.

Using the Color Selection Tools

In Tutorial 2, you learned about the different color modes available in Photoshop. In particular, you focused on RGB, which is the standard mode for Web content, and CMYK, which is the standard for printed output. No matter which color mode you use, you select colors in Photoshop using similar methods. In fact, before you use any of the drawing or painting tools on the Tools panel in Photoshop, you need to select the colors you want to use. Photoshop includes many color selection tools, including the Color panel, the Color Picker dialog box, the Eyedropper Tool, and the Swatches panel. Which selection tool you use depends on the task at hand. For example, if you want the color of a vector object you add to match one of the colors in a digital image, you can use the Eyedropper Tool. If you want to ensure that a color is appropriate for the Web or for printing, you can use the Color Picker or the Color panel, both of which display icons to let you know if your color will be available when the image is uploaded or printed.

In Photoshop, you can specify the foreground color and the background color. See Figure 4-3.

Figure 4-3	Default foreground and background colors

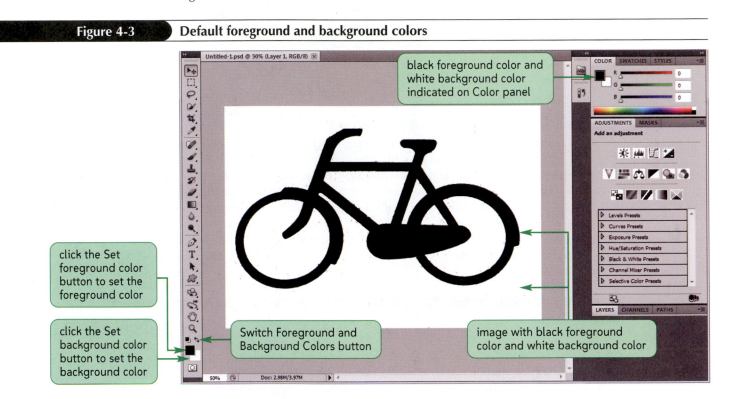

click the Set foreground color button to set the foreground color

click the Set background color button to set the background color

Switch Foreground and Background Colors button

black foreground color and white background color indicated on Color panel

image with black foreground color and white background color

Photoshop uses the foreground color when you work with the drawing tools on the Tools panel. By default, the foreground color is black. The background color is the color Photoshop uses to extend the canvas or, when combined with the foreground color, to create a **gradient fill**, which is a gradual blending of the foreground and background colors or of other colors determined by a gradient preset. Photoshop also uses the background color to fill empty areas of an image. By default, the background color is white.

Setting the Foreground Color with the Eyedropper Tool

If you are working on a composition and want to select a color for text or a vector object based on a color or colors in a photograph, the Eyedropper Tool is a good choice for setting the foreground color. See Figure 4-4.

Figure 4-4	Sampling colors with the Eyedropper Tool

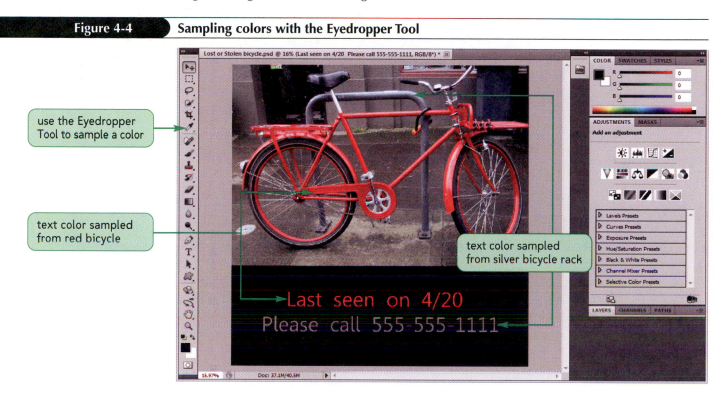

use the Eyedropper Tool to sample a color

text color sampled from red bicycle

text color sampled from silver bicycle rack

In the poster shown in Figure 4-4, the Eyedropper Tool was used to sample the color of the bicycle for the top line of text. It was used again to sample the color of the bicycle rack for the bottom line of text. When you sample a color, you pick up the color values for a single pixel, or for an average of pixel colors in a specified area. You can then use the sampled color to fill a vector object, to specify the color for text, or to fill a selection with the color.

You sample a color with the Eyedropper Tool by selecting the layer that contains the color, activating the Eyedropper Tool, and then clicking the location on the image where the color appears. To refine your selection, you can use the settings on the options bar to sample the color of a single pixel, called a point sample, or to sample the average of colors in an area of pixels, for example, a 3 × 3 pixel average or even a 101 × 101 pixel average, as shown in Figure 4-5.

TIP

You can also select a sample area by selecting the Eyedropper Tool, right-clicking the image, and then choosing a sample size from the shortcut menu.

Figure 4-5   Sample size causes variations in color

101 x 101 average sample size

sample location

color taken from point sample is a light orange

color taken from 101 x 101 pixel sample size is a darker orange because the sample includes shadows

Figure 4-5 shows the different results achieved by clicking the image at the same spot, but sampling areas of different dimensions. The first color sample includes only the light orange of a single sampled pixel. The second sample is a darker orange because the sample is 101 × 101 pixels, and includes shadows. The sampled color can vary significantly at different sample sizes, so it's a good idea to experiment with a few settings if you aren't satisfied with the initial sampling.

You can also designate whether you want to sample the color on the current layer only, or on all of the layers in the document by clicking the Sample arrow on the options bar, and then clicking Current Layer or All Layers. If you sample all layers, Photoshop combines the colors to come up with the sample.

If you want to see the RGB and CMYK color values when you are sampling a color from an image, open the Info panel, and then, with the Eyedropper Tool selected, move the mouse over different areas of the image. As you do, the numbers displayed on the Info panel change to reflect the color you are pointing to. You can open the Info panel by clicking Window on the Application bar and then clicking Info, or by pressing the F8 key.

REFERENCE

Using the Eyedropper Tool

- On the Tools panel, click the Eyedropper Tool.
- On the options bar, specify the Sample Size, and specify Current Layer or All Layers as the Sample.
- Switch to the image you want to obtain a sample from, or point to the sample area on the current image, and click the color you want to sample.
- Apply the sample using the Paint Bucket Tool, or add it to the Swatches panel by clicking a blank area on the Swatches panel.

Lee is experimenting with ideas for a store logo and would like you to take one of her ideas a bit further. She has given you a simple graphic of four bicycles, currently filled with white, and she would like you to experiment by making them different colors. Her idea is that a multicolored image will emphasize the variety of bicycles available at the shop. You'll color the first bicycle using a color sample from the Eyedropper Tool. You'll apply the sampled color to the bicycle with the Paint Bucket Tool, which replaces the color of not only the pixel you click but also all adjacent pixels with a similar color. In other words, if you click the white bicycle, the Paint Bucket Tool will fill the pixel you click—plus all of the white pixels on the layer—with the new color, and it will leave the nonwhite pixels the same.

To sample a color using the Eyedropper Tool:

1. Start Photoshop while pressing the **Ctrl+Alt+Shift** keys. When you are prompted to delete the Adobe Photoshop Settings File, click **Yes**. On the Application bar, right-click **Essentials**, and then click **Reset Essentials** to reset the default work-space layout.

2. Navigate to the Photoshop4\Tutorial folder included with your Data Files, and open **Tricycle.jpg** and **FourBikes.psd**.

3. Select the **FourBikes.psd** tab, if necessary, and on the Application bar, click the **Arrange Documents** button , and then click **Fit On Screen**.

4. Switch to the **Tricycle.jpg file**, and on the Tools panel, click the **Eyedropper Tool** , and then click the green handlebar in the area shown in Figure 4-6.

Figure 4-6 **Color sampled in one image will be applied to another**

- sample size is set to Point Sample
- Eyedropper Tool is selected
- click here to sample green color
- tricycle green is now the foreground color

The foreground color icon changes to green on the Tools panel and on the Color panel. (Don't be concerned if your color doesn't exactly match the color in the figure.)

Make sure you select the specified layer in this step and all other layer selection steps. Selecting an incorrect layer will apply the color to the wrong part of the image.

5. Switch to the **FourBikes** file, expand the **Layers** panel, if necessary, make the **Top Left** layer the active layer, and then click the **Paint Bucket Tool** on the Tools panel.

   Notice that the pointer shape changes to a paint bucket.

   Trouble? If you can't see the Paint Bucket Tool , point to the Gradient Tool on the Tools panel, press and hold the mouse button to display the hidden tool, and then click the Paint Bucket Tool .

6. Click the **top-left bicycle**. Photoshop fills the bicycle with the sampled green color.

   Trouble? If the background or a different bicycle is filled with the green color when you click, you did not select the Top Left layer or you were pointing at the area around the bicycle rather than the bicycle itself. Press the Ctrl+Z keys, or click Edit on the Application bar and click Undo Paint Bucket to undo the change, and then repeat Step 6.

Setting the Foreground Color on the Color Panel

You can also use the Color panel to select a color for the foreground. On the Color panel, RGB color values are displayed if you're working in RGB mode; CMYK color values are displayed if you're working in CMYK mode. See Figure 4-7.

Figure 4-7 **Color panel showing RGB color values**

By default, the color values for the foreground color in RGB mode are R=0, G=0, and B=0 because those are the RGB values for black, the default foreground color. When you change the foreground color, those values change. You can modify the foreground color on the Color panel by entering new color values for R, G, and B; by dragging the color sliders for R, G, and B; by clicking a color in the color ramp; or by clicking the Set foreground color icon on the Color panel to open the Color Picker (Foreground Color) dialog box.

You can also use a combination of these methods to achieve the exact color you want. For example, you might click a green color in the color field, and then use the color sliders to adjust the levels to achieve the shade of green you want. Keep in mind, however, that some of your color manipulations might result in a color that either won't print properly or is not Web safe. A Web-safe color is one that is displayed properly in a Web browser. If a color is not Web safe, the image is dithered as it is uploaded to a browser to achieve a similar color effect. Dithering is the process of mixing two colors to achieve an approximation of the unavailable color. If you are creating a composition for the Web, your best bet is to use Web-safe colors because dithering slows the upload time of your image in most browsers. Similarly, if you are working on an image for print, you need to ensure that your color choice is within the **gamut**, or range of colors allowed by the CMYK mode. A color that won't print properly is considered out of gamut because it is a color not included in the complete set (or gamut) of print-safe colors. See Figure 4-8.

Figure 4-8   Out of gamut color correction

In Figure 4-8, the selected foreground color is out of gamut for printing, as indicated by the triangle with the exclamation point. You can choose a new color yourself, or you can click the square to the right of the warning to have Photoshop substitute a similar color that is in gamut.

You'll use the Color panel to select a light blue color for the next bicycle.

To set a color using the Color panel:

1. On the Layers panel, click the **Bottom Left** layer to select it.

2. On the Color panel, point to the **color ramp**. When the pointer is over the ramp, it changes to the Eyedropper pointer ✐.

3. On the color ramp, click a **light blue** color. The foreground color icon changes to light blue on the Tools panel and on the Color panel.

4. Point to the **bottom-left bicycle** in the image, and then click on the white area of the bicycle. Photoshop fills the bicycle with the light blue color. See Figure 4-9.

Figure 4-9   **Using the Color panel**

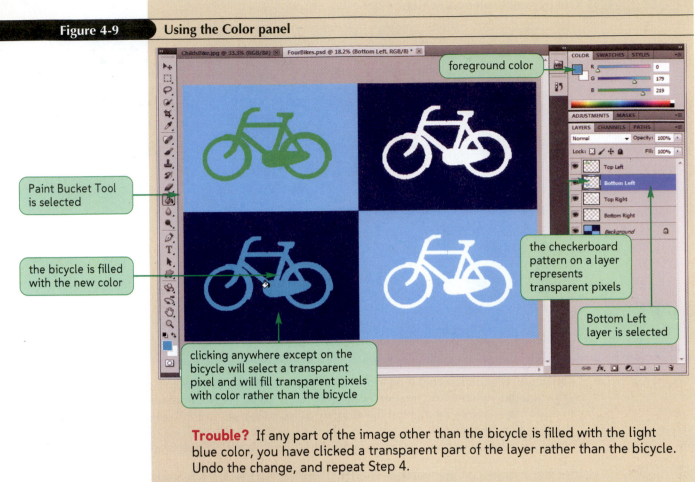

Paint Bucket Tool is selected

the bicycle is filled with the new color

foreground color

the checkerboard pattern on a layer represents transparent pixels

Bottom Left layer is selected

clicking anywhere except on the bicycle will select a transparent pixel and will fill transparent pixels with color rather than the bicycle

Trouble? If any part of the image other than the bicycle is filled with the light blue color, you have clicked a transparent part of the layer rather than the bicycle. Undo the change, and repeat Step 4.

Notice that the pointer shape is still a paint bucket because the Paint Bucket Tool is still selected on the Tools panel.

You can also use the Color Picker to set a color for the foreground. To select a color in the Color Picker, click in the color ramp to display shades of that color in the color field. You can then use the color field to click a particular shade of the current color. See Figure 4-10.

Figure 4-10   Color Picker (Foreground Color) dialog box

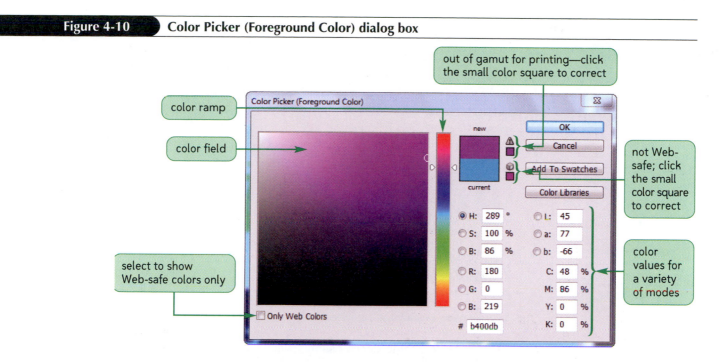

color ramp

color field

out of gamut for printing—click the small color square to correct

not Web-safe; click the small color square to correct

color values for a variety of modes

select to show Web-safe colors only

When you select the color, the Color Picker displays the color's values using different color modes, including HSB (Hue, Saturation, and Brightness), RGB, CMYK, and the color's hexadecimal color values. In a hexadecimal color value, the first pair of characters defines the red used in the color, and the next two pairs define green and blue, respectively. Hexadecimal color values are used to specify colors in **HTML (HyperText Markup Language)**, a programming language used to create Web pages. The Color Picker also displays Lab color mode values. **Lab color mode** describes colors as most people actually see them, rather than as they are interpreted by a device such as a monitor or a printer. Lab colors are considered **device independent** because a Lab color should look the same to the human eye no matter which device it's displayed on.

In addition to color values, the Color Picker also displays icons that let you know if a color is either out of gamut, not Web safe, or both. To ensure that any color you choose is Web safe, select the Only Web Colors check box before selecting your color. If a color is out of gamut, click the "Click to select in gamut color" icon under the "Warning: out of gamut for color printing" icon to substitute a similar in-gamut color.

You'll use the Color Picker dialog box to select a yellow color for the third bicycle.

To set the foreground color using the Color Picker dialog box:

1. On the Layers panel, click the **Top Right** layer.

2. On the Tools panel, click the **Set foreground color** icon ▮. The Color Picker (Foreground Color) dialog box opens.

3. Click the **Only Web Colors** check box to select it, if necessary. The dialog box changes to display only Web-safe colors in the color field.

4. On the color ramp, click the **yellow color**, and then in the color field, click a bright yellow. See Figure 4-11. Note that your color values might not match the values shown in the dialog box.

Figure 4-11 Color Picker with Web-safe colors displayed

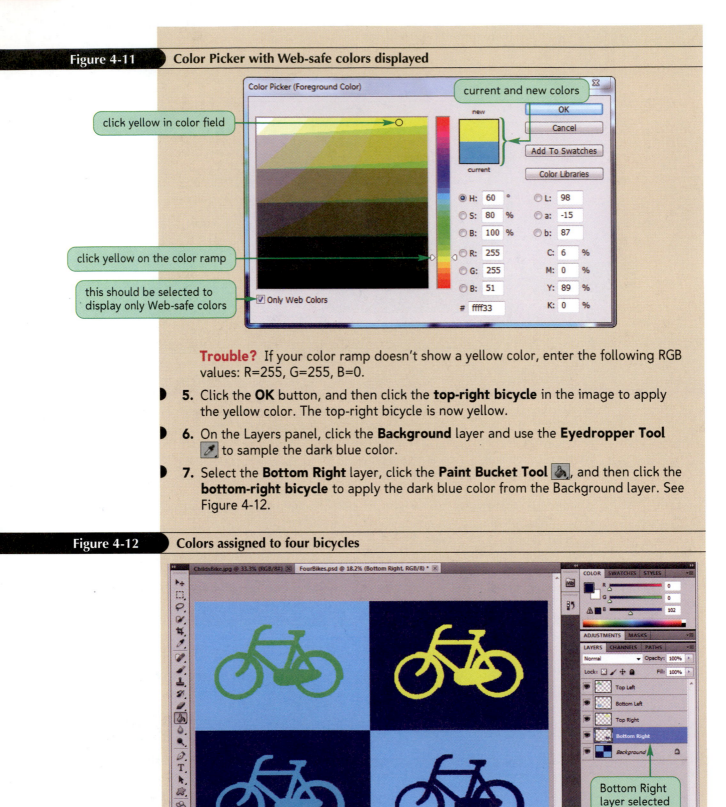

Trouble? If your color ramp doesn't show a yellow color, enter the following RGB values: R=255, G=255, B=0.

5. Click the **OK** button, and then click the **top-right bicycle** in the image to apply the yellow color. The top-right bicycle is now yellow.

6. On the Layers panel, click the **Background** layer and use the **Eyedropper Tool** to sample the dark blue color.

7. Select the **Bottom Right** layer, click the **Paint Bucket Tool**, and then click the **bottom-right bicycle** to apply the dark blue color from the Background layer. See Figure 4-12.

Figure 4-12 *Colors assigned to four bicycles*

All of the bicycles have been assigned a color. You'll continue to work with color by assigning a new background color to see if you can add interest to the logo.

Changing the Background Color

Photoshop uses the background color in combination with the foreground color to create some of the gradient presets covered later in this tutorial. You can also use the background color when you increase the canvas size of a composition, as you did in Tutorial 2. However, Photoshop only provides a background color option for increased canvas size if your composition has a Background layer. When you create a new file, Photoshop uses the current background color if you select Background from the Background Contents list in the New dialog box.

You can specify the background color in Photoshop using the same methods you use to specify foreground color. You can use the Color Picker (Background Color) dialog box, the Color panel, and the Eyedropper Tool.

You can easily switch foreground and background colors by clicking the Switch Foreground and Background Colors button on the Tools panel. You can reset Photoshop to the default foreground and background colors by clicking the Default Foreground and Background Colors button on the Tools panel or by pressing D.

Lee thinks that the four-bicycle logo idea might be overkill, but wants to see if adding a border to it helps to tone the colors down a bit. She suggests that you increase the size of your poster by adding a border that alternates the two colors she used on the original Background layer. To do so, you'll use the Increase Canvas Size command two times, using a different method to choose a background color each time you do.

To change the background color:

1. Make the **Background** layer active on the Layers panel.

2. On the Color panel, click the **Set background color** icon ▢, which is partially hidden by the Set foreground color icon ■. The color values for the current background color (white) are displayed.

   Trouble? If the Color Picker (Background Color) dialog box opens, click Cancel.

3. On the Tools panel, click the **Eyedropper Tool** ✐, and then click in the top left quadrant of the image, on the light blue color. The background color icon changes to the light blue.

4. On the Application bar, click **Image**, and then click **Canvas Size**.

5. In the Canvas Size dialog box, click the **Relative** check box to select it, if necessary, type **2** in the Width box, select **inches** as the unit of measurement, if necessary, and then type **2** in the Height box. You'll leave the Anchor setting as is so the canvas is extended equally on all four sides of the image.

6. Select **Background** from the Canvas extension color list, if necessary, and then click the **OK** button to close the Canvas Size dialog box. The canvas now has a border that uses the light blue color.

7. On the Tools panel, click the **Switch Foreground and Background Colors** icon ⇄. The background color icon changes to dark blue.

   Next, you'll extend the canvas again using the new background color.

8. On the Application bar, click **Image**, and then click **Canvas Size**.

TIP

You can also press the X key to switch the foreground and background colors.

9. In the Canvas Size dialog box, click the **Relative** check box to select it, if necessary, type **2** in the Width box, and then type **2** in the Height box.

10. Select **Background** from the Canvas extension color list if necessary, and then click the **OK** button to close the Canvas Size dialog box. The canvas now has a second border that uses the dark blue color.

11. On the Application bar, click the **Arrange Documents** button 🔲 ▾, and then click **Fit On Screen**. See Figure 4-13.

Figure 4-13 ▸ **Extending the canvas with the background color**

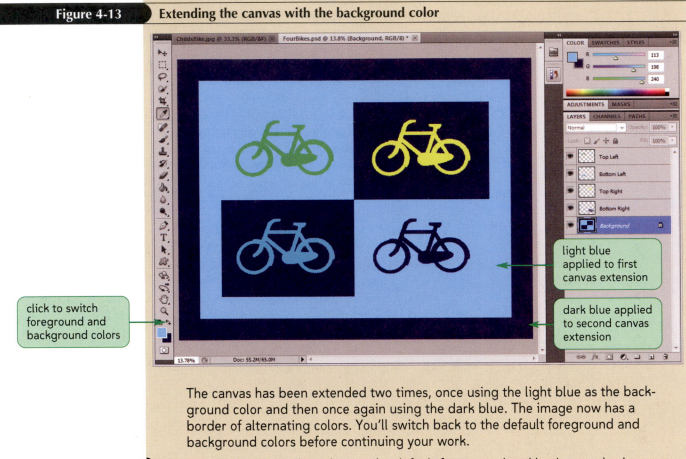

click to switch foreground and background colors

light blue applied to first canvas extension

dark blue applied to second canvas extension

The canvas has been extended two times, once using the light blue as the background color and then once again using the dark blue. The image now has a border of alternating colors. You'll switch back to the default foreground and background colors before continuing your work.

12. Press **D** to return Photoshop to the default foreground and background colors, black and white.

13. Save the file as **FourColors.jpg**, using the default JPEG Options, in the Photoshop4\Tutorial folder, and then close the file. Photoshop saves the file as a JPEG and flattens the image into a single layer.

14. Close FourBikes.psd and Tricycle.jpg without saving the files.

PROSKILLS

Problem Solving: Making Your Work Accessible to the Color Blind

As someone using digital imaging to convey messages, you will often be faced with the challenge of trying to ensure that your work is accessible to the largest number of people possible. It's a good idea to keep in mind that some people are **color blind**, which means they don't see certain colors the same way the majority of the population sees them. There are many kinds of color blindness. Some color-blind people can't distinguish between red and green; others can't distinguish between blue and yellow; others don't see color at all (though this is extremely rare). There are a number of ways that you can create designs that accommodate the color blind:

- Avoid putting red and green or blue and yellow directly next to each other in a composition, if possible.
- Use textures in addition to colors to help distinguish between objects in a composition.
- Add borders to delineate separate areas in a composition or on a Web page.
- Underline text that you want to stand out, rather than relying solely on a color change.
- Vary the fonts for text that uses different colors.
- Use shapes as backgrounds for different parts of a composition.

Each of these suggestions is a helpful aid for reaching a color-blind audience, but they also present additional challenges, such as images that are too busy (because of multiple fonts and shapes), or images that aren't aesthetically pleasing to a wider audience. By following these guidelines and using the tools in Photoshop to help you solve some of these problems, you can create compositions that reach the widest possible audience.

Lee asks you to work on an ad that she has started for a Web campaign. She suggests you use the Swatches panel and display a library of Web-safe colors to do your work.

Working with the Swatches Panel

The Swatches panel provides a library of commonly used colors that you can easily access to modify your images. The panel appears behind the Colors panel in the default Essentials workspace. You can also open the Swatches panel from any other workspace by clicking Swatches on the Window menu. See Figure 4-14.

Figure 4-14   **Default Swatches panel**

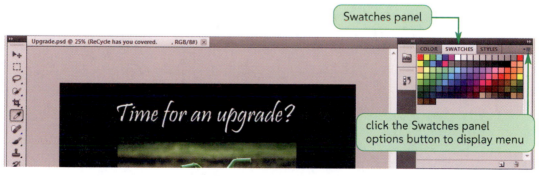

Swatches panel

click the Swatches panel options button to display menu

You can add colors to the Swatches panel so your customized palette of swatches gives you easy access to colors that you use often. To create a subset of colors with which to work, you can delete colors from the Swatches panel. You can also save the customized panel as a preset. In addition, Photoshop provides a long list of color palettes that you can choose to display on the Swatches panel based on your designing or printing needs.

You have the option of loading or replacing a swatches **library**, or palette of swatches, on the Swatches panel. When you load a library, it is added or **appended** to the current library of swatches at the bottom of the panel. When you replace a library, the new library takes the place of the current library on the panel, and you are prompted to save the current library if you have made any modifications to it. Whether you choose to load or replace a swatches library depends on the work you're doing. If you want to continue to work with the current swatches but need additional choices, loading a library is your best bet. If you want to restrict your choices to a single library, replace the current library. You can also customize the display of swatches on the Swatches panel to display small or large thumbnails, or to display the choices in a list.

Photoshop provides numerous libraries or color palettes that you can display on the Swatches panel. You choose a color palette based on your current project. For example, if you are creating graphics for a newspaper, you should consider displaying the ANPA color palette on the Swatches panel. ANPA stands for American Newspaper Publishers Association, and the ANPA palette displays colors commonly used in newspaper layout applications. If you are working on a printed piece, choose one of the PANTONE or other CMYK libraries. You can also display Web-safe swatches so you can be sure that any vector objects you create for a Web site will be assigned the appropriate colors.

To select a color swatch, click a swatch to choose it as the foreground color, or press the Ctrl key and then click the swatch to choose it as the background color.

Lee wants you to revise an ad she's created for the store's Web site. She would like you to add colored rectangles behind the white text in the ad but also wants you to ensure that the colors are Web safe. You'll use the Swatches panel to assign colors using Web-safe presets.

> **TIP**
>
> To restore the default Photoshop swatches, click the panel options button, and then click Reset Swatches.

To customize the display of the Swatches panel:

▶ 1. Reset the Essentials workspace, click the **Swatches** panel tab, and then open **Upgrade.psd** from the Photoshop4\Tutorial folder provided with your Data Files. Photoshop displays the default Swatches panel presets using the Small Thumbnails display.

▶ 2. On the Swatches panel, click the **panel options** button ▤, and then click **Large List**. Photoshop displays the swatches in a list. Each swatch includes a thumbnail of the color, as well as the swatch name or color value.

Next, you'll change the Swatches panel palette to Web Spectrum to ensure that you only include Web-safe colors in your ad.

To change the palette to Web Spectrum colors on the Swatches panel:

▶ 1. On the Swatches panel, click the **panel options** button ▤ to display the list of presets, and then click **Web Spectrum**. Photoshop asks if you want to replace the current color swatches or append them to the swatches already on the panel.

▶ 2. Click the **OK** button to replace the colors on the panel with the Web Spectrum colors. The Swatches panel changes to display the new colors.

Trouble? If you don't have the Web Spectrum palette, choose a different Web-safe palette from the menu.

3. Drag the scroll box to just before the halfway point on the scroll bar, place the Eyedropper pointer 🖊 over the green swatch that displays the hexadecimal values **#006600** for the green color, and then click. The foreground color changes to green.

   Trouble? If the background color changes instead of the foreground color, click the Color panel tab, and then click the Set foreground color icon 🟦 on the Color panel. Repeat Step 3.

4. On the Tools panel, click the **Rectangle Tool** 🔲 on the options bar, click the **Shape layers** button 🔲 to select it, if necessary, and then draw a rectangle over the "Time for an upgrade?" text. When you release the mouse button, a green rectangle appears.

5. Expand the Layers panel, if necessary, click the **Shape 1** layer on the Layers panel, and then drag it under the text layer on the Layers panel so "Time for an upgrade?" is displayed on top of the rectangle. See Figure 4-15.

Figure 4-15	Shape layer under text layer

confirm that Shape layers is selected

this swatch is selected

swatch color is applied to the rectangle

Rectangle Tool

swatch color is now foreground color

6. Draw a rectangle over the "ReCycle has you covered" text.

7. To restore the original swatches, click the Swatches **panel options** button 🔳, click **Reset Swatches**, and then click the **OK** button.

8. Click the Swatches **panel options** button 🔳, and then click **Small Thumbnail**.

9. Save the file as **ColorUpgrade.jpg**, using the default JPEG Options, in the Photoshop4\Tutorial folder, and then close Upgrade.psd without saving it.

Adding Colors to the Swatches Panel

You can add the current foreground color to the Swatches panel by positioning the mouse pointer over a blank area of the Swatches panel so a Paint Bucket pointer appears, and then clicking. You can also use the Create new swatch of foreground color button at the bottom of the Swatches panel, or the New Swatch command on the panel options menu. Once you add a color to the Swatches panel, you can apply it as you would apply any other color.

When you add a color to the panel, it is saved with the Swatches panel as a preference. If at some point you reset your preferences, you will lose any modifications to the Swatches panel. To save a modified Swatches panel permanently, you need to save it in a library.

Lee has given you a photograph that she plans to use in a number of different campaigns, and she would like you to save some of the colors in the photograph as swatches on the Swatches panel.

To add sampled colors to the Swatches panel:

1. Reset the default Essentials workspace, and then open **RedBicycle.jpg** from the Photoshop4\Tutorial folder.

2. Press **D** to restore the default foreground and background colors, if necessary.

3. On the Tools panel, click the **Eyedropper Tool** 🖉.

4. Select the **Background** layer, if necessary, and then click the red chain guard on the bicycle.

5. Click the **Swatches** panel tab, move the mouse pointer to a blank (gray) area at the bottom of the swatches area, until it becomes a Paint Bucket pointer ⬧, and then click. The Color Swatch Name dialog box opens, as shown in Figure 4-16.

| Figure 4-16 | Naming a color swatch |

6. Type **RedBike** in the Name box, and then click the **OK** button. The new swatch appears as the last swatch on the panel.

7. Place the mouse pointer over the new swatch until the tool tip "RedBike" appears. The new swatch has the name you assigned.

8. Sample the orange lock on the bicycle and add it to the Swatches panel as **Lock**. The new swatch appears to the right of the RedBike swatch on the panel.

9. Sample the silver bicycle rack in the image and add it to the Swatches panel as **Rack**. The new swatch appears to the right of the Lock swatch on the panel.

You'll save the modified swatches as a preset so you can use the set again in the future.

Saving Modified Swatches as a Preset

If you have swatches that you plan to reuse, for example, swatches based on a color model that you will use consistently with one campaign or for one client, it is a good idea to save them as a preset so you can reload them at any time.

To save swatches as a preset and then load them:

1. Click the Swatches **panel options** button ▾≡, and then click **Save Swatches**. The Save dialog box opens.

2. Navigate to the Photoshop4\Tutorial folder, type **MySwatches** in the File name box, and then click **Save**. Photoshop saves the swatches with an .aco extension in the Tutorial folder.

   You'll replace the MySwatches palette with the default palette, and then practice opening the custom palette you created.

3. Click the Swatches **panel options** button ▾≡, click **Reset Swatches**, and then click the **OK** button. Photoshop reloads the default swatches.

4. Click the Swatches **panel options** button ▾≡, click **Load Swatches**, navigate to the Photoshop4\Tutorial folder, click the **MySwatches** file to select it, and then click **Load**. The saved customized swatches are displayed on the Swatches panel.

You can delete colors that you don't need from the Swatches panel. When you delete a swatch from a library, you need to save the library for the deletion to be permanent. If you delete a swatch by mistake, close the library without saving it and then reopen it.

You'll delete two of the colors from the Swatches panel that you know you'll never use, and you'll keep the RedBike swatch in the customized library.

To delete a color from the Swatches panel:

1. Point to the **Lock** swatch at the bottom of the Swatches panel, press the **Alt** key so a scissors pointer ✂ appears, and then click. The swatch is deleted from the Swatches panel.

   Trouble? If you delete a different swatch accidentally, reload the My Swatches library without saving changes to the open library.

2. Repeat Step 1 to delete the Rack swatch.

3. Reset the swatches, and save changes to the current custom swatches before closing them. Saving your changes will ensure that the customized swatches include RedBike so you can use it in future Photoshop sessions.

   Trouble? If you are given the choice of replacing or appending the current swatches with the default, click the Replace button.

4. Close RedBicycle.jpg without saving it.

Working with the Styles Panel

You can take the time to apply individual effects to layers in Photoshop to achieve a certain look for text or a vector object, or you can choose from a library of professionally designed styles on the Styles panel. The Styles panel, which appears behind the Swatches panel in the Essentials workspace, includes a library of layer presets that let you change the look of a layer by applying multiple effects with a single click of the mouse. Using a style is a quick and easy way to apply multiple effects at the same time—for example, a **bevel effect**, which gives an object the appearance of a third dimension, and a gradient or a shadow. See Figure 4-17.

Figure 4-17   Style applied from Styles panel

- Styles panel
- presets for buttons, images, layer fills, and textures
- Bevel and Emboss style applied to layer

TIP

You can change the library of styles displayed on the Styles panel by selecting a new library of style presets from the Styles panel options menu.

The default Styles panel library includes presets for buttons, images, layer fills, and textures. You can also choose a library with styles designed only for a particular object—for example, a library created solely for buttons or solely for text. When you assign a style to a layer, the letters *fx* appear to the right of the layer name, and the effects used in the style are listed beneath the layer on the Layers panel.

Lee would like her bicycle shop sign to be simple. She wants you to develop a sign that would consist of a bicycle silhouette that will appear on a hinged sign sticking out over the shop door—no words, just the sign. To show Lee the full effect of the sign you design, you'll place it in a photograph of the shop; later in the tutorial, you'll even draw the hinge upon which it will hang.

To work with the Styles panel:

1. Reset the Essentials workspace, restore the default foreground and background colors, and then click the **Styles** tab in the Color panel tab group to display the Styles panel. The Styles panel appears at the top of the panel group.

   If you hover over a style thumbnail, Photoshop displays the name of the style. However, it is difficult to tell from the names exactly what effects will be applied. To see what a style does, you need to apply it to a layer.

2. Open **BikeSign.psd** from the Photoshop4\Tutorial folder, display it at 100% magnification in the Document window, and pan the image so the bicycle and the white background rectangle are near the center of the window.

   The file Lee provided you includes three layers: The background is a photograph of the storefront; the top layer is a plain bicycle silhouette on a transparent background; and the layer beneath the bicycle is a plain white rectangle.

3. Resize the Layers panel so you can see all three layers, and then click the **Bicycle** layer to select it, if necessary.

4. Point to the first thumbnail on the Styles panel. Photoshop displays the style name, Default Style (None), when you point to the thumbnail. You can click this thumbnail at any point to undo any style you have applied to the layer.

5. Point to the thumbnail in the second row, fourth column, called Blanket (Texture), and then click. Photoshop applies the Blanket style to the bicycle. Notice that *fx* appears to the right of the layer name, and a list of effects appears indented under the layer name. Clicking a different style will replace this style with the new style.

6. Point to the thumbnail in the third row, fifth column, called Sunset Sky (Text), and then click to apply this style to the bicycle. See Figure 4-18.

Figure 4-18   Applying the Sunset Sky (Text) style

Although this style was designed for text, it can be applied to any object. It includes three effects: Drop Shadow, Bevel and Emboss, and Gradient Overlay. You can hide any of these individual effects just as you can hide layers.

7. On the Layers panel, click the **Eye** icon ▣ to the left of Drop Shadow to hide that effect. The bicycle no longer has a shadow.

8. Click in the column to turn the effect back on.

9. Hide the Gradient Overlay effect. The bicycle has returned to its original color, but with the drop shadow and the bevel and emboss effect still applied.

10. Click in the column to turn the effect back on.

11. Save the file as **SunsetBike.psd** in the Photoshop4\Tutorial folder.

You can leave a style preset as it is, or you can modify it to create a custom style preset. You'll modify the Sunset Sky (Text) style to see if you can achieve a better effect for the sign.

Using the Layer Style Dialog Box

You can modify a layer style using the Layer Style dialog box. For example, you might want to change the width of an outline (called a **stroke**) or the angle of a shadow. You can access the Layer Style dialog box by double-clicking the *fx* label to the right of the layer name, or through the Layer command on the Application bar. See Figure 4-19.

Figure 4-19 **Layer Style dialog box**

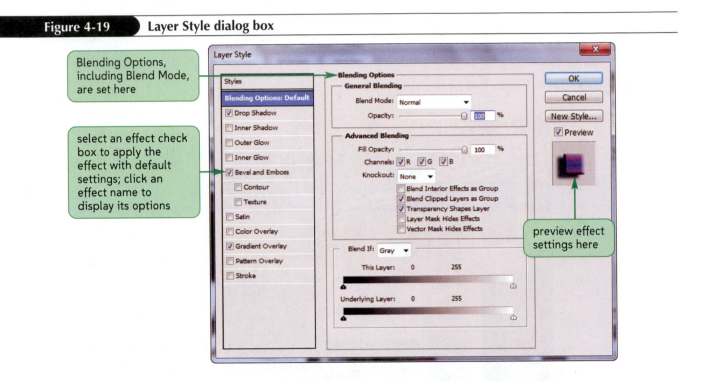

By default, the right side of the Layer Style dialog box displays blending options, such as the blending modes covered in Tutorial 3, and the fill opacity. However, the dialog box also includes a number of other options that are not visible when you first open the dialog box. In fact, the Layer Style dialog box behaves in ways you might not have seen before. On the left side of the dialog box, under Blending Options: Default, you can click a check box to select an option such as Drop Shadow or Outer Glow and apply the default settings for that option. When you do, the effect is applied, but you are not given the opportunity to modify the effect. However, if you click the name of the effect rather than the check box, you select the effect and the right side of the Layer Style dialog box changes to display options for the selected effect.

The effects available in the Layer Style dialog box are listed and described in the table in Figure 4-20.

Figure 4-20   **Effects in Layer Style dialog box**

Layer Style	Effect
Drop Shadow	Places a shadow behind the layer; you can specify the angle and opacity of the shadow and its distance from the layer object, among other things
Inner Shadow	Gives the layer an indented or recessed appearance by placing a shadow inside the edges of the layer content
Outer Glow	Adds a glow outside the layer content
Inner Glow	Adds a glow inside the layer content
Bevel and Emboss	Combines highlights and shadows to create a beveled effect that makes an object look three-dimensional
Satin	Adds shading to the object's interior to give it the appearance of satin
Color Overlay	Fills the layer content with color
Gradient Overlay	Fills the layer content with a gradient
Pattern Overlay	Fills the layer content with a pattern
Stroke	Outlines the object—usually text—with a color, gradient, or pattern

You've presented a draft of your sign to Lee, and she thinks it would be more effective without the gradient overlay and drop shadow. You'll experiment with different layer styles to see if you can achieve a better effect.

TIP

You can also double-click a layer thumbnail to open the Layer Style dialog box.

To use the Layer Style dialog box and save the new style:

1. Double-click **fx** to the right of the Bicycle layer name. The Layer Style dialog box opens.

2. If necessary, drag the dialog box by its title bar so you can see the bicycle.

3. In the Layer Style dialog box, click **Drop Shadow**. The Drop Shadow effect is selected and its settings are displayed in the dialog box.

   You can change the blend mode of the shadow, its opacity, and its angle. If you would like the angle that you set to apply to all other effects so they are consistent, select the Use Global Light check box. You can also change other shadow options, such as the distance from the object it is shadowing, and its size.

4. Decrease the Distance setting for the drop shadow from 10 pixels to **5** pixels. The shadow is closer to the bicycle.

5. Click the **Drop Shadow** check box to deselect it. See Figure 4-21.

Figure 4-21 Deselecting Drop Shadow

Drop Shadow is deselected

no drop shadow on bicycle image

Preview area shows your changes

deselecting an effect in the dialog box hides it on the Layers panel

In the Layer Style dialog box, the Preview area shows the effect without the drop shadow, and in the Document window, the bicycle on the sign no longer has the shadow.

6. Click the **Gradient Overlay** check box to deselect it. The bicycle appears in its original color, but it still has the Bevel and Emboss effect applied. You'll save this style so you can use it again in the future.

7. On the right side of the Layer Style dialog box, click the **New Style** button, type **BikeSign** in the Name box, select the **Include Layer Effects** check box to select it, if necessary, and then click the **OK** button.

8. Click the **OK** button to close the Layer Style dialog box. The image of the bicycle on the sign now includes the new style you created.

9. Save the file as **EffectSign.jpg**, using the default JPEG Options, in the Photoshop4\Tutorial folder, close SunsetBike.psd without saving it, and then exit Photoshop.

In this session, you learned how to use the color selection tools, including the Color panel, the Color Picker, and the Eyedropper Tool. You sampled colors, applied them to objects, and added them to the Swatches panel. You also worked with styles and made changes in the Layer Style dialog box to enhance parts of your image.

In the next session, you'll modify the image further so you can show Lee what your sign will look like hanging above the entrance of the store.

REVIEW

Session 4.1 Quick Check

1. By default, Photoshop uses the _____ color when you draw or paint with one of the tools found on the Tools panel.
2. You can use the _____ Tool to sample a color.
3. A color that will be displayed properly in a browser is called _____.
4. _____ is the process of mixing two colors to achieve an approximation of an unavailable color.
5. The range of colors used in a color mode is called the _____.
6. Sometimes colors are defined by _____ values, which are unique strings of six letters and numbers.
7. The _____ panel displays a library of commonly used colors.

SESSION 4.2 VISUAL OVERVIEW

The gradient fill style determines how the colors are laid out in the gradient. For example, they can be linear, or **radial** (emanating out like a bull's eye).

In the Gradient Fill dialog box, you can select the gradient, which can combine multiple colors.

You can let underlying layers show through by setting the opacity of a fill layer.

You can experiment with the angle of a fill to achieve different effects.

A **fill layer** is a layer filled with a solid color, a pattern, or a gradient. This gradient fill uses multiple colors.

Pattern fills include many different texture options.

A gradient fill layer blends the foreground color with transparent pixels, or blends two or more other colors.

FILL LAYERS, SHAPES, AND PAINTING

Use the options bar to set the **diameter**, or width, of the brush tip.

Brush tip choices include leaves, flowers, and other natural objects.

You can display the panel options menu to choose from many different Brush preset libraries.

To create an exact brushstroke, create a work path and then stroke the path.

Clicking once with a brush adds a single stroke.

A brushstroke uses the style that is applied to the layer on which it is painted.

The Brush Presets panel lets you preview how brush tips will look when you stroke the canvas.

Adding Fill Layers

You can add a fill layer to a Photoshop file using the Create new fill or adjustment layer icon at the bottom of the Layers panel. You can use fill layers to colorize black-and-white photographs, or to produce interesting effects—for example, placing an image so it has a gradient or patterned background. When you add a fill layer, you set its opacity to determine how much of an effect it will have on underlying layers. You can also move it on the Layers panel so it applies to some layers and not others, as shown in Figure 4-22.

Figure 4-22   **Adding a solid color fill layer**

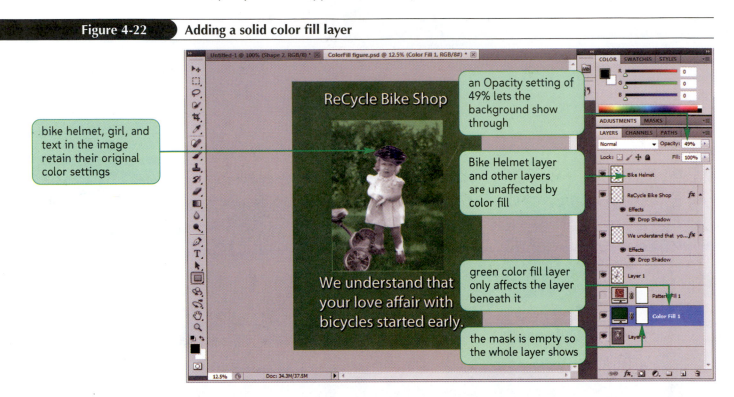

Photoshop links every fill layer to a layer mask. A **layer mask** hides part of a layer so it doesn't show through. By default, the layer mask for a fill layer is empty so the whole layer shows through. You'll learn more about layer masks and vector objects later in this session. You'll also work more with masks in Tutorial 5.

In Figure 4-22, the green, solid color fill layer is set at 49% opacity, and has been placed beneath the girl and tricycle layer so it affects only the black-and-white bottom layer, Layer 0, which is the only layer beneath it on the Layers panel. At this opacity, the fill layer makes the background photograph look as if it has been shot through a green-colored lens filter. If the fill layer were set to 100% opacity, it would completely hide the bottom layer.

You can add a gradient fill layer to produce an immediate and powerful effect in a composition without changing the pixels in any other layer. You can choose from many gradient presets in Photoshop, each with a different effect. The default gradient combines the foreground color with transparent pixels. See Figure 4-23.

Figure 4-23   Gradient Fill dialog box

click to see a list of available gradients

click to change the gradient style

change the gradient angle here

changing the gradient scale affects its impact on the image

When you work with gradients, you can apply one of the many presets, or you can modify a gradient by making changes in the Gradient Fill dialog box. Given the number of choices, you could very easily spend hours playing with gradients to find the one that works best with your composition. Later in this session, you'll experiment with a few settings to see what works best in the image you're modifying.

A pattern fill layer works in much the same way both the solid fill and gradient fill layers work. When you add the layer, it appears on its own layer on the Layers panel. Just as gradients and other layers in Photoshop include presets, so do pattern fill layers. When you first add a pattern fill layer, Photoshop applies the default pattern at 100% opacity. You can change the opacity, and you can drag the pattern fill layer to change which layers it affects. To change the pattern, you use the Pattern Fill dialog box shown in Figure 4-24.

Figure 4-24   Pattern Fill dialog box

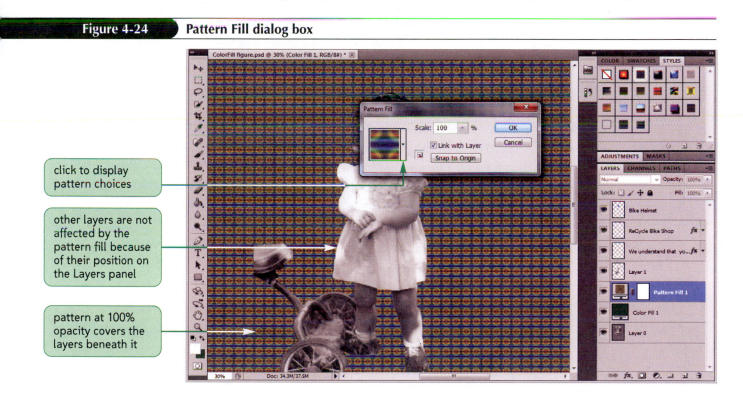

click to display pattern choices

other layers are not affected by the pattern fill because of their position on the Layers panel

pattern at 100% opacity covers the layers beneath it

You can choose from additional presets in the Pattern Fill dialog box by selecting a different preset group. For example, you can choose Rock Patterns, Nature Patterns, Color Paper, and different texture pattern sets. You can also modify the scale of a pattern. For example, if you modify the scale of a rock pattern, the size of the rocks in the pattern will increase by the percentage you specify in the dialog box.

Creating a Solid Color Fill Layer

Because a solid color fill layer is separate from the content it affects, it provides flexibility you wouldn't have by adjusting the color directly in the image itself. Once you add the layer, you can adjust its opacity and blending mode to achieve a variety of effects.

You've found an image of a bicycle on a beach that you think Lee might want to use in her summer ad campaign. You'll experiment with a solid color fill layer to enhance the image and create a more dramatic effect.

To create a solid color fill layer:

1. Start Photoshop while pressing the **Ctrl+Alt+Shift** keys. When you are prompted to delete the Adobe Photoshop Settings File, click **Yes**. On the Application bar, right-click **Essentials**, and then click **Reset Essentials** to reset the default workspace layout.

2. Open **FillLayers.psd** from the Photoshop4\Tutorial folder, expand the **Layers** panel, if necessary, and then select the **Tire** layer.

3. At the bottom of the Layers panel, click the **Create new fill or adjustment layer** icon ⊘, and then click **Solid Color**. The Pick a solid color dialog box opens. This dialog box is essentially the same as the Color Picker dialog box you worked with earlier.

4. In the Pick a solid color dialog box, click the **Only Web Colors** check box to select it, if necessary, select any blue color, and then click the **OK** button. The color layer appears on top of the image so nothing shows through. You can change the opacity of the fill layer so the layers beneath it show through.

5. On the Layers panel, change the Opacity to **50%**. The bicycle tire image shows through the blue layer; however, this is not quite the effect you were looking for.

6. Drag the **Color Fill 1** layer down below the Tire layer. See Figure 4-25.

Figure 4-25   Adding a fill layer

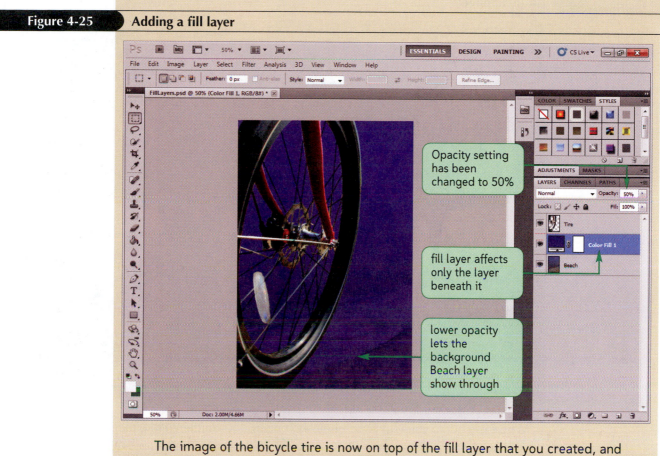

The image of the bicycle tire is now on top of the fill layer that you created, and the effect is much more dramatic.

7. On the Layers panel, change the blending mode to **Color Burn**. The layer fill effect is much different than it was using the Normal blending mode.

8. Save the file as **TireOnBlue.psd** in the Photoshop4\Tutorial folder, and leave the file open.

Creating a Gradient Layer

You can also add a gradient layer to a composition. Gradients are an easy way to add dramatic effects to your compositions, as shown in Figure 4-26.

Figure 4-26 Gradient effects

When you add a gradient layer, Photoshop opens the Gradient Fill dialog box. The default gradient combines the foreground color with transparent pixels, using a Linear style with a 90-degree angle for the gradient. Changing any of these settings changes the look of the gradient. For example, you can change the Style setting to Radial, Angle, Reflected, or Diamond. You can also choose from other gradient presets by clicking the Gradient arrow in the dialog box to display the Gradient picker. See Figure 4-27.

Figure 4-27 Gradient picker in the Gradient Fill dialog box

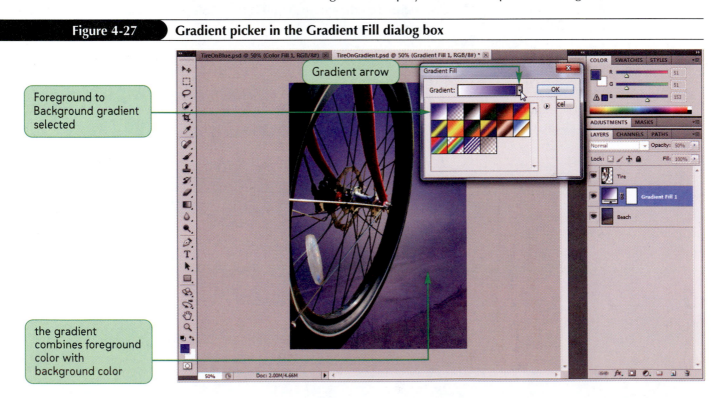

Gradient arrow

Foreground to Background gradient selected

the gradient combines foreground color with background color

The Gradient picker displays a variety of gradient presets, some that use the background and foreground colors and others that have different color combinations, including foreground to transparent. If you apply a gradient and then decide you want to change it, you can double-click the gradient thumbnail on the layer to reopen the Gradient Fill dialog box.

Next, you'll see if you can achieve a different effect using a gradient fill layer, and you'll save the file with a new name so the pattern fill file is still available.

To add a gradient layer:

1. Delete the Color Fill 1 layer, and then save the file as **TireOnGradient.psd** in the Photoshop4\Tutorial folder.

2. Change the foreground color to a Web-safe blue, and make the background color black.

3. Select the **Beach** layer, click the **Create new fill or adjustment layer** icon at the bottom of the Layers panel, and then click **Gradient**. The Gradient Fill dialog box opens, and the default gradient is applied to the image.

4. Click the **Gradient** arrow to display the Gradient picker. The first gradient choice on the list creates the gradient using the foreground color and the background color, in this case, blue and black.

5. Click the first gradient choice to see the effect. The effect is dramatic, but it completely covers the beach image.

6. In the Gradient Fill dialog box, click the **OK** button, and then on the Layers panel, change the opacity of the layer to **50%**.

7. Double-click the **gradient thumbnail**. The Gradient Fill dialog box opens again. Click the **Gradient** arrow, click the **Spectrum** gradient (the first gradient in the third row), and then click the **OK** button. The Spectrum gradient is applied to the image using the gradient layer.

8. Save TireOnGradient.psd, and leave the file open.

You'll try a different effect by choosing from the pattern layers available in Photoshop.

Creating a Pattern Layer

Although there are only two patterns listed in the default Pattern Fill dialog box, there are many patterns to choose from if you select a different library of presets. Pattern galleries include Artist Surfaces, Color Paper, Nature Patterns, and Rock Patterns, among others. When you select a pattern library, you are prompted to either replace the current patterns or append the list to the current pattern list, just as you were prompted to replace or append styles in Session 4.1.

You'll experiment with adding pattern layers to see the effects you can achieve.

To add a pattern layer:

1. Delete the Gradient Fill 1 layer, and then save the file as **TireOnPattern.psd** in the Photoshop4\Tutorial folder.

2. Select the **Beach** layer, click the **Create new fill or adjustment layer** icon [icon] at the bottom of the Layers panel, and then click **Pattern**. The Pattern Fill dialog box opens, and Photoshop applies the default pattern fill to the image.

3. In the Pattern Fill dialog box, click the **pattern** thumbnail to open the Pattern pre-set picker, and then click the **More options** arrow [icon] to open the menu.

4. Click **Color Paper** on the menu, and then click the **OK** button to replace the current patterns with the selected patterns.

   Trouble? If you are prompted to save changes to the current patterns before replacing them, click the No button.

   The Color Paper patterns are displayed in the preset picker.

5. Scroll down the list and then click the **Red Textured** pattern to select it. See Figure 4-28.

Figure 4-28 **Pattern picker on Pattern Fill dialog box**

The pattern appears in the dialog box and is applied to the image. The effect is interesting, but it's not the effect you had in mind. You'd like to lend a sense of outdoor adventure to the image.

6. Display the menu again, click **Rock Patterns**, and then click the **OK** button. The rock patterns replace the paper patterns.

7. Click **Stones** (the second pattern) to select it, change the scale to **500%**, and then click the **OK** button. Because the pattern replaces the Beach layer in the composition, you can delete the Beach layer to decrease the file size.

8. Delete the Beach layer, and then save TireOnPattern.psd and close the file.

Adding Shape Layers Versus Filling Pixels on a Layer

You've already seen that Photoshop includes a number of drawing tools that you can use to enhance a composition. Now that you know what a fill layer is, and understand what a mask does, you can delve more deeply into options available to you when using the drawing tools. See Figure 4-29.

Figure 4-29   Shape layer versus Fill pixels

When you draw a vector shape such as the rectangle you added in Session 4.1 or the pink flower shown in Figure 4-29, you are adding both a fill layer that defines the color of the shape and a mask linked to that fill layer that determines the outline of the shape and specifies where the color will show through. Any layer with this combination (a fill and a shape outline) is called a **shape layer**. As you saw earlier, shape layers are a form of nondestructive editing because they don't alter the pixels on the layer or layers beneath them.

You can also add a raster shape to a layer using the same drawing tool but a different option on the options bar. The Fill pixels option places the shape you draw directly on a layer as a raster or bitmap object, overwriting the pixels beneath it. The yellow Starburst shape in Figure 4-29 appears directly on the green Background layer that contains it. It consists of pixels that are painted over the original green pixels on the layer. Adding the Starburst to the Background layer was an example of destructive editing.

The third option for adding a shape is the Paths option, which is covered later in this tutorial. If you draw a shape with the Paths button selected on the options bar, you are creating a temporary work path.

Adding a Shape Layer

You have already added a rectangle shape to an image. In this section, you'll learn the different kinds of shapes you can add to a composition. To add a shape layer, click one of the shape tools on the Tools panel to select it. When the tool is selected, the options bar lets you choose to draw a shape layer (a vector object), to draw a path, or to fill the drawn object with pixels (a bitmap, or raster, object). Figure 4-30 describes the vector, path, and fill options on the options bar, as well as the options for creating complex shapes by combining, intersecting, and excluding shapes as you draw.

Figure 4-30	Shape options bar buttons

Button	Name	Effect
	Shape layers	Adds a vector shape on a new layer
	Paths	Creates a temporary work path
	Fill pixels	Adds a bitmap shape that overwrites underlying pixels
	Create new shape layer	Adds a new shape layer rather than creating the new shape on the current shape layer
	Add to shape area	Combines new shape with current shape on same layer
	Subtract from shape area	Uses new shape to subtract from existing shape
	Intersect shape areas	Creates a shape that consists of the intersection of the new shape and the previous shape or shapes on the layer
	Exclude overlapping shape areas	Excludes any overlapping shape areas

To draw a shape, you must first activate the desired drawing tool on the Tools panel, and then select the Shape layers option on the options bar. Make sure the Create new shape layer option is selected on the options bar, and then drag the mouse pointer on the canvas to draw the object. As you draw, an outline of the object appears. When you release the mouse button, the object is filled with the foreground color and appears on its own layer. To specify drawing options, click the Geometry options button on the options bar to choose additional specifications. For example, if you are drawing a rect-angle, you can constrain it to a square by selecting the Square option button. You can also specify a fixed or proportional size, or select the From Center check box so you can start your drawing at the center and drag outward. See Figure 4-31.

Figure 4-31	Geometry options

click the Geometry options button to display options for current shape tool

click to draw a square

select to draw an object from the center

You can continue to add vector layers and draw additional shapes, or you can modify the existing vector layers using one of the buttons on the options bar. See Figure 4-32.

Figure 4-32   Adding, subtracting, and intersecting

inside rectangle
subtracts from
outside rectangle

two shapes added
together to create a
single shape

only the intersection
of these two shapes
is filled with the
layer color

outlines of shapes
will disappear when
layer is deselected

For example, to add to the vector object, click the Add to shape area option on the options bar, and then draw an additional shape. The shape appears on the same layer, and is combined with the existing shape to create a new shape.

You can subtract from the shape you have drawn by clicking the Subtract from shape area option on the options bar, and then drawing a new shape. When you release the mouse button, the new shape you drew is subtracted from the original shape so the under-lying background color shows through. You can also leave the Create new shape layer button selected on the options bar and press the Alt key to subtract from the shape layer.

You can click the Intersect shape areas option to create a shape that is the intersec-tion of two or more shapes that you draw. If you click the Exclude overlapping shape areas option, intersecting areas are transparent, and areas outside of the intersections are opaque (or filled).

Next, you'll add a vector shape to an image. Then, you'll copy the style that you cre-ated for the bicycle in the previous session and apply it to the sign in the image as well, so you can show Lee what your sign will look like over the doorway of the store.

To draw a vector shape:

1. Open **BikeSign2.psd** from the Photoshop4\Tutorial, and display it at 100% mag-nification. Restore the default background and foreground colors, and select the **Background** layer on the Layers panel.

2. On the Tools panel, click the **Rectangle Tool** 🔲, and on the options bar, click the **Shape layers** button 🔲. Draw a rectangle so it contains the bicycle, as shown in Figure 4-33.

Figure 4-33 Drawing a rectangle shape layer

rectangle around bicycle

3. Change the name of the new layer from Shape 1 to **Sign**. Next, you'll change the color of the sign's background rectangle.

4. On the Layers panel, right-click the **Sign** layer, and then click **Rasterize Layer**. The Sign layer is no longer a vector object; it is now made up of pixels that you can manipulate with the image-editing tools in Photoshop.

5. Make the **Background** layer active, use the **Eyedropper Tool** to sample the blue color of the storefront, select the **Sign** layer, and then use the **Paint Bucket Tool** to apply the sampled color to the sign.

   The rectangle of the sign is now the same color as the storefront. Next, you'll copy the style applied to the Bicycle layer and paste it on the Sign layer.

6. Right-click the **Bicycle** layer, click **Copy Layer Style** on the menu, right-click the **Sign** layer, and then click **Paste Layer Style**. The sign now has the Bevel and Emboss effect that you applied to the bicycle. See Figure 4-34.

Figure 4-34 Applying the BikeSign style

bicycle effects

same effects copied to rectangle sign

Because the Drop Shadow and Gradient Overlay effects are hidden but still listed on the Bicycle layer, they are listed and hidden on the Sign layer as well. If you wanted to, you could delete these unused effects; however, you'll leave them hidden for now.

7. Save the file as **BikeSignFinal.psd** in the Photoshop4\Tutorial folder, and leave the file open.

Lee has asked you to work on an image of a tricycle that she plans to use in one of her ads. The tricycle has a brand label on it that she does not want to appear in the ad. You'll use the vector tools and options to hide the label and replace it with a geometric shape.

To modify a vector shape by subtracting:

1. Open **Tricycle.jpg** from the Photoshop4\Tutorial folder, reset the Essentials workspace, restore the default foreground and background colors, reset all tools, and display the image in the Document window at 100% magnification.

2. Sample the red color on the back of the tricycle.

3. On the Tools panel, click the **Rectangle Tool**. On the options bar, click the **Geometry options** button ⬛, and then click **Square**.

4. Click the **From Center** check box to select it. This option allows you to draw the square by clicking at its center point and then dragging outward to define its dimensions.

5. Click the center of the tricycle's label.

6. Drag to draw a square over the label on the back of the tricycle, and release the mouse button when you have covered the label. The square fills with red when you release the mouse button.

7. On the Layers panel, click the **Create a new layer** icon ⬛ and then select the **Background** layer. Sample the green color from the handlebars, make the new layer active and draw a green square that covers the red square you just drew.

8. On the Tools panel, select the **Custom Shape Tool** ⬛, on the options bar, click the **Custom Shape picker** button ⬛, and then click the **Flower 5** shape option in the second row.

9. On the options bar, click the **Geometry options** button ⬛, click the **From Center** check box, and then click the **Geometry options** button ⬛ again to close the list.

10. On the options bar, click the **Subtract from shape area** button ⬛. Now any shape you draw on the current layer will be subtracted from the existing shape where the two shapes overlap.

11. Position the mouse pointer ⊢ over the center of the green square you just drew. The mouse pointer now has a minus sign to the right of the crosshairs, indicating that the shape you draw will subtract from the previous shape.

12. Draw the flower shape centered within the green square, and then on the Layers panel, click the **Background** layer to select it. See Figure 4-35.

Figure 4-35   **Subtracting a shape**

the flower shape is subtracted from the green square to expose the red square beneath

The red square you covered with the green square is now partially visible because the flower shape you drew is subtracted from the green square shape.

13. Save the file as **AddTrike.psd** in the Photoshop4\Tutorial folder and then close the file.

You can switch from one option to another on the options bar as you draw to create a complex shape that is the result of adding, subtracting, and intersecting geometric objects. Next, you'll use a combination of standard shapes and add them together to create a drawing of a fish on an image of a submerged bicycle. Lee hopes to use the image in a campaign she's calling "Time for a Replacement?" to encourage people to replace their old bicycles.

To modify a vector shape by adding and excluding:

1. Open **Submerged.jpg** from the Photoshop4\Tutorial folder, display it at 100% magnification, and specify a blue foreground color.

2. Pan to the lower-right side of the image. Display the ruler, and drag a horizontal guide to about 11 ½ inches on the vertical ruler, and drag a vertical guide to about 15 ½ inches on the horizontal ruler.

3. On the Tools panel, select the **Ellipse Tool** .

   Trouble? If you can't find the Ellipse Tool, right-click the Custom Shapes Tool , and then click Ellipse Tool on the list of hidden tools.

4. On the options bar, click the **Geometry options** button , and then click the **From Center** check box.

5. Drag to draw an ellipse that is about 3 inches wide and 1 inch high, centered at the intersection of the two guides. See Figure 4-36.

Figure 4-36	Drawing an ellipse

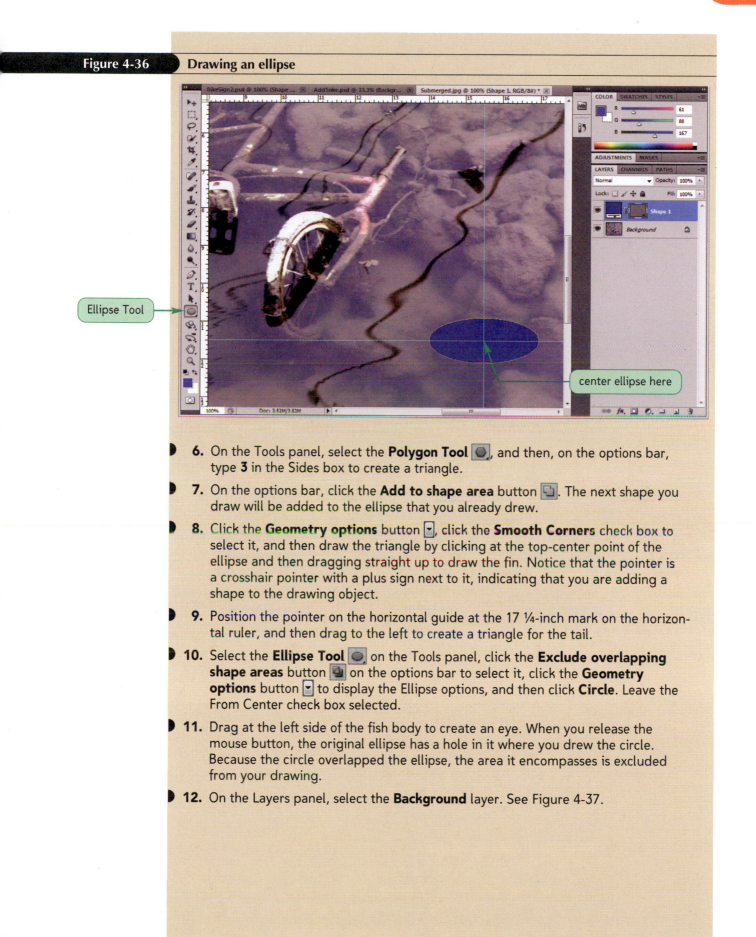

Ellipse Tool

center ellipse here

6. On the Tools panel, select the **Polygon Tool** , and then, on the options bar, type **3** in the Sides box to create a triangle.

7. On the options bar, click the **Add to shape area** button . The next shape you draw will be added to the ellipse that you already drew.

8. Click the **Geometry options** button , click the **Smooth Corners** check box to select it, and then draw the triangle by clicking at the top-center point of the ellipse and then dragging straight up to draw the fin. Notice that the pointer is a crosshair pointer with a plus sign next to it, indicating that you are adding a shape to the drawing object.

9. Position the pointer on the horizontal guide at the 17 ¼-inch mark on the horizontal ruler, and then drag to the left to create a triangle for the tail.

10. Select the **Ellipse Tool** on the Tools panel, click the **Exclude overlapping shape areas** button on the options bar to select it, click the **Geometry options** button to display the Ellipse options, and then click **Circle**. Leave the From Center check box selected.

11. Drag at the left side of the fish body to create an eye. When you release the mouse button, the original ellipse has a hole in it where you drew the circle. Because the circle overlapped the ellipse, the area it encompasses is excluded from your drawing.

12. On the Layers panel, select the **Background** layer. See Figure 4-37.

Figure 4-37   **Drawing the fish**

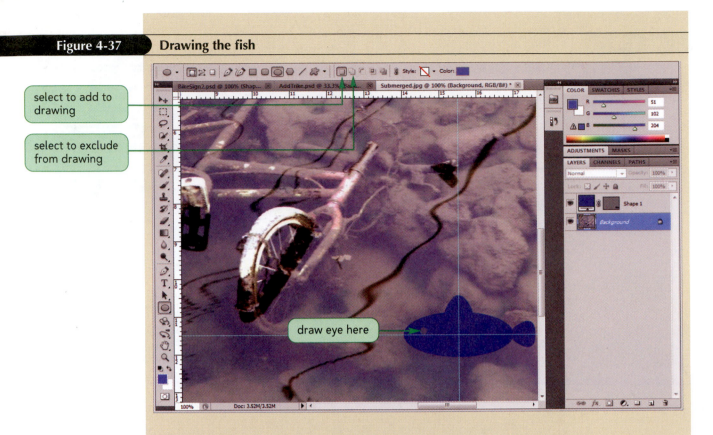

select to add to drawing

select to exclude from drawing

draw eye here

▶ **13.** On the Layers panel, click the **Shape 1** layer, click the **Move Tool** on the Tools panel, and then click **Show Transform Controls** on the options bar. The transform controls surround the fish as a single object.

▶ **14.** Merge the two layers on the Layers panel, save the file as **SleepingWithFishes.jpg**, using the default JPEG Options, in the Photoshop4\Tutorial folder, and then close the file.

Next, Lee wants you to cover the label on the tricycle with a red color instead of using the flower label you created. You'll draw a bitmap shape over the background pixels to remove the label permanently.

Drawing a Bitmap or Raster Shape Using Fill Pixels

To draw a bitmap shape, select the tool with which you want to draw, for example, the rectangle or ellipse, and then click the Fill pixels button on the options bar. As implied by the name of the option, when you draw the shape using Fill pixels, you are modifying the pixels in the area of your drawing by filling them with the foreground color. Drag the mouse pointer on the canvas to draw the object. As you draw, an outline of the object appears. When you release the mouse button, the object appears filled with the foreground color on the current layer, replacing the pixels beneath it.

To draw a bitmap shape:

▶ **1.** Open **Tricycle.jpg** from the Photoshop4\Tutorial folder, and save it as **CoverTrike.jpg**, using the default JPEG Options, in the same folder.

▶ **2.** Sample the red from the tricycle to set it as the foreground color.

▶ **3.** On the Tools panel, click the **Rectangle Tool** .

4. On the options bar, right-click the **Rectangle** button ▣, click **Reset All Tools**, and then click the **OK** button.

5. On the options bar, click the **Fill pixels** button ▣. The pixels in the Background layer will be hidden by the pixels you add to the canvas as fill.

6. Click the **Geometry options** button ▾, and select the **Square** and **From Center** Geometry options.

7. Drag a square over the label on the back of the tricycle, starting from the center of the label. When you release the mouse button, the new pixels replace the original pixels on the Background layer. Once you save the file and exit Photoshop, you will not be able to undo this change.

8. Save CoverTrike.jpg, and then close the file.

Using the Brush Tool

The Brush and Pencil Tools in Photoshop let you paint or draw on your images. If you are using a mouse, you have less control over your brushstrokes and pencil strokes than you would if you were using a Tablet PC with a **stylus**, which lets you write or draw directly on the screen. However, both tools are still valuable image-editing tools.

The Brush Tool produces strokes that are **anti-aliased**—that is, even though you are working with pixels, your brushstrokes will have a smooth rather than a jagged appearance because Photoshop adds pixels to blend the edges into the background. Because anti-aliasing adds pixels, anti-alias settings increase file size. The **hardness** of the Brush Tool is related to the amount of anti-aliasing applied to the brushstroke. A setting of 100% uses the least anti-aliasing, but still produces smooth edges. The Pencil Tool is never anti-aliased; as a result, it can sometimes produce jagged or pixelated edges. See Figure 4-38.

| Figure 4-38 | Brush and pencil strokes |

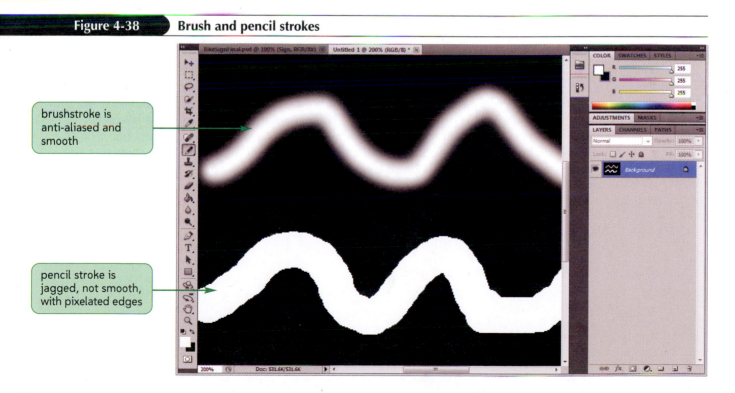

brushstroke is anti-aliased and smooth

pencil stroke is jagged, not smooth, with pixelated edges

In Figure 4-38, the top stroke was drawn with the Brush Tool and the bottom stroke was drawn with the Pencil Tool. Both strokes have identical diameter (width) and hardness settings. However, notice how different they look. The brushstroke is smooth because it is anti-aliased. The pencil stroke has hard edges and is not anti-aliased; in fact, you can distinguish the individual pixels along the edges. In this session, you'll focus on the Brush Tool, but the skills you learn can also be applied to the Pencil Tool.

Choosing Brush Settings and Adding Brushstrokes

When you select the Brush Tool, the options bar displays the Brush Tool options shown in Figure 4-39.

Figure 4-39   **Brush Tool options**

Button	Name	Use To
⬇	Tool Preset picker	Display the presets for the Brush Tool, such as "Airbrush soft round 50% flow," "Paintbrush Oval 45 pixels Multiply," and "Transparent Red Spray Paint"
13	Brush Preset picker	Specify the size and hardness for the brush or choose from a variety of presets, including Chalk, Dune grass, Stars, and certain preset brush hardness and size settings
🖌	Toggle the Brush panel	Expand and collapse the Brush panel display
Mode	Mode	Choose a blending mode for the brush
Opacity	Opacity	Set brush opacity
🎨	Tablet pressure	Control brushstroke opacity based on the pressure you place on the tablet rather than Brush panel opacity settings
Flow	Flow	Set the flow rate, or the amount of paint on the brush; a low percentage paints as if you have just dipped the brush lightly in paint, and a high percentage saturates the brush
🖌	Enable airbrush mode	Turn on airbrush mode
🎯	Tablet pressure controls size	Control brushstroke size based on the pressure you place on the tablet rather than Brush panel opacity settings

The Brush Preset picker displays a library of brush settings. You can set the diameter of the brush (measured in pixels) as well as the hardness of the brush. A brush with a high hardness setting will paint on the canvas in much the same way a physical paint brush with hard bristles will paint. Strokes will appear firm and full, with little space showing between the virtual bristles. A brush with a low hardness setting will paint like a brush with softer bristles. See Figure 4-40.

Figure 4-40   **Working with brush presets**

Tool Preset picker button

Brush Preset picker button

default brush presets

brushstrokes with different diameters and 100% hardness

brushstrokes with equal diameters, but with hardness decreasing from 100 to 0

You can also use the Brush Preset picker to choose from a variety of presets. However, the Brush Presets panel is a more convenient way to work with presets, and is covered later in this tutorial.

To paint with the Brush Tool, set the foreground color you want to use, select the layer on which you want to paint, click the place you want to begin your brushstroke, and then drag the mouse to complete the stroke. When you have finished the first stroke, release the mouse button. You can repeat this procedure for each stroke in your composition.

You can also paint in straight lines with the Brush Tool by using the click-Shift-click method. To draw a straight line, click the place on the canvas where you want to begin the stroke. Release the mouse button. Position the mouse over the point where you want to end the stroke and then Shift-click. Photoshop fills in the area between the first place you clicked and the last place you Shift-clicked with a straight brushstroke.

You'll use the Brush Tool to add a chalky border to an image of a submerged bicycle, much like the outline police might add at a crime scene. Lee is planning to use the image for her "Time for a Replacement?" campaign.

To paint using the Brush Tool:

1. Reset the Essentials workspace, restore the default foreground and background colors, reset all tools, and then open **PoliceLine.psd** from the Photoshop4\Tutorial folder.

2. Click the **Layers** panel tab, if necessary, to display the layers, and then select the **Background** layer, if necessary.

3. On the Tools panel, click the **Brush Tool** . The options for the Brush Tool appear on the options bar.

4. Press **X** to switch the foreground and background colors and set the foreground color to white.

5. On the options bar, click the **Brush Preset picker** button ⊡. The Preset picker displays the default size (13 pixels) and hardness (0%) for the Brush Tool.

6. Change the brush size to **25** pixels, and then drag the brush pointer ⬡ around the submerged bicycle as if you are outlining the victim's body at a crime scene. See Figure 4-41.

| Figure 4-41 | Adding a brushstroke |

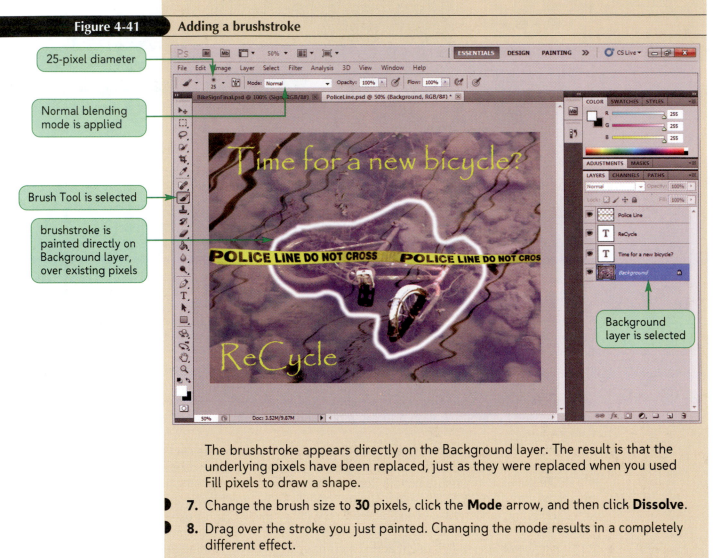

25-pixel diameter

Normal blending mode is applied

Brush Tool is selected

brushstroke is painted directly on Background layer, over existing pixels

Background layer is selected

The brushstroke appears directly on the Background layer. The result is that the underlying pixels have been replaced, just as they were replaced when you used Fill pixels to draw a shape.

7. Change the brush size to **30** pixels, click the **Mode** arrow, and then click **Dissolve**.

8. Drag over the stroke you just painted. Changing the mode results in a completely different effect.

9. Save the file as **PoliceLine1.jpg**, using the default JPEG Options, in the Photoshop4\Tutorial folder, and then close the original file without saving it.

Next, you'll use the Brush Tool to add straight lines to your sign image to create a hinge upon which to hang the sign. Because you'll add the lines to a layer that has a Bevel and Emboss effect, the lines you draw will also have a Bevel and Emboss effect.

To draw straight lines with the Brush Tool:

1. Open **BikeSignFinal.psd** from the Photoshop 4\Tutorial Folder, display it at 100% magnification in the Document window, and then select the **Sign** layer if necessary.

2. Set the foreground color to **black**, and reset all of the tools.

3. Open the **Brush Tool Preset** picker and set the size of the brush to **10** pixels and the hardness to **100%**.

4. On the Layers panel, select the **Sign** layer, if necessary, position the brush pointer ⬚ just to the left of the upper-left corner of the sign and then click. Photoshop adds the first point in the straight line you'll draw.

5. Position the brush pointer ⬚ at the left of the lower-left corner of the sign, press and hold the **Shift** key, and then click.

   Photoshop draws a straight brushstroke along the left side of the sign. Notice that it has the same Bevel and Emboss effect you applied to the Sign layer because you are drawing the brushstroke on the Sign layer. To "attach" the sign to the storefront, draw another straight brushstroke from the upper-left corner to the storefront.

6. Position the brush pointer ⬚ just to the left of the upper-left corner of the sign and then click.

7. Position the brush pointer ⬚ at the center of the wall between the windows, press and hold the **Shift** key, and then click. The sign appears to be attached to the building by a wrought iron hanger. See Figure 4-42.

Figure 4-42 **Painting in a straight line**

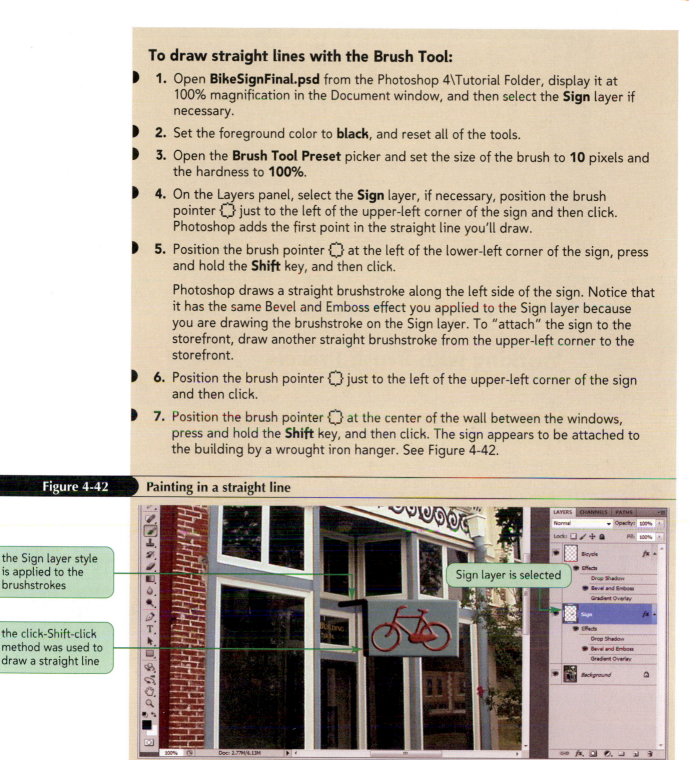

the Sign layer style is applied to the brushstrokes

the click-Shift-click method was used to draw a straight line

Sign layer is selected

8. Save BikeSignFinal.psd, and keep the file open.

Teamwork: Knowing When to Call in Help

No matter how good your digital image-editing skills are, there will be times when you need to reach out to another person on your team to help you do your best work. Not only are teams useful for providing feedback on the work you do, but every good team has people who specialize in different areas. Being a Photoshop expert doesn't necessarily mean you have the artistic skills to create vector drawings at a professional level. Furthermore, Photoshop is certainly not the best drawing tool for any professional composition you create—Illustrator is. When you need to create a challenging graphic for your composition, it is a good idea to call in a graphic designer or a visual artist when you need help. For example, if you need a vector drawing for a comp you are working on for a client, you could fumble around with the drawing tools in Photoshop and create a pretty good drawing—but why not shoot for excellent instead? This is an example of where calling on an expert from your team will result not only in the best final product, but will also show that you have the decision-making and problem-solving skills necessary to get a job done right, the team player mentality to advance your organization's interests, and the potential to lead that team in the future.

Working with Brush Presets

The Brush and Pencil presets offer a great variety of brushstrokes and pencil shapes for you to choose from. The most convenient way to work with presets is to use the Brush panel or the Brush Presets panel. The Brush panel displays the brush tip shape and lets you modify size, angle, and roundness settings. The Brush Presets panel previews the brush tip shape and shows you what a brushstroke will look like. In this section, you'll work with the Brush Presets panel. It appears by default in the Painting workspace, so you'll switch to that workspace. See Figure 4-43.

Figure 4-43   **Working with Brush presets**

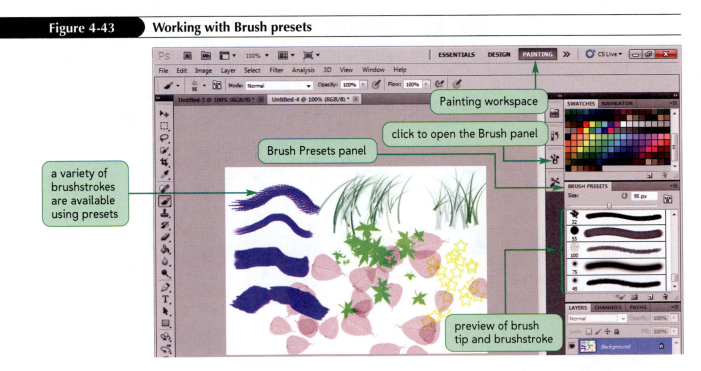

With the Brush Tool, not only can you choose brush tips with different diameters and hardness settings, but you can also choose different paints as well. For example, you can choose a preset that mimics oil paint, one that mimics spray paint, or one that mimics chalk. You can also choose brush tips that paint leaves, stars, and other shapes.

Loading Other Presets

There are numerous libraries of presets in Photoshop, and as a result, you have hundreds of choices for brushes. As you become more experienced in Photoshop, you'll develop a sense of which brushes you need for which effects, but as a novice, it's a good idea to experiment with as many presets and preset modifications as possible. Loading a brush preset library is basically the same as loading any other library. You do it from the panel options menu, and, as with the Color, Swatches, and Styles panels you've already worked with, you need to determine whether you want to append the library to the current library, or use it to replace the current library. You can also modify any preset in any library and save it as a custom preset or, if you decide that you don't want to keep the changes you have made to a set of brush presets, you can reset the Brush panel by clicking Reset Brushes on the panel options menu.

To load a preset library:

1. On the Layers panel, click the **Bicycle** layer, on the Application bar, click the **workspace switcher**, and then click **Painting** to display the most commonly used panels for painting. The Brush Presets panel opens on the right. The Brush panel is minimized to an icon.

2. On the Brush Presets panel, click the **panel options** button , and then click **Assorted Brushes**.

3. Click the **OK** button to replace the current brushes with the new brushes. Click the **No** button if asked to save the current brushes.

4. On the Tools panel, click the **Brush Tool** , and on the Brush Presets panel, scroll down until you see the Dashed Circle 2 preset shown in Figure 4-44, and then click the **Dashed Circle 2** preset to select it.

| Figure 4-44 | Selecting the Dashed Circle 2 brush preset |

5. Add a new layer to the Layers panel, set the foreground color to white, and then click in the front tire of the bicycle. The brush adds a dashed circle to the image.

6. Click in the rear tire to add the dashed circle there as well.

7. Save the file.

Using a Brush Preset to Stroke a Path

When you draw a shape in Photoshop, you can use the Paths option on the options bar to specify that the shape is a temporary work path. A **work path** provides a temporary outline on a layer. You can use the outline to define a path for a variety of tasks, including erasing the area defined by the path, or stroking the path with the Brush or Pencil Tool. To create a work path and apply a stroke to it, you select the desired shape tool on the Tools panel, draw the shape, and then use the Stroke Path command on the shortcut menu to display a list of tools you can use for the stroke. If you select the Brush option from the list, Photoshop uses the current brush settings to draw a brushstroke around the work path. Once you have added the stroke, you can delete the work path from the Paths panel or save it for future sessions.

You'll create a circular work path and stroke it with a concentric circle brushstroke to show Lee an idea you have about painting a design on the store window.

TIP

To display a list of preset names rather than sample strokes, select the Text Only option from the Brush Presets panel options menu.

To create a work path and apply a stroke:

1. In the Brush Presets panel, select the **32-pixel Concentric Circles** preset (the fifth option in the list), and then click in the center of the left store window. Photoshop adds a single brushstroke to the window (a concentric circle).

2. On the Tools panel, select the **Ellipse Tool**, and on the options bar, click the **Paths** button.

3. Click the **Geometry options** button, select the **Circle** and **From Center** options, and then click in the center of the circle you just painted and drag out to create the shape.

4. Right-click the work path. See Figure 4-45.

Figure 4-45 Path shortcut menu

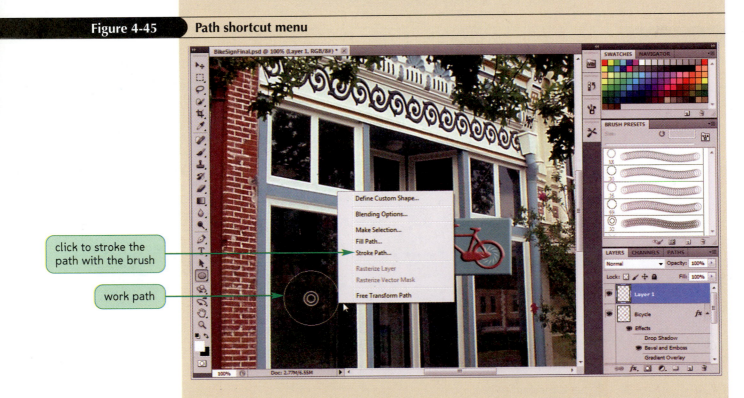

click to stroke the path with the brush

work path

Photoshop displays options for working with the work path. You can fill the path, make it a selection, or you can stroke it.

5. On the shortcut menu, click **Stroke Path** on the shortcut menu, click the **Tool arrow**, click **Brush**, and then click the **OK** button to accept Brush as the tool you'll use to stroke the path. Photoshop adds a brushstroke that follows the path of the circle you drew. You can save the path for future sessions, or delete it. You'll delete it.

6. In the Layers panel group, click the **Paths** tab. Photoshop lists a single work path on the Paths panel.

7. Select the **Work Path** path, if necessary, and then press the **Delete** key. The path is deleted from the panel and from the image, but the circular brushstroke remains. See Figure 4-46.

Figure 4-46   **Brushstroke on path**

Brush preset strokes the path

path is deleted from Paths panel

Creating a Custom Preset

You can create a custom preset and save it so you can use it in future Photoshop sessions. To create a custom preset, select the brush preset you want to modify and change the settings, such as diameter and hardness, until you achieve the effect you want. When you are satisfied with your changes, you can use the New Brush Preset command on the options menu to save the custom preset. You can then save any of your new presets as a library using the options menu. Photoshop adds an .abr extension to any brush preset library you save. If you decide that you don't want to keep the changes you have made to a set of brush presets, you can reset the Brush panel without saving your changes.

Lee is happy with the storefront work you have shown her so far and is planning to use your image of the storefront in an upcoming ad. However, she would like you to create the effect of motion in the image to add some excitement. You'll use a customized preset to add blowing leaves to achieve the effect.

To create a new brush preset:

1. Reset the Painting workspace, and reset the background and foreground colors.

2. Zoom out to 50% magnification, select the **Background** layer, if necessary, sample the green color from the Rose of Sharon bush on the right side of the image, and then press **B** to activate the Brush Tool.

3. On the Brush Presets panel, click the **panel options** button ▼≣, and reset the brushes on the Brush Presets panel, and then scroll through the list of brush presets until you see the Scattered Maple Leaves brush preset (which is 74 pixels by default).

4. Click the **Scattered Maple Leaves** preset to select it, and on the Brush Presets panel, change the size to **85** pixels.

5. Click repeatedly in the area of the maple tree (the upper-left portion of the image) to add leaves to the tree, and then click a few times below the tree to achieve the effect of falling leaves on a windy day. See Figure 4-47.

Figure 4-47   **Creating falling leaves with brush preset**

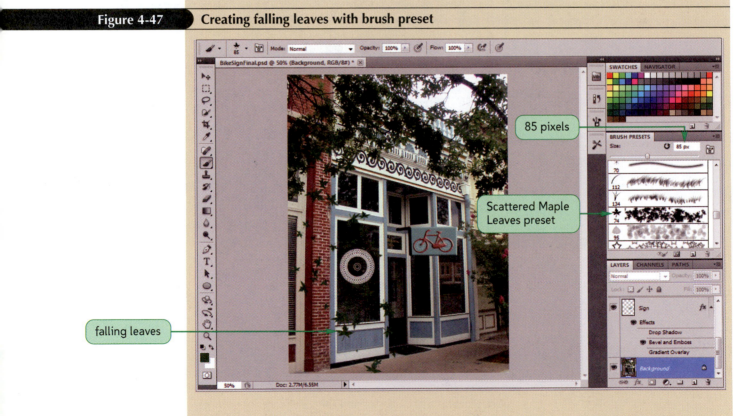

85 pixels

Scattered Maple Leaves preset

falling leaves

6. On the Brush Presets panel, click the **panel options** button ▾☰, and then click **New Brush Preset**.

7. Type **85 px maple leaves** in the Name box, click the **Capture Brush Size in Preset** check box to select it, if necessary, and then click the **OK** button to save the new preset.

8. Save the BikeSignFinal.psd file, close the file, and then exit Photoshop.

INSIGHT

Making a Brush Preset from an Image

You can create a custom brush preset by selecting part of an image and using the Define Brush Preset command on the Edit menu. Photoshop adds the new preset to the Brush panel and shows a preview of the brushstroke at the bottom of the panel. Note that if you open an image but don't select an area, Photoshop uses the entire image as the preset, which might not be your intention. You might want to save a custom brush preset to create an effect that you plan to use in multiple files. Rather than repeating the same steps for every file, you can use the brush preset to add the desired effect.

In this session, you learned how to add color, gradient, and pattern fill layers to your compositions. You also learned how to add shapes to a layer, and how to modify them by adding and subtracting shapes. You worked with brushes and brush presets. In the next tutorial, you'll learn how to select, remove, and tweak content, and work further with layer masks to create more sophisticated images.

REVIEW

Session 4.2 Quick Check

1. A fill that combines one color and transparent pixels or two or more colors to create a special effect is called a _____.

2. True or False. You cannot apply a blending mode to a Fill layer.

3. To constrain a rectangle to a square, click the _____ options button, and then click Square.

4. True or False. To use multiple shape tools to draw a complex shape, click the Add to shape area button on the options bar.

5. True or False. If you use the Fill pixels option and draw directly on an image, you are altering the pixels beneath your drawing.

6. To draw or paint a straight line, you can click at the beginning of the line, press the _____ key, and then click at the end of the line.

7. You can save the modifications you make to a brush as a brush _____.

PRACTICE

Review Assignments

Data Files needed for the Review Assignments: Accident.psd, TrafficCone.jpg

Lee likes the sign you proposed for the entrance to her store, and would like you to submit some ideas for signs to place in various sections of the store. For starters, she'd like a sign directing people to the area for bicycle repairs. Because she thinks the bike shop sign worked fine with no words, she would like you to do something similar for the in-store signs. Complete the following steps:

1. Start Photoshop while pressing the Ctrl+Alt+Shift keys. When you are prompted to delete the Adobe Photoshop Settings File, click Yes. On the Application bar, right-click Essentials, and then click Reset Essentials to reset the default workspace layout, and then reset all of the tools.

2. Open **Accident.psd** and **TrafficCone.jpg** located in the Photoshop4\Review folder included with your Data Files, and arrange the Document windows so the images are displayed side by side.

3. Add a new empty layer to Accident.psd and fill it with yellow, using a point sample of the yellow color from the police cone. If the color is out of gamut, adjust it so it is in gamut.

4. Arrange the layers on the Layers panel so the bicycle and rider show in the image.

5. Take an 11 × 11 Average sample of the red color at the top of the police cone and then make the rider's body and head red. Do not change the color of the bicycle.

6. Close TrafficCone.jpg without saving it.

7. On a new shape layer, draw a ½ inch wide red rectangle the same color as the rider all along the left side of the image, from top to bottom. On the same shape layer, draw a ½ inch wide red rectangle all along the right side of the image, using the Add to shape area option on the options bar.

8. Draw a ½ inch high rectangle along the top of the image, but exclude the overlapping shape areas. Draw a ½ inch high rectangle along the bottom of the image, but exclude the overlapping shape areas. (*Hint*: The result will be yellow squares in all four corners.)

9. Apply the Basic Drop Shadow style to the rider and bicycle, and then adjust the style so the shadow's Distance setting is 6 pixels. Save the new style with Layer Effects and Layer Blending Options as **6pixdrop**.

10. Convert the color mode to CMYK, and merge the layers.

11. Save the file as **Accident1.psd** in the Photoshop4\Review folder, and close the file.

12. Create a new 7" x 5" file with the default Photoshop settings. Draw four rectangles 3½ inches wide and 2½ inches high, each on a different shape layer. (*Hint*: You can draw a single rectangle and then duplicate it three times.) Arrange the rectangles so they cover the canvas completely.

13. On the Swatches panel, switch to one of the CMYK libraries, and then apply one CMYK color to the upper-left and lower-right rectangles and a different color to the upper-right and lower-left rectangles to achieve a checkerboard effect.

14. Using the Custom Shape Tool, draw the Registration Target 2 symbol (located in the Symbols library) in the upper-left rectangle using any color. Constrain the symbol to a circle so it resembles a bicycle wheel. Draw a target symbol of the same size in each of the other rectangles so you have four "wheels" in four rectangles. (*Hint*: You can duplicate the layers if you'd like.)

15. Apply any styles you'd like to the symbols you've drawn. You can also apply styles to the rectangles.

16. Flatten the image and save the file as **Wheels.psd** in the Photoshop4\Review folder, and then close it. Submit the results of the preceding steps to your instructor either in printed or electronic form, as requested.

Use your skills to create a composition for a technology business.

APPLY

Case Problem 1

Data Files needed for this Case Problem: TekSell.jpg, CD.jpg

TekSell   Founded in 2008, TekSell is an online technology retail business that sells computer hardware and software. TekSell's owner, Jose Ruiz, has hired you to create a new look for the company's Web site. For your initial meeting with Jose, you plan to present a few ideas for the page background and possible navigation buttons. In this exercise, you'll create a sample button and a proposed page background. Complete the following steps:

1. Start Photoshop while pressing the Ctrl+Alt+Shift keys. When you are prompted to delete the Adobe Photoshop Settings File, click Yes. On the Application bar, right-click Essentials, and then click Reset Essentials to reset the default workspace layout.

2. Open **TekSell.jpg** located in the Photoshop4\Case1 folder provided with your Data Files.

3. Place **CD.jpg** from the Photoshop4\Case1 folder in the TekSell.jpg file and size it so it is 10% of its original width and height. It should appear at the center of the composition.

4. Add a gradient fill layer that affects only the Background layer. This will be the "look" you are proposing for the Web page background. Open the Color Harmonies 1 gradient presets and apply the Orange, Blue gradient from that group. Change the angle of the gradient to 180 degrees. Set the opacity of the gradient fill layer to 80%.

5. Use the Swatches panel to make the foreground color Pure Yellow, and then select the Brush Tool.

6. In the Painting workspace, select the Flowing Stars brush preset, and then change its size to 215 pixels. On a new layer placed at the top of the Layers panel, paint stars on the left side of the image.

7. In the Essentials workspace, apply the Sun Faded Photo style to the CD layer. Your proposal will include using the image of the CD as a navigation button on the Web site. Modify the style you just applied so it has a Bevel and Emboss effect with a Size setting of 50 pixels.

8. Change the name of Layer 1 to **Stars**, and change its opacity to 50%.

9. Flatten the image and save it as **TekSellWeb.jpg**, using the default JPEG settings, in the Photoshop4\Case1 folder. Submit the results of the preceding steps to your instructor either in printed or electronic form, as requested.

Use your skills to create two cover options for an architecture magazine.

APPLY

Case Problem 2

Data Files needed for this Case Problem: ArchiText.psd

Architext Meena Patel is the publisher of Architext, a magazine for architects, where you have recently been hired as a graphic designer. The fall issue of the magazine will include photographs and articles about a series of architecturally interesting buildings from a single city, anywhere in the world. Meena has presented a challenge to you and your colleagues: Submit a mock-up of a cover that uses a photograph of a city building and presents it in a unique way; the winner's work will be published on the cover of the fall issue. To stand out from the others who will be competing, you'll create a second version of the cover that uses mostly drawn objects instead of a photograph. Complete the following steps:

1. Start Photoshop while pressing the Ctrl+Alt+Shift keys. When you are prompted to delete the Adobe Photoshop Settings File, click Yes. On the Application bar, right-click Essentials, and then click Reset Essentials to reset the default workspace layout.

2. Open **ArchiText.psd** located in the Photoshop4\Case2 folder provided with your Data Files, and save it as **ArchiText2.psd** in the same folder.

⊕ EXPLORE

3. Open a Web browser of your choice and go to *www.morguefile.com*. This site includes links to images that are free, require no attribution, and can be modified (or remixed). Search the site for images of buildings from the city of your choice. For example, search for images of buildings in Chicago by typing **Chicago** as your search term. Select an image in any format with which you would like to work. Before you download the image, check the licensing information to make sure that it can be remixed without attribution and used for commercial purposes. Download the image and save it as **CityShot.jpg** in the Photoshop4\Case2 folder.

4. Return to Photoshop and place the **CityShot.jpg** image in the **ArchiText2.psd** file. Size the placed image so it fits properly in the composition, with the original text still showing.

5. Apply a style to the "ArchiText" text and modify it until it suits your composition. Save the modified style as ArchiStyle, and then apply it to "the city issue" text.

6. Add a Pattern or Gradient layer to the composition, change its settings as desired, and position it so it only affects the Background layer.

7. On a new layer, use the Brush Tool to add brushstrokes or special effects to your cover using one or more brush presets. Make sure to position the layer so the strokes appear where you want them to. Save Architext2.psd, and close it.

8. Create a new file with any background color using the same dimensions as the cover, 8 ½ × 11 inches. Use the CMYK color mode, 300 ppi, and 8-bit color. Save the file as **ArchiText3.psd** in the Photoshop4\Case2 folder.

9. Use any combination of layers, brushstrokes, drawing tools, and color selection tools to create a page that you'll submit as an alternate cover idea. See Figure 4-48 as an example.

Figure 4-48   Sample cover

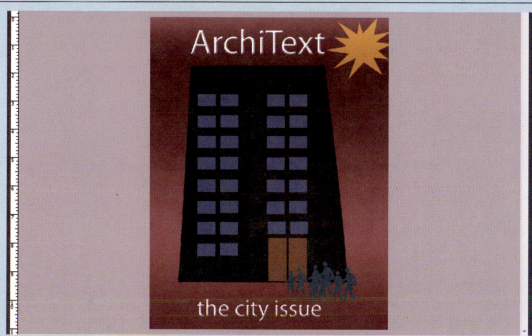

Your file should include a drawing that uses addition, subtraction, intersection, and exclusion. (*Hint*: Draw a building with windows and doors.) Be sure to include the magazine title and subtitle, as shown in Figure 4-48.

10. Flatten the image, and then save the file and close it.

11. Submit the results of the preceding steps to your instructor either in printed or electronic form, as requested.

Extend what you've learned to use the Mixer Brush to modify an image.

CHALLENGE

Case Problem 3

Data Files needed for this Case Problem: Easel.jpg

TeachOut   David Jasper is the creative director for TeachOut, a company that provides distance learning solutions for schools, universities, and technical training centers. You have been hired to work with David on a series of ads to emphasize that although TeachOut is a serious business, its goal is to make learning fun. For your first project, you'll use the Mixer Brush to paint on an easel to produce an image reminiscent of preschool finger painting. Complete the following steps:

1. Start Photoshop while pressing the Ctrl+Alt+Shift keys. When you are prompted to delete the Adobe Photoshop Settings File, click Yes. On the Application bar, right-click Essentials, and then click Reset Essentials to reset the default workspace layout.

2. Open **Easel.jpg** located in the Photoshop4\Case3 folder provided with your Data Files, and save it as **TeachOut.psd** in the same folder.

3. Add a shape layer with a white rectangle, sized to fit on the easel. Rasterize the rectangle, and then rotate it and position it so it appears to be a canvas sitting on the easel in the image. Add a shadow to the rectangle shape to give it depth and a realistic look.

⊕ **EXPLORE**

4. Use Photoshop Help to research the Mixer Brush. Make sure you understand the settings on the options bar, including Wet, Load, Mix, and Flow.

⊕**EXPLORE** 5. Create a new file with the default Photoshop settings to experiment with the Mixer Brush before you paint on the canvas in the TeachOut.psd file. Try different combinations of colors and different brushes until you understand how the options bar settings affect the mixture of colors. Save the file as **Scrap.psd** in the Photoshop4\Case3 folder, and then close the file.

⊕**EXPLORE** 6. Switch back to TeachOut.psd, and using Figure 4-49 as a guide, paint an image in the style of a child's finger painting.

Figure 4-49	Sample finger painting

Your painting should demonstrate that you understand how to mix colors with the Mixer Brush, and how to achieve different effects with different Wet, Load, Mix, and Flow levels. You should use at least five different colors, at least three color combinations (mixes), and three different brushes. (*Hint*: If you paint outside of the canvas by accident, use the Eraser Tool to erase the paint so it is contained within the canvas edges.)

7. Change the dimensions of the document by extending the canvas one inch on all sides; sample one of the mixed colors as the canvas extension color.

8. When you are satisfied with your artwork, flatten the image and then save it.

9. Submit the results of the preceding steps to your instructor either in printed or electronic form, as requested.

APPLY

Use your skills to create an original composition for a landscaping company.

Case Problem 4

There are no Data Files needed for this Case Problem.

Prettyscapes Prettyscapes is a landscaping company with 15 employees in Boise, Idaho. Business has been growing lately, and Maya Morrisson, the owner, is interested in attracting creative talent. Maya has asked you to come up with a composition for a help wanted ad that conveys whimsy and creativity. She will provide the text. You'll use the color, drawing, and brush tools in Photoshop to show what a landscape designer might do when presented with an empty lot.

1. Start Photoshop while pressing the Ctrl+Alt+Shift keys. When you are prompted to delete the Adobe Photoshop Settings File, click Yes. On the Application bar, right-click Essentials, and then click Reset Essentials to reset the default workspace layout.

2. Create a new file with a white background of any dimensions.

3. Open a Web browser of your choice and go to *www.morguefile.com* or to *www.creativecommons.org*. If you use Creative Commons, click the Find link and then, on the Search page, confirm that the use is for commercial purposes, and modify, adapt, or build upon check boxes are selected. Enter **landscape** as your search term. Select an image with which you can work. Before you download the image, check the licensing information to make sure that it can be remixed without attribution and used for commercial purposes.

4. Download the image and save it as **Landscape.jpg** in the Photoshop4\Case 4 folder included with your Data Files.

5. Return to Photoshop and place the **Landscape.jpg** image in your newly created file, and size it to fit.

6. On one part of the image, use the drawing tools to draw a house with windows and a door. To create the drawing, use at least two of the add, subtract, intersect, and exclude options.

7. Use blending modes, opacity, styles, and other adjustments to modify the various shapes in your drawing. (*Hint*: For some effects, you might need to rasterize your drawn objects.)

8. Use any tools you choose to draw a brick walkway leading to the house.

EXPLORE

9. Open one of the brush preset libraries you haven't yet used, and choose brush tips that will let you create bushes and flower beds around the house.

10. Add objects such as butterflies to your drawing using various brush presets. Make sure to vary your color choices.

11. Put any finishing touches on your composition that you'd like, flatten the image, and then save the file as **LandscapeWhimsy.psd** in the Photoshop4\Case4 folder.

12. Submit the results of the preceding steps to your instructor either in printed or electronic form, as requested.

ENDING DATA FILES

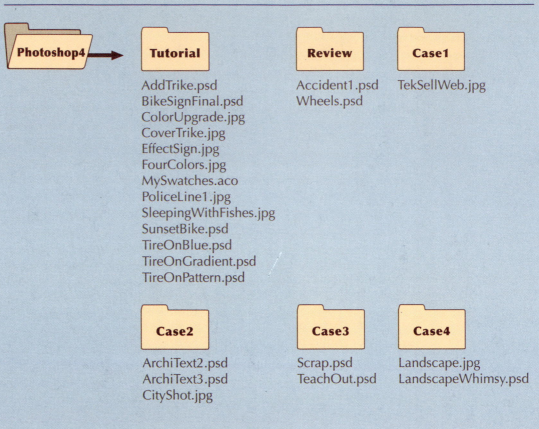

Photoshop4 →

Tutorial

AddTrike.psd
BikeSignFinal.psd
ColorUpgrade.jpg
CoverTrike.jpg
EffectSign.jpg
FourColors.jpg
MySwatches.aco
PoliceLine1.jpg
SleepingWithFishes.jpg
SunsetBike.psd
TireOnBlue.psd
TireOnGradient.psd
TireOnPattern.psd

Review

Accident1.psd
Wheels.psd

Case1

TekSellWeb.jpg

Case2

ArchiText2.psd
ArchiText3.psd
CityShot.jpg

Case3

Scrap.psd
TeachOut.psd

Case4

Landscape.jpg
LandscapeWhimsy.psd

TUTORIAL 5

OBJECTIVES

Session 5.1
- Modify, grow, transform, and refine a selection
- Apply an adjustment to a selection
- Copy and paste a selection
- Create complex selections
- Select a color range in an image
- Step backward and forward
- Use the History panel and the History Brush Tool

Session 5.2
- Use the Lasso Tool, the Magnetic Lasso Tool, and the Quick Selection Tool
- Save and reload a selection
- Apply Content-Aware and other fills to a selection
- Add a stroke to a selection
- Work with filters and masks

Selecting and Modifying Content

Compositing Photos

Case | *Food for Change*

Food for Change, a nonprofit organization in Hartford, Connecticut, brings sustainable food systems into urban areas. Its founder, Azar Miller, created the organization in 2002, after noticing that many dirt lots around Hartford were not being used. When he learned that the city owned most of these lots, he approached city leaders with a proposal: With the help of urban and suburban youth, he would transform the lots into gardens for growing vegetables and fruits. At the same time, he would work to build a cultural bridge between urban and suburban youth, educate them about good nutrition, and send them into the city schools to promote urban and rooftop gardening and good nutrition. In return, the city would provide an initial investment for starting the project as well as support and resources for fund-raising as the project grew.

You have recently been hired by Azar to transform many of the photographs he's taken over the years into compositions that he can use in brochures and fund-raising materials and on the Food for Change Web site. To make the changes that Azar has in mind, you will explore several Photoshop selection tools. In addition to modifying and refining selections, you will learn how to apply an adjustment to a selection. You will also learn how to undo and redo actions using the Edit menu, the History panel, and the History Brush Tool. You will examine Photoshop's Content-Aware fill feature, and you will save and reload selections. Finally, you will experiment with filters, fills, and masks.

STARTING DATA FILES

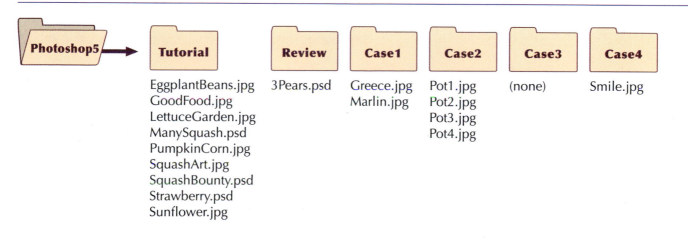

Photoshop5 →	Tutorial	Review	Case1	Case2	Case3	Case4
	EggplantBeans.jpg	3Pears.psd	Greece.jpg	Pot1.jpg	(none)	Smile.jpg
	GoodFood.jpg		Marlin.jpg	Pot2.jpg		
	LettuceGarden.jpg			Pot3.jpg		
	ManySquash.psd			Pot4.jpg		
	PumpkinCorn.jpg					
	SquashArt.jpg					
	SquashBounty.psd					
	Strawberry.psd					
	Sunflower.jpg					

SESSION 5.1 VISUAL OVERVIEW

Use the commands on the Select menu to select all of the pixels in a layer, to deselect or reselect a selection, or to invert a selection.

Click one of the Marquee Tools and then drag on the canvas to create an **active selection** enclosed by an animated series of dashed lines or curves called a **marquee**.

Using the History Brush Tool, you can paint over your composition and uncover part of the history state that is set as the source on the History panel.

Making adjustments to an image or combining different image files (or parts of image files) and/or vector objects in a single file is called **compositing**.

You can select areas of an image to cut and paste either back into the image or into another file.

SELECTING CONTENT

The History panel displays the last 20 **history states**, or previous versions of the file; you can return to a history state using the History panel.

This history state is set as the **source** for the History Brush Tool.

You can save a **snapshot**, or a picture of what the composition looked like at any given history state.

You can make a selection, and then fill the selected pixels with color; the unselected area filled with black is the mask, and it protects everything not included in the selection from changes.

Save a version of the document in its own file using the Create new document from current state icon.

Use the Create new snapshot icon to produce a snapshot of the current history state.

Selecting Content for Compositing

When you work in Photoshop, much of your work will involve compositing, creating images by combining parts of different image files in a single file, or modifying an image to create a unique composition. For example, you might select a tree from one image and copy it to a photograph of an empty lot. If you do this repeatedly, you can grow a digital forest in no time. Or, you might put two people who appear in separate images into one image by selecting, copying, and pasting them into the same composition. You can also create a complex composition by starting with a single photograph to which you then apply multiple effects. Photoshop has numerous tools that let you select not only layers, but also areas of pixels in a layer. These selection tools allow you to apply different effects to different areas of an image. In Tutorial 3, you dragged a rectangular marquee around part of an image to select it, and then used the Copy and Paste commands to add your selection to another file. However, there are many more tools available for making selections, as shown in Figure 5-1.

Figure 5-1   **Photoshop selection tools**

Icon	Tool	Use
	Rectangular Marquee Tool	Drag to select a rectangular area; select Fixed Ratio to draw a rectangle with a height/width ratio you specify, or select Fixed Size to specify the exact dimensions of the rectangle. You can also press the Shift key while drawing the selection to constrain the marquee to a square.
	Elliptical Marquee Tool	Drag to select an elliptical area; select Fixed Ratio to draw an ellipse with a height/width ratio you specify, or select Fixed Size to specify the exact dimensions of the ellipse. You can also press the Shift key while drawing the selection to constrain the marquee to a circle.
	Single Row Marquee Tool	Drag to select a row of pixels (one pixel high) across an image
	Single Column Marquee Tool	Drag to select a column of pixels (one pixel wide) down an image
	Lasso Tool	Drag on an image to make a freehand selection
	Polygonal Lasso Tool	Click on an image multiple times to create straight-edged selections to form the shape of a polygon
	Magnetic Lasso Tool	Drag a marquee whose border snaps to defined edges on an image—for example, a white object on a dark background
	Quick Selection Tool	Drag the pointer to paint your selection; as you drag, the selection grows. You can determine the sensitivity of the selection by specifying Tolerance.
	Magic Wand Tool	Select an area based on a specific color; the Tolerance setting determines the color range that the tool will select.

In fact, the variety and power of the selection tools in Photoshop give you a great deal of creative license when you composite, or compose, an image. You can select an object in an image, cut it completely out of the image, and then fill in the cutout area with another object, a fill, or a gradient. You can also make a selection and apply filters and special effects only to the selection or to everything in the image *except* the selection. Figure 5-2 shows a composition created by selecting part of an image (the pumpkin on the left).

Figure 5-2   **Selecting, copying, and adjusting selected pixels**

this pumpkin is part of the original image

this pumpkin is a copy of the original that was resized and then modified with the Color Balance adjustment

The selection was copied to the Clipboard, pasted into the right side of the composition, and then resized to create the appearance of two pumpkins. While the pumpkin on the right was still selected, a Color Balance adjustment was applied only to the selection, which is why that pumpkin is more orange than the pumpkin on the left, even though they are actually the same pumpkin. As you can see from this simple example, the possibilities for working with selections in Photoshop are limitless.

PROSKILLS

Verbal Communication: Understanding a Client's Needs Up Front

Before you begin working on a digital composition for a client, you need to ensure that you fully understand what the client is looking for. To do so, you need to set up strong and reliable lines of communication, which will involve you not only offering your advice and expertise, but also listening to what the client is *really* saying. Helping your client clearly communicate his or her needs to you is essential before you dive into any project. For example, if your client asks you to create an ad for a magazine, that information should be just a starting point. You need to ask clarifying questions, such as: Is the ad aimed at a certain demographic or group? Is the magazine a conservative business magazine, an interior decorating magazine, or is it for teens—with an emphasis on pop culture? Are you trying to convey a certain mood? Should the text be in a particular font or color? Listen carefully, and give your client time to fully explain their vision for the ad. Even after your client has provided more details, it's a good idea to make sure you really understood what you were told. It can be helpful to use phrases such as "What I understood is" or "Let me see if I heard you correctly" to be sure you really know what's required. By asking clarifying questions and restating your understanding of the client's needs, you can iron out many potential wrinkles ahead of time. That will save you time and effort in the short term, and in the long run, it will result in a happy client who will be more likely to request your services again—and recommend you to others.

Azar would like you to work on a few compositions that show the bounty of the Food for Change program so he can present them at a government funding conference next month. He has some photographs from last summer, but he is concerned that some don't show the extent or variety of the food grown by the program, while others won't grab a viewer's attention. You'll work with the selection tools to enhance and compose images for the conference. You'll also work with the selection tools to apply effects to parts of your composition while leaving other parts unchanged.

Selecting with the Rectangular or Elliptical Marquee Tool

The Rectangular and Elliptical Marquee Tools allow you to specify an exact rectangular or elliptical area by dragging on an image. When you drag, Photoshop outlines the area you are selecting, and when you release the mouse button, a marquee indicates that the selection is active. You can press the Shift key as you drag to constrain the proportions of the marquee selection—for example, to constrain an ellipse to a circle or a rectangle to a square.

When you use either the Rectangular or Elliptical Marquee Tool, you can specify settings on the options bar for the tool, as shown in Figure 5-3.

Figure 5-3   **Using Marquee Tool options to create a complex selection**

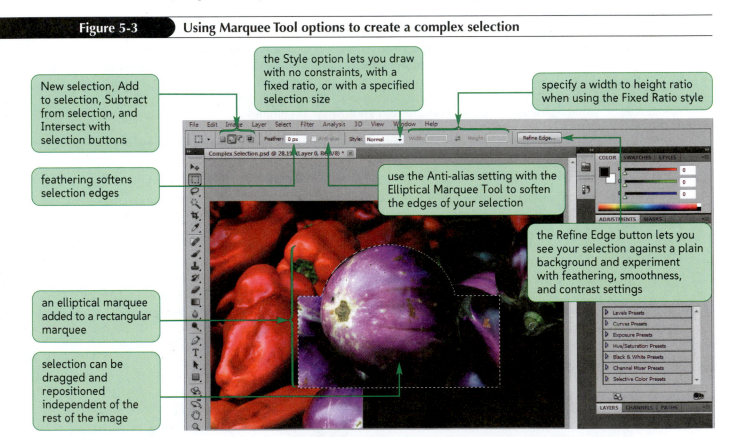

The first group of settings should be familiar to you from Tutorial 4. The New selection, Add to selection, Subtract from selection, and Intersect with selection buttons behave like similar buttons (New shape, Add to shape, Subtract from shape, and Intersect with shape options) you worked with when you created vector drawings. These buttons let you create complex selections by building on and subtracting from existing selections. For example, the selection of the eggplant in Figure 5-3 was created by drawing the first part of the selection (enclosing the eggplant) with the Elliptical Marquee Tool, clicking the Add to selection button on the options bar, and then using the Rectangular Marquee Tool to add the rectangular area to the selection. The entire selection was then dragged up and to the left on the image, uncovering the black background beneath.

The next setting on the options bar is Feather, which you can use to soften or blur the edges of a selection. The higher the Feather setting, the softer the edges of the selection will be, which can help blend a selection into a composition. You can also modify the Feather setting in the Refine Edge dialog box to preview the setting before finalizing the selection.

The Anti-alias setting is available only with the Elliptical Marquee Tool. Turning on this setting softens the pixelated edges of the curves in your selection. It is not available for the Rectangular Marquee Tool because the edges of the Rectangle are drawn horizontally and vertically along lines of pixels, so no jagged edges appear.

You can also specify the Style of your selection. The default is the Normal style, which lets you drag a rectangle or an ellipse with no constraints. You can use Fixed Ratio to specify the width to height ratio of a selection. For example, a fixed ratio of Width 1 and Height 1 would draw a square or a circle. The Fixed Size option lets you specify the exact dimensions of the selection in pixels so when you click on the image, the selection marquee is created automatically. You can then drag it to its correct position. The last option on the Marquee options bar, Refine Edge, opens the Refine Edge dialog box, where you can fine-tune and preview your selection by modifying a number of options, including smoothness and feathering, all in one place.

Specifying a Fixed Ratio or Fixed Size Selection

With the Photoshop selection tools, you aren't confined to dragging on the canvas to create the selection marquee you need. You can instead specify a fixed ratio or fixed size selection when you have very specific needs, and then simply click the canvas and drag the marquee into position to create it. These fixed options allow you to be extremely precise.

REFERENCE

Specifying a Fixed Ratio Selection

- On the Tools panel, select the Rectangular Marquee or the Elliptical Marquee Tool.
- On the options bar, click the Style arrow, and then click Fixed Ratio.
- Type ratio values in the Width and Height boxes.
- Click on the canvas, and drag to make your selection.
- Move the marquee as desired to place it where you want it.

You'll work with a photograph of squash to create a unique, beveled image that Azar will use during his workshops around the city to emphasize that the work that Food for Change is doing is just one piece of a larger hunger and nutrition puzzle in urban areas.

To specify a fixed ratio selection:

1. Start Photoshop while pressing the **Ctrl+Alt+Shift** keys. When you are prompted to delete the Adobe Photoshop Settings File, click **Yes**. On the Application bar, right-click **Essentials**, and then click **Reset Essentials** to reset the default Essentials workspace layout.

2. Navigate to the Photoshop5\Tutorial folder included with your Data Files, and open **SquashBounty.psd**. Press **Ctrl+1** to display the photograph at 100% magnification.

3. Display the Essentials workspace, if necessary, display the rulers, expand the Layers panel, and then click the **Rectangular Marquee Tool** on the Tools panel to select it, if necessary.

4. On the options bar, click the **Style** arrow, and then click **Fixed Ratio**. By default, Photoshop sets both the Width and Height boxes to 1, which would create a square.

5. Type **3** in the Width box, and then type **2** in the Height box. When you drag the selection, it will have a width to height ratio of 3 to 2.

6. Select the **Squash** layer and then, starting at about 1" on the vertical and horizontal rulers, drag down and to the right until you're at about 3 1/2" on the vertical ruler. Photoshop creates a selection marquee with a width to height ratio of 3 to 2.

7. On the Application bar, click **Edit**, and then click **Cut**. The selection is cut from the image, and the black background shows through.

8. On the Application bar, click **Edit**, and then click **Paste**. The selection is pasted onto the center of the image on its own layer, named Layer 1.

9. On the Layers panel, double-click the **Layer 1** thumbnail to open the Layer Style dialog box, and then click **Bevel and Emboss** to select the style and display its properties.

10. In the Structure section, change the Structure Depth to **1000%**, set the size to **5 px**, if necessary, and then click the **OK** button. The cut-and-pasted selection now has a bevel and emboss effect. See Figure 5-4.

| Figure 5-4 | Cutting and pasting a selection |

the selection has been cut and pasted on a new layer in the center of the canvas

Bevel and Emboss effect applied

Trouble? If you can't see the Structure Depth option, you have selected the Bevel and Emboss check box, but you haven't highlighted Bevel and Emboss. Click Bevel and Emboss, and then complete Step 10.

11. Save the file as **SquashBevel.psd** in the Photoshop5\Tutorial folder, and then close it.

You selected an area of an image using the Rectangular Marquee Tool with a fixed ratio setting. You cut and pasted the selection onto its own layer, and then applied a layer effect. Next, you'll work with a fixed size selection to modify an image of a pumpkin by selecting it and making a copy of the selection that you modify.

REFERENCE

Specifying a Fixed Size Selection

- On the Tools panel, select the Rectangular Marquee Tool or the Elliptical Marquee Tool.
- On the options bar, click the Style arrow, and then click Fixed Size.
- Type the fixed width and height values you want in the Width and Height boxes. Make sure to specify *px* for pixels or *in* for inches.
- Click the canvas, and draw the selection marquee.
- Move the marquee as desired to place it where you want it.

Next, you'll use the Elliptical Marquee Tool to select an area with a fixed size. You'll make a copy of one pumpkin and then paste it into the composition so two pumpkins appear in the image. Azar will use the before and after versions of the image to demonstrate that it is only with contributions from the public that the bounty at Food for Change can grow and multiply.

To specify a fixed size selection:

1. Open **PumpkinCorn.jpg** from the Photoshop5\Tutorial folder provided with your Data Files. On the Tools panel, select the **Elliptical Marquee Tool** ⬭.

   Trouble? If you don't see the Elliptical Marquee Tool ⬭ on the Tools panel, click and hold the Rectangular Marquee Tool ⬚ to display the hidden tools, and then click the Elliptical Marquee Tool ⬭.

2. On the options bar, change the Feather setting to **5 px**, select the **Anti-alias** check box, if necessary, click the **Style** arrow and then click **Fixed Size**. The Width and Height boxes become available.

3. Type **1200 px** in the Width box, and type **1100 px** in the Height box.

   The ellipse you draw will have a width of 1200 pixels and a height of 1100 pixels. Because you selected Anti-alias, the edges of the selection will be smooth rather than jagged or pixelated.

4. Click anywhere on the pumpkin. Photoshop immediately draws an elliptical selection marquee in the size you specified. Drag the **marquee** so it is centered over the pumpkin.

Make sure you specify pixels (*px*) and not inches (*in*). Using inches will cause Photoshop to freeze up as it attempts to draw an ellipse well beyond the bounds of the canvas.

Notice that the marquee is slightly smaller than the pumpkin. You can expand a selection using commands on the Select menu, which you'll do in the next section.

Modifying a Selection

Once you have made a selection, you can modify it. The Select menu includes many commands for changing the nature and dimensions of your selection. The Grow command selects adjacent pixels of a similar color. If some of the pixels are missed by the Grow command, you can use the Magic Wand Tool and the Add to selection button on the options bar to select the missing pixels. The Grow command is a good choice when the object you are selecting is quite distinct from the background it is on, but may not work as well when the background has colors within range of the object's colors. You can use the Expand command to expand the selection by a specified number of pixels. The Expand command is useful if the object you are selecting has a regular shape.

You can make a selection larger or smaller, or even distort or warp a selection, using the Transform Selection command on the Select menu. Photoshop encloses your selection in a rectangle with eight handles—one handle on each corner and one handle on each side. You can resize the selection by dragging the handles. To constrain the proportions of the selection so you don't distort it, press the Shift key while you drag. When you drag, the size of the marquee changes. You can accept the transformation by clicking the Commit transform button on the options bar or by pressing the Enter key.

REFERENCE

Expanding or Growing a Selection

- Use a tool from the Tools panel to make a selection.
- On the Application bar, click Select, point to Modify, and click Expand to open the Expand Selection dialog box.
- Type a pixel value in the Expand By box, and then click the OK button.
or
- Use a tool from the Tools panel to make a selection.
- On the Application bar, click Select, and then click Grow.

Next, you'll expand and then grow the current selection to encompass the whole pumpkin.

To expand and grow the selection:

1. On the Application bar, click **Select**, and then point to **Modify**. Photoshop displays a list of commands for modifying your selection.

2. Click **Expand**. The Expand Selection dialog box opens. You can enter a pixel value to specify the size of the expansion.

3. In the Expand By box, type **100**, and then click the **OK** button. The selection marquee expands to encompass more of the pumpkin. Because the selection is still not large enough to cover all of the pumpkin, you will try the Grow option next.

4. On the Application bar, click **Select**, and then click **Grow**. The selection expands to include most of the pumpkin.

Notice that the selection is no longer an ellipse because the Grow command grew the selection by finding similarly colored pixels. However, there are still some small areas that are unselected. You'll use the Magic Wand Tool to add those stray pixels to your selection.

To use the Magic Wand Tool to add pixels to the selection:

1. On the Tools panel, point to the **Quick Selection Tool** , press and hold the mouse button, and then click the **Magic Wand Tool** .

2. On the options bar, confirm that the Tolerance is **32** and that the **Anti-alias** and **Contiguous** check boxes are selected.

3. On the options bar, click the **Add to selection** button . See Figure 5-5.

TIP

You can also press and hold the Shift key to temporarily select the Add to selection button on the options bar. Press and hold the Alt key to temporarily select the Subtract from selection button.

Figure 5-5   **Adding pixels to the selection with the Magic Wand Tool**

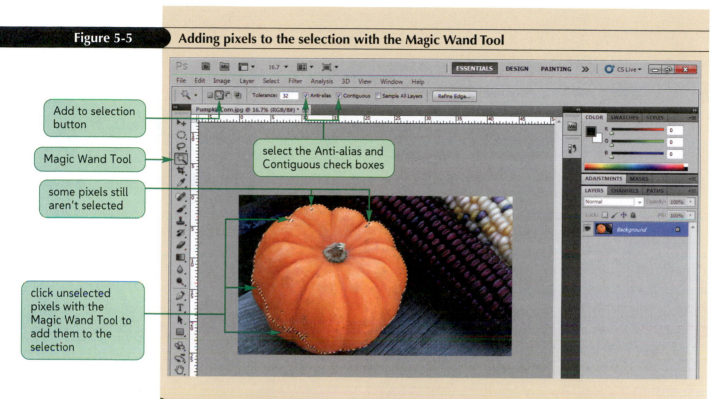

Add to selection button

Magic Wand Tool

some pixels still aren't selected

click unselected pixels with the Magic Wand Tool to add them to the selection

select the Anti-alias and Contiguous check boxes

4. Click all of the pixels in the pumpkin that are not currently selected to add them to the selection. The wand pointer ⚡ includes a plus sign, indicating that you are adding to the selection.

All of the pixels in the pumpkin should now be selected.

Trouble? If clicking the missing pixels doesn't add them to the selection, you have clicked one of the other options on the options bar, such as Subtract from selection. Click the Add to selection button and then repeat Step 4.

Applying an Adjustment to a Selection

In Tutorial 3, you applied adjustments to entire layers. Photoshop also lets you adjust individual areas of an image using selections. When a selection is active, you can apply an adjustment to it, and the adjustment will affect only the selected area of the image.

You'll change the color balance of the selected pumpkin so the orange is intensified. You'll then copy and paste the selection so you have two pumpkins of different shades of orange.

To apply a Color Balance adjustment to the selection:

1. Open the **Adjustments** panel, and then click the **Color Balance** icon ⚖.

2. Drag the Cyan Red slider all the way to the right so the value in the box is **100**. The selection marquee disappears, but it is still active. The color of the pumpkin changes to a bright orange. The unselected area of the image is unchanged.

3. On the Layers panel, select the **Color Balance 1** layer, if necessary, and then on the Tools panel, click the **Move Tool** ⊹.

> **4.** Point to the pumpkin, press and hold the mouse button, and drag to the right, as shown in Figure 5-6.

Figure 5-6 **Applying a color adjustment to a selection and moving the adjustment**

the color adjustment is applied to the selection so it moves with the selection

unselected area is masked in black

color adjustment on its own layer

The selection, along with the Color Balance adjustment, now appears to the right of the pumpkin. (The green outline around the Color Balance adjustment was added to Figure 5-6 to highlight the adjustment.) The colored adjustment has moved because the adjustment was applied to the selection, not to the pixels in the image.

When you made your selection and applied the adjustment, what you were actually doing was creating a mask, much like you created a mask in Tutorial 4 when you added a shape to a layer. A mask is the inverse of a selection—it masks, or protects, everything not included in the selection. As you can see on the Color Balance 1 layer, your selection (in the shape of the pumpkin) is shown in white on the thumbnail to the right in the Color Balance thumbnail. The rest of the thumbnail is black, indicating that anything you do to the selection will not affect the black areas.

You'll undo the move action you just performed, and then you'll reselect the pumpkin so you can copy and paste it in another part of the image.

To copy and paste the pumpkin selection:

1. On the Application bar, click **Edit**, and then click **Undo Move**.

2. On the Layers panel, click the **Background** layer to select it.

3. On the Application bar, click **Select**, and then click **Reselect**. The Reselect command activates the most recent selection.

4. On the Application bar, click **Edit**, click **Copy**, click **Edit** again, and then click **Paste** to paste a second copy of the pumpkin onto the image on its own layer.

5. On the Layers panel, move the **Layer 1** layer above the Color Balance 1 adjustment layer.

6. Using the Move Tool, point to the pumpkin and then drag it to the right so the two pumpkins are side by side. You will need to drag part of the pumpkin off the canvas. See Figure 5-7.

TIP

You can also press Shift+Ctrl+D to reselect a selection. Press Ctrl+D to deselect a selection.

| Figure 5-7 | Two versions of the same pumpkin |

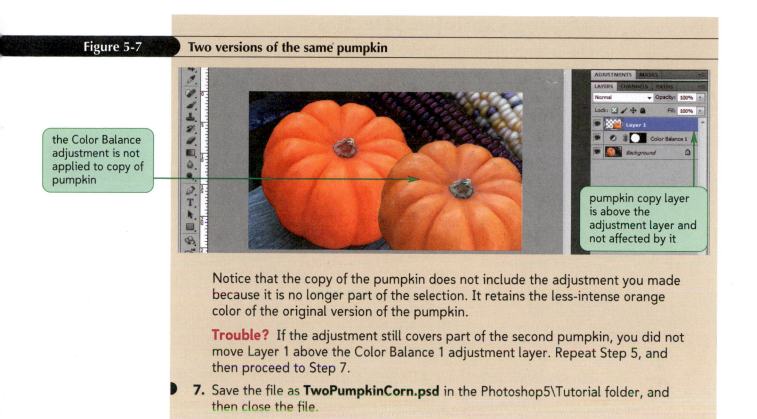

the Color Balance adjustment is not applied to copy of pumpkin

pumpkin copy layer is above the adjustment layer and not affected by it

Notice that the copy of the pumpkin does not include the adjustment you made because it is no longer part of the selection. It retains the less-intense orange color of the original version of the pumpkin.

Trouble? If the adjustment still covers part of the second pumpkin, you did not move Layer 1 above the Color Balance 1 adjustment layer. Repeat Step 5, and then proceed to Step 7.

7. Save the file as **TwoPumpkinCorn.psd** in the Photoshop5\Tutorial folder, and then close the file.

Now that you have added more interest to this image, you will give this file to Azar so he can use the image in his fund-raising presentation. In the next section, you will learn how to use selection tools to make more complex selections.

INSIGHT

Refining a Selection

Once you have made a selection, you can click the Refine Edge button on the options bar to further refine the selection. Using Refine Edge, you can better see if you have picked up any unwanted pixels in your selection, and you can fine-tune the selection. Clicking Refine Edge opens the Refine Edge dialog box, which shows your selection against a white background by default. You can change the View Mode to a black background or another option depending on the colors of the selection. You can also adjust edge settings, such as Smooth, Feather, and Contrast, and you can shift the edge to expand the selection or contract it.

Creating Complex Selections

As you continue to work in Photoshop, you'll find that many of the individual selection tools will work just fine in certain cases. But what happens if the area or areas you need to select are very complex? If they are, you might find that a single selection tool just won't do the job. Just as you did with the Magic Wand Tool earlier, you can use the buttons on the options bar to add to and subtract from selections. This Photoshop feature is useful if you want to make a complex selection that includes irregularly shaped areas containing pixels with a variety of colors.

REFERENCE

Adding to a Selection to Create a Complex Selection

- Activate one of the selection tools on the Tools panel, and set its options on the options bar.
- Drag on the canvas to make the first selection.
- On the options bar, click the Add to selection button.
- Use the same tool or select a different one, and drag on the canvas to make a selection that will be added to the first.
- Repeat until you are satisfied with the final selection.

For one of your projects for Azar, you need to select just part of an image of a strawberry plant to use in a flyer. To do so, you'll create a complex selection using both the Rectangular Marquee Tool and the Elliptical Marquee Tool.

To create a complex selection and paste it into a new file:

1. Open **Strawberry.psd** from the Photoshop5\Tutorial folder, zoom to fit the image on screen, reset all of the tools, and display the rulers, if necessary.

2. On the Tools panel, click the **Elliptical Marquee Tool** ⬭, and on the options bar, confirm that the **New selection** button �«is selected and that the Feather setting is **0 px**.

3. On the options bar, click the **Style** arrow, and then click **Fixed Size**.

4. Specify a Width of **700** pixels and a Height of **700** pixels, click the canvas to create the selection, and then drag the selection until it is positioned as shown in Figure 5-8.

Figure 5-8   Positioning a selection

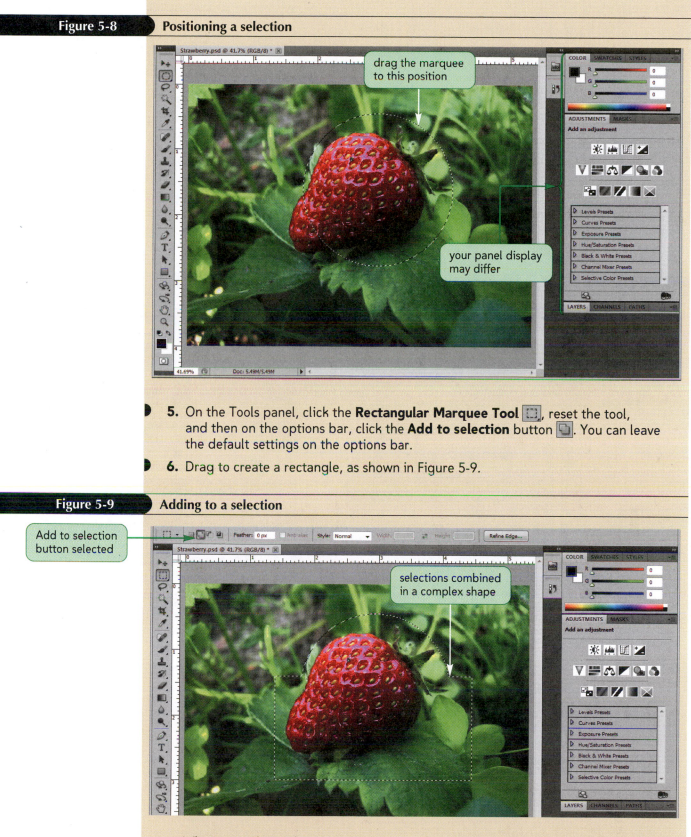

5. On the Tools panel, click the **Rectangular Marquee Tool** ▦, reset the tool, and then on the options bar, click the **Add to selection** button ▣. You can leave the default settings on the options bar.

6. Drag to create a rectangle, as shown in Figure 5-9.

Figure 5-9   Adding to a selection

When you release the mouse button, the two selections are combined into a single selection.

7. Copy the selection to the Clipboard.

8. Press **X** to switch the foreground and background colors so the background color is black.

9. On the Application bar, click **File**, click **New**, and then create a new file using the Default Photoshop Size preset, the RGB Color mode, and a Resolution setting of 300 ppi. Click the **Background Contents** arrow and then click **Background Color** to create a black background. Paste your selection into the new file.

   The strawberry and part of the strawberry plant are pasted as a new layer, labeled Layer 1, into the file.

10. On the Layers panel of the new file, double-click the **Layer 1** thumbnail to open the Layer Style dialog box. Apply an Outer Glow effect to the layer with **75%** opacity; in the Elements section, set the Size to **150** pixels, and click the **OK** button. See Figure 5-10.

| Figure 5-10 | Complex selection pasted in new file with Outer Glow effect applied |

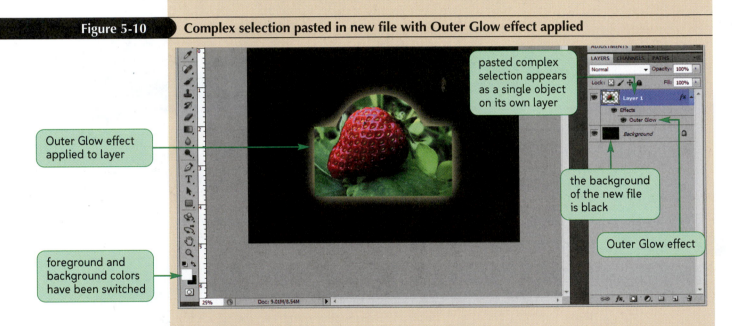

Outer Glow effect applied to layer

pasted complex selection appears as a single object on its own layer

the background of the new file is black

Outer Glow effect

foreground and background colors have been switched

11. Save the new file as **StrawberryGlow.psd** in the Photoshop5\Tutorial folder, and then close the file.

Selecting a Color Range

There may be times when one of the colors in an image is not quite what you want it to be. To solve this problem, you can select a color range in an image, and then adjust the color of the pixels that are in that color range—without affecting any other part of the image. In the Color Range dialog box, you can select either a sampled color or any of the RGB (red, green blue) or CMY (cyan, magenta, yellow) colors. When you use the Color Range command to select a color in an image, Photoshop surrounds the pixels containing the color with a selection marquee. See Figure 5-11.

Figure 5-11   Selecting a color range

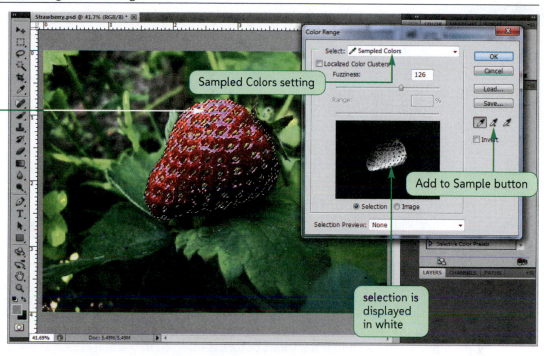

red colors in strawberry are selected; seeds are not red, so they are not selected

Sampled Colors setting

Add to Sample button

selection is displayed in white

Figure 5-11 shows a selection based on selecting a range of sampled red colors. Notice that the selection is much more complex than you could make yourself using the selection tools on the Tools panel. When you select a color range using sampled colors, you can expand your selection to include pixels that are variations in shades of the original sampled color, or even completely different colors. To do so, select the first color and then click the Add to Sample button in the dialog box. You can subtract from a sample by clicking the Subtract from Sample button and then clicking the color or shade on the canvas that you want to subtract from the selection. You can also click the Localized Color Clusters option to extend the selection only to pixels near the sampled color. Once you select the color range you want, close the dialog box, and then modify the selection as desired—for example, by adjusting its hue, saturation, and brightness (HSB) or by applying an adjustment layer to the pixels that are part of the selection but not to the image as a whole.

Azar wants you to work with the image of the strawberry to create a "before" version of an unripe berry, and then an "after" version—the red berry in the image. He'd like to use the two images, plus an image of an empty patch of dirt, in a flyer he's preparing for donors as a way of showing what a difference their contributions can make to the program.

To select using a color range:

1. On the Application bar, click **Select**, and then click **Deselect** to deselect the previous selection. Press **D** to return to the default foreground and background colors.

2. Click **Select**, and then click **Color Range**. Drag the dialog box to the right so the strawberry is visible. See Figure 5-12.

Figure 5-12   **Using the Color Range dialog box**

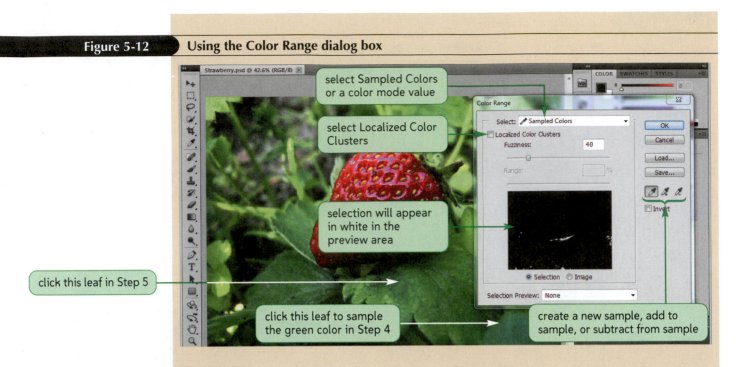

3. Confirm that **Sampled Colors** is selected in the Select box at the top of the dialog box, and then click different areas of the leaves and stems on the canvas. As you do so, the preview changes to show what areas of the image would be selected based on the sampled color.

To see the effect of selecting localized color clusters, you'll select that option in the dialog box.

4. Click the **Localized Color Clusters** check box to select it, and then click the green leaf at the lower-right corner of the image. The leaf and only a few other green areas are selected in the preview.

5. Click the large leaf just above and to the left of the leaf you just clicked. A few more leaves are now selected, but not the leaf you originally selected because it is a different shade of green.

6. Deselect the **Localized Color Clusters** check box. Notice that more of the green areas in the image are selected, and the selection covers a larger area.

7. In the Color Range dialog box, click the **Select** arrow, and then click **Greens**. Almost all of the image except the strawberry and the dirt areas are selected.

8. Click the **Select** arrow, and then click **Reds**. The strawberry is selected. See Figure 5-13.

Figure 5-13   **Selecting pixels in the red color range**

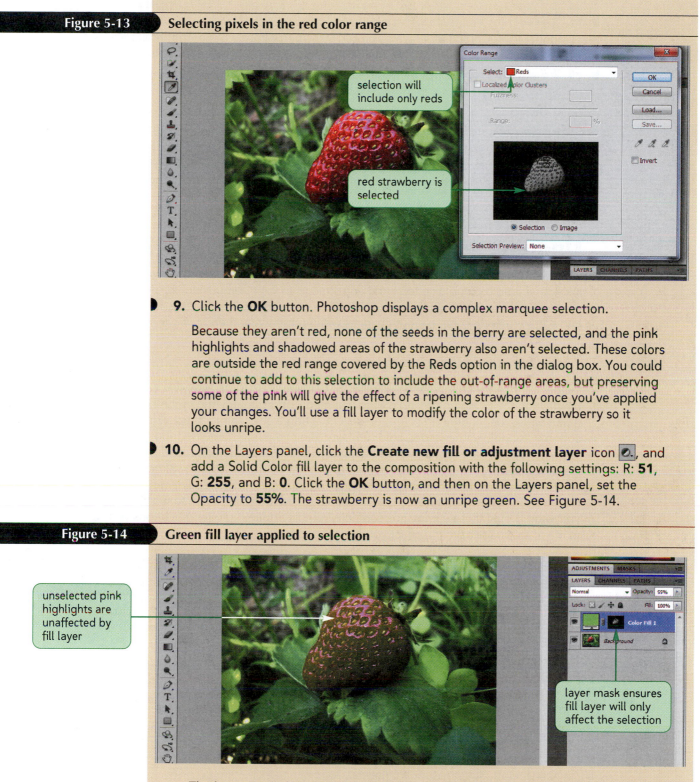

9. Click the **OK** button. Photoshop displays a complex marquee selection.

   Because they aren't red, none of the seeds in the berry are selected, and the pink highlights and shadowed areas of the strawberry also aren't selected. These colors are outside the red range covered by the Reds option in the dialog box. You could continue to add to this selection to include the out-of-range areas, but preserving some of the pink will give the effect of a ripening strawberry once you've applied your changes. You'll use a fill layer to modify the color of the strawberry so it looks unripe.

10. On the Layers panel, click the **Create new fill or adjustment layer** icon, and add a Solid Color fill layer to the composition with the following settings: R: **51**, G: **255**, and B: **0**. Click the **OK** button, and then on the Layers panel, set the Opacity to **55%**. The strawberry is now an unripe green. See Figure 5-14.

Figure 5-14   **Green fill layer applied to selection**

The layer mask thumbnail on the fill layer indicates which parts of the image are affected by the new fill layer. The thumbnail displays the selection in white.

> **11.** To see more clearly how the new layer has changed the image, hide and then unhide the **Color Fill 1** layer. The red strawberry image beneath the fill layer is unchanged.
>
> **12.** Save the file as **UnripeStrawberry.psd** in the Photoshop5\Tutorial folder, and then close it.

The tasks Azar is giving you are getting more and more complex. You'd like to make sure you can keep track of all of your changes to a composition and not alter any files permanently until you are happy with what you've done. You'll learn about and then use undo and redo techniques to keep track of your actions so you can proceed with confidence.

Undoing and Redoing Actions

Once you master selections, you have the tools to be more creative than ever. You can apply even more complex effects and adjustments to your compositions—not just to layers, but to pixels selected in a layer. With this newfound creative license, it is helpful to know how to undo some of your changes while preserving others.

Stepping Backward and Forward

When you make a change or an adjustment that you want to reverse, you can undo it by clicking the Undo command on the Edit menu. The actual name of the Undo command varies, depending on your most recent action. For example, if your most recent action was adding a new solid color fill layer, the command name is Undo New Color Fill Layer. If you have just drawn a rectangle on the canvas, the command name is Undo Rectangle Tool. Using the Undo command, you can undo only the most recent action.

Photoshop has two additional commands on the Edit menu, Step Forward and Step Backward, that let you undo a series of changes, and then redo them to whatever point you want. Using these commands can help you determine if the modifications you've made to an image have the effect you had planned.

To step forward and backward in a file:

> **1.** Open **SquashArt.jpg** from the Photoshop5\Tutorial folder. On the Application bar, click the **Arrange Documents** button ▦▾, and then click **Fit On Screen**.
>
> **2.** Activate the **Elliptical Marquee Tool** ⬭, and click the green squash. Drag the selection to center it over the squash, if necessary. Don't worry if you haven't encompassed the entire squash with the marquee, or if your marquee is too large. You'll learn how to make an exact selection of an irregular object later in this tutorial.
>
> **3.** On the Application bar, click **Select**, and then click **Transform Selection**. A rectangle appears around the selection, and handles appear on the rectangle.
>
> **4.** Drag the handles on the rectangle until the ellipse encompasses the squash pretty well, and then click the **Commit transform** button ✔ on the options bar.
>
> **5.** Using any paintbrush with any diameter and any color, paint three separate strokes over the selection, starting above the marquee and ending below the marquee. See Figure 5-15.

Figure 5-15   Altering the pixels within a selection marquee

painting is confined to selection

marquee contains the brushstrokes

As you paint, notice that none of your painting spills over the selection border. The selection contains your actions, and only lets you affect the pixels within the marquee.

6. On the Application bar, click **Edit**. The top menu choice is Undo Brush Tool. The third choice is Step Backward. As you have seen, you can only undo one action (in this case, the last action taken using the Brush Tool). However, you can step backward up to 20 times.

7. Click **Step Backward**. Your third brushstroke disappears from the image.

8. On the Application bar, click **Edit**, and then click **Step Backward**. The second brushstroke disappears.

9. On the Application bar, click **Edit**, click **Step Forward**, click **Edit**, and then click **Step Forward** again. Both brushstrokes reappear. You undid and then redid two actions.

10. On the Application bar, click **Edit**, and then click **Step Backward**. The last brushstroke to reappear disappears again.

TIP

You can also press Alt+Ctrl+Z to step backward. Press Shift+Ctrl+Z to step forward.

Using the Step Backward and Step Forward commands works well if you're only dealing with a few actions, but what happens when you've made multiple changes to a file, and want to quickly go back to a previous state? This is where the History panel comes in.

Reverting to a Previous State Using the History Panel

The History panel provides a more flexible way to reverse changes to a composition. By default, the History panel records your 20 most recent actions and lists them in order. Each item on the list is called a history state. A snapshot of the file's original state appears at the top of the list. As you work, you can create additional snapshots to make it easy to return to a particular history state after you have made a series of changes. If you perform more than 20 actions, the earliest history states drop off the History panel, and are no longer visible or reversible. See Figure 5-16.

Figure 5-16 Using the History panel

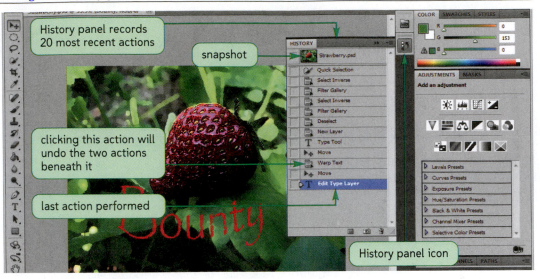

You can click a history state on the History panel to revert your image to the state it was in when you performed that action. When you do, the states beneath that action appear dimmed on the History panel. However, they are still stored in memory, so if you want to redo all of the actions at once, you can simply click the bottom command on the panel. For example, in Figure 5-16, the last action on the list is the Edit Type Layer. If you click the Warp Text history state two rows up, Photoshop will undo the two actions beneath it on the panel. If you click the Edit Type Layer history state again, Photoshop will redo the final two actions on the History panel.

It's important to note, though, that if you select a history state and then perform a different action, all of the steps beneath the history state you selected are no longer in memory and are erased from the panel. Furthermore, once you close a document, all of the states and snapshots are erased and won't be available the next time you open the file.

REFERENCE

Reverting to a Previous History State Using the History Panel

- Click the History icon to the left of the Color panel, or on the Application bar, click Window, and then click History to open the History panel.
- Edit the image you are working with, and at the bottom of the History panel, click the Create new snapshot icon as needed to record specific history states.
- Click a history state or a snapshot to revert to that state.

You'll experiment with the History panel, and then modify the image of the squash so Azar can use it in his nutrition presentation "The Squash Stands Alone," which is an outreach program that encourages schoolchildren to eat more vegetables.

To use the History panel to revert to History states, delete History states, and create snapshots:

1. Click the **History** icon to the left of the Color panel. The History panel opens, and a snapshot of the file's original state appears at the top of the list.

2. Point to the bottom edge of the History panel until you see a double-headed arrow ↕, and then drag down until all of the history states appear on the panel.

3. Add another brushstroke to the selection. See Figure 5-17.

Figure 5-17   History states recorded on the History panel

original state of file

Brush Tool actions recorded on the History panel

most recent action is highlighted as current state

third brushstroke

Notice that an additional Brush Tool history state now appears at the bottom of the panel. Because it is your most recent action, it is highlighted.

4. On the History panel, click the **Free Transform Selection** state. All of the Brush Tool states appear dimmed on the History panel, and all of the brushstrokes disappear from the composition.

5. Click the filename **SquashArt.jpg** next to the snapshot at the top of the History panel. The file reverts to its original state, with no selection marquee.

6. Click the top **Brush Tool** state. One brushstroke appears on the image along with the selection marquee, but the other two brushstrokes do not appear on the image.

7. At the bottom of the History panel, click the **Create new snapshot** icon. A snapshot of the image in the selected state appears on the History panel beneath the image of the file in its original state. See Figure 5-18.

Figure 5-18   **Storing a state as a snapshot**

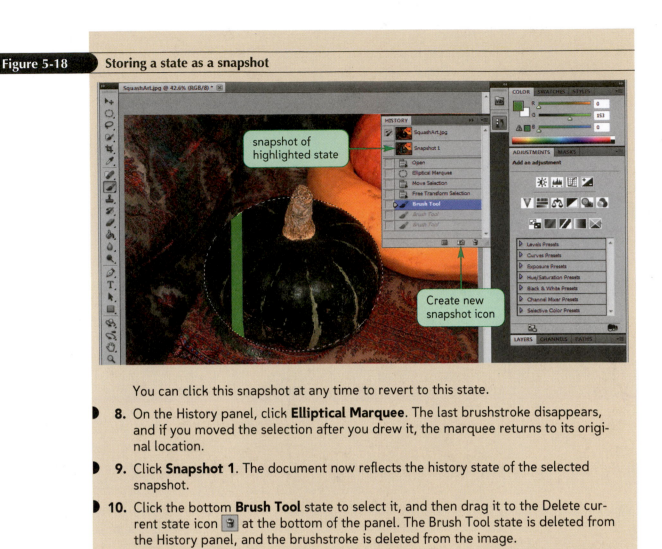

You can click this snapshot at any time to revert to this state.

8. On the History panel, click **Elliptical Marquee**. The last brushstroke disappears, and if you moved the selection after you drew it, the marquee returns to its original location.

9. Click **Snapshot 1**. The document now reflects the history state of the selected snapshot.

10. Click the bottom **Brush Tool** state to select it, and then drag it to the Delete current state icon 🗑 at the bottom of the panel. The Brush Tool state is deleted from the History panel, and the brushstroke is deleted from the image.

11. Click the top **Brush Tool** state on the History panel, click the **Delete current state** icon 🗑 at the bottom of the panel, and then click the **Yes** button in the dialog box to confirm the deletion. Both of the remaining brushstrokes disappear from the image, and both of the Brush Tool states disappear from the History panel.

You'll learn more about the Quick Selection Tool in the next session, but for now, you'll use the Quick Selection Tool to add the stem to the squash selection, and then apply an effect to the inverse of the selection so the squash stands out.

12. On the Tools panel, click the **Quick Selection Tool** 🖌, on the options bar, click the **Add to selection** button 🖌, and then click the stem until it is fully selected.

13. On the Application bar, click **Select**, and then click **Inverse**. Everything but the squash is selected in the image.

14. Add a yellow color fill layer to the image with **45%** opacity, and then close the History panel. See Figure 5-19.

Figure 5-19   **Adding an effect to an inverse selection**

squash unaffected by color fill

squash is masked from color fill layer

color fill is added to selected area

The squash stands out, while the rest of the image is shaded in yellow.

15. Save the file as **SquashStandsAlone.psd** in the Photoshop5\Tutorial folder, and then close the file.

You can also use the History Brush Tool to return an image to a previous state—or even a partial version of a previous state.

Using the History Brush Tool

The History Brush Tool works in tandem with the History panel to give you very detailed control over the edits you've made to a file. You might be familiar with the phrase *to airbrush history*. In historical terms, airbrushing history means deliberately hiding the parts of a historical record that you think are unfavorable. You can think of the History Brush Tool in a similar way. Imagine that you have made multiple changes to a composition, and each change is recorded as a state on the History panel. Some of your changes are perfect; you want to keep them the way they are. Others work for some areas of the image but not for others. In Normal mode, the History Brush Tool lets you paint over individual areas you want to revert to a previous state while leaving other areas alone. When you paint over those areas, the brush erases the state or states on top of the image to return to the state you have chosen as the source for your brush.

To use the History Brush Tool, on the History panel, click in the empty box to the left of a state that you want to "uncover" with the brush. This sets the source for the History Brush Tool. You can then choose a brush tip for your brush, set the diameter, and set the Opacity and Flow percentages. If you want to paint with the selected state exactly as it appeared before the additional changes, make sure that the Opacity and Flow settings are 100% and the Mode setting is Normal so all of the details revert to the way they looked in that state.

REFERENCE

Using the History Brush Tool to Return Part of an Image to a Previous History State

- Click the History icon to the left of the Color panel, or on the Application bar, click Window, and then click History to open the History panel.
- Click to the left of an action on the panel to mark it with the Sets the source for the history brush icon and to make it the source for the brush.
- On the Tools panel, click the History Brush Tool.
- On the options bar, specify History Brush Tool options such as brush diameter, mode, opacity, and flow.
- Paint over the part of the image you want to return to the source state.

To use the History Brush Tool to return part of an image to a previous state:

1. Open **LettuceGarden.jpg** from the Photoshop5\Tutorial folder, click the **Arrange Documents** button on the Application bar, and click **Fit On Screen**. Reset the Essentials workspace, reset the foreground and background colors, open the History panel, and drag the bottom edge of the History panel down to resize it so there is room to show multiple history states. If necessary, drag the History panel so it doesn't cover any part of the image.

2. On the Tools panel, select the **Brush Tool**.

3. On the Application bar, click **Window**, and then click **Brush Presets** to open the Brush Presets panel.

4. On the Brush Presets panel, click the **panel options** icon, click **Special Effect Brushes**, and then click the **OK** button to replace the current brushes with the Special Effect Brushes.

   Trouble? If you are prompted to save changes to the current brushes, click the No button.

5. In the Brush Preset picker, click the **Azalea** brush, and change the size of the brush to **20** pixels.

6. Set the foreground color on the Color panel to R=**170**, G=**90**, and B=**165**, and set the background color on the Color panel to R=**196**, G=**130**, and B=**171**. The Azalea brush uses both the foreground and background colors in its strokes.

7. Click the **Brush Presets** icon to the left of the Color panel to collapse the Brush Presets panel.

8. Paint over the two narrow gardens near the top of the image, as shown in Figure 5-20, by dragging back and forth and up and down with the mouse pointer. Keep the mouse button depressed the entire time so only one Brush Tool state is recorded on the History panel.

Figure 5-20   Recording painting actions on the History panel

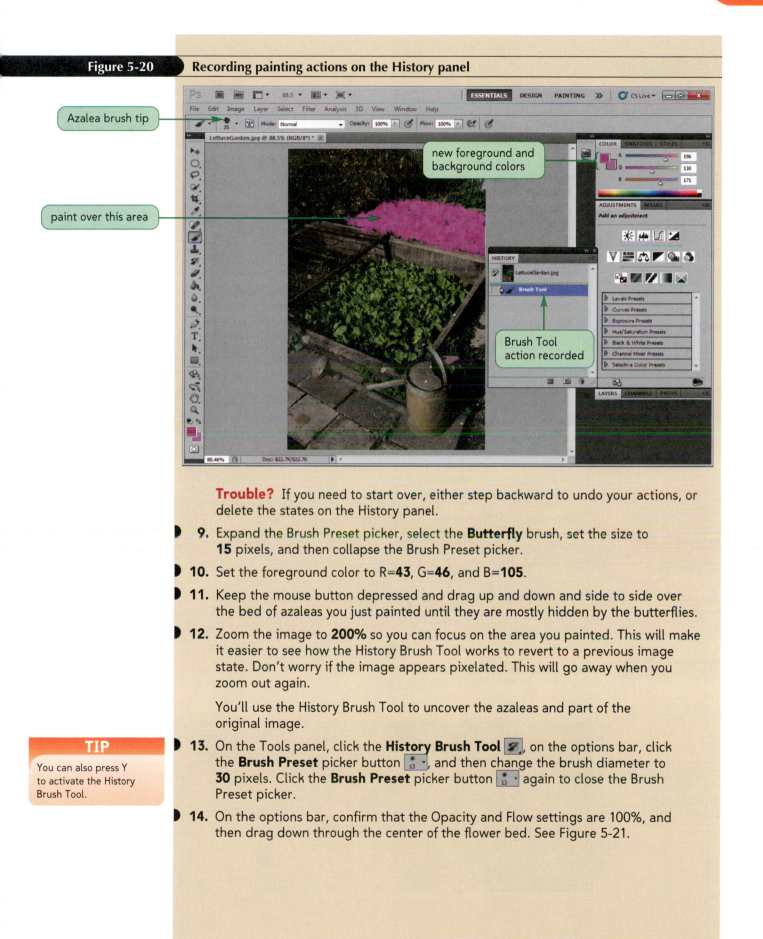

Azalea brush tip

new foreground and background colors

paint over this area

Brush Tool action recorded

Trouble? If you need to start over, either step backward to undo your actions, or delete the states on the History panel.

9. Expand the Brush Preset picker, select the **Butterfly** brush, set the size to **15** pixels, and then collapse the Brush Preset picker.

10. Set the foreground color to R=**43**, G=**46**, and B=**105**.

11. Keep the mouse button depressed and drag up and down and side to side over the bed of azaleas you just painted until they are mostly hidden by the butterflies.

12. Zoom the image to **200%** so you can focus on the area you painted. This will make it easier to see how the History Brush Tool works to revert to a previous image state. Don't worry if the image appears pixelated. This will go away when you zoom out again.

You'll use the History Brush Tool to uncover the azaleas and part of the original image.

TIP

You can also press Y to activate the History Brush Tool.

13. On the Tools panel, click the **History Brush Tool**, on the options bar, click the **Brush Preset** picker button, and then change the brush diameter to **30** pixels. Click the **Brush Preset** picker button again to close the Brush Preset picker.

14. On the options bar, confirm that the Opacity and Flow settings are 100%, and then drag down through the center of the flower bed. See Figure 5-21.

Figure 5-21 Using the History Brush Tool

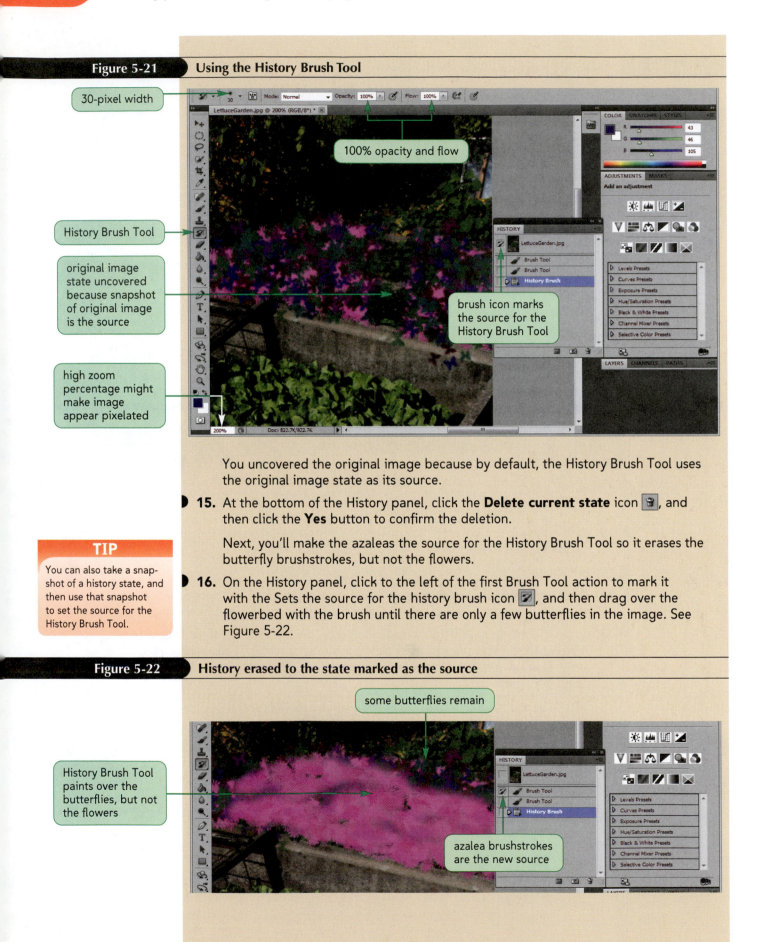

30-pixel width

100% opacity and flow

History Brush Tool

original image state uncovered because snapshot of original image is the source

brush icon marks the source for the History Brush Tool

high zoom percentage might make image appear pixelated

You uncovered the original image because by default, the History Brush Tool uses the original image state as its source.

▶ **15.** At the bottom of the History panel, click the **Delete current state** icon 🗑 , and then click the **Yes** button to confirm the deletion.

Next, you'll make the azaleas the source for the History Brush Tool so it erases the butterfly brushstrokes, but not the flowers.

TIP

You can also take a snapshot of a history state, and then use that snapshot to set the source for the History Brush Tool.

▶ **16.** On the History panel, click to the left of the first Brush Tool action to mark it with the Sets the source for the history brush icon 🖌 , and then drag over the flowerbed with the brush until there are only a few butterflies in the image. See Figure 5-22.

Figure 5-22 History erased to the state marked as the source

some butterflies remain

History Brush Tool paints over the butterflies, but not the flowers

azalea brushstrokes are the new source

The History Brush Tool erases the butterfly brushstroke, but not the flowerbed you painted. This is because you set the Azalea brushstroke state as the source for the brush.

▶ 17. Save the file as **Flowerbed.jpg**, using the default JPEG Options, in the Photoshop5\Tutorial folder, close the file, and then exit Photoshop.

INSIGHT

Using the Art History Brush Tool

The Art History Brush Tool also uses history states to paint on an image, but the effect is completely different from the effect of the History Brush Tool. The Art History Brush Tool creates stylized artwork by essentially transforming a digital photograph into a painting using the colors of the source. Its results are often unpredictable, and if you choose to use the Art History Brush Tool, you should take the time to experiment with different Mode, Opacity, Style, and Tolerance settings. Minor variations in any of these settings can create very different results.

In this session, you experimented with a variety of Photoshop selection tools. You learned how to apply an adjustment to a selection and how to copy and paste selections. You created complex selections, and explored how to select a color range in an image. You also spent time undoing and redoing actions with the Edit menu, the History panel, and the History Brush Tool. In the next session, you'll explore additional selection tools, and work with filters, fills, and masks.

REVIEW

Session 5.1 Quick Check

1. A(n) _____ encloses part of an image in a series of animated dashed lines or curves.
2. True or False. The Rectangular Marquee Tool has an Anti-alias setting.
3. The _____ _____ setting on the options bar lets you specify a width and a height for your selection.
4. Which command increases the size of a selection by a specified number of pixels?
5. By default, the History panel stores up to _____ history states.
6. True or False. When you save a file, all history states are saved with the file.
7. Which tool can you use in conjunction with the History panel to return part of an image to a previous state?

SESSION 5.2 VISUAL OVERVIEW

The Magnetic Lasso Tool selects the outline of a complex object on a high contrast background and adds **fastening points** that define the selection marquee based on the frequency you specify.

The Stained Glass effect has been applied to the Eggplant selection.

An RGB image has a composite RGB color channel and three individual color channels (Red, Green, and Blue).

The Glass effect has been applied to the Beans selection.

Color channels appear on the Channels panel and store information about the colors in your image.

Selections can be saved as **alpha channels**, which store selections as masks; white indicates the selection, while black indicates the masked area.

You can load a saved selection by selecting it from the Channel list.

LASSO TOOLS AND FILTERS

Use selections and the Filter Gallery to apply multiple effects to the same image.

Each folder in the Filter Gallery contains multiple filter effects.

Filters come with multiple settings that you can modify before applying the filter.

You can preview the selected filter effect before applying it.

Click a folder icon to expand or collapse the folder.

Working with the Lasso Tools and Fills

The Lasso Tools give you many options for selecting content on your canvas. Photoshop includes three Lasso Tools, each with unique benefits. To use the Polygonal Lasso Tool, click a starting point for your selection, and then continue to click around the selection. As you do, Photoshop connects the points you click with straight lines. You can close your selection and activate the marquee by double-clicking. The Magnetic Lasso Tool is attracted to the defined edges of whatever object you first click on. As you move the mouse pointer, it adds points along the selection based on a frequency you specify. You can add extra points and change direction by clicking. You use the regular Lasso Tool in much the same way you would draw with a brush or pencil. You simply drag on the image to create your free-form selection. When you release the mouse button, Photoshop creates the marquee. If you release the mouse button before returning to your starting point, Photoshop draws a straight line to the starting point from the point at which you stopped dragging to complete the selection. A selection made with the Lasso Tool isn't as exacting as other selection methods, but you'll find you use it often as a starting point. As you become more experienced with Photoshop, you'll be able to determine which particular tool is the best one for your selection needs.

Filling a Selection Using the Content-Aware Fill Feature

Photoshop CS5 has a new feature called a Content-Aware fill that allows you to remove objects from a photograph and replace them with similar versions of the surrounding pixels. For example, you might have a beautiful photograph of a sandy beach, with one problem: There's a piece of trash right in the middle of it. You can use one of the Lasso Tools to select the trash and some of the sand surrounding it. When you use the Content-Aware fill, Photoshop makes the trash disappear and replaces it with the sand. Because the feature generates the fill randomly, if you're not happy with the first result, you can repeat it.

Azar has given you a photograph that he wants to use in his Live Green, Eat Green slide show. The photograph is of green beans and an eggplant, but Azar wants you to change so it only shows the green beans and no other vegetables. You'll select the eggplant using the Lasso Tool, and then you'll fill the selection using the Content-Aware fill.

To use the Lasso Marquee Tool and fill the selection with content:

1. Start Photoshop while pressing the **Ctrl+Alt+Shift** keys. When you are prompted to delete the Adobe Photoshop Settings File, click **Yes**. On the Application bar, right-click **Essentials**, and then click **Reset Essentials** to reset the default Essentials workspace layout.

2. Navigate to the Photoshop5\Tutorial folder, and open **EggplantBeans.jpg**.

3. Click the **Lasso Tool** 🔾 on the Tools panel and drag a selection completely around the eggplant, and then release the mouse button.

   You don't need to be too exacting when you make the selection, but make sure the eggplant is completely selected, and that the selection includes some of the beans beyond the eggplant. A selection marquee appears around the eggplant. See Figure 5-23.

Figure 5-23   **Selecting with the Lasso Tool**

Lasso Tool

selection made with Lasso Tool

4. On the Application bar, click **Edit**, and then click **Fill**. The Fill dialog box opens.

5. In the Contents section, select **Content-Aware** from the Use drop-down menu, if necessary. Set the Blending Mode to **Normal**, set the Opacity to **100%**, and then click the **OK** button. See Figure 5-24.

Figure 5-24   **Selected area filled with surrounding content**

eggplant has been replaced by surrounding pixels

Photoshop uses the data in the area surrounding the selection to fill the selection.

6. On the Application bar, click **Select**, and then click **Deselect** to clear the selection.

The image has been transformed from a photograph of an eggplant and green beans to a photograph of green beans. There is no evidence that the eggplant was ever there.

Trouble? If you aren't satisfied with the way Photoshop filled in the area, repeat Steps 3 through 6. Because the results are randomly generated, the fill will look different every time.

7. Save the file as **GreenBeans.jpg**, using the default JPEG Options, in the Photoshop5\Tutorial folder, and then close it.

Problem Solving: Using an Image Without a Model Release

Problem solving is the ability to identify a gap between an existing state and a desired state. It's a critical skill to develop because no matter what your career, you're bound to encounter problems that take a creative thinker (you) to solve them. For example, imagine that you have the perfect landscape photo for a travel ad you're creating. The image includes a stunning landscape, beautiful architecture, and an old man riding his bicycle along the cobblestone road. Can you use the photograph?

The answer isn't simple. Basically, it depends. If you're using the photograph for a commercial purpose, as in this travel ad example, you would need to ask the man to sign a model release form giving you permission to use his likeness in your piece. However, if the man isn't recognizable—for example, if you've photographed his back, or if his face is cloaked in shadow, you really don't need his permission. But, imagine that the man in the image is fully recognizable, and that using his image is a problem you need to solve. Even without his permission, you still have a number of options. You can modify the photograph so the man is unrecognizable—for example by using Photoshop to add shadows to his face. You can also use the Content-Aware fill feature to replace the man and his bicycle with pixels from the cobblestone road. In other words, when you're experienced in digital image editing, you'll find more than one way to solve any image problem you may encounter.

Selecting Content with the Magnetic Lasso Tool

The Magnetic Lasso Tool is hidden under the Lasso Tool on the Tools panel. It's aptly named, because it appears to use a virtual magnet to select the edges of an object in an image. When you work with the tool, it is as if the object you are selecting is metal and the marquee is a magnet.

As the tool draws a marquee, it drops fastening points along the marquee to hold the selection in place. The **frequency** determines the distance between fastening points. On the options bar, you can specify a Frequency setting between 0 and 100. For a more refined selection, increase the frequency of the fastening points. You can also specify a detection Width, which is the distance from the pointer, in number of pixels, within which you want the tool to detect edges. The Contrast setting, which ranges from 1% to 100%, determines how sensitive the tool is to edges. A low Contrast setting detects low contrast edges, whereas a high setting detects edges with a sharp contrast. Unlike with the Lasso Tool, you do not hold down the mouse button when making a selection using the Magnetic Lasso Tool. You click to set the first fastening point, and then move the mouse pointer to outline the selection. As you do, Photoshop adds fastening points at the frequency you specified. You can add fastening points manually by clicking as you make your selection. You can delete the most recent fastening point by pressing the Backspace key. When you have finished making your selection, you can modify its pixels or fill it with surrounding content or with a pattern, color, or gradient. To fill a selection, you can use the Fill command on the Edit menu, which fills a selection on the current layer, rather than adding the fill to a separate layer as you did earlier in this tutorial.

Using the Magnetic Lasso Tool

- On the Tools panel, select the Magnetic Lasso Tool.
- On the options bar, click the New selection, Add to selection, Subtract from selection, or Intersect with selection button.
- Specify a Feather setting, and select or deselect the Anti-alias check box.
- Specify a Width for edge detection, the Contrast percentage for detecting either low contrast or high contrast edges, and the Frequency at which fastening points will appear.
- Click on the image to set the first fastening point, and then move the mouse pointer along the edges of your selection.
- Click at the last fastening point to close the selection marquee.

Azar has an image of a sunflower that he wants to use after his Live Green, Eat Green slide in the presentation, where he includes various recipes, including one for green beans, garlic, and sunflower seeds. The image has a gray sky, and he has asked you to make it blue. You'll select the sky and then apply a blue fill to the selection.

To use the Magnetic Lasso Tool and fill the selection with color:

1. Open **Sunflower.jpg** from the Photoshop5\Tutorial folder, and then, on the Tools panel, click the **Magnetic Lasso Tool** .

2. On the options bar, confirm that the Feather setting is **0 px**, select the **Anti-alias** check box, if necessary, set the Width to **1 px**, set the Contrast to **100%**, and set the Frequency to **100**. A frequency of 100 will drop fastening points very close together along the edges of the selection.

3. Start by clicking the upper-left corner of the image, move the mouse pointer to the right until you reach the upper-right corner, and then move the mouse pointer down until you reach the lower-right corner. Stay at the edge, or even slightly outside of the image, so the fastening points are along the edges of the photograph.

4. Move the pointer slowly along the edges of the flower until you reach the upper-left corner at the first fastening point. Click to close the selection marquee. The marquee encloses the sky in a selection. See Figure 5-25.

   Trouble? If you find that the selection marquee strays from the outlines of the sunflower, use the Magic Wand Tool and the Add to selection and Subtract from selection buttons to refine your selection.

TIP

You can restart a selection by pressing the Esc key, and then clicking the first fastening point again.

Figure 5-25	Using the Magnetic Lasso Tool

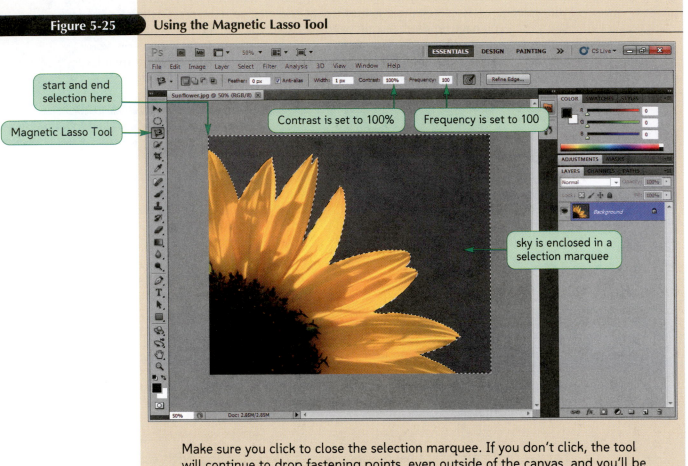

start and end selection here

Magnetic Lasso Tool

Contrast is set to 100%

Frequency is set to 100

sky is enclosed in a selection marquee

Make sure you click to close the selection marquee. If you don't click, the tool will continue to drop fastening points, even outside of the canvas, and you'll be unable to choose any commands or tools.

5. On the Application bar, click **Edit**, and then click **Fill**. In the Fill dialog box, click the **Use** arrow, and then click **Color** to open the Choose a color dialog box, where you can select a color for the fill.

6. In the Choose a color dialog box, change the RGB settings as follows: R=**51**, G=**102**, B=**153**, and then click the **OK** button.

7. Under Blending in the Fill dialog box, scrub over the word *Opacity* to change the setting to **50%**, and then click the **OK** button to close the Fill dialog box.

8. On the Application bar, click **Select**, and then click **Deselect** to clear the selection. See Figure 5-26.

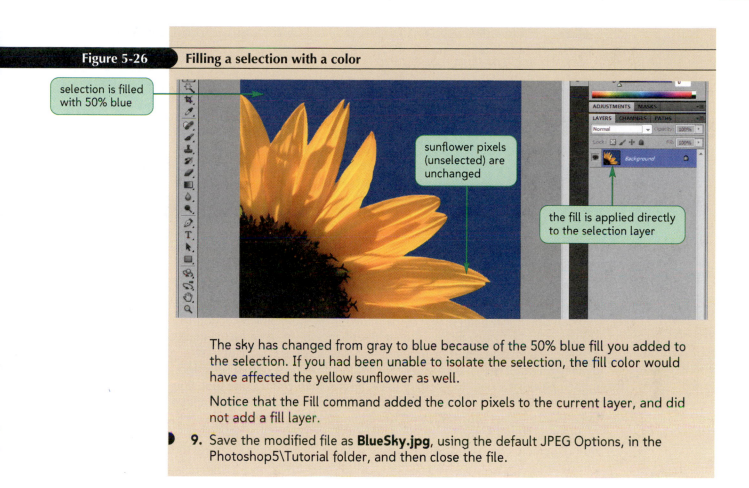

Figure 5-26   Filling a selection with a color

selection is filled with 50% blue

sunflower pixels (unselected) are unchanged

the fill is applied directly to the selection layer

The sky has changed from gray to blue because of the 50% blue fill you added to the selection. If you had been unable to isolate the selection, the fill color would have affected the yellow sunflower as well.

Notice that the Fill command added the color pixels to the current layer, and did not add a fill layer.

9. Save the modified file as **BlueSky.jpg**, using the default JPEG Options, in the Photoshop5\Tutorial folder, and then close the file.

Saving and Reloading a Selection

You can save a selection with a file so you can use it the next time you open the file. For example, if you want to experiment with many different effects on a single selection, you can save the first effect in a file with a new name, reopen the original file, load the saved selection, and then try a different effect. Photoshop saves the selection as a new layer on the Channels panel, which you'll explore later in this tutorial. See Figure 5-27.

Figure 5-27   Loading a selection

click the Channel arrow to load a saved selection

create a new selection or add to, subtract from, or intersect with an existing selection

You can choose a selection from the Channel list in the Load Selection dialog box. You can use the saved selection to add to, subtract from, or intersect with an active selection. You can also simply load the selection you saved with the file.

REFERENCE

Saving and Loading a Selection

- On the Tools panel, activate any selection tool and make a selection on the image.
- On the Application bar, click Select, and then click Save Selection.
- In the Save Selection dialog box, type a name for the selection in the Name box, and then click the OK button.
- On the Application bar, click Select, and then click Load Selection.
- In the Source section of the Load Selection dialog box, click the Channel arrow, and then click the name of the selection you want to load.
- In the Operation section of the Load Selection dialog box, click New Selection, Add to Selection, Subtract from Selection, or Intersect with Selection.
- Click the OK button.

Selecting with the Quick Selection Tool

You can select part of an image by painting it with the Quick Selection Tool. The Quick Selection Tool expands to select the edges of any object in an image that you paint over to enclose it in a selection marquee. It works well when you want to select areas with defined edges. It is also a good tool for adding pixels to a partial selection, as you did in the first session with the stem of the squash. When you use the tool, you can specify its diameter. A larger diameter gives you less control over the tool, but if you are selecting a large area, it's more efficient. You can also select Sample All Layers to create the selection using all of the layers in the file rather than just the active layer. If you select Auto-Enhance, Photoshop automatically reduces the roughness around the border of the selection.

Azar has asked you to create two images that showcase the quality of last summer's tomato crop for Food for Change. To do so, you'll create two compositions. In one, you'll use the Quick Selection Tool to make a selection and then select the inverse so you can change all of an image except the tomatoes to black and white to make them stand out. In the second composition, you'll place a stroke or outline around the tomatoes to make them stand out in the image.

To use the Quick Selection Tool and save the selection:

1. Open **GoodFood.jpg** from the Photoshop5\Tutorial folder, and then zoom in on the tomatoes in the image so you can work with them.

2. Reset all of the tools, reset the Essentials workspace, and then, on the Tools panel, click the **Quick Selection Tool** 🖊. By default, the New selection button 🖊 is selected on the options bar, and the brush size is set to 30 pixels.

3. Open the Brush Preset picker and drag the slider to the left to change the brush size to **20** pixels. Close the Brush Preset picker.

4. Point to the top of the tomato on the top, click and drag the mouse down to the bottom of that tomato. Photoshop selects most of the tomato, but it also selects some of the shadow. See Figure 5-28.

TIP

You can also press the [key to reduce the brush size in 5-pixel increments.

Figure 5-28   **Using the Quick Selection Tool**

Add to selection button selected automatically after first selection

Quick Selection Tool

selection includes shadow

your selection may be different

brush tip

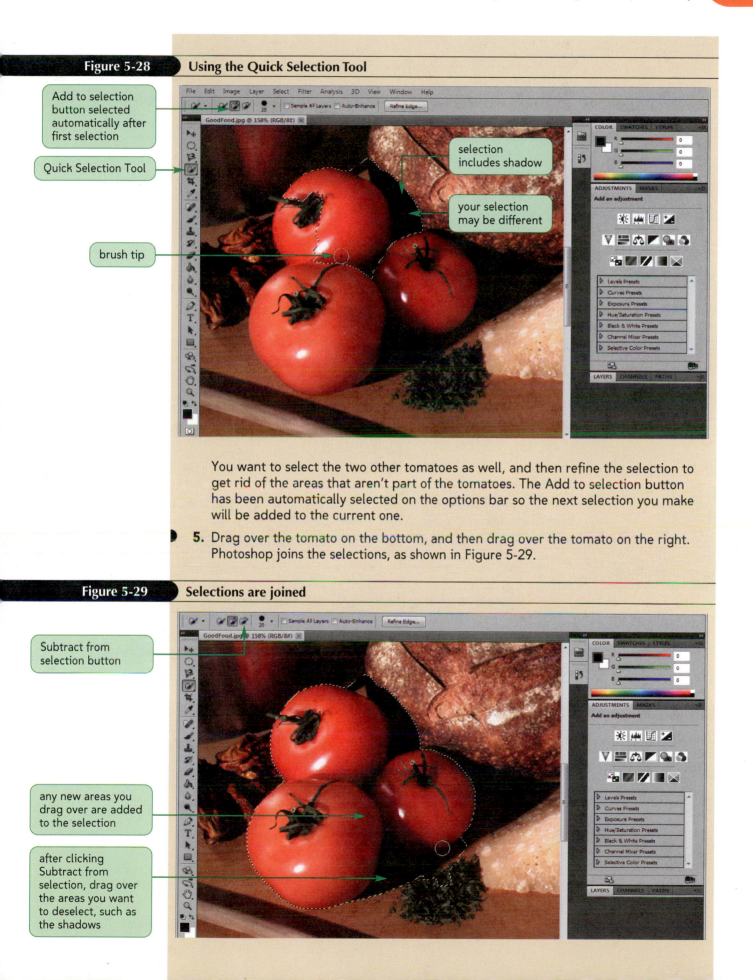

You want to select the two other tomatoes as well, and then refine the selection to get rid of the areas that aren't part of the tomatoes. The Add to selection button has been automatically selected on the options bar so the next selection you make will be added to the current one.

5. Drag over the tomato on the bottom, and then drag over the tomato on the right. Photoshop joins the selections, as shown in Figure 5-29.

Figure 5-29   **Selections are joined**

Subtract from selection button

any new areas you drag over are added to the selection

after clicking Subtract from selection, drag over the areas you want to deselect, such as the shadows

You can subtract from your selection using the Subtract from selection button on the options bar.

6. On the options bar, click the **Subtract from selection** button , and then drag in the areas you want to deselect.

   Trouble? If you accidentally deselect part of one of the tomatoes, you can use the Add to selection button to add it back to the selection.

   Photoshop deselects the shadowed parts of the selection so now the marquee encompasses only the tomatoes. You'll save this selection to use later.

7. On the Application bar, click **Select**, click **Save Selection**, and then in the Save Selection dialog box, type **tomatoes** in the Name box. Click the **OK** button. The selection is saved with the file so you can use it later.

8. Save the file as **GoodFood1.psd** in the Photoshop5\Tutorial folder.

Next, you'll select the inverse of the tomato selection so you can apply an effect that makes the tomatoes stand out.

To select the inverse of the selection:

1. Zoom out so you can see the entire image. On the Application bar, click **Select**, and then click **Inverse**. Photoshop changes the selection so all of the image *except* the tomatoes is now selected.

2. On the Application bar, click **Image**, click **Adjustments**, and then click **Black & White**.

3. In the Black and White dialog box, change the Reds setting to **30%**, and then click the **OK** button.

4. On the Application bar, click **Select**, and then click **Deselect**. See Figure 5-30.

Figure 5-30 | **Applying the Black and White Adjustment to a selection**

only the tomatoes appear in color

All of the areas in the image except the tomatoes are now black and white. Using this kind of effect in a composition immediately draws attention to the area of the image on which you want the viewer's eyes to focus.

5. Save the file as **BlackWhiteRed.psd** in the Photoshop5\Tutorial folder, and close it.

Next, you'll work with the same image, and apply a different effect so you have two options to show to Azar at your next meeting.

Stroking a Selection

You can make a selection stand out by **stroking** it, or drawing a border around it. To do so, you select an area of the image with any of the selection tools or load a saved selection and use the Stroke option on the Edit menu. In the Stroke dialog box, you can specify the Width, Color, and Location of the stroke, as well as its Blending mode and Opacity.

You'll add a stroke to the tomato selection you saved earlier to see if you like the effect.

To load the saved tomatoes selection and add a stroke to the selection:

1. Open **GoodFood1.psd** from the Photoshop5\Tutorial folder. Photoshop displays the original image of the tomatoes. Although you can't see the selection you saved earlier, it has been saved with the file.

2. On the Application bar, click **Select**, and then click **Load Selection**.

3. Confirm that **tomatoes** appears in the Channel box under Source, and then click the **OK** button. Photoshop selects the three tomatoes in the image using the marquee you saved with the file. You'll expand the selection, and then you'll add a stroke to the selection to make it stand out.

4. On the Application bar, click **Select**, click **Modify**, and then click **Expand**.

5. In the Expand by box, in the Expand Selection dialog box, type **20** and then click the **OK** button to expand the selection by 20 pixels.

6. On the Application bar, click **Edit**, and then click **Stroke**.

7. In the Stroke section of the Stroke dialog box, specify a Width of **20 px**, and select a **yellow** color. Under Location, click the **Outside** option button. Under Blending, click the **Mode** arrow, click **Lighter Color**, and then set the Opacity to **80%**. See Figure 5-31.

Figure 5-31	Stroking a selection

- stroke width
- stroke color
- stroke location
- stroke blending mode and opacity

8. Click the **OK** button, and then deselect the tomatoes. See Figure 5-32.

Figure 5-32   Selection with stroke added

stroke applied to the tomatoes selection

9. Save the file as **Stroke.psd** in the Photoshop5\Tutorial folder, and then close the file.

When you next meet with Azar, you'll show him the two versions of the file to see which one he prefers. Next, you'll explore filters and masks.

Working with Filters and Masks

Photoshop includes more than enough filter options to fill a book. In this session, you'll focus on just a few of the available filters. However, once you understand how to apply them, you'll be able to experiment with many more. You can access all of the available filters from the Filter menu. Some commands open a dialog box specific to the filter; other commands are applied when you click them. Still other commands open the Filter Gallery, where you can modify and preview different filters.

You can apply a filter effect to an entire image, to a layer, or to a selection on a layer. In this session, you'll apply different filters to different selections. When you apply an effect to a selection, you are actually working with a mask. The mask ensures that the filter is only applied to the selected area. Sometimes filter results can be a little over the top, but if you experiment with them, you'll see the variety and creativity you can achieve using these tools.

Understanding Masks

If you have ever painted a room, you know that there's a certain amount of preparation that has to take place before you actually put your paintbrush in the paint and the brush on the wall. Certain areas of the room—for example, the doors, windows, and molding—need to be protected, and to protect these areas, you'll most likely use masking tape. Photoshop carries the metaphor of masking tape into the digital image-editing world. Masking an area keeps it safe from any digital paint you apply. You saw a masking effect in Session 5.1 when you selected an area on an image, and then added brushstrokes: The brushstrokes were contained in the selection and did not spill over onto the rest of the image.

You might be wondering what a mask actually looks like in Photoshop. Masks are stored on the Channels panel, which appears behind the Layers panel in the Essentials workspace. See Figure 5-33.

Figure 5-33	Channels panel

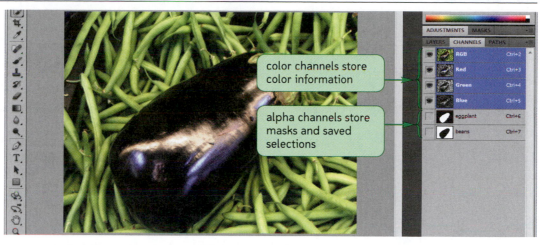

color channels store color information

alpha channels store masks and saved selections

The Channels panel stores a variety of information, including color information. In an RGB image, Red, Green, and Blue color channels appear. For a CMYK file, the Channels panel would display Cyan, Magenta, Yellow, and Black channels. You can show and hide these color channels as you work with an image file.

When you saved a selection earlier in this tutorial, Photoshop saved it as a mask, also called an alpha channel, on the Channels panel. On any alpha channel thumbnail, the masked part of the image is black, indicating that it is protected, and the unmasked part of the image is white, indicating that it is editable. In Figure 5-33, notice that in addition to the color channels, there are two other channels. One, called eggplant in the figure, masks the green beans. It was created by selecting the eggplant, and then saving the selection. The other, called beans, masks the eggplant. It was created by inverting the original selection, and then saving the selection. You'll continue to work with masks in this tutorial as you apply filters from the Filter Gallery.

INSIGHT

Working with Color Channels

The color channels on the Channels panel give you a high level of control over color adjustments. You can use them to change the color balance in an image by modifying them individually. For example, you can modify the Red channel to achieve one effect or the Blue channel to achieve another. If you have a photograph with too much red in it, you can select the Red color channel on the Channels panel and modify its settings individually to reduce the red output. Having this kind of flexibility when you modify a photograph helps to ensure that you get exactly the effect you want.

Using the Liquify Filter

The Liquify filter is available directly from the Filter menu. You can use the Liquify filter to distort or correct an image. You can create swirls; you can stretch certain areas; you can even bloat or pucker the image. The tools on the left side of the dialog box give you a variety of options for using the Liquify filter, as shown in Figure 5-34.

Figure 5-34   **Liquify Tools**

Icon	Name	Description
	Forward Warp Tool	Pushes pixels ahead of the pointer as you drag
	Reconstruct Tool	Undoes any distortion you've applied
	Twirl Clockwise Tool	Twirls pixels clockwise; hold down the Alt key to twirl pixels counterclockwise
	Pucker Tool	Moves pixels toward the center of the mouse pointer as you click
	Bloat Tool	Moves pixels away from the center of the mouse pointer as you click
	Push Left Tool	Moves pixels to the left when you drag up and to the right when you drag down
	Mirror Tool	Creates the appearance of a reflection; for example, can add the appearance of a tree reflected in a pond
	Turbulence Tool	Scrambles pixels to create cloud and wave effects
	Freeze Mask Tool	Protects an area from changes
	Thaw Mask Tool	Thaws an area with freeze mask applied
	Hand Tool	Pans an image
	Zoom Tool	Zooms in and out on an image

As you work, you can change tools to create different effects on different parts of an image. For example, you might use the Turbulence Tool to create special effects in a cloudy sky or to add a current to still water.

The Freeze Mask Tool in the Liquify dialog box is especially useful if you want to avoid liquifying parts of an image while working on other parts. It has a similar effect to inverting a selection to exclude it before applying an adjustment or effect. You use the Freeze Mask Tool to paint a mask on the image. As with other masks in Photoshop, any area that is masked is protected. You can use the Zoom Tool and the Hand Tool to zoom and pan the image to paint an accurate mask. If you paint beyond the boundaries of the mask you want to create, you can "thaw" the mask by clicking the Thaw Mask Tool and painting over the part of the mask you want to erase.

REFERENCE

Using the Liquify Filter

- Select the area you want to work with; if you want to liquify the whole layer, don't make any selection.
- On the Application bar, click Filter, and then click Liquify.
- Use the Freeze Mask Tool to freeze any areas you don't want to liquify.
- Select a tool on the left side of the Liquify dialog box, and drag the mouse pointer over the image to warp, bloat, pucker, or otherwise liquify your image.
- Use the Thaw Mask Tool to thaw any frozen areas, and use additional tools to add more liquify effects, if desired.
- Click the OK button to apply the effects, and close the dialog box.

Azar is planning a Halloween fund-raiser, and would like to send a postcard to patrons as an invitation. He supplies you with an image of squash, and asks you to apply an unusual eye-catching effect to the image. You'll use the Liquify filter to swirl the colors in the image around the large squash in the center. You'll then add a stroke to the squash to make it "pop."

To work with the Liquify filter:

1. Open **ManySquash.psd** from the Photoshop5\Tutorial folder, and save it as **Liquify.psd** in the same folder.

2. Hide the Boo! layer, select the **Background** layer, and then use any of the selection tools you have learned about to select the large squash on the left side of the image. Add to and subtract from the selection as necessary.

   Trouble? If you're having difficulty making exact selections, remember that you can refine your selection using the add and subtract buttons on the options bar.

3. On the Application bar, click **Select**, and then click **Inverse**. Everything but the squash is selected in the image.

4. On the Application bar, click **Filter**, and then click **Liquify**. The Liquify dialog box opens. See Figure 5-35.

| Figure 5-35 | Liquify dialog box |

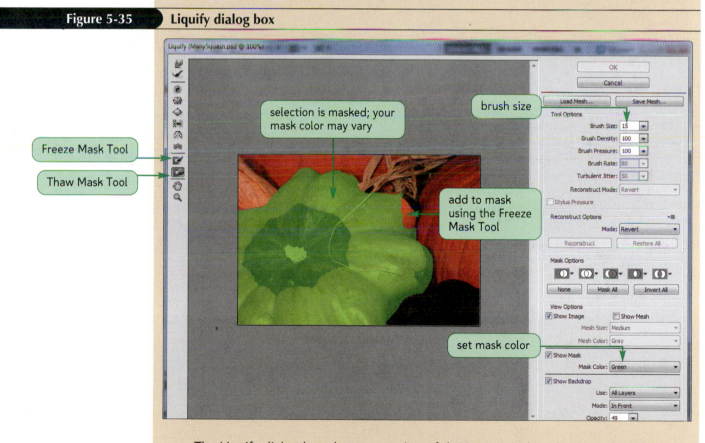

The Liquify dialog box shows a preview of the image, with tools along the left side and settings for each tool along the right. In Figure 5-35, the squash is painted over with a green mask, though your mask color and opacity settings might vary. Your goal is to liquify the area around the squash to give it an impressionistic effect, while leaving a realistic squash image in the middle.

In the figure, the mask of the squash is imperfect. There is a part of the squash that isn't masked. You'll use the Freeze Mask Tool to correct any similar oversights on your mask.

5. On the Tools panel of the Liquify dialog box, click the **Freeze Mask Tool** . The pointer shape for the Freeze Mask Tool is a circle with a plus sign in it ⊕.

6. Change the brush size to **15**. You'll leave the other settings as is. Notice that the settings include Mask Color and Opacity.

7. Drag over the squash to paint the mask repairs. As you paint, use the Hand Tool and the Zoom Tool to ensure that you paint every pixel of the squash to protect it from the filter changes. If the current brush size is inconvenient for you, use a different size.

8. If you make any errors while you paint, click the **Thaw Mask Tool** and paint over your mistakes to erase them, and then click the **Freeze Mask Tool** and continue painting. When you have finished applying the mask, your image should resemble Figure 5-36.

| Figure 5-36 | **Masked area in Liquify dialog box** |

You are now ready to liquify the unmasked parts of your image.

9. On the Tools panel of the Liquify dialog box, click the **Forward Warp Tool** , set the brush size to **20**, point to the upper-left side of the image, and then drag the mouse pointer to the right.

    The part of the image beneath the pointer is dragged to the right, as if it is made of putty. Notice that the warp has even uncovered part of the background, which is made up of transparent pixels. To correct this warp, you can use the Reconstruct Tool.

10. Click the **Reconstruct Tool** , and then drag to paint over the warp you just created. Continue to drag until the image returns to its original state. The Reconstruct Tool works in much the same way the History Brush Tool works. The history state you are reverting to is the state the image was in when you issued the Liquify command.

11. Click the **Twirl Clockwise Tool** 🌀, and set the Brush Size to **80**.

12. Point to the upper-left corner of the image, and press and hold the mouse button. Look carefully inside the pointer: The image beneath the pointer has become a whirlpool, and is rotating clockwise.

13. Drag the pointer over the image, and watch the distortions take shape.

14. Continue to experiment with the different Liquify options by clicking different Liquify Tools. If you are dissatisfied with a result, use the Reconstruct Tool.

15. Click the **OK** button to liquify your image, and then deselect the squash. Unhide the **Boo!** layer. See Figure 5-37.

TIP

Any transparent pixels you uncover will be white on the canvas.

| Figure 5-37 | Liquified image |

unmasked areas have been liquified

squash is unaffected by Liquify filter

The area surrounding the squash has an impressionistic, painted effect, but the squash itself is unchanged by the filter because you masked it.

16. Save Liquify.psd, and then close it.

Working with the Filter Gallery

The Filter Gallery includes nearly 50 filters that you can apply to an image. The filters can provide artistic effects—for example, turning your image into a colored pencil drawing or pastel painting, or distortions—making your image appear to glow or to be covered by a pane of glass. Figure 5-38 shows just a few of the effects you can achieve with filters from the gallery. All of the filters have been applied to the same image.

Figure 5-38 **Four different filters applied to same image**

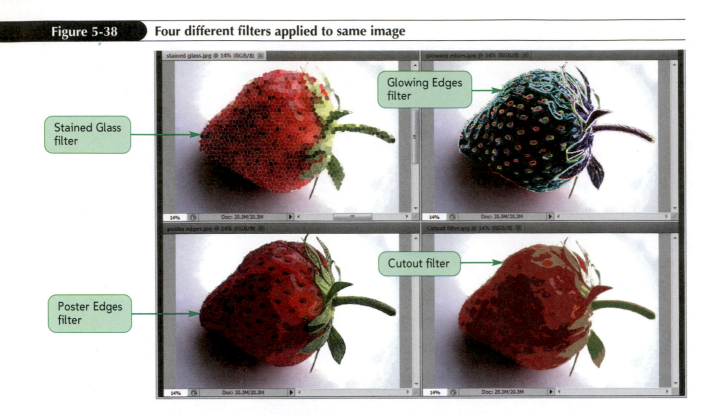

The Filter Gallery includes six categories of filter: Artistic, Brush Strokes, Distort, Sketch, Stylize, and Texture. Some filters, like the Sketch filters, use the current foreground and background colors to produce an effect. In addition, each filter has its own custom settings, which you can manipulate on the right side of the dialog box. You can also combine filters for unique effects by clicking the New effect layer icon at the bottom of the dialog box, or you can delete an effect by clicking the Delete effect layer icon. As you make changes to the filter or include additional filters, you can preview everything in the left pane of the dialog box. To see more or less of the image, you can click the Zoom Out or Zoom In icons at the bottom of the dialog box or type a zoom percentage. You can also pan the image by dragging the scroll box at the bottom of the preview area.

To use the Filter Gallery:

1. Open **EggplantBeans.jpg** from the Photoshop5\Tutorial folder. Reset the default foreground and background colors.

2. Use your choice of selection tools to select the eggplant and the eggplant stem in the image.

3. Click the **Channels** tab to display the Channels panel, and if necessary, collapse the Adjustments panel group.

4. On the Application bar, click **Select**, click **Save Selection**, type **Eggplant** in the Name box in the Save Selection dialog box, and then click the **OK** button. Photoshop adds the selection as an alpha channel on the Channels panel. Notice that the eggplant appears white on the channel thumbnail, and the rest of the image is black. This indicates that everything in the image except the eggplant is masked.

5. Click to the left of the Eggplant mask thumbnail so an Eye icon appears. Photoshop paints the masked area directly on the image using a translucent shade of red. See Figure 5-39.

Figure 5-39   **Showing the mask on the image**

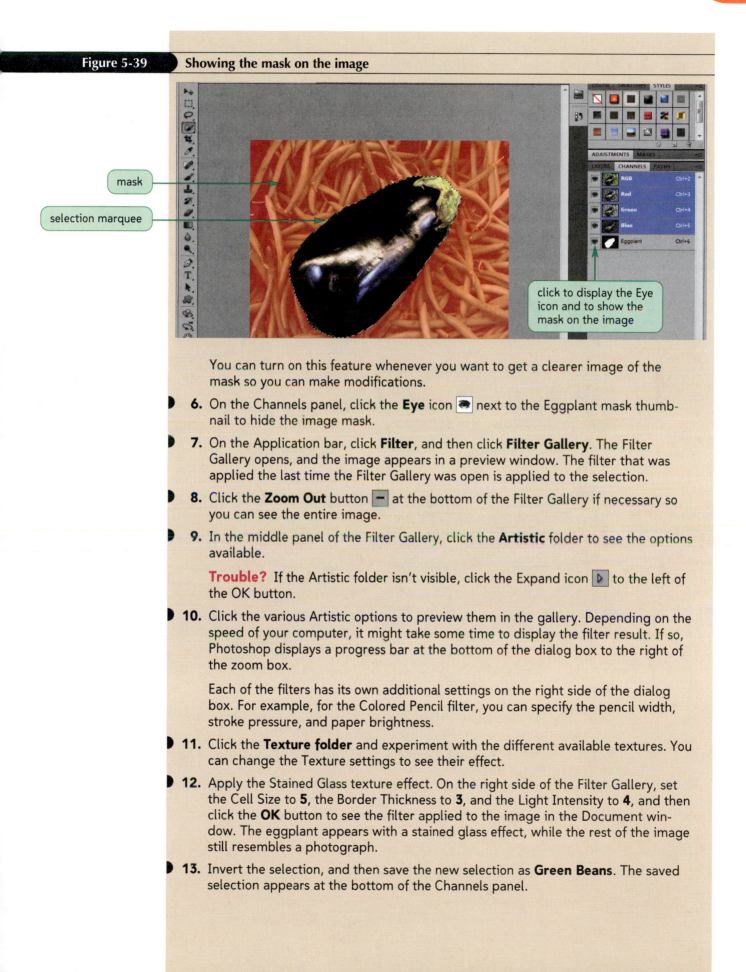

mask

selection marquee

click to display the Eye icon and to show the mask on the image

You can turn on this feature whenever you want to get a clearer image of the mask so you can make modifications.

6. On the Channels panel, click the **Eye** icon 👁 next to the Eggplant mask thumbnail to hide the image mask.

7. On the Application bar, click **Filter**, and then click **Filter Gallery**. The Filter Gallery opens, and the image appears in a preview window. The filter that was applied the last time the Filter Gallery was open is applied to the selection.

8. Click the **Zoom Out** button ➖ at the bottom of the Filter Gallery if necessary so you can see the entire image.

9. In the middle panel of the Filter Gallery, click the **Artistic** folder to see the options available.

   Trouble? If the Artistic folder isn't visible, click the Expand icon ▷ to the left of the OK button.

10. Click the various Artistic options to preview them in the gallery. Depending on the speed of your computer, it might take some time to display the filter result. If so, Photoshop displays a progress bar at the bottom of the dialog box to the right of the zoom box.

    Each of the filters has its own additional settings on the right side of the dialog box. For example, for the Colored Pencil filter, you can specify the pencil width, stroke pressure, and paper brightness.

11. Click the **Texture folder** and experiment with the different available textures. You can change the Texture settings to see their effect.

12. Apply the Stained Glass texture effect. On the right side of the Filter Gallery, set the Cell Size to **5**, the Border Thickness to **3**, and the Light Intensity to **4**, and then click the **OK** button to see the filter applied to the image in the Document window. The eggplant appears with a stained glass effect, while the rest of the image still resembles a photograph.

13. Invert the selection, and then save the new selection as **Green Beans**. The saved selection appears at the bottom of the Channels panel.

14. Open the Filter Gallery. Photoshop applies the Stained Glass effect to the new selection because the Filter Gallery keeps the settings of the previous filter. You'll change the effect.

> **Trouble?** If Photoshop applies a stained glass effect to the rest of the image without opening the gallery, you have selected the wrong Filter Gallery command. Photoshop lists your most recent filter command at the top of the menu. Selecting it will just apply the same settings to the new selection. Undo the change, and then click the Filter Gallery command that is followed by ellipses (...).

15. In the Filter Gallery, select the **Ocean Ripple** filter in the Distort folder. Set the Ripple Size to **2**, set the Ripple Magnitude to **10**. See Figure 5-40.

Figure 5-40   **Image with two filters applied**

Ocean Ripple filter

Stained Glass filter applied to eggplant

Stained Glass filter

set ripple size and magnitude

Ocean Ripple filter applied to beans

16. Click the **OK** button to close the Filter Gallery.

You used selection masks, the Channels panel, and two filter effects to change a photograph into a completely different composition.

17. Save the file as **EggplantFilters.psd** in the Photoshop5\Tutorial folder, close the file, and exit Photoshop.

In this session, you learned how to use the Lasso Tools and the Quick Selection Tool to make selections. You learned how to save selections on the Channels panel and how to load selections to reuse them. You experimented with fills, including the Content-Aware fill, and you learned how to work with filters, including the Liquify filter and some of the filters in the Filter Gallery.

REVIEW

Session 5.2 Quick Check

1. Which tool lets you drag on the canvas to create a free-form selection marquee?
2. The _____ fill feature lets you remove objects from an image and replace them with randomly generated versions of surrounding pixels.
3. What are fastening points?
4. True or False. Photoshop stores saved selections on the Layers panel.
5. The _____ Selection Tool works well if you want to select an area of an image with clearly defined edges.
6. To reuse a selection that you have saved, use the _____ Selection command on the _____ menu.
7. To select the unselected pixels in your image, use the _____ command on the Select menu.
8. Use the _____ Mask Tool in the Liquify dialog box to paint a mask on the part of an image you want to protect.

Practice the skills you learned in the tutorial using the same case scenario.

PRACTICE

Review Assignments

Data Files needed for the Review Assignments: 3Pears.psd

Azar would like to include images in this year's annual report that emphasize his message that Food for Change not only unites urban and suburban youth, but also encourages cross-cultural understanding. He has given you an image of three pears, and wants you to modify it so each pear has a different effect or filter, representing the variety of youth his program serves. Complete the following steps:

1. Start Photoshop while pressing the Ctrl+Alt+Shift keys. When you are prompted to delete the Adobe Photoshop Settings File, click Yes. On the Application bar, right-click Essentials, and then click Reset Essentials to reset the default Essentials workspace layout.

2. Open **3Pears.psd**, located in the Photoshop5\Review folder provided with your Data Files.

3. Select the Background layer, and then select the first pear in the image, using the Elliptical Marquee Tool with a fixed size of 150 pixels by 200 pixels. Then, use the Quick Selection Tool to select the whole pear. Make sure to include the stem when you make your selection. (*Hint*: You might need to change the default brush size of the Quick Selection Tool.)

4. Save the selection as **Pear1**, and then deselect the pear.

5. Select the second pear and stem, but don't select the dark shadow of the first pear that falls on the second pear. Save the selection as **Pear2**, and then deselect the pear.

6. Select the third pear and stem, but not the dark shadow of the second pear on the third pear. Save the selection as **Pear3**.

7. Load the Pear1 selection, add a new solid color fill layer, and add a red color fill at 50% opacity.

8. Open the History panel and take a snapshot of the current file.

9. Apply a Liquify filter to the second pear using the Pear2 selection. (*Hint*: Make sure to select the Background layer first. Try the Twirl Clockwise Tool with a brush size of 25, a brush density of 90, a brush pressure of 100, and a brush rate of 100.)

10. Load the Pear3 selection, and apply the Glass Filter with a Frosted Texture, a Distortion setting of 4, a Smoothness setting of 1, and a 150% Scaling setting, and then add a color fill to the selection with a color setting of R=0, G=255, B=204 and a 10% opacity.

11. Save the file as **Diversity.psd** in the Photoshop5\Review folder.

12. Revert the file to the snapshot you took in Step 8, then save the file as **RedPear.psd** in the same folder.

13. Load both the Pear1 and Pear2 selections. (*Hint*: When loading the second selection, make sure to select the Add to Selection option button in the Load Selection dialog box.) Then add to the combined selection by selecting the Pear1 shadow that falls on Pear2.

14. Make the background color on the Tools panel black, and then copy the selection to the Clipboard.

15. Create a new file using the Default Photoshop Size preset, select the Background Color as the Background Contents, and then click the OK button.

16. Paste the Clipboard contents into the new file, and drag the two pears to the bottom of the canvas so the left pear rests along the bottom edge.

17. Using Myriad Pro 30 pt font in white, add the text **Our Pears Are a Work of Art** to the top of the canvas.

18. Save the file as **ArtPears.psd** in the Photoshop5\Review folder, and then close the file.

Use your skills to select parts of an image to create interesting effects.

APPLY

Case Problem 1

Data Files needed for this Case Problem: Greece.jpg, Marlin.jpg

Lake Shares Shirley Beaghan is the marketing director for Lake Shares, an online time-share company specializing in waterfront properties. She wants you to take two images shot on a beach in Greece and combine them to create a whimsical image for the Web site. You'll use selection tools and filter effects. Complete the following steps:

1. Start Photoshop while pressing the Ctrl+Alt+Shift keys. When you are prompted to delete the Adobe Photoshop Settings File, click Yes. On the Application bar, right-click Essentials, and then click Reset Essentials to reset the default Essentials work-space layout.

2. Open **Greece.jpg** and **Marlin.jpg** located in the Photoshop5\Case1 folder provided with your Data Files.

3. Select the marlin and copy it to the Clipboard and then, using Figure 5-41 as a guide, paste it into the Greece image four times. Resize and reposition three of the copies of the marlin so they appear to be jumping out of the water beyond the beach umbrella.

Figure 5-41   **Sample Case Problem 1 solution**

4. Reposition the fourth copy of the marlin above the umbrella, and transform and rotate it so it is slightly larger than the fish in the water and appears to be jumping into the photograph from the right side of the image.

5. Open the Liquify dialog box, use the Mask All button under Mask Options to mask the entire image, and then thaw the part of the mask that covers the canvas of the umbrella. (*Hint*: Remember that if you thaw outside the lines of the umbrella, you can use the Freeze Mask Tool.)

6. Apply any of the Liquify filters to the umbrella.

7. Use the Color Range command to select the water, and add a bright green color fill layer to the selection. Make sure to lower the opacity so some of the texture of the water shows through.

8. Select the sky above the cloud line and change its color and opacity.
9. Apply any other effects to other parts of the image, and then save the image as **BeachShow.psd** in the Photoshop5\Case1 folder.

Using Figure 5-42 as a guide, combine images in a single composition.

CREATE

Case Problem 2

Data Files needed for this Case Problem: Pot1.jpg, Pot2.jpg, Pot3.jpg, Pot4.jpg

PierCeramics   You are the owner of PierCeramics, a ceramics studio on Sanibel Island in Florida. You have many photographs of your work, and think you might be able to turn those photographs into digital art to sell along with your pottery. You'll experiment with selections, filters, and effects using four photographs of your pottery. Complete the following steps:

1. Start Photoshop while pressing the Ctrl+Alt+Shift keys. When you are prompted to delete the Adobe Photoshop Settings File, click Yes. On the Application bar, right-click Essentials, and then click Reset Essentials to reset the default Essentials workspace layout.
2. Create a new file with a custom canvas size of 13 inches wide and 10 inches high with a resolution of 72 ppi, using the RGB color mode.
3. Open **Pot1.jpg**, **Pot2.jpg**, **Pot3.jpg**, and **Pot4.jpg** located in the Photoshop5\Case2 folder provided with your Data Files.
4. Using Figure 5-42 as a guide, select and paste a copy of each pot into the new file. Use the Move Tool to move the pots where you want them in the composition, and create a background effect that you like using Color Fill and/or Pattern Fill layers.

| Figure 5-42 | Sample Case Problem 2 solution |

5. Take a snapshot of the file with the four pots, and rename the snapshot **No filters**.
6. Duplicate each pot, and apply a filter to the duplicate.

7. Apply a different filter to each pot, but leave the copies of the original pots unchanged. In Figure 5-42, the pot on the top has two filters applied, one for the exterior, and one for the interior (the opening at the top), and the original, unretouched pot appears behind it.

8. Take a snapshot of the current state on the History panel.

9. Save the file as **FilterPots.psd** in the Photoshop5\Case2 folder.

10. Hide the background effects you added so the pots appear in front of transparent pixels, and create a new document based on the current History state. (*Hint*: Use the Create new document from current state icon at the bottom of the History panel.)

11. Flatten the new document image and discard the hidden layers. Save the new file as **NoBackground.psd**, and then close the file.

12. Return to the state you recorded in the snapshot in Step 8, and then save FilterPots.psd in the Photoshop5\Case2 folder and close it.

Extend your skills to transform images for a bookstore.

CHALLENGE

Case Problem 3

There are no Data Files needed for this Case Problem.

GoBooks   Gary Smith is the owner of a small bookstore in Shawano, Wisconsin. He has asked for your help in developing a poster for the storefront window for the month of January that shows that books can take you anywhere—even when you're snowed in. Your focus for the first poster is children's books. You'll use one landscape image from the Web, and at least three additional images to create the poster. Complete the following steps:

1. Start Photoshop while pressing the Ctrl+Alt+Shift keys. When you are prompted to delete the Adobe Photoshop Settings File, click Yes. On the Application bar, right-click Essentials, and then click Reset Essentials to reset the default Essentials workspace layout.

2. Go to *www.morguefile.com* and search for a landscape or cityscape with which you would like to work. You'll be adding filters and effects to change a real landscape into a storybook landscape. Before you download any images, check the licensing information to make sure that they can be remixed without attribution and used for commercial purposes. Download the landscape image you have chosen.

3. At *www.morguefile.com*, find images of at least two "characters" for your poster. Your characters can be animals, insects, plants, statues, tea pots—whatever you feel comfortable working with. Download the character images you have chosen.

4. Confirm that all of the images you have downloaded are the same resolution before you combine them. If they aren't, change their resolution before combining the files.

5. Using WordPad, which is available from the Accessories menu of the All Programs menu in Windows 7, create a new document and keep a record of the steps you take to create the final image. You don't need to record steps that you later undo. Save the document as **Process.rtf** in the Photoshop5\Case3 folder.

6. Using the skills you learned in this tutorial, create a composition that you think would catch a customer's eye. The focus of this exercise is to mix realistic photographic images with images that have been altered to look painted or computer-generated. Use selection tools, filters, fills, and the drawing tools for your composition. Use the Brush Tools and the History Brush Tool to refine your work.

⊕ **EXPLORE**

7. In any font, add a headline to the poster that reads **Go Books Go Anywhere**.

8. Warp the title text. To do so, click the Create warped text icon on the options bar, and then click a Style setting such as Bulge.

EXPLORE 9. Transform or warp at least one of the characters you place in the landscape, either by resizing, rotating, or warping it. (*Hint*: To warp a selection, make an initial selection, click Select on the Application bar, and then click Transform Selection. On the options bar, click the Switch between free transform and warp modes button. When you are in warp mode, warp the selection by dragging one of the handles on the selection.)

EXPLORE 10. Use Puppet Warp to change the position of the limbs of one of your characters. (*Hint*: On the Application bar, click Edit, and then click Puppet Warp to add pins to one of the animals or objects in the poster and manipulate them. For example, click to place pins in knee joints or elbows, and then drag to warp the limb.) In Figure 5-43, the zebra's legs have been manipulated with the Puppet Warp feature.

| Figure 5-43 | Sample Case Problem 3 solution |

11. Save Process.rtf in the Photoshop5\Case 3 folder.
12. Save the file as **GoBooks.psd** in the Photoshop5\Case3 folder, and exit Photoshop.

Using Figure 5-44 as a guide, apply multiple filters to an image.

CREATE

Case Problem 4

Data Files needed for this Case Problem: Smile.jpg

DBF Dental   Aisha Gomez is the marketing manager for DBF Dental, a dental supply company in Chicago, Illinois. The company's customer base includes dentists and orthodontists in Iowa, Wisconsin, Indiana, and Minnesota. Recently, another dental supply company has moved into the area. However, there have been reports of inferior products from some of your former customers who switched suppliers. Aisha wants you to develop a new campaign that addresses this issue and tries to win back the customers. You'll comp an image that uses humor to address the problem. Complete the following steps:

1. Start Photoshop while pressing the Ctrl+Alt+Shift keys. When you are prompted to delete the Adobe Photoshop Settings File, click Yes. On the Application bar, right-click Essentials, and then click Reset Essentials to reset the default Essentials workspace layout.
2. Open **Smile.jpg** from the Photoshop5\Case4 folder.

3. Go to www.morguefile.com or www.creativecommons.org, and search for any other image files you think you might need, such as the kinds of tools shown in the example in Figure 5-44. Before you download any images, check the licensing information to make sure that they can be remixed without attribution and used for commercial purposes.

4. Create a new file with a background color of your choosing, and place any tool images that you downloaded on the canvas.

5. Comp an image that uses the unexpected or the humorous to get your point across, as shown in the example in Figure 5-44.

Figure 5-44   **Sample Case Problem 4 solution**

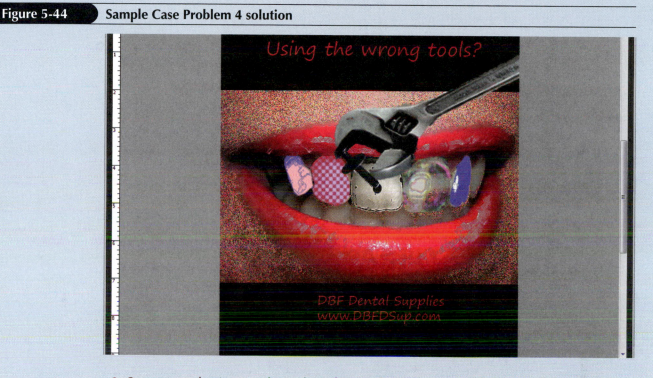

6. Save your selections as channels and name them. For example, save each tooth as its own selection.

7. Save at least two layer comps that show different ideas or arrangements. If you want to comp different filter effects for the same selection, make sure to apply the effect to its own layer so you can turn it on and off.

8. When you have finished editing the file, save it as **DBFDental.psd** in the Photoshop5\Case4 folder.

ENDING DATA FILES

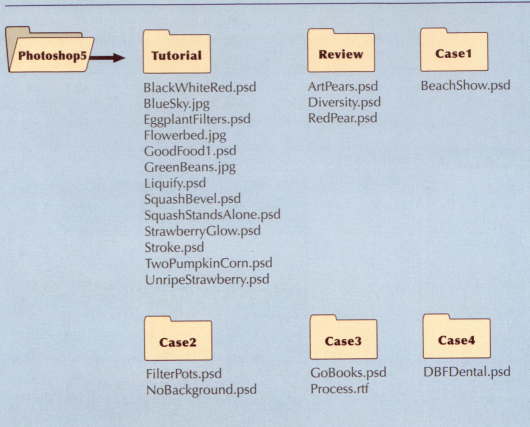

Photoshop5 ➔ **Tutorial**

BlackWhiteRed.psd
BlueSky.jpg
EggplantFilters.psd
Flowerbed.jpg
GoodFood1.psd
GreenBeans.jpg
Liquify.psd
SquashBevel.psd
SquashStandsAlone.psd
StrawberryGlow.psd
Stroke.psd
TwoPumpkinCorn.psd
UnripeStrawberry.psd

Review

ArtPears.psd
Diversity.psd
RedPear.psd

Case1

BeachShow.psd

Case2

FilterPots.psd
NoBackground.psd

Case3

GoBooks.psd
Process.rtf

Case4

DBFDental.psd

TUTORIAL 6

OBJECTIVES

Session 6.1
- Work with text layers and the Type Tools
- Use the Design workspace to enter and modify point type and paragraph type
- Assign fonts and other text formats
- Work with vertical text
- Check spelling, and find and replace text

Session 6.2
- Apply a style to text
- Set tracking and scaling for individual characters
- Specify a baseline shift
- Bend text to a closed path
- Apply a clipping mask to fill text with an image, pattern, and gradient

Designing with Text

Using Text and Text Effects

Case | RC Investments

You have taken a summer internship with a small investment firm called RC Investments, which was founded in 1979 by Rhiann Clarke's father, Richard. In 2009, Rhiann took over the company, which helps middle income people manage their assets by developing an investment strategy best suited to their needs. Rhiann was the sole employee when she took over the firm, but word of mouth has helped her grow the firm to five investment professionals. She has asked you to create a marketing campaign to help her increase the firm's client base. You'll use the Photoshop Design workspace and many of the text tools and features to create comps that you'll present to her for the proposed campaign. You'll add text to images and modify text fonts; you'll also adjust the scaling and tracking, alignment, and rotation of text. Finally, you'll apply styles to text, and fill text with images, gradients, and color.

STARTING DATA FILES

Photoshop6 →

Tutorial

Money.psd
RCPath.psd
RCVertical.tif
RightChoicePlace.psd
RightChoiceStart.psd

Review

RCRetire.jpg

Case1

Fireworks.jpg
Shuttle.jpg

Case2

Gourmet.jpg

Case3

Luxury.jpg

Case4

Soccer.jpg

SESSION 6.1 VISUAL OVERVIEW

Use settings on the Paragraph panel to align text at the left, right, or center edges of a text bounding box.

A **point**, abbreviated as pt, is 1/72 of an inch.

The Hyphenate setting determines whether a word breaks across two lines.

To add interest to the copy in a composition, you can apply effects to the text; for example, this text is outlined by a black stroke.

You can format text in a variety of ways, including all caps and italic.

TEXT LAYERS AND PANELS

The Design workspace displays panels, such as the Character and Paragraph panels, that are useful for working with text.

You can specify font family and font style on the Character panel.

Left-aligned text lines up at the left edge of the text box you draw with the Horizontal Type Tool.

To fine-tune the appearance of text, adjust the **tracking**, which is the spacing between all of the characters in selected text or a paragraph.

The **font size** is the height of the text measured in points.

For more control, you can modify the **kerning**, which is the spacing between a pair of characters.

Quickly apply text styles by clicking a style button.

Scale text vertically or horizontally by changing the percentage settings.

You can **center-align** text in a paragraph so that each line of text is balanced on an imaginary vertical line through the center of the bounding box.

Text in Photoshop is stored on **text layers**.

Text effects change the appearance of text and are listed on the Layers panel grouped with the layer to which they apply.

Introducing Text Layers

Photoshop is first and foremost a digital image-editing tool, but it also provides a variety of text tools that let you format and arrange text in a document in much the same way you would format text in a page layout application. As a result, you can be confident that when you do need to add text to an image, you can achieve the full effect you want using Photoshop. When you add text to a Photoshop image, it is added as a vector object. This means that you can resize it, rotate it, stretch it, change its color, or apply a style to it without affecting its resolution. You can also stroke vector text to add an outline that makes it stand out. However, if you want to use the full set of image-editing tools available in Photoshop, you need to rasterize text to change it to a bitmap object. This gives you the flexibility to fill the text with an image, apply filters, and use other image-editing features; however, once you rasterize text, you can no longer edit it as text.

The Photoshop interface uses the terms *text* and *type* interchangeably. The tools you use to add text are called **Type Tools**, but text is stored on text layers. See Figure 6-1.

Figure 6-1	Text layers in a composition

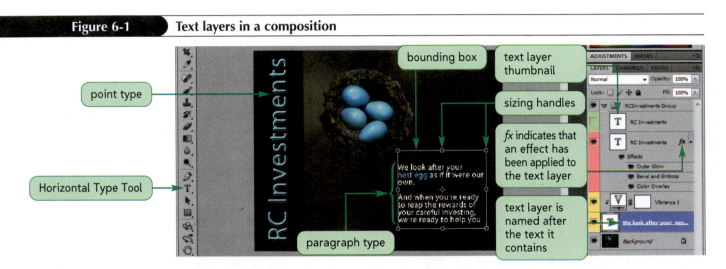

Text layers follow the same hierarchy rules as other layers on the Layers panel. A text layer on the canvas appears on top of any layers that it is on top of on the Layers panel. You can clip adjustments to text layers and set their opacity and blending modes. You can also select text layers, and move, group, copy, and delete them.

A text layer is distinguished on the Layers panel by a Text thumbnail, which is a square with the letter *T* in it. By default, a text layer takes as its name the text that is included on the layer, but you have the option to rename the layer just as you can rename any other layer. When you apply an effect to a text layer, an *fx* appears to the right of the layer name on the Layers panel, and the details of the effect are listed beneath the layer name.

If you show transform controls when a layer is selected, you will see that the text is contained in a bounding box. You can manipulate the bounding box in the same way you manipulate any other object. You can drag a handle to resize it, or use the rotate pointer to rotate it.

Photoshop lets you enter two kinds of text: point type (also called character type) and paragraph type. **Point type** or **character type** is text that you type after selecting one of the Type Tools and clicking directly on the canvas to type. At the point you click, Photoshop adds a **baseline**, which is the line on which the text will rest as you type. The baseline extends with each new character. You can move to a new line by pressing the Enter key, and Photoshop will add a new baseline on the new line. When you have finished entering point type and move to a new task, Photoshop encloses the point type in a bounding box that you can see if you select the layer again and turn on transform controls.

Paragraph type is text that is contained in a bounding box whose dimensions you specify by activating a Type Tool and then clicking on the canvas and dragging. Once you define the dimensions of the bounding box, you can start to type, and the text will appear in the box. As you type, text wraps to a new line when it reaches the border of the bounding box. If you type more text than can fit in the bounding box, it is hidden unless you change the dimensions of the bounding box by dragging a transform control.

After you select a Type Tool, you can use the options bar to define the font, font style, font size, and anti-aliasing method for the text, as well as its alignment. See Figure 6-2.

Figure 6-2	Type Tool options

Icon	Tool	Description
⟨T⟩	Toggle text orientation	Switches between the Horizontal and Vertical Type Tools
Myriad Pro ▼	Set the font family	Lets you choose from and preview a list of fonts installed on your computer; the font name in the box varies depending on the last font selection
Regular ▼	Set the font style	Applies styles such as bold, italic, and bold condensed
T 12 pt ▼	Set the font size	Allows you to select from a list of font sizes or type a custom size in the text box
aa Sharp ▼	Set the anti-aliasing method	Sets the anti-alias method, which determines the smoothness of text; settings include None, Sharp, Crisp, Strong, and Smooth
▤, ▤, ▤	Left align text, Center text, and Right align text	Aligns text within a text bounding box on the canvas
▬	Set the text color button	Opens the Select text color dialog box where you can use the color ramp and color field to select a color or enter color values; the color of this icon varies depending on the last text color selection
⤸	Create warped text	Opens the Warp Text dialog box, where you can apply a style and/or horizontal and vertical distortions
▤	Toggle the Character and Paragraph panels	Toggles between the Character and Paragraph panels

INSIGHT

Using the Design Workspace

When you are working with a lot of text in a composition, you'll find that the Design workspace has many of the tools you'll need. The Design workspace provides character formatting tools on the Character panel and paragraph formatting tools on the Paragraph panel. The Character and Paragraph panels appear in the Design workspace in their own tab group, stacked with some of the panels you are already familiar with, including Swatches, Styles, Layers, and Channels. You can switch between the Character and Paragraph panels depending on whether you are formatting individual characters, words, or entire paragraphs.

You'll use both point type and paragraph type to work on the compositions you will propose that Rhiann use in the firm's marketing campaign.

Adding and Modifying Point Type

Photoshop lets you add two different kinds of point type: horizontal and vertical. **Horizontal type** flows from left to right along a horizontal line. You create horizontal type using the Horizontal Type Tool on the Tools panel. **Vertical type** runs from top to bottom along a vertical line. You can rotate horizontal type 90 degrees so it has a vertical orientation in your composition, but when you do so, the characters themselves are also rotated 90 degrees. If you want the characters in vertical type to have a horizontal orientation, you need to enter the type using the Vertical Type Tool. See Figure 6-3.

| Figure 6-3 | Horizontal and vertical type |

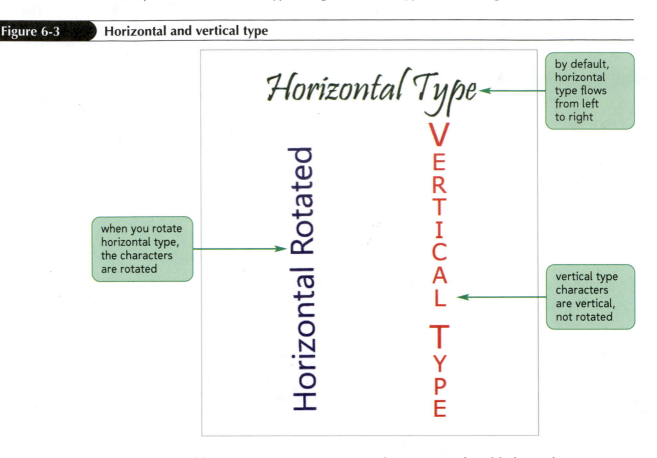

When you add point type, you are in text mode. In **text mode**, a blinking white **cursor**, or vertical line, appears at the end of the text that you type, indicating that you can continue to type with the same settings. A horizontal white baseline also appears under the text as you type. The type rests on that line unless you specify a baseline shift, which you will do later in this tutorial.

Once you add a point type layer, you can modify it. For example, you can change its font, font size, color, or style. Styles include Regular, Italic, Bold, and Bold Italic. If a font family doesn't include a style that you want to apply, you can apply a **faux style**, which is a style generated by Photoshop when an attribute, such as bold, is unavailable in a font family. For example, the Pristina font includes only regular characters. If you want to make a Pristina character bold, you have to use the Faux Bold button on the Character panel to have Photoshop generate a bold version of the character.

REFERENCE

Adding Point Type to an Image

- On the Tools panel, click the Horizontal Type Tool or the Vertical Type Tool.
- On the options bar, specify the font, font style, font size, anti-aliasing method, alignment, and color.
- Click the canvas at the location you want the text to appear, and type the text.
- On the options bar, click the Commit any current edits button.

You'll create a new composition as the basis for the ad you will present to Rhiann, and you'll add point type to it.

To add point type to a new file:

1. Start Photoshop while pressing the **Ctrl+Alt+Shift** keys. When you are prompted to delete the Adobe Photoshop Settings File, click **Yes**. On the Application bar, right-click **Essentials**, click **Reset Essentials** to reset the default Essentials workspace layout, and then reset all of the tools.

2. On the Application bar, click **File**, and then click **New**. Create a new RGB file that is 18 inches wide and 12 inches high, with a resolution of 72 ppi and a white background.

3. On the Application bar, click **File**, and then click **Place**. Navigate to the Photoshop6\Tutorial folder included with your Data Files, and place **RightChoiceStart.psd** on the left side of the composition. Place **RightChoicePlace.psd** on the right side.

4. Display the rulers, and then add vertical guides at 2 inches and 13 ½ inches on the horizontal ruler. Add two horizontal guides at 3 ½ inches and 10 inches on the vertical ruler.

5. On the Tools panel, click the **Horizontal Type Tool** T. The options bar displays settings for the Horizontal Type Tool.

6. On the options bar, click the **Set the font family** arrow Myriad Pro. Photoshop lists the fonts available on your system. To the right of the font name, you can see a preview of the font. See Figure 6-4.

Figure 6-4	Available fonts

Set the font size arrow

Set the font family arrow

font name

Left align text button

vertical guide

preview of the font

horizontal guide

7. On the font family list, click **Pristina**, click the **Set the font size** arrow T 12 pt ▼, click **60 pt**, and then click the **Left align text** button ☰, if necessary. Click the **Set the text color** button ■ to open the Select text color dialog box. The pointer changes to the Eyedropper pointer ✎. Use the pointer to sample the color from one of the lighter feathers on the bird's back, and then click the **OK** button to close the dialog box.

Trouble? If you don't have Pristina, click a different font to select it.

You are now ready to type text that will have the settings you specified.

8. Click at the intersection of the top horizontal guide and the left vertical guide, and type **Who's**. See Figure 6-5.

Figure 6-5 **Adding point type**

Trouble? If your font color doesn't match the figure exactly, don't worry. The idea is to choose a font color that works with the image. If you want the color to match, set the RGB settings as follows: R=205, G=118, B=86.

Because the text is left-aligned, it starts where you clicked with the mouse. Photoshop adds the text on its own layer. Any new text you enter will be added to that text layer after you click the Commit any current edits button ✔, which tells Photoshop that you have finished entering text.

9. Press the **spacebar**, type **watching over**, and then on the right side of the options bar, click the **Commit any current edits** button ✔.

10. Click at the intersection of the lower horizontal guide and the left vertical guide, type **your nest egg?**, and then click the **Commit any current edits** button ✔.

Because you didn't change any of the options on the options bar, the new text has the same formatting and size as the first text you entered.

TIP

You can click the Cancel any current edits button on the options bar to delete the text entry before committing it.

You'll be making a lot of changes to the text you enter in your new composition, so you'll switch to the Design workspace for easy access to tools that let you work with text.

To switch to the Design workspace and modify the point type:

1. On the Application bar, click the **Design** button to display the Design workspace.

2. Expand the **Layers** panel, if necessary. On the Layers panel, double-click the **your nest egg?** text thumbnail ⊤. The text is highlighted on the image. Double-clicking the thumbnail is a quick and efficient way to select the text on a layer.

   You'll change the color of the *your next egg* text so it stands out more than the color you originally assigned.

3. On the Character panel, click the **Color** box, change the color of the text to white by typing RGB values of R=**255**, G=**255**, and B=**255** in the Select text color dialog box, click the **OK** button, and then click the **Commit any current edits** button ✔ on the options bar. The text is now white.

4. On the canvas, double-click within the word **your**. Double-clicking within a word selects it. See Figure 6-6.

Figure 6-6   **Double-clicking a word to select it**

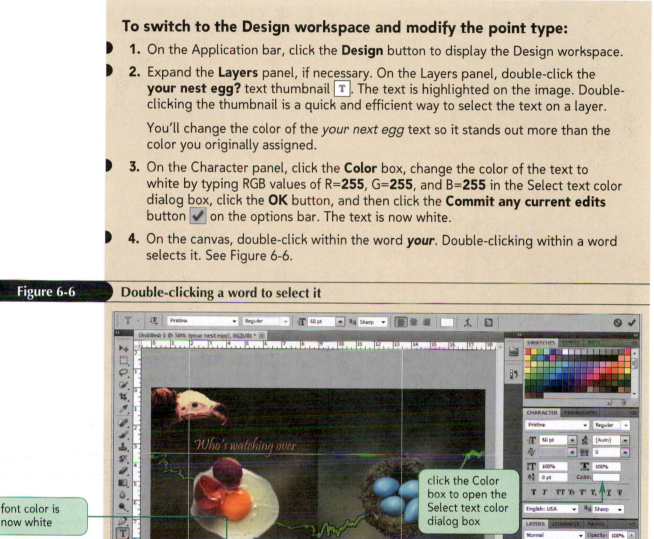

font color is now white

double-clicking within a word selects it

click the Color box to open the Select text color dialog box

When a word is selected, you can edit it by typing new text, or you can change its format using the options bar or the Character panel. See Figure 6-7 for a table of the formatting options available on the Character panel.

Character panel formatting options

Format	Description
Faux Bold	Generates and applies a bold version of the selected character(s)
Faux Italic	Generates and applies an italic version of the selected character(s)
All Caps	Displays selected text in all capital letters
Small Caps	Displays selected text in small capital letters
Superscript	Displays the selected character(s) in superscript, above the baseline
Subscript	Displays the selected character(s) in subscript, below the baseline
Underline	Formats the selected character(s) with a line underneath
Strikethrough	Draws a line through the selected character(s)

5. On the Character panel, click the **Faux Bold** button [T], click the **Underline** button [T], and then click the **Commit any current edits** button [✔]. The word *your* is now underlined and in bold.

6. On the Layers panel, double-click the **Who's watching over** text thumbnail [T] to select the words *Who's watching over*, click the **White** swatch on the Swatches panel to change the text to white, and then click the **Commit any current edits** button [✔].

   You could have also clicked the Color button on the Character panel to select the new color, but the Swatches panel provides an easier way to assign a standard text color because it avoids the dialog box.

You can also use the Character panel to format the text as all caps or small caps. The **all caps** format changes any text you type, whether you type it as uppercase or lowercase, to all capital letters in the current point size. The **small caps** format changes the text you type to all capital letters, but at the same height as the lowercase letters. You'll add some additional text, and then change the formatting of that text to add interest to the composition.

To center text and format it as small caps:

1. At the intersection of the guides above the bird's nest, click to make the insertion point active, and then, on the options bar, click the **Center text** button [▤]. Type **RC Investments**. When the Center text option is selected on the options bar, any text that you type spreads out from the center point, which is the point where you click the mouse. See Figure 6-8.

Figure 6-8   Adding centered point type

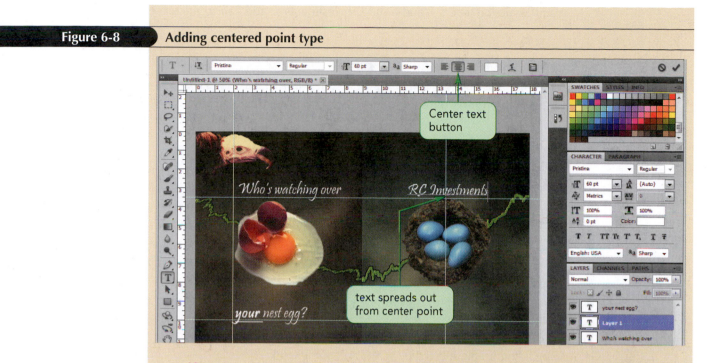

You can use small caps in a layout to add sophistication to your text, or to make it stand out from the other text. You'll apply it to the word *Investments* in the company name.

2. Highlight **Investments** by dragging the mouse over the word. On the Character panel, click the **Small Caps** button Tr, and then click the **Commit any current edits** button ✔. The capital *I* in the word is the same size as the capital *R* and capital *C*. However, the letters you typed as lowercase (*nvestments*) are formatted not as lowercase, but as small capital letters.

3. Using the same settings, type **The Right Choice** beneath the nest at the intersection of the guides, and then click the **Commit any current edits** button ✔.

Scaling Text Using the Character Panel

Using the Character panel, you can also scale text on a text layer. Scaling has an effect similar to changing the font size, but scaling gives you the flexibility to scale width and height separately.

You'll scale the letters *R* and *C* in RC investments to add flair to the text on the canvas.

To scale the RC Investments text:

1. On the Layers panel, select the **RC Investments** layer, select *RC* on the canvas, and then on the Character panel, click in the **Vertically scale** box and type **200**. Click in the **Horizontally scale** box, and type **200**. The selected text is now twice its original height and twice its original width.

2. Click to the right of the letters *RC* and then press the **Enter** key. Photoshop adds a line break, and the *Investments* text moves to a new line below *RC*. Pressing the Enter key while the Text Tool is active adds another line with the same point text settings as the current line. Notice that the *Investments* text is still centered at the vertical guide because the Center text button is still selected on the options bar.

3. Select the *I* in *Investments* and make it **200%** wider and **200%** taller. Select the last *s* in *Investments* and make it **200%** wider and taller, and then click the **Commit any current edits** button.

4. Use the Move Tool to move the *RC Investments* text above the nest, as shown in Figure 6-9.

| Figure 6-9 | Adding a line break, increasing scale, and moving text |

5. Save the file as **RCI.psd** in the Photoshop6\Tutorial folder.

Scaling Text Using the Move Tool

You can also use the Move Tool to scale text using the transform controls. The transform controls, also called selection handles, let you resize contents of the selected layer by dragging. You drag a side control to make the text wider or narrower, and you drag a top or bottom control to make the text taller or shorter. You can maintain the width to height ratio by pressing the Shift key while dragging a corner handle.

Scaling Text Using the Move Tool

- On the Layers panel, select the text layer you want to scale.
- On the Tools panel, select the Move Tool.
- On the options bar, select the Show Transform Controls check box.
- Press and hold the Shift key, and drag a corner handle to scale text uniformly.

or

- Drag any handle to change the size of the text in the direction you drag.
- Press the Enter key, or on the options bar, click the Commit any current edits button.

You'll use the Move Tool and the Shift key to scale the text on the The Right Choice layer uniformly.

To use the Move Tool to scale text:

1. On the Layers panel, select **The Right Choice** layer.

2. Click the **Move Tool** , if necessary, and then on the options bar, select the **Show Transform Controls** check box, if necessary.

3. Press and hold the **Shift** key, and then drag the upper-right transform control up and to the right until you reach the right edge of the canvas. Release the mouse button, and then the Shift key. See Figure 6-10.

| Figure 6-10 | Resizing text by dragging transform controls |

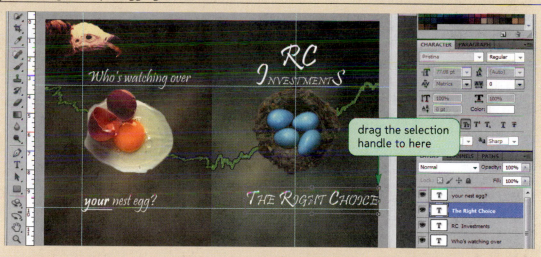

drag the selection handle to here

Trouble? If the text doesn't have similar proportions to Figure 6-10, you released the Shift key before releasing the mouse button. Cancel the transformation by clicking the Cancel any current edits button on the options bar, and then repeat Step 3.

4. Click the **Commit any current edits** button .

5. With the **The Right Choice** layer still selected, move the text so it is centered on the vertical guide.

6. Save the RCI.psd file and close it.

You can also draw attention to the text in a composition by adding it using a vertical orientation, so it is read top to bottom. Next, you'll experiment with adding vertical text to an image Rhiann has given to you.

Working with Vertical Point Type

Using vertical instead of horizontal type is another way to draw attention to a word or words in a composition. Obviously, you wouldn't apply vertical text to entire paragraphs. That would just frustrate your audience. However, a company name or catch phrase running vertically in a composition is an excellent way to make it stand out.

You will create another sample RC Investments ad using vertical type for the company name to add interest to the layout. You'll work with two kinds of vertical text. First, you'll enter horizontal type and rotate it 90 degrees to see if you like that effect. Then, you'll enter text using the Vertical Type Tool, which adds the text from top to bottom.

To rotate horizontal type to a vertical position:

1. Open **RCVertical.tif** from the Photoshop6\Tutorial folder provided with your Data Files, and then save it as **RCDetails.psd** in the same folder.

2. Restore the default foreground and background colors, if necessary, and then switch the foreground and background colors so the foreground color is white and the background color is black.

3. Extend the canvas so you add an additional 2 inches to the left side of the canvas. Use the black background color. (*Hint*: Click the Relative check box and anchor the existing image on the right.) The canvas now includes a 2-inch wide black bar along the left side. This is where you'll place the company name.

4. On the Application bar, click the **Arrange Documents** button ▣▾, and then click **Fit On Screen**.

5. On the Tools panel, click the **Horizontal Type Tool** T, and then use the Character panel to set the font to **Myriad Pro** and the font size to **60 pt**. Click the **Small Caps** button Tr to deselect it. Leave the other settings on the Character panel as they are.

6. On the options bar, click the **Left align text** button ▤, and display the rulers, if necessary.

7. Click the canvas at about 7 inches on the vertical ruler and 1 inch on the horizontal ruler, and then type **RC Investments**. See Figure 6-11.

Figure 6-11   **Entering font settings for horizontal type**

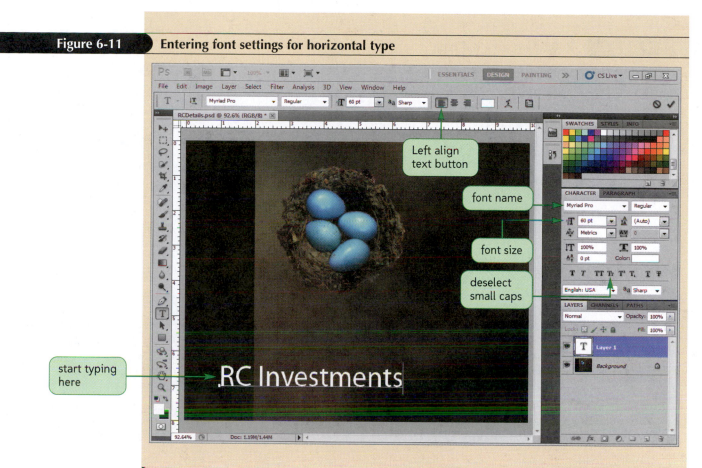

8. Click the **Commit any current edits** button ✔. The text appears along the bottom of the image.

9. Press **V** to activate the Move Tool ▶⊕, show the transform controls if necessary, and then position the mouse pointer near the upper-right transform control so it appears as a curved double-headed arrow ↰.

10. Drag the control up and to the left until the text is at about a 45-degree angle. As you drag, the text rotates counterclockwise. See Figure 6-12.

TIP

Pressing the Shift key while rotating the text constrains the rotation to increments of 15 degrees.

Figure 6-12   **Rotating horizontal type**

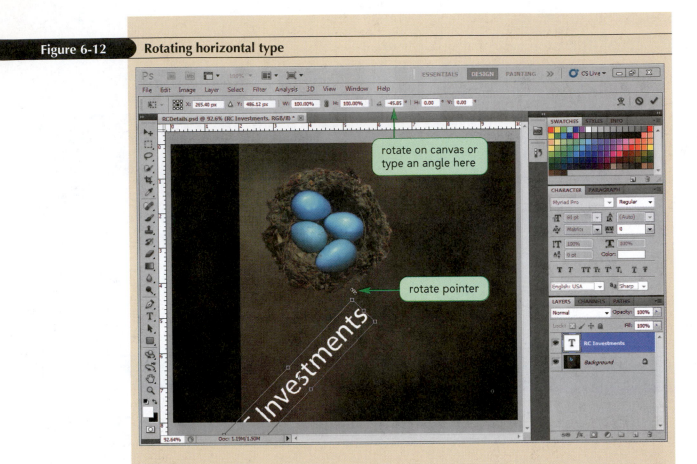

There will be times when you'll want to eyeball an angle of rotation until you're happy with how it looks in the image. However, if you know the angle of rotation that you want, it is easier to type it on the options bar or use the Shift key to rotate in increments.

11. On the options bar, type **-90** in the Set rotation box ⊿ ☐ °.

   Specifying a negative number rotates the text in a counterclockwise direction. Typing a positive number rotates the text in a clockwise direction.

12. On the options bar, click the **Commit any current edits** button ✔, and then drag the text until it appears centered in the black bar.

13. On the options bar, deselect the **Show Transform Controls** check box so you can see the full effect of the text rotation. See Figure 6-13.

Figure 6-13   Horizontal type rotated to vertical position

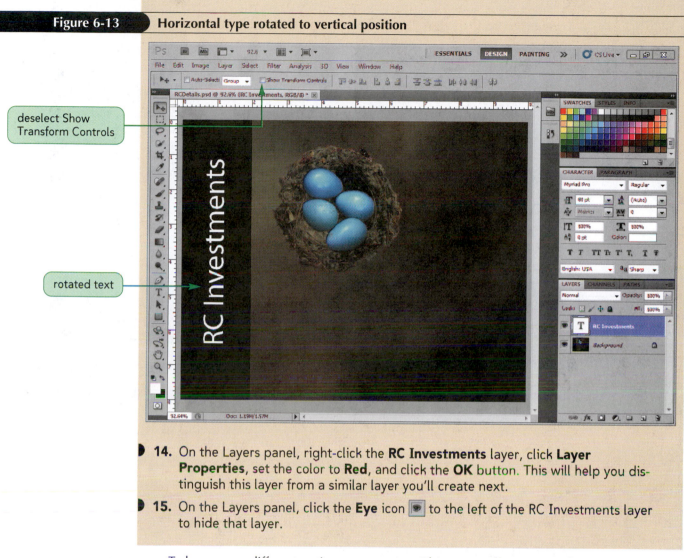

deselect Show Transform Controls

rotated text

14. On the Layers panel, right-click the **RC Investments** layer, click **Layer Properties**, set the color to **Red**, and click the **OK** button. This will help you distinguish this layer from a similar layer you'll create next.

15. On the Layers panel, click the **Eye** icon 👁 to the left of the RC Investments layer to hide that layer.

To have some different options to present to Rhiann, you'll create another RC Investments layer that has vertical text in the black bar, only this time, you'll use the Vertical Type Tool.

To use the Vertical Type Tool to enter vertical type:

1. On the Tools panel, click the **Vertical Type Tool** ↓T.

   Trouble? If you can't find the Vertical Type Tool ↓T, right-click the Horizontal Type Tool T, and then click the Vertical Type Tool ↓T on the list.

2. Click the canvas at about 1 inch on the horizontal ruler and ½ inch on the vertical ruler. On the options bar, click the **Top align text** button ▥, if necessary, set the font size to **48**, and then type **RC Investments**. As you type, Photoshop enters subsequent letters beneath the previous letters, so the text has a vertical orientation. It also centers the letters along a vertical baseline. See Figure 6-14.

Figure 6-14   **Entering vertical type**

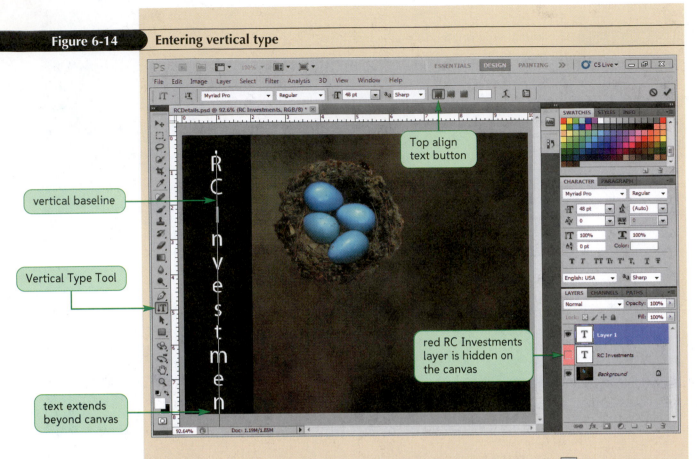

vertical baseline

Vertical Type Tool

text extends beyond canvas

Top align text button

red RC Investments layer is hidden on the canvas

3. On the options bar, click the **Commit any current edits** button ✔.

Notice that the text has extended beyond the canvas. You'll adjust the tracking of the text to fix this problem.

Adjusting the Tracking of Vertical Text

In Photoshop, you can modify text tracking, which is the spacing between characters. The settings on the Character panel allow you to increase or decrease the spacing between the characters in selected text.

The RC Investments text is too spread out, so you will adjust the tracking so it all fits on the canvas. You'll also adjust the scaling of one of the characters so the characters line up better vertically.

To adjust the tracking and the scaling of the RC Investments text:

1. On the Layers panel, right-click the new **RC Investments** layer, click **Layer Properties**, set the color to **Green**, and click the **OK** button.

2. Double-click the **green RC Investments** text thumbnail T, and then on the Character panel, click in the **Set the tracking for the selected characters** box AV, select any existing value, and type **-170**. All of the characters now fit on the canvas, but the result still isn't satisfactory because it appears as if there is no space between *RC* and *Investments*.

3. Select the *C* and the *I*, and then on the Character panel, click in the **Set the tracking for the selected characters** box [AV], highlight -**170**, and then type **100**. There is now more space between the words, but the text flows off the page again.

4. Select all of the text, and then, in the Set the font size box [T] on the Character panel, type **40** to decrease the font size to 40 points. The text now fits on the canvas, but the letter *m* seems out of place because it's much wider than the other letters in *Investments*.

5. Select the *m*, and then on the Character panel, type **75** in the Horizontally scale box [T] to make it narrower, and then commit the change.

   The text still needs work because the *I* in *Investments* is now too far from the *n*. You'll adjust the tracking between the *I* and the *n*.

6. Select the letters *In* within the word *Investments*, click the **Set the tracking for the selected characters** box [AV] arrow, and then click -**100**. The *I* and the *n* move closer together. Commit the change.

7. If necessary, use the Move Tool to drag the text layer so it is centered in the black bar, as shown in Figure 6-15.

Figure 6-15	Centering the vertical text

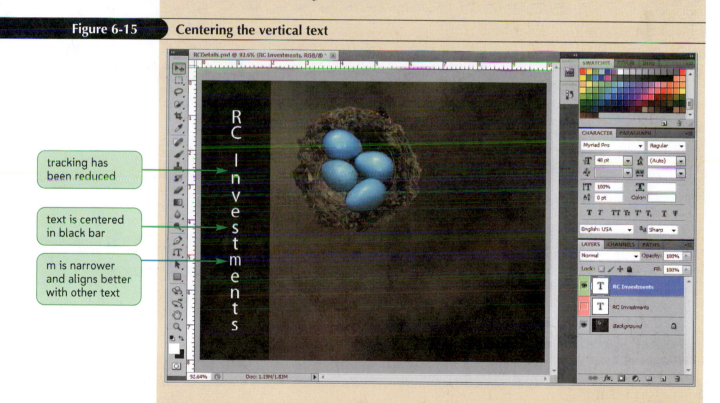

tracking has been reduced

text is centered in black bar

m is narrower and aligns better with other text

8. Hide the green RC Investments layer, and display and select the **red RC Investments** layer. On the canvas, select the *RC Investments* text.

9. On the Character panel, increase the vertical scale of the RC Investments text to **130%**, and increase the tracking to **60**. See Figure 6-16.

Figure 6-16 Centering the vertical text

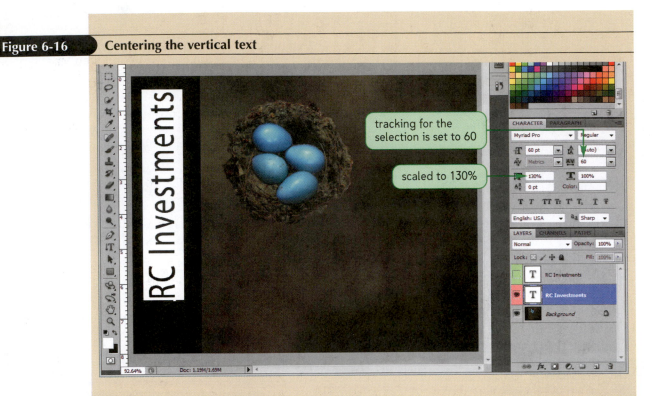

10. Commit the change, and then open the Layer comps panel, and save the current view as a new layer comp called **Rotated**. Base it on Visibility and Position.

11. Hide the red RC Investments layer, display the **green RC Investments** layer, and save the current view as a new layer comp called **Vertical**, based on Visibility and Position. Minimize the Layer Comps panel group.

12. Save RCDetails.psd, and leave the file open.

Working with Paragraphs

You can also work with paragraphs in a Photoshop composition. Paragraph text lets you predefine the size of the text box before you type, which is often essential when you are working with a fixed layout. To create paragraph text, click the Horizontal Type Tool, and then drag on the canvas to create the bounding box that will hold the text. When you first enter it, Paragraph text behaves differently than point text. For example, if you type beyond the edges of the bounding box, the text will not appear, although as you'll see in the following steps, it's still being recorded by Photoshop.

REFERENCE

Adding Paragraph Text

- On the Tools panel, select the Horizontal Type Tool, and on the options bar, specify the formatting options for the paragraph text.
- Click on the canvas, and drag to create a bounding box to hold the paragraph.
- Click in the bounding box, and type the text.
- When finished entering text, click the Commit any current edits button on the options bar.

To enter paragraph type in a bounding box:

1. Position guides at 1 inch and 3 inches on the vertical ruler and 6 ½ inches and 9 inches on the horizontal ruler.

2. On the Layers panel, click the **Background** layer, and then on the Tools panel, click the **Horizontal Type Tool** T , and reset all of the tools.

3. Click the canvas at the upper-left intersection of the guides, and then drag a bounding box down to the 3-inch mark on the vertical ruler and over to the 9-inch mark, as shown in Figure 6-17.

Figure 6-17 | **Creating a bounding box**

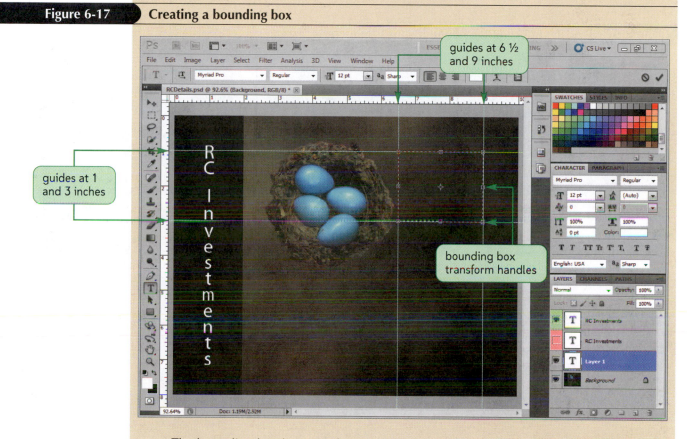

The bounding box has transform handles like other objects in Photoshop. An insertion point appears in the upper-left corner of the bounding box, although it might be difficult to see.

Trouble? If your bounding box doesn't fit in the guides exactly, press the Escape key and repeat Step 3. If it still doesn't fit the guides, your text might wrap differently than the text shown in the figures.

4. On the Character panel, set the font to **Myriad Pro**, if necessary, click the **Set the font size** arrow T 12 pt , and then click **18 pt**. If necessary, set the vertical scale to **100**.

5. On the Swatches panel, click the **Pure Yellow Green** swatch. The Color box on the Character panel displays the new color.

Trouble? If you can't find the Pure Yellow Green swatch, click any bright green swatch on the panel.

6. Type **At RC Investments, we have your best interests at heart.** As you type, notice that the text wraps to fit in the bounding box you drew.

7. Press the **spacebar**, and then type **Your nest egg is our nest egg, and your child's future is our future as well.**

8. Press the **Enter** key. Pressing the Enter key starts a new paragraph and moves the cursor to a new line, just as it does in a word-processing program.

9. Type **Come to us for guidance on your best options for** in the bounding box. The word *guidance* is hyphenated, and the rest of the text is hidden. See Figure 6-18.

Figure 6-18   **Text beyond the bounding box is hidden**

Trouble? If your text wraps differently, or fits the text box differently, don't worry. If there is even a slight difference in the size of the bounding box, line breaks will vary.

When you enter point type, the bounding box expands to fit the text as you add it to the canvas. However, with paragraph type, the text you type must fit in the bounding box to show up on the canvas. To display more text, you need to change the size of the bounding box.

10. Position the mouse pointer over the center bottom handle of the bounding box, and then drag the handle down to about the 6-inch mark on the vertical ruler. The rest of the text that you typed is now visible.

You'll continue to type, and will intentionally misspell the word *education* as *edcuation* so you can correct it when you check spelling later.

11. Type **edcuation savings accounts, individual retirement accounts, and more.**

12. On the Application bar, click **View**, point to **Show**, and then click **Guides** to hide the guides. Select all of the text and change the font to **20 pt**, and then commit the change. See Figure 6-19.

Figure 6-19   **Paragraph text after the bounding box has been extended**

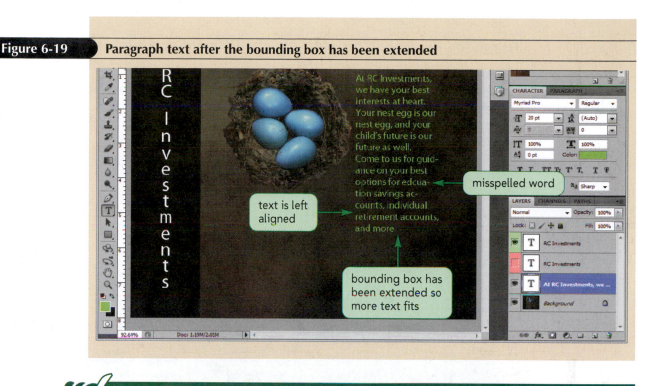

Decision Making: Knowing When to Justify

When formatting paragraph text, you can choose to left-align, right-align, center, or justify it. When you left-align a paragraph, text appears **flush left**, or straight along the left margin, and has a ragged right edge, like the paragraphs in this book. In Photoshop, and in word-processing programs, text is left-justified by default. When you right-align text, it appears **flush right** along the right margin, and has a ragged left edge. When you center text, both the left and right edges are ragged, and each line is centered, resulting in lines of different lengths. When you **justify** text, it is aligned flush along both the left and the right margins. This gives your paragraphs neat, symmetrical margins, but it can introduce other problems, such as loose or tight lines. In a **loose line**, text is so spread out that it is distracting to the eye because of all of the white space. White space flowing from line to line, called a **river**, can draw a reader's attention away from the content. In a **tight line**, some words are so close together that they are difficult to distinguish. In general, justifying text in a narrow column results in a great number of loose lines and is, therefore, not advised. Most programs, including Photoshop, provide tools that let you fix the tracking and kerning of loose lines to reduce the white space between words and characters in justified text, but making adjustments line by line can be very time consuming.

So when do you use justified text, and when do you use some other alignment option? In fact, there's no simple answer. You need to determine your needs on a case-by-case basis. In general, justified text is considered formal, while unjustified text is less so. Other considerations are column width and page design. For example, how do the graphics on the page look next to justified or unjustified text? As you become more experienced working with text, you'll develop a sense of what works best in a given situation. You'll also need to weigh other factors, such as the time it takes to adjust tracking, kerning, and hyphenation in a particular design. Once you have weighed all of these factors, you'll have the information you need to make the right decision for a given project.

Next, you'll use the Paragraph panel to adjust the alignment of the paragraphs and the space between paragraphs to see if that improves the layout. You'll also turn off hyphenation to see how different line breaks affect the readability of the text.

To use the Paragraph panel to adjust alignment and hyphenation:

1. Click the **Paragraph panel** tab to display the Paragraph panel.

2. On the canvas, click in the first line of the first paragraph, and then on the Paragraph panel, click the **Center text** button ▤. The text in the first paragraph is centered, and both the left and right margins are ragged. Notice that clicking the Center text button only affects the current paragraph.

3. Click in the second paragraph, and on the Paragraph panel, click the **Justify last left** button ▤. See Figure 6-20.

Figure 6-20   Adjusting text alignment

The text is justified, or evenly spread between the margins of the bounding box, with the last line aligned at the left margin. Three of the words in the second paragraph are hyphenated.

Trouble? If you don't see three hyphenated words, your bounding box is a different size. Continue with the remaining steps.

4. On the Paragraph panel, click the **Hyphenate** check box to deselect it. The words that were hyphenated in the second paragraph have now moved to the next line of text, without hyphenation, and the remaining text spreads out to maintain the justification. Notice that there are now more loose lines and rivers of blank space.

5. On the Paragraph panel, click in the **Add space before paragraph** box ▤, and type **20**. Photoshop adds a 20-point vertical space before the second paragraph.

   Even with the space before the second paragraph, the text doesn't work well as it is currently formatted. Some of the words are too spread out, which makes the paragraph look sloppy. You'll use the center align option for the second paragraph so the characters and words are spaced for easier reading and so it matches the formatting of the first paragraph.

6. Click in the second paragraph, if necessary, and then on the Paragraph panel, click the **Center text** button ▤. The text is centered, without hyphenation.

7. Commit the changes to the paragraph text. See Figure 6-21.

Figure 6-21   **Paragraphs centered and separated by space**

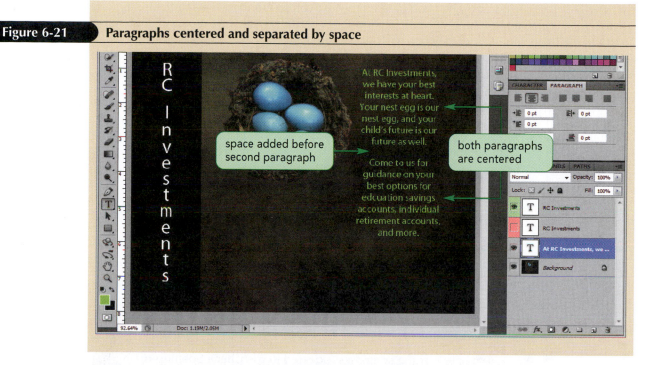

Using Advanced Justification Settings

INSIGHT

You can use advanced justification settings by selecting Justification from the Paragraph panel options menu. Advanced justification settings let you specify Minimum, Desired, and Maximum values for word and letter spacing, as well as glyph spacing. Word spacing is the space between words. You typically add space between words by pressing the spacebar. Using advanced justification settings, you can adjust the width of that space. Letter spacing is the distance between letters. 100% puts the width of a regular space between letters; 0% packs letters tightly together with no space between them. **Glyph spacing** determines the width of individual characters. Each font family has predetermined widths for characters, but you can override that setting by specifying a value between 50% to 200%.

Next, you'll format individual words in the paragraphs to make them stand out from the rest of the paragraph. You'll do this using the Character panel and the Swatches panel.

To format the paragraph text:

1. Double-click the word *heart* in the first paragraph.

2. On the Swatches panel, click any **red swatch**. The word *heart* is formatted in a red font.

3. In the fourth line of the first paragraph, double-click the word ***our***, and then on the Character panel, click the **Set the font style** arrow Regular, and then click **Italic**.

4. At the bottom of the Character panel, click the **Underline** button, and then click outside the word *our* to deselect it. The word *our* is italicized and underlined, while the rest of the words retain their original formatting.

Even though you entered the text you just formatted as paragraph type, you can format it the same way you format point type. In fact, after you commit either paragraph type or point type, they behave in the same manner.

Checking Spelling and Replacing Text

When you enter a lot of text in a bounding box, you'll sometimes find that you've made typing errors. You might be used to word-processing programs that mark misspelled words as you type. Photoshop doesn't have that feature, so you need to use the Check Spelling option on the Edit menu on the Application bar. You can also replace one word or phrase with another using the Find and Replace feature in Photoshop. This command is also on the Edit menu.

To check spelling in the paragraph text:

1. Click at the beginning of the first paragraph, to the left of the word *At*.

2. On the Application bar, click **Edit**, and then click **Check Spelling**. The Check Spelling dialog box opens, indicating that *edcuation* is not in the dictionary. Photoshop suggests that you replace the word with the correctly spelled version, *education*.

   Trouble? If the spelling suggested in the Check Spelling dialog box is not the spelling you want, or is not the word you intended, you can either type the correct spelling in the Change To box, or scroll down the list of suggestions and select one of the alternate words.

   Trouble? If a dialog box with a "Spell check complete." message appears, you either have no errors in your text, or you have not clicked at the beginning of the first paragraph. Photoshop starts at the insertion point and goes to the end of the bounding box. If the insertion point is in the middle of the text, it checks only the second half of the text entry.

3. Click the **Change** button. Photoshop corrects the spelling of *education* and indicates that the spelling check is complete.

   Trouble? If Photoshop finds additional misspelled words, correct them as necessary before closing the dialog box.

4. Click the **OK** button to end the spelling check.

You can also replace text using the Find and Replace Text command, which opens the Find and Replace Text dialog box. See Figure 6-22.

Figure 6-22   **Find And Replace Text dialog box**

You can type the word you want to replace in the Find What box, and then type the new word in the Change To box. The Find Next button finds the next instance of the word you want to replace. The Change button replaces the word. The Change All button replaces all instances of the Find What word in one step. To change one instance of the word you want to replace and then move to the next, click the Change/Find button. You can also specify whether you want to search forward through the text, whether you want to search all layers, and whether the search should be case sensitive and should look for whole words. For example, if you specify *day* as the word to find, Photoshop will find *today*, *Monday*, and *daylight* in addition to *day*. If you specify Whole Word Only, Photoshop will only find *day*.

While the Find and Replace feature is most useful in situations in which you are working with large segments of text, you will experiment with it by replacing the word *guidance* with the word *advice* in the ad you are working on for Rhiann.

To find and replace text:

1. Click at the beginning of the first paragraph. On the Application bar, click **Edit**, and then click **Find and Replace Text**. The Find And Replace Text dialog box opens.

2. In the Find What box, type **guidance**, and then in the Change To box, type **advice**.

3. Click **Find Next**. Photoshop highlights the instance of *guidance* in the paragraph.

4. Click the **Change** button to change *guidance* to *advice*.

5. Click the **Done** button, and then on the Layers panel, click the **Background** layer to deselect the paragraph text.

6. Save RCDetails.psd. If you are not taking a break before the next session, leave the file open.

In this session, you learned about text layers, and you worked with horizontal point type, vertical point type, and paragraph type. You explored the Design workspace, and experimented with a variety of text formatting and alignment options. In the next session, you will work with some more advanced text formatting options, including applying text styles, specifying baseline shifts, and bending text to a path. You will also fill text with an image, a pattern, and a gradient.

REVIEW

Session 6.1 Quick Check

1. Paragraph type is contained in a(n) _____ box.
2. Point type is entered along a(n) _____ that expands to accommodate new text.
3. The _____ workspace is designed for text editing and formatting.
4. True or False. Vertical type entered with the Vertical Type Tool has the same appearance as text that is entered with the Horizontal Type Tool and then rotated counterclockwise 90 degrees.
5. You can adjust the space between words and characters by changing the _____ setting on the Paragraph panel.
6. When you _____ text, it is spread out or compressed on each line so the right and left margins aren't jagged.

SESSION 6.2 VISUAL OVERVIEW

Selecting the Paths button when you draw a shape tells Photoshop that you're creating a work path.

Shift the baseline of a character or characters in a line of text to create a special effect.

Typing text along a path gives it a unique shape.

On the Character panel, you can use the **baseline shift** feature to raise characters a specified number of points above or below the baseline.

Use the Styles panel to apply preset effects to text.

Use the Pen Tool to draw a path along which you can bend text.

Fill text with an image, pattern, or gradient with a clipping mask.

CREATING UNIQUE TEXT

When you **warp** text, it is distorted horizontally and/or vertically and is sometimes skewed as if viewed from a different angle.

Warped text layers display a thumbnail indicating that the text is warped.

The underlined text on this layer indicates that the layer is a **clipping mask**, which will mask the layer or layers above it. In this case, the image of the hundred dollar bill will be masked by the *Money Matters* text.

The spacing between the *Money* paragraph and the *Matters* paragraph has been reduced by 45 points.

Creating Unique Text

When you enter text in Photoshop, you can combine formatting options such as font, color, and alignment to get the look you want. However, there may be times when you want a unique look that isn't possible simply using the standard formatting tools. With the options available on the Styles panel, the baseline shift feature, and the text warping and bending capabilities of Photoshop, you have more powerful tools to work with to achieve interesting and unique results for your text. In addition, the ability to raster-ize text and treat it as a digital or bitmap image opens up countless other possibilities as you use Photoshop's digital image-editing tools to create eye-catching text in your compositions.

Applying a Style to Text

The Styles panel has dozens of possible formatting presets that you can apply with the click of a button. In fact, Photoshop has style presets designed specifically for text, which are accessible via the Styles panel options menu. Using the style presets allows you to experiment with different looks for the text in your composition without having to set a variety of individual effects such as shadow, bevel and emboss, and gradient fills.

The RC Investments text is too plain to draw attention to the company name in the layout on which you're working. You'll apply a text style to the company name, and then see if formatting the paragraph text with preset styles makes the layout more interesting.

To apply a style to the text:

1. If you took a break after the last session, start Photoshop while pressing the **Ctrl+Alt+Shift** keys. When you are prompted to delete the Adobe Photoshop Settings File, click **Yes**. On the Application bar, right-click **Design**, and click **Reset Design**.

2. Click the **Styles** panel tab, click the **panel option** button ▾≣, and click **Reset Styles**. Click the **OK** button when prompted to replace the current styles with the default styles.

   Trouble? If you are prompted to save changes to the current set of styles, click No.

3. Navigate to the Photoshop6\Tutorial folder, and open **RCDetails.psd**, if necessary.

4. Hide the guides, if necessary, and then hide the green RC Investments layer if necessary. Unhide and click the **red RC Investments** layer to select it. On the Styles panel, click the **panel options** button ▾≣, click **Text Effects 2**, and then click the **OK** button to replace the current styles with style presets designed spe-cifically for text.

5. On the Styles panel, click the **Swamp Bevel with Shadow** icon ▤ (the first effect). This effect gives the text a raised, three-dimensional look.

6. Click **Dented Metal with Shadow** icon ▣ (third row, fourth column). This effect gives the text a shiny, metallic look.

7. Click the **By Candle Light** icon ▤ (the last effect on the panel). This effect adds a drop shadow, a bevel and emboss effect, and a gradient overlay. Each effect in the style is listed beneath the RC Investments layer on the Layers panel. See Figure 6-23.

Figure 6-23   Applying a style

Trouble? If you can't see the By Candle Light style, click the down scroll arrow on the Styles panel until you can see it.

8. Select the **At RC Investments...** layer, and then apply the **By Candle Light** style to both paragraphs. Although the style made the company name stand out well on the black background, when it is applied to the paragraph, it makes it difficult to read.

9. Apply the **Dented Metal with Shadow** style. See Figure 6-24.

Figure 6-24   Dented Metal style applied to both paragraphs

The Dented Metal style also makes the paragraph text difficult to read. For paragraphs with a lot of text, the simpler the better. You can get a message across much more effectively if the text itself takes center stage rather than its formatting.

10. Delete the paragraph text style you added by dragging the **fx** symbol at the right of the At RC Investments... text layer name to the **Delete** icon 🗑 at the bottom of the Layers panel. The text returns to the green formatting you applied earlier.

11. Save RCDetails.psd, and close it.

Scaling and Tracking Text to Achieve Balance

You can also create unique text by scaling individual characters to give words and phrases different shapes, and to achieve balance in a layout. When you adjust the tracking between characters, text shifts left or right on the text layer, changing its relation to the center point. When you change the horizontal scale of a letter or letters, you're not only changing the shape of the word, you're also shifting the text on either side as you widen or narrow the selected characters.

To adjust scaling and tracking to add shape and balance a text object:

1. Open **RCPath.psd** from the Photoshop6\Tutorial folder, and save it as **RightPath.psd** in the same folder; then press the **Ctrl+0** keys to fit the image on screen. Display the rulers, if necessary. This file includes images and text.

2. Double-click the **Safe & Sound** text thumbnail ⊤ to select all of the text, and then click on the canvas to the left of the ampersand (&) to place the insertion point.

   Trouble? If your system doesn't have the font provided in the file, accept the suggested font substitution.

3. Double-click the **&** to select it. See Figure 6-25.

TIP

You can also triple-click text on a selected layer directly on the canvas to select all of the text in the text object.

Figure 6-25   Single character selected in text edit mode

square indicates the beginning of a text object

baseline is displayed

selected text includes & and the space after it

The & and the space after it are selected. The baseline appears under the text, and the small square on the left side of the baseline indicates where the text object starts. You'll make the ampersand larger to give the text a unique shape.

4. Change the font size of the & from 36 points to **48** points, and then commit the change. See Figure 6-26.

Figure 6-26 **Mixed font sizes**

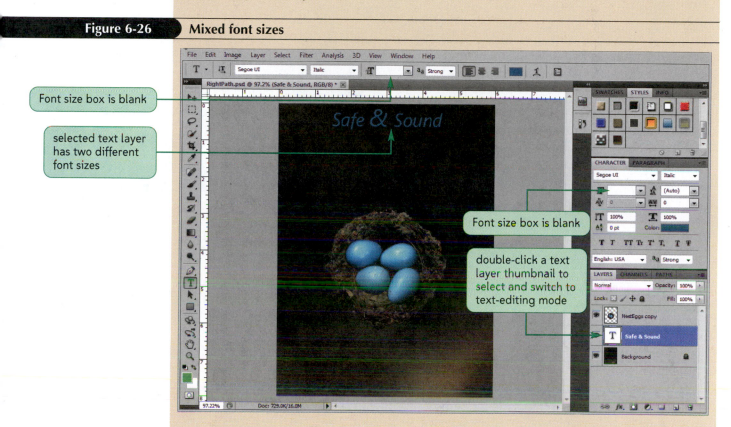

Font size box is blank

selected text layer has two different font sizes

Font size box is blank

double-click a text layer thumbnail to select and switch to text-editing mode

Because this text layer now has more than one font size applied, the Set the font size boxes are blank on the Character panel and on the options bar.

Trouble? If you can't see the Set the font size box on the options bar, make sure the Horizontal Type Tool is still selected on the Tools panel.

5. Press **V** to activate the Move Tool, and then show the transform controls, if necessary. See Figure 6-27.

Figure 6-27 Centering text

center transform control

Horizontal scaling box

Notice that the center transform control, which marks the center of the text, is to the right of the ampersand. You'll change the horizontal scaling of the word *Safe* and change the tracking of individual letters and spaces to make the text more balanced around the center point.

6. On the Layers panel, double-click the **Safe & Sound** text thumbnail [T], and then drag on the canvas to select all of the letters in the word *Safe*.

7. On the Character panel, horizontally scale the word *Safe* to **120%**.

8. On the canvas, select the **e** in *Safe* and the space after the word *Safe,* and set the tracking to **-40**.

9. Select the space after the **&** and select the **S** in *Sound*, and decrease the tracking to **-80**. Click the **Commit any current edits** button ✔, then press **V** to activate the Move Tool and show the transform controls, if necessary. The text is now more evenly balanced around the center point. See Figure 6-28.

TIP

You can also scrub the Set the tracking for the selected characters icon on the Character panel to adjust the tracking value by increments of 20.

Figure 6-28 Balanced text

Safe is 20% wider

tracking is reduced between the e and the space

tracking is reduced between the space and the S

text is more balanced around center point

10. Save RightPath.psd, and keep the file open.

Understanding Optical and Metric Kerning

Kerning makes text easier to read by adding or subtracting space between pairs of characters. Just looking at the text on this page, you can probably see that some character pairs are closer together than others based on the shapes of the characters. Many of the font families you'll work with come with predefined kern pairs that handle letter pairings that might otherwise be problematic—for example, the letter *W* might be kerned differently when paired with the letter *o* than when paired with the letter *i* simply for readability. When this kerning is built in to a font family, it's called **metrics kerning**. However, some fonts don't have built-in kerning, or they have kerning for some character pairs but not others. When this is the case, you can choose the **optical kerning** option in Photoshop, and Photoshop will adjust the spacing between character pairs based on the shapes of the characters. To work with metrics and optical kerning, you can choose either Metrics or Optical, rather than a number setting, from the Set the kerning between two characters list on the Character panel.

Next, you'll change the baseline shift of the ampersand in the *Safe & Sound* text to give the text in the composition a more interesting shape.

Specifying a Baseline Shift

So far, all of the point text you have entered has been placed on the default baseline, indicated by *0 pt* in the Set the baseline shift box on the Character panel. However, you can assign a positive number to the baseline to shift characters up above the baseline by the specified number of points. You can assign a negative number to shift characters so they sit beneath the baseline.

To specify a baseline shift for the ampersand:

1. Press **T** to activate the Horizontal Type Tool, and then select the **&** on the Safe & Sound layer.

2. On the Character panel, type **10** in the Set the baseline shift box A| 0 pt |. The ampersand moves above the rest of the text, 10 points above the baseline. Now the ampersand is too close to the top edge of the image, and looks out of place. You'll try a different setting, this time below the baseline.

3. On the Character panel, set the baseline shift to **-15**, and commit the change. See Figure 6-29.

Figure 6-29   Baseline shift

original baseline

baseline for the ampersand has shifted down

baseline shift value

A negative baseline shift value moves the selection below the baseline of the other characters.

4. Save the file as **Baseline.psd** in the Photoshop6\Tutorial folder, and keep the file open.

Warping Text

You can warp text to give it a unique shape. When you warp text, characters fill the shape of the warp style you specify. Characters no longer have a consistent font size, and depending on the warp, they might also be slightly skewed in perspective—for example, they might look as if they are being squashed or stretched vertically, horizontally, or diagonally. See Figure 6-30, which shows some of the default warp styles available in Photoshop, including Flag, Squeeze, and Bulge.

Figure 6-30   **Warping text**

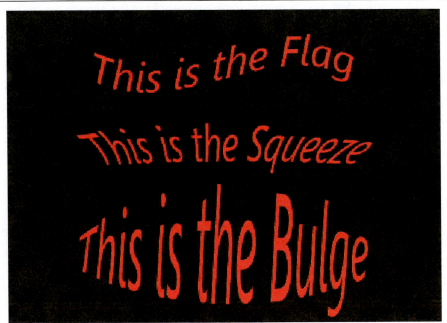

When you warp text, you can use the default settings for the specified warp, or you can modify the extent of the warp by changing the Bend percentage, or the Horizontal or Vertical Distortion. As you change the values in the Warp Text dialog box, you can see them being applied on the canvas.

You'll warp the Safe & Sound text to see if the effect works in your composition.

TIP

You can also click Layer on the Application bar, point to Type, and then click Warp Text to open the Warp Text dialog box.

To warp the Safe & Sound text:

1. On the Layers panel, select the **Safe & Sound** text layer, if necessary.

2. On the options bar, click the **Create warped text** button [⊥]. The Warp Text dialog box opens.

3. Drag the Warp Text dialog box to the right so you can see all of the canvas.

4. In the Warp Text dialog box, click the **Style** arrow, and then click **Arc Lower**. See Figure 6-31.

Figure 6-31   Arc Lower warp applied to the Safe & Sound text

5. Change the Bend to **-20** and the Horizontal Distortion to **-60**. The Bend setting determines the amount of distortion applied to the text. By specifying a negative number, you reduced the distortion. The Horizontal Distortion setting changes the perspective of the warp.

6. Press the **Alt** key and then click the **Reset** button in the Warp text dialog box. Photoshop removes the warp and the settings go back to their defaults. You'll try a different warp setting to see if it works better in the composition.

7. Click the **Style** arrow, and then click **Rise**.

8. Change the Bend setting to **0**. A Bend setting of 0 applies no distortion, so the text is not affected by the warp.

9. Drag the **Bend** slider to change the Bend setting to **+100**.

   As you experiment with warp effects, you can move the text around the image without closing the dialog box. This feature lets you get the effect you want in the most efficient way.

10. On the canvas, drag the text to the upper-left corner of the canvas. See Figure 6-32.

Figure 6-32 **Rise warp applied to the Safe & Sound text**

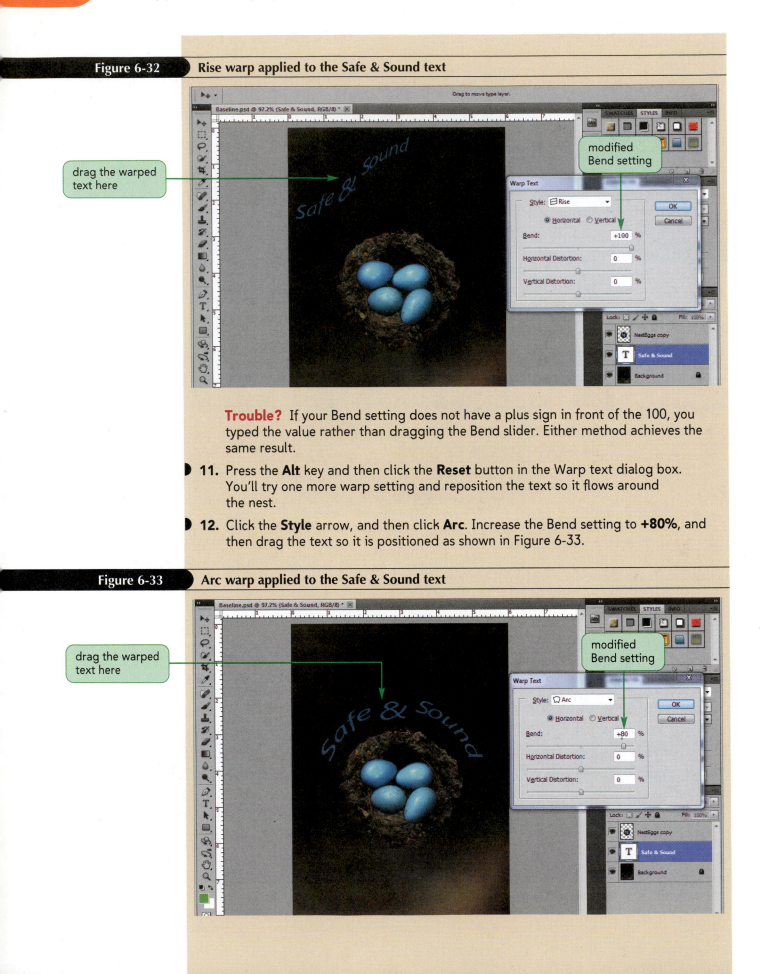

Trouble? If your Bend setting does not have a plus sign in front of the 100, you typed the value rather than dragging the Bend slider. Either method achieves the same result.

11. Press the **Alt** key and then click the **Reset** button in the Warp text dialog box. You'll try one more warp setting and reposition the text so it flows around the nest.

12. Click the **Style** arrow, and then click **Arc**. Increase the Bend setting to **+80%**, and then drag the text so it is positioned as shown in Figure 6-33.

Figure 6-33 **Arc warp applied to the Safe & Sound text**

13. Click the **OK** button to close the Warp Text dialog box. The warp is applied to the text, and on the Layers panel, the text now has a different icon, indicating that the text is warped.

14. On the Layers panel, position the pointer over the **Safe & Sound** text thumbnail. Photoshop displays an "Indicates warped text layer" tip.

15. Save the file as **Arc.psd** in the Photoshop6\Tutorial folder, and leave it open.

INSIGHT

Working with Placeholder Text

If your Photoshop comp includes text, you might not be the one who writes the text. Instead, you might need to get the text for your piece from some other department, such as editorial or marketing. If this is the case, and the text is not readily available, consider using **placeholder text** or **dummy text**, which lets you work with fonts and font sizes in text boxes to plan your layout. Many compositors use *lorem ipsum* text as placeholder text in templates. **Lorem ipsum** text is a standard series of Latin words. Oddly enough, if you do use lorem ipsum text, what you are doing is called **greeking**.

Adding Text Along a Path

TIP

To add and delete anchor points, you use the Add Anchor Point and Delete Anchor Point Tools, which are hidden beneath the Pen Tool on the Tools panel.

If the warp options in Photoshop aren't what you need for your composition, you can draw a path on the canvas and then add text to it so the text follows the path. When you create text on a path, the path becomes the baseline for any text you enter. Photoshop provides a number of tools for creating paths. You can use the Pen Tool or the Freeform Pen Tool to create an **open path** with separate start and end points and then manipulate individual points on the path until it takes the shape you need. Using the Pen and Freeform Pen Tools often creates an initial path that is inexact. Getting the path to conform to the shape you actually want can be time consuming, as it requires adding, deleting, and moving **anchor points**, the points that define the path.

Drawing tools like the Ellipse Tool, the Rectangle Tool, and the Custom Shape Tool provide an easier way than the Pen Tools to create interesting paths for text. When you draw a path with one of these tools, you are creating a **closed path**, or a path in which the start point and the end point are one and the same. You can use the drawing tools individually, or you can combine them to create a complex path shape. In Figure 6-34, the elliptical path was created using the Ellipse Tool, and the other two paths were drawn with the Pen Tool.

Figure 6-34 Sharp angles and curves in a path

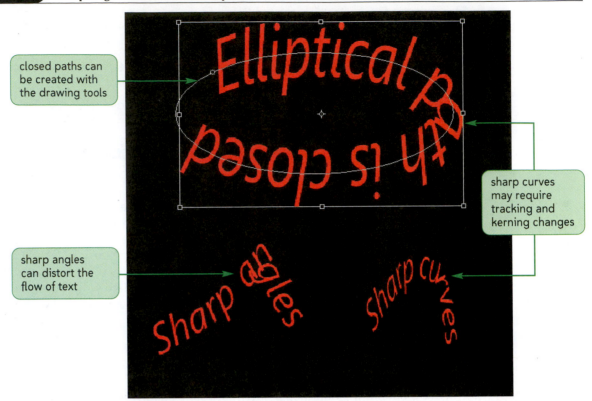

Figure 6-34 shows two of the pitfalls of drawing text on a path. Typing text along a path with a sharp angle can distort the flow of text and throw characters on top of each other. Typing text along a curved path often requires tracking and kerning adjustments so the text flows smoothly.

Rhiann would like you to try a different promotional phrase on the image of the nest on which you've been working. In addition, she'd also like you to wrap the text completely around the nest. You'll use the Ellipse Tool to create a closed path along which you'll enter the new text.

To create the closed path and add text to it:

1. On the Layers panel, hide the Safe & Sound layer, and then select the **Background** layer.

2. On the Tools panel, click the **Ellipse Tool** 🔘.

3. On the options bar, click the **Paths** button 🖉. Selecting the Paths button ensures that the shape you draw will be a path rather than a shape on the layer.

4. On the options bar, click the **Geometry options** arrow ▾, click the **Fixed Size** option button, type a width of **4.25** inches and a height of **4.25** inches, and then press the **Enter** key. These settings will create a path in the shape of a circle.

5. Click the canvas at about 2 ½ inches on the vertical ruler and 1 inch on the horizontal ruler. Photoshop adds a path in the shape of a circle around the image of the nest.

6. To center the path over the nest, on the Tools panel, click the **Path Selection Tool** , point to the path, and then drag it to the location shown in Figure 6-35.

Figure 6-35	Closed path for text

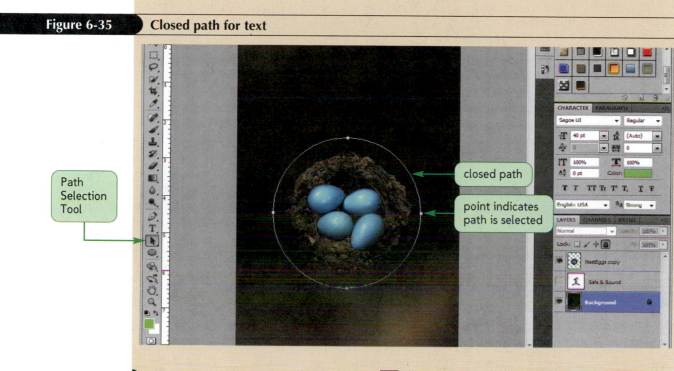

Path Selection Tool

closed path

point indicates path is selected

7. Activate the **Horizontal Type Tool** , and on the options bar, select **Segoe UI** as the font, set **Regular** as the font style, set the font size to **40** points, set the antialiasing to **Strong**, and set the color to a Web-safe **green**. If necessary, set the tracking to **0**.

8. Click the left side of the path, just under the anchor point, and then type **RC Investments: The Right Choice for Your Nest Egg**. The text follows the shape of the path you drew. See Figure 6-36.

Figure 6-36   **Text along a closed path**

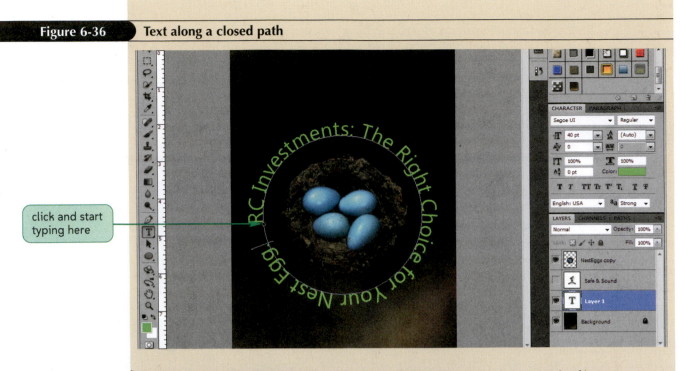

click and start typing here

9. Select the **Background** layer to deselect the path, and then save the file as **CirclePath.psd** in the Photoshop6\Tutorial folder, and close it.

PROSKILLS

Written Communication: Adding Copy to a Composition

If it is your responsibility to write the text in a layout yourself, you need to gather the information and details you'll need for the copy ahead of time. To do so, you can discuss the copy with managers or subject matter experts in other departments. Or, if the piece is for an external customer, contact the customer for details about their product or service. Once you have written the copy, you'll most likely need to get it approved by the department responsible for external communications, such as the Public Relations Department or the Marketing Department. You'll also need to have someone edit the text, and when the composition is complete, you should have someone proofread the copy to check for errors.

You need to consider the context in order to make decisions about text layout and formatting. Will your composition appear in a newsletter that uses a particular font set? If so, you'll need to use a font from that set—unless, of course, your goal is to draw attention to the image in a way that is out of the ordinary. You also need to consider the nature of the brand you're writing about. If your piece is an ad, is there a specific font that the company always uses in its advertisements so the text itself is recognizable as part of the brand? Once you understand what the expectations are for written communication in your organization, you can use your image- and text-editing skills to create impressive, attention-grabbing layouts.

Rhiann would like to eventually work with a Web developer to create an ad that appears along the right side of some of the more popular search engines. Her idea is that three words, "Money Changes Everything", will appear one by one to grab the viewer's attention. She wants each word to have a different effect, and has asked you to create a comp that shows her some options.

Filling Text with an Image, Pattern, or Gradient

Another way you can give text a unique look is to fill it with an image, pattern, or gradient. To fill text with an image, you apply a clipping mask to the image you want the text to display. A clipping mask lets you define a mask for a layer based on the shape of another layer. When you fill text with an image, pattern, or gradient, you are actually specifying that everything *except* the text should mask the underlying image. As a result, the graphic or pattern shows through the letter shapes.

To fill the Money text with an image:

1. Open **Money.psd** from the Photoshop6\Tutorial folder, and save it as **MoneyClip.psd** in the same folder. Reset the background and foreground colors to the default colors, and then switch the background and foreground colors.

2. Hide the NestEggs layer, and select the **Background** layer, if necessary. On the Tools panel, click the **Horizontal Type Tool** [T], and on the options bar, select **Onyx**, **Regular**, **100 pt**, and **Strong**.

3. Click on the canvas and type **Money**, and then drag the text layer if necessary so the text appears at the upper-left of the canvas. The white text is difficult to see, so you'll make it more visible by adding a black stroke.

4. On the Layers panel, double-click the **Money** layer to open the Layer Style dialog box, and then add a **3-pixel**, **Normal**, **Outside black** stroke to the text, as shown in Figure 6-37.

Figure 6-37	Stoke added to text

Stroke effect will add emphasis to the image you will place within the letters

clipping mask will be applied to this image

Stroke effect

5. On the Layers panel, unhide the **NestEggs** layer and select it.

6. On the Application bar, click **Layer** and then click **Create Clipping Mask**. Photoshop uses the NestEggs image layer to fill the *Money* text. See Figure 6-38.

TIP

You can also press the Alt+Ctrl+G keys to create a clipping mask.

Figure 6-38 Clipping mask applied

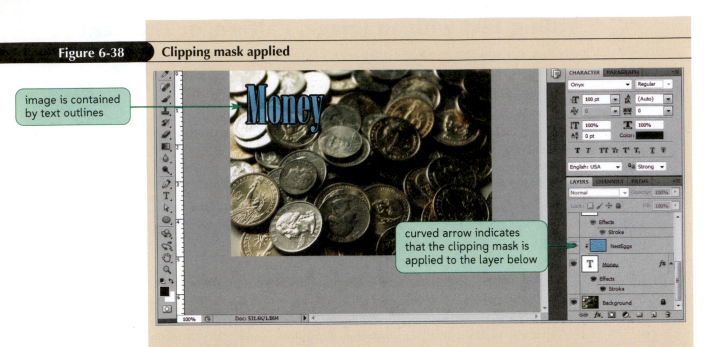

image is contained by text outlines

curved arrow indicates that the clipping mask is applied to the layer below

7. Right-click the **NestEggs** layer, and then click **Release Clipping Mask**. The image you used to mask the text now appears on top of the canvas, covering everything beneath it on the Layers panel, including the text and the background.

8. Press the **Ctrl+Z** keys to undo Step 7. The mask is reapplied.

9. Save the file, and keep it open.

You can also use a clipping mask to fill text with a gradient or a pattern. To do so, add a gradient or pattern layer above the text you want to fill, and then create the clipping mask. You'll experiment with pattern and gradient clipping mask effects to see which one will work best for RC Investments.

To fill the text with a pattern and a gradient:

1. Add a layer above the NestEggs clipping mask, activate the **Horizontal Type Tool** T, and then type **Changes** in the middle of the canvas. You'll copy the layer style you applied to the Money layer and apply it by pasting it on the Changes layer.

2. Right-click the **Money** layer, and click **Copy Layer Style**. The layer style is copied to the Clipboard.

3. Right-click the **Changes** layer, and then click **Paste Layer Style**. The Changes layer now has a 3-pixel black stroke.

4. At the bottom of the Layers panel, click the **Create new fill or adjustment layer** icon, and then click **Pattern**.

5. In the Pattern Fill dialog box, click the **pattern** thumbnail to open the Pattern preset picker, click the **More** button to display the list of available preset libraries, click **Nature Patterns**, and then click the **Append** button to append the new presets to the current set of patterns.

6. Select the **Yellow Mums** preset (the first preset in the third row), and then click the **OK** button. The layer is now filled with a pattern of yellow flowers.

   Trouble? If the Yellow Mums preset is not in the third row, position the mouse pointer over the preset thumbnails until you see *Yellow Mums*.

7. Right-click the **Pattern Fill 1** layer, and then click **Create Clipping Mask**. The *Changes* text is filled with the pattern you selected. See Figure 6-39.

Figure 6-39   **Pattern-filled text**

text contains pattern

pattern with clipping mask applied

8. Add a layer above the Pattern Fill 1 clipping mask, activate the **Horizontal Type Tool** T, if necessary, type **Everything** on the lower-right side of the canvas, and commit the change.

   Because the layer style from the Money layer is still on the Clipboard, you can paste it on this layer as well.

9. Right-click the **Everything** layer, and then click **Paste Layer Style**. The Everything layer now has a 3-pixel black stroke.

10. At the bottom of the Layers panel, click the **Create new fill or adjustment layer** icon ⊘, and then click **Gradient**.

11. In the Gradient Fill dialog box, click the **Gradient** arrow, click the **Blue, Red, Yellow** gradient (the last gradient in the first row), and then click the **OK** button to accept the default settings for the gradient and add a gradient fill layer above the Everything layer.

    Trouble? If you don't see the Blue, Red, Yellow gradient, select a different gradient for the fill.

12. Right-click the **Gradient Fill 1** layer, and then click **Create Clipping Mask**. The *Everything* text is filled with the gradient you selected. See Figure 6-40.

Figure 6-40   **Gradient mask applied**

text filled with a gradient

Gradient Fill layer with clipping mask applied

13. Save the MoneyClip.psd file, close it, and then exit Photoshop.

Session 6.2 Quick Check

REVIEW

1. On which panel can you adjust the horizontal and vertical scale of text?
2. What is a baseline shift?
3. When you change the shape of text by applying a predefined style with bend and distortion settings, you are _____ the text.
4. A path that has the same beginning and ending point is called a _____ path.
5. True or False. A path can be used as the baseline for text typed on a layer.
6. The individual points along a path are called _____ points.
7. When you fill text with a gradient, pattern, or image, you are using a(n) _____ mask.

Practice the skills you learned in the tutorial using the same case scenario.

PRACTICE

Review Assignments

Data Files needed for the Review Assignment: RCRetire.jpg

Rhiann wants you to create an ad directed specifically at baby boomers and their retirement accounts. She provides you with an image and asks you to add text that will capture the attention of potential customers and educate them about RC Investment opportunities. Complete the following steps:

1. Start Photoshop while pressing the Ctrl+Alt+Shift keys, click Yes to delete the Settings File when asked, select and then reset the Design workspace layout, and reset all tools.

2. Open **RCRetire.jpg** from the Photoshop6\Review folder provided with your Data Files and save it as **RCRetirement.psd** in the same folder.

3. Using the Horizontal Type Tool, drag a bounding box on the lower-right side of the canvas, starting at about 6 ½ inches on the horizontal ruler and 4 inches on the vertical ruler, and ending at the bottom right of the canvas. Use a Papyrus, Regular, 24 pt, Strong, left-aligned black font, and type the following two paragraphs (*Note:* The three spelling errors—*liesure, conselors, carreer*—are intentional):

   At RC Investments, we believe that retirement is not an end, but a beginning, a time to spread your wings and take flight, or to settle in to a life of liesure and relaxation--a life you and your investment firm have worked hard to achieve.

   Our investment conselors were there for you when you started your carreer, and we're here for you now. RC Investments. The Real Choice. The Right Choice.

4. Format both paragraphs with no hyphenation, and justify them so the last line of each paragraph is centered.

5. Add a 12-point space before the second paragraph to separate it from the first paragraph.

6. Put each of the last three phrases in its own paragraph. (*Hint:* You can press the Enter key to add a paragraph break.)

7. Adjust the tracking of the text if necessary to improve its appearance by avoiding loose and tight lines and rivers of white space. (*Note:* Determining when the paragraphs are acceptable will be an individual choice.)

8. Use the Move Tool to change the dimensions of the bounding box and reposition it on the canvas. Adjust the size of the bounding box so it is about 6 inches wide and 6 inches tall, and place it so the center of the top of the bounding box is immediately under the sun on the right side of the image.

9. Add a new text layer using the same options, but change the font to 48 point. Type **Dreams Take Flight** on the canvas as point type. Apply the Rise warp style and change the bend to 100%. Reposition the text layer so it starts just above and to the right of the bird and rises to the upper-right corner of the canvas.

10. Select the Dreams Take Flight text, and format it with an underline.

11. Apply the Bright Red Bevel style (from the Text Effects 2 preset library) to the Dreams Take Flight layer.

12. Check the spelling in the document, and correct any misspelled words.

13. Add a vertical type layer using Poplar Std, 48-point font, and type **RC Investments** along the left side of the canvas. Increase the horizontal scale of the text to 250%. Reduce the horizontal scale of the letter *m* to 200%, and then increase the tracking between the letter *C* and the letter *I* to about 160.

14. Use a clipping mask to apply a Red Textured pattern fill to the company name.

15. Apply a Drop Shadow and a Bevel and Emboss effect to the RC Investments layer text using the default settings.

16. Save RCRetirement.psd, and exit Photoshop.

17. Submit the results of the preceding steps to your instructor either in printed or electronic form, as requested.

Case Problem 1

Data Files needed for this Case Problem: Shuttle.jpg, Fireworks.jpg

Concord High School   You've recently been hired as a teaching assistant at Concord High School in Ohio. You'll be working with the school's physics teacher, Dr. Marie Cash. She has asked you to create a series of slides meant to pique students' interest in physics. You'll add text with different special effects to an image and save a series of layer comps to see which options will work best in the slide show. Complete the following steps:

1. Start Photoshop while pressing the Ctrl+Alt+Shift keys, click Yes to delete the Settings File when asked, select and then reset the Design workspace layout, and reset all tools.

2. Open **Shuttle.jpg** from the Photoshop6\Case1 folder provided with your Data Files, and save it as **Physics.jpg** in the same folder.

3. Using the Horizontal Type Tool, choose a font that you think is appropriate for a clipping mask—with a font size that is at minimum 200 points. Type **E = MC2** near the top of the image.

4. Apply a superscript effect to the *2* in the *E = MC2* text.

5. Scale the text horizontally so it fills the width of the image.

6. Add a new layer at the top of the Layers panel, and place the **Fireworks.jpg** file from the Photoshop6\Case1 folder on the new layer.

7. Fill the $E = MC^2$ text with the Fireworks image you just added. You may need to drag the Fireworks layer to get the effect you want.

8. Add any adjustment to the composition, and then save a layer comp called **Fireworks**, and hide any adjustment layers and the Fireworks layer.

9. Duplicate the E = MC2 layer. (*Hint*: Right-click the E = MC2 layer on the Layers panel, and select Duplicate Layer.) Move the copy beneath the original on the Layers panel. Using the Layer Properties dialog box, make the original E = MC2 layer red and the copy green. Then, hide the red E = MC2 layer.

10. Add a stroke to the green layer text, and then warp the green layer using the style of your choice. Fill the text with a pattern from the Rock Patterns preset group. Create a layer comp, and save it as **PhysicsRocks**.

11. Hide all layers except the Background layer and the adjustment layer, and then type **Physics** so it runs vertically on the left side of the canvas. (*Hint*: Use the Vertical Type Tool.) Fill the word with a gradient.

12. Type the following paragraph at the top of the canvas in 16 point, Times New Roman in any color you choose:

    You might not believe it yet, but physics is fun! Or should we say phun? What other disciplines have put a man on the moon and the shuttle into orbit? And who would argue that gravity doesn't keep us grounded?

    So put on your space suits, your x-ray specs, and your thinking caps and get ready for the ride of a lifetime!

13. Check the spelling of the text you typed, but leave the spelling of *phun*.

14. Adjust the alignment and the paragraph spacing until you're satisfied with the results.

15. Format *physics is fun!* in all caps, and format the vertical Physics as small caps.

16. Save Physics.jpg as **Physics.psd** in the Photoshop6\Case1 folder, and exit Photoshop.

17. Submit the results of the preceding steps to your instructor either in printed or electronic form, as requested.

Use your skills to create a logo for a catering business.

APPLY

Case Problem 2

Data Files needed for this Case Problem: Gourmet.jpg

No Fuss Gourmet   You've recently started your own catering business. You specialize in intimate parties, and consider food your art form. You've decided to start advertising online, and you need to create a logo for the business. You'll experiment with the text features of Photoshop to come up with the best look for your business, and then you'll place the logo with an image to see the full effect. Complete the following steps:

1. Start Photoshop while pressing the Ctrl+Alt+Shift keys, click Yes to delete the Settings File when asked, select and then reset the Design workspace layout, and reset all tools.

2. Create a new file of any size, with any background color. Make sure you have enough space to experiment with at least two different logo ideas. Because you are creating the logo for the Web, you can work with a file that is 72 ppi.

3. Create two possible logos with the name of the company—No Fuss Gourmet—using different fonts, styles, fills, and effects. Adjust character spacing, font, and styles as necessary to come up with the best effect. Combine text with shapes to achieve the effect you want. Change layer order as necessary to build the logo.

4. Save the file as **Logos.psd** in the Photoshop6\Case2 folder provided with your Data Files.

5. Open **Gourmet.jpg** from the Photoshop6\Case2 folder, and save it as **NoFuss.psd** in the same folder.

6. Choose your favorite logo from Logos.psd, merge the layers you used to create it, and copy it to the NoFuss image. Resize it as necessary to achieve the best effect. You can use Figure 6-41 as an example, but your composition should be unique.

Figure 6-41   Sample Case Problem 2 solution

7. Create a rectangle of any color on the right side of the image and format it with any effects you want. Type the following paragraph text over the rectangle:

   At No Fuss Gourmet, we provide fabulous food without all the fuss. We come to your house, we set up your dinner, we serve, we clean, and we leave. Food with flair, food with flavor, but no fuss!

8. Format *No Fuss Gourmet* as small caps, and change the font color. In the last sentence, format *no fuss* as all caps.

9. Check the spelling in the paragraph, and replace *fabulous* with *fine*.

10. Turn off hyphenation, and justify the paragraph settings as desired.

11. On the left side of the composition, add short sample quotes from customers using warped text. Format the text with any style or stroke.

12. Save NoFuss.psd and Logos.psd, and exit Photoshop.

13. Submit the results of the preceding steps to your instructor either in printed or electronic form, as requested.

Use your skills to add text to an image for an ad campaign.

APPLY

Case Problem 3

Data Files needed for this Case Problem: Luxury.jpg

Goldilocks Inn   Goldilocks Inn is a small bed and breakfast in Ripton, Vermont. The proprietor Betsy Hemmings, hoping to attract both tourists and the parents of local college students, has asked you to create an ad for a page in the college calendar. Complete the following steps:

1. Start Photoshop while pressing the Ctrl+Alt+Shift keys, click Yes to delete the Settings File when asked, select and then reset the Design workspace layout, and reset all tools.

2. Open **Luxury.jpg** from the Photoshop6\Case3 folder provided with your Data Files, and save it as **Goldilocks.psd** in the same folder.

3. Extend the canvas so it measures 11 inches wide and 8 ½ inches high. The canvas extension should be a color that you think works well with the image supplied. Anchor the image in a corner when you extend the canvas.

4. Using a font or fonts of your choosing, type the name of the inn on two different layers. For one layer, use a vertical orientation and for the other, use a horizontal orientation. You'll save layer comps so you have a couple of choices to show to Betsy. Save the horizontal composition as a layer comp named **Horizontal** and the vertical composition as a layer comp named **Vertical**.

⊕ EXPLORE

5. Using the Vertical layer comp, apply a style to the text. Modify the style by changing at least one of its attributes. (*Hint*: Double-click an individual effect on the Layers panel to open the Layer Style dialog box with the settings for that effect displayed.)

6. The image includes five pillows. Use the Type Tools to type the word **Comfort** five times, one time on each pillow. Each instance should use a different text effect. For example, warp the text, type it along a path, apply a style to it, or change its scale in some way. Rotate individual instances until you have the effect you want for each pillow.

7. At the bottom of the image, type the following paragraph text:

   At Goldilocks Inn, we offer all the comforts of home, with none of the hassles. Dine in our four-star dining room and enjoy the company of other guests. Or request a table in a romantic corner. Sip cognac by the common fireplace in the evening or relax in our outdoor hot tub year-round. Take a cooling dip in our pool, or heat up in the sauna.

   Goldilocks Inn is all about comfort. Comfort, comfort, and affordability. And oh, did we mention comfort?

8. Check the spelling of the paragraph text.

9. Format the inn name in all caps.

10. Format the second paragraph in a way that distinguishes it from the first paragraph, and specify the alignment and justification for each paragraph as desired.

11. Type the word **AHH!** somewhere on the composition, and fill it with a pattern.

12. Save the file, and then convert the image to CMYK mode, rasterize, and flatten it.

13. Save the flattened file as **Flat.tif** in the Photoshop6\Case3 folder, using the default TIFF settings.

14. Submit the results of the preceding steps to your instructor either in printed or electronic form, as requested.

Extend your skills to create an ad for a soccer academy.

CHALLENGE

Case Problem 4

Data Files needed for this Case Problem: Soccer.jpg

Soccer Academy   You are a recent college graduate who played soccer in college. You have had trouble finding a job, so you decide to start your own business using the skills you have: a degree in marketing, experience in soccer, and a flair for Photoshop. Your "soccer academy" offers classes for women who are interested in playing in recreational leagues. You'll go to their homes or to a soccer field of their choice and teach them shooting, dribbling, and strategy skills. You'll create a logo for your new business, as well as a poster that you'll hang at local community and childcare centers. Complete the following steps:

1. Start Photoshop while pressing the Ctrl+Alt+Shift keys, click Yes to delete the Settings File when asked, select and then reset the Design workspace layout, and reset all tools.

2. Open **Soccer.jpg** from the Photoshop6\Case4 folder provided with your Data Files, and save it as **Academy.psd** in the same folder.

3. Extend the canvas size so there are 2 additional inches on the top and 4 additional inches on the bottom. Use black for the canvas extension color.

4. Add white vertical text along the left side of the image using the Ravie, Regular, 30-point font. Type **Soccer Academy**, and position the text so its vertical baseline is at about 1 inch on the horizontal ruler.

5. Increase the tracking between the *r* in *Soccer* and the *A* in *Academy*.

6. Decrease the horizontal scale of the *m* in *Academy*, and increase the vertical scale of the *S* in *Soccer*, the *A* in *Academy*, and the *d* in *Academy*.

7. Create a duplicate layer of the Soccer Academy layer and name it **Soccer Academy copy**. Hide the original layer.

EXPLORE

8. Change the vertical alignment so the text runs sideways from top to bottom. (*Hint*: Click the Character panel options button, and deselect Standard Vertical Roman Alignment.) Reposition the text to your liking, and then rename the layer **Sideways**.

9. Hide the Sideways layer, select and display the Soccer Academy layer, click the Character panel options button, and select Change Text Orientation. Reposition and resize the text so it fits in the top black bar. Adjust tracking so the letters aren't crowded.

10. Shift the baseline of *cc* down and shift the baseline of *de* up.

11. Type the following text in a paragraph:

    New to soccer? Have a ball while getting fit. Call us for a fun workout while learning the fundamentals of the most popular sport in the world.

    You name the place and the time and we'll be there. If you don't have access to a field in your neighborhood, let us know and we'll arrange a meeting place.

⊕ **EXPLORE** 12. In Help, look up Adobe Every-line Composer. To see how it works, apply it to the paragraphs you typed. If you still need to make changes, align and/or justify the text to your liking.

13. Add **555-555-5555** as a phone number somewhere on the poster. Type it along a path that you specify.

14. Type **Have a Ball!** on the image so it follows the curve of the soccer ball and is in front of the grass but does not run on to the person's leg.

⊕ **EXPLORE** 15. To create a logo, select the soccer ball on the Background layer and copy it to a new layer. Rearrange the layers so the Have a ball layer is on top of the new layer, and then merge the two layers. (*Hint*: Select both layers, right-click, and then click Merge Layers.) Create a new file with any color background and drag the new logo layer you just merged into the file. See Figure 6-42 for an example.

| Figure 6-42 | Sample logo file |

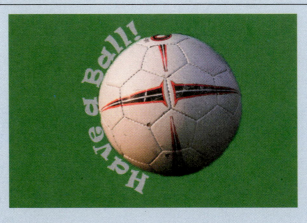

16. Save the new file as **FinalLogo.jpg** in the Photoshop6\Case4 folder.

17. Save Academy.psd, and exit Photoshop.

18. Submit the results of the preceding steps to your instructor either in printed or electronic form, as requested.

ENDING DATA FILES

Photoshop6 →

Tutorial
Arc.psd
Baseline.psd
CirclePath.psd
MoneyClip.psd
RCDetails.psd
RCI.psd
RightPath.psd

Review
RCRetirement.psd

Case1
Physics.jpg
Physics.psd

Case2
Logos.psd
NoFuss.psd

Case3
Flat.tif
Goldilocks.psd

Case4
Academy.psd
FinalLogo.jpg

ProSkills

Teamwork

Working with a Team to Create a Campaign

Teamwork involves the collaborative process by which team members work together to achieve a common goal. You may often find that you need to reach out to managers, to fellow employees, and to people in other departments within your organization to achieve a goal. You might also need to collaborate with a customer or with organizations outside of your company.

Knowing how to be a team player is a critical skill because many organizations rely heavily on teams to complete work tasks. Learning the different roles team members play, how they complement each other for efficient task completion, and how to lead and motivate a team toward achieving a goal can mean the difference between success and failure. Whether your team is ad hoc and short-lived, or ongoing and strategic, the ability to work effectively on a team is a professional skill you need to develop.

What Is a Team?

The Web sites of this country's most desirable employers tell potential employees they'll be working on teams from the start. At Google, the Advertising Sales team members "collaboratively shape solutions that drive their [clients'] strategic initiatives." Apple's corporate retail team is "the backbone behind Apple's retail revolution." For KPMG, one of the world's leading professional services organizations, you may be part of a multi-disciplinary team or on a team that is "at the heart of our organization." But what exactly is a team?

More than just people thrown together, a team consists of individuals who have skills, talents, and abilities that complement each other and, when joined, produce synergy—results greater than those a single individual could achieve. It is this sense of shared mission and responsibility for results that makes a team successful in its efforts to reach organizational goals.

Types of Teams

In organizations, there are a variety of team types. Some are formal, while others are more informal. Some meet in person; others have members who have never met face-to-face. Depending on the work, the type of teams you work on will vary.

Formal teams are organized within the company as part of its official structure. These teams can be either horizontal or vertical. A horizontal team has members from roughly the same level in the organization. When people on a team come from different functional areas of the company—finance, information systems, sales—they are often called a cross-functional team, project team, special-purpose team, or task force because they usually have a specific problem to solve within a limited time frame. After the problem is solved, the team disbands. A vertical team, sometimes called a functional team, has a manager and subordinate workers from the same department in the company's hierarchy. The manager is in charge and directs the workers as they complete their tasks. This type of team has a much longer life because the work is not single-goal oriented. Functional teams work together to accomplish their everyday tasks.

Informal groups sometimes form in the workplace when the members themselves join forces to solve a problem, work on a task, or simply meet to talk over lunch. Because they are not appointed by management and their duties are not specifically outlined in

ProSkills

job descriptions, there is little or no direct accountability or reporting of results to the organization. For example, a group that organizes to clean up the stretch of highway outside the office building won't have management directing its efforts.

A virtual team is one whose members rarely, if ever, meet in person to work on team tasks. Instead, technology makes it possible for members to be geographically distant yet work as if everyone was in the same room. Some common examples of technologies used in virtual teamwork include:

- Corporate networks, such as intranets, as well as File Transfer Protocol (FTP) sites
- Teleconferencing—both audio and video
- Groupware and collaboration software tools, such as those found in Adobe Creative Suite and Microsoft Office 2010
- Social networks, blogs, and wikis
- Email, voice mail, and fax

Virtual teams often must work rapidly to accomplish tasks, so knowing how best to use these technologies is critical. Some virtual teams also have high turnover because members will join when their expertise is needed and then leave upon completion of their contribution. The leader may change as well, depending on the stage of work the team is completing.

The Importance of Technology in Teamwork

Each time you work in a group, decide at the outset how the team will use different technologies to communicate and document work activities. Determine how the team will organize and combine deliverable documents or presentation materials. Use whatever technology tools make the most sense for your team, your task, and your skills.

The Roles of Team Members

If a team is to be successful, individual members must see the value in their respective contributions and what the team as a whole gets out of each member's contribution. This means two important requirements must be met: task performance and social satisfaction. Task performance usually is handled by one or more members who are task specialists. Task specialists spend a lot of time and effort ensuring that the team achieves its goals. They initiate ideas, give opinions, gather information, sort details, and provide motivation to keep the team on track. Social satisfaction is handled by individuals who strengthen the team's social bonds through encouragement, empathy, conflict resolution, compromise, and tension reduction. Have you ever been on a team where the tension was high, and someone stepped in to tell a joke or tried to soften the blow of criticism? That person held the role of managing social satisfaction. Both the task specialist and social satisfaction specialist are important roles on teams. These are not the only roles, however. Other roles include team leaders, work coordinators, idea people, and critics. The roles of individual team members are not always mutually exclusive. For example, the task specialist might also be the team leader, and the idea person might also fill the social satisfaction role. As you begin working with your team in this exercise, watch how these roles are filled and how they change as your team completes its work. Perhaps you'll want to discuss upfront which role each member is comfortable filling to see how complementary your collective skill sets turn out to be. What if a role is not being filled on your team? Then you'll need to figure out, as a team, how to move forward so you

ProSkills

can complete your work successfully. The following are tips that everyone should respect as work on a team begins:

- Remember that everyone brings something of value to the team.
- Respect and support each other as you work toward the common goal. When criticism or questions arise, try to see things from the other person's perspective.
- If someone needs assistance, find ways to encourage or support that person so the team is not affected.
- Deal with negative or unproductive attitudes immediately so they don't damage team energy and attitude.
- Get outside help if the team becomes stuck and can't move forward.
- Provide periodic positive encouragement or rewards for contributions.

Create a Campaign for a Business

Many organizations use Photoshop for both internal and external publications, including Web and print pieces. In this exercise, you'll work with your team members to design a logo as well as print and Web marketing pieces for a fictional business. As you decide on your business, keep the following in mind: Your main tool for this exercise will be Photoshop; therefore, the business should lend itself to striking visuals so that you have photographs and other images to manipulate for the exercise. In other words, a travel agency would probably be a better candidate than a company that provides typing services.

As a group, you'll create the following three pieces: a company logo consisting of both text and a drawing or photograph; a Web banner with text and graphics for the company's home page; and a magazine ad that includes point text and paragraph text, as well as a digital image that has been modified using special effects, adjustment layers, and the Brush Tool. The ad will consist of multiple layer comps, with the goal of presenting the comps to the group so you can come to a consensus on the best design. To create and design these pieces, your group will use the Photoshop skills and features presented in Tutorials 1 through 6.

1. Meet with your team to brainstorm and come to a consensus on what your business will be. Coming to a consensus is a necessary part of any work a team undertakes, so make sure everyone is happy with the choice. Once you have chosen a business, discuss what products and/or services it provides.

2. As a group or individually, use the Web to research businesses similar to the one your group chose. Print the home pages of the similar businesses you find, and, if you can find banner ads on other Web pages, print those. What logos do the businesses use? What kind of language do they use in their ads? Do they use a particular font and color scheme? Do you think their branding is effective?

3. As a group, discuss what color scheme might work best to promote your business and create a recognizable brand. Do you want complementary, monochromatic, analogous, or neutral colors? Any member who proposes a color scheme should begin a group discussion on the reasons for that color scheme, and what kind of audience might respond to the scheme.

ProSkills

4. Have each team member create a logo for the business, and set a deadline for its completion. The logo should include both text and graphics, and to create it, team members should use the Drawing Tools, the Type Tools, special effects, warped text or text along a path, and multiple layers. The logo should be created in the RGB color mode at 300 ppi. It will be saved at lower resolutions and in different color modes later in the exercise. The logo can include a digital image, but it must be either your own image, in the public domain, or available for commercial, royalty-free use.

5. In a team meeting, have each member present his or her logo. Spend time discussing the effectiveness of each one. At the end of the discussion, choose the two logos (we'll call them Logo1 and Logo2) that best represent the products, services, and perceived brand of the company.

6. Split the team into two groups. Team members in Group 1 will work with Logo1, and those in Group 2 will work with Logo2. Every team member should leave the meeting with a digital copy of the logo their group will be using.

7. Each team member should create a new file based on one of the Photoshop Web presets. The new file should include the placed logo and any supporting text for a Web banner for the company's home page. It can be a horizontal or vertical banner, and can include horizontal or vertical type. The final version of the file should be saved using the RGB color mode in JPG format and should have a resolution of 72 ppi.

8. Each group should meet separately and individual team members should present their banners to each other. Each group should then create one file and place each member's banner JPG on a separate layer in the file. Each layer will comprise its own layer comp, which means that all other layers must be hidden when the layer comp is created. The name of the layer comp should be the name of the team member who created that particular banner. The layer comp Comment field should list what the group considered the strengths of each banner design.

9. Each group should choose its favorite banner and save the combined banner file with the favorite banner layer on top and visible, and all of the other layers hidden. In order to preserve the individual layers, the file should be saved in PSD format.

10. As a final step, the groups should rejoin and all the team members should combine their efforts to lay out a magazine ad using one of the logos, point text, and paragraph text. The ad should include text along a path and/or warped text. The paragraph text can be placeholder text or can be written specifically for the ad. Either the point text or the paragraph text should include at least one character that uses a baseline shift. The ad should demonstrate knowledge of how to adjust colors, how to use fill layers, blending modes, opacity, masks, and filters, and how to use the Brush Tool and the History Brush Tool. Team members can work together to come up with the best design. When there is a consensus, save the ad in PSD format at 300 ppi for a CMYK print piece, and then save it in Grayscale at the appropriate resolution and as the appropriate file type for a newspaper ad.

11. Submit your team's completed files to your instructor as requested. Files should include the two logo files in digital format, the Web banner file in digital format with the multiple Web banner layers, and the magazine ad in CMYK PSD format and Grayscale JPG format. The team should also provide written documentation that describes the role of each team member and his or her contributions to the team. This documentation should include descriptions of any challenges the team faced while completing this exercise and how the team members worked together to overcome those challenges.

TUTORIAL 7

OBJECTIVES

Session 7.1
- Use the Ruler Tool to straighten and crop images
- Crop images using the Crop Tool
- Adjust images with the auto correction tools
- Correct images using the Threshold and Curves adjustments

Session 7.2
- Retouch images with the Spot Healing Brush and Healing Brush Tools
- Work with the Dodge, Burn, and Sponge Tools
- Create focus in an image with the Blur and Sharpen Tools
- Adjust color and luminosity in Lab color mode

Correcting, Adjusting, and Retouching

Adjusting and Retouching Photographic Images

Case | *Hooked*

Hooked is a small ecoadventure company, based in New Braunfels, Texas, that provides guided zip line tours that enable adventurers to experience the canopy of the hill country of Texas from a whole new perspective. The tour takes place on a course consisting of a series of steel zip lines connected by platforms. Every tour is led by an experienced guide who is an expert in finding and explaining the local ecosystems to guests. The tour also focuses on showing visitors how people are affecting the native Texas landscape, and guides discuss ways in which each person can help to preserve native ecosystems.

You have been hired by Dayne Brenneman, the owner of Hooked, to create a new promotional brochure using photographs he has given you. In this tutorial, you'll crop images using the Straighten and Crop Tools, and you'll correct images with Photoshop's auto correction tools. You'll also make adjustments to images using the Threshold and Curves adjustments as well as the Dodge, Burn, Sharpen, Sponge, and Healing Tools. Finally, you'll use the Lab color mode to create color and luminosity adjustments.

STARTING DATA FILES

Photoshop7 → **Tutorial**

Flying.psd
Hanging.psd
HeadChristy.psd
HeadKathyJim.psd
LookUp.psd

Review

Resting.psd

Case1

JamJam.psd

Case2

GroupSushiBar.psd
ManInside.psd

Case3

ArtistJohnVasquez.psd
ArtistJasonPrice.psd
ArtistsMarkJennyCope.psd

Case4

AlterProject.psd

SESSION 7.1 VISUAL OVERVIEW

Using the Image menu, you can access **auto correction tools**, which use mathematical algorithms and preset values to adjust images.

The Crop Tool enables you to crop your image using the Rule of Thirds grid.

The Ruler Tool provides a variety of helpful measurements when you draw a line between two points, and it can be used to position elements precisely within a composition; you can also use the Ruler Tool to quickly straighten an image.

The **Rule of Thirds** states that you should divide every image into nine equal parts, using two vertical lines and two horizontal lines. To achieve the greatest visual interest, energy, and tension, you should position significant elements along the lines or, for even more power, where they intersect.

File   Edit   Image   Layer   Select   Filter   Analysis   3D   View   Window   Help

X: 0.00   Y: 0.00   W: 0.00   H: 0.00   A: 0.0°   L1: 0.00   L2:   Use Measure

hooked brochure72.psd @ 77.7% (Curves 1, RGB/8) *

hooked
eco adventure tours

77.65%   Doc: 1.39M/4.77M

CROPPING AND CORRECTION TOOLS

The Straighten button is used to rotate an image so that an important element in the image is straightened within the frame; it is used with the Ruler Tool.

The Adjustments panel provides an easy way to create adjustment layers, such as a Curves adjustment layer.

Selecting the Auto adjustment is the same as selecting Auto Color from the Image menu, but in this case, the adjustment is applied to an adjustment layer so it is not destructive.

The **Curves adjustment** alters image contrast and tone by taking selected input tones and stretching or compressing them using anchor points.

The **Threshold adjustment** changes an image to high-contrast black-and-white output by specifying a threshold level at which lighter pixels are changed to white and darker pixels are changed to black.

Adjustment layers are displayed above the layer, or layers, they affect.

Because each adjustment is on its own layer, the adjustments are nondestructive and can be changed at any time.

Photoshop as Digital Darkroom

One of Photoshop's most powerful applications is as a darkroom that enables you to digitally correct, enhance, and retouch your photographic images. Just as traditional photographers adjusted their images when they were developing film and printing photographs, modern photographers use Photoshop to optimize the composition, color, contrast, and tone of photographic images. In this section, you'll explore a range of Photoshop tools that enable you to correct your compositions and photographs.

Straightening and Cropping

The first step in creating a breathtaking photo is to frame the image in a way that is visually appealing. This process takes some thought. You must identify what elements you want to incorporate in the photo, and then you must determine how much of the background you want to include in your final product. Determining the position of the main elements within the photo is also an important part of creating a good photographic image.

When working with images in Photoshop, look at the original image and determine on which elements you would like the viewer's eye to focus, and then remove distracting elements from the image. You can often do this easily by cropping those elements from the image. By making calculated decisions regarding what is included in your photographs, you can control the message that you are creating.

INSIGHT

Archiving Original Photos

Remember that many of the changes that you make in Photoshop are destructive and alter an image permanently. Having an archival file of original artwork ensures that you can find and use the original, unaltered image again in the future. In addition, many photographers and graphic design professionals use tools such as Adobe Bridge to keep track of photographs and to create identifying information, such as tags and metadata, that make it easier to search for those images. Maintaining organized archives of your original work should become a regular part of your work routine.

Straightening and Cropping with the Ruler Tool

As its name suggests, the Ruler Tool provides a variety of measurements when you draw a line between two points in the work area. Designers often use these measurements to position elements precisely within a composition. You can also use the tool to straighten an image by quickly aligning key elements of the image with a horizontal or vertical line that you draw using the tool. This feature is helpful because it enables you to rotate an image to create a composition that is oriented around elements on which you would like the observer to focus.

The Straighten feature of the Ruler Tool is useful in many circumstances. For example, if you have an image of a building that is positioned at an angle, you can use the Ruler to draw a line that is parallel to the roofline of the building, and then you can use the Straighten button to rotate the photograph so the roofline of the building is parallel to the top of the image.

Dayne has an image of one of his employees hanging from a zip line that he would like to use in the brochure. However, the employee is positioned at the edge of the image and is positioned at an angle that might not work well in the brochure. You'll use the Ruler Tool to straighten and crop the image so the angle of the rope is parallel to the side of the image, thus creating a more dramatic and focused composition.

TIP

When you use the Straighten button, the image is also cropped to remove any blank areas from the composition.

Straightening an Image

- On the Tools panel, click the Ruler Tool.
- On the canvas, draw a line that is parallel to the key element to which you want to orient the image.
- On the options bar, click the Straighten button.

To use the Ruler Tool to straighten the image:

1. Start Photoshop while pressing the **Ctrl+Alt+Shift** keys. When you are prompted to delete the Adobe Photoshop Settings File, click **Yes**. On the Application bar, right-click **Essentials**, and then click **Reset Essentials** to reset the default work-space layout. Reset all tools.

2. Navigate to the Photoshop7\Tutorial folder included with your Data Files, and open **Hanging.psd**.

3. Save the file as **HangStraight.psd** in the Photoshop7\Tutorial folder, and then press the **Ctrl+0** keys to fit the image on screen.

4. On the Tools panel, click the **Ruler Tool** , which is hidden under the Eyedropper Tool . The pointer changes to the ruler pointer . Place the pointer just above the image, slightly to the left of the rope, from which the man is hanging.

5. Click and drag the mouse down and to the right to create a line parallel to the rope. Release the mouse button after the line exits the image. See Figure 7-1.

TIP

You can also activate the Ruler Tool by pressing the Shift+I keys.

Figure 7-1   **Ruler line drawn parallel to the rope**

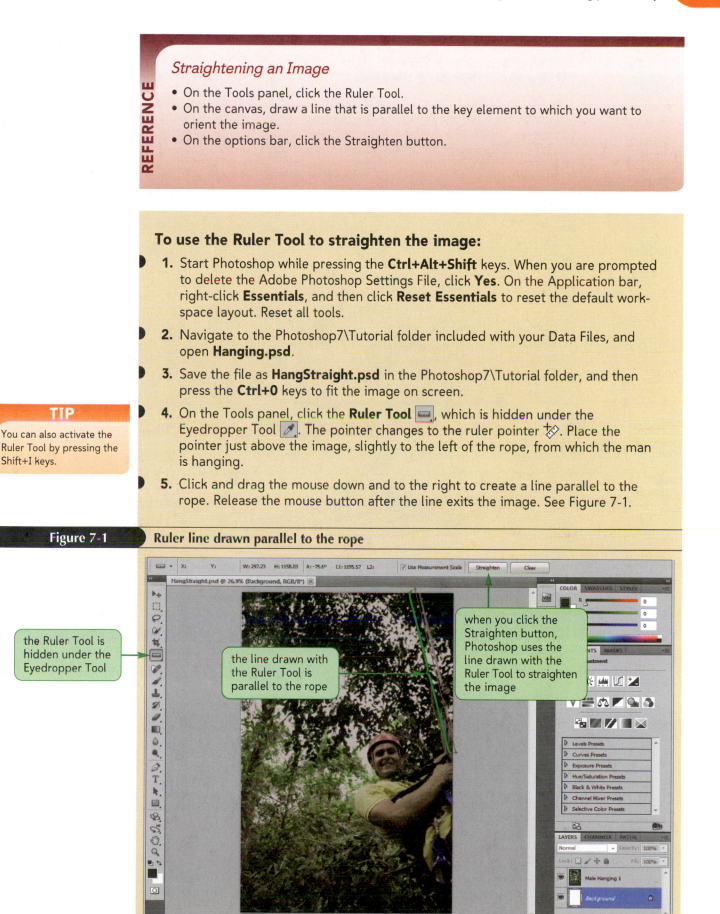

the Ruler Tool is hidden under the Eyedropper Tool

the line drawn with the Ruler Tool is parallel to the rope

when you click the Straighten button, Photoshop uses the line drawn with the Ruler Tool to straighten the image

When you click the Straighten button, the image will be rotated to make this line parallel to the sides of the image.

6. On the options bar, click the **Straighten** button. Photoshop rotates the image until the ruler line (and the rope) is at a 90-degree angle to the bottom of the image. Then, the image is automatically cropped to eliminate any blank areas of the background that appeared when the image was rotated. See Figure 7-2.

Figure 7-2   **Straightened and cropped image**

image has been rotated to place the ruler line at a 90-degree angle to the bottom of the image

any areas showing the white background have been cropped

When Photoshop crops the composition area of a straightened image, it does not delete the areas of the image that lie outside the cropped area. This enables you to move the image around slightly if you feel that different positioning will create a better composition.

7. On the Application bar, click **Edit**, and then click **Undo Crop**. Without the cropping, you can see how Photoshop rotated the image on the canvas.

8. On the Application bar, click **Edit**, and then click **Redo Crop** to view the cropped image again.

Dayne thinks this image would work better in the brochure if the man, who is the focus of the composition, is slightly higher in the frame. To do so, you will use the Move Tool to shift the image up.

To move the straightened image:

1. On the Layers panel, select the **Male Hanging 1** layer, if necessary, and then on the Tools panel, click the **Move Tool** 🢒⊹.

2. Click inside the image, and drag the mouse up and to the right until you have the maximum amount of the man displayed in the image without showing any of the white background. See Figure 7-3.

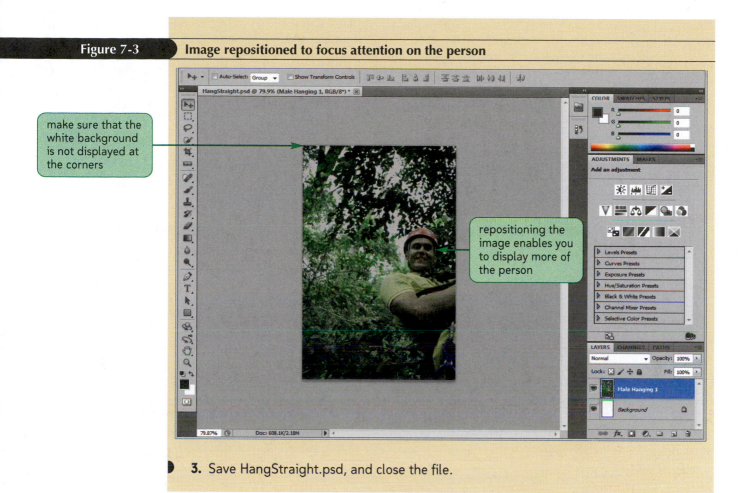

Figure 7-3   **Image repositioned to focus attention on the person**

make sure that the white background is not displayed at the corners

repositioning the image enables you to display more of the person

3. Save HangStraight.psd, and close the file.

This straightened and cropped image will work well in the new Hooked brochure. Dayne has some additional images that he needs your help with, including one that needs to be cropped to create more interest.

Cropping with the Crop Tool

Using the Crop Tool, you can drag a grid, called the Crop Guide Overlay, over an image and then adjust the visible area of the overlay to determine where you will crop the image. The portion of the image that falls in the darkened area outside the Crop Guide Overlay will be cropped. By default, the Crop Guide Overlay is divided into three equal horizontal sections and three equal vertical sections. This creates a grid with nine sections that you can drag and reposition over the image. This enables you to easily use the Rule of Thirds when making cropping decisions.

The Rule of Thirds provides important guidance in helping you achieve good photographic composition. The rule suggests that you should imagine every image as being divided into a grid of nine equal parts. To achieve the greatest visual interest, energy, and tension, you should position significant elements along these lines or, for even more power, where they intersect.

Employing the Rule of Thirds prevents designers from making the common mistake of placing the main object in a photograph directly in the center of the composition, which can be less visually interesting. The rule is like a set of training wheels; it enables you to create reasonably good compositions even before you have fully developed your skills. However, there is more to good composition than just following the rules. To consistently create exceptional compositions, you need to understand why the rules work, and you need to take some time to think about each composition as an independent creation. It is also important to understand when to break the rules.

Examining the compositions that you create using the Rule of Thirds can provide you with insight into what a good composition looks like. Take some time with each image you create and think about how the image makes you feel. Then, try to identify what elements in the image reinforce that feeling and which elements are distractions. Examining the compositions of successful artists can also provide you with insights. The understanding that you develop from these exercises will enable you to develop your design muscles and to create your own personal style.

Dayne has provided you with another image that he wants to use in the brochure. In this image, the employee is centered in the frame surrounded by a great deal of background imagery; consequently, the composition is not that interesting. You'll employ the Rule of Thirds and crop the image using the Crop Tool to create a more interesting composition that focuses on the employee rather than on the background.

REFERENCE

Cropping an Image

- On the Tools panel, click the Crop Tool.
- Click in the image and drag the mouse to display the Crop Guide Overlay.
- On the options bar, click the Crop Guide Overlay arrow, and then click Rule of Thirds, if necessary.
- Using the side and corner selection handles, adjust the Crop Guide Overlay until the areas of the image that you want to crop are in the darkened area outside the Crop Guide Overlay.
- Using the Rule of Thirds to optimize the composition, further adjust the grid to ensure that important items are located on the grid lines and intersection points.
- Press the Enter key or click the Commit button on the options bar to crop the image.

To crop the image with the Crop Tool:

1. Open **LookUp.psd** from the Photoshop7\Tutorial folder provided with your Data Files.

2. Save the file as **LookUpCrop.psd** in the Photoshop7\Tutorial folder, and then press the **Ctrl+0** keys to fit the image on screen.

3. On the Tools panel, click the **Crop Tool** 🔲. The pointer changes to the crop pointer 🔲.

   Trouble? If there are values in the Width and Height boxes on the options bar, delete those values before moving to Step 4.

4. Place the pointer at the upper-left corner of the image. Click and drag the mouse down to the lower-right corner of the image. Release the mouse button. The Crop Guide Overlay is displayed over the image.

5. On the options bar, click the **Crop Guide Overlay** arrow, and then click **Rule of Thirds**, if necessary. See Figure 7-4.

TIP

You can also activate the Crop Tool by pressing the Shift+C keys.

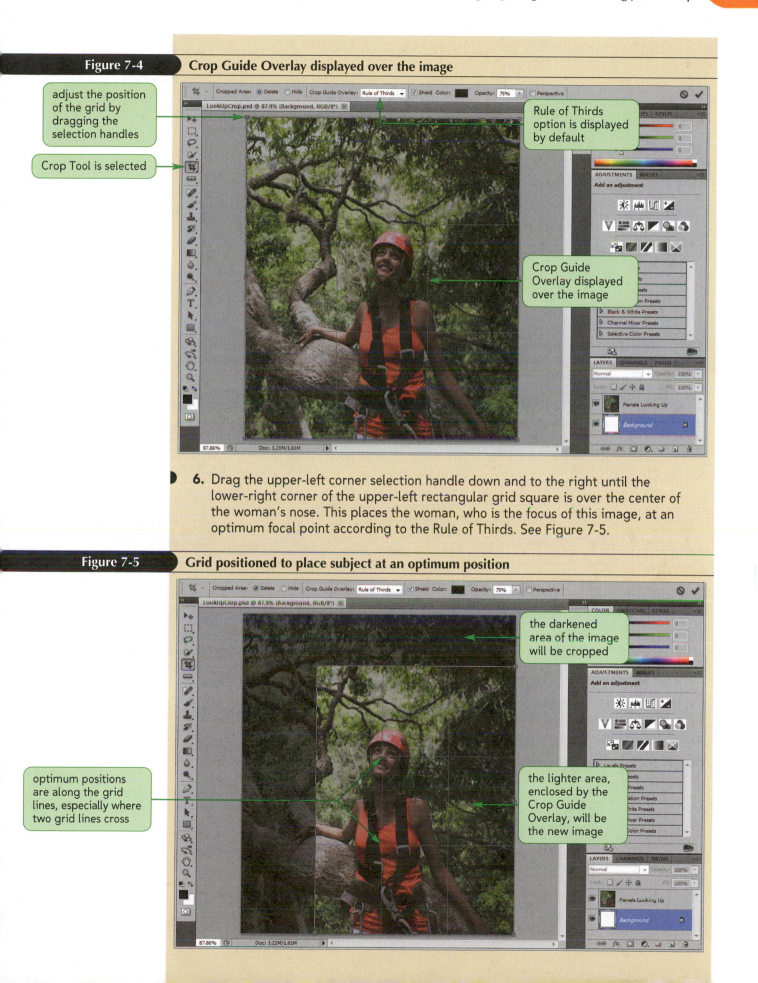

Figure 7-4   Crop Guide Overlay displayed over the image

adjust the position of the grid by dragging the selection handles

Crop Tool is selected

Rule of Thirds option is displayed by default

Crop Guide Overlay displayed over the image

6. Drag the upper-left corner selection handle down and to the right until the lower-right corner of the upper-left rectangular grid square is over the center of the woman's nose. This places the woman, who is the focus of this image, at an optimum focal point according to the Rule of Thirds. See Figure 7-5.

Figure 7-5   Grid positioned to place subject at an optimum position

the darkened area of the image will be cropped

optimum positions are along the grid lines, especially where two grid lines cross

the lighter area, enclosed by the Crop Guide Overlay, will be the new image

7. Place the pointer inside the highlighted grid area and drag the entire grid to the left until the woman's nose is aligned with the lower-right corner of the center-top rectangle. This placement is even better because the woman's gaze is now focused into the image.

8. Press the **Enter** key to crop the image. See Figure 7-6.

Figure 7-6 ▶ **Cropped image**

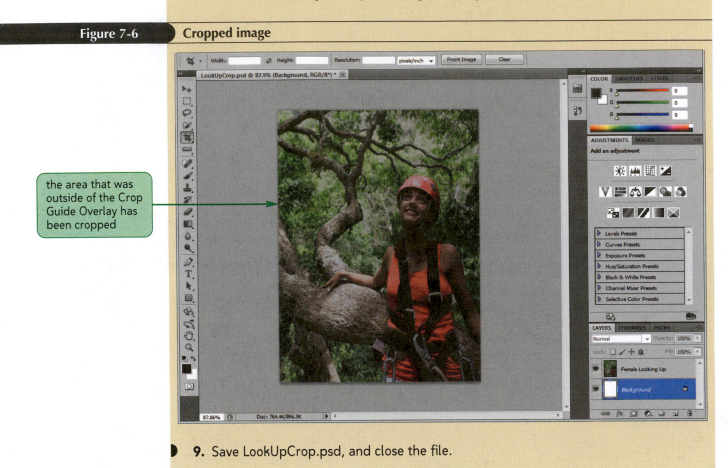

the area that was outside of the Crop Guide Overlay has been cropped

9. Save LookUpCrop.psd, and close the file.

By cropping the image, you have made the young woman the focus of the composition. Placing her on a grid line with her gaze focused into the composition, as if she is looking at something that is slightly out of the frame, creates visual interest and energy and causes the viewer to engage in the image, wondering what she is focused upon. Dayne likes what you have done with this image, and he plans to use it in the brochure. Next, you'll adjust some images using auto adjustments.

Auto Correction Tools

The Auto Color, Auto Contrast, and Auto Tone Tools in Photoshop allow you to quickly correct the color, contrast, and tone in an image, using the tools alone or in combination. The auto correction tools use mathematical algorithms and preset values to adjust images. The following is a summary of the three tools:

• **Auto Tone:** Adjusts the black-and-white points in an image. Portions of the shadows and highlights in each channel are clipped, and the lightest pixels in each color channel are mapped to pure white while the darkest pixels in each color channel are mapped to pure black. The remaining colors are redistributed proportionally.

- **Auto Contrast:** Adjusts the contrast of an image as a whole, without adjusting individual color channels. Contrast is created by clipping shadow and highlight values of the image and then mapping the lightest pixels to pure white and the darkest pixels to pure black.
- **Auto Color:** Adjusts the color and contrast of an image by adjusting highlights, midtones, and shadows. Highlights and shadows are clipped by .5 percent and midtones are neutralized. You can use Auto Color to neutralize color casts created by the Auto Tone correction.

The values and settings for each auto correction tool can be adjusted in the Auto Color Correction Options dialog box, but it is a good idea to use the default settings until you have a good understanding of how these tools work. The obvious shortfall in this, and any general approach to correction, is that the character and details of specific images are not factored into the corrections. Because of this, you are sometimes left with average-looking images. The other problem with using the auto correction tools is that the adjustments are destructive. However, the auto correction tools are a great place to start, especially when you are trying to develop an understanding of what an image with good color, contrast, and tone looks like.

TIP

To prevent the auto correction tools from taking large blocks of color, such as an image border, into account when calculating correction values, first select the area of the image you want to correct and then apply the auto correction.

INSIGHT

Understanding Components of Color

Understanding some of the components of color will help you to do a better job when you adjust or manipulate photographic images. **Hue** is essentially what we think of or perceive as an object's color. Generally, when you refer to an object as being red, or blue, you are referring to the object's hue. Hue is expressed as the measurement, in degrees, of the location of a color around the standard color wheel. **Saturation** is the expression of purity or strength of a color. If a color has 0 percent saturation, it is gray, whereas a pure color has a saturation of 100 percent. Colors that have a 100 percent saturation value are located at the outside of the color wheel, and saturation decreases as the pure color is blended or diluted while you move toward the middle of the wheel. **Brightness** is a measurement of the lightness or darkness in a color and is also measured as a percentage. A brightness value of 0 percent is black and a brightness value of 100 percent is white.

The third image that Dayne would like to use in the brochure needs some adjustment to its color, contrast, and tone. You'll use the auto correction tools in an attempt to quickly improve the image.

To correct the image with the auto correction tools:

1. Open **Flying.psd** from the Photoshop7\Tutorial folder.

2. Save the file as **FlyingAuto.psd** in the Photoshop7\Tutorial folder, and then press the **Ctrl+0** keys to fit the image on screen.

3. On the Layers panel, select the **Fly Guy** layer, and create three duplicate layers of the Fly Guy layer. Name the new layers **Fly Guy Tone**, **Fly Guy Contrast**, and **Fly Guy Color**. Collapse the Adjustments panel group so all of the layers are displayed. See Figure 7-7.

Figure 7-7   **Duplicate layers created and renamed**

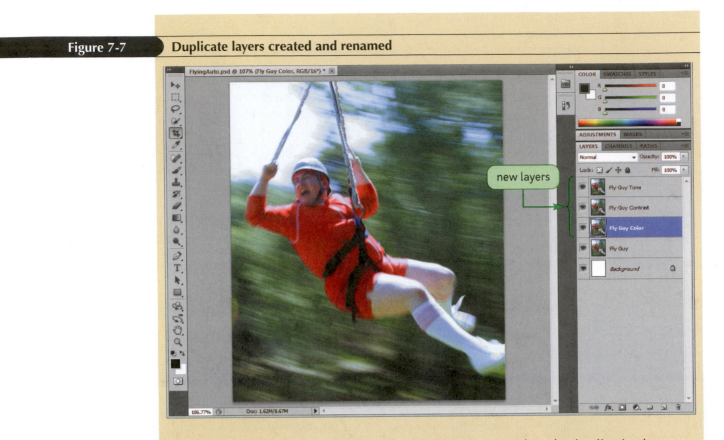

new layers

4. On the Layers panel, select the **Fly Guy Tone** layer, and on the Application bar click **Image**, and then click **Auto Tone** to apply the tone adjustment. The image now has deeper blacks, brighter whites, and greater contrast. See Figure 7-8.

Figure 7-8   **Auto Tone correction applied**

Auto Tone, Auto Contrast, and Auto Color are located in the Image menu

the contrast of the colors in the image has increased

the darkest color in each color channel is mapped to absolute black

the lightest color in each color channel is mapped to absolute white

5. On the Layers panel, click the **Eye** icon next to the Fly Guy Tone layer to hide that layer.

6. Select the **Fly Guy Contrast** layer, and on the Image menu, click **Auto Contrast** to apply the contrast adjustment. The contrast of the entire image is increased. See Figure 7-9.

| Figure 7-9 | Auto Contrast correction applied |

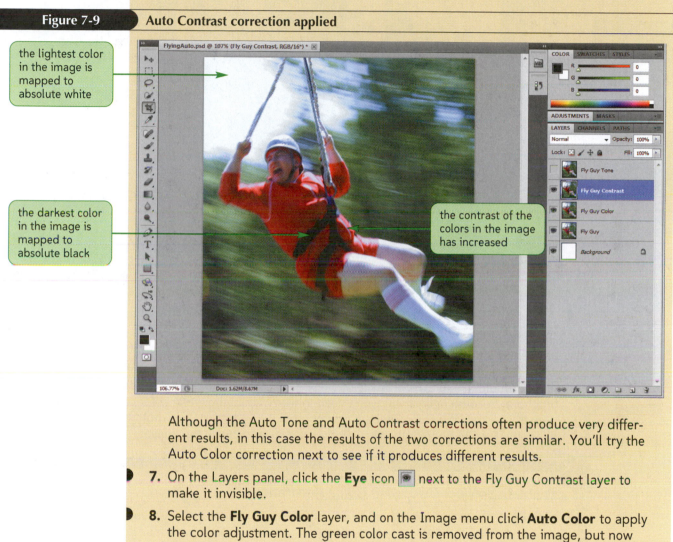

the lightest color in the image is mapped to absolute white

the darkest color in the image is mapped to absolute black

the contrast of the colors in the image has increased

Although the Auto Tone and Auto Contrast corrections often produce very different results, in this case the results of the two corrections are similar. You'll try the Auto Color correction next to see if it produces different results.

7. On the Layers panel, click the **Eye** icon next to the Fly Guy Contrast layer to make it invisible.

8. Select the **Fly Guy Color** layer, and on the Image menu click **Auto Color** to apply the color adjustment. The green color cast is removed from the image, but now there is too much red visible in the skin tones. See Figure 7-10.

Figure 7-10 | **Auto Color correction applied**

there is a little too much red in the skin tones of the image

the green color cast has been removed from the image

9. Compare the changes made to each layer, and then save and close the file.

None of the auto corrections were perfect. Auto Tone and Auto Contrast left a green color cast to the image, and Auto Color made the skin tones too red. Dayne has decided that he would like to use the image of the guy cut out from the background in the brochure. Because of this, you won't need to worry about the green color cast, which primarily distorts the colors in the background of the image, so you would be able to use either the Fly Guy Tone or the Fly Guy Contrast layer to create the image.

PROSKILLS

Problem Solving: Displaying Color Accurately

Before you can accurately adjust or correct the color in your projects, you must create an environment in which you can reliably evaluate compositions in the context of their intended output. You do this by creating a work flow process that integrates color management into every phase.

The first step in creating an effective color management work flow is to calibrate and profile your monitors for accurate display. **Calibrating** a monitor adjusts the display to conform to known specifications, and creating a color profile enables you to save those settings so your monitor display is consistent over time. Although all monitors display images using RGB color, every monitor is calibrated to display colors slightly differently. This fact becomes evident when you look at a wall of monitors in a department store. In addition, to inherent color display differences, users can make adjustments to the brightness and contrast of most monitors. Because of these variables, it can be difficult to know how the adjustments you make to images will affect your final product. Both the Windows and Mac OS provide a basic monitor calibration utility; however, for professional results, you can purchase a third-party calibration software that would provide additional measuring devices and greater accuracy. By making use of high-quality color calibration tools, you can ensure that throughout your design process, your decisions regarding color will be based on accurate input and output information.

Next, you'll explore how adjustment layers enable you to create remarkable, precise, nondestructive adjustments to the tone, contrast, and color of your images.

Correcting Images with the Adjustments Panel

The Adjustments panel provides an array of powerful tools that enable you to correct images nondestructively by making corrections on adjustment layers rather than to the image itself. As with the auto adjustment tools you just used, you can use adjustment layers alone, or in combination, but each adjustment creates its own independent adjustment layer, which you can tweak repeatedly until you get the look you desire. In addition, changing the order in which adjustment layers are stacked will also change their effect on the image because layers that are lower in the stacking order are applied before layers that are higher in the stacking order.

Now that you have a basic understanding of tone, contrast, and color, it is a good time to take a deeper look at how you can use the power and precision of the adjustments on the Adjustments panel to create spectacular images. Figure 7-11 provides a description of all the available options on the Adjustments panel.

Figure 7-11	Major tools in the Adjustments panel

Adjustment	Use To
Brightness/Contrast	Quickly adjust the brightness and contrast of the image.
Levels	Manipulate the intensity level of shadows, midtones, and highlights using sliders and histograms.
Curves	Adjust the contrast and tone of images using curve controls.
Exposure	Adjust the tonal range of 32-bit high dynamic range (HDR) images (this tool also works less effectively with 8-bit and 16-bit images); the Exposure Tool uses a linear color space, not the image's current color space, to make adjustments. When used with HDR images, this can uncover details that would otherwise be lost in shadow or highlight.
Vibrance	Adjust the saturation or intensity of color in an image (not available in CMYK).
Hue/Saturation	Adjust the hue, saturation, and lightness of an entire image or individual colors.
Color Balance	Alter the range of colors used in an image.
Black & White	Convert color images to gray scale and control how individual colors convert; can also be used to add a color tint to a grayscale image (not available in CMYK).
Photo Filter	Reproduce the effects of various camera lens filters.
Channel Mixer	Adjust the amount of information to include from each channel when creating a grayscale image.
Invert	Invert image colors to their opposites on the color wheel or invert values in noncolor images.
Posterize	Specify the number of tonal (or brightness) levels for each channel of an image to create a special effect where the image contains large, flat areas of color.
Threshold	Change an image to high-contrast black-and-white output by specifying a threshold level where lighter pixels are changed to white and darker pixels are changed to black.
Gradient Map	Convert an image to gray scale by mapping the image colors to a specified gradient fill.
Selective Color	Target specified colors, and adjust the amount of cyan, magenta, yellow, and black in the specified color.

Using the Threshold Adjustment

As explained in Figure 7-11, the Threshold adjustment changes an image to a black-and-white image. The slider enables you to adjust the **threshold level**, which is the pixel value above which all lighter pixels are changed to white and below which all darker pixels are changed to black. Moving the slider all the way to the right changes all pixels to white and moving the slider all the way to the left changes all pixels to black.

Primarily, this adjustment is used to create special effects. For example, you might change a photograph, which has millions of colors, to a two-color, black-and-white image and then adjust the threshold level to create a dramatic composition. You could then use the Selective Color adjustment to change white and black to different colors, as shown in Figure 7-12.

| Figure 7-12 | Image with Threshold and Selective Color adjustments |

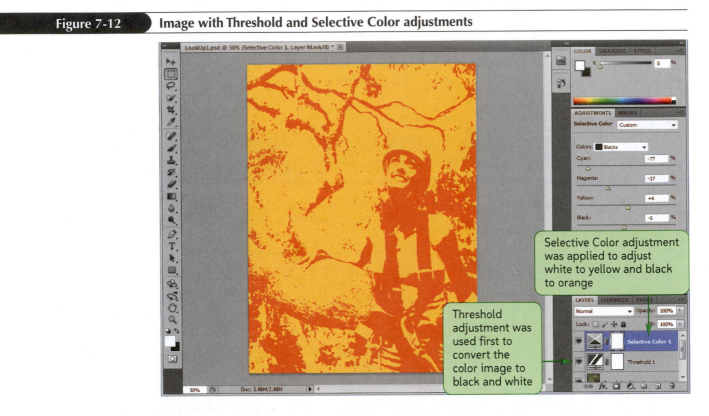

You can also use the Threshold adjustment to locate the darkest and lightest points in an image. To find the darkest pixels in your image, move the slider all the way to the left. Then, move it slightly toward the middle until some black pixels are displayed on the white background. The first points to display are the darkest points in the image. Once you have located the darkest pixels in the image, you can add a color marker to the image that will enable you to locate that point in the future. To find the lightest pixels in the image, reverse the preceding process, moving the slider all the way to the right and then back to the left until the first white pixel appears.

Once you identify the darkest or lightest pixels in an image, you can use the Color Sampler Tool to create color markers in your image. **Color markers** are identifiers that are only visible in Photoshop and that enable you to locate specific areas of color while you are adjusting your image. When you select a pixel with the Color Sampler Tool, the Info panel opens; however, you may want to open the Info panel prior to selecting a pixel. As you move the tool over the image in the Document window, the Info panel displays the RGB values, CMYK values, and the X and Y values (the values that correspond to placement along the X and Y axes of a graph) of the pixels over which you are moving the pointer.

Although Dayne was happy with the way you cropped the image of the young woman in the tree, he noted that the image looks a bit dull. He would like you to do some additional work to make the photo more vibrant and dynamic. Your first step in creating a more dramatic image is to locate the darkest and lightest points in the image. You'll use the Threshold adjustment to locate these points. You'll use the Color Sampler Tool with the Threshold adjustment to create color markers that enable you to identify the darkest and lightest pixels in your image. Then, you'll increase the contrast of the image using the Curves adjustment by setting the darkest pixels to absolute black and setting the lightest pixels to absolute white.

REFERENCE

Marking Lightest and Darkest Pixels with the Threshold Adjustment

- Select the layer you want to adjust.
- Open the Adjustments panel, and select the Threshold adjustment tool.
- On the Adjustments panel, move the Threshold Level slider all the way to the left and then slide it back toward the middle until some black pixels are displayed.
- On the Tools panel, select the Color Sampler Tool, and then Shift-click the black pixels to create a marker over those pixels that will enable you to locate them again.
- Move the Threshold Level slider all the way to the right, and then slide it back toward the middle until some white pixels are displayed.
- Shift-click the white pixels to create a marker over those pixels.

To locate the lightest and darkest points in the image:

1. Open the **LookUpCrop.psd** file that you saved in the Photoshop7\Tutorial folder, and then press the **Ctrl+0** keys to fit the image on screen.

2. On the Layers panel, select the **Female Looking Up** layer.

3. Expand the Adjustments panel, if necessary, and then click the **Threshold** icon ▨. The image is converted to black and white, and an adjustment layer named Threshold 1 is added above the Female Looking Up layer.

4. On the Adjustments panel, slide the **Threshold Level** slider to the left until the Threshold Level value reads **1**. The image is almost entirely white.

5. Slowly move the slider back to the right until several pixels of black are displayed together.

6. On the Application bar, click **Window**, and then click **Info** to open the Info panel.

7. On the Tools panel, click the **Color Sampler Tool** ▨, which is hidden beneath the Ruler Tool that you used earlier in this tutorial. Place the bottom edge of the eyedropper over the black pixels, make sure that a value of 0 is displayed beside R, G, and B in the 8-bit section of the Info panel, and click to add color marker 1 to the image. See Figure 7-13.

Figure 7-13   Threshold adjustment with color marker 1 inserted

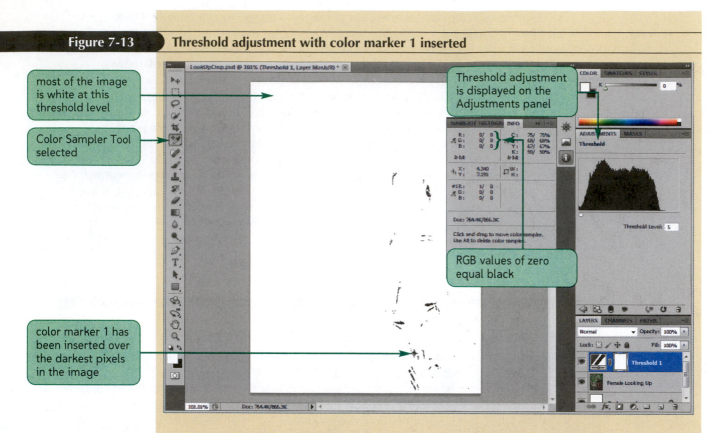

most of the image is white at this threshold level

Color Sampler Tool selected

Threshold adjustment is displayed on the Adjustments panel

RGB values of zero equal black

color marker 1 has been inserted over the darkest pixels in the image

Trouble? If the layout of your Info panel does not match that shown in Figure 7-13, click the panel options icon ⊟ at the top of the Info panel, and then click Panel Options. In the Info Panel Options dialog box, click the Mode arrow, select Actual Color, and then click the OK button.

8. On the Adjustments panel, slide the **Threshold Level** slider all the way to the right, and then slide it back to the left to display some white pixels.

9. Click the white pixels to place color marker 2 to mark the lightest pixels in the image. This time, the RGB values should all be 255.

10. On the Layers panel, drag the **Threshold 1** layer to the **Delete layer** icon 🗑 to delete it, and then close the Info panel group. The color markers remain on the image. Notice that they are located over the darkest and lightest pixels in the image. See Figure 7-14. The location of your color markers might vary slightly.

| Figure 7-14 | Color markers 1 and 2 inserted |

color marker 2 marks the lightest pixels in the image

color marker 1 marks the darkest pixels in the image

Now that you have identified the darkest and lightest pixels in the image, you'll use the Curves adjustment to correct the contrast, tone, and colors of the image.

Enhancing Images with the Curves Adjustment

The Curves adjustment is a robust adjustment that alters image contrast and tone by taking selected input tones and stretching or compressing their values using anchor points. Initially, the tonal range of any image is represented by a straight diagonal line that is displayed in the center of the Curves graph on the Adjustments panel. In this graph, the values of **Input tones** (the original value of the tones in the image when the Curves adjustment layer is first created) are represented horizontally, and the values of **Output tones** (the values of the same tones after adjustments are made) are represented vertically. The representation is a diagonal line because the original Input tones are equal to the Output tones— indicating that no adjustments have yet been made. As you alter the tones, anchor points are added to the line, and the line changes to a curve to visually represent the altered Output values of the tones you stretch or compress. There are several different ways to adjust an image using the Curves adjustment. See Figure 7-15.

Figure 7-15   **Curves adjustment**

You'll use the Curves adjustment on the Adjustments panel to enhance the LookUpCrop.psd image. First, you'll use the eyedroppers on the Adjustments panel to set the white point and black point of the image. When you set the white point, you click on a point in the image (in this case, you'll click in color marker 1), and that point changes to absolute white. When you set the black point, you click on a point in the image (in this case, you'll click in color marker 2), and that point changes to absolute black. The remaining pixels in the image adjust proportionately and the contrast in the image is increased. If an image is dull or flat, this adjustment produces a more rich and vibrant image.

REFERENCE

Setting the White and Black Points of an Image

- Select the layer you would like to adjust.
- Open the Adjustments panel, and select the Curves adjustment tool.
- On the Adjustments panel, click the "Sample in image to set black point" icon, and click the darkest point in the image to change the value of that point to absolute black.
- Click the "Sample in image to set white point" icon, and click the lightest point in the image to change the value of that point to absolute white.
- Save the image.

To set the white point and black point of the image:

1. On the Adjustments panel, click the **Curves** icon 🔲. An adjustment layer is added above the Female Looking Up layer on the Layers panel.

   Trouble? If the Curves adjustment layer appears below the Female Looking Up layer on the Layers panel, the Female Looking Up layer was not selected. Drag the Curves 1 adjustment layer above the Female Looking Up layer on the Layers panel.

2. Click the **Sample in image to set black point** icon 🖊, and then click in color marker 1 in the image. The darkest pixels are set to absolute black. You will only notice a small change in the image because the darkest pixels were already close to absolute black.

3. Click the **Sample in image to set white point** icon 🖊, and then click in color marker 2 in the image. The lightest pixels are set to absolute white, and the contrast of the image is increased, creating a more vibrant composition. The diagonal line in the Curves graph on the Adjustments panel changes position to reflect the change in the value of the lightest pixels in the image. See Figure 7-16.

Figure 7-16	Image with white point and black point adjusted

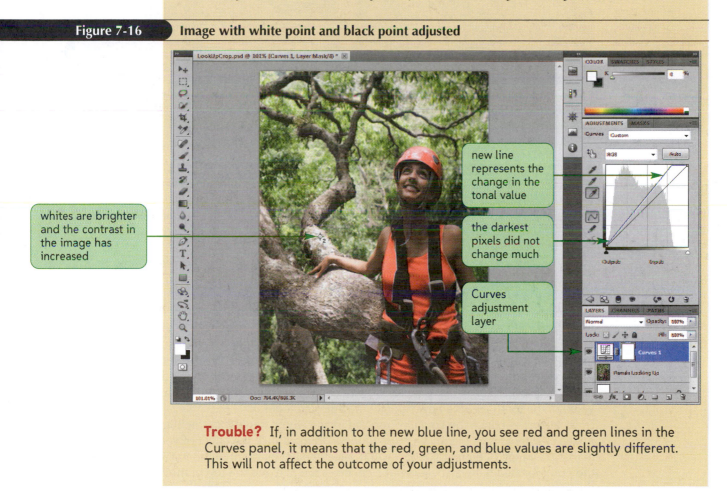

whites are brighter and the contrast in the image has increased

new line represents the change in the tonal value

the darkest pixels did not change much

Curves adjustment layer

Trouble? If, in addition to the new blue line, you see red and green lines in the Curves panel, it means that the red, green, and blue values are slightly different. This will not affect the outcome of your adjustments.

You can also use the Curves adjustment to change the highlights, midtones, and shadows of an image. The midtones of the image are represented by the center area of the Curves grid, and making adjustments to that area of the line will have the strongest effect on the midtones of the image. Highlights are represented by the area above the center of the grid, and making adjustments to that area of the line will have the strongest effect on the highlights of the image. Finally, the shadows are represented by the area below the center of the grid, and making adjustments to that portion of the line will have the strongest effect on the shadows of the image. See Figure 7-17.

Figure 7-17 Highlights, midtones, and shadows on the Curves graph

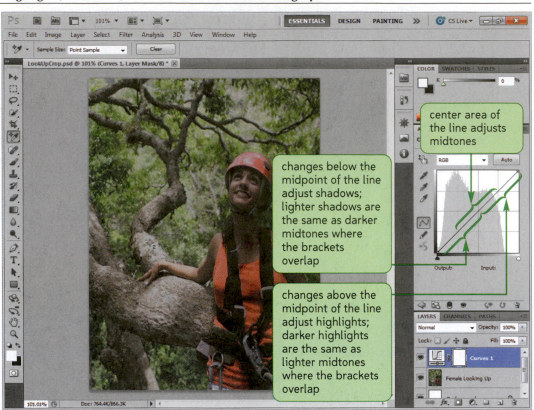

center area of the line adjusts midtones

changes below the midpoint of the line adjust shadows; lighter shadows are the same as darker midtones where the brackets overlap

changes above the midpoint of the line adjust highlights; darker highlights are the same as lighter midtones where the brackets overlap

Note that there is not a cutoff point between where highlights end and midtones begin, or between where midtones end and shadows begin. The areas of overlap, shown in Figure 7-17, demonstrate that the high midtones are also the low highlights. This way of thinking is in line with the way your eyes view things. Most people do not distinguish a specific point at which shadow begins; rather, when you look at something, you see a range of tonalities that flow subtly from lighter to darker.

One way to locate the tones that fall into a certain area of the grid is to select the "Click and drag in image to modify the curve" icon. The pointer changes to an eyedropper, and as you move the pointer over the image, a circle is displayed over the diagonal line. When the circle is displayed over the midpoint of the line, located at the center of the grid, you have located the center of the midtones in the image. When the circle is displayed on the line over the third vertical grid line, you have located the center of the highlights. If you click in the image and drag up and down, you can adjust the value of the tones represented by that point on the line. The line will become curved to reflect the changes you make. The curve represents the change in value between the original Input value of the tones and the new value of the adjusted tones.

To further enhance the LookUpCrop.psd image, you'll lighten the highlights in the image slightly to give the image more fullness. To maximize the effect of your adjustment across the range of highlight tones, you'll select the center point of the highlights. This is the point located halfway between the center of the line and the top of the line, where the vertical and horizontal grid line intersect under the line.

To adjust the highlights of the image:

1. On the Adjustments panel, click the **Click and drag in image to modify the curve** icon.

2. Place the pointer in the image, around the area of the young woman's right elbow and then move the pointer along her arm until the circle is located over the third vertical grid line in the Curves panel. See Figure 7-18.

Figure 7-18   Modify the curve by dragging in the image

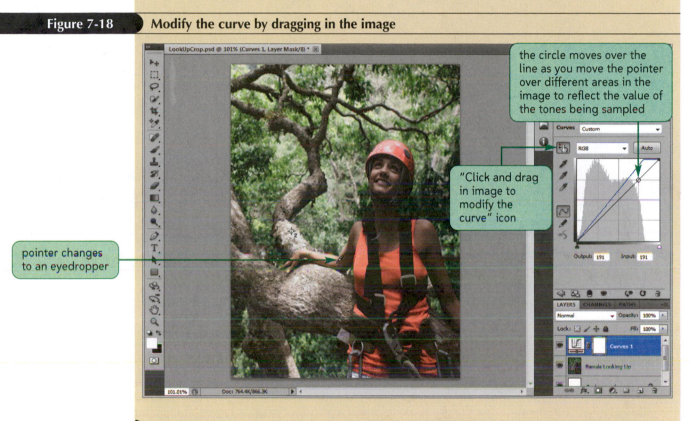

pointer changes to an eyedropper

the circle moves over the line as you move the pointer over different areas in the image to reflect the value of the tones being sampled

"Click and drag in image to modify the curve" icon

3. Click in the image and drag the pointer up slightly until the Output value shown below the Curves graph on the Adjustment panel is **220** and the Input value is **194**, and then release the mouse button. As the curve is stretched upward, the tones of the image, especially the highlights where the anchor is located, become lighter. See Figure 7-19.

Figure 7-19   **Highlights of the image adjusted**

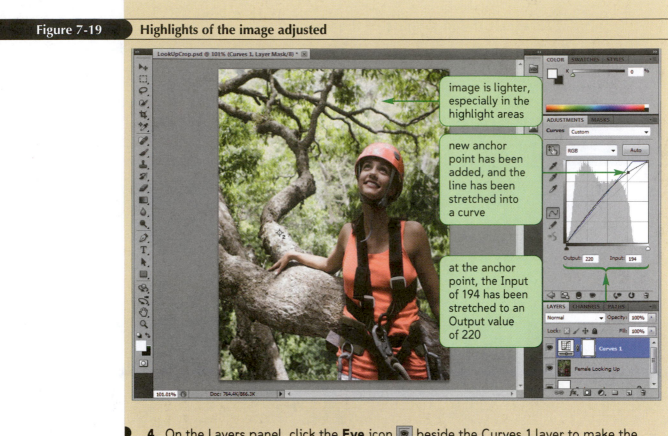

image is lighter, especially in the highlight areas

new anchor point has been added, and the line has been stretched into a curve

at the anchor point, the Input of 194 has been stretched to an Output value of 220

4. On the Layers panel, click the **Eye** icon [eye] beside the Curves 1 layer to make the layer invisible. Notice how this affects the way the image looks.

5. On the Layers panel, click the empty **Eye** icon box [box] to make the layer visible.

You can also create and edit anchor points to modify the curve. You'll create a new anchor point at the first vertical grid line, which is the center of the shadow tones, and you'll move the anchor point down to darken the shadows of the image. By selecting the center point of the shadow tones to create your adjustment point, you ensure that your adjustments will have an effect on the lighter and darker shadow tones in the image. If you were to select a point that was in the darker range of the shadow tones, your adjustments would affect the deepest shadows more than the lightest shadows while a higher point would affect the lightest shadows more drastically. Making this adjustment will give some depth and richness to all of the darker tones in the image.

To create and modify anchor points:

1. On the Adjustments panel, click the **Edit points to modify the curve** icon [curve], if necessary, and then click on the curve where it crosses the first vertical grid line on the left.

2. Drag the anchor point down until the Output is **63** and the Input is **63**. Notice how the darker tones add a richness to the image. See Figure 7-20.

Figure 7-20   **Image with darker shadows**

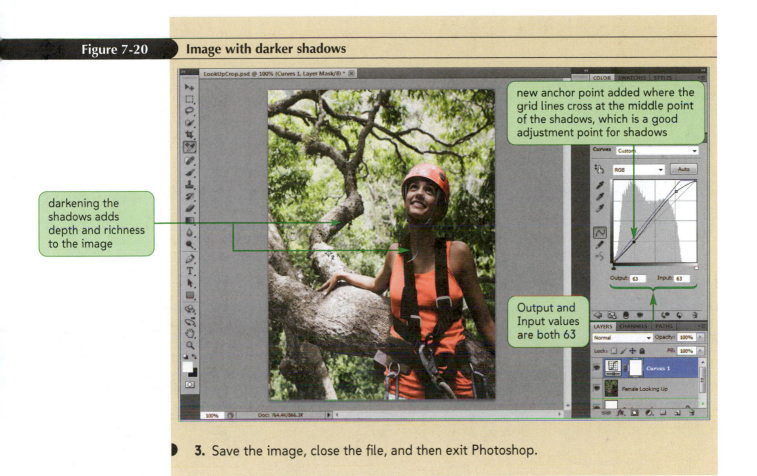

darkening the shadows adds depth and richness to the image

new anchor point added where the grid lines cross at the middle point of the shadows, which is a good adjustment point for shadows

Output and Input values are both 63

3. Save the image, close the file, and then exit Photoshop.

Dayne is thrilled with the images that you have corrected thus far and with the progress of the project. He has approved the adjusted images for use in the brochure.

In this session, you learned that the first step in creating a professionally corrected image is to rotate and crop the image. You learned how to rotate and crop images, and you learned how to use the Rule of Thirds. The second step in the image-correction process is to perform color and tonal corrections. In this session, you adjusted images with the auto correction tools and went on to perform more complex corrections with the Threshold and Curves adjustment tools. The final step in image correction is to use retouching tools to correct smaller imperfections and flaws in the image. In the next session, you'll retouch some of the images for the brochure.

REVIEW

Session 7.1 Quick Check

1. What is the Rule of Thirds?
2. What is the quickest way to adjust the color of an image?
3. True or False. The Auto Tone, Auto Contrast, and Auto Color correction tools make nondestructive edits to your images.
4. _____ are layers in which you can make nondestructive edits to images and compositions.
5. The Threshold adjustment enables you to create _____ images.
6. The _____ adjustment enables you to alter contrast and tone by taking selected input tones and stretching or compressing them using anchor points.
7. What is hue?

SESSION 7.2 VISUAL OVERVIEW

Dramatic color and luminosity adjustments can be made in Lab color mode via the Image menu.

When a tool is selected, the options for that tool are available in the options bar.

The Healing Brush Tool and the Spot Healing Brush Tool can be used to remove slight imperfections from an image.

The Blur and Sharpen Tools enable you to draw the viewer's focus to a particular area of the image.

The Dodge Tool lightens portions of images without distorting skin tones.

The Burn Tool darkens parts of your image without distorting skin tones.

The Sponge Tool adjusts the saturation in an image.

The Spot Healing Brush Tool removes small imperfections by automatically sampling the area surrounding a selection and blending the selection pixels together so texture and tone cause the problem area to disappear into the surrounding image.

RETOUCHING TOOLS

The Rule of Thirds was used to add interest and energy to both of these images.

Retouching tools are tools that can be used to remove small imperfections from an image (such as a distracting highlight on a person's face) or to correct larger areas of an image that still need help after color and tonal corrections are made to the entire image.

When you can use the Healing or Spot Healing Brush Tool on a blank layer above the layer you would like to affect, the adjustments are nondestructive.

Repairing and Retouching Images

Almost any photograph can benefit from a little retouching. Photoshop offers a virtual first aid kit full of tools that enable you to smooth backgrounds, fix blemishes, and patch problems. There are also tools for red-eye correction and tools that help you adjust skin tone and sharpness. In this session, you'll use Photoshop's retouching tools to improve some photographs of the tour guides that Dayne provided for the Hooked brochure.

Repairing Images with the Spot Healing Brush Tool

The Spot Healing Brush Tool is used to remove slight imperfections or problems from an image by automatically taking samples from the area surrounding the part of the image that is being retouched and blending them together so texture and tone cause the problem area to disappear into the surrounding image. This brush is frequently used to fix blemishes and other small imperfections. You can apply the Spot Healing Brush Tool directly to the image that you want to correct; however, this creates a destructive edit. A better choice is to create a blank layer above the image that you want to retouch and then apply the brush to that layer with the Sample All Layers check box checked. In this scenario, the alteration is created in the blank layer and is nondestructive. The settings on the options bar for the Spot Healing Brush Tool include the following:

- **Brush:** The brush you select determines the shape and size of the area that will be affected. It is best to select a round brush that is slightly larger in diameter than the area you would like to repair.
- **Mode:** The Mode setting controls the blending mode, which determines how pixels in the image are affected by the tool. The blending modes available with the Spot Healing Brush Tool are a subset of those available when you are blending layers.
- **Type:** The Type setting enables you to select how the pixels used to heal the problem area are selected. The Proximity Match option uses the pixels just outside the edges of the brush area to heal the brush area. The Create Texture option creates texture by examining the pixels within the brush area; this option is often used when the problem area is surrounded by a great deal of detail. The Content-Aware option is a good starting point. Like the Content-Aware filter that you have already used, the Content-Aware Type setting takes information into account using intelligent algorithms that give you the best shot at a clean fix.
- **Sample All Layers:** This setting enables you to gather healing information from all of the layers in the document. If you want to use this setting, it must be checked when you apply the Spot Healing Brush Tool to an empty layer above the image.

Dayne would like to use some shots of the Hooked tour guides in the brochure. You'll use the Spot Healing Brush Tool to fix a shiny spot on the head shot of Christy, one of the Hooked tour guides.

REFERENCE

Applying the Spot Healing Brush Tool to an Image

- Create an empty layer above the layer that you would like to adjust.
- Select the empty layer, and on the Tools panel, select the Spot Healing Brush Tool.
- On the options bar, select a brush size that is slightly larger than the area you would like to alter, select a blending mode, select a type, and check the Sample All Layers check box. Confirm that the empty layer is the active layer.
- Place the brush over the area of the image you would like to heal, and press the Enter key.
- Save your adjusted image.

To correct an imperfection with the Spot Healing Brush Tool:

1. Start Photoshop while pressing the **Ctrl+Alt+Shift** keys. When you are prompted to delete the Adobe Photoshop Settings File, click **Yes**. On the Application bar, right-click **Essentials**, and then click **Reset Essentials** to reset the default workspace layout. Reset all tools.

2. Navigate to the Photoshop 7\Tutorial folder, and open **HeadChristy.psd**.

3. Save the file as **HeadChristyHeal.psd** in the same folder, press the **Ctrl+0** keys to fit the image to the screen, and then on the Layers panel, select the **Christy Headshot** layer to select it, if necessary.

4. On the Layers panel, click the **Create a new layer** icon ▣ to add a new layer above the Christy Headshot layer; name the new layer **Heal Shine**.

5. On the Tools panel, click the **Spot Healing Brush Tool** 🖌.

6. On the options bar, click the **Brush picker** button ▾, and set the brush size to **80 px**. Select **Normal** as the blending mode, if necessary, select **Content-Aware** as the Type, and click the **Sample All Layers** check box to select it.

7. Place the pointer over the shiny circular spot on Christy's right cheek and click. The image is corrected. See Figure 7-21.

   Trouble? If your selection does not produce results that you like, undo the adjustment by pressing the Ctrl+Z keys, and repeat Step 7.

Figure 7-21   Spot Healing Brush Tool applied to image

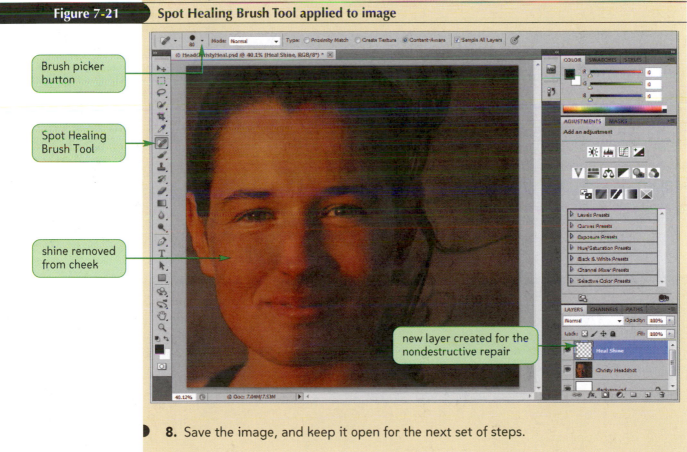

Brush picker button

Spot Healing Brush Tool

shine removed from cheek

new layer created for the nondestructive repair

8. Save the image, and keep it open for the next set of steps.

Repairing Images with the Healing Brush Tool

The Healing Brush Tool is like the Spot Healing Brush Tool's bigger, tougher brother. It has all of the capabilities of the Spot Healing Brush Tool, and it enables you to select the pixels that will be used as a sample to create the healing effects. This is a better choice when you are working with larger or more complex areas because it provides you with more control.

The Healing Brush Tool can be found on the Tools panel under the Spot Healing Brush Tool. Additional options for the Healing Brush Tool include the following:

- **Source:** You can select the source for the sample pixels that you will use to heal your image. With the Sampled option, you Alt-click in the image, or in any image that is open in Photoshop, at the point where you would like your pixel sample to begin. The Pattern option allows you to select one of the patterns in the Pattern picker as the source for your brush.
- **Aligned:** When the Aligned check box is selected, your sample point stays aligned to your pointer even if you release the mouse and move to a different area. If the Aligned check box is not checked, the original sample point is used each time you start to paint with your healing brush.
- **Sample:** The Sample drop-down list enables you to select the layer, or layers, that the tool will use when sampling pixels. Choices include Current Layer, Current & Below, or All Layers.

First, you'll experiment with using a pattern as the source for the Healing Brush Tool so you can get a sense of how you can use this brush option. Then, you'll use the Healing Brush Tool to smooth some of the wrinkles under Christy's eyes.

To add a pattern using the Healing Brush Tool:

1. On the Layers panel, create a new layer below the Heal Shine layer and name the new layer **Fix Squint Wrinkles**.

2. On the Tools panel, click the **Healing Brush Tool** .

3. On the options bar, use the Brush picker to select a brush size of **138 px**. Set the Mode to **Multiply**, select **Pattern** for the Source, and click the **Pattern** thumbnail to open the Pattern picker.

4. In the Pattern picker, click the **Bubbles** pattern (the first pattern) to select it.

   Trouble? If you do not see Bubbles in your list of patterns, you may have a different Pattern group open. On the right side of the Pattern picker, click the More options arrow . Click Patterns, and click the OK button to replace the current patterns. Do not save changes to the current patterns.

5. On the options bar, click the **Aligned** check box to select it, and in the Sample list, click **Current & Below**.

6. Ensure that the Fix Squint Wrinkles layer is active, and paint over Christy's forehead area. Although the pattern is very visible as you paint, when you release the mouse button, the Healing Brush Tool uses the settings you specified to blend the pattern with the layers below it, creating a unique, translucent effect. Congratulations—you have turned Christy into an alien. See Figure 7-22.

Figure 7-22   **Pattern applied using the Healing Brush Tool**

blending mode set to Multiply

Bubble pattern selected

Healing Brush Tool

new layer created for nondestructive repair

Patterns can be useful and sometimes fun. However, in this case, the effect is not suitable for the Hooked brochure. Next, you'll remove the Bubble pattern from the image, and use the Healing Brush Tool to remove the wrinkles under Christy's eyes.

To remove wrinkles using the Healing Brush Tool:

1. On Application bar, click **Edit**, and then click **Step Backward** until the bubble pattern is removed from Christy's face.

2. On the options bar, change the brush diameter to **50 px**, select **Normal** for the Mode, and select **Sampled** for the Source. Now, you'll select a pixel source.

3. Zoom the image to **100%**, and pan the image, if necessary, so that Christy's right eye is displayed in the Document window. (Note that Christy's right eye appears on the left side of the image.)

4. Select the **Healing Brush Tool** 🖌, again, if necessary. Place the pointer at the outer edge of Christy's right eye, below the wrinkled area, and then Alt-click to select the pixels for your source.

5. Place the pointer over the outside of the wrinkled area of the right eye and paint over the wrinkles to smooth them. Remember that your source pixels started on the outside of the eye. When you paint, start at the outside of the eye and move inward. See Figure 7-23.

TIP

Select pixels as close as possible to the area you want to heal to provide the most realistic and accurate results.

Figure 7-23   **Wrinkles under right eye smoothed with the Healing Brush Tool**

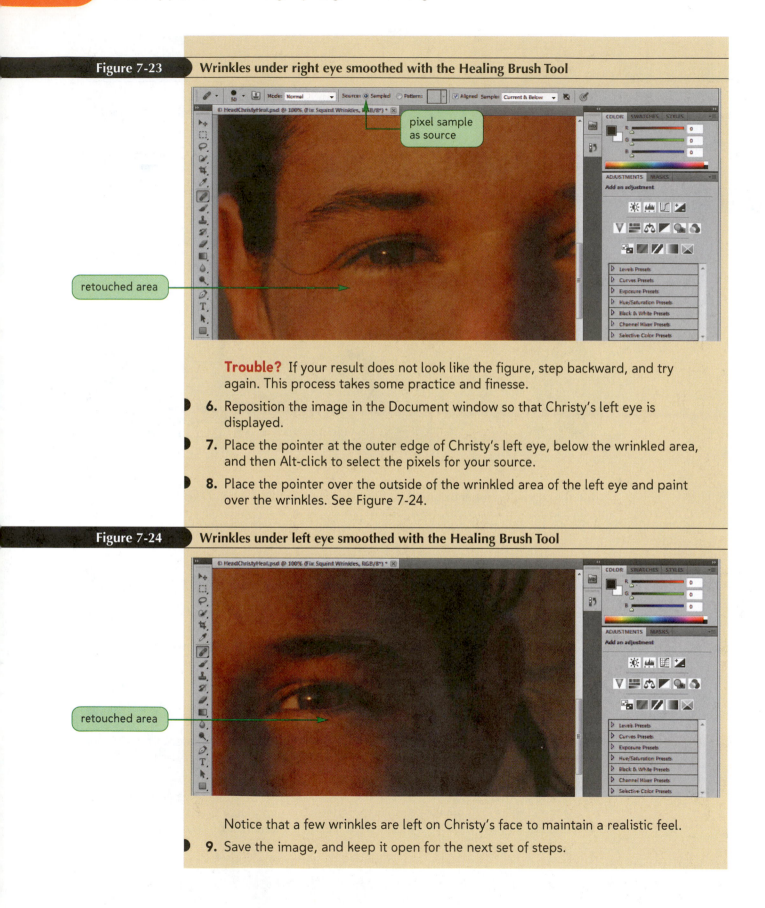

pixel sample as source

retouched area

Trouble? If your result does not look like the figure, step backward, and try again. This process takes some practice and finesse.

6. Reposition the image in the Document window so that Christy's left eye is displayed.

7. Place the pointer at the outer edge of Christy's left eye, below the wrinkled area, and then Alt-click to select the pixels for your source.

8. Place the pointer over the outside of the wrinkled area of the left eye and paint over the wrinkles. See Figure 7-24.

Figure 7-24   **Wrinkles under left eye smoothed with the Healing Brush Tool**

retouched area

Notice that a few wrinkles are left on Christy's face to maintain a realistic feel.

9. Save the image, and keep it open for the next set of steps.

Next, you'll use the Dodge and Burn Tools to adjust the brightness and darkness of specific areas in an image.

Retouching with the Dodge Tool

The Dodge Tool allows you to brighten small areas of an image, such as areas that are in a shadow. When the Protect Tones option is selected, shadow clipping is minimized, and the tool attempts to brighten without shifting the hue of affected colors. This produces more realistic and subtle adjustments, especially when working with skin tones. The Dodge Tool also gives you control over the tonal region to which changes are applied. You can brighten the highlights, midtones, or shadows of an image discreetly, and that provides you with added control. When painting with the Dodge Tool, you can also adjust the exposure of the brush. This has the effect of adjusting the opacity of the changes.

Although it is an effective tool, the Dodge Tool is a destructive tool. If you use the Dodge Tool, you should make a copy of the layer you will adjust and apply the changes to that copy, preserving the original layer in case the changes go awry. When you paint with the Dodge Tool, each time you pass over an area with the brush, it increases the effect of the dodge.

Because there are other, nondestructive tools that enable you to adjust the brightness of an image, a good rule to use is: If the area you want to brighten is more than 25 percent of the image, you should consider using a nondestructive tool. For example, you could use the Brightness/Contrast adjustment layer with a mask that prevents it from affecting the areas you want to remain unchanged.

You'll use the Dodge Tool to brighten some of the shadows on Christy's face and hair.

REFERENCE

Brightening an Image with the Dodge Tool

- Open an image in Photoshop, and select the layer you would like to adjust, if necessary.
- Duplicate the layer, and then select the duplicate layer to make it active.
- Select the Dodge Tool, and on the options bar, select a brush, brush size, Range, and Exposure, and then click the Protect Tones check box to select it.
- Paint the areas of the image that you would like to lighten until you achieve the desired effect.
- Save your image.

To lighten shadows in the photograph:

1. On the Layers panel, duplicate the **Christy Headshot** layer, and use the default layer name, Christy Headshot copy.

2. On the Layers panel, select the **Christy Headshot copy** layer to select it, if necessary and then press the **Ctrl+0** keys to fit the image on screen.

3. On the Tools panel, click the **Dodge Tool** 🔍.

4. On the options bar, click the **Brush picker** button ▾, and set the brush size to **350 px**.

5. On the options bar, select **Shadows** from the Range list, set the Exposure to **30%**, and then click the **Protect Tones** check box to select it, if necessary.

TIP

Each pass over an area increases the effect of the tool, so use multiple passes only in areas that need additional lightening.

6. Paint the right half of the image (which is the left side of Christy's face) to lighten the shadows on Christy's face. Try to target the darker areas, so you do not end up with too much artificial lightness in the lighter areas.

   The changes that you made to the Fix Squint Wrinkles layer are not affected by the Dodge Tool, so the adjustments on that layer do not blend with the image. You'll zoom into the area to examine the problem.

7. Zoom in to 100%, and reposition the image, if necessary, so that Christy's left eye is displayed in the Document window. See Figure 7-25.

Figure 7-25   **Shadows brightened with the Dodge Tool**

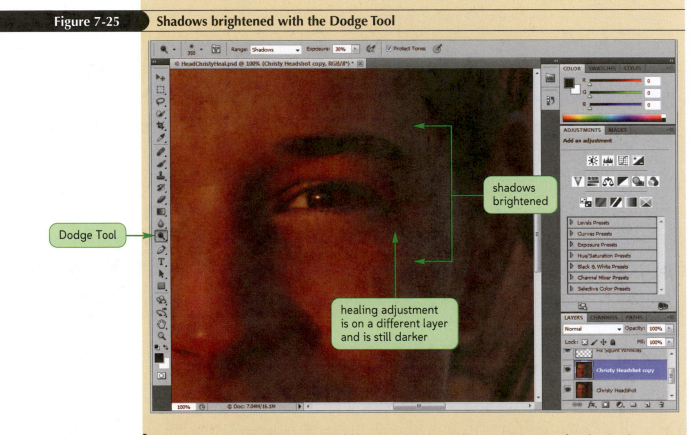

8. Select the **Fix Squint Wrinkles** layer, and use the same settings for the Dodge Tool to adjust the area around Christy's left eye.

9. Press the **Ctrl+0** keys to fit the image on screen.

10. Examine the image and look for any area where the shadows are distracting, or where they do not seem natural. See Figure 7-26.

Figure 7-26   **Fix Squint Wrinkles layer brightened but some harsh shadows remain**

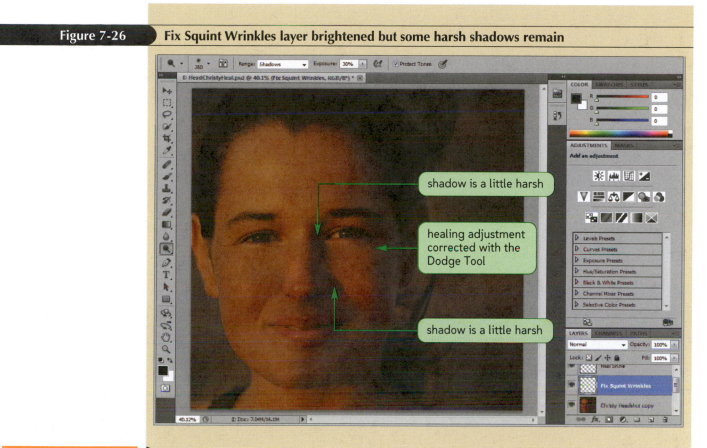

shadow is a little harsh

healing adjustment corrected with the Dodge Tool

shadow is a little harsh

11. On the Layers panel, select **Christy Headshot copy** layer to select it, and then use the Dodge Tool to correct any small areas where the shadows seem harsh.

12. Save the file, and close it.

When you compare Christy's initial head shot photograph with the final retouched photograph, you can see the great improvement in the final product. See Figure 7-27.

Figure 7-27   **Compare starting image with retouched image**

shadows lightened

wrinkles removed

shine healed

Next, you'll use the Burn Tool to darken an image background to draw focus to the subject of the photo.

Retouching with the Burn Tool

The Burn Tool allows you to darken small areas of an image in the same way that the Dodge Tool allows you to brighten them. The Burn Tool can be found on the Tools panel under the Dodge Tool, and it has all of the features and limitations of the Dodge Tool. Although it produces the opposite outcome, darkening instead of brightening, it works in the same way.

INSIGHT

Making Small Changes with Big Results

When using tools such as Dodge and Burn, keep in mind that the effects of the changes you make are cumulative and, therefore, making several subtle changes can create a large impact on the final image. For example, if you are correcting an image of a person, darkening the highlights of the image might make only a small change. However, once you have darkened the highlights, the midtones, and the shadows as needed, and you have brightened the highlight, midtones, and shadows, as needed, the photo will usually have a much different look. For this reason, it is a good idea to make small changes to all of the areas that need retouching, then, once you have examined the image, you can repeat the process until you achieve the look you desire.

Dayne has provided another head shot of two tour guides; however, the image is flat because the shadows of the image are not very different from the midtones. You'll add depth to the image by creating more dramatic shadows. Because it is an excellent tool for darkening areas of an image, while maintaining skin tones, you'll use the Burn Tool.

To darken areas of the photograph:

1. Open **HeadKathyJim.psd** from the Photoshop7\Tutorial folder, and save it as **HeadKathyJimDark.psd** in the same folder.

2. On the Layers panel, duplicate the **Kathy and Jim** layer, and use the default layer name Kathy and Jim copy. You'll work in the Kathy and Jim copy layer.

3. On the Application bar, click **View**, and then click **Fit on Screen**.

4. On the Tools panel, select the **Burn Tool** , which is hidden under the Dodge Tool .

5. On the options bar, select the **Brush picker** , and set the diameter to **100 px**.

6. Select **Highlights** from the Range drop-down list, set the Exposure to **10%**, and then click the **Protect Tones** check box to select it, if necessary.

7. Paint Jim's face and neck to darken the highlights.

8. On the options bar, select **Shadows** from the Range list, and set the Exposure to **10%**, if necessary. Paint both faces in areas where you would like to darken the shadows, like on the sides of the faces. See Figure 7-28.

Figure 7-28   **Burn Tool used to darken an image**

darken image with the Burn Tool

9. Turn the visibility of the Kathy and Jim copy layer off and on to see how your changes have affected the image.

10. Save the file, and keep it open for the next set of steps.

Although the changes that you have made to the image are subtle, they have created a better photographic composition by removing the highlights that caused the viewer to focus more on Jim than on Kathy and by creating more depth in the image by intensifying the shadows. As you continue to retouch the image, the effects of the small changes will add up to create big results. Next, you'll use the Sponge Tool to increase the saturation of the image.

Retouching with the Sponge Tool

The final tool in the Dodge Tool family is the Sponge Tool. The Sponge Tool has the same settings and nuances as the Dodge and Burn Tools, and it is used to increase or decrease saturation in a small part of an image. This is helpful because adjusting image brightness can sometimes wash the color out of an image. When this happens, you can use the Sponge Tool to add a little saturation where needed. You'll use the Sponge Tool to add some saturation to the head shot.

To add saturation to areas of the image:

1. On the Layers panel, ensure that the Kathy and Jim copy layer is selected and visible.

2. On the Tools panel, click the **Sponge Tool** , which is currently hidden under the Burn Tool .

3. On the options bar, set the brush diameter to **150 px**, set the Mode to **Saturate**, set the Flow to **15%**, and click the **Vibrance** check box to select it, if necessary.

4. Paint Jim's face and neck to create a more realistic skin tone.

5. Change the Flow setting to **5%**, paint Kathy's face, and then paint Jim's shirt to make the shirt look a more vibrant yellow.

6. Now that the color in your image is saturated, examine your image, and use the Dodge and Sponge Tools on any small areas that still need work. See Figure 7-29.

| Figure 7-29 | The Sponge Tool increases the saturation in washed-out areas |

the Sponge Tool is used to add or decrease image saturation

Turn the visibility of the Kathy and Jim copy layer off and on to see how your changes have affected the image. Notice how the addition of this subtle change has increased the overall intensity of the changes to the image.

7. Save the file, and keep it open for the next set of steps.

You'll continue retouching this image using the Blur Tool to defuse the areas of the background that might distract the viewer's focus from Kathy and Jim's smiling faces.

Retouching with the Blur Tool

The Blur Tool is another tool that can be used to retouch images and to redirect focus within compositions. You can use blur to defuse detail in an area of an image, to soften imperfections, or to create a soft focus around an object on which you would like the viewer's eye to focus. As with most tools in Photoshop, the possibilities that can be achieved with the Blur Tool are as endless as your imagination. Like the healing tools, the Blur Tool can be used nondestructively in a blank layer above the image, or it can be applied directly to the image, creating a destructive edit. Whenever possible, you should choose to edit nondestructively. If you do not want to sample all of the layers below your healing tool when you make your correction, you must make a destructive edit directly to the layer that you would like to affect. To do so, you should duplicate the layer that you would like to affect and then use the healing tool on the duplicate layer. This will ensure that you can return to the unaffected layer, if necessary. The Blur Tool is a good choice if you only want to alter small areas of your image. If you are going to add blur to an entire image, consider using Blur filters, which provide more control. Like the healing brushes, the Blur Tool has Brush and Mode settings, and it has a Strength setting that is similar to the Exposure setting of the Dodge and Burn Tools.

You'll create a new layer and then use the Blur Tool to soften the harshness of the light on Kathy and Jim's heads to draw focus to their faces.

REFERENCE

Blurring an Area of an Image

- Select the layer you would like to adjust.
- If you want to sample all of the layers below the layer you want to adjust, create a new blank layer above the layer you would like to adjust.
- If you do not want to sample all of the layers below the blur layer, make a duplicate layer and edit the duplicate layer directly.
- Select the Blur Tool, and on the options bar, select a brush, brush size, Blending Mode, and Strength, and then click the Sample All Layers check box to select it.
- Paint the area that you want to blur until you have achieved the desired effect.
- Save the image.

To soften the image using the Blur Tool:

1. Create a new empty layer above the Kathy and Jim copy layer, and name the layer **Blur**. Zoom in to **150%** so you can see the image in more detail.

2. On the Tools panel, click the **Blur Tool** 🔘.

3. On the options bar, set the brush diameter to **100 px**, set the Mode to **Darken**, set the Strength to **50%**, and click the **Sample All Layers** check box to select it.

4. On the new layer, paint around the top and side edges of the image until the hair and background soften and the light becomes more muted. This creates a halo effect with the light, which makes your image look more polished and professional.

5. To check your progress, show and hide the Blur layer as you go so you can view the changes you have made to the look of the image. When you feel you have achieved the desired effect, stop. See Figure 7-30.

Figure 7-30   **Image softened with the Blur Tool**

the Blur Tool was used to soften the focus and defuse the harsh light around the hair line

6. Save your image, and keep it open for the next set of steps.

INSIGHT

Keeping Up with New Developments

Designers constantly push the limits of what technology can accomplish, and new techniques for using the current design tools are in a state of continuous development. As a result, what is considered contemporary and fresh in aesthetic design is constantly shifting and evolving. One of the responsibilities of designers is to continue to grow and develop their craft. This does not mean that you should simply mimic the latest trends, but rather that you should be aware of new developments and that you should be able to incorporate current techniques and best practices into your design intelligently. One way to continue your development is to dedicate a few hours, each week, to reading design-related trade magazines and Web sites. The Adobe Design Center (*http://adobe.com/designcenter*) is Adobe's community forum for designers. The design center provides resources such as tutorials, opinions, training, articles, and design galleries. Another method for furthering your professional development is to occasionally take a class or attend a seminar. Whatever steps you take, remember that you are responsible for your continuing development as a design professional.

Retouching with the Sharpen Tool

Like the Blur Tool, the Sharpen Tool can be used to retouch images and redirect focus within compositions. The Sharpen Tool is primarily used to intensify detail in an area of an image where you would like the viewer's eye to focus or to sharpen areas of the image that have a soft focus. For example, a common, industry technique is to use the Sharpen Tool over the eyes of a subject to increase clarity and detail. This technique can produce stunning results and can add depth and drama to your images. The Sharpen Tool can also be used nondestructively, in an empty layer above the image, or it can be applied directly to the image, creating a destructive edit. The Sharpen Tool is found under the Blur Tool on the Tools panel, and is a good choice if you only want to alter small areas of your image. You'll use the Sharpen Tool to sharpen Jim's eyes in Kathy and Jim's head shot.

To sharpen an area of the image using the Sharpen Tool:

1. On the Layers panel, create an empty layer above the Blur layer, and name the layer **Sharpen**. Position the image so that both of Jim's eyes are visible in the Document window.

2. On the Tools panel, select the **Sharpen Tool** △, which is currently hidden under the Blur Tool ⬤.

3. On the options bar, set the brush diameter to **10 px**, set the Mode to **Normal**, if necessary, set the Strength to **50%**, click the **Sample All Layers** check box to select it, and click the **Protect Detail** check box to select it.

4. Make sure the Sharpen layer is selected on the Layers panel, and in the image, paint Jim's eyes until they become sharp enough to be slightly dramatic.

5. To check your progress, show and hide the Sharpen layer as you go so you can view the changes you have made to the look of the image. When you feel you have achieved the desired effect, stop. See Figure 7-31.

TIP

You can use the Darken mode to increase the intensity of the Sharpen Tool.

Figure 7-31   **Eyes sharpened using the Sharpen Tool**

the sharpness of Jim's eyes draws attention to them

6. To see the cumulative effect of all of the changes that you have made, fit the image in the Document window, hide all of your new layers so the Kathy and Jim layer is visible, and then show each of the new layers in order to see how the final composition compares with the original.

7. Save the image, and close it.

Working with the Lab Color Mode

As you learned in Tutorial 4, Lab (Luminosity, A and B channels) is another color mode that, like RGB and CMYK, can be used in Photoshop. Lab color is based on human color perception, and it contains values for the range of color that can be seen with the average human eye. It is unique because it is considered to be a device-independent color model that describes how color looks rather than how much of each pure color a device must mix to achieve the color. Lab color separates color into three channels:

- The Luminosity channel contains all of the lightness and darkness information for the image. In fact, with a few adjustments, you can use the Luminosity channel to create an amazing black-and-white image.
- The A channel contains the red and green color information for the image.
- The B channel contains the yellow and blue color information for the image.

Because of the way Lab color interprets color, you can use it to create amazing color and luminosity adjustments to your images. For instance, you can adjust the lightness and darkness values in an image without affecting the colors, or you can adjust a color value without affecting the brightness. You can move in and out of Lab color mode without damaging your images, but Photoshop merges adjustment layers when you move from Lab to another color mode. Because of this, it is especially important to work with a copy of your original images when you are working in Lab.

Dayne thinks the cropped version of the LookUp.psd image looks so good he would like to use it on a promotional postcard he is creating. Because the cropped version of the image is not the right dimensions for use in the postcard layout, Dayne would like you to adjust the original image so the person creating the postcard can crop it for use in her layout. You will use the Lab color mode to adjust the image.

To adjust the image using Lab color mode:

1. Open **LookUp.psd** from the Photoshop7\Tutorial folder. (Do not use the LookUpCrop.psd file that you already changed.)

2. Save the file as **LookUpLAB.psd** in the same folder, and change the view to **Fit on Screen**.

3. On the Application bar, click **Image**, point to **Mode**, and then click **Lab Color**.

4. A small dialog box opens, and Photoshop asks you if you want to flatten the image. Click the **Don't Flatten** button.

5. On the Layers panel, make sure the **Female Looking Up** layer is selected, click the **Create new fill or adjustment layer** icon ⬤., and then click **Curves**.

6. On the Adjustments panel, select **Lightness** from the channel list, if necessary. Click the bottom point of the curve and drag it up until the Output is **5** and the Input is **0**. See Figure 7-32.

TIP

The Lightness channel controls the Luminosity in Lab color mode in the Curves adjustment.

Figure 7-32   **Adjusting an image in Lab color mode**

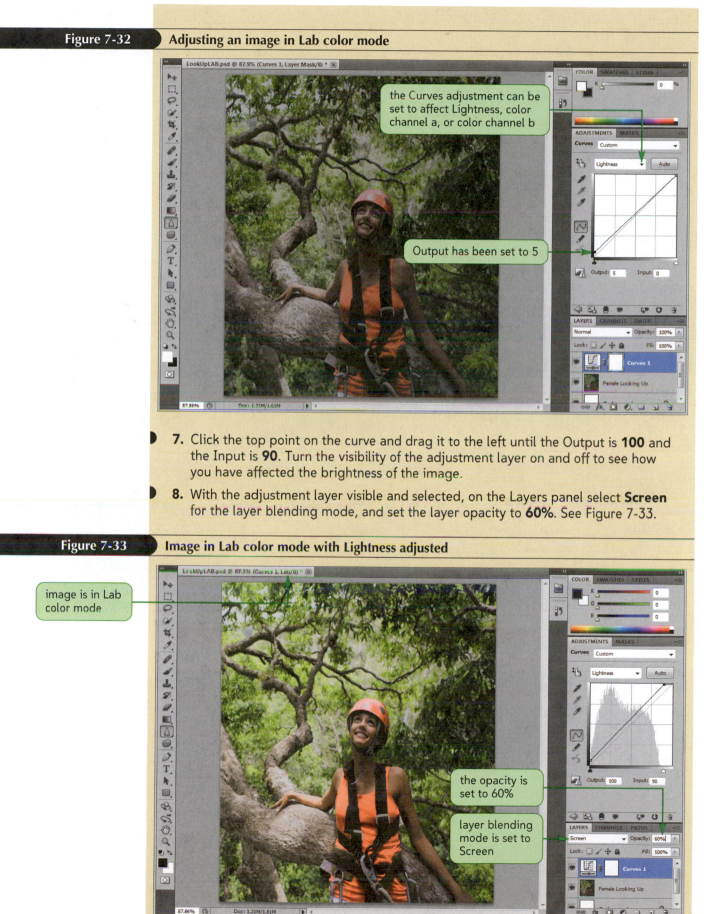

the Curves adjustment can be set to affect Lightness, color channel a, or color channel b

Output has been set to 5

7. Click the top point on the curve and drag it to the left until the Output is **100** and the Input is **90**. Turn the visibility of the adjustment layer on and off to see how you have affected the brightness of the image.

8. With the adjustment layer visible and selected, on the Layers panel select **Screen** for the layer blending mode, and set the layer opacity to **60%**. See Figure 7-33.

Figure 7-33   **Image in Lab color mode with Lightness adjusted**

image is in Lab color mode

the opacity is set to 60%

layer blending mode is set to Screen

9. On the Adjustments panel, select **b** from the channel list, and then click the bottom point of the curve and drag it to the right until the Output is **-128** and the Input is **-87**.

10. Click the top point of the curve and drag to the left until the Output is **127** and the Input is **87**, and then turn the visibility of the Curves 1 layer off and on to see how you have affected the image. Notice how vibrant the colors are.

11. With the adjustment layer visible, on the Application bar, click **Image**, point to **Mode**, and then click **RGB Color**. Click the **Flatten** button in the dialog box to merge the adjustment layer.

The image is flattened and is in RGB color mode again. See Figure 7-34.

Figure 7-34	Final image with adjustments

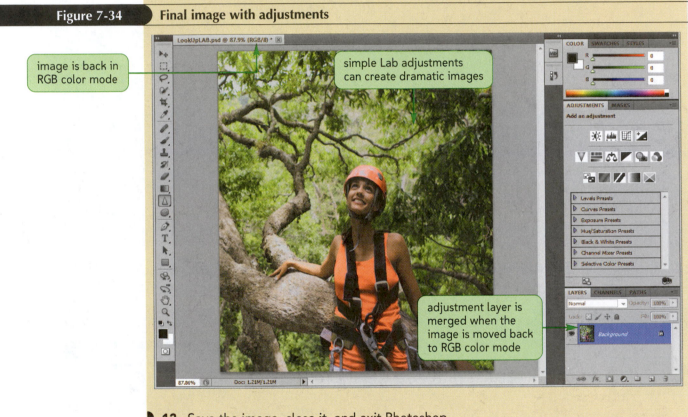

image is back in RGB color mode

simple Lab adjustments can create dramatic images

adjustment layer is merged when the image is moved back to RGB color mode

12. Save the image, close it, and exit Photoshop.

Now that the images have been corrected, you will be able to use them in the Hooked brochure. Once they are in place, additional small adjustments may be necessary, but all of the hard work is finished.

In this session, you worked on the final phase of image adjustment: retouching. You learned to correct blemishes and small image problems with the Spot Healing Brush Tool and the Healing Brush Tool. You used the Dodge, Burn, and Sponge Tools to adjust areas of relative lightness, darkness, and saturation within an image. You used the Blur and Sharpen Tools to create areas of focus, and you used Lab color mode to create dynamic color and luminosity adjustments.

PROSKILLS

Decision Making: Making It Real

Once you learn the tricks for making images look perfect, it is easy to fall into the trap of needing to create a perfect-looking world where every chin is sharp, and every flaw has been neatly removed. But that perfect world does not exist, and images or compositions that look "too perfect" have the artificial feel that manufactured reality can produce. To serve your client's interest, you must use a light touch in creating aesthetically pleasing, yet interesting and believable imagery. Remember that the product you create should be driven by the client's desired goals for the campaign. The end product is only a success if it serves your client's interest.

REVIEW

Session 7.2 Quick Check

1. Why would you use the Spot Healing Brush Tool?
2. True or False. The Dodge Tool can be used to make areas of an image darker.
3. The _____ Tool is used to increase or decrease saturation in a small area of an image.
4. You use the Burn Tool to make areas of an image _____.
5. _____ color mode is used to adjust color and luminosity in images.
6. What tools can you use to draw focus to an area of an image?

*Practice the skills
you learned in
the tutorial using
the same case
scenario.*

PRACTICE

Review Assignments

Data File needed for the Review Assignments: Resting.psd

Your design team will be adding more images to the brochure and other collateral materials that have been created for Hooked. Dayne would like you to crop, adjust, and retouch the remaining images. Remember that retouching is an art. Use discretion when cleaning up flaws to ensure that the images retain an authentic look. Complete the following steps:

1. Start Photoshop while pressing the Ctrl+Alt+Shift keys. When you are prompted to delete the Adobe Photoshop Settings File, click Yes. On the Application bar, right-click Essentials, and then click Reset Essentials to reset the default workspace layout. Reset all tools.

2. Open **Resting.psd** located in the Photoshop7\Review folder provided with your Data Files, and save it as **RestingAdjust.psd** in the same folder.

3. Set your view to Fit on Screen, and show the rulers with the units set to inches.

4. Use the Crop Tool to add a Crop Guide Overlay that covers the entire image, and then set the Crop Guide Overlay to Rule of Thirds. Notice that the man is aligned with the right grid line, which follows the Rule of Thirds.

5. Drag the bottom of your grid up to crop the image horizontally just below the man's right knee (which is on the left side of the image). Drag the top of the grid down 1/2 inch from the top of the image, and crop the image. The man should still be aligned with the right grid line.

6. Apply Auto Contrast to the image to correct the contrast and tone of the image.

7. Duplicate the Background layer, and title the new layer **Resting with Changes**. Hide the Background layer.

8. Zoom in on the face, and select the Burn Tool with a 20 pixel brush in the Highlights Range at 10% Exposure, with the Protect Tones option selected. Paint the overexposed areas of the chin, nose, and forehead so the image has consistent color over the entire face.

9. Select the Dodge Tool with a 20 pixel brush in the Highlights Range at 10% Exposure, with the Protect Tones option selected. Paint the right side of the man's face to add subtle highlights to the image.

10. Create a new blank layer above the Resting with Changes layer, and name the layer **Healing**.

11. Select the Spot Healing Brush Tool with a 10 pixel brush in Screen Mode with the Content-Aware Type and Sample All Layers options selected. Remove the distracting highlight on the man's nose.

12. Create a new blank layer above the Healing layer, and name the layer **Sharpen**.

13. Select the Sharpen Tool with a 15 pixel brush in Normal Mode at 50% Strength, with the Sample All Layers and Protect Detail options selected. Paint over the man's eyes to sharpen them.

14. Save the file, and exit Photoshop.

15. Submit the results of the preceding steps to your instructor either in printed or electronic form, as requested.

APPLY

Use your skills to add some interest to images in a poster.

Case Problem 1

Data File needed for this Case Problem: JamJam.psd

The Jam Jam   Every April, the spring thaw brings hundreds of competitors out to Washington Park in Portland, Oregon, for a funky day of jamming and jamming. The Jam Jam started as a way to teach Portland residents to use locally grown, seasonal fruits in new and interesting ways. Jenny Conn, the event organizer, was quoted as saying, "By encouraging people to jam, we are showing them how to use fruit that is in season in a way that will enable them to enjoy it at other times of the year." Since its inception, the jam has become something of a local event promoting local gardening, local bands, and local art. This year, your firm has volunteered to create marketing materials for the Jam Jam. The Art Department has created a poster and, after review, Jenny has asked you to create a little drama by punching up some of the images in the poster. Complete the following steps:

1. Start Photoshop while pressing the Ctrl+Alt+Shift keys. When you are prompted to delete the Adobe Photoshop Settings File, click Yes. On the Application bar, right-click Essentials, and then click Reset Essentials to reset the default workspace layout. Reset all tools.

2. Open **JamJam.psd** located in the Photoshop7\Case1 folder provided with your Data Files, and save it as **JamJamAdjust.psd** in the same folder. (*Hint*: If a dialog box appears stating that you need to update fonts, click OK. This will not affect the end result.)

3. Select the Jam 3 layer, change the image to the Lab Color mode, and do not flatten the layers when prompted.

4. On the Channels panel, ensure that all of the channels are visible so you can effectively adjust the lightness of the Jam 3 layer.

5. On the Layers panel, add a Curves adjustment layer, and clip the adjustment layer to the Jam 3 layer only. (*Hint*: Use the "This adjustment affects all layers below" icon on the Adjustments panel to clip the adjustment layer to the Jam 3 layer.)

6. Select the bottom point on the curve and drag it right until the Input value is 16.

7. Click in the center of the curve to add a new anchor point, and then drag the point down and to the left until the Output value and the Input value are both 25.

8. On the Layers panel, select the new Curves 1 layer and the Jam 3 layer, and from the Layer menu, select Merge Layers to merge the new adjustment layer with the Jam 3 layer. Rename the newly merged layer **Jam 3**. (Remember that adjustment layers created in the Lab color mode are lost when you move from Lab color mode to RGB color mode.)

9. Change the image back to RGB color mode, and choose not to flatten the layers when prompted.

10. Select the Jam 1 layer, and add a new Brightness Contrast adjustment layer with the Brightness set to 30 and the Contrast set to 35.

11. Select the Jar Left layer, and create a new Posterize adjustment layer with the Levels set to 7. Clip the adjustment layer to the Jar Left layer only.

12. Return to the adjustment list on the Adjustments panel, create a Hue/Saturation adjustment layer, and set the adjustment layer to affect only the Jar Left layer. Check the Colorize check box, set the Hue to 183, set the Saturation to 100, and set the Lightness to 20.

13. Select the Jar Right layer and repeat Step 11 and Step 12, substituting the following settings in Step 12: Hue 45, Saturation 100, Lightness 25.

14. Save the file, and exit Photoshop.

15. Submit the results of the preceding steps to your instructor either in printed or electronic form, as requested.

Use your skills to adjust images for a media campaign for a new restaurant.

APPLY

Case Problem 2

Data Files needed for this Case Problem: ManInside.psd, GroupSushiBar.psd

The Cell   The Cell is probably the only restaurant in Chicago where customers don't get dirty looks for talking on their phones. This new Asian-fusion restaurant and lounge actually encourages its patrons to talk it up. The concept for a restaurant that caters to cell phone junkies is the brain child of Denise Duke. Duke was an executive at a local marketing firm, and she spent her days tied to the phone. "One day, I was at lunch and realized that half the restaurant was working, like me, and the other half was annoyed. It occurred to me that, in downtown Chicago, you could create a cell phone friendly restaurant that would solve everyone's problem." Your company is working on a media campaign for The Cell. Your job is to take the images that Denise gave you and make them pop by adding color and some dramatic flair. Complete the following steps:

1. Start Photoshop while pressing the Ctrl+Alt+Shift keys. When you are prompted to delete the Adobe Photoshop Settings File, click Yes. On the Application bar, right-click Essentials, and then click Reset Essentials to reset the default workspace layout. Reset all tools.
2. Open **ManInside.psd** located in the Photoshop7\Case2 folder provided with your Data Files, and save it as **ManInsideCrop.psd** in the same folder.
3. Using the Ruler Tool, draw a line across the image that runs parallel to the top edge of the table, and then straighten the image.
4. Using the Crop Tool with the Crop Guide Overlay set to Rule of Thirds, crop the image by dragging the top of the grid down to the 1 inch mark on the vertical ruler.

⊕ EXPLORE

5. Create a Vibrance adjustment layer above the Man Inside Table layer, and increase the Vibrance and the Saturation settings so the image does not appear to be washed out. (*Hint*: Remember that because this adjustment is done in an adjustment layer, you can change the settings as many times as you would like. Play with the adjustment until you achieve the look you want.)
6. Save the image.
7. Open **GroupSushibar.psd** located in the Photoshop7\Case2 folder provided with your Data Files, and save it as **GroupAdjust.psd** in the same folder.

⊕ EXPLORE

8. Examine the image and compare it to the ManInsideCrop.psd image that you just corrected. Create an Exposure adjustment layer and adjust the GroupdAdjust.psd image so it will complement the image of the man sitting by himself when the images are used together in marketing materials. (*Hint*: Remember that image adjustment takes thought and judgment. Your images should have similar or complementary colors, tones, and saturation, and they should have a similar look and feel.)
9. Create a copy of the Group Sushi Bar layer, and hide the original layer.
10. Select the Burn Tool with a 40 pixel brush in the Highlights Range at 10% Exposure. Paint any highlights on the Group Sushi Bar copy layer that are overexposed.
11. To draw attention to the cell phone in the foreground, use the Sharpen Tool to sharpen the phone.
12. Save your image, close both files, and exit Photoshop.
13. Submit the results of the preceding steps to your instructor either in printed or electronic form, as requested.

CHALLENGE

Extend your skills to adjust images to fit with a Web site's stylized look.

Case Problem 3

Data Files needed for this Case Problem: ArtistJohnVasquez.psd, ArtistsMarkJennyCope.psd, ArtistJasonPrice.psd

Graffiti Street   Graffiti Street is a section of East Hardmon Street in Detroit, Michigan, that has opened its walls as canvas for local graffiti artists. It is the concept of urban planner and local artist, David Galvan. As an urban planner, David was looking for a cost-effective way to revitalize the dilapidated walls of East Hardmon Street when he happened upon an amazing graffiti mural painted by local artist Daryl Huffington. The project solved several problems: It provided local artists with a legal space to create; it provided the city with an inexpensive way to revitalize a dilapidated area of town; and it created a sense of pride and ownership in the community.

You are part of a team creating a Web site that will provide information about the project. David has provided several images of the artists with their artwork. He has selected a very stylized urban look for the photography that will be used on the Web site. The imagery is slightly overexposed and oversaturated, mimicking the look of some contemporary magazine imagery. This is a look that will appeal to the target audience of the site. You'll adjust and retouch the artist images so they fit with that look. Complete the following steps:

1. Start Photoshop while pressing the Ctrl+Alt+Shift keys. When you are prompted to delete the Adobe Photoshop Settings File, click Yes. On the Application bar, right-click Essentials, and then click Reset Essentials to reset the default workspace layout. Reset all tools.

2. Open **ArtistJohnVasquez.psd** located in the Photoshop7\Case3 folder provided with your Data Files, and save it as **ArtistJohnVasquezFix.psd** in the same folder.

3. Show and hide the Exposure 1 layer to view the adjustments and the original image. Notice the settings that were used in the adjustment layer to achieve the desired look. The Exposure adjustment was used to create a stylized look, rather than to make a necessary correction.

4. Create a new a new blank layer under the Exposure 1 layer, and name the layer **Heal**. The stylized adjustments have created harsh red circles under John's eyes and a bit of distracting redness on his nose. You'll retouch the image to remove the circles and distracting redness.

5. Use the Spot Healing Brush Tool to retouch the area under John's eyes and on his nose. (*Hint*: Make sure the Sample All Layers check box is checked, and do not overcorrect the image. Using the Screen Mode with the Spot Healing Brush Tool will help you create a softer correction.)

6. Save the image, and leave it open.

7. Open **ArtistsMarkJennyCope.psd** located in the Photoshop7\Case3 folder provided with your Data Files, and save it as **ArtistsMarkJennyCopeFix.psd** in the same folder.

⬥ EXPLORE

8. Create an Exposure adjustment layer above the Mark and Jenny Cope layer, and adjust the Exposure, Offset, and Gamma Correction values to match the Graffiti Street style. Switch between this image and the ArtistJohnVasquezFix.psd image to evaluate the changes to the ArtistsMarkJennyCopeFix.psd image.

9. Use your judgment to evaluate the image and locate any problem areas. Add a new layer above the Mark and Jenny Cope layer, and name the new layer **Heal**. Use the Spot Healing Brush Tool, the Burn Tool, and the Dodge Tool to correct any problems.

10. Save the image, and leave it open.

11. Open **ArtistJasonPrice.psd** located in the Photoshop7\Case3 folder provided with your Data Files, and save it as **ArtistJasonPriceFix.psd** in the same folder.

⊕ EXPLORE   12. Create an Exposure adjustment layer and adjust the Exposure, Offset, and Gamma Correction values to match the Graffiti Street style. Use the previously corrected images to evaluate the changes to the new image.

⊕ EXPLORE   13. Use the Quick Select Tool to select Jason's shirt in the image. On the Layers panel, click in the Exposure 1 layer mask thumbnail, located beside the Layer thumbnail, and, then in the Document window, fill the selected area with black. The white T-shirt remains unaffected by the adjustments. (*Hint*: Any area that is filled with black in the mask for your adjustment layer will not be affected by the adjustment layer.)

14. Create a new layer above the Jason layer, and name the layer **Heal**.

15. Use the healing brushes to retouch any problem areas in the image.

16. Duplicate the Jason layer, and then hide the original layer.

17. Use the Dodge and Burn Tools to correct any remaining problem areas in the image.

18. Save the image, close all three files, and exit Photoshop.

19. Submit the results of the preceding steps to your instructor either in printed or electronic form, as requested.

Use your skills to create something that expresses your point of view.

CREATE

Case Problem 4

Data File needed for this Case Problem: AlterProject.psd

The Digital Alter   The Digital Alter project is a collective art project that provides artists with a group of images and asks each artist to combine, adjust, and alter the images so the final artwork has some sort of personal meaning that reflects the artist's point of view. You have been invited, by project coordinator Juana Lewis, to participate in the project. The images have been broken into four categories, each of which has been placed in a group in the AlterProject.psd file, so the file is organized and easy to understand and use. Groups include Backgrounds, Fruits, Stars, and Birds. Examine the images that have been provided and use one image from each group to create something new. See Figure 7-35 for an example, but remember that the final artwork is supposed to reflect your personal point of view. This example is also included in the AlterProject.psd file on the Example layer.

Figure 7-35   Digital Alter project example

background

bird

fruit

star

Complete the following steps:

1. Start Photoshop while pressing the Ctrl+Alt+Shift keys. When you are prompted to delete the Adobe Photoshop Settings File, click Yes. On the Application bar, right-click Essentials, and then click Reset Essentials to reset the default workspace layout. Reset all tools.

2. Open **AlterProject.psd** located in the Photoshop7\Case4 folder provided with your Data Files, and save it as **MyAlterProject.psd** in the same folder.

3. Delete the existing Background layer.

4. Open the Backgrounds group folder, and examine the images provided by Digital Alter.

5. Repeat Step 4 for the Fruits, Stars, and Birds folders.

6. Think about the images in each folder, how they look, what they represent to you, and how you might combine them together to create something unique.

7. Hide all of the group folders, and examine the image on the Example layer to get an idea of how you might work with the individual images to create a new composition, and then hide the Example layer.

8. Select one image/layer from each group. Copy each layer, and move the copy out of its folder group to the main area of the Layers panel below all of the folder groups.

9. Move the background layer that you selected to the bottom of the stack of images, and then hide the other layers.

10. Switch to Lab color mode, and use a Levels or Curves adjustment layer to alter the look of your background layer.

11. Merge the adjustment layers with the background layer, and switch back to RGB color mode.

12. Rename the newly merged layer, if necessary, and then continue to adjust and manipulate the background until you achieve the look you desire.

13. Select the bird layer, and alter the layer as needed to achieve the look you desire. Use at least one adjustment layer and either the Sharpen Tool or the Blur Tool. Rename the layer, if necessary, as you work to ensure your workflow is not confusing.

14. Select the stars layer, and alter the layer as needed to achieve the look you desire. Use at least one adjustment layer and either the Healing Brush Tool or the Spot Healing Brush Tool. Rename the layer, if necessary, as you work to ensure your workflow is not confusing.

15. Select the fruit layer, and alter the layer as needed to achieve the look you desire. Use at least one adjustment layer and either the Dodge Tool, the Burn Tool, or the Sponge Tool. Rename the layer, if necessary, as you work to ensure your workflow is not confusing.

16. Examine what you have created and adjust as needed to create a cohesive composition that reflects your point of view.

17. Save the file, and exit Photoshop.

18. Submit the results of the preceding steps to your instructor either in printed or electronic form, as requested.

ENDING DATA FILES

Tutorial

FlyingAuto.psd
HangStraight.psd
HeadChristyHeal.psd
HeadKathyJimDark.psd
LookUpCrop.psd
LookUpLAB.psd

Review

RestingAdjust.psd

Case1

JamJamAdjust.psd

Case2

GroupAdjust.psd
ManInsideCrop.psd

Case3

ArtistJohnVasquezFix.psd
ArtistJasonPriceFix.psd
ArtistsMarkJennyCopeFix.psd

Case4

MyAlterProject.psd

Advanced Input/ Output and Color Management

Working with the Camera Raw Plug-In and Color Management Tools

Case | *FW Museum Store*

The FW is a Western art museum located in the heart of Fort Worth, Texas. The Museum Store is located in the FW lobby, enabling visitors to commemorate their visit to the museum by purchasing a variety of collection reproductions, items created by local artisans, and an array of Western accoutrements.

Sadie Downing, the FW Museum Store administrator, has asked your firm to create a one-page promotional insert promoting an upcoming sale on handmade, artisanal jewelry. The insert will be distributed with Museum Store print catalogs and via a promotional email campaign. Sadie would also like your firm to create a series of Web banners that will publicize the upcoming sale on the home page of the FW Museum Store Web site.

In this tutorial, you'll work with original camera raw files in the Camera Raw plug-in, and save them as Smart Objects. You'll explore a histogram and pixel clipping. You'll learn about color management, including monitor calibration. You'll examine color settings and soft proof parameters, and you'll convert the color profile of a document. Finally, you'll optimize and save a file for use on the Web.

STARTING DATA FILES

Photoshop8

Tutorial
FeaturedItemBox.psd
Insert.psd
MG4835.CR2
MG4998.CR2

Review
MG4820.CR2

Case1
Auto.tif
Music.tif
Skateboard.tif

Case2
Basket.CR2
Snake.CR2

Case3
ThisTooWillPass.tif
YouCompleteMe.tif

Case4
BacMuffins.tif
BacSushi.tif

SESSION 8.1 VISUAL OVERVIEW

The Document window tools in the Camera Raw dialog box enable you to move, resize, rotate, and perform slight retouching to an image.

Camera raw files open in the Camera Raw dialog box. **Camera raw** (sometimes called **RAW**) files are large files that contain unprocessed and uncompressed grayscale picture data and metadata from the image sensor of a digital camera, an image scanner, or a motion picture film scanner.

You can zoom, pan, and crop an image in the Camera Raw Document window; you can also preview changes that you make using the Camera Raw tools.

A **Smart Object** is a layer in a Photoshop image file that contains either vector or raster image data and that preserves a link to the image's source content, enabling you to open and edit the image source.

Clicking this linked text takes you to the Camera Raw Workflow Options dialog box; the **workflow options** in Camera Raw enable you to set output parameters such as Space, Depth, Size, and Resolution.

WORKING WITH CAMERA RAW

When Preview is checked, your changes are displayed in the Document window.

Open a camera raw file from Mini Bridge by right-clicking the file and selecting Open in Camera Raw.

The Shadow clipping warning icon and the Highlight clipping warning icon will change to different colors if some shadow colors or highlight colors are out of spectrum and cannot be reproduced. **Clipping** occurs when pixel values fall outside of the range that can be reproduced in the color space in which you are working.

A **histogram** is a visual representation of the number of pixels an image has at each luminance (the perceived brightness) value.

The RGB values of the pixel located under the pointer are displayed here.

The White Balance adjustment tools allow you to correct a color cast created by the temperature of the lighting used when an image was taken.

The Tonal Adjustment tools help you create a more dynamic and professional image.

With the Saturation Adjustment tools, you can adjust the vividness of the color in an image.

Working with Camera Raw Files

When you take pictures with a high-end digital camera, you can specify that the images be saved in the camera's RAW format. A camera raw file is the digital equivalent of a photo negative. Because the major camera manufacturers have each developed their own proprietary processes for creating camera raw files, there are actually hundreds of different camera raw formats and file extensions that vary between manufacturers and sometimes even between camera models. In the past, this made working with camera raw files somewhat difficult unless you used the software that came with your camera to process the images and to save them in other, usable image formats. Fortunately, Adobe provides the Camera Raw plug-in, which is a third-party software that works with Photoshop to allow you to open and process many different camera raw files. You can find a list of cameras and camera raw files that Camera Raw supports at *www.adobe.com/go/learn_ps_cameraraw*.

The Photoshop Camera Raw Plug-in

The Photoshop **Camera Raw plug-in** enables Photoshop users to construct images from camera raw file data and to adjust and process those images. Each type of camera raw file saves image information in a slightly different way, and with the Camera Raw plug-in you can open and adjust all supported types of camera raw image files. However, you cannot use the Camera Raw plug-in to save images in a camera raw format. Instead, when you use Camera Raw to make adjustments to camera raw images, you can specify that the adjustment data is saved outside of the camera raw file, in one of two ways:

- **In the Camera Raw database:** A Camera Raw database file is located by default in the folder titled Documents and Settings/[*your user name*]/Application data/Adobe/CameraRaw. When you choose the Camera Raw database option, all of the adjustment data for the file is stored in the database, enabling you to move the camera raw file to different locations on your computer. If you need to move the image file to a storage location outside your computer, such as a CD or another computer, you must export the information from the database to an XMP file. Therefore, this option is a poor choice if you are working in a team or from more than one computer.
- **As a companion file called a sidecar XMP file:** An **XMP file** is a separate file that is saved in the same folder as the camera raw file and holds all of the adjustment data. The original camera raw image data is not altered; rather, the adjustment data is saved outside of the original file. This means that all of the edits are nondestructive, and you can continue to use the camera raw file as your digital negative or as an archival file. Camera Raw saves the XMP file using the name of the original camera raw file along with an .xmp extension. When you open a camera raw file that you have adjusted, all of your adjustment data is automatically pulled from the XMP file and applied to the camera raw file. If you delete the XMP file, you will lose all of the adjustment data, and when you next open the camera raw file, it will appear as it did before you made any changes. When you move a camera raw file to another storage location, you must remember to move the XMP file with it or you will not be able to view any adjustments. To create another file from a camera raw file, you output the file to Photoshop where you must save it in a different file format, such as a JPEG or TIF. Saving changes to a camera raw file in an XMP file is a good option whenever you might need to work on a file on more than one computer; because of this, it is the preferred option for people who work in teams.

To get set up before you begin working on the catalog image files, you'll adjust your Photoshop settings to specify that you save adjustment data as a sidecar XMP file.

TIP

When Camera Raw is open, you can access the Preferences dialog box by clicking the Open preferences dialog button on the toolbar or by pressing the Ctrl+K keys.

To adjust Camera Raw preferences:

1. Start Photoshop while pressing the **Ctrl+Alt+Shift** keys. When you are prompted to delete the Adobe Photoshop Settings File, click **Yes**. On the Application bar, right-click **Essentials**, and then click **Reset Essentials** to reset the default workspace layout. Reset all tools and tool presets.

2. On the Application bar, click **Edit**, point to **Preferences**, and click **Camera Raw**. The Camera Raw Preferences dialog box opens. See Figure 8-1.

Figure 8-1   Camera Raw Preferences dialog box

your version number may vary

this option instructs Camera Raw to save changes in an XMP file

3. In the "Save images settings in" box, click **Sidecar ".xmp" files**, if necessary.

4. Click the **OK** button to close the dialog box, and save the changes.

Make sure you click the Sidecar ".xmp" files option, or your adjustments will not be saved in the same folder as your Data Files.

Exploring the Camera Raw Workspace

When you open a camera raw image, the image is displayed in the Camera Raw dialog box, which is divided into a Document window and an Adjustments panel. The Document window is where the image is displayed and, when the Preview check box is selected, where your changes are displayed. Above the Document window, you'll find a toolbar with a variety of viewing and retouching tools that enable you to manipulate the way you see the image and to correct small blemishes and problems in your image. For an overview of these tools, see Figure 8-2.

Figure 8-2	Viewing and retouching tools in the Camera Raw dialog box

Tool Name	Icon	Use To
Zoom Tool		Control how much of an image is displayed in the Document window; clicking in the viewing area zooms in to the next higher zoom preset value while Alt-clicking zooms out. Dragging in the viewing area with the Zoom Tool enables you to zoom in on an area of an image so it fills the screen.
Hand Tool		Pan an image to display a different area of the image when the entire image is not visible in the viewing area.
White Balance Tool		Adjust the colors in an image to correct for color cast created by flash and ambient light; select an object from your image that should be displayed as gray or white, and the White Balance Tool will correct the color cast of the image and return the object to true white or gray.
Color Sampler Tool		Select up to nine points from which you can sample color; when you select a pixel with the Color Sampler Tool, the RGB values for that point are displayed at the top of the viewing area, enabling you to see the values of the selected pixels while you make adjustments to your photo.
Targeted Adjustment Tool		Make color and tonal corrections by dragging on the image rather than using the sliders; you can adjust the Parametric Curve, Hue, Saturation, Luminance, and Grayscale Mix. Dragging down in an area decreases the value of colors in the image that are located in that area, while dragging upward increases their value.
Crop Tool		Adjust the borders of the image created from the camera raw file; because this does not affect the original file, you can readjust the image at any time.
Straighten Tool		Adjust the horizontal and vertical orientation of an image based on a line you drag in the viewing area; anything outside of the newly created borders of the image will be cropped.
Spot Removal		Repair a selected area of an image with sample pixels from another area of the image.
Red Eye Removal		Darken the red pupils that sometimes occur when a flash is used in photography.
Adjustment Brush		Make adjustments to areas of an image by setting the brush options and then painting over the areas of the image that you would like to alter; when the Adjustment Brush is selected, the tool options are displayed below the histogram on the Adjustments panel. Options include exposure, brightness, contrast, saturation, clarity, sharpness, and color.
Graduated Filter		Adjust a region of your image by setting filter options and then dragging across the image to select the region that the filter will affect; options include exposure, brightness, contrast, saturation, clarity, sharpness, and color.
Open preferences dialog		Open the Camera Raw Preferences dialog box.
Rotate image 90° counter clockwise		Rotate the image displayed in the viewing area 90° in a counterclockwise direction; each time you click, the image rotates 90°.
Rotate image 90° clockwise		Rotate the image displayed in the viewing area 90° in a clockwise direction; each time you click, the image rotates 90°.

Next, you'll open a camera raw file provided by the catalog photographer and examine the Document window in the Camera Raw dialog box. Then, you'll crop the image using the Camera Raw Crop Tool.

Opening a File in Camera Raw

- On the Application bar, click File, click Open, navigate to the camera raw file, and double-click the file to open it in the Camera Raw dialog box.

or

- Open Bridge, navigate to the camera raw file, right-click the file, and select Open in Camera Raw.

To open the camera raw file:

1. Navigate to the Photoshop8\Tutorial folder included with your Data Files, and open **MG4835.CR2**. The file opens in the Camera Raw dialog box. See Figure 8-3.

Figure 8-3   **Camera Raw dialog box**

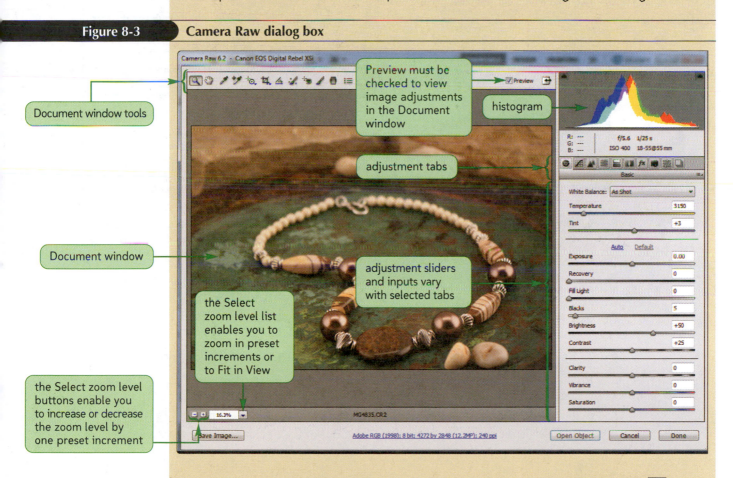

Document window tools

Preview must be checked to view image adjustments in the Document window

histogram

adjustment tabs

Document window

adjustment sliders and inputs vary with selected tabs

the Select zoom level list enables you to zoom in preset increments or to Fit in View

the Select zoom level buttons enable you to increase or decrease the zoom level by one preset increment

2. On the toolbar located above the Document window, click the **Zoom Tool**, if necessary, and then click in the Document window to increase the magnification of the image to **25%** (which is one of the preset values).

3. Click in the Document window, and drag to select the front of the necklace. The selected area expands to fill the Document window, as shown in Figure 8-4.

Figure 8-4   Selected area of the image fills the Document window

use the Zoom Tool to select an area of the image to magnify

the selected area of the image fills the Document window

4. On the toolbar above the Document window, click the **Hand Tool** [hand icon], click in the image, and then drag the image to the right, so you can see how to pan the image within the Document window.

5. In the Select zoom level list located below the Document window, click **Fit in View**. The entire image is displayed in the Document window.

6. On the toolbar, click and hold the **Crop Tool** [crop icon] to display its shortcut menu, and then click **Custom**. The Custom Crop dialog box opens.

7. Select **Ratio** from the Crop list, if necessary, type **1** in the first box and **.8** in the second box, and then click the **OK** button.

   The crop ratio is now set for the Crop Tool. Next, you'll crop the image.

8. Place the pointer at the upper-left corner of the necklace, and click and drag the mouse down and to the right until the front of the necklace is in the area that will not be cropped. Release the mouse button. See Figure 8-5.

Figure 8-5   **Crop Tool in the Document window**

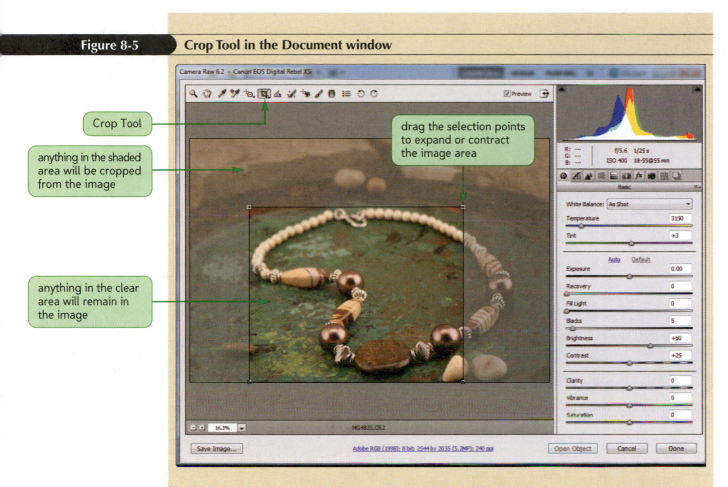

Crop Tool

anything in the shaded area will be cropped from the image

drag the selection points to expand or contract the image area

anything in the clear area will remain in the image

9. Drag the upper-right selection handle up and to the right until the entire necklace is in the image area. See Figure 8-6.

Figure 8-6   Adjusted crop area

the entire necklace is now included in the clear area of the image; the rest of the image will be cropped

▶ **10.** On the toolbar, click the **Hand Tool** to view the cropped image.

Specifying Workflow Options

As noted previously, the way you work in the Camera Raw plug-in is slightly different from the way you work in Photoshop and other graphics programs because any adjustments that you make in Camera Raw are stored outside of the original file, in an XMP file or the camera raw database, and are only applied when you create other files from your original camera raw file by outputting the file to Photoshop. Once you output your file to Photoshop, the adjustments you made in Camera Raw are incorporated into the file, and you must save the file as a different file type, such as PSD, PDF, TIFF, or JPEG.

Another difference is that images are always opened in Camera Raw with the full size, resolution, and color specifications and bit depth with which your digital camera captured them, and because you do not make destructive adjustments to camera raw files, there is never a need to adjust these settings while you are working in Camera Raw. You can, however, use the Workflow Options dialog box in Camera Raw to adjust these parameters for files you output from the Camera Raw plug-in. You access the Workflow Options dialog box by clicking the link below the Document window. The workflow settings are very similar to the settings you input when you create a new document in

Photoshop, and they are applied when a file is output from Camera Raw to Photoshop. The Camera Raw workflow options include the following:

- **Space:** RAW files usually use camera-native specifications for color; however, Camera Raw enables you to specify a target color profile for image output. Selecting Space settings is like selecting a color mode and color profile when you create a new document in Photoshop.
- **Depth:** You can set the bit depth for an image in Camera Raw, as you have already done in Photoshop. You can choose to open a file in Photoshop as an 8Bits/Channel or a 16 Bits/Channel image.
- **Size (or Crop Size):** With this setting, you can select the pixel dimensions of images you import into Photoshop. By default, the size is set to the dimensions of the image. Once you have cropped an image, the label changes to Crop Size, indicating that the image will be output at the cropped size. This is similar to setting the width and height of a new document in Photoshop.
- **Resolution:** You can adjust the resolution at which an image is printed. This setting does not affect the pixel dimensions; it is the same as setting Resolution for a document in Photoshop.
- **Sharpen For:** This option allows you to specify sharpening settings for output to Screen, Glossy Paper, or Matte Paper. Typically, this setting is left to the default option—None.
- **Open in Photoshop as Smart Objects:** When this box is checked, camera raw images opened in Photoshop will open as Smart Object layers.

PROSKILLS

Decision Making: Determining Project Parameters

To make good work flow decisions during a project, you must have a clear understanding of what you need to provide as a final product. Decisions regarding color model, size, resolution, file type, delivery method, and so forth should be determined during the planning phase of the project. Get input from all of the people who will receive versions of the final product to ensure that you create an end product that will satisfy all of your client's needs. For example, if your project includes professional print output, ask the printer to specify the required image size, resolution, and file type. If you are creating a Web version of the materials, ask the Web designer similar questions. It is a good idea to create a complete project plan prior to beginning any work on your project. Even if you are just retouching an image, take a few moments to make sure you understand exactly what you need to provide as an end product. Taking the time to make decisions regarding project parameters prior to beginning work will enable you to streamline your process and to provide superior final results.

When Sadie hired your team to create this project, she contacted her printer who provided all of the parameters for the project. You'll use that information to set the Camera Raw workflow options before you save your adjustments.

REFERENCE

Setting Workflow Options in Camera Raw

- In the Camera Raw dialog box, click the linked text at the bottom of the Document window.
- In the Workflow Options dialog box, set the Space, Depth, Size, Resolution, and Sharpen For settings, as desired.
- Click the Open in Photoshop as Smart Objects check box to select it so that camera raw images opened in Photoshop will open as Smart Object layers.

To set workflow options in Camera Raw:

1. At the bottom of the Document window, click the linked text (as called out in the Session 8.1 Visual Overview). The Workflow Options dialog box opens.

2. In the Space box, select **Adobe RGB (1998)**, if necessary, and in the Depth box select **8 Bits/Channel**. In the Resolution box, type **300** and make sure the **pixels/inch** setting is selected. Click the **Open in Photoshop as Smart Objects** check box to select it, if necessary. See Figure 8-7.

Figure 8-7 Camera Raw Workflow Options dialog box

these dimensions will vary depending on the size at which you cropped the image

check to open the Camera Raw file as a Smart Object layer in Photoshop

3. Click the **OK** button to accept changes and return to the Camera Raw dialog box.

Saving Adjustments to a Camera Raw File

After you make adjustments to a camera raw file, you can save the adjustments by clicking either the Done button or the Open Object button at the bottom of the Camera Raw dialog box. When you click Done, the changes are saved in an XMP file, and the Camera Raw dialog box closes without a copy of the image being opened in Photoshop. If you select Open Object, the adjustments are saved in an XMP file, the Camera Raw dialog box closes, and a copy of the image is opened as a Smart Object layer in a Photoshop document. To save a copy of the image that opened in Photoshop, you must save the file as a PSD in Photoshop. This will not affect the original camera raw file, which can only be accessed via the Camera Raw plug-in, but it will make your image accessible for other uses.

Unlike most Smart Objects, which are linked to an original source file, a Smart Object that is created from a camera raw file is linked to a copy of the camera raw file that is embedded in the Photoshop file. When you double-click the Smart Object layer, it will open the embedded camera raw file in the Camera Raw dialog box. You can make edits to the embedded camera raw file and when you exit Camera Raw the adjustments will flow through to your Smart Object in your PSD file, but they will not affect the original camera raw file. Further, additional adjustments to your original camera raw file will not affect the Smart Object or its embedded camera raw file. As with regular Smart Objects, you can make nondestructive adjustments to the Smart Object layer from within Photoshop. However, if you would like to make pixel-altering adjustments, like dodging, or burning, you must convert the Smart Object into a regular layer by rasterizing it.

Next, you'll save your adjustments and open a copy of the image of the necklace as a Smart Object layer in a document in Photoshop so you can create versions of the image that you will use for print and for the Web. You'll save the document as a PSD file, and then you'll open the embedded camera raw file in Camera Raw to ensure that the Smart

Object is linked to the embedded camera raw file. Finally, you'll open the folder where your Data Files are stored, and you'll locate the XMP file that was created when you adjusted your camera raw file by cropping it.

To open the camera raw file as a Smart Object:

1. In the Camera Raw dialog box, click the **Open Object** button.

   Trouble? If you see an Open Image button instead of the Open Object button, you did not check the Open in Photoshop as Smart Objects check box in the Workflow Options dialog box. Open the Workflow Options dialog box, and check the Open in Photoshop as Smart Objects check box, and click the OK button to save your change. Then click the Open Object button. Or, simply Shift-click the Open Image button to open the file as a Smart Object.

   The adjustments to the camera raw file are saved in an XMP file, and a copy of the image is opened as a Smart Object layer in a document in Photoshop. See Figure 8-8.

TIP

When you click the Open Object button, the camera raw file opens in Photoshop, but the image will still need to be saved in Photoshop.

Figure 8-8   **Image opened as a Smart Object**

image opened as a Smart Object layer in Photoshop

the filename does not have a file extension, indicating that it has not yet been saved

a small portion of a rock is visible in the frame; you will crop this later

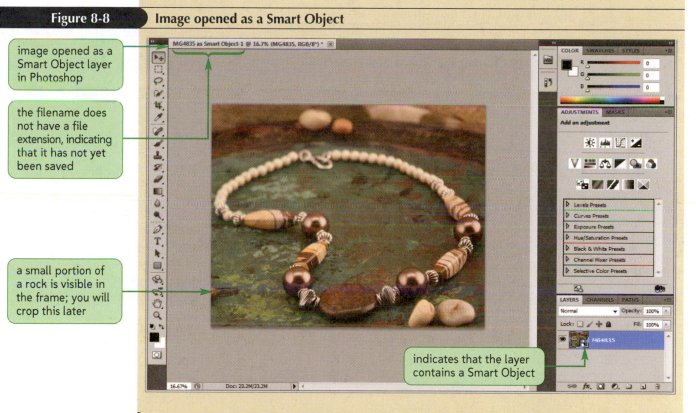

indicates that the layer contains a Smart Object

2. Save the file as **MG4835SO.psd** in the Photoshop8\Tutorial folder.

3. On the Layers panel, double-click the thumbnail for the Smart Object layer. The embedded camera raw file opens in the Camera Raw dialog box.

4. Click the **OK** button to return to Photoshop.

   The Progress dialog box appears, indicating that Photoshop is updating the Smart Object to synchronize it with the embedded camera raw file and display any changes that you made to the original files. You must save the PSD file again even if you have not made changes.

▶ **5.** On the Application bar, click **File**, and then click **Save**.

▶ **6.** On the Windows 7 taskbar, click the **Windows Explorer** icon 🖼️, and navigate to the Photoshop8\Tutorial folder. Locate the MG4835.xmp file; this is the sidecar file where the adjustments to your original camera raw file are stored.

▶ **7.** Close the folder window.

Sadie would like to use this image in the insert, but she feels that the small portion of the brown rock that appears at the left of the cropped image is distracting. She would like you to adjust the cropping so that the rock is removed from the frame. This will involve cropping a portion of the necklace from the frame, but it will create a less cluttered and, therefore, more aesthetically appealing composition.

When you adjust the size of the camera raw file embedded in the Smart Object layer of your PSD file, the size of the width and height of your PSD file does not change; therefore, an area of your Document window will not be filled by your image. To fill the document area with the image, you can either crop the document area to the size of the image or you can stretch the image to fill the document area.

You'll open the Smart Object in Camera Raw and adjust the cropping to remove the portion of the rock that is displayed at the left of the frame. Then, you'll return to Photoshop and use Free Transform to stretch the cropped image to fill the canvas. Finally, you'll examine your original camera raw file to see if the changes you made to the embedded document affect the original file.

To crop image in the camera raw file embedded in the Smart Object:

▶ **1.** On the Layers panel, double-click the thumbnail for the Smart Object layer to open the embedded camera raw file in the Camera Raw dialog box.

▶ **2.** On the toolbar located above the Document window in the Camera Raw dialog box, click the **Crop Tool** 🔲 to display the entire image and the adjustable cropping area.

▶ **3.** Click and drag the upper-left selection handle down and to the right until the rock, located at the left of the visible area, is no longer within the cropped area of the image.

▶ **4.** Click the **OK** button to save the adjustment and update the Smart Object. See Figure 8-9.

Figure 8-9	Updated Smart Object

asterisk indicates that changes have been made to the document since it was last saved

the cropped Smart Object no longer fills the Document window

You'll use Free Transform to stretch the image to fill the Photoshop Document window. When you make adjustments to the Smart Object in Photoshop, it does not affect the embedded camera raw file.

5. On the Application bar, click **Edit**, and then click **Free Transform**. Photoshop adds selection handles to the image in the Document window.

6. Click and drag the upper-right selection handle up and to the right until it is in the upper-right corner of the document.

7. Click and drag the lower-left selection handle down and to the left until it is in the lower-left corner of the document.

8. Press the **Enter** key. Notice that the cropped area has not changed but the image now fills the canvas. See Figure 8-10.

Figure 8-10   **Cropped Smart Object transformed to fill the canvas**

canvas is no longer visible

the cropped area remains the same, but it now fills the canvas

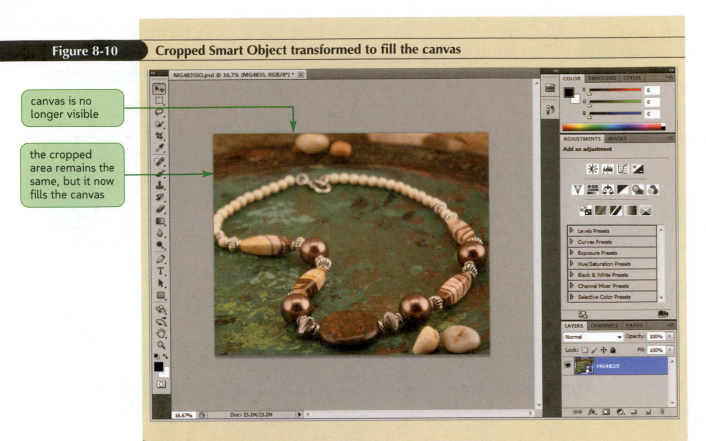

9. Save the image, and close the file.

10. Navigate to the Photoshop8\Tutorial folder, and open the **MG4835.CR2** file, which is the file you originally worked with.

    The file opens in the Camera Raw dialog box. Notice that the new Crop adjustment was not applied to this file.

11. Click the **Cancel** button to close the Camera Raw dialog box.

INSIGHT

Using Mini Bridge (or Bridge) with Camera Raw

You can use Mini Bridge (or Bridge) to view and manage your camera raw files, just as you would with other image files. Camera raw files are displayed in the same way that your other image files are displayed, and you can open a camera raw file by right-clicking it and selecting Open in Camera Raw or by simply double-clicking the camera raw file. In Bridge, you can open a camera raw file without opening Photoshop by right-clicking the file and selecting Open in Camera Raw. If you double-click a camera raw file in Bridge, it will open the image in the Camera Raw plug-in and it will also open Photoshop. Bridge also enables you to apply, copy, and clear settings between files and to see file metadata. It enables you to batch process your files and to apply settings to files without opening the Camera Raw dialog box.

Before you can use Camera Raw to create a professional image, you must understand the Camera Raw retouching and adjustment tools, and you need to learn a bit about the language photographers use so that you will understand how your adjustments will affect your photographic image. Next, you'll spend some time exploring the Adjustments panel in the Camera Raw dialog box.

Making Basic Adjustments to RAW Images

The Adjustments panel in the Camera Raw dialog box is set up a bit differently than the Adjustments panel in Photoshop, but it enables you to create some similar adjustments. The Camera Raw Adjustments panel is located on the right side of the Camera Raw dialog box, and it provides a robust array of tools for adjusting your RAW images. The histogram, which is displayed above the Adjustments panel, provides a visual representation of how the adjustments you make are affecting the image. Because camera raw files contain so much more data than image files that you work with in Photoshop, and because the Camera Raw plug-in was created specifically to enable you to make the fine adjustments necessary for correcting professional photographic images, you can usually achieve better results adjusting images in Camera Raw rather than in Photoshop. Using the information provided by the histogram and the adjustment tools available in Camera Raw provides you with a great deal of control over image output. For an overview of the tabs on the Adjustments panel, see Figure 8-11.

Figure 8-11	Adjustments panel tabs

Tab	Icon	Description
Basic		General adjustments to white balance, tone, and saturation are performed using the Basic tab; the other tabs are used for fine-tuning images.
Tone Curve		Like the Curves Adjustment in Photoshop, the Tone Curve tab is used to fine-tune tonal adjustments.
Detail		The Detail tab contains the Sharpening and Noise Reduction adjustments. Sharpening adjusts the edge definition of images, and Noise Reduction adjusts the artifacts that are sometimes visible in photographic images.
HSL/Grayscale		Fine adjustments to hue, saturation, and luminance, as well as conversion to gray scale, are made on the HSL/Grayscale tab.
Split Toning		Fine adjustments to the highlights and shadows of an image are made on the Split Toning tab.
Lens Corrections		Perspective and lens flaws can be corrected automatically or manually on the Lens Corrections tab.
Effects		The Grain and Vignette effects are located on the Effects tab. The Grain effect creates artifacts that simulate film grain, and Vignette effects create dark or light edges around images, creating a circular frame that is used to draw the viewer's eyes toward an object of focus located near the center of the frame.
Camera Calibration		The Camera Calibration tab enables you to adjust how Camera Raw will process the colors of your camera raw images.
Presets		The Presets tab enables you to create and name custom presets, which you can use to adjust images.
Snapshots		The Snapshots tab enables you to record the state of an image at any point while you are in Camera Raw. Once you have created a snapshot of an image, you can restore the image back to the settings that were applied when the snapshot was taken, at any time during the editing process.

The Basic tab is displayed on the Adjustments panel by default when a file is opened in the Camera Raw dialog box because its controls enable you to make general adjustments to your image, including white balance, tone, and saturation adjustments. Almost all images benefit from Basic tab adjustments. Once you have cropped an image so that the composition is appealing, your next step should always be to make adjustments to the image using the adjustments on the Basic tab. All of the images that you are working on for the catalog insert will need basic adjustments. In the next section, you'll examine the histogram and the Basic tab to see how your adjustments affect your images.

Understanding the Histogram

The histogram that appears above the Adjustments panel displays a great deal of useful information, but it can be a bit tricky to interpret what you see. It is important to understand that the histogram is a simple bar graph that has two axes. The horizontal x-axis represents all of the possible brightness (also called luminance) values that can be displayed in an image starting at 0 (complete darkness) on the left and running to 255 (the brightest white) on the right. This means that the center of the x-axis represents the midtones of the image. The vertical y-axis represents the number of pixels in the image that display a particular luminance value, starting with 0 pixels at its lowest point and moving upward. Understanding this information can tell you a lot. For example, when a large number of high Y values in an image are concentrated at the left of the x-axis, the image is probably underexposed and, therefore, looks dark. If a large number of high Y values in an image are concentrated at the right of the image, it is probably overexposed, and looks blown out—or white.

The histogram also has three channels of color: red, green, and blue. White is displayed when all three of the channels overlap. Yellow, magenta, or cyan appears when two channels overlap.

A histogram that displays a fairly wide curve or arc for each channel is representative of an image that uses the full tonal scale; for such an image, the histogram shows the highest number of pixels at the midtone values, along with some pixels that display shadows and some pixels that display highlights. When making adjustments to images, designers often try to spread out pixel values fairly evenly across the histogram. A histogram that has wide areas of zero value across channels is an image that does not use a full tonal range. Images that display this type of histogram are often dull. Finally, a histogram that displays tall spikes is likely to produce clipping.

Remember that clipping occurs when the pixel values fall outside of the range that can be reproduced in the color space in which you are working. Areas that are overly bright are clipped to output white, whereas areas that are overly dark are clipped to output black. Whenever clipping occurs, detail is lost in areas of the image containing the clipped color values.

Now that you understand how to interpret a histogram, you can see that when spikes occur at the left of the histogram, there is potential for shadow clipping because the spikes are occurring on the side of the x-axis that displays darker values. Conversely, spikes at the right of the histogram indicate potential highlight clipping.

Clipping warnings are displayed in the top corners of the histogram. When pixel values fall outside of the reproducible range, the black clipping warning triangles in the histogram change in color to correspond with the color(s) being clipped. The clipping warning icons display red, green, or blue if only red, green, or blue values are being clipped. White is displayed when all three of the channels are being clipped, and yellow, magenta, or cyan appears when two channels are being clipped. The Shadow clipping warning icon is displayed at the left of the histogram and the Highlight clipping warning icon is displayed at the right. If you click on a clipping warning triangle icon, the clipped pixels will be colored in the Document window—highlights in red and shadows in blue—enabling you to identify problems and to adjust your image more effectively.

You'll select the Highlight clipping warning icon to display pixels in your image that will be clipped.

To display clipped pixels:

1. On the Application bar, click **File**, click **Browse in Mini Bridge**, and navigate to the Photoshop8\Tutorial folder. Right-click the **MG4998.CR2** file, and click **Open in Camera Raw**. The file opens in the Camera Raw dialog box.

2. In the upper-right corner of the histogram, click the red **Highlight clipping warning** icon ▲. The pixels that will be clipped are displayed in red in the image. See Figure 8-12.

Figure 8-12   Highlight clipping displayed in red

3. Click the **Highlight clipping warning** icon ▲ again. The red is removed from the display.

White Balancing an Image

Lighting is an important factor in taking a good photograph, and one of the important components of light that can affect your photographs is color temperature. Every light source has a color temperature that is measured in Kelvins. High color temperature measurements (5000K or more) produce light that is considered to have a cool color because it has a bluish tint. Florescent lights, found in many office buildings, are a good example of cool-colored light. Lower color temperature measurements (2700K to 3000K) produce light that is considered to have a warm color because it has a yellowish or reddish tint. The sun and fire are good examples of warm-colored light. Tungsten lights, often used by photographers when lighting in a studio, also have a warm color.

The color temperature of lights has a minimal effect on us in our daily lives because our eyes do an excellent job of recognizing what we are supposed to see, making things look fairly normal to us. However, the sensor that interprets light on a digital camera does not do as good of a job dealing with color temperature. Because of this, photographs often have a color cast. A **color cast** is a tint that affects an entire photograph. For example, a photograph that was taken in the sun might have a yellowish color cast; a photograph taken under florescent lighting might have a bluish color cast.

Camera Raw enables you to correct the color cast created by the color temperature of lighting by white balancing your images. When you **white balance** an image, you locate objects in the image that should be white or gray and then make corrections that account for the color temperature of the lighting and that remove color casts from the image. In Camera Raw, the White Balance list has several preset options you can use to make general white balance corrections to your images, including the following:

- **As Shot:** Uses a camera's white balance settings
- **Auto:** Uses image data to calculate white balance adjustments
- **Daylight, Cloudy, and Shade:** Adjust white balance to compensate for a specified lighting condition
- **Tungsten, Florescent, and Flash:** Adjust white balance to compensate for the color temperature of the lighting used when a photograph was taken
- **Custom:** Enables you to create custom white balance settings

In addition, you can create small adjustments by moving the Temperature and Tint Sliders on the Adjustments panel in the Camera Raw dialog box.

Next, you'll adjust the white balance settings to compensate for the tungsten lighting that the photographer used while shooting the image for the insert. Remember that tungsten lights have a color temperature of around 3200K, which produces a warm color. You'll experiment with white balance settings, and then you'll adjust to compensate for tungsten lighting. By white balancing the image, you'll remove the yellowish color cast from the photograph.

TIP

It is a good idea to make white balance corrections before you make any other tonal corrections.

REFERENCE

White Balancing an Image

- On the Adjustments panel in the Camera Raw dialog box, click the White Balance arrow, and then select the option for the type of lighting that was used when the photograph was taken.
- At the top of the Camera Raw dialog box, click the Preview check box to uncheck it, and then click it again to check it, to see the effects of the White Balance option you selected.
- If the White Balance option you selected did not remove the color cast from the image, select a different White Balance option.

To white balance the image:

1. On the Basic tab of the Adjustments panel in the Camera Raw dialog box, click the **White Balance** arrow, and then click **Flash**. See Figure 8-13.

Figure 8-13   **Image with white balance adjusted to compensate for flash**

Because the color temperature of flash lighting is cool, the white balance adjustment made the image warmer, which has a poor effect on your image because it was shot with warm-colored tungsten light. The correction created a very yellow image.

2. On the Adjustments panel, click the **White Balance** arrow, and then click **Tungsten**. See Figure 8-14.

Figure 8-14 **Image with white balance adjusted to compensate for tungsten**

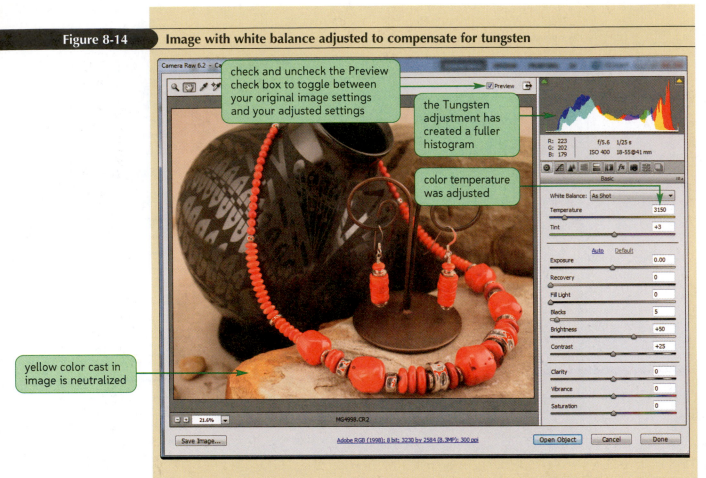

3. Click the **Preview** check box to uncheck it and see your original image settings.

4. Click the **Preview** check box again to check it and see your adjusted image settings. Notice how the yellowish color cast has been removed from the image.

Once you have adjusted the white balance of an image, you should make tonal corrections to the image. Tonal adjustments enable you to create a more dynamic and professional image. If the image is too bright, you can create a richer image by adding shadows and darker midtones. If the image is too dark, you can lighten the image to see more detail in areas of shadow. If an image is flat, you can increase contrast to create a more dynamic range of colors in the image.

Next, you'll make tonal adjustments to the image you just white balanced.

Making Basic Tonal Adjustments

Like Photoshop, Camera Raw has an Auto adjustment option, located at the top of the tonal adjustments section of the Basic tab, which analyzes the camera raw data and makes adjustments based on generalized rules of best practice. The Auto adjustment can be a good place to start, but, like Photoshop's Auto adjustments, the Auto adjustments in Camera Raw are often too general. It is a better idea to become familiar with the tonal adjustment tools on the Basic tab, which allow you to make changes by dragging the sliders, entering values in the boxes, or selecting the numbers in the box and pressing the up or down arrow. See Figure 8-15.

Figure 8-15   Making tonal adjustments using the tools on the Basic tab

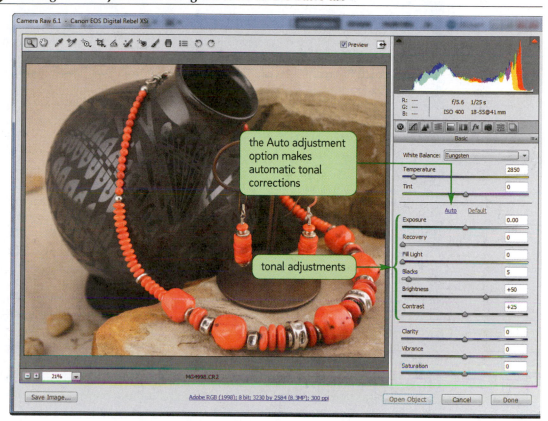

The Basic tab includes the following tonal adjustment tools:

- **Exposure:** Exposure adjusts the overall brightness/darkness of the image and has a greater effect on the image highlights. (Increments are equivalent to a camera's f-stop adjustments.)
- **Recovery:** The Recovery Tool is used to recover highlight details by bringing highlight values down; it enables Camera Raw to reconstruct some detail in areas where some color channels were clipped to white.
- **Fill Light:** The Fill Light Tool is used to recover shadow details by bringing shadow values up without brightening blacks. Like Recovery, the Fill Light Tool enables Camera Raw to reconstruct some detail in areas where some color channels were clipped to black.
- **Blacks:** Concentrating its effects on the shadows in an image, this tool adjusts the input levels that are mapped to black. When you increase the Blacks value, you increase the range of dark colors in the image that are set to black. It is similar to setting and adjusting the black point in Photoshop. Increasing the Blacks value can be used to create the illusion that the image has greater contrast.
- **Brightness:** Like Exposure, the Brightness Tool is used to adjust the brightness/darkness of an image; however, it creates the changes by compressing highlights while expanding shadows, when you move right—or the reverse, when you move left.
- **Contrast:** Contrast enables you to adjust the image by increasing or decreasing the opposition of relative lightness to relative darkness in the midtones of your image.

INSIGHT

Image Style

Before you begin making tonal adjustments to images that you will use in a project, it is important to identify what look you are trying to create. It is not enough to create beautiful images. To produce a strong final project, all the images must work well together. You should make general decisions about cropping, lightness, darkness, and color saturation before you begin adjusting images. Consider how you want objects to appear within the frame of the image. Cropping an image tightly around an object gives the object an exaggerated importance, whereas making an object a small part of a large composition can provide a sense of environment. Decide what you want to accomplish with the images in your project, and then make decisions regarding the cropping with those goals in mind. Image lightness and darkness can affect the drama and intensity of your composition as well as how the image looks in the overall composition. Consider how you would like the images to make the viewer feel and consider what styles are popular with your target audience. Also, consider the color of your composition background. Lighter images will pop on a dark background and may blend into a lighter background, whereas darker images may blend into a dark background and pop on a lighter background.

After you have considered all of these elements, make decisions about the lightness and darkness of your images. Saturation can be used to create a stylized look. Images that have heavily saturated colors look full and rich. Christmas catalogs often use images with oversaturated colors to create a rich, festive look. Reducing image saturation also creates a stylized look. Western landscape photographers sometimes reduce the saturation of their images to intensify the vast openness of their photographic compositions. When making saturation decisions, think about the subject matter of your photographs. How will saturation affect the look of the images in your composition? What will be most effective in creating the look you are trying to achieve? Once you have an overall plan in place, you can adjust the images that you will use in your project. When you are finished, you should also compare the final images to ensure that when combined they will create a cohesive composition.

Because the tonal adjustment tools have a cumulative effect on your image, it is best to start with exposure adjustments and then work your way through the Basic tab, as needed. For the FW Museum Store project, your team has decided to crop all of the images fairly closely to emphasize the details of the jewelry. Images must be cropped with a 1 to .8 ratio to fit into the layout created by other members of your team. (The current image has already been cropped to reflect these dimensions.) Images should be light, and earth tones should be juxtaposed with vibrant, saturated colors. Next, you'll make tonal adjustments to your image.

To make basic tonal adjustments to the image:

1. On the Adjustments panel, click the **Auto** link. Notice that the adjustments are fairly heavy-handed and that the image is now fairly dark. In the histogram, the Highlight clipping warning is off, but now some shadow clipping is occurring.

2. Click the **Shadow clipping warning** icon ⬆. Pixels in the image that will be clipped are now displayed in a dark blue. See Figure 8-16.

Figure 8-16   Auto adjustment with shadow clipping visible

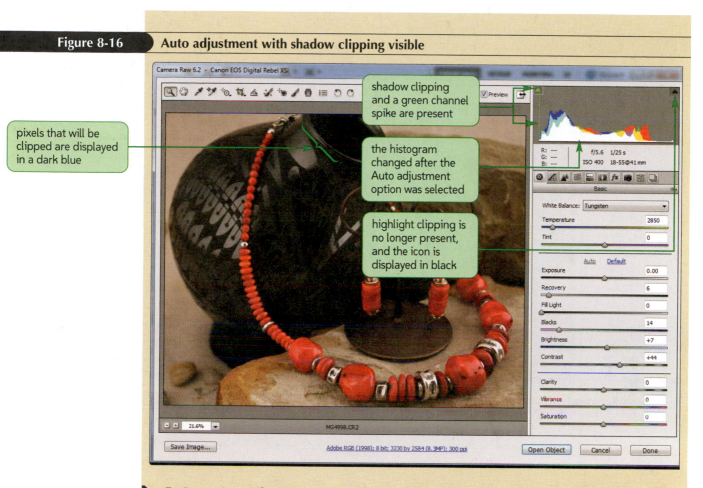

pixels that will be clipped are displayed in a dark blue

shadow clipping and a green channel spike are present

the histogram changed after the Auto adjustment option was selected

highlight clipping is no longer present, and the icon is displayed in black

3. Press the **Ctrl+Z** keys to undo the Auto adjustment, and then drag the **Exposure** slider left until **-0.25** is displayed in the box. This adjustment darkens the image in a less dramatic way than the Auto correction. Notice how the histogram changes as you drag the slider.

You do not want to decrease the exposure of the entire image any further because it will make the image too dark, but it would be nice to see some of the detail that is currently lost in the highlights of the image, especially on the silver beads. To accomplish this, you'll increase the Recovery value. This will darken only the highlight tones of the image, so you will be able to see more of the details in those areas.

4. To recover some of the detail in the silver beads, drag the **Recovery** slider to the right until **20** is displayed in the box. See Figure 8-17.

Figure 8-17 **Image with Recovery increased**

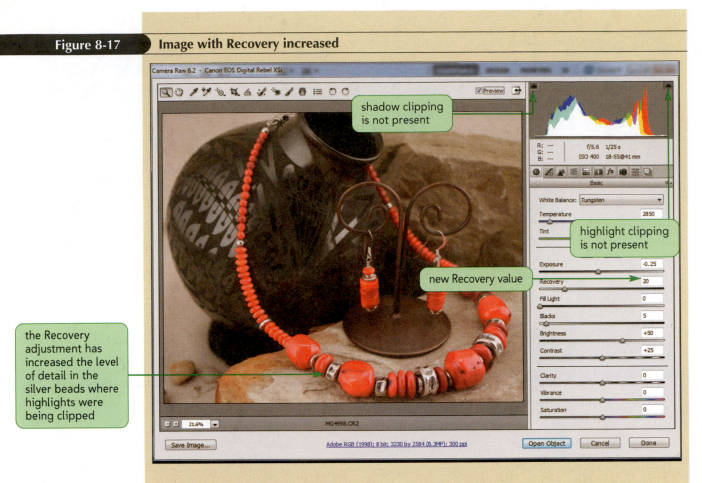

shadow clipping is not present

highlight clipping is not present

new Recovery value

the Recovery adjustment has increased the level of detail in the silver beads where highlights were being clipped

5. Click the **Preview** check box to uncheck it and view your original settings, and then click it again to recheck the box.

6. Increase the Blacks value to **20** to increase the number of colors in the image that are displayed as black.

   With this adjustment, the image becomes too dark, and shadow clipping warnings are displayed again.

7. Double-click the **Blacks** slider to return to the original Blacks original value of **5**, and notice how the shape of the histogram has changed.

Your image is looking better, but it is not perfect. Next, you'll adjust the clarity, vibrance, and saturation of your image to enhance the look of the final image.

Clarity, Vibrance, and Saturation Adjustments

The remaining controls on the Basic tab all affect the saturation of color in your images. As you learned in Tutorial 7, the saturation is the vividness or purity of the color. Adjustments to the Clarity value have the greatest effect in the midtones of an image. Increasing the Clarity value increases the sharpness and detail of an image by increasing local contrast of the image, especially in the midtones. Decreasing the Clarity value can make an image seem smoother and less detailed. Adjustments made using the Vibrance Tool change the saturation of all of the lower-saturated colors in an image and have a small effect on colors that are already high in saturation. Finally, the Saturation Tool adjusts the saturation of all colors equally. Next, you'll use the Clarity and Vibrance sliders to adjust the saturation of your image.

To adjust the color saturation of the image:

1. Type **-100** in the Clarity box. Notice that some of the detail has been removed from the image. See Figure 8-18.

Figure 8-18   Clarity decreased to soften the image

the background is soft because detail is removed when Clarity is decreased

decreased Clarity value

Adjusting the clarity has made the image too soft; some of the details have been lost.

2. Double-click the **Clarity** slider to return the Clarity value to its previous setting.

3. Increase the Vibrance value to **+30**. Although the increase has a minimal effect on the saturated red beads, it increases the saturation of the more neutral earth tones of the rock and background. Notice that shadow clipping has returned.

4. Decrease the Blacks value to **0** to remove shadow clipping. See Figure 8-19.

Figure 8-19 | **Image with the Vibrance and Blacks values adjusted**

increasing Vibrance has a minimal effect on highly saturated colors, such as the red in the beads

saturation is increased in colors with lower saturation values

Blacks decreased to prevent shadow clipping

increased Vibrance value

5. Click the **Done** button to save your adjustments and close the Camera Raw dialog box, and then exit Photoshop.

Opening JPEG and TIFF Files in Camera Raw

You can also open and work with JPEG and TIFF files in the Camera Raw plug-in with Mini Bridge (or Bridge) by right-clicking on the image and selecting Open in Camera Raw. When you open these files in Camera Raw, you have access to all of the tools and controls that you have when you work with camera raw files; however, some of the settings are different. For example, the White Balance options only include As Shot, Auto, and Custom because JPEG and TIFF files, unlike camera raw files, do not include metadata about how the images were shot. The biggest drawback with using these file types in Camera Raw is that you cannot achieve the same effect with adjustments because the files do not have as much image data as uncompressed and unprocessed camera raw files. This is especially true with JPEG images because JPEG is not a lossless format.

Saving Camera Raw Files as DNG files

The **Digital Negative (DNG)** file format was created by Adobe as a potential solution to the problems introduced by all of the competing proprietary camera raw formats. DNG files contain all of the uncompressed raw data that proprietary raw files contain, and when you save a camera raw file as a DNG, it does not lose any of the information that was stored in the original file. Unlike camera raw formats, DNG is nonproprietary (it is not owned by a single company) and is publicly documented (the code is available for free to the general public) and widely supported. This means that software does not need camera-specific knowledge to read DNG files and because of this, it is more likely that DNG files will be usable in the future. DNG files are often used as archival files, but you can also use them for working files. You work with DNG files in Camera Raw just as you work with camera raw files, and the adjustment data can be embedded nondestructively within the file, so you do not need multiple files for an image. The point at which you will convert camera raw files to DNG files depends upon the work flow process that you or your team have selected.

In this session, you learned about the camera raw file format, and you used the Camera Raw plug-in to crop and adjust camera raw files. You also saved adjustments to your camera raw files, and you opened images as Smart Object layers in Photoshop.

REVIEW

Session 8.1 Quick Check

1. _____ files are large files that contain unprocessed and uncompressed grayscale picture data and metadata from the image sensor of a digital camera, an image scanner, or a motion picture film scanner.

2. True or False. There is only one type of camera raw file, and it has the file extension .raw.

3. What is the name of the software plug-in that enables you to open and adjust camera raw files?

4. What file type accompanies a camera raw file and contains image adjustment data?

5. What is a histogram?

6. True or False. You can measure the temperature of light.

7. DNG stands for _____ file format.

SESSION 8.2 VISUAL OVERVIEW

Change your working space color profiles and adjust your color management policies by selecting Color Settings from the Edit menu.

From the View menu, you can access Proof Setup options that allow you to specify output settings to simulate color blindness or a particular type of output, such as CMYK. Then, select Proof Colors from the View menu to view a **soft proof** of your work, which simulates the way it will look when output.

The Save for Web & Devices dialog box enables you to optimize and save a copy of an image for display on the Web.

As you change the file type and the compression quality, you can see how the file size and the Web download time are affected.

The Optimized tab in the Save for Web & Devices dialog box displays an image as it will appear with the compression settings you have selected.

COLOR MANAGEMENT AND OUTPUT

If you have the Adobe Creative Suite, the Unsynchronized warning appears in the Color Settings dialog box if you do not have the same color settings for all of your CS5 software.

The Color Settings dialog box enables you to select color profiles for your various working space color models. A **color model** is a set of mathematical values that numerically represent color.

You can select or change color management policies here. **Color management** is the process of creating controlled, consistent, and accurate color throughout the work flow process—from input, through display, creation, adjustment, and output.

When you mouse-over an element in the Color Settings dialog box, a description of that element is displayed here.

A **working space** is a color space used to define and edit colors while you are in an Adobe application. A **color space** is a three-dimensional representation of the specific plotted points of color designated by the numerical values of colors that can be produced by a color model.

Creating Successful Output

Photoshop enables you to create artwork for output to a variety of media, including desktop printers, professional printers (both offset and digital), and the Web. In addition, because Photoshop is not primarily used as a layout program, the artwork that you create and manipulate in Photoshop is often output to other programs that are used to create the final product. For example, for one project you might get photographic images of products from a digital camera and manipulate those images in Camera Raw and Photoshop. Afterward, you might output a high-resolution version of the images to use in a print catalog that will be created in InDesign, which is Adobe's layout program, and a low-resolution version of the images to use in a Web site created in Dreamweaver, which is Adobe's Web design program. The path that a project travels from original input through final output is called the **design chain**. It is important to understand the design chain so you can create a work flow process that intelligently controls variables and maximizes the potential for professional output. See Figure 8-20.

Figure 8-20   The design chain

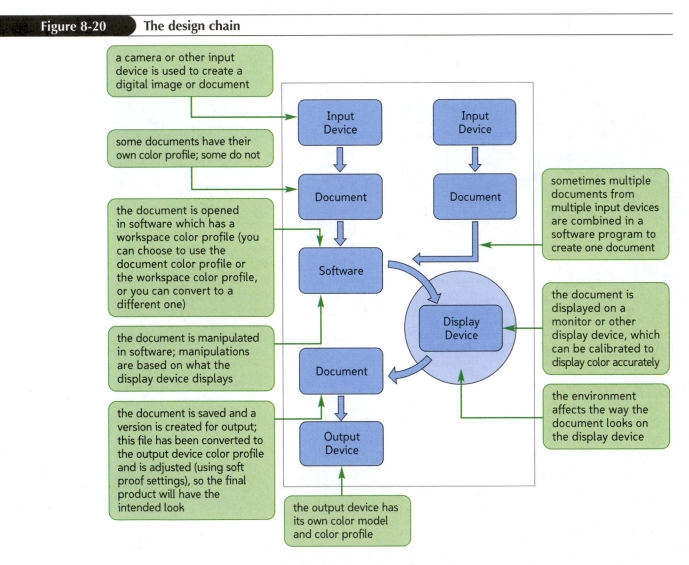

To understand the effect that the links in a design chain have on the end product, think of the children's game, telephone. In this game, people stand in a line and the first person in the line whispers a message to the person to her right. As the process is repeated and the message moves down the chain of people, the original information becomes distorted as the message is reinterpreted and "output" by each person in the chain. Finally, when the message reaches the end of the line, the person at the end of the chain "outputs" the end product, which is usually nothing like the original message. Some of the links in your design chain, such as your monitor, affect every project; while other links, such as print profiles, are specific to a particular output.

Because you are working on professional projects, it is important that you learn about color management. In this session, you'll learn to manage all of the links in your design chain so you can create high-quality output.

PROSKILLS

Problem Solving: Gathering Important Information

To maximize your chances for creating professional output, it is critical that you obtain all relevant specifications and parameters for your final output before you even get started. Problems can often be anticipated and avoided when you have the information you need to make informed decisions before you start your project. If you are working with a professional printer, you should ask for information regarding color profiles and output preferences. It is also important to decide when in your process you will move between color spaces. Each time you move between RGB and CMYK, you degrade your files during the conversion. For this reason, you should try to make conversion your final step, and you should keep a copy of the files with the working color space so you can return to your original working environment to make changes. Finally, your entire team should be aware of the requirements so you are all working with the same settings in place. Gathering all of the relevant information before you begin your project will enable you to avoid many common problems and will enable you to create a better end product.

Basic Color Management

Color management is the process of creating controlled, consistent, and accurate color throughout the work flow process—from input, through display, creation, adjustment, and, finally, output. The goal of color management is to display accurate color that matches across different media and display devices—regardless of color mode, color gamut capabilities, or output limitations. Whenever your creative process includes at least one device that attempts to reproduce or interpret the color output from another device, you can benefit from some color management.

At the professional level, color management can be quite complex, but there are some simple things that you can control on any level that will enable you to better manage your colors and create more professional output.

Calibrating Your Monitor

The first step in creating an effective color management work flow is to calibrate your monitor by adjusting the display to conform to known specifications. Next you should create a color profile, which enables you to save those settings so your monitor display is consistent over time. Remember that all monitors display images using RGB color, but every monitor is calibrated to display colors slightly differently, In addition, users can complicate things by making additional adjustments to the brightness and contrast of their monitors. Professional calibration results are usually only obtained by purchasing and using a third-party calibration software that provides additional measuring devices and greater accuracy, such as the Datacolor Spyder3 (*www.datacolor.com*) or the Pantone hueyPRO (*www.pantone.com*). However, Windows provides a basic monitor calibration utility that provides a baseline calibration.

Adjusting Ambient Lighting

Ambient lighting levels and reflections on your monitor can have a significant impact on your perception of color. For instance, red objects look blacker in blue light. It is important to consider the ambient lighting and color in your work environment and adjust it before making calibration adjustments to your monitor. For optimum results, you should work in a neutrally colored room, under subdued lighting, and no strong direct light should reach the screen. It is ideal to have the overall ambient illumination lower than the brightness output of the screen, with light sources positioned away from the screen, and windows covered completely to maintain consistent illumination. The purpose of this is to ensure that dark areas of the screen appear dark to the eye. If you are going crazy, you can install daylight-balance fluorescent or filtered halogen lights to a color temperature of 5000 degrees Kelvin. You should make these changes before you calibrate, and you should calibrate your monitor under your regular working conditions. When your working conditions change, you should recalibrate.

You'll calibrate your monitor using the Windows calibration tool, which walks you through the steps for setting the gamma, brightness, contrast, and the color balance for your monitor. Before you begin, you should understand what you are adjusting:

- **Gamma:** Gamma is a measure of the nonlinear relationship between red, green, and blue color values that are sent to the display and the luminance (or light energy) that is actually emitted from the monitor. Gamma generally affects midtones and has no effect on black or white. When gamma is set too high, the midtone display is too dark, and when it is set too low, the midtone display is too light. You'll adjust the gamma of your monitor using an on-screen slider provided in the Windows calibration tool.
- **Brightness:** Some monitors have a brightness control, whereas others do not. The brightness control might be a physical button that is located on the monitor, or it might be located in a menu on your monitor. The icon for the brightness control is a circle with lines around it that looks like a sun. In most cases, the brightness control actually adjusts the black level of the monitor by adjusting the red, green, and blue signals. When brightness is adjusted properly, black objects are displayed as true black on the monitor. To adjust the brightness of your monitor, you must locate the brightness control on your monitor and use it to adjust an image that is displayed in the Windows calibration tool. If your monitor does not have a brightness control, you will need to skip this step when calibrating your monitor.
- **Contrast:** Some monitors have a contrast control, whereas others do not. The icon for the contrast control is a circle that is divided in half vertically with black filling the left half of the circle and white filling the right half of the circle. The contrast control might be a physical button that is located on the monitor, or it might be located in a menu on your monitor. Adjusting the contrast control affects the luminance that is produced for a white input signal. When contrast is set correctly, the highlight values on your monitor will be bright but not unpleasant to look at. To adjust the contrast of your monitor, you must locate the contrast control on your monitor and use it to adjust an image that is displayed in the Windows calibration tool. If your monitor does not have a contrast control, you will need to skip this step in calibrating your monitor.
- **Color balance:** When you adjust the color balance of your monitor, you are actually adjusting the color temperature to remove any color cast that might be visible on your monitor. As with images, monitors with a lower color temperature will have a warm color cast to their display, whereas monitors with a higher color temperature will have a cool color cast to their display. Although some monitors have color settings, it is a good idea to leave those set to the factory default and to use the sliders in the Windows calibration tool to adjust the color balance of your monitor.

You'll use the Windows 7 Display Color Calibration Wizard to adjust your monitor. If you have a professionally calibrated monitor, do not complete the following steps; instead, read the steps and move to the next section.

REFERENCE

Calibrating a Monitor

- Click the Start button on the Windows 7 taskbar, click Control Panel, click Appearance and Personalization, and then click Display.
- In the Display window, click Calibrate color.
- Follow the directions provided by the Display Color Calibration Wizard.
- Save the new settings.

To calibrate your monitor:

1. On the Windows 7 taskbar, click the **Start** button 🏁, and then click **Control Panel**.

2. In the Control Panel window, click **Appearance and Personalization**, and in the Appearance and Personalization window, click **Display** to open the Display window.

3. In the Display window, click **Calibrate color** from the list on the left to open the Display Color Calibration Wizard. If necessary, click the **Maximize** button 🔲 to maximize the window. See Figure 8-21.

Figure 8-21   Windows 7 Display Color Calibration Wizard

4. Click the **Next** button to move to the next screen, and then read the on-screen information, which instructs you to locate the menu button on your monitor.

5. Once you have located the physical menu button, click it to display the menu on your monitor screen. What you see and what you can control from the menu will vary from monitor to monitor. If necessary, move the position of the menu that is displayed on screen, so it does not cover the Next button at the bottom of the screen.

6. Set your monitor display to the factory default color settings, and click the **Next** button to move to the next screen.

   Trouble? If you cannot locate the button that opens the on-screen menu, look for buttons located on the side or bottom edge of your monitor. If you still cannot locate the button, ask your instructor or technical support staff, look through the documentation that came with your monitor, or search online for documentation for your monitor.

7. Read the information explaining how to adjust the gamma for your monitor. Take a careful look at the Good gamma image, as shown in Figure 8-22.

Figure 8-22   **Good gamma as displayed by the Display Color Calibration Wizard**

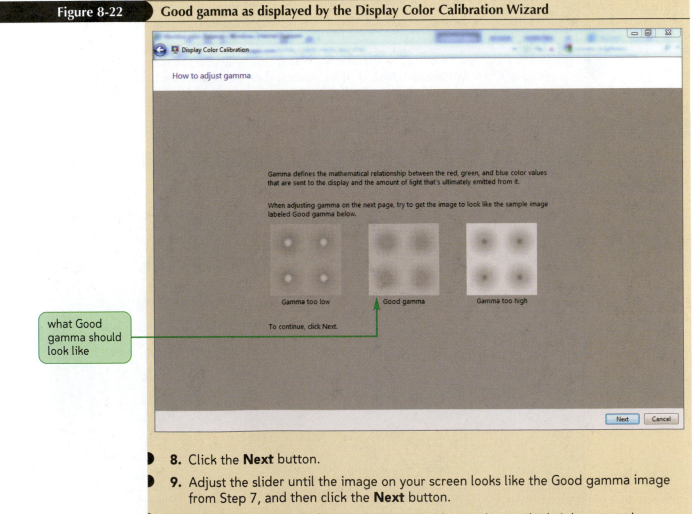

what Good gamma should look like

8. Click the **Next** button.

9. Adjust the slider until the image on your screen looks like the Good gamma image from Step 7, and then click the **Next** button.

10. Read the on-screen information explaining how to locate the brightness and contrast controls, and then locate the brightness and contrast controls for your monitor. Click the **Next** button.

Trouble? If you cannot find brightness or contrast controls for your monitor, click the Skip brightness and contrast adjustment button, and move to Step 17.

11. Take a careful look at the Good brightness image, as shown in Figure 8-23.

Figure 8-23   **Good brightness as displayed by the Display Color Calibration Wizard**

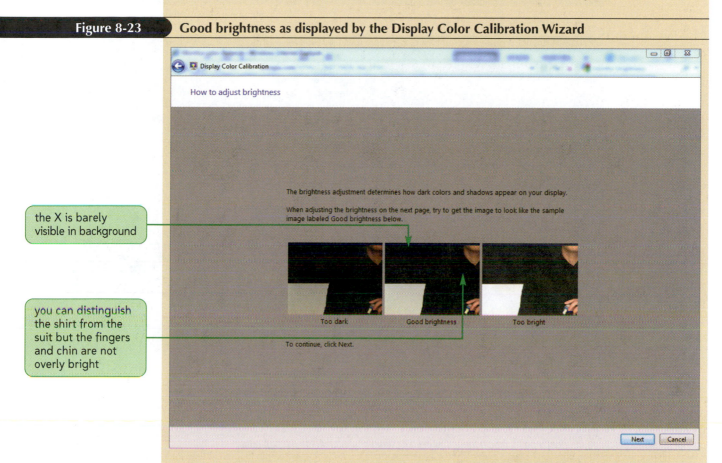

the X is barely visible in background

you can distinguish the shirt from the suit but the fingers and chin are not overly bright

12. Click the **Next** button.

13. Use the brightness control on your monitor to adjust the image on your screen so it matches the Good brightness image from Step 11, and then click the **Next button**.

Trouble? If your screen does not match the image, do the best you can. Some monitors will not be able to match the image exactly.

14. Read the on-screen information to learn more about contrast, and take a careful look at the Good contrast image, as shown in Figure 8-24.

Figure 8-24 Good contrast as displayed by the Display Color Calibration Wizard

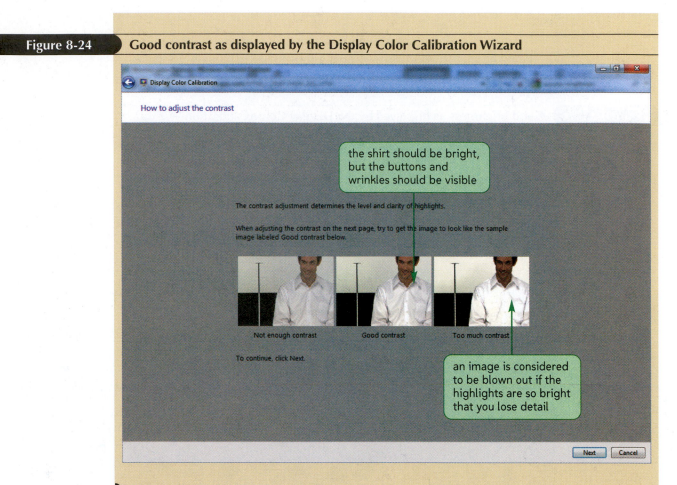

15. Click the **Next** button.

16. Use the contrast control on your monitor to adjust the image to match the Good contrast image from Step 14, and click the **Next** button.

Trouble? If your screen does not match the image, do the best you can. Some monitors will not be able to match the image exactly.

Trouble? If your monitor does not have a contrast control, skip Step 16, and move to Step 17.

17. Read the on-screen information to learn more about color balance, and take a close look at the neutral grays image, as shown in Figure 8-25.

Figure 8-25 **Good color balance as displayed by the Display Color Calibration Wizard**

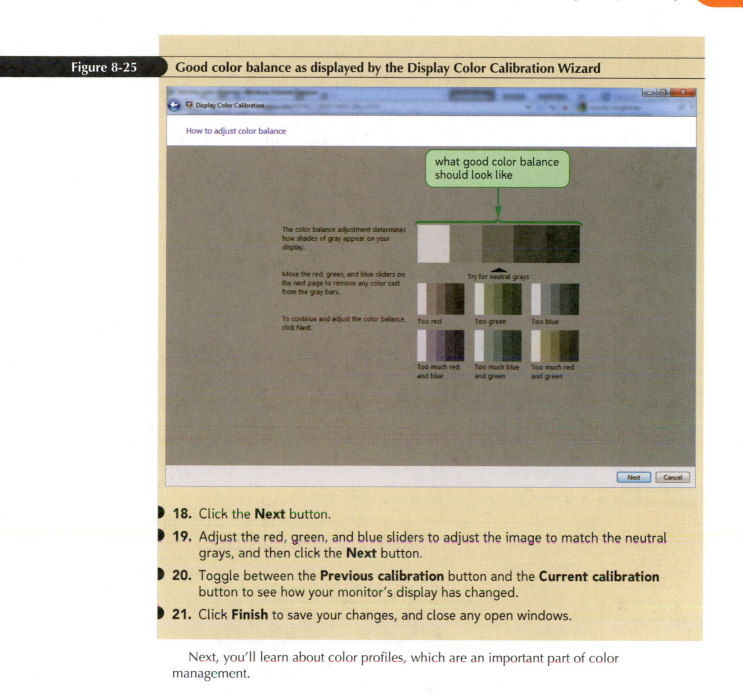

18. Click the **Next** button.

19. Adjust the red, green, and blue sliders to adjust the image to match the neutral grays, and then click the **Next** button.

20. Toggle between the **Previous calibration** button and the **Current calibration** button to see how your monitor's display has changed.

21. Click **Finish** to save your changes, and close any open windows.

Next, you'll learn about color profiles, which are an important part of color management.

Setting Your View for Soft Proofing

Because you will often work in one color mode and then output to another color mode, Photoshop provides a view that enables you to see your artwork as it will appear when output to another color mode. Simulating output settings is called soft proofing. Although the changes to output that you see when soft proofing are often small, it is still very important to make sure that you do not skip this step because even small changes in the display of color can make the difference between an amateur or professional composition.

You can also create a soft proof that enables you to see your artwork as a person who is color blind would see the work. This is a great feature because it enables you to ensure that someone with color blindness will be able to view all of the important information you are trying to convey. Photoshop has settings that simulate the two most common forms of color blindness: protanopia (reduced sensitivity to red) and deuteranopia (reduced sensitivity to green).

A member of the FW Museum Store project team created the insert that will be printed for placement in catalogs and that will also be displayed on the Web. You'll open that file, which was created in RGB, and you'll adjust your Proof Settings to specify output settings that simulate protanopia color blindness. Then, you'll view a soft proof of the file. You'll also specify output settings that simulate CMYK output, and you'll view a soft proof with those settings.

To view a soft proof:

1. Start Photoshop while pressing the **Ctrl+Alt+Shift** keys. When you are prompted to delete the Adobe Photoshop Settings File, click **Yes**. On the Application bar, right-click **Essentials**, and then click **Reset Essentials** to reset the default workspace layout. Reset all tools and tool presets.

2. Navigate to the Photoshop8\Tutorial folder included with your Data Files, and open **Insert.psd**.

   Trouble? If you get a message about missing fonts, click the OK button, and let Photoshop make the substitution.

3. Save the file as **InsertCMYK.psd** in the Photoshop8\Tutorial folder, and then press the **Ctrl+0** keys to fit the image on screen.

4. On the Application bar, click **View**, point to **Proof Setup**, and then click **Color Blindness - Protanopia-type** to select it, if necessary. This tells Photoshop to simulate the way someone with protanopia will see the artwork.

5. Select **Proof Colors** from the View menu to check it, if necessary, and view a soft proof of the document. See Figure 8-26.

Figure 8-26   Soft proof that simulates protanopia color blindness

check the soft proof to make sure that text does not disappear into the background

Next, you'll adjust your settings to proof for CMYK output.

6. On the Application bar, click **View**, point to **Proof Setup**, and then click **Working CMYK**. The document is now displayed as a soft proof for CMYK output. See Figure 8-27.

Figure 8-27   **Soft proof that simulates CMYK output**

insert document viewed as a soft proof for printing

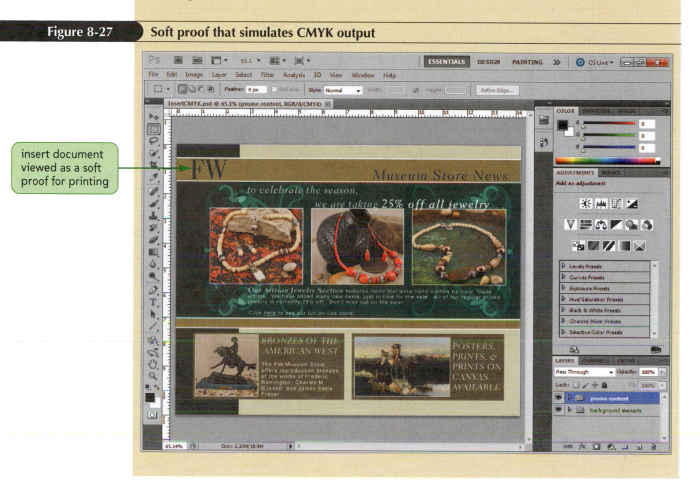

You should check your View settings every time you open a document in Photoshop because these settings affect the way your compositions look and, therefore, affect your output. It is a good idea to get into the habit of unchecking Proof Colors on the View menu when you first view a document so you can see the document displayed with its own settings or with the workspace settings if it has no profile of its own.

The soft proof presets that Photoshop provides use the color profiles specified in your Color Settings to create the soft proof you view.

Understanding Color Profiles

The **International Color Consortium (ICC)** is a group of industry professionals who are dedicated to the development of cross-platform standards for color communication and consistency. The ICC color profile is the vehicle they have created to communicate color information across platforms and devices that support ICC standards. An **ICC profile** (or just **color profile**) is a data file that characterizes an input, display, or output device and provides color management systems with the information needed to intelligently convert color data between native device color spaces and device-independent color spaces using ICC standards.

To clearly understand what color profiles do, it is important to understand a few industry terms that remain frequent sources of confusion:

- **Color model:** Color models, such as RGB, CMYK, and Lab, are sets of mathematical values that numerically represent color. When a color model is device dependent, different devices interpret the exact numeric values differently and most devices can reproduce or display only portions of the color model.
- **Color space:** A color space is a three-dimensional representation of the specific plotted points of color designated by the numerical values of colors that can be produced by a color model. A color space enables you to map the values of a color in a color model to a specific, concrete color in the real world. The standards we use for colors that correspond to a specific coordinate in a color space are those created by the ICC.
- **Gamut:** The range of color that a device can produce or display, or the range of color a color model can represent is called the gamut. The gamut of a device or process is the portion of the color space that can be represented or reproduced. When a color cannot be displayed or reproduced, it is said to be "out of gamut."
- **Color profile:** To create consistent color across devices, a color profile maps the color model to an absolute color space and communicates information about the portion (or gamut) of the color model a device can reproduce or display as well as how to most accurately translate from one color model to another so your image's colors are as consistent and accurate as possible.
- **Color mode:** In Photoshop, you can specify a color mode in which to work. Examples of modes include Grayscale, RGB, and CMYK. When you select a specific color mode in Photoshop, you are selecting a color model, and, where applicable, you are selecting a color profile that is associated with that color model. Color profiles are specified in the Color Settings dialog box.

To sum it up, ICC profiles use the standards created by the ICC to create data files that specify a color model, mapped to a specific color space with concrete values that are defined by ICC standards. This enables users to reproduce and display accurate specific colors. Furthermore, profiles specify additional information, which enables accurate and consistent translation, display, and reproduction of color—across software, between color models, and between devices.

Setting Profiles and Color Management Policies

ICC profiles are used across the design chain. You can create monitor profiles, working space profiles, input profiles, document profiles, and output profiles. The file formats that support ICC profiles include PDF, PSD, JPEG, Photoshop EPS, and TIFF. In addition to selecting a file format that supports profiles, you must make sure the Embed Color Profile or ICC Profile check box is checked when you save the file. When you calibrated your monitor, Windows saved a profile that enables your monitor to provide a more accurate display.

Photoshop provides some color setting presets that enable you to set your working space profiles and color management policies for some general purposes. Using preset settings is a good place to start. In the Color Settings dialog box, you can select a working space color profile for each color model. When you create a new document in Photoshop, it will have the color profile that you have associated with the color model you select for the document. If you open a document in Photoshop and that document has an embedded color profile that does not match your working space color profile, or if it does not have a color profile at all, Photoshop relies on your color management policy settings to decide how to handle the color data for that file.

You can also save your own custom settings, and they will appear in the Settings list along with the preset Adobe settings. This becomes important when you start working with professional printers who provide custom color profiles.

Next, you'll examine the Color Settings dialog box, and you'll adjust your settings.

TIP

It is a good idea to preserve embedded profiles when opening documents.

To adjust color settings in Photoshop:

1. On the Application bar, click **Edit**, and then click **Color Settings** to display the Color Settings dialog box.

2. Click the **Settings** arrow, and then click **North America Prepress 2** from the Settings list, if necessary. See Figure 8-28.

Figure 8-28 Color Settings dialog box

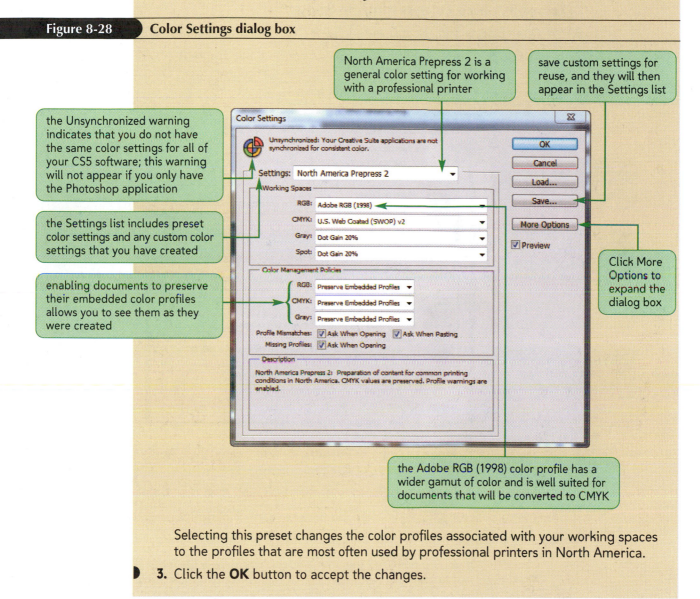

North America Prepress 2 is a general color setting for working with a professional printer

save custom settings for reuse, and they will then appear in the Settings list

the Unsynchronized warning indicates that you do not have the same color settings for all of your CS5 software; this warning will not appear if you only have the Photoshop application

the Settings list includes preset color settings and any custom color settings that you have created

enabling documents to preserve their embedded color profiles allows you to see them as they were created

Click More Options to expand the dialog box

the Adobe RGB (1998) color profile has a wider gamut of color and is well suited for documents that will be converted to CMYK

Selecting this preset changes the color profiles associated with your working spaces to the profiles that are most often used by professional printers in North America.

3. Click the **OK** button to accept the changes.

Using Bridge to Synchronize Color Settings

If you have Adobe's Creative Suite 5, you can synchronize the color settings for all of the Creative Suite 5 applications using Bridge. If you only have Photoshop, you will not have this option, but it is important to understand that you should maintain consistent color management policies across all of the software that you use. Keeping applications synchronized helps you to maintain consistent color and color management policies. The icon and message that is displayed at the top of your Color Settings dialog box tells you if all of your applications are in sync. When applications do not have synchronized color settings, a warning message is displayed at the top of the Color Settings dialog box.

If you have the entire suite of applications, your colors settings are not synchronized because you have just changed the Photoshop settings. You'll open Bridge and synchronize the color settings for all of your applications. If you do not have the entire Adobe Create Suite, do not open Bridge. Read the following steps, and then complete the steps in the Trouble following Step 4.

To synchronize color settings in Bridge:

1. Open Bridge and select **Creative Suite Color Settings** from the Edit menu.

   The Suite Color Settings dialog box is displayed. See Figure 8-29.

Figure 8-29 Setting Creative Suite color settings from Bridge

indicates that the Creative Suite applications are not synchronized

select North America General Purpose 2, if it is not selected

click Apply to apply your changes to all of the Creative Suite applications

2. Select **North America General Purpose 2**, if necessary, click **Apply**, and then close Bridge.

3. On the Application bar in Photoshop, click **Edit**, and then click **Color Settings**.

   The color setting has been changed back to North America General Purpose 2.

4. Click the **OK** button to close the Color Settings dialog box.

   Trouble? If you do not have the entire Adobe Creative Suite, click Edit on the Photoshop Application bar, and then click Color Settings. Click the Settings arrow, and then click North America General Purpose 2 from the Settings list. Then, click the OK button to accept the changes.

Converting a Color Profile

You should keep documents in their native color space while you work with them and convert them to the output color model and profile, if necessary, only when you are finished with adjustments. This ensures that your composition is not degraded by moving between color models. Save the converted composition with a new name to ensure that you have a copy of the composition with its original profile. In the future, if you need to make changes, you should go back to the original composition, make changes, and repeat the process. To change the color profile, use the Convert to Profile option on the

Edit menu. This is the preferable method because Photoshop converts the colors to the color space of the new profile by shifting the color numbers. This is done to preserve the original appearance of the document as much as possible. The Convert to Profile dialog box is broken into three sections:

- **Source Space:** The Source Space profile is the color profile that is currently attached to the document.
- **Destination Space:** When you click the Advanced button, the Convert to Profile dialog box allows you to select the color model to which you will convert the document, and then you can select the color profile for the selected color model.
- **Conversion Options:** The Convert to Profile dialog box also provides you with additional conversion options. It is a good idea to leave these alone until you have a solid understanding of color management.

You can assign a new profile by selecting a different color model from the Mode menu, but this is not recommended. When this method is used, the color numbers in the document stay the same and, because of this, the new profile may change the appearance of a document dramatically.

You'll convert the InsertCMYK.psd document to the CMYK color model, and you'll select a new color profile.

To convert the document to a new color profile:

1. On the Application bar, click **Edit**, and then click **Convert to Profile**.

2. In the Convert to Profile dialog box, click the **Advanced** button.

   Trouble? If you see a Basic button rather than an Advanced button on the right side of the Convert to Profile dialog box, then the Advanced options are already displayed. Skip Step 2.

3. Under Destination Space, click **CMYK**, if necessary, to select it, click the **Profile** arrow next to the CMYK option, and then click **Working CMYK - U.S. Web Coated (SWOP) v2**. See Figure 8-30.

| Figure 8-30 | Convert to Profile dialog box with Advanced options displayed |

the Source Space profile is the profile that is currently attached to the document

select a Destination Space color model, and then select a profile for the selected model

when you work with professional printers, they may ask you to adjust the Conversion Options

click Basic to display only the Basic options

4. Click the **OK** button to convert the profile of the document. See Figure 8-31.

Figure 8-31	InsertCMYK.psd document with new profile

the new color model is displayed here

notice that the layers were collapsed when the document was converted and that Photoshop renamed the new layer

5. Save the file, and close the document.

Printing at Home

Most users generally print their documents to a desktop printer, such as an inkjet, laser, or dye sublimation printer. The following are a few tips that can help you achieve better results with your desktop prints:

- Crop, edit, and resize your image or composition before printing. You will do a better job of resizing than your printer will. Also, remember that the resolution should be somewhere between 200 and 400 ppi.
- Work with lossless file formats whenever possible. PSDs, PDFs, and TIFFs files are good files for printing, and they can all be tagged with profiles.
- If you are working in RGB, you should not convert your document to CMYK when printing to a desktop printer because most of these printers apply a built-in RGB-to-CMYK converter to all images automatically. If your images are already CMYK, they will be converted a second time and you can end up with very unpredictable results.
- As always, ensure that your monitor is calibrated and that you have color management in place.
- Research your printer online, and download the printer profile recommended for your printer and the paper on which you are printing. Paper does matter, when printing, because different papers have slightly different brightness and the paper's finish affects the way in which the toner is absorbed into the paper. You should consider changing your printer profile when you change the type of paper on which you are printing.

TIP

Often, you can find specific printer profiles at the Web sites of paper manufacturers.

- Create a custom Color Settings profile for your printer, using the printer profile you downloaded, and remember to select your new profile in the Proof Setup. Then, check the Proof Colors command on the View menu to soft proof your document while you are working.
- In the Print dialog box, select Document under Color Management to use the document color profiles when printing, select Photoshop Manages Color, and select the Printer profiles that match the printer and paper you are using to print. It is also a good idea to check the Printer Settings and make sure that the color management in the printer is turned off so no conflicts occur.

With a little practice, you will achieve consistent, high-quality printing on your home printer.

Printing at a Professional Print Shop

Most of the time, you will not send files from Photoshop straight to a professional printer; instead, you will use the images you adjust in Photoshop as part of a layout you create in Illustrator or InDesign. However, even in these cases, you will often convert the color profile for these images prior to placing them in another program. The best thing you can do to achieve professional output when working with a service bureau is to contact the printer and ask them questions. Every printer is different, and most are extremely happy to provide you with all of the information that you will need to create professional output. Following are some of the questions you might want to ask:

- How will your document be printed? Because digital presses use toner and commercial offset presses use ink, it is a good idea to know what type of press will be used.
- Should you convert to CMYK, or should you leave your files in RGB? Some RIP (Raster Image Processor) programs convert to CMYK, whereas others prefer a CMYK file to start with.
- What color profile should you use? Do they have one for you to download? This may change with every job because it is partially dependent on the paper on which you will be printing.
- What file format would the printer prefer to receive? Today, many printers prefer to receive a PDF file, and most printers have preferences for specs for compatibility, compression, output, and so forth. The preferences vary from printer to printer so it is important to ask.

Remember that in order for all of this information to help you produce professional output, you must first have your monitor calibrated, and you must have color management built into your internal work flow.

Saving for the Web

Unlike images created for print, the name of the game when creating images for the Web is balance; you must find the right balance between image quality and file size. Because of this, the file formats that are used for the Web are all compressed file formats. The most common image formats used on the Web are GIF, JPEG, and PNG. Because all of these image formats are compressed, you should save your image in its original uncompressed file format, and then make a copy of the image to use on the Web. This enables you to return to your original image to make changes and prevents the possibility of degrading the images over time. Because size matters, for some projects, you might decide to cut a large image into pieces to decrease the size of the image. For example, if you create a layout design for a Web page in Photoshop, you would not save the entire image as a background for your Web page. Instead, you would create an image for the logo and an image for each button and for each image on the page. This approach will create several images that will load quickly, and it will enable a Web designer to add interactivity to some of the graphics in the page. The easiest way to create graphics for use on the Web is use the Save for Web & Devices dialog box in Photoshop to save a Web version of your image. To create a high-quality Web version of an image, do the following:

- **Resize the image:** Images are displayed at 72 ppi on screen. You can adjust the width and height of the image in pixels at 72 ppi, or you can set the resolution to 72 ppi and then visually adjust your image size. It is important to consider the size of the average monitor when creating Web graphics. Common sizes for Web pages are 1024 × 768 and 760 × 480.
- **Select a file format:** Decide which file format you would like to use to compress the image. Remember that each format has pros and cons. For example, JPEG is a good choice for photographic images, and PNG supports gradient transparency.
- **Save a copy:** Use Save for Web & Devices to save a copy of your image for use on the Web. Using this dialog box to save a copy will provide you with adjustment options for optimizing your compressed image. It is very important to balance image quality and file size because this will affect the users' experiences with the Web site. Your goal should be to create the smallest possible file size while maintaining good quality in your image.

You will use the Save for Web & Devices dialog box to save a copy of the new banner for use in the FW Museum Store Web site. You will save the banner as a JPEG because there is a photographic image in the file. Once you select JPEG, you will set the quality to Low. If you can see artifacts or blurriness in the image, you will raise the quality to Medium and you will continue this process until you find the lowest quality that still displays a professional looking image.

REFERENCE

Saving a JPEG Image Using Save for Web & Devices

- On the Application bar, click File, and then click Save for Web & Devices.
- In the Save for Web & Devices dialog box, select the Optimized tab, if necessary. Select JPEG from the file format list, check the Embed Color Profile check box to include the color profile with the image, and select Low from the Compression quality list.
- Zoom in on the image to check for artifacting. Select a different compression quality, if necessary, to remove the artifacting—balancing image quality with file size and download time.
- At the bottom of the Save for Web & Devices dialog box, click the Save button to open the Save Optimized As dialog box. Navigate to the folder where you want to save the file, and then click the Save button.

To save a copy of the image for the Web banner using the Save for Web & Devices dialog box:

1. Open **FeaturedItemBox.psd** from the Photoshop8\Tutorial folder provided with your Data Files, and set View to **Fit on Screen**.

   Trouble? If you get a message about some text layers containing fonts that are missing, click the OK button and let Photoshop make the substitution. You will not open or adjust the text for this document so this will not affect you.

2. On the Application bar, click **File**, and then click **Save for Web & Devices**. The document is displayed in the Save for Web & Devices dialog box.

3. Select the **Optimized** tab, if necessary, select **JPEG** from the file format list, check the **Embed Color Profile** check box to include the color profile with the image, and select **Low** from the Compression quality list.

4. Using the zoom controls at the lower-left corner of the Save for Web & Devices dialog box, zoom the image to **200%** to get a better look. Notice the artifacting around letters and around the beads. See Figure 8-32.

Figure 8-32   **Low-quality JPEG with artifacting**

on the Optimized tab you can view your image as you adjust the compression

select JPEG from the file format list

select Low from the Compression quality list

check to embed the color profile with the image

notice the artifacting around the letters and the beads

as you change the quality, you can see how it affects the file size and the download time

zoom controls

5. Select **Medium** from the quality list.

Some of the artifacts disappear, but there are still some pixelated spots in the image.

6. Select **High** from the quality list, examine the image, and then select **Very High**. Leave the quality at Very High, and zoom out to **100%** to see the entire image. See Figure 8-33.

Figure 8-33 | Very High-quality JPEG with larger file size

7. At the bottom of the Save for Web & Devices dialog box, click the **Save** button to open the Save Optimized As dialog box. Navigate to the Photoshop8\Tutorial folder, and then click the **Save** button.

   It is not necessary to rename the image because it will be saved with a different file extension (.jpg) and will not save over your Photoshop document.

8. Close FeaturedItemBox.psd without saving it, and exit Photoshop.

In this session, you learned about color management and how it impacts every aspect of your design. You calibrated your monitor, examined your color settings, and synchronized the color setting for all of your CS5 Suite software. You also set your soft proof parameters and learned to soft proof documents. Finally, you converted the color profile of a document, and you saved a copy of an image for use on the Web.

REVIEW

Session 8.2 Quick Check

1. The path that a project travels from original input through final output is called the _____ _____.

2. You can use the Windows _____ Wizard to calibrate your monitor.

3. Name at least three file formats that can include ICC color profiles.

4. _____ _____ is the process of creating controlled, consistent, and accurate color throughout the work flow process—from input, through display, creation and adjustment, and, finally, output.

5. When should you convert your document's color profile?

6. _____ _____ is a three-dimensional representation of the specific plotted points of color designated by the numerical values of colors that can be produced by a color model.

7. What are the two things that you must balance when saving a copy of an image for use on the Web?

Practice the skills you learned in the tutorial using the same case scenario.

PRACTICE

Review Assignments

Data File needed for the Review Assignments: MG4820.CR2

In addition to the FW Museum Store catalog insert, Sadie would like you to create a version of the insert to place on the Web and to send to customers as a newsletter. You'll adjust images of some new products to add to the Web version of the insert, and then you'll soft proof the insert and correct it for Web distribution. Finally, you'll need to provide Sadie with a file that can be distributed on the Web. Complete the following steps:

1. Start Photoshop while pressing the Ctrl+Alt+Shift keys. When you are prompted to delete the Adobe Photoshop Settings File, click Yes. On the Application bar, right-click Essentials, and then click Reset Essentials to reset the default workspace layout. Reset all tools and tool presets.

2. Set your color settings to North America General Purpose 2, if necessary, and then select Internet Standard RGB from the Proof Setup menu, if necessary.

3. Navigate to the Photoshop8\Review folder included with your Data Files, and open the **MG4820.CR2** file.

4. Select the Crop tool, and then create a custom ratio of 1 to .8. Crop the image closely around the necklace.

5. Change the White Balance setting to Tungsten, and then adjust the tonal controls until you create a clear, vibrant image that will work well with the other product images you adjusted in the tutorial. (*Hint*: View the other product images, if necessary, and notice that all of the images are filled with neutral earth tones and only one or two vibrant colors.)

6. Make sure that neither the Highlight nor Shadow clipping warning is displayed at the top of the histogram. If warnings appear, adjust the image until they are gone.

7. Increase the clarity of the image so that the softer parts of the necklace become clearer.

8. Make any other adjustments that you feel the image needs, click the Open Object button to save your changes, and then open the image as a Smart Object in Photoshop.

9. Change the View to Fit on Screen, and then save the image as **MG4820.psd** in the Photoshop8\Review folder.

10. Using the Proof Setup options and the Proof Colors command on the View menu, view the image as it will appear when displayed in a Web page. If you see problems, open the Smart Object in Camera Raw, adjust it, and view it again as a soft proof. Repeat this process as needed until your soft proof looks the way you would like it to look and then save the file.

11. In the Image Size dialog box, set the resolution to 72 ppi image, using a 300-pixel width. Use Save for Web & Devices to optimize the image and to save a copy as **MG4820.jpg** in the Photoshop8\Review folder.

12. Close the MG4820.psd file without saving the changes because you do not want to change the resolution of the original image.

13. Open the **MG4820.psd** file again, select Working CMYK under Proof Setup, and then check Proof Colors, if necessary. Notice the difference in the vibrancy of the colors in the image.

14. Open the MG4820 Smart Object. Adjust the image in Camera Raw, and then click the OK button. View the soft proof of the image. Repeat as necessary to achieve the look you desire, then save the file, and exit Photoshop.

15. Submit the results of the preceding steps to your instructor either in printed or electronic form, as requested.

Use your skills to correct, adjust, proof, and convert images.

APPLY

Case Problem 1

Data Files needed for this Case Problem: Music.tif, Auto.tif, Skateboard.tif

Old School   Based in the Dotty Lynn Recreation Center in Sacramento, California, the Old School offers unconventional evening classes that pair adult and youth students who have similar interests in student-led classes. The classes are structured so the first four weeks are taught by older members of the class who share their experiences, techniques, and historical perspective on the subject. The last four weeks are taught by the younger members of the class who present current trends, technologies, and techniques. The Old School has been very well received in the greater Sacramento community. The school's most popular classes include skateboarding, music appreciation, and automotive repair/restoration.

Matthew Palmer, the founder of the Old School, has hired your firm to create posters to promote the fall class schedule. When you adjust photographs that will be used in the poster, you'll use the color profiles provided to your team by the printer. You'll also need to convert the files for print. Complete the following steps:

1. Start Photoshop while pressing the Ctrl+Alt+Shift keys. When you are prompted to delete the Adobe Photoshop Settings File, click Yes. On the Application bar, right-click Essentials, and then click Reset Essentials to reset the default workspace layout. Reset all tools and tool presets.

2. Set your color settings to North America General Purpose 2, if necessary.

3. Open Mini Bridge, navigate to the Photoshop8\Case1 folder provided with your Data Files, and open the **Music.tif** file in Camera Raw.

4. Select Auto from the White Balance list, and then adjust the other settings on the Basic tab until you have created an image that you find aesthetically pleasing.

5. If necessary, click the Shadow and Highlight clipping warning icons located above the histogram to view pixels in the image that are out of gamut, and make further adjustments to remove clipping.

EXPLORE

6. Use the HLS/Grayscale tab or the Tone Curve tab to adjust the hue, saturation, or luminance, if necessary. (*Hint*: The Tone Curve tab works in the same way that the Curves adjustment works in Photoshop.) Remember that small adjustments are usually enough to create big results.

7. Open the image as a Smart Object in Photoshop, and then view a soft proof of the image.

8. If the soft proof does not have the desired look, open the Smart Object in Camera Raw, adjust the image, and view the image in Photoshop again.

9. Repeat Step 8 until the image has the desired look when you view a soft proof.

10. Save the image as **MusicAdjust.psd** in the Photoshop8\Case 1 folder, and then use Convert to Profile to convert the image to CMYK, and save a copy as **MusicAdjust.tif** in the same folder. Uncheck the Layers check box in the Save As dialog box, and make sure that the ICC Profile check box is checked to ensure that the image is tagged with a color profile. Use the following settings in the TIFF Options dialog box; Image Compression: None, Pixel Order: Interleaved, Byte Order: IBM PC, Layer Compression: Discard Layers and Save a Copy. This is the image you will provide to the team that is laying out the posters.

11. Close the MusicAdjust.psd file without saving it.

12. Repeat Steps 3–11 for the Auto.tif image and the Skateboard.tif image. Use **AutoAdjust** and **SkateboardAdjust** as the filenames for the PSD and TIFF files that you create.

13. Submit the results of the preceding steps to your instructor either in printed or electronic form, as requested.

Use your skills to adjust images in Camera Raw and save copies for the Web.

APPLY

Case Problem 2

Data Files needed for this Case Problem: Snake.CR2, Basket.CR2

Tom Little, Ferrier/Artisan   Tom Little is a farrier and artisan who has lived in Sedona, Arizona, for the past 19 years. Using old lariats, he creates baskets, which he shapes by hand, joining them together by melting the rope with an electric soldering iron. No glue is involved in his unique process. Tom also creates snakes from old blacksmith tools called rasps, which he heats on his forge and twists to shape and beat with a hammer to form realistic scales.

Tom has had some photographs of his work taken by a professional photographer, and he has asked you to crop, adjust, and correct the images so he can use them in online newsletters that he sends to collectors, festivals, and stores that might be interested in his unique works of art. Because the images will be used online, you will create a compressed JPEG copy of each image that he will use in the newsletter. For an example of a corrected image, see Figure 8-34.

Figure 8-34   **Sample Case Problem 2 solution**

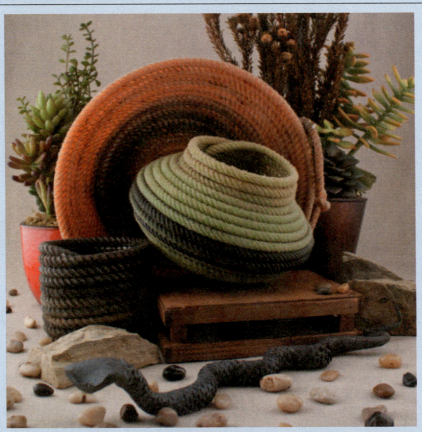

Complete the following steps:

1. Start Photoshop while pressing the Ctrl+Alt+Shift keys. When you are prompted to delete the Adobe Photoshop Settings File, click Yes. On the Application bar, right-click Essentials, and then click Reset Essentials to reset the default workspace layout. Reset all tools and tool presets.

2. Navigate to the Photoshop8\Case2 folder included with your Data Files, and open **Snake.CR2** in Camera Raw.

3. In the Camera Raw dialog box, select the Crop Tool, and then select 1 to 1 from the Ratio list (select the 2 to 3 ratio option for the Basket.CR2 image). Draw a square around the snake and the baskets, and make sure that you do not include any of the edges of white tent in the square. (*Hint*: In the Snake.CR2 image, it is okay to crop some of the tips of the plants from the shot; in the Basket.CR2 image, you may need to crop some of the basket edges.)

4. Select the Hand Tool to view your cropped image.

5. Select Tungsten from the White Balance list, and then adjust the tonal adjustments, clarity, and vibrance on the Basic tab until you are satisfied with the look of the image.

6. Zoom in on the image, and locate any debris that is located within the image area. (*Hint*: In the Snake.CR2 image, there are a few pieces of dirt to the right of the snake; in the Basket.CR2 image, there is a little dirt on the canvas in the left foreground.)

⊕ EXPLORE

7. On the Document window toolbar in the Camera Raw dialog box, select the Spot Removal Tool, and select Heal from the Type list on the Adjustments panel. Using a Radius of 5 and an Opacity setting of 100, place the pointer in the image area over the spot that you would like to remove, and click. Two circles are drawn in the image area.

⊕ EXPLORE

8. Drag the red circle so it is over the spot that you would like to remove, if necessary, and then drag the green circle to an area of the background that is similar to the area where the spot is located, but which is spot free. The spot disappears from the image. (*Hint*: If the circles are too large, place the pointer over the edge of a circle, then drag in to make the circles smaller, or drag out to make the circles larger.)

9. Repeat Steps 7–8 until all of the debris is removed from the image. Select Fit in View from the Select Zoom Level list, and select the Hand Tool to view the image without the circles.

10. Make any adjustments that you feel are necessary, and then click Open Object to open the image as a Smart Object in Photoshop.

11. Save the image as **Snake.psd** in the Photoshop8\Case2 folder. Then, adjust the image size so the image is 400 pixels by 400 pixels, with a resolution of 72 ppi. Use the Save for Web & Devices to optimize and save a JPEG copy of the image as **Snake.jpg** in the Photoshop8\Case2 folder. (For the Basket.jpg, use width: 600; height: 400; and resolution: 72 ppi.)

12. Close Snake.psd without saving.

13. Repeat Steps 2–12 for the Basket.CR2 image, saving the image as **Basket.psd** and **Basket.jpg**.

14. Submit the results of the preceding steps to your instructor either in printed or electronic form, as requested.

Extend your skills to explore some other Camera Raw tools.

CHALLENGE

Case Problem 3

Data Files needed for this Case Problem: ThisTooWillPass.tif, YouCompleteMe.tif

Petcentric   Petcentric is a line of greeting cards for pets. Have you ever wanted to say "I'm sorry" to your parrot or "I'm thinking about you" to your boxer? Now you can with Petcentric cards. Owner Bobby May came up with the idea when her bull dog, Nicky, was in the hospital with a virus. "She looked so sad. I just wanted to bring her something to say get well, and there was nothing out there. I thought if I feel this way, there are surely other crazy pet owners who are feeling the same thing." One year later, her first line of cards hit the shelves, and Petcentric cards have been a success from the start.

The Petcentric line of cards uses humorous images of animals with bold bursts of color, and tongue-in-cheek sentiments to distinguish it from other lines of cards. You will adjust some images that will be used by another member of your team to create final cards. For an example of a Petcentric card image, see Figure 8-35.

Figure 8-35   Sample Case Problem 3 solution

Complete the following steps:

1. Start Photoshop while pressing the Ctrl+Alt+Shift keys. When you are prompted to delete the Adobe Photoshop Settings File, click Yes. On the Application bar, right-click Essentials, and then click Reset Essentials to reset the default workspace layout. Reset all tools and tool presets.

2. Use Mini Bridge, navigate to the Photoshop8\Case3 folder provided with your Data Files, and open **ThisTooWillPass.tif** in Camera Raw.

EXPLORE 3. To raise the saturation values of the collars, select the Targeted Adjustment Tool on the toolbar, and select Saturation from the Targeted Adjustment Tool list. Place the pointer over the blue collar and drag upward until the blue in the collar has increased significantly. Repeat the process on the pink collar. Then, to lower the saturation values in the rest of the image, place the pointer over one of the dog's face or body, and drag down until the dogs appear to be grayscale, leaving only the collars in color.

EXPLORE 4. Select Luminance from the Targeted Adjustment Tool list, and decrease the luminance of the collars by dragging down on the collars, as needed, to intensify the color. Then, decrease the luminance of the dogs as needed to create a more dramatic image.

5. Use the Adjustment tabs to make any other necessary adjustments. (*Hint*: Increasing the clarity and vibrance will enhance the intensity of the color-saturated areas.)

6. Open the image as a Smart Object in Photoshop, and save the image as **ThisTooWillPass.psd** in the Photoshop8\Case3 folder, and close the image. Another member of the team will now be able to convert the image and place it in a layout program to create the final card.

EXPLORE 7. Open **YouCompleteMe.tif** from the Photoshop8\Case3 folder in Camera Raw, and use the Hue setting in the Targeted Adjustment Tool to change the background color to turquoise.

8. On the Basic tab, decrease the clarity of the image to give the image a soft glow. Use the sliders on the Basic tab to make any additional corrections to the image. Remember that you are creating a humorous image with a bold burst of color.

9. Open the image as a Smart Object in Photoshop, and save the image as **YouCompleteMe.psd** in the Photoshop8\Case3 folder. Close the file, and exit Photoshop.

10. Submit the results of the preceding steps to your instructor either in printed or electronic form, as requested.

Using Figure 8-36 as a guide, create images that have a similar look and feel.

CREATE

Case Problem 4

Data Files needed for this Case Problem: BacMuffins.tif, BacSushi.tif

Baconality   Baconality is a restaurant located in Atlanta, Georgia, that is dedicated to all things bacon. The concept for a bacon-centric restaurant was created by two frat brothers, John Waynes and Bob Hansel, after a late-night breakfast where they agreed that bacon was a single ingredient that almost every person loves. From that after-hours epiphany, Baconality was born.

John has hired your firm to create an online version of the menu for Baconality, and he has provided you with a few professional photographs of menu items. Although the images have come from different sources, it is important that you create a unified look and feel when you adjust them. This will enable the online menu to have a cohesive look. Take some time before you begin editing to determine what unifying elements you will emphasize to ensure that the images work together. Consider the following items:

- Number of items in the shot
- Relative closeness of items in the shot
- Space around items in the shot
- Focus and depth
- Color and saturation of each image

For some examples of images that would work well in the online menu, see Figure 8-36.

Figure 8-36   Sample Case Problem 4 solutions

Complete the following steps:

1. Start Photoshop while pressing the Ctrl+Alt+Shift keys. When you are prompted to delete the Adobe Photoshop Settings File, click Yes. On the Application bar, right-click Essentials, and then click Reset Essentials to reset the default workspace layout. Reset all tools and tool presets.

2. Use Mini Bridge to navigate to the Photoshop8\Case4 folder provided with your Data Files, and examine both images in the folder.

3. Consider which elements are similar in each image, and which elements are unique to an individual image. Then, write a short paragraph outlining your findings and your plan for creating a unified look.

4. Determine how you will adjust the images to create a unified look and feel.

5. Use Mini Bridge to open one of the images in Camera Raw.

6. Adjust the image as needed according to your plan. Then, open the image as a Smart Object in Photoshop, and save a copy as a PSD file, using the same filename, in the Photoshop8\Case4 folder.

7. Adjust the image size so the image is 400 pixels x 400 pixels at 72 ppi. (*Hint*: Do not save the original image at this size in case you need to make adjustments later.)

8. Use Save for Web & Devices to create an optimized and compressed JPEG copy of the image for use in the online menu, using the same filename, and save the image in the Photoshop8\Case4 folder.

9. Repeat Steps 2–8 for the remaining image.

10. Submit the results of the preceding steps to your instructor either in printed or electronic form, as requested.

ENDING DATA FILES

Photoshop8 →

Tutorial
FeaturedItemBox.jpg
InsertCMYK.psd
MG4835.CR2
MG4835.xmp
MG4835SO.psd
MG4998.CR2
MG4998.xmp

Review
MG4820.CR2
MG4820.jpg
MG4820.psd
MG4820.xmp

Case1
AutoAdjust.psd
AutoAdjust.tif
MusicAdjust.psd
MusicAdjust.tif
SkateboardAdjust.psd
SkateboardAdjust.tif

Case2
Basket.CR2
Basket.jpg
Basket.psd
Basket.xmp
Snake.CR2
Snake.jpg
Snake.psd
Snake.xmp

Case3
ThisTooWillPass.psd
YouCompleteMe.psd

Case4
BacMuffins.jpg
BacMuffins.psd
BacSushi.jpg
BacSushi.psd

OBJECTIVES

Session 9.1
- Define project goals and write a statement of purpose
- Create a viewer profile and identify the target audience
- Research audience interests, competition, branding, and identity
- Identify output specifications

Session 9.2
- Gather materials and develop a concept and metaphor
- Understand layout theories and create a layout
- Select a color palette, typographical style, typeface, and fonts
- Decide on a graphic style and create graphics
- Determine a photographic style
- Create output files and archive project files

Planning, Creating, and Delivering a Complete Project

Creating a Web Banner Ad Campaign

Case | *FlashFlock*

FlashFlock is a nonprofit organization made up of nature photographers, activists, artists, and flash mob enthusiasts from around the world who have decided to take the flash mob back to its roots. The group started when George Lemming and Rick Loon created the FlashFlock Web site to publicize an exhibition of photos showing animal flash mobs staged in urban settings. The site and the movement grew from there as it became embraced by the guerilla art community, which seeks to incite public and political commentary through the creation or exhibition of unauthorized public art. The FlashFlock Web site is home to thousands of animal flash mob photos as well as a series of juried art galleries and a digital platform for member activism, art criticism, and public relations. The FlashFlock concept has expanded to include nature photos, both organic and engineered, digitally enhanced animal flock images, and even synthetic animal herd images in a variety of settings.

George has asked your firm to create collateral materials for this year's FlashFlock nature photography festival. Your team, led by Jessica Tate, will work with George and Rick to plan, develop, create, and execute the Web banner campaign advertising the FlashFlock Festival.

As a junior member of the team, you'll work with Jessica to learn about each phase of the process, and you'll create an alternate version of some of the materials, which she will review.

STARTING DATA FILES

Photoshop9 →	Tutorial	Review	Case1	Case2	Case3	Case4
	BannerSamp1.jpg	BannerText2.rtf	CatLogo.gif	ElGalLogo.ai	LogoBlack.png	Logos.psd
	BannerSamp2.jpg	Graphics.psd	Vision.rtf	Mailer.psd	LogoWhite.png	Specs.rtf
	BannerText.rtf	Penguins.jpg	WebSite.tif	Mailer1Image.jpg	Promo1.png	
	FFLogo.psd			Planning.rtf	Promo2.png	
	Fish.jpg				Vision.rtf	
	Graphics.psd					
	WebHome.jpg					

SESSION 9.1 VISUAL OVERVIEW

A **viewer profile** is a set of data describing the characteristics of the target audience.

The **target audience** is the group of people whom you would most like to view and respond to the final output.

Target audience

The **vision** includes the client's ideas and overall plan for a project.

The **client** is the person for whom you are creating a project.

Client meetings

Vision

The **project goals** are a short prioritized list of goals, written in active voice, that you would like to accomplish with a project.

Goals and statement of purpose

A **statement of purpose** is a precise statement that articulates the vision and aspirations for a project.

PLANNING A PROFESSIONAL PROJECT

A **search engine** is a Web site whose primary function is to retrieve Web pages based on a search for specified keywords or phrases.

Market research is the careful investigation and study of the data about the target audience and the competition.

Output

Brand is the combination of symbols, name, colors, and slogans associated with a product, service, or organization.

Client branding and identity

Brand identity is the way that an organization would like the public to perceive a brand.

Brand image is the way the public perceives an organization and its products or services.

Market research and technical research

Competition

Technical research involves gathering all relevant technical specifications for a project, including the file size, resolution, and color profile required for the output files.

Target audience

Planning and Delivering a Professional Project

Creating a professional project involves much more than just opening Photoshop and using its tools to make a composition. In the real world, creating a graphic design project is a process that has many important steps. Understanding the entire process will help you create successful professional projects.

The design process usually starts with a series of meetings with a client. (If you are working on an internal company project, the person for whom you are creating the project is your client.) During the meetings, you must ascertain your client's vision for the project. You should also help the client develop specific goals, define a target audience, and articulate his or her aesthetic preferences. Once you have gathered this information, you will need to do some research to discover what the competition is doing and to determine what is popular with the target audience. For example, what styles are popular with the target audience? What do people in the target audience like to do for recreation? Where do they spend their time and money? How do they speak? How do they dress? What interests them? You should also review the client's current and historic advertising and marketing materials and find any information regarding the client's brand and identity. For example, what colors, logos, and graphic styles are identified with the client? What image is the client trying to create? Does the general public see the client in the way the client would like to be seen?

You should work with the client to determine final output file types, color models, color profiles, and resolution. Then, you will need to gather all of the necessary content for the project, including text, images, logos, and any other artwork that the client already has.

After the planning and research is complete, you can begin the process of creating the composition. This part of the process includes creating a layout and possibly mocking up a rough draft to show the client. If you are planning a campaign or another large project, you should select a concept and a metaphor to help unify the various elements. You must select colors, typefaces, and a graphic style for the project before creating any graphic elements. Moving on, you'll need to develop a style for your photographs; you can then crop, adjust, and retouch photos, as necessary, to fit that style. Then, you'll be ready to add them to the composition. Finally, you'll need to carefully review what you have done and make any necessary adjustments.

After you have presented the completed project to your client and made any necessary adjustments, you'll need to have your client approve (or "sign off on") the design. This ensures that you and your client both agree that the project is complete and that you are both happy with the results. If the client decides to make changes after signing off on the project, you can consider those changes to be a new project—with new deadlines and a new budget. After you get your client's sign-off on the project, you can create all of the final output files and deliver them to the client. Then, you should clean up your internal working files and create an archive of the project.

Now that you have an understanding of the process, your team will begin planning the FlashFlock banner ad campaign.

Planning a Design Project

Whether you are part of an in-house design team or are an independent designer hired to create a project for a client, you must determine the project vision, goals, purpose, and target audience for the project. You obtain this information from the client and through the research you conduct during the planning phase. This process usually requires several meetings with the client and a considerable amount of time.

Client meetings and research time are a crucial part of the planning process because it is impossible to design a project that will effectively meet a client's needs until you determine exactly what those needs are. You should explain clearly to the client what information you will need and how his or her contributions will add value to the final project. Throughout the project, be sure to show your work to the client and other team members for feedback and evaluation.

There are many possible paths in any creative process. As you gain experience in planning, designing, and creating projects, you will find that some things work better than others. As part of your training, Jessica has asked you to come up with your own ideas about the FlashFlock banner project goals, target audience, and so on. You'll then compare them with those approved by George. You'll evaluate how your findings, proposed goals, and project plan are similar to and different from the final FlashFlock project plan; you'll then consider the benefits and drawbacks of each option.

INSIGHT

Developing Your Professional Design Skills

Becoming an expert on Photoshop and other design software is an important first step in becoming a successful designer. Just as a successful carpenter must be able to use the tools of her trade, a designer must have expert skills in working with the software that is one of the tools of his trade. However, expert use of tools is not enough to make you an expert designer. To become a professional, you must also develop expertise in additional areas, including marketing principles, aesthetic/art theory, and project management. To extend the carpenter metaphor—a carpenter building a table for someone's home must understand how the size and shape of the room, the style of the house, and the aesthetic preferences and lifestyle of the client will affect what design would work best for that client.

A designer must understand how to create a project that will fulfill the client's vision and goals, reach and connect with the target audience, and produce the desired results when output to its final format. In addition, a good designer must understand classic design theory and current aesthetic trends to be able to create solid designs that effectively communicate with the target audience. A good designer must also be able to use her own sense of aesthetics to create successful, original projects. For example, without an understanding of the effective use of white space, a designer might create layouts filled with graphic elements that do not give the composition a sense of space and flow. Without an understanding of what styles are popular with a particular age group, the designer might not be able to create a composition that catches the attention of people in that group. You develop these skills by taking classes in classic art theory, reading trade magazines, working for professional designers, and using what you learn to create new projects.

Understanding the Client's Vision

When a client comes to you with a project, that client has a need that he wants to address. Usually, the client has an idea of what the project should look like, communicate, and achieve. However, there are often many details that the client has not considered. Clients seek your expert skills and knowledge, and they rely on you to know what questions to ask and to guide them in making decisions throughout the design process. Your first task is to discover the client's vision for the project by asking him to explain, in detail, what he would like you to create.

George and Rick have provided your team with a document that explains their initial vision of the project. Read the statement shown in Figure 9-1.

Figure 9-1 **FlashFlock vision statement**

FlashFlock Banner Ad Project Vision Statement

We would like your firm to create a series of banner ads that will advertise our annual fall FlashFlock Festival. Below, we have provided some information about the festival along with our ideas and parameters for the campaign.

FlashFlock Festival

This is a juried online festival that is open to the general public. This year we would like to increase participation among younger viewers—specifically targeting college students and artists age 18–25. There is no charge for entry, and people will be able to fill out an online form to enter.

There are several categories of photographs that can be entered, including:

- Organized flash flock: Photographs of organized animal flash mobs
- Organic flash flock: Photographs taken of herds/flocks/gaggles of animals in their natural environment
- Staged flash flock: Photographs that have been digitally altered to produce a flash flock with real or synthetic animals

All photographs will be judged on artistic composition, humor, social commentary, and audacity. Winners will be featured on the FlashFlock Web site and will receive a $200 cash prize and a package of photographic equipment worth $500. Artists may enter up to three photographs in each category. The above information, as well as additional details, will be posted on our Web site.

Banner Ads

Banner ads will be used in the body of our Web site, on other Web sites, and in advertisements on our social media pages. Banners should contain the FlashFlock logo and one of the following taglines:

- Come fly with us
- Get your flock on
- We let the cows out
- Murders in numbers
- Gaggle your tail off

The ads should contain one or more photos that we will provide, and they should generate interest in the festival—causing the viewer to click on the banner to get more information. Banner ads do not need to provide in-depth information about the festival because that will be provided on the site. All of the banners should look good on our Web site and should be consistent with the FlashFlock look.

Although the vision statement provides a good deal of information, it does not contain all of the information that your team will need from George and Rick. For example, they do not mention what size the banner ads should be, and they have not clearly articulated their goals for the project. This sometimes happens because a client has not thought of these questions. Once you have gotten your client to explain their initial vision for the project, you'll pose questions that they must answer—with your guidance.

Next, your team will determine the goals for the project.

Establishing Goals for the Project

The next question you should ask when guiding a client through the planning process is: What are the primary goals and purpose of the project? A design project can have one goal or many goals. The goals should be in alignment with the client's vision for the project. If a client's goals do not fit with the original project vision, you should help the client work to envision a project that will accomplish his goals. It is a good idea to brainstorm with the client to create a list of all of the possible goals you can think of for the project. For example, the goals of a commercial project might include the following:

- Provide information about a product.
- Sell a product.
- Increase brand recognition.
- Provide help or operational instructions.

These examples are very general; the goal list for an actual project should be much more specific. For example, the first two bullets should state what the product is and the third bullet should include a specific measurement of brand recognition and what the targeted increase is.

After you have a list of possible goals, review the list and place the goals in order of importance from most important to least important. For example, the commercial project goals might be reordered as follows:

- Sell a product.
- Increase brand recognition.
- Provide information about a product.
- Provide help or operational instructions.

Review your list again. Combine goals, if possible, and then reprioritize as needed. Your final list for a given project should include no more than five goals. Some of the lower-priority goals might actually be part of higher-priority goals. For example, in some cases, providing help or operational instructions might be incorporated into the general goal of providing information about the product. There is a limit to the number of goals that a project can effectively achieve; therefore, you will probably want to focus on the top two or three goals for any given project. Remember that goals are most effective if they are the result of collaboration with the client. After all, just as you are an expert on design, the client is an expert on his or her business. Also remember that what you can accomplish with a project varies with the size and scope of the project. For example, you can communicate much less information with a banner than you can with a printed brochure.

PROSKILLS

Written Communication: Writing Effective Goals for Your Project

Creating a strong list of project goals requires careful thought. Keep in mind the following guidelines as you develop the list of goals for a project:

- Write goals in active voice rather than passive voice, using verbs that move the action along and that identify you, your team, or the client as the actors. For example; *sell products* rather than *product sales will increase*.
- Use action verbs to help you select achievable goals rather than concepts. For example, brand recognition is a concept, not a goal; *increase brand recognition* is a goal. Action verbs include words such as *achieve*, *increase*, and *provide*.
- Be specific when you are creating goals. Identify specific products, programs, or outputs, and when possible, specify an identifiable and measurable amount of change. For example: *Increase sales of "Widget A" by 10 percent*. By creating specific goals, you are able to evaluate your success in the future.
- Create individual goals that touch on different aspects of the product or service or event that you are promoting. For example, in addition to selling products, you might want to advertise reliable support.

Learning to write clear, achievable, and specific goals will enable you to guide your clients through the process of creating a project that accomplishes their most important goals. As you gain experience in project management and design, your ability to identify and articulate goals will continue to improve.

After your list of goals is final, review the list, and develop a one-sentence statement of purpose that speaks to the core purpose of the project. This is your chance to help the client hone his or her original vision of the project by creating a precise statement that defines the vision and aspirations for the project. For example, a good statement of purpose for a banner ad campaign for an e-commerce Web site might be: "With this banner ad campaign, we intend to increase public awareness of our site and our brand by 10 percent, to drive customers to our site, to increase our sales of quality widgets by 5 percent, and to connect with new clients with the intention of building lifelong customer relationships."

Next, using the information from the initial vision statement, you'll develop a list of goals and a statement of purpose for the FlashFlock banner ad campaign.

To create a list of goals and a statement of purpose for the project:

1. Review the initial FlashFlock vision statement, and then, using WordPad, which is available from the Accessories menu of the All Programs menu in Windows 7, create a new document and write down 10 to 15 possible goals. Save the document as **Goals.rtf** in the Photoshop9\Tutorial folder.

2. Review the list to be sure that all statements are in active voice and use action verbs.

3. Prioritize the goals in order of importance, based on your understanding of the vision statement.

4. Review your list, combining goals, if possible, and reprioritizing them, as necessary.

5. Review the top five goals. Make sure that your list of goals will help achieve what FlashFlock wants to accomplish.

6. Write a one-sentence statement of purpose for the FlashFlock project based on your final list of goals, and add it to the Goals document.

   Jessica worked with George to create a list of goals for the banner ad campaign, and then she prioritized and combined them. From her list of goals, she developed a statement of purpose, using the top five goals for the project.

7. Compare your goals and statement of purpose with Jessica's, which are shown in Figure 9-2. Consider how her list and statement are similar to and different from yours. Also, consider how this might affect the project.

8. Save the Goals.rtf file, and close it.

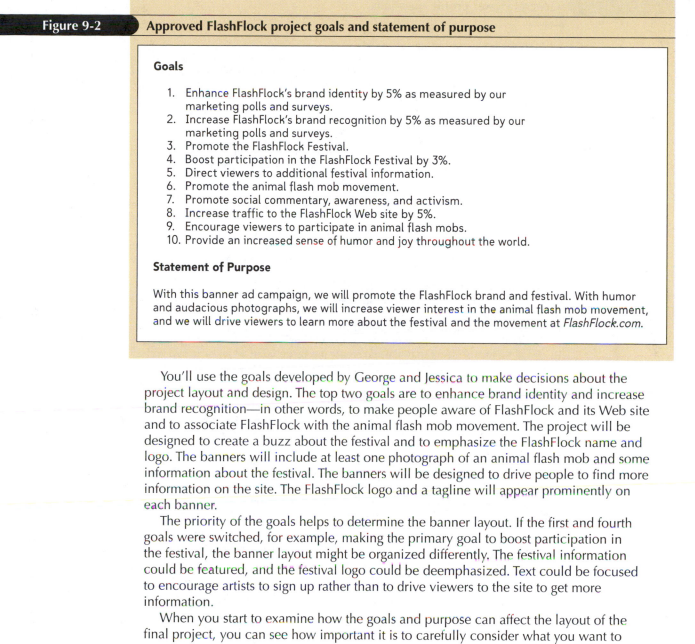

Figure 9-2   Approved FlashFlock project goals and statement of purpose

Goals

1. Enhance FlashFlock's brand identity by 5% as measured by our marketing polls and surveys.
2. Increase FlashFlock's brand recognition by 5% as measured by our marketing polls and surveys.
3. Promote the FlashFlock Festival.
4. Boost participation in the FlashFlock Festival by 3%.
5. Direct viewers to additional festival information.
6. Promote the animal flash mob movement.
7. Promote social commentary, awareness, and activism.
8. Increase traffic to the FlashFlock Web site by 5%.
9. Encourage viewers to participate in animal flash mobs.
10. Provide an increased sense of humor and joy throughout the world.

Statement of Purpose

With this banner ad campaign, we will promote the FlashFlock brand and festival. With humor and audacious photographs, we will increase viewer interest in the animal flash mob movement, and we will drive viewers to learn more about the festival and the movement at *FlashFlock.com*.

You'll use the goals developed by George and Jessica to make decisions about the project layout and design. The top two goals are to enhance brand identity and increase brand recognition—in other words, to make people aware of FlashFlock and its Web site and to associate FlashFlock with the animal flash mob movement. The project will be designed to create a buzz about the festival and to emphasize the FlashFlock name and logo. The banners will include at least one photograph of an animal flash mob and some information about the festival. The banners will be designed to drive people to find more information on the site. The FlashFlock logo and a tagline will appear prominently on each banner.

The priority of the goals helps to determine the banner layout. If the first and fourth goals were switched, for example, making the primary goal to boost participation in the festival, the banner layout might be organized differently. The festival information could be featured, and the festival logo could be deemphasized. Text could be focused to encourage artists to sign up rather than to drive viewers to the site to get more information.

When you start to examine how the goals and purpose can affect the layout of the final project, you can see how important it is to carefully consider what you want to accomplish. Taking the time to establish goals and expectations from the very beginning will make a world of difference in the final output.

Ascertaining the Target Audience

The target audience for a design project is the group of people whom you would *most* like to view and respond to the final output. You identify the target audience by creating a viewer profile, which is a set of data describing the viewer you are trying to reach. The data is gathered from a list of questions, such as those shown in Figure 9-3. Creating a viewer profile helps you define the characteristics of your target audience.

Figure 9-3 General viewer profile questions

1. **What is the age range of the viewer?**
   - You can create a project that appeals to any range of ages. The age range will depend on the project goals. Generally, the group members are linked because they share a commonality such as a habit, a characteristic, or a developmental stage.
2. **What is the gender of the viewer?**
   - Projects can be targeted at males only, females only, or both. Not all projects are targeted at a specific gender.
3. **What is the education level of the viewer?**
   - Education level will be a range. Designate education level either by the current year in school (e.g., senior in high school) or the degree earned, if out of school (e.g., associate's degree).
4. **What is the economic situation of the viewer?**
   - Economic situation refers to the annual income level of the viewer, as well as other extenuating economic factors, such as parental support or student loans. For example, the viewer may be a student who has only a part-time job. As a student, the viewer may have a lower income bracket, earning only $20,000 a year, but extenuating economic factors, such as parental support and student loans, may affect the viewer's buying power.
5. **What is the geographic location of the viewer?**
   - Projects can be targeted at users in a specific city, a specific region, or a specific country.
6. **What is the primary language of the viewer?**
7. **What is the ethnic background of the viewer?**
   - Most projects that you will create are targeted at a viewer group with diverse cross sections of ethnic backgrounds; however, sometimes ethnicity is a factor in your target audience. For example, ads in *Jet* magazine are typically targeted at African-American viewers.
8. **Are there other unifying characteristics that are relevant to the viewer?**
   - If you know that the target group has a common characteristic that may be of use in designing the project, list it here. Unifying characteristics are useful if they are related to the topic or purpose of the project or if they could affect the goals of the project. Unifying characteristics could include things such as: target viewers have diabetes (for an educational diabetes disease-management brochure), target viewers ride dirt bikes (for a Web banner advertising motorcycle helmets), target viewers listen to club music (for an advertisement in *Rolling Stone*), and so on.

Jessica asks you to create a profile that identifies the target audience of the FlashFlock banner ad campaign.

To identify the target audience for the project:

1. Using WordPad, create a new document, and answer the viewer profile questions included in Figure 9-3. Review your answers to ensure that the target audience you identified reinforces FlashFlock's vision, final goals, and purpose, as shown in Figure 9-1 and Figure 9-2. If it does not, adjust either your target audience or your goals (depending on which is more flexible) so that the two are compatible and so that the project will produce the best possible outcome.

2. Compare your answers to the user profile questions with those compiled by Jessica and George, as shown in Figure 9-4.

Figure 9-4   FlashFlock banner ad target audience

1. Age: 18 to 25
2. Gender: Male and female
3. Education level: Some college, especially art school and liberal arts
4. Economic situation: One- and two-income households with incomes ranging from $35,000 to $90,000+ or college students who have financial support (households with enough disposable income or financial support to afford computer with high-speed, home Internet service, preferably those who have access to photographic equipment and digital-editing software)
5. Geographic location: United States, but we hope to encourage participation internationally
6. Primary language: English
7. Ethnic background: No specific ethnicity targeted
8. Other unifying characteristics: Primary target viewer is an adult who enjoys art and who appreciates social satire, preferably those who appreciate wry and silly humor

   3. Save the document as **Target.rtf** in the Photoshop9\Tutorial folder, and close the file.

Sometimes clients and designers are hesitant to identify the target audience because they think it will limit the reach of the project. However, a very broad target audience can be even more restrictive than a very narrow target audience. A project that must appeal to many different groups of people must be more generic in some ways. For example, if the new FlashFlock banner ad campaign was intended to appeal to an older audience (50 to 60 years of age) as well as to a college-aged audience (18 to 29 years of age), it should only include elements that will be attractive and communicate effectively to both age groups. You can see how this might exclude some stylistic options, such as graphics, wording, and color that would be appropriate for a project with a target audience that includes only a college-aged group.

Some projects must appeal to a broad target audience. Consider the Internal Revenue Service (IRS) Web site, *www.irs.gov*. The IRS site and much of its collateral material, such as brochures, are designed for a very diverse target audience. Knowing that the target audience for the IRS Web site and collateral materials is broad and that the goal of the various materials is to dispense information, designers working on these projects must create text-based materials with few graphic elements that will be accessible to the broadest possible group of users. IRS materials are very effective at achieving their goals. However, the primarily text-based designs would not be effective if the main goal was entertainment because although rich in informational content, the materials are not very entertaining.

After you have identified a target audience, you can use the information from the viewer profile as a basis to research and make more advanced decisions about viewer wants, needs, and so on. When used appropriately, the viewer profile is a great tool for focusing a design project so it achieves the project goals and communicates effectively with the target audience. However, be careful with stereotypes. It is easy to draw general conclusions about a target audience without backing up those assumptions with research. This can lead to an output that does not actually appeal to your intended audience, or worse yet, offends them. For example, think about a television commercial you've seen that is supposed to appeal to your gender and/or age group. What was your reaction to a commercial that has the right look but underestimates your intelligence or misinterprets your styles and habits? Use the target audience information as a starting point for your research so that you can create a project that will communicate effectively with your audience.

Conducting Research

Market research is the careful investigation and study of data about a target audience's preferences, needs for a particular product or service, and personal habits. Market research also involves evaluating the products and services of competitors, as well as the marketing efforts they put behind those products and services. The viewer profile provides information that enables you to identify your target audience. After you have created the viewer profile and you understand who you are targeting, you need to investigate the habits, interests, likes, and dislikes of that group of people as well as what competitors are doing to attract them.

Technical information—such as the screen size and the speeds of the computer and Internet connection used by the target audience—tells you the technical limitations for an effective banner ad campaign. In a commercial campaign, information about the spending habits of the target audience tells you the potential profitability of the campaign. In campaigns for other types of organizations, such as nonprofit groups, spending habits sometimes help you to identify need. Information on the interests of the target audience tells you what will appeal to the target audience and what elements you might include in the campaign to draw in viewers. Information on the needs of the target audience tells you what you can do to provide value to the target audience. Information about the culture and the customs of the target audience tells you what colors, symbols, fashions, and styles will be effective in communicating with the target audience. Finally, information about the competition tells you what the competition believes effectively attracts and communicates with the target audience, which can be useful in your decision making. Large advertising and design agencies spend a substantial amount of money subscribing to services (such as *www.ipsos-asi.com* and *www.imarketinc.com*) that provide in-depth market analysis of products or services and their target audiences, but the average individual designer has to rely on his or her own research.

Studying the Target Audience and the Competition

TIP

Three common search engines are Google (*www.google.com*), Yahoo! Search (www.yahoo.com), and Bing (www.*bing.com*).

The fastest way to obtain information about the habits, interests, and likes of a target audience is to use a search engine to locate Web sites with statistics and other data about the target audience's lifestyle, needs, and preferences. Jessica and George spent some time using search engines to gather information online and compiled the data shown in Figure 9-5.

Figure 9-5	Statistics and information about the FlashFlock target audience

- 68.7 percent of average U.S. households use computers with Internet access. (63.5 percent of all households use high-speed broadband connections, and 4.7 percent have 56Kbs or less dial-up connectivity.) In the target income range, 58.7 percent to 78.7 percent of people use broadband Internet service, and in the target age range, 69.3 percent to 80.8 percent of people use broadband Internet service.
  (*www.ntia.doc.gov/reports/2010/NTIA_internet_use_report_Feb2010.pdf*)
- Artists held about 221,900 jobs in 2008. About 60 percent were self-employed.
  (*www.bls.gov/oco/ocos092.htm*)
- Median annual wages of salaried photographers were $29,440 in May 2008.
  (*www.bls.gov/oco/ocos092.htm*)
- Data underscore the relationship between arts lessons and participation in all modes of arts activities as an adult. Specifically, a person who has had any arts lessons is 32 percent more likely to create art, 33 percent more likely to participate in media-based arts, and 29% more likely to attend an art event or performance—taking into account demographics variables.
  (*www.nea.gov/research/2008-SPPA-BeyondAttendance.pdf*)
- Approximately 15% of adults in the U.S. participate in the arts via electronic media only.
  (*www.nea.gov/research/2008-SPPA-BeyondAttendance.pdf*)
- As virtually all research on participation has demonstrated, educational attainment is the strongest predictor of cultural engagement. (DiMaggio and Ostrower 1992; Peterson et al. 2000)

The information that Jessica compiled gives you some understanding of the target audience's habits and likes. Now, you'll switch your focus from the habits of the target audience to what you can do with your design to attract the target audience. Because this is a Web-based project, you'll investigate Web sites that the target audience might frequent as well as Web sites of FlashFlock competitors. Jessica has selected some sites based on the information gathered about the target audience, including its habits and preferences. For future projects, you can use the information you gather about a project's target audience to make assumptions about which sites to explore. By exploring sites that are popular with the target audience as well as the sites of competitors, you can familiarize yourself with graphic styles to which the target audience is accustomed. You can get a better understanding of what colors, symbols, fashions, styles, and slang terms have been effective in communicating with the target audience.

While you are exploring the Web sites, pay close attention to their designs. What colors do the sites use? Is there anything unique about a particular site? What aspects of each site might appeal to the target audience? How is the space used? Is the content presented using straightforward language or using slang specific to the target audience? Is there a lot of text on each page, or is the text broken into smaller segments?

If you were creating a magazine ad, you would still use the Web to research your target audience, but you would also need to look at other ads in the magazine in which you would be advertising, as well as other magazines and print materials that might appeal to your target audience. You would also need to spend time reviewing magazine ads of competitors. The same principles are true for brochures and other forms of output.

You'll examine some sites that might attract the FlashFlock target audience as well as the Web sites of competitors. For each piece of information you find, note the name and URL of the Web page in case you need to refer to that source in the future.

> **TIP**
>
> For nonprofit organizations, competitors are other organizations that target your viewers.

To use a search engine to research the target audience and the competition:

1. Create a new document in WordPad, and name the document **Research.rtf**. Save the document in the Photoshop9\Tutorial folder.

2. Start your Web browser, type **bing.com** in the address bar, and then press the **Enter** key. The Bing home page opens.

   Trouble? If the Bing search engine is unavailable for some reason, type the URL for another search engine in the address bar, and then press the Enter key.

3. In the Enter your search term box at the top of the page, type **art activism**, and then click the **Search** button to start the search.

4. Review the list of Web sites, click the link for a Web site that you think looks promising, and then explore that site.

5. In the Research.rtf document, type **Art activism** as a heading, and then create a bulleted list of the pertinent information you find, especially information regarding aesthetics and use of language. Make sure to include the name and URL of the Web page in case you need to refer to that source in the future.

   Trouble? If the site does not seem relevant, continue with Step 6.

6. On the browser toolbar, click the **Back** button ← to return to the search results.

7. Repeat Step 4 through Step 6 to gather information from other Web sites until you have documented at least three distinct insights, statistics, or facts.

8. Repeat Step 3 through Step 6 using the term **art as social commentary** until you have gathered three new insights, statistics, or facts.

9. In your browser, go to the Web site, *www.thisridiculousworld.com*. This is a competing site, which has produced satirical social commentary in China since 2007.

10. Explore the site, and in the Research.rtf file, type **www.thisridiculousworld.com** as a heading then make note of any pertinent information. You should have at least one short paragraph of information about this site.

11. Repeat Step 9 and Step 10 for the following sites:

    • *www.telluridephotofestival.com*

    • *www.guerrillagirls.com*

12. Save the Research.rtf file, and close it.

Next, you'll turn your research inward to review some of the FlashFlock marketing materials.

Reviewing the Client's Branding, Identity, and Marketing Materials

Like all people, businesses, and organizations, FlashFlock has a public image. In marketing and design, brand image is the way that the public, especially your target market, perceives your organization and its products or services. Originally, a brand was a symbol that enabled people to distinguish one person's cattle from another's. As the marketing industry grew, the term *brand* was used to describe the symbol, name, colors, and slogans associated with an organization, product, or service. Now, an organization's brand includes a separate component referred to as *identity*. Brand identity refers to the way that an organization would like the public to perceive the brand. It includes everything that the organization creates, presents, and cultivates as an outward expression of the brand. Organizations usually spend a great deal of time, energy, and money to create a brand identity that is in line with the goals, mission, and ideals they want the public to associate with their brand; however, organizations do not have complete control over how they are viewed. Everything that a company does contributes to the public's perception of who that company is and what they stand for. When the public's brand image is in line with the organization's brand identity, the organization's marketing efforts are considered successful.

Maintaining a well-planned brand image helps an organization in many ways. It helps the public to remember the organization and to associate it with specific goals, ideas, products, and/or services. This enables the organization to spend marketing dollars on focused campaigns instead of reminding the public who they are and what they do. When a focused campaign reinforces brand identity, it increases the strength of the brand, creating even more bang for the buck.

When an organization sends mixed or unclear messages, or when they change what they are trying to be too often, the organization can suffer from a lack of identity. When this occurs, the public either does not have an image of the organization, or they have an image that is muddy and unclear. In either case, an organization is forced to increase the amount of marketing funds spent just reminding the public of who they are and what they do. Because of this, organizations that maintain a strong brand and brand identity have an advantage.

Before you create a project for an organization, you need to understand the organization's brand, brand identity, and brand image. The layout, colors, fonts, and graphic style that you select when you create your project should reinforce the organization's brand and brand identity. In other words, your project should look like it goes with the design, colors, and graphic style of the materials used by the organization, and your project should support the brand identity. If the organization has not spent time creating a strong, consistent brand and brand identity, it is your job to explain the importance of brand identity, to help your client make brand and identity decisions, and then to create a project that will reinforce those decisions. As you can see, there is a lot of work involved in creating a professional project.

FlashFlock has a logo and a set of taglines that they use across all of their materials. Their marketing materials and their Web content have a witty, tongue-in-cheek style, and their designs have a consistent graphic style. George has provided a few of the organization's existing marketing materials for you to examine. You'll look at the materials and consider the look, style, and colors to provide you with ideas that you'll use when you start to create the banner ad campaign.

To examine the materials that George provided:

1. Start Photoshop while pressing the **Ctrl+Alt+Shift** keys. When you are prompted to delete the Adobe Photoshop Settings File, click **Yes**. On the Application bar, right-click **Essentials**, and then click **Reset Essentials** to reset the default workspace layout. Reset all tools.

2. Navigate to the Photoshop9\Tutorial folder included with your Data Files, and open **BannerSamp1.jpg**. See Figure 9-6.

Figure 9-6   **Existing FlashFlock banner ad 1**

background graphic elements match the style of the logo

banner uses a gradient jewel tone for a background

the text is white and fonts are all sans serif

the FlashFlock logo has a simple, flat, graphic style

other than the photograph and the background, the design elements, including the border, are all white

3. Notice the colors used and the graphic style of the banner ad and the logo.

4. Examine the layout. Is the banner filled with text and images, or is it open and airy?

5. Consider the photograph. Is there a style to the image? Is the image saturated with color, or is it washed out? Are a few items close to the screen, or are you viewing an entire scene?

6. Repeat Step 2 through Step 5 using **BannerSamp2.jpg**, which shows another of FlashFlock's current banner ads. See Figure 9-7.

Figure 9-7 | Existing FlashFlock banner ad 2

background graphic elements match the style of the logo

banner uses a gradient jewel tone for a background

the text is white and fonts are all sans serif

the FlashFlock logo has a simple, flat, graphic style

other than the photograph and the background, the design elements, including the border, are all white

join the flock at FlashFlock.com ... home to the biggest animal flash mob movement the world has ever seen.

FlashFlock come fly with us

7. Repeat Step 2 through Step 5 using **WebHome.jpg**, which shows the existing FlashFlock Web site home page. See Figure 9-8.

Figure 9-8	Existing FlashFlock Web site home page

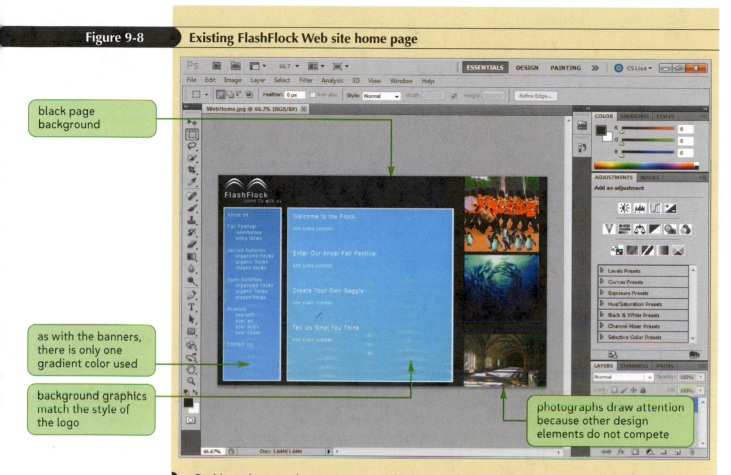

black page background

as with the banners, there is only one gradient color used

background graphics match the style of the logo

photographs draw attention because other design elements do not compete

8. Now that you have seen several existing pieces of FlashFlock marketing material, write a paragraph describing the materials that FlashFlock is currently using to create its brand and identity. Open WordPad, create a new document, and save the document in the Photoshop9\Tutorial folder as **CurrentBrand.rtf**.

9. What are the unifying elements that you notice? Are any elements unique to only one of the pieces that you examined? Describe how the materials make you feel about the FlashFlock brand, and identify design elements that work well for you, as well as any elements that you don't think work.

10. Indicate what layout and design elements you think would work well in the new banner campaign, and explain how you might make the new banners different from the old banners while maintaining a consistent brand identity.

11. Close all three images, and then save and close the WordPad document.

Now that you have spent time setting goals, identifying your target audience, and doing research, it is time to make decisions regarding your final output files for the project.

Determining Output

The final step before you can begin to create your project is to do some research to determine how you should deliver the final files. You should answer the following questions:

- What file type, size, and resolution should be used?
- What color model and color profile are needed for final output?
- What delivery method should be used for the final output files?
- Should the final working files (probably PSD files) also be included with the final output files?

It is important that you make these decisions prior to beginning work to ensure that you create files that have adequate size and resolution and to ensure you soft proof using the correct color model and profiles so that you can produce accurate colors. In this case, you'll be producing FlashFlock banner ads for display on the Web.

You can make some assumptions regarding output files, based on the technical parameters of the project. Web resolution is 72 ppi, and that is the resolution at which you'll create the FlashFlock project. The banners will be displayed on Web sites and on social media pages—including Facebook pages. Currently, the maximum width at which you can display graphics on Facebook is 480 pixels; therefore, you will use 480 pixels as the width of your banners. Your color space will be RGB because the Web is displayed on monitors, and as you have already learned, monitors use red, green, and blue pixels to produce color. Finally, you'll use the sRGB color profile because it defines the color space of the standard monitor used to view images on the Web.

Jessica and George have made the decisions regarding the remaining output specifications. The height of the banner will be 275 pixels, and the images will be compressed and delivered as JPEGs because that file format will create small files that can be displayed on the Web; the JPEG format will also do a good job of compressing the photographic images that will be included in the banners.

Next, you'll create a new Photoshop file with the correct size, resolution, color model, and color profile.

To create a Photoshop document for the project:

1. On the Application bar, click **File**, and then click **New**.

2. In the New dialog box, type **FFBanners** in the Name box.

3. In the Width box, type **480**, and select **pixels** from the drop-down list. In the Height box, type **275**, and select **pixels** from the drop-down list, if necessary.

4. In the Resolution box, type **72**, if necessary, and select **pixels/inch** from the drop-down list. Select **RGB Color** and **8 bit** from the Color Mode list to select the RGB color model. In the Background Contents box, select **White**.

5. Click the **Advanced** arrow to expand the dialog box to show the advanced settings, and then in the Color Profile box, select **sRGB IEC61966-2.1**. See Figure 9-9.

Figure 9-9   **New dialog box**

Color Mode should be set to RGB Color

the sRGB color profile is best-suited for Web display

6. Click the **OK** button to create the new document.

7. On the Application bar, click **File**, and then click **Save As**.

8. In the Save As dialog box, confirm that the ICC Profile check box is checked.

9. Save the file as **FFBanners.psd** in the Photoshop9\Tutorial folder included with your Data Files.

10. Close the file, and exit Photoshop.

The ICC Profile check box in the Save As dialog box must be checked to save the document with a color profile.

Your team has completed the planning phase of the project. You have defined project goals and written a statement of purpose. You created a viewer profile, identified your target audience, and researched your target audience and the competition. You've also started the Photoshop document that you'll use to create your composition for the project. Now you are ready to begin creating the banners. In the next session, you'll work through the creation and delivery process.

REVIEW

Session 9.1 Quick Check

1. True or False. You should create a plan before you begin to create a design for a project.
2. What is the purpose of listing project goals?
3. How many goals can a project achieve effectively?
4. What is a target audience?
5. What happens if you draw general conclusions about the target audience without backing up those conclusions with research?
6. Why should you conduct market research?
7. What is a brand?

SESSION 9.2 VISUAL OVERVIEW

The **concept** is the general underlying theme that unifies the various elements of a composition to create a cohesive look and feel.

A **project metaphor** is a visual extension of a project concept.

Create a concept and metaphor

Gather materials

Look and feel refers to the way all the elements of the design interact to create an experience for a viewer.

FlashFlock
gaggle your tail off. . .

hey old school, swim on by www.flashflock.com ...

jump in the bowl with the other contestants

...you might win or you might get schooled

Organize & archive files

Review design & create output

Design is an exacting form of art that has a specific and defined purpose.

CREATING A PROFESSIONAL PROJECT

Layout is the position of elements in a composition.

Balance is the feeling of equilibrium that is felt when looking at a composition as a whole.

Create layout

The **color palette** is the set of colors used to create a composition.

Harmonious colors are colors that are pleasing to look at, create a sense of balance, and stimulate a viewer to explore a composition.

Select color palette

Typography is the art and technique of type arrangement, design, and modification.

Select typefaces & add text

Graphic style is the look of the graphic elements in a composition, including lines, shapes, textures, borders, logos, illustrations, buttons, and so forth.

Design graphic style & add graphics

Design photographic style & add images

Designing a Project

Design is a form of art that has a specific and defined purpose. The phrase *look and feel* is used to describe the overall impact of the characteristics of the design of a graphic project. It refers to the way that all the elements of the design interact to create an experience for the viewer. The look and feel of a particular design is achieved from a mixture of many smaller choices, including which colors, typefaces, graphic style, and layout are selected for the design. Jessica will make all of the choices regarding the aesthetic design elements in the project. You'll create the project and, as you did in the planning phase, you'll create alternative designs as part of your training. As you make decisions, consider how each element impacts the design and the target audience. To combine all these elements effectively, you'll need to create a concept and metaphor for the project, but first you must gather all of the materials that you will use in the project.

Gathering or Acquiring Materials

It is a good idea to assemble all of the content and materials that you will use in a project before you jump into the layout process. You need to know what you have to work with so that you can determine the best layout and design potentials. For example, if you need to include a large quantity of text in a composition, you will need to create a different layout than you would for a composition that only contains a small amount of text.

Ask the client to assemble all of the materials that they have. When you are assembling client materials, get any text content that the client would like to use in a digital format, such as a Word document. You'll also need any photographic images and logos the client already has that will be used for the project. Make sure that the images and graphic elements that you'll be using in the project are of adequate size and resolution and, if possible, get a version that is in the same color model.

Jessica has helped George collect all of the materials that he has available for the project. They have gathered the existing files that you have reviewed to gain an understanding of FlashFlock's branding and identity. George has provided a copy of the logo as a PSD file and a copy of the photographs as JPEG files (these were the best files they had available). Jessica and George have provided a document containing the text that George would like to include in the banner. You'll examine the new image files and read the text George has created so that you'll have an understanding of the elements that will be included in the new campaign. See Figure 9-10 to review the photographs that George has selected for the campaign.

Figure 9-10 Images that will be used in the new campaign

To review the tagline and text that George would like to use with each image in the campaign, see Figure 9-11.

Figure 9-11   Text for the new FlashFlock campaign

Banner 1

Tagline: gaggle your tail off…

Content:

hey old school, swim on by www.flashflock.com … jump in the bowl with the other contestants … you might win or you might get schooled

Image:

Fish.jpg

Banner 2

Tagline: murders in numbers…

Content:

hey you in the tuxedo…loosen up and dive in to www.flashflock.com … enter the contest and you might just be the next emperor

Image:

Penguins.jpg

Banner 3

Tagline: we let the cows out…

Content: yo scalie … why don't you slink on down to www.flashflock.com … enter the competition and you could be the hippest liz in the lounge

Image:

Lizards.jpg

Now that you have what you need to start, you can begin creating a concept and metaphor for the composition.

Developing a Concept and Metaphor

A good concept is the basis for developing an aesthetically cohesive composition or campaign. A concept unifies the various elements of a composition and contributes to the cohesiveness of the look and feel. To develop a concept, review some of the artwork and Web sites that appeal to the target audience and look for common underlying themes. Next, make a list of words that describe what you would like the banners to convey. Try to think of words that will reinforce the project goals and communicate something to the target audience. Finally, write down the concept. Examples of a possible concept for a project include *growth*, *speed*, or *stability*.

After you have developed a concept, you need to create a metaphor for the project. A **metaphor** is a comparison in which one object, concept, or idea is represented as another. For example, the expression "at that moment, time was molasses" and Shakespeare's famous observation that "all the world's a stage" are metaphors. A project metaphor should be a visual extension of the project's concept, which reinforces the vision and the site goals. The metaphor helps to create a unified design.

The metaphor you choose for your project does not have to be concretely represented in the composition. For example, if the concept is fluidity, the metaphor might be a river. The actual composition does not need to be designed to look like a river, but instead could integrate elements that are commonly identified with rivers, such as a series of small, partially transparent, wavy lines in the background, a flowing theme in the graphic design, and cool colors such as muted blues and silvers. The river metaphor is an instrument to focus all of the aesthetic choices.

For the FlashFlock banner campaign, Jessica came up with a list of words to describe FlashFlock and the campaign: *fun, underground, campy, organic, technical, creative, human, artificial, sarcastic, playful, intelligent, hip, outsider,* and *enlightening.* Some words apply to a look that is popular with the target audience (*campy, underground,* and *outsider*); other words apply to the undertone George would like to create (*playful, enlightening, artificial,* and *organic*). Next, Jessica reviewed the research and spent some time considering how to pull it all together to create a campaign that will accomplish the stated goals, reinforce FlashFlock's branding and identity, and appeal to the target audience. Finally, she worked with George to develop the concept—*artistically motivated scientific experimentation fostering artificially engineered, temporary, symbiotic, interspecies habitats for the purpose of enlightenment and fun.* Based on that concept, they chose a metaphor of "mashups." In later sections, you'll see how the mashups metaphor helps to shape the site design by providing a foundation for color choice, font choice, graphics choice, and layout.

To continue your training, Jessica asks you to develop an alternate concept and metaphor for the project.

To develop an alternate concept and metaphor for the project:

1. Open WordPad, create a new document, and save the document in the Photoshop9\Tutorial folder as **Concept.rtf**.

2. In the WordPad document, list at least five words that describe FlashFlock and the banner campaign.

3. Review your notes regarding artwork and imagery that appeal to the target audience.

4. Choose a project concept, and then write a short description of the concept and why you selected it.

5. Choose a project metaphor, and then write a short description of the metaphor and why you selected it.

6. Write a paragraph that explains how you could integrate the concept and the metaphor into the banner campaign.

7. Save the Concept.rtf file, and close it.

Now you have a foundation that will help you create a cohesive project; you can make design choices that support the project metaphor. You have also experimented with creating a metaphor of your own. This experience will help you when you create a project on your own. Next, you'll begin working on the layout for the FlashFlock banner ad.

Creating a Layout

The term *layout* comes from traditional print design. Layout is the position of elements in a composition—in this case, on the computer screen. You need to decide where in the composition to place the text, logo, artwork, and so on. The layout should support the project goals and metaphor. It should be easy for a viewer to interpret, and it should appeal to the target audience. Finally, it should be consistent. For example, the logo should be located in the same place in all of the banners to create a unified look across the compositions in your campaign. Most important, layout should conform to the basic tenets of sound artistic design by employing balance, unity, and rhythm. You need to consider the space as a whole—in addition to the individual elements in the composition.

Balance and Space

Balance is achieved by arranging objects so that their visual weight is balanced in the overall composition. The two main approaches to balance are symmetrical and asymmetrical. **Symmetrical balance** evenly distributes the visual weight of objects in a composition around the central horizontal and vertical axes of the canvas. See Figure 9-12.

Figure 9-12   **Symmetrical balance**

the left side is a mirror image of the right side

objects are centered around the horizontal and vertical axes

Radial symmetry creates balance in a composition by distributing objects around one center point. See Figure 9-13.

Figure 9-13   **Radial symmetry**

objects are distributed around the imaginary center point of the composition

In juxtaposition, **asymmetrical balance** (also referred to as *informal balance*) is created by distributing visually disproportionate objects in the composition so that the visual weight of the objects achieves balance with respect to one another instead of with the canvas axes. Informal balance is often more visually compelling than symmetrical balance because it better incorporates the white space (or negative space) of the canvas into the design. See Figure 9-14.

Figure 9-14   **Asymmetrical balance**

objects are scattered around the image

in this case, objects are laid out using the Rule of Thirds

balance is achieved because the total visual weight of objects is equal

White space is the empty space in the canvas, and it is an important part of a well-designed composition. (White space can be filled with the background color.) If graphic elements, text, and images fill every inch of the canvas, viewers can become disoriented. Visually, they may not be able to move easily through the composition or to ascertain the meaning or emotion that the artist was trying to convey. Leaving white space opens up the composition and enables the viewer to more easily navigate the canvas. White space can also be used to draw attention to important components of a composition. Separating important elements, such as headings or taglines, from other page content with a little white space helps the viewer to distinguish those elements more quickly.

One tool for achieving an open design that integrates white space into the layout is a frequently used design concept that you are already familiar with—the Rule of Thirds. Remember, the Rule of Thirds states that the most interesting compositions are those in which the strongest element is off center. You can implement this technique in compositional design in a way that is similar to the technique you used to crop images. For instance, the composition in Figure 9-14 was created following the Rule of Thirds to produce a composition that has energy and visual interest. To use the Rule of Thirds when designing a composition, divide the page into thirds both horizontally and vertically, and then place the objects in the composition on the lines. No object should take up more than two-thirds of the canvas. For example, in most advertisements the logo takes up no more than one third of the canvas, leaving the other two-thirds of the canvas for the remaining content.

Rhythm and Unity

Rhythm is achieved in a composition by repeating or alternating objects or elements on the canvas. For example, a color that is repeated in different places in the canvas helps create a sense of rhythm or flow. **Unity** is a quality achieved by ordering elements in a design so that each contributes to an overall unified composition. The same concept applies across a campaign. See Figure 9-15.

Figure 9-15   **Rhythm and unity in a composition**

white space is used to open the composition

repetition of colors and shapes, as well as a consistent graphic look create a sense of unity in the compositions and across the campaign

patterns and shapes are repeated, but altered slightly across the campaign

colors are repeated within the canvas

Repeating or alternating objects or elements across a campaign helps unify the individual compositions into a cohesive project. Using one graphic style throughout the project, repeating colors throughout the project, and creating balance and symmetry between objects in the compositions all help to create unity in the design.

Creating a Wireframe of Your Layout

Often, two or three effective layouts are possible for a given project. Initially, designers create rough sketches of possible layout designs. Sometimes designers create wireframes of the layout. A **wireframe** is a bare-bones mock-up that is created in a graphics program instead of being drawn by hand. Wireframes include only rough placeholder images, such as boxes with text, to indicate where a graphic or image will be placed. The purpose of creating a wireframe is to show placement of the logo, images, text, and other elements to the client before creating the actual artwork.

Jessica has developed a rough wireframe of the layout for the FlashFlock banner campaign that she will present to George and Rick for their approval. See Figure 9-16.

Figure 9-16 Wireframe

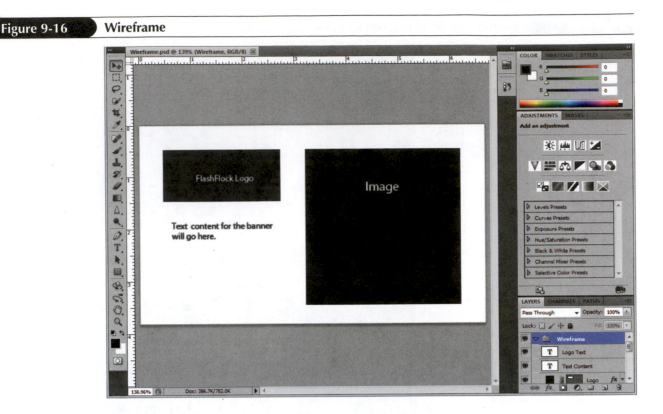

Jessica used asymmetrical balance when creating the sketch, and she placed the logo in the upper-left corner of the page, where the viewer's eye usually focuses first. This was done to support the top two goals of the campaign: enhance brand identity and increase brand recognition. The text content will be located below the logo, and a photograph will be located at the right center of the page.

Based on the alternate concept and metaphor you created, you will create a wireframe of another possible layout. You'll use the Rectangle Tool in Photoshop to create shapes that represent the logo and the image you will include in your composition. You'll use placeholder text to designate where the text will be placed. If Jessica likes your layout, both layouts will be presented to George and Rick at the next meeting. You'll create the wireframe in the Photoshop composition that you created and saved in the first session. Remember to consider the goals, target audience, and research, as well as the current FlashFlock marketing materials. Also remember to employ the concepts that you have learned regarding space, balance, and harmony.

To create a wireframe of your layout:

1. Navigate to the Photoshop9\Tutorial folder included with your Data Files, and open **FFBanners.psd**. Make sure it is displayed at **100%**, and then save the file as **Wireframe.psd** in the Photoshop9\Tutorial folder.

2. On the Tools panel, click the **Rectangle Tool** , and draw a black rectangle (2.25 inches wide by 1 inch high) that will represent the FlashFlock logo and tagline. Move it where you want it within the composition. Type **FlashFlock Logo** in the rectangle to label the shape.

3. Repeat Step 2 for the photographic image and any additional elements that you would like to include in the banner.

4. Because the banners include only a small amount of text, it is not necessary to use lorem ipsum text to mark where the content will be placed. Instead, in the location where you would like to display text in the banner, type **Text content for the banner will go here.**

5. Once all of the elements are on the canvas, review your layout. Does it follow the Rule of Thirds? Identify the type of balance that your composition uses and locate the white space in the composition. Finally, consider how effective this layout will be at communicating with your target audience and achieving the goals you have set for the campaign. Consider how it works with FlashFlock's current materials to reinforce branding and identity.

6. Make any necessary adjustments that you identified in your review, and then save and close your file.

Once you and your client have narrowed down the options to one or two layouts, you'll need to create comps (comprehensive drawings, or in this case digitally created comprehensive compositions) from the sketch or wireframe. Comps are the fully developed, detailed compositions from which you'll eventually create your final output files.

There are usually several rounds of creation and client feedback built into the design process. In the first round of design, you'll create a comp for each selected layout to show to the client at a meeting where you review the work. During the review process, you'll work with the client to select elements that are working. Often, you will end up combining elements that the client likes from different layouts in this round. In the second round of design, you'll create a single comp based on the input and discussion from your first review. Again, you'll present the comp to the client and you'll work together to fine-tune the composition. This process may occur one or two more times while you make slight changes to achieve sign-off on your finished product.

Now you'll continue the creation process by selecting colors for the composition.

TIP

The exact number of layouts, comps, and rounds of changes should be specified in the proposal that you submit to win a project.

Selecting Colors

Color is an interesting component of design because it sets the tone for the composition. The colors you choose affect the emotional response that a viewer has to the composition. Before selecting colors for a project, you will need a basic understanding of color theory as it applies to design. You have already learned about the concepts of additive (RGB) and subtractive (CMYK) color, and you have learned about color management, color profiles, and out-of-gamut color. You have also learned that the three components of color are brightness (or luminosity), saturation, and hue.

The Kuler panel is a tool that Adobe provides to help you select color palettes. You will work with the Kuler panel to learn more about how colors work in relation to each other and within the framework of a composition. You'll use the Kuler panel and your new insights to select a color scheme for the project. The selection of good color is not a science, so remember to take the rules you have learned as guidelines; use them along with your judgment and experience to select a color scheme for your projects. See Figure 9-17 to view the Kuler panel.

Figure 9-17   The Kuler panel

the Kuler panel is a tool for selecting color palettes (called themes)

color wheel

the large circle with a white outline is the base color for the palette

the five circles mark the five colors in the palette

the five circles correspond to the five swatches

Selecting Harmonious Colors

One of the goals of color selection is to create a harmonious composition. In general, **harmony** is a pleasing arrangement or combination of parts that creates an engaging end product that is balanced and filled with dynamic equilibrium. The term *harmony* can be used to refer to anything from the parts in a musical composition to the flavors of ice cream in a banana split. Harmonious colors are pleasing to look at. They create a sense of balance and are engaging, stimulating the viewer to explore the composition. Harmony is subjective, but there are some rules or formulas that can help you to select color combinations that are considered by experts and scholars to be harmonious. All of these formulas are based on the location of colors on a standard artistic color wheel.

Remember that complementary colors are colors that are located directly across from each other on the standard color wheel, such as red and green. See Figure 9-18.

Figure 9-18	Complementary colors

this color palette consists of two complementary colors and three tints (or shades) of those colors

Colors that are opposite one another on the color wheel have the maximum amount of contrast. Creating a composition with complementary colors maximizes the contrast in the composition, which creates a vibrant, visually stimulating composition. The maximum number of colors you should use when creating a composition is five. In addition to two complementary colors, the additional three colors in a complementary color palette should be tints (lightened by mixing with white) or shades (darkened by mixing with black) of the two complementary colors, as shown in Figure 9-18.

Because they produce vibrant effects, color schemes based on complementary colors are frequently seen in advertising. The potential danger with these color schemes is that they can be jarring; the colors must be employed intelligently to produce a visually appealing composition. For example, a color scheme of red and green is often used over a white or black canvas so the colors do not overwhelm the viewer. Another approach is to select one color as the dominant color and use the other color sparingly, as an accent. As you work with color, you will develop a sense of how to use complementary colors in your compositions.

When selecting a color for small text, avoid selecting the color that is the complement of your background because the stark contrast of the text against the background can make it difficult for the viewer to read the text. When using vibrant colors, high contrast sometimes creates excessive brightness at the edges of the text and sometimes very high contrast can cause fine lines to disappear against the background. For an example, see Figure 9-19.

Figure 9-19	Complementary colors and text

complementary colors can make small text hard to read

swatch and text are the same color

A **triad color palette** divides the color wheel into three sections, enabling you to select three colors that are spaced at an equal distance from each other on the color wheel from each other. See Figure 9-20.

Figure 9-20 | **Triad color palette with warm colors as the dominant colors**

triad color palette with two warm colors and one cool color

This provides you with three colors for your palette; the other two colors should be selected from the tints, shades, and tones of the original three colors. The triad color scheme provides less contrast than a complementary color scheme, but it still has balance because the colors are equidistant from each other on the color wheel. Again, there is a danger when you use this type of color scheme that the colors will not be harmonious because they are all competing for the viewer's attention. It is a good idea to select one or two dominant colors for this color scheme and to use the other color or colors as accents. A nice way to use this type of color scheme is to select two warm colors (colors that have higher color temperatures—such as reds, oranges, and pinks) to be your dominant colors, and then select one cool color (colors that have lower color temperatures—such as greens, blues, and purples) to be your accent color. This will create a warm, active composition that uses cool accents to provide a bit of contrast and visual interest. You can also do the opposite by selecting two cool colors as dominant colors and one warm color as an accent. This will create a cool, flowing composition that uses warm accents to provide contrast and visual interest. See Figure 9-21.

Figure 9-21   Triad color palette with cool colors as the dominant colors

triad color palette with two cool colors (blue and green) and one warm color (red)

You may recall that analogous color palettes have at least three colors that are located beside each other on the color wheel, with an identifiable common hue, such as yellow, yellow-orange, and orange. See Figure 9-22.

Figure 9-22   Analogous color palette

analogous color palette with warm and cool tones

The additional two colors in an analogous color palette can be other colors that are located next to the colors you selected on the color wheel, or they can be tints or shades of those colors. Analogous color schemes are harmonious because the colors blend with each other. When the colors in an analogous color scheme are all tints or shades of the same hue, it is referred to as a monochromatic color scheme. See Figure 9-23.

Figure 9-23 **Monochromatic color palette**

monochromatic color palettes in warm colors are sometimes visually jarring

cool colors work well in a monochromatic color palette

When designing with an analogous color scheme, one of the colors is usually used as the dominant color in the composition, while the other two or more colors are used as accents. When using an analogous color scheme, you need to ensure that your composition does not become bland and visually uninteresting. To avoid this, you should step back from your composition frequently during the design process and take a fresh look. Try to visualize the composition as though you are seeing it for the first time and consider how a viewer will feel when looking at the composition. Because analogous color schemes tend to blend together, designers often use black or white in the composition to make the analogous colors pop. See Figure 9-24.

Figure 9-24 **Monochromatic color palette with black**

black adds drama to the composition

dominant color

There are many other techniques for selecting color combinations. Once you are comfortable using complementary and analogous color schemes, try researching other ways to use color.

Additional Guidelines for Color Selection

In addition to selecting a color scheme for your project, you need to consider how to use the colors within the composition. Here are a few guidelines that will provide some guidance:

- **Keep it simple:** With color choice, more is definitely not better. Everyone has seen a Web site or flyer that looks as if it erupted from a rainbow. Too many competing colors cause the eye to race around the page, leaving the user dazed and confused. Remember that you want to create a harmonious composition.
- **Remember branding, identity, and project goals:** Your color palette must reinforce the organization's branding and identity. It also must work with the project goals and metaphor you selected for the composition.
- **Consider the mood you want to create:** Colors create a mood. Studies show that colors have certain psychological effects on people. For example, blue is calming; red is hot or intense. Think about what your target audience might associate with a color when choosing your palette.
- **Keep the target audience in mind:** Different cultures do not always have the same psychological associations with specific colors. For example, people in the United States associate white with purity and red with danger, whereas some countries associate white with death and red with marriage. If a composition has a global or foreign target audience, you might need to research the customs and symbols of the target culture(s).
- **Examine your colors in the composition:** When two colors are placed side by side, they interact with one another. This is called **simultaneous contrast**, and it affects the way you interpret what you see when you look at a composition. This is especially true if you are using a warm color and a cool color because warm colors—such as red, yellow, and orange—are active. They seem to advance out into space, and an object that is colored with a warm color will appear to be larger than the same object that is colored with a cool color. Cool colors—such as blue or green—are passive. They seem to recede from view and appear to fall back in space. To identify potential problems with color interaction, it is important that you look at your composition as a whole to see how the colors are affecting each other and how they are affecting the balance of the composition.

By creating different versions of the same layout using different accent colors, you can visualize the way that different color combinations affect the composition. See Figure 9-25 for examples.

Figure 9-25   **Color interactions affect the composition**

black replaced with a warm, red color

small pink areas disappear against the intense red

red and pink compete for focus

pinks are the same in all three compositions

original black and pink composition

black replaced with a cool blue-green color, a near complement to the pinks

the cool color recedes and the warm color advances

Using Art as an Inspiration When Choosing a Color Palette

Another way to develop an effective color palette is to look to works of art for inspiration. Think of what emotions and feelings you want to evoke with the composition, and then find a painting, photograph, or other work of art that stirs those feelings in you. Evaluate the colors the artist used. Consider how the colors interact. Try to pinpoint colors that are causing the emotion. Consider how that color palette would work with your metaphor. Think about how you might use that color palette in your composition.

Using the Kuler Panel

Adobe provides the Kuler panel to help you create harmonious color schemes, which Kuler refers to as themes. The Kuler panel is an add-on piece of software—like Camera Raw—that is included with Photoshop. From the Kuler panel, if you have an Internet connection, you can use the Browse tab to view color themes that were created by other artists and then uploaded to the Kuler Web site (*kuler.adobe.com*). In the default view, the Browser tab displays the Highest Rated themes. These are the themes that members of Kuler's online community have given the highest aggregated ratings, using a five-star rating system. See Figure 9-26.

Figure 9-26   **Kuler panel with the Browse tab displayed**

If you find a theme in the Browse tab that you like, you can add the palette to your Swatches panel, or you can edit the theme in the Create tab where you can adjust the colors to create your own custom theme. See Figure 9-27.

Figure 9-27   **Kuler panel with Create tab displayed**

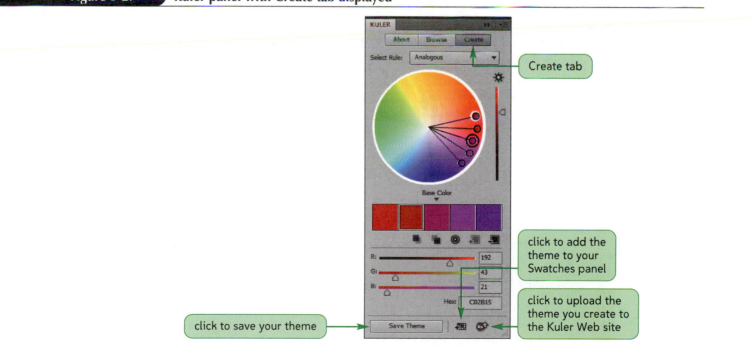

From the Create tab, you can adjust themes that were created by other artists, you can create and save your own themes using the color theory rules that you just learned, and you can adjust themes that you have previously created. You can also upload the themes you create to the Kuler Web site where other artists can view them and comment on them. One drawback of the Kuler panel is that it uses RGB colors, so it sometimes creates themes with colors that are out of gamut for printing.

To gain experience in creating color schemes, you'll open the Kuler panel and use the Browse tab to view color themes created by other artists. Then, you'll use the Create tab to experiment with the different rules that you learned about creating color palettes. If you do not have Internet access, you will not be able to complete the steps that include the Browse panel but you can still create your own color palettes using the Create panel. If you cannot complete the steps, read them and examine the figures.

Before you begin working with color, it is a good idea to check your Color Settings to ensure that they are set to display color using the color profile that you selected when you did your planning. This will ensure that colors are displayed as accurately as possible, regardless of your Color Management Policies settings.

REFERENCE

Using the Kuler Panel

- On the Application bar, click Window, point to Extensions, and then click Kuler.
- On the Kuler panel, click the Browse tab, select Highest Rated from the Choose which themes you wish to display list, and select All Time from the Limit themes by their creation date list.
- Select a theme that you like, and then click the Add selected theme to swatches icon.
- Click a theme's arrow, and then click Edit This Theme to open the Create tab and edit the selected theme.

To explore the Kuler panel:

1. On the Application bar, click **Edit**, and then click **Color Settings**. Select **North America General Purpose 2** from the Settings list, if necessary, and click the **OK** button to close the dialog box.

2. On the Application bar, click **Window**, point to **Extensions**, and then click **Kuler**. The Kuler panel opens in the Photoshop window.

3. On the Kuler panel, click the **Browse** tab, select **Highest Rated** from the Choose which themes you wish to display list, and select **All Time** from the Limit themes by their creation date list.

   The Browse tab is connected to the Kuler Web site, which is constantly updated with new styles. If you are connected to the Internet, the list displayed on your screen will probably vary each time you use the tab to browse for new color themes.

   Trouble? If you are not connected to the Internet, you might see the list of themes that was displayed the last time the computer was connected to the Internet or you might not see any themes at all. You might also see a message indicating that no Internet connection was detected. Click the OK button to acknowledge the message, and then read but do not keystroke the following steps.

4. Select a theme that you like, and then click the **Add selected theme to swatches** icon ▦.

5. Click the **Swatches** panel to display it. Notice that the colors from the theme you selected have been added to the end of your swatches. See Figure 9-28.

Figure 9-28   Theme added to Swatches panel

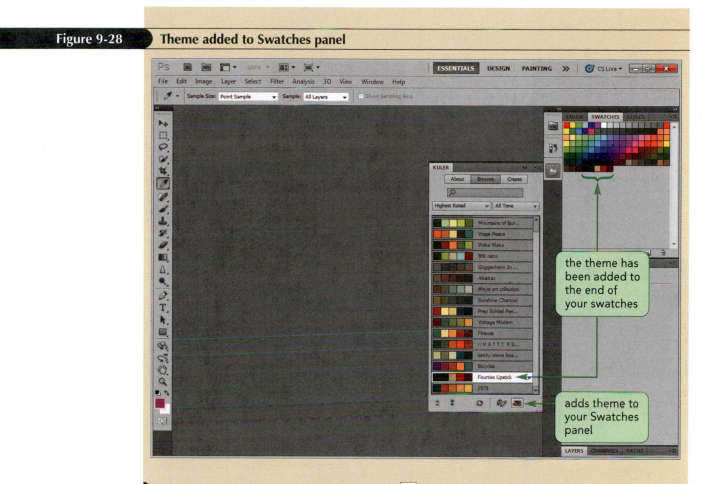

the theme has been added to the end of your swatches

adds theme to your Swatches panel

6. Select another theme, click its arrow ▶, and then click **Edit This Theme**. The Create tab opens, and the theme you selected is displayed.

Next, you'll customize this theme to create your own custom color theme. When creating a custom theme, you can start with an existing theme or you can simply open the Create tab and start experimenting, using the rules that you have learned.

REFERENCE

Creating a Theme on the Kuler Panel

- On the Create tab of the Kuler panel, select a rule from the Select Rule list.
- Click the Base Color swatch located below the color wheel, if necessary.
- Drag the Base Color circle around the color wheel until you find the base color you want to use.
- Select the other circles on the color wheel, and move them around to select the four other colors for your theme.
- Adjust the shade of any color by dragging the Control brightness by increasing or decreasing black slider located at the right of the color wheel up or down.
- Click the Save Theme button, and in the Name box, type a name for the theme.
- Click the Save button.

To create your own themes:

1. On the Kuler panel, select **Analogous** from the Select Rule list, and then click the **Base Color** swatch located below the color wheel, if necessary.

   The Base Color indicator on the color wheel of the Kuler panel is a circle that is surrounded by a white border.

2. Drag the **Base Color** circle around the color wheel until a shade of red is displayed in the circle.

   You can also select the Base Color by typing a specific hexadecimal color code in the Hex box at the bottom of the Kuler panel.

3. Select one of the circles, other than the Base Color circle, and drag it until all of the circles are fairly close together. See Figure 9-29.

Figure 9-29 Adjusted analogous color palette

4. Adjust the shade of the color by dragging the **Control brightness by increasing or decreasing black** slider located at the right of the color wheel to the top.

5. Drag the bottom color circle about halfway toward the center of the color wheel to lighten the tint of this color swatch. See Figure 9-30.

Figure 9-30   **Adjusted analogous color palette**

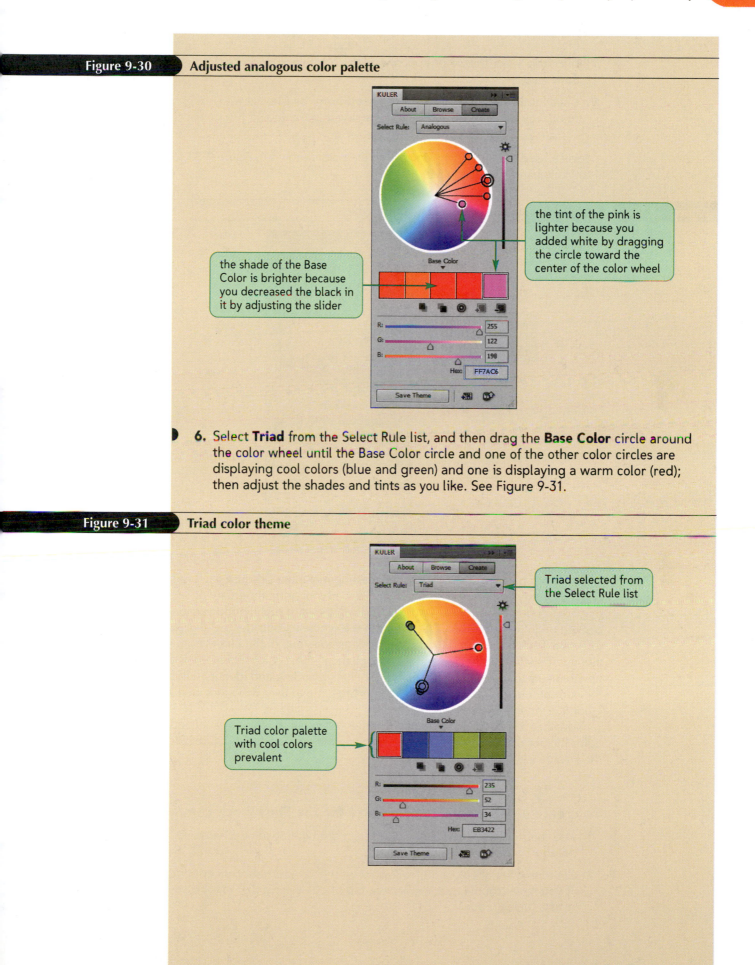

the tint of the pink is lighter because you added white by dragging the circle toward the center of the color wheel

the shade of the Base Color is brighter because you decreased the black in it by adjusting the slider

6. Select **Triad** from the Select Rule list, and then drag the **Base Color** circle around the color wheel until the Base Color circle and one of the other color circles are displaying cool colors (blue and green) and one is displaying a warm color (red); then adjust the shades and tints as you like. See Figure 9-31.

Figure 9-31   **Triad color theme**

Triad selected from the Select Rule list

Triad color palette with cool colors prevalent

7. Click the **Save Theme** button, and in the Name box, type **Test**. Click the **Save** button.

8. Click the **Browse** tab, and select **Saved** from the Choose which themes you wish to display list. Your new theme is displayed in the tab so you can access it later.

Jessica used the Kuler panel to choose the colors shown in Figure 9-32 for the new FlashFlock banner ad campaign.

Figure 9-32	FlashFlock banner ad campaign color theme

each banner will use one hue from this color theme

This color palette fits nicely into the mashup metaphor because each of these colors is created by mixing other colors together. They are not normal primary or secondary colors that are frequently used in advertising. Instead, they are slightly odd versions of the colors you might expect to see. This provides the synthetic, outsider feel that Jessica wants to evoke. Each banner in the campaign will use one hue of the colors from the palette along with white for the text and graphic elements. This color scheme will allow the new banners to reinforce the current FlashFlock branding and identity without repeating the current look exactly. Finally, the colors are fun and they will work well with other graphic elements in the banners.

Now that you have had a chance to experiment with the Kuler panel and create some color themes using the rules that you learned, you'll create an alternate color palette for the FlashFlock banner ad campaign.

To create an alternate color palette for the FlashFlock campaign:

1. Use the rules you have learned to select the type of color scheme you'll create as an alternate FlashFlock color palette.

2. Envision a set of colors that will work with your alternate concept and metaphor. If you have trouble, use the Browse tab of the Kuler panel to look at themes other artists have created.

3. On the Create tab of the Kuler panel, select the type of color theme you would like to create from the Select Rule list.

4. Move the **color** circles and the **Control brightness by increasing or decreasing black** slider until you have a color theme that you like.

5. Examine the theme and consider the psychological associations of the colors. Do these fit with your goals? Do the colors work with the concept and metaphor, the FlashFlock branding and identity, and the project goals?

6. When you are finished making adjustments, click the **Save Theme** button, and save the theme as **FlashFlockAlt**.

7. Open WordPad, create a new document, and save the document in the Photoshop9\Tutorial folder as **Color.rtf**.

8. Write a paragraph explaining how the palette you selected works with FlashFlock's current branding and identity and how it supports the project goals, your alternate concept, and metaphor. Describe where and how you intend to use the colors in the project, and then save and close the document.

9. On the Application bar, right-click **Essentials**, and click **Reset Essentials** to close the Kuler panel and return the workspace to its default view.

INSIGHT

The Web-Safe Color Palette

The **Web-safe color palette** consists of 216 colors. When many computers could display only 256 colors at a time, the Web-safe color palette provided Web designers a reliable color palette. Because current computers can display over 16 million colors, most designers have disregarded the Web-safe color palette. All colors, including the Web-safe colors, have hexadecimal color codes, and all well-coded HTML uses hexadecimal color codes to refer to a specific color.

Adding Colors to Your Composition

You are ready to add colors to your composition, using the FFBanners.psd file that you created in the first session. You'll create a new layer group for the first banner, and then you'll create a gradient background using white and one color from the color palette. Before you begin working with color in your composition, it is a good idea to check your Color Settings to ensure that the Working Spaces setting displays RGB color using the color profile that you selected when you did your planning. This will ensure that colors are displayed as accurately as possible regardless of your Color Management Policies settings. This is also the point at which you would normally adjust your Proof Setup setting, so you can soft proof your work, if necessary. In this case, that step is overkill because you are working in RGB and you know that your document color profile is the same as your Working Spaces color profile, so we will skip that step.

To create gradient banner backgrounds:

1. Press the **Shift+Ctrl+K** keys to open the Color Settings dialog box and select **North America General Purpose 2** from the Settings list, if necessary. This changes the Working Space setting for RGB to sRGB IEC61966-2.1, which is the color profile you selected when you created the document. Click the **OK** button to close the dialog box.

2. Open the **FFBanners.psd** file that you saved in the Photoshop9\Tutorial folder, and set the document to display at **100%**, if necessary. Select **Rulers** from the View menu to show the rulers, and collapse the Adjustments panel group.

3. On the Layers panel, click the **Create a new group** icon ▢, and name the new group **Banner 1**.

4. With the Banner 1 group selected on the Layers panel, click the **Create a new layer** icon ▣ to create a new layer inside of the Banner 1 folder, and name the new layer **Banner Background**.

5. On the Color panel, click the **Set foreground color** icon ■, and in the Color Picker dialog box, type **9c005e** in the # box at the bottom of the dialog box. Click the **OK** button. The new foreground color is the berry color from Jessica's color palette.

6. On the Tools panel, click the **Gradient Tool** ▣, and then on the options bar, click the **Click to open Gradient picker** arrow ▾.

7. In the Gradient picker, double-click the first option, **Foreground to Background**, to select it, and close the Gradient picker.

8. On the options bar, click the **Linear Gradient** icon ▣, select **Normal** from the Mode list, **100%** from the Opacity list, and click the **Dither** check box to select it, if necessary.

9. With the Gradient Tool still selected, start at the top of the canvas, and drag the mouse straight down the canvas, past the bottom edge to around the 5 inch mark on the ruler. Release the mouse button. The background is now a gradient. See Figure 9-33.

Figure 9-33   **Gradient background of Banner 1**

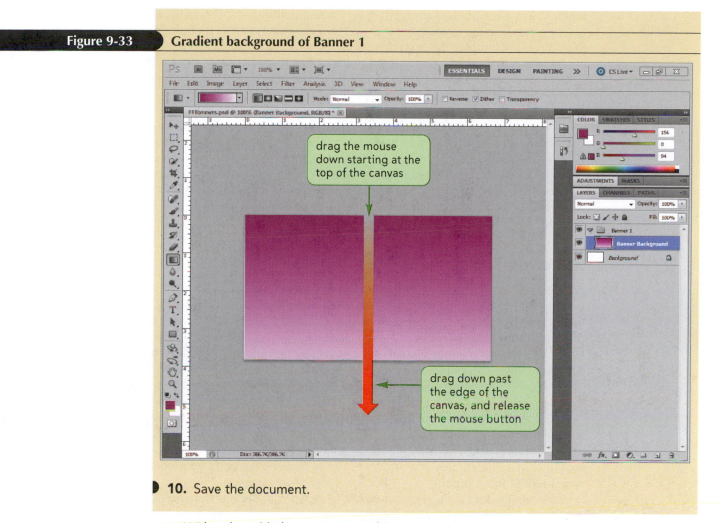

10. Save the document.

With color added to your composition, you're ready to select typefaces and add the text to the composition.

Selecting Fonts and Adding Text

Typography is the art and technique of arranging, designing, and modifying type. From the time of the first printing press, designers and typographers have used text as part of aesthetic design. You have learned the basics skills of type arrangement, including adding text to a canvas; adjusting text colors; selecting point sizes; and adjusting leading, tracking, kerning, and so forth. Now, you'll learn how to use text effectively as part of your composition.

Selecting the Appropriate Typographical Style

In traditional **text typography**, the goal of text design and layout is to create a cohesive, readable, and visually pleasing document, using an unobtrusive typographical style. This approach to working with text is appropriate when your project is a traditional printed work with a large amount of text, or when the goal of your project is to communicate information efficiently, such as in an IRS pamphlet. It is also an approach you should consider when adding paragraph text to a composition. For example, in a magazine article, this style would be appropriate for the text in the main body of the article, so it is easy for the viewer to read, but it would probably not be the first choice for the title text. When you employ the text typography approach, you use typeface, color, and size of text to create a logical, hierarchical structure that helps the viewer move through the content. This approach can be used to distinguish relative importance of content or to categorize content.

Another approach to typography is **display typography**. In this approach, the designer is less concerned with the readability of a large body of text, and more concerned about using the text in an artistic manner to communicate a succinct, potent message to the viewer. Designers often employ the display typography approach when creating a composition. However, both approaches are appropriate in different circumstances, and you can combine the approaches to create a more effective and well-rounded composition.

Now that you understand how your approach affects your design, you'll select typefaces for the FlashFlock project.

Selecting Typefaces and Font Styles

A **typeface** is a unified set of alphanumeric symbols that are designed with stylistic unity. Most typefaces include letters, numerals, punctuation, and symbols—sometimes in multiple languages. Typefaces are usually grouped together into a collection or family of fonts. A **font** actually refers to a designated set of letters, numbers, and symbols in a single size and style in one typeface. For example, the Helvetica typeface might include 12-point Helvetica bold font and 9-point Helvetica italic font, among many other fonts. However, in the modern age, people often use the words typeface and font interchangeably. In fact, digital typeface designers are often referred to as font designers.

Because of this blurring of the traditional lines, Photoshop refers to the typeface as the font family and to the font as the font style. And, in some instance, such as certain articles within Help, Photoshop uses the general term font to refer to all aspects of the font, including font family and font style. We will use Photoshop's terminology for the remainder of this tutorial.

Selecting the font is the most important typographical decision you will need to make for a project. Selecting the right font family and font style is important in creating an effective design because a font conveys a wealth of subtle information and often creates an impression about the content before it is even read. Just think about the different fonts that might be used on designs that present current news and events, offer Far East travel information, or advertise science fiction movies. Font selection also has an effect on the readability of the text. Because of this, different fonts are appropriate for different applications and in different circumstances. In fact, some industries have specific standards and specifications for selection of appropriate fonts. It is important to understand the font characteristics and the project requirements when selecting a font for your project.

The three general categories of font are serif, sans serif, and mono. **Serif fonts** are fonts in which a delicate, horizontal line called a serif finishes the main strokes of each character; an example would be the horizontal bars at the top and bottom of an uppercase M. The most common serif font is Times New Roman. Serif fonts are usually used in traditional printing for body text in books, newspapers, and magazines because historically, people believed that serif fonts were easier to read. Recent studies have disproven this fact, but the history and perception still persist.

Sans serif fonts are those in which the serifs are absent. (*Sans* means *without* in French, so *sans serif* means *without serif*.) The most common sans serif font is Helvetica. Sans serif fonts are commonly used on Web sites and in other digital media, even for body text. Because of their prevalence in contemporary digital design, they have also become popular for headlines and headings in contemporary print.

A third category, mono, is sometimes used. *Mono* is short for *monospaced*. A **monospaced font** is one in which each letter takes exactly the same width in the line; for example, the letter *i* (a thin letter) takes the same amount of space as the letter *m*. A common monospaced font is `Courier`. Monospaced fonts are serif fonts, but they are considered a separate font family because of their unique characteristic. Fonts that are not monospaced are **proportional fonts** because each letter takes up a different width on the line, proportional to the width of each letter. For example, the letter *i* takes less space than the letter *m*. Both the serif font Times New Roman and the sans serif font Helvetica are proportional.

The font selection for the FlashFlock banner campaign was fairly simple because FlashFlock has a very minimalist approach to design. In addition, because FlashFlock is primarily a Web-based organization, they have traditionally used sans serif fonts. The FlashFlock logo font family (typeface) is Arial Rounded MT Bold and the font style (font) is Regular. All other text is always displayed using the Arial font family, and all text is displayed in white (hexadecimal color #ffffff). See Figure 9-34.

Figure 9-34   **Font family and font style used by FlashFlock**

logo uses Arial Rounded MT Bold font

all other text uses Arial font family

all text is displayed in white (hexadecimal #ffffff)

Jessica has decided that for the purposes of branding and identity, you will follow those guidelines for the banner ad campaign. This style also supports the mashup metaphor because it is contemporary and minimalist.

Selecting Fonts for Use as Text on the Web

When you are creating a design for a Web page, it is important to remember that although you are creating a picture of what the Web page will look like, the actual page will be made using a combination of graphic images, text, and computer code. In a Web page, a font must be installed on the end user's computer for the page to be displayed using that font. If you use a font that is not found on a viewer's computer, the page will be displayed in the default font the end user has chosen for his or her browser. To avoid possible font substitutions, you can create a graphic that is a picture of the text; you place the graphic in the Web page as you would any other image. For example, most logos that you see displayed on Web pages are actually images that change appearance when the user drags the mouse over the image. This technique works for a small amount of text, such as a title or heading. However, you cannot change all text to graphic images because it would make the pages slow to load in a browser, and it would prevent the text from wrapping to accommodate the size of the viewer's screen.

Web design programs, such as Adobe Dreamweaver, arrange fonts into groups, as shown here:

Verdana, Geneva, sans-serif
Georgia, Times New Roman, Times, serif
Courier New, Courier, monospace
Arial, Helvetica, sans-serif
Tahoma, Geneva, sans-serif
Trebuchet MS, Arial, Helvetica, sans-serif
Arial Black, Gadget, sans-serif
Times New Roman, Times, serif
Palatino Linotype, Book Antiqua, Palatino, serif
Lucida Sans Unicode, Lucida Grande, sans-serif
MS Serif, New York, serif
Lucida Console, Monaco, monospace
Comic Sans MS, cursive

These groups provide designers with the best chance for achieving the desired look for a page. Each group contains the most common names for the selected font; these include the most common PC name, the most common Mac name (when different), and the generic font family name.

When you apply a font grouping to text, you actually apply computer code that contains all three choices, ensuring maximum potential for aesthetic continuity across all platforms and all computers. When a browser displays a page, it checks the user's computer for the first font in the group. If the computer doesn't have that font, the browser checks for the second font in the list, and then, if necessary, the third font.

Once you have selected your font family and font style and you have set the font size and font color, you can fine-tune the text by making small adjustments to spacing, kerning, and so forth, as needed. Because you will be using FlashFlock's existing font family, font style, and font color, there is no need to make an alternate font selection, just remember to use what you have learned here when you select fonts for projects in the future. Next, you'll add text to Banner 1.

To add text to your composition:

1. Drag a vertical guide ¼ inch from the left side of the canvas and a horizontal guide ¼ inch from the bottom of the canvas.

2. On the Tools panel in Photoshop, select the **Horizontal Type Tool** T, and starting at the left guide, approximately one-third of the way down the page, draw a box that is 2 ¾ inches wide with the bottom of the rectangle against the bottom guide. See Figure 9-35.

Figure 9-35 **Text box in the new banner**

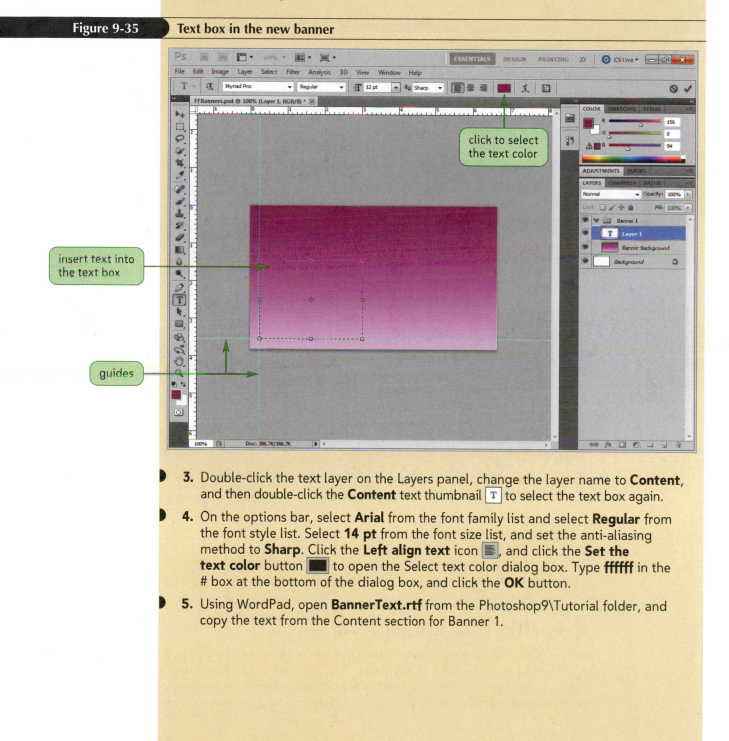

click to select the text color

insert text into the text box

guides

3. Double-click the text layer on the Layers panel, change the layer name to **Content**, and then double-click the **Content** text thumbnail T to select the text box again.

4. On the options bar, select **Arial** from the font family list and select **Regular** from the font style list. Select **14 pt** from the font size list, and set the anti-aliasing method to **Sharp**. Click the **Left align text** icon ▤, and click the **Set the text color** button ▆ to open the Select text color dialog box. Type **ffffff** in the # box at the bottom of the dialog box, and click the **OK** button.

5. Using WordPad, open **BannerText.rtf** from the Photoshop9\Tutorial folder, and copy the text from the Content section for Banner 1.

6. In Photoshop, paste the text into the box, and add a line break between each chunk of text by clicking at the end of the line and pressing the **Enter** key. See Figure 9-36.

Figure 9-36   **Text content in the new banner**

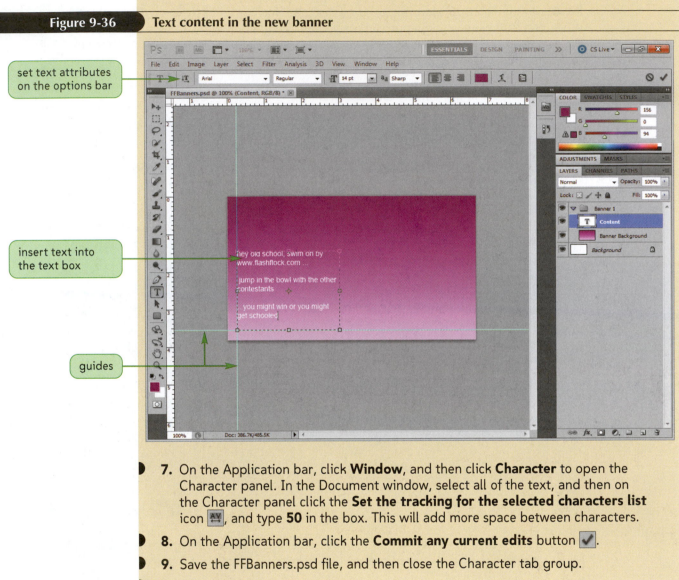

7. On the Application bar, click **Window**, and then click **Character** to open the Character panel. In the Document window, select all of the text, and then on the Character panel click the **Set the tracking for the selected characters list** icon ⁞AV⁞, and type **50** in the box. This will add more space between characters.

8. On the Application bar, click the **Commit any current edits** button ✔.

9. Save the FFBanners.psd file, and then close the Character tab group.

10. Close the BannerText.rtf file.

Next, you'll select a graphic style, create any graphics that you need, and add graphics to the composition.

Creating a Graphic Style

Now it is time to determine the graphic style for your project. The graphics in a composition provide the personality of the project. They are like accessories that either pull the composition together or detract from its overall look. Graphic style refers to the look of the graphic elements in the project, including lines, shapes, textures, borders, logos, illustrations, buttons, and any other elements you draw or create digitally that are not text or photographs. There are several elements to consider when you are creating the graphic style for your composition. Here are a few questions that you can ask yourself to get the creative juices flowing and to help you decide upon a graphic style for your project:

- Will the graphics be flat like a two-dimensional drawing you see in magazine ads or comics, or will they have depth that is created by using shadows, highlights, gradient colors, and perspective? Remember that a simple graphic style can be as sophisticated and powerful as a complex graphic style, and it can be just as successful if it reinforces your goals and works with your metaphor.
- Will the graphic elements be flowing—like wavy lines, swirls, and circles—or will they have sharp angles and breaks?
- Will you use flat colors, gradients, textures, or some combination?
- Will your graphics look realistic—like they are attempting to re-create something from the real world, or will they look artificial, like they are symbolic of real-world objects?
- Are there other words that you can use to describe what you would like the graphic style to convey to the viewer—such as *grungy* or *crisp*?

Finally, remember that the choice not to use any graphic elements in your composition is a stylistic choice as well, and it can be just as powerful a choice if it helps you to accomplish your goals.

After you have decided upon a graphic style, you are ready to create the graphic elements that you'll use in your composition. Graphics can be helpful in many ways. They can help you reinforce the organization's branding, identity, project goals, and metaphor. You can use graphics (such as symbols) to communicate information, you can use graphics (such as those used in the background of FlashFlock's current ads) to break up space, and you can use graphics (such as customized bullet points or stylized backgrounds for featured content) to add logic to the composition. You can also use graphics to help the flow of the composition by guiding the viewer's eye from one element to the next. The possibilities are endless.

Based on the FlashFlock banner ad goals, color palette, typeface choices, layout, and metaphor, Jessica selected a graphic style that includes flat, white, stylized graphic elements that will be inserted into the background of the composition to add movement to the composition, which is otherwise very static. The elements will be stylized or manufactured representations of organic elements, which will reinforce the mashup metaphor and will work with the current FlashFlock aesthetic. Although the older FlashFlock banners and marketing materials used linear elements, this campaign will use curved elements repeated with varying opacities to soften the composition and to add some repetition to the composition by mimicking the lines of the logo. Each banner will include a slightly different graphic repeated as a background element layered over the gradient background. The curves will guide the viewer's eye up to the FlashFlock logo in each banner to help reinforce the goals for the project. This will provide unity to the campaign while maintaining visual interest in the individual compositions. See Figure 9-37 for a sample of the three graphic background elements.

Figure 9-37 Graphics patterns created for the campaign

Jessica is also considering adding a thin white border around the outside of the banners. She would like you to create two versions of the banner—one with the border and one without it—so that she can present both to George and Rick. However, first you'll design an alternate graphic style to go with your alternate concept/metaphor, layout, and color palette for the FlashFlock banner ad campaign by answering the above questions and writing a paragraph explaining the style and how it works with your alternate project metaphor and goals as well as FlashFlock's branding and identity.

To design an alternate graphic style:

1. Review the alternate concept, metaphor, layout, and color palette that you developed for the banner ad campaign. Also, review the research that you gathered about what appeals to the target audience.

2. Open WordPad, create a new document, and save the document in the Photoshop9\Tutorial folder as **AltGraphics.rtf**. Consider how you would like to use graphics in the campaign, and answer the questions in the bulleted list presented earlier in this section regarding graphic style.

3. Write a few sentences that describe the graphic style for the campaign. Explain how this graphic style supports your metaphor, works with the FlashFlock aesthetic, and reinforces the campaign goals.

4. Save and close the AltGraphics.rtf document.

Once you have designed a graphic style, you will create graphics and add them to your composition. You should examine and prepare graphic files before you add the graphics to your composition. It is a good idea to convert your graphics to the correct color model and, when possible, the correct color profile, before you add them to your composition so you can access the colors of the converted graphic. In addition, if the converted graphic needs color correction because of the way the converter compensated for out-of-gamut colors, you can return to the original graphic to make any necessary color adjustments, and then create a new converted version of the graphic file before you add it to the composition. Following this work flow will allow you to achieve the best possible results because you will be able to adjust the colors of the converted graphic without affecting the other elements in the final composition.

When possible, you should add the graphics to your composition as Smart Objects to enable you to continue to edit them at their original size and in their original format. This is especially helpful if you have created the graphics in another Adobe software program, such as Illustrator. Adding the file as a Smart Object enables you to open, edit, and save the file in the original program (if you have that program installed on your computer), and to view the alterations in your composition.

Now, you'll add the graphic element that Jessica created to the FlashFlock banner and you'll add the other graphic element, the FlashFlock logo, to the banner. Once you do this, you might need to adjust the text slightly to create an aesthetically pleasing composition.

To add graphics to your composition:

1. In Photoshop, open **Graphics.psd** from the Photoshop9\Tutorial folder, and set the document to display at **100%**, if necessary.

2. On the Application bar, click **Edit**, and then click **Convert to Profile**. Review the Source Space profile for the document. This document already has the color profile that you decided to use when you were planning (sRGB IEC61966-2.1) because Jessica created the graphic specifically for this project.

3. Now that you have confirmed that the color profile is correct, click **Cancel** to close the Convert to Profile dialog box without making any changes.

4. On the Application bar, click the **Arrange Documents** icon ▦ ▾, and then click the horizontal **2 Up** icon ▤. The file containing the graphics for the banners opens in one pane, and the FFBanners document is displayed in the other. See Figure 9-38.

Figure 9-38   **Graphics.psd and FFBanners.psd open in the Document window**

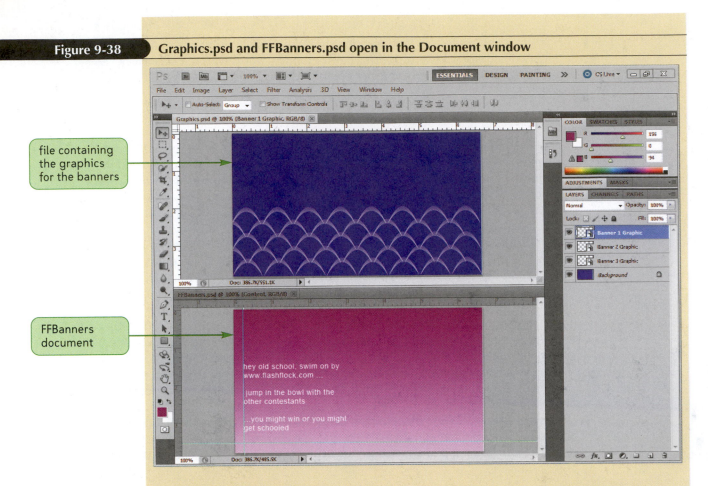

file containing the graphics for the banners

FFBanners document

5. Select the **Graphics.psd** document, if necessary, and then drag the **Banner 1 Graphic** layer from the Layers panel to the FFBanners.psd Document window.

    A copy of the Banner 1 Graphic layer is added to the FFBanners.psd document. It appears at the top of the Layers panel for the FFBanners.psd document.

6. On the Tools panel, select the **Move Tool** ⊞, and move the graphic in the FFBanners.psd Document window until it is centered at the bottom of the document (it should appear in essentially the same position as it does in the Graphics.psd document). See Figure 9-39.

Figure 9-39   **Graphic in the new banner**

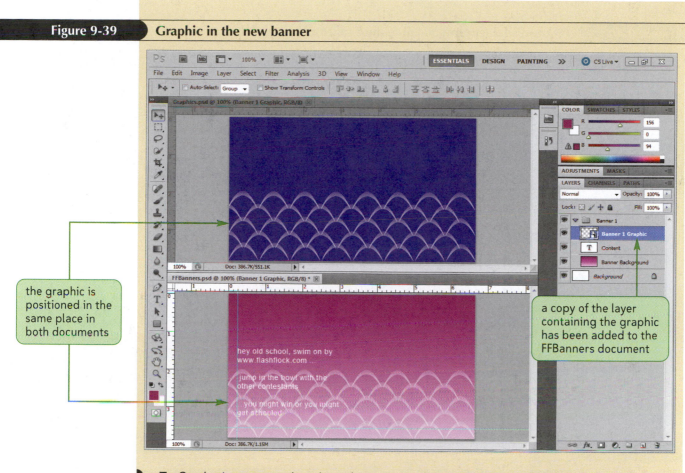

the graphic is positioned in the same place in both documents

a copy of the layer containing the graphic has been added to the FFBanners document

7. On the Layers panel, reduce the opacity of the new layer to 40% to ensure that the graphic does not compete with the text for the viewer's attention.

8. Save the FFBanners.psd document, and close the Graphics.psd document without saving it.

   Now you'll add the FlashFlock logo to the FFBanners document as a Smart Object.

9. In a Windows Explorer window, navigate to the Photoshop9\Tutorial folder, select the **FFLogo.psd** file, drag it over the FFBanners.psd Document window in Photoshop, and release the mouse button. Press the **Enter** key to place the object.

   The entire Photoshop file is placed as a Smart Object in the banner. See Figure 9-40.

Figure 9-40   **FFLogo.psd document added to the banner as a Smart Object**

the graphic is positioned in the center of the document

a copy of the FFLogo.psd document was added as a Smart Object

▶ 10. On the Layers panel, double-click the **FFLogo** layer thumbnail to open the FFLogo.psd document in a new Document window.

Trouble? If a dialog box appears with information regarding saving the file, click the OK button.

Trouble? If a message about missing fonts appears, click the OK button.

▶ 11. On the Layers panel, in the FFLogo.psd Document window, show the **Gaggle Your Tail Off** layer and hide the We Let The Cows Out layer and the Background layer. See Figure 9-41.

Figure 9-41   **FFLogo.psd document with changes**

new tagline visible

graphic with Background layer hidden

▶ 12. Save the FFLogo.psd file, and close it.

The Smart Object is now displayed in the FFBanners.psd document with the changes made.

▶ 13. In the FFBanners Document window, drag a horizontal guide ¼ inch from the top of the canvas, and then drag the logo so that the left tip of the wings are positioned against the left guide and the top of the wings are positioned against the top guide. See Figure 9-42.

Figure 9-42   **Logo positioned correctly in the composition**

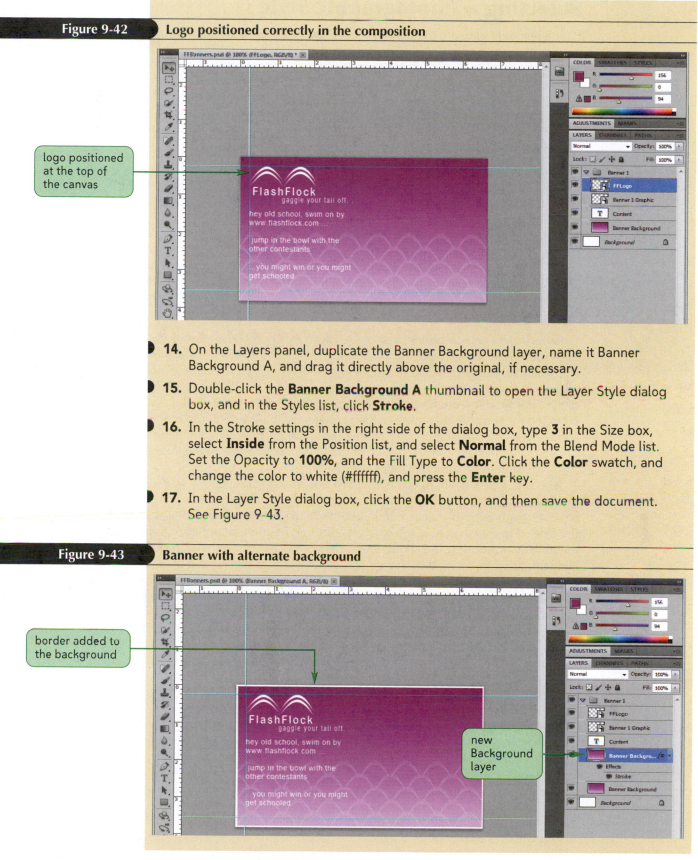

logo positioned at the top of the canvas

14. On the Layers panel, duplicate the Banner Background layer, name it Banner Background A, and drag it directly above the original, if necessary.

15. Double-click the **Banner Background A** thumbnail to open the Layer Style dialog box, and in the Styles list, click **Stroke**.

16. In the Stroke settings in the right side of the dialog box, type **3** in the Size box, select **Inside** from the Position list, and select **Normal** from the Blend Mode list. Set the Opacity to **100%**, and the Fill Type to **Color**. Click the **Color** swatch, and change the color to white (#ffffff), and press the **Enter** key.

17. In the Layer Style dialog box, click the **OK** button, and then save the document. See Figure 9-43.

Figure 9-43   **Banner with alternate background**

border added to the background

new Background layer

Now that the graphic elements have been added to the composition, you are ready to select your photographic style, retouch an image, and add it to your composition.

Selecting a Photographic Style

Photographic images are the final element that you add to a composition. As you have seen in previous tutorials, photographs can be blended or combined with other elements as part of a composition, or they can be placed in a composition as individual elements. When you adjusted and retouched photographs, you learned about image brightness, contrast, saturation, cropping, and exposure. All of those elements can be used to create a style for all of the photographs in a composition to give a unified, cohesive look to the project. Answering the following list of questions will help you to develop an intelligent photographic style for the project:

- What would you like to communicate with the photographs in the composition, and how can you accomplish those communication goals with the images you have?
- What looks will appeal to your target audience and reinforce your identity and metaphor?
- Will you cut elements from the images, or will you use the entire image?
- How will images be cropped? Will they be cropped tightly, like product shots? How will you adjust and retouch your images? Will you process your images to create a distinct artificial look, possibly by oversaturating the color or overexposing the images? Or, will you use digital adjustments to enhance the natural look of the photos?
- Will images have borders?

Images are a very important part of the FlashFlock brand and identity because the Web site is devoted to photography. Although some of the animal flash mobs are artificially created using digital software, the images attempt to maintain the look of realistic professional nature photos. This is a major contributing factor to the underlying humor of the FlashFlock brand. Because of this unique circumstance, Rick and George have provided the final versions of all of the photographs that you will use in the banner campaign. The photographs support your metaphor because they are depicting collisions of nature and the urban environment or urban concepts. Some of the images are even digital mashups of real photographic elements.

Jessica has already made some aesthetic decisions regarding how you will use the images in the banners. You'll add a border around all of the images to frame them and separate them from the background elements of the banners. The photographs will be the single largest element in the banners. This signifies their importance to the brand and identity. By positioning the photos to the right of the banner and making it the largest element, Jessica is using the viewer's natural tendency to first look at the upper left of a composition then to move right, then down (like the motion of reading) to reinforce the campaign goals visually. The viewer first sees the logo (which is fairly large in scale), then moves to the photograph, and finally to the text.

Because FlashFlock already has a specific photographic style, you will not need to create an alternate style for this project. You should use what you have learned from the decisions that Jessica, George, and Rick have made when you create projects in the future.

Even though you do not need to adjust, resize, crop, or retouch the photographs, you should prepare them before you add them to your composition. When possible, you should add the images to your composition as Smart Objects to enable you to continue to edit the images at their original size. This is especially helpful if you have high-quality camera raw images because those files enable you to achieve better results than you can achieve by adjusting compressed images. Regardless of the file type of the photograph, it is a good idea to convert your images to the correct color model and the correct color profile (for file formats that support color profiles) before you add them to your composition. This will allow you to make any necessary color adjustments to the original image file before you add it to the composition and will enable you to achieve the best possible results with the final composition.

To convert the image and add it to your working document:

1. Open **Fish.jpg** from the Photoshop9\Tutorial folder, and save the image as **FishAdjust.jpg** in the same folder, using Maximum quality for compression.

2. On the Application bar, click **Edit**, and then click **Convert to Profile**.

   The Source Space Profile for this image is Adobe RGB (1998) D65 WP 2.2 Gamma. Although this is in the RGB color model, it does not use the color profile that you selected when planning the project, so you'll select the correct color profile and convert the document.

3. In the Convert to Profile dialog box, select **sRGB IEC61966-2.1** from the Destination Space Profile list, and click the **OK** button.

   In this case, the changes to the document are so slight that they might not be perceptible, but the change is necessary to maintain consistency with color profiles across all of the documents in your project.

   Next, you'll convert the layer to a Smart Object, and you'll add a copy as a Smart Object to a layer of the FFBanners.psd document.

4. On the Application bar, click the **Arrange Documents** icon ![icon], and then click the horizontal **2 Up** icon ![icon] to display both images in the Document window. Click in the **FishAdjust.jpg** Document window to select it, if necessary.

5. On the Layers panel, right-click the **Background** layer of the FishAdjust.jpg document, and click **Convert to Smart Object** on the shortcut menu. On the Layers panel, rename the layer **Fish**. See Figure 9-44.

| Figure 9-44 | Color Profile converted with layer converted to a Smart Object |

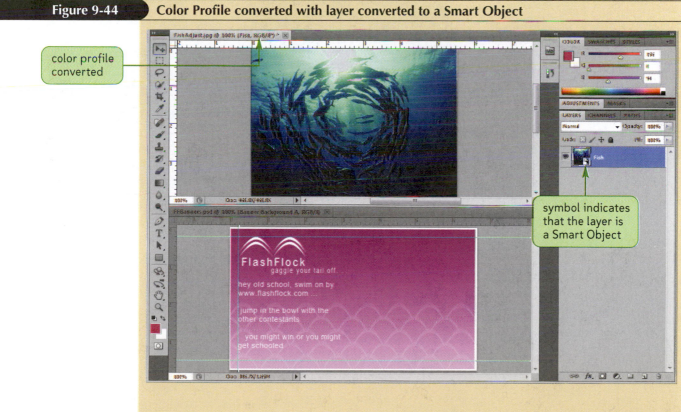

color profile converted

symbol indicates that the layer is a Smart Object

6. Save the FishAdjust.jpg document as **FishAdjust.psd** in the Photoshop9\Tutorial folder.

7. On the Layers panel, select the **Fish** layer, and drag it over the FFBanners.psd document in the Document window. Release the mouse button to add the image to the document as a Smart Object, and then close the FishAdjust.psd file. See Figure 9-45.

Figure 9-45   **Fish layer added to the composition as a Smart Object**

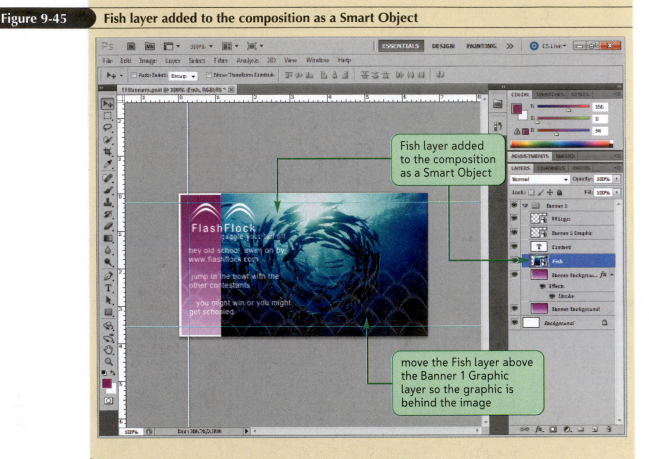

Fish layer added to the composition as a Smart Object

move the Fish layer above the Banner 1 Graphic layer so the graphic is behind the image

8. On the Layers panel, drag the Fish layer above the Banner 1 Graphic layer, if necessary, and then drag a vertical guide ¼ inch from the right border of the canvas.

9. Place the mouse pointer inside the image and drag the image down and to the left until the top border of the image is aligned to the top guide and the right border of the image is aligned to the right guide.

10. Press the **Ctrl+T** keys to activate Free Transform so that you can adjust the size of the image. See Figure 9-46.

Figure 9-46   **Fish layer selected with Free Transform**

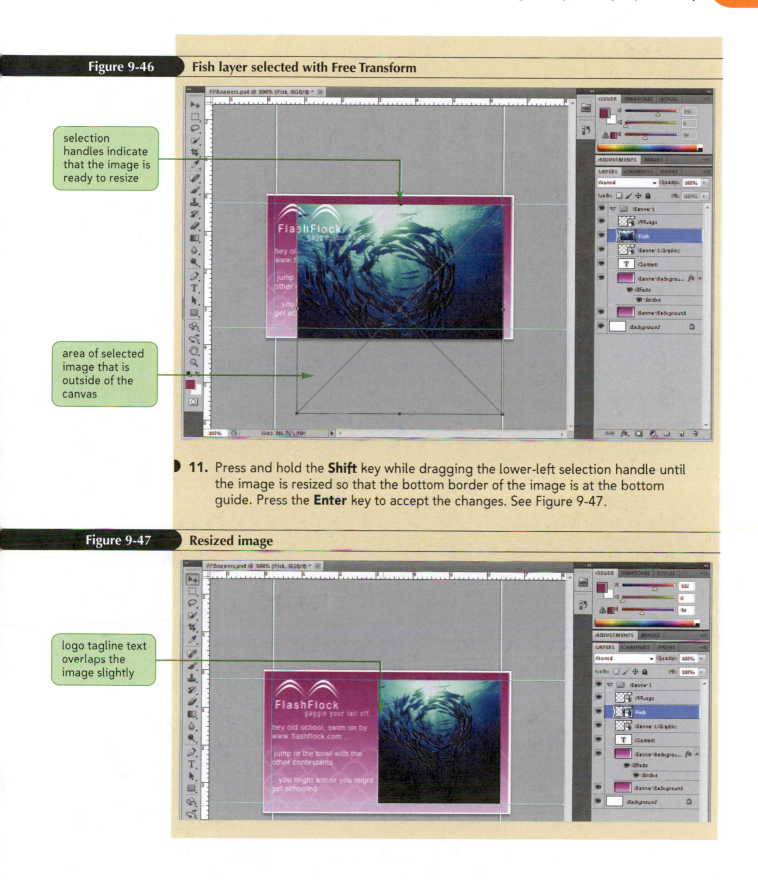

selection handles indicate that the image is ready to resize

area of selected image that is outside of the canvas

▶ **11.** Press and hold the **Shift** key while dragging the lower-left selection handle until the image is resized so that the bottom border of the image is at the bottom guide. Press the **Enter** key to accept the changes. See Figure 9-47.

Figure 9-47   **Resized image**

logo tagline text overlaps the image slightly

Now that all of the elements are in the composition, you can make your final adjustments and corrections. You'll add a border around the image, and you'll adjust elements in the composition so the image and tagline text do not overlap. You could accomplish this by shrinking the size of the logo or by shrinking the size of the image. Because your top goals for the campaign involve brand and identity recognition, you'll shrink the image and not the logo. Then, you'll reposition the resized image so it is centered between the guides. Finally, you'll hide the guides and examine your completed composition.

To make final adjustments:

1. On the Layers panel, double-click the **Fish** layer to open the Layer Style dialog box. In the Styles list, click **Stroke**, and use the following settings: Size: **3**, Position: **Inside**, Blend Mode: **Normal**, Opacity: **100%**, and Fill Type: **Color**. Double-click the **Color** swatch, and change the color to **white** (#ffffff). Click the **OK** button to close the Select stroke color dialog box, and then click the **OK** button to close the Layer Style dialog box.

2. Press the **Ctrl+T** keys, and then press and hold the **Shift** key while dragging the upper-left handle down until there is approximately ⅛ inch of space between the last period in the tagline and the edge of the image. Press the **Enter** key to accept the transformation.

3. Move the image until it is equal distance between the top and bottom guides. Press the **Ctrl+;** keys to hide the guides. See Figure 9-48.

| Figure 9-48 | Completed Banner 1 |

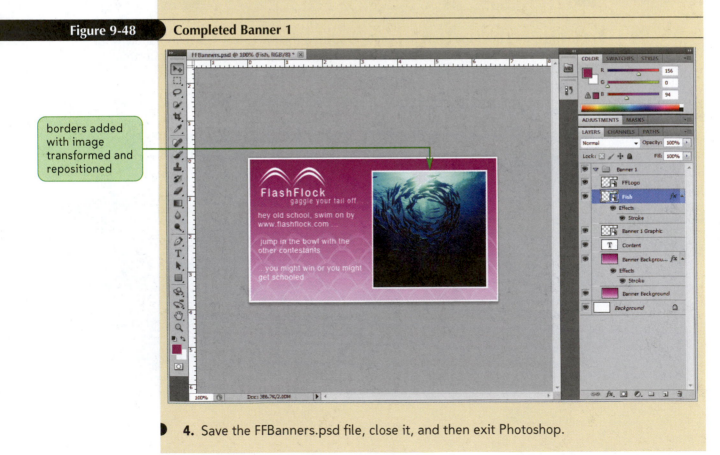

borders added with image transformed and repositioned

4. Save the FFBanners.psd file, close it, and then exit Photoshop.

Creating Output Files and Wrapping Up

You have completed your first composition, but you have not finished your work on the campaign. Once you have presented the comps to the client and you have made any necessary changes based on that review, the client will need to approve the project. At this point, you can create all of the output files that you will need. You can look back at your plan to see the exact size, resolution, color model, color profile, and file formats required for your output files. When all of the files have been created, you will provide them to the client or to the person who was specified in the plans, such as the printer. Then, you should gather all project working files from the members of your team into one folder. Make sure that everything is labeled in a way that will make sense in the future, and then you can archive the project. Every company has its own way of archiving files from projects that are no longer active. Follow your company's guidelines to ensure that anyone who needs these files in the future can locate and understand them.

Jessica plans to present both versions of Banner 1 to George and Rick. Once they approve the first banner, you'll create two additional banners for the campaign. Because the campaign is still in progress, you will not create output files or archive your working files.

PROSKILLS

Teamwork: Broadening Your Understanding to Strengthen Your Team

It is a good idea to gain a general understanding of all the components involved in creating an effective project. No matter what your role is, understanding the project as a whole and understanding what is required of your teammates makes you better equipped to do your job, and it makes you a more valuable member of the team.

Employers look for people who can understand the big picture and can contribute to the project in ways that may move beyond the scope of their current position. For example, if you design projects that will be displayed on the Web, it is a good idea to gain a basic understanding of HTML, even if you are not a programmer. Graphic designers benefit from this knowledge because they are better able to create useful Web site and banner ad designs when they understand the breadth and limits of HTML code. Project managers are better able to facilitate successful projects when they understand the various steps involved in creating a graphic design and the time it takes to complete each activity. The possibilities are endless; the more you know, the more valuable you become to the team.

REVIEW

Session 9.2 Quick Check

1. What is design?
2. What is the purpose of selecting a concept and metaphor?
3. Name two types of balance.
4. _____ _____ is the empty space in the canvas.
5. _____ is the art and technique of type arrangement, design, and modification.
6. _____ colors are pleasing to look at, creating a sense of balance and engagement.

Practice the skills you learned in the tutorial using the same case scenario.

Review Assignments

Data Files needed for the Review Assignments: FFBanners.psd, BannerText2.rtf, Graphics.psd, Penguins.jpg

George and Rick have signed off on Banner 1, and they are excited to see the other banners for the campaign. They selected the version that has the white border. You'll create an additional banner for the campaign using all of the aesthetic guidelines Jessica already set. Jessica is also considering making some additional materials to go with this banner, and she would like you to use the Kuler panel to select a monochromatic color palette using the background color from the new banner as the Base Color. Complete the following steps:

1. Start Photoshop while pressing the Ctrl+Alt+Shift keys. When you are prompted to delete the Adobe Photoshop Settings File, click Yes. On the Application bar, right-click Essentials, and then click Reset Essentials to reset the default workspace layout. Reset all tools and then collapse the Adjustments panel group.

2. Navigate to the Photoshop9\Tutorial folder, and open **FFBanners.psd**, which is the file in which you created Banner1. Save the document in the Photoshop9\Review folder as **FFBanners2.psd**.

3. Unhide the guides that you previously added to the file. (*Hint*: To view guides, press the Ctrl+; keys.) Drag an additional horizontal guide to the top of the photograph, drag another to the bottom edge of the photograph, drag a third to the top of the text, and then drag a fourth to the top of the graphic element in the background. You will now have a total of six horizontal guides and two vertical guides, which will enable you to place the objects in the same positions in the other banners.

4. Create a new layer group, drag it above the Banner 1 folder, and name it **Banner 2**. Drag the FFLogo layer above the Banner 2 group because it will be used in both banners. Hide the Banner 1 group.

5. Create a layer in the Banner 2 group and name it **Banner Background B**; use the Color Picker to set the foreground color to #b29a00 and to set the background color to #ffffff, if necessary.

6. Select the Gradient Tool, with the following settings: Gradient: Foreground to Background, Linear Gradient, Mode: Normal, and Opacity: 100%. Check Dither, and uncheck Reverse and Transparency, if necessary. Drag the mouse straight down the canvas to create the gradient banner background. (*Hint*: The logo and tagline will be visible once the background has been created.)

7. Copy the layer style from the Banner Background A layer in the Banner 1 group, and paste it on to the Banner Background B layer in the Banner 2 group.

8. Double-click the thumbnail image in the FFLogo layer, and then click the OK button in any dialog boxes that appear to open up the original logo Smart Object file.

9. Click beside the Murders In Numbers layer to make it visible, and hide the Gaggle Your Tail Off layer. Save and close the FFlogo.psd document, and view the updated logo in the FFBanners2 file.

10. Duplicate the text layer in the Banner 1 group, and drag the copied layer above the Banner Background B layer in the Banner 2 group. Double-click the thumbnail image for the copied layer to select the text in the Document window, and then delete the text. (Copying the Banner 1 layer ensures that the text area in Banner 2 is the exact same size as the text area in Banner 1.)

11. Open the **BannerText2.rtf** document located in the Photoshop9\Review folder, and copy the text in the Content section for Banner 2. Paste the text into the text box in the Photoshop window, and add a line break between each chunk. If any word breaks over two lines and is hyphenated, press the Enter key to create a line break and move the word to the next line. Close the BannerText2.rtf file.

12. Open the **Graphics.psd** file located in the Photoshop9\Review folder, select the horizontal 2 Up option from the Arrange Documents list, and drag the Banner 2 Graphic layer into the FFBanners2.psd file. Then, drag the layer into the Banner 2 group, above the Banner Background B layer.

13. Use the Move Tool to position the graphic using the guides, so it appears in the same position as it did in the Graphics document. Close the Graphics.psd document, and set the Banner 2 Graphic layer to display at 50% opacity. (You do not need to check the color profile because you did that when you created Banner 1.)

14. Open **Penguins.jpg** from the Photoshop9\Review folder, and convert the color profile to sRGB IEC61966-2.1. Then, convert the layer to a Smart Object, and name it **Penguins**. Save the file as **Penguins.psd** in the same folder.

15. Select the horizontal 2 Up option from the Arrange Documents list, drag the Penguins layer into the FFBanners.psd document, and then close the Penguins.psd document. Move the Penguins layer above the Banner 2 Graphic layer, if necessary.

16. Transform the image, and shrink it to the correct dimensions. (*Hint*: Remember to hold down the Shift key while you move the selection handle to keep the same image proportions while you shrink it.)

17. Copy the layer style from the Fish layer in the Banner 1 group, and paste the layer style on the Penguins layer.

18. Save the FFBanners2.psd document, and close it.

19. Open the Kuler panel to the Create tab. Select the Base Color swatch, type **b29a00** into the Hex text box, and then select Monochromatic from the Select Rule list.

20. Adjust the colors in the color palette by adjusting the position of the color circles on the color wheel and by adjusting the Control brightness by increasing or decreasing black slider until you have a color palette with which you are satisfied.

21. Save the theme as **FF Additional**.

22. Submit the results of the preceding steps to your instructor either in printed or electronic form, as requested.

Use your skills to plan a design project for an indie record label.

APPLY

Case Problem 1

Data Files needed for this Case Problem: Vision.rtf, CatLogo.gif, WebSite.tif

Catalyst Records   Catalyst Records is an indie record label founded in 2000 by Sara Lynn. Catalyst is based in Washington, D.C., and most of the bands affiliated with the label originated as part of the underground D.C. music scene, which centers around low-fi dub music (a genre of music that uses low-fidelity recording equipment to achieve interesting sounds) and post punk discord. Since the label created a Web site, some of its bands have developed a national following. Sara believes that this success is due in part to exposure from the Catalyst Web site. She would like to take this momentum to the next level by creating a banner ad that will be displayed on other sites that cater to the indie music scene. She has asked your company to create the banner, and you have been selected as the project manager. Your first task is to research and plan the project. Once your planning and research are complete, you will meet with Sara to get her input before you begin the design phase of the project. Complete the following steps:

1. Open the **Vision.rtf** file located in the Photoshop9\Case1 folder provided with your Data Files, and read the document to gain insight into Sara's vision for the project.

2. Open WordPad, create a new document, and save the document in the Photoshop9\Case1 folder as **CatPlan.rtf**.

3. In the CatPlan document, create a list of 10 goals for the project, in order of importance. Write the goals in the active voice. Combine goals where possible, and narrow your list to five goals for the ad.

4. Use what you have learned about Catalyst from Sara's Vision.rtf document, as well as your goals, to write a statement of purpose summarizing what you would like to accomplish with the ad.

5. Identify your target audience, and develop a viewer profile by answering the list of questions from Figure 9-3 in the tutorial. Write each question followed by your answer.

6. Use a search engine to locate statistics and additional information about your target audience, their interests, and your competitors. Search for the terms *low-fi music* and *dub music*. For each term, write down at least two statistics or insights you gather from the search results. Include the URL next to each statistic so that you can locate the information again in the future. Also, find at least two statistics or findings about each of the following: your target audience, aesthetics that may appeal to them, and about your competitors.

7. Start Photoshop while pressing the Ctrl+Alt+Shift keys. When you are prompted to delete the Adobe Photoshop Settings File, click Yes. On the Application bar, right-click Essentials, and then click Reset Essentials to reset the default workspace layout. Reset all tools.

8. Open **CatLogo.gif** from the Photoshop9\Case1 folder. Examine the logo, and then close it.

9. Open **WebSite.tif** from the Photoshop9\Case1 folder. Examine the file, and then close it.

10. Write a few sentences about Catalyst's branding and identity, and indicate how you will incorporate the current aesthetic into the banner ad design.

11. Use a search engine to determine the standard size for horizontal banner ads, and then determine the exact height, width, resolution, color space, and file format that you will use for your final output files. Document those specifications in the CatPlan document.

12. Save your work, and exit Photoshop, if necessary.

13. Submit the results of the preceding steps to your instructor either in printed or electronic form, as requested.

Using Figure 9-49 as a guide, create a mailer for a boutique.

CREATE

Case Problem 2

Data Files needed for this Case Problem: Planning.rtf, Mailer1Image.jpg, Mailer.psd, ElGalLogo.ai

El Gallinero   El Gallinero is a boutique located in the quaint harbor town of Portland, Maine. The shop imports and sells a stunning array of Mexican art and handcrafts. The owner, Tika, has long been known as the *Chicken Goddess*, a name she got when she started raising specialty breed show chickens. "I have a love of all things Mexican and all things chicken, so calling the store El Gallinero, which means *the roost*, was a natural choice." Tika would like you to create a postcard-sized mailer that she can print out on her color laser printer and mail as part of her store marketing campaign. She has worked with a consultant who planned the project extensively and has provided all of the information that you will need to design and create the mailer. See Figure 9-49 for an example of a possible mailer design.

Figure 9-49   El Gallinero mailer

Complete the following steps:

1. Open **Planning.rtf** located in the Photoshop9\Case2 folder. Read the document and visit the Web sites listed in the Research – Competitors section to familiarize yourself with the planning and research for the project.

2. Start Photoshop while pressing the Ctrl+Alt+Shift keys. When you are prompted to delete the Adobe Photoshop Settings File, click Yes. On the Application bar, right-click Essentials, and then click Reset Essentials to reset the default workspace layout. Reset all tools.

3. Open **Mailer1Image.jpg** from the Photoshop9\Case2 folder to see the image that Tika has provided for you to use in the mailer.

4. Open **Mailer.psd** from the Photoshop9\Case2 folder, and save as **ElMailer1.psd**. Hide the guides, examine the Background layer, and then show the guides. (*Hint*: The term *bleed* is a print term defining the area outside of the borders of the final composition, into which the background extends. Standard bleed is ¼ inch around each edge. This area provides the printer with a small amount of space to move around paper and account for slight deviations when cutting print materials. Cuts are generally made at the inside border of the bleed area, and the area just inside the bleed is usually reserved for noncrucial print elements, such as backgrounds. Print is usually not allowed in the outside ¼ inch bordering the bleed to ensure that slight deviations in cutting do not affect important design components.)

5. Select the horizontal 2 Up option from the Arrange Documents list, so you can view the image and the mailer document while you are making aesthetic decisions for the composition.

 EXPLORE   6. Open a Windows Explorer window, and navigate to the **ElGalLogo.ai** file located in the Photoshop9\Case2 folder. Drag the ElGalLogo.ai file over the ElMailer1.psd document in the Photoshop Document window. Click the OK button in the Place PDF dialog box, and press the Enter key to insert the logo as a Smart Object in the ElMailer1 document.

7. Examine the logo to help you determine the look and feel for the mailer.

8. Create a concept and metaphor for the mailer, and then look up the term *bleed* in a search engine if you need additional insight on how this should be laid out.

9. Create a layout for the mailer, and create a wireframe of the layout.

10. Open the Create tab of the Kuler panel, and create a color theme for the mailer. Save the theme as **Mailer**. Add the theme to your Swatches panel, and then close the Kuler panel. (*Hint*: Consider the colors in the logo and image when creating your theme. You can enter the hexadecimal code for a color from the image or logo as the Base Color to get started.)

11. Add colors to the background and anywhere else that they are needed. (*Hint*: Once you have added a background, you can use the guides to show you where the bleed area is and where it is safe to place text.)

12. Develop a graphic style, and then create graphic elements and add them to your composition; also transform and adjust the logo graphic as necessary so it works in your composition.

13. Add layer styles, adjustment layers, and masks as needed to create the look you have envisioned.

14. Add the Mailer1Image.jpg image to your composition and adjust it as necessary to make it work with your layout and design.

15. Add the copy text from the Planning document to the composition, and then adjust the color and style of the text to fit your composition.

16. Review your composition, and make any necessary adjustments.

17. Save your image, close all open files, and exit Photoshop.

18. Submit the results of the preceding steps to your instructor either in printed or electronic form, as requested.

Use your skills to plan a project for a small pub.

APPLY

Case Problem 3

Data Files needed for this Case Problem: Vision.rtf, Promo1.png, Promo2.png, LogoBlack.png, LogoWhite.png

The Rookery   The Rookery is a small, English-style pub in Nashville, Tennessee, that specializes in serving traditional fish and chips. The owner, Brian Botan, has decided to run a special on the pub's famous fish and chips, and he would like your company to create the insert that he can place in the menu. If this first promotion works well, Brian would like your company to provide a new insert once a month. You have been selected to head the project, and your first job is to read Brian's vision and to create a plan, which you will present to Brian. Complete the following steps:

1. Open **Vision.rtf** from the Photoshop9\Case3 folder, and read the document to gain insight into what Brian would like to accomplish with the project.

2. Start Photoshop while pressing the Ctrl+Alt+Shift keys. When you are prompted to delete the Adobe Photoshop Settings File, click Yes. On the Application bar, right-click Essentials, and then click Reset Essentials to reset the default workspace layout. Reset all tools.

3. Open the following images from the Photoshop9\Case3 folder: **Promo1.png**, **Promo2.png**, **LogoBlack.png**, and **LogoWhite.png**. Examine the files to get an idea of the Rookery's style, and then close the files and exit Photoshop.

4. Open WordPad, create a new document, and save the document in the Photoshop9\Case3 folder as **Plan.rtf**.

5. In the Plan document, create a list of 10 goals for the insert, and put them in order of importance. Combine goals where possible, make sure they are in active voice, and narrow your final list to five goals for the insert.

6. Use what you have learned about the Rookery from Brian's Vision document and your goals to write a statement of purpose summarizing what you would like to accomplish with the ad.

7. Identify your target audience and develop a viewer profile by answering the list of questions from Figure 9-3 in the tutorial. Write each question followed by your answer.

8. Use a search engine to locate statistics and additional information about your target audience, their interests, and your competitors. Search for the following terms: *English pubs*, *pub food*, and *English pub advertisements* (try searching for images on this one). Write down at least two statistics or findings about each term. Include the URL by each statistic, so you can locate the information again in the future. Also, find at least two statistics or findings about your target audience, about aesthetics that may appeal to them, and about the Rookery's competitors.

9. Write a few sentences about the Rookery's branding and identity and how you will incorporate the current aesthetic into the insert design, and save your work.

10. Submit the results of the preceding steps to your instructor either in printed or electronic form, as requested.

Using Figure 9-50 as a guide, create something that expresses your point of view.

CREATE

Case Problem 4

Data Files needed for this Case Problem: Specs.rtf, Logos.psd

Montana Science and History Museum   The Montana Museum of Science and History is a medium-sized museum in Billings, Montana, run by director Andy Hall. Andy has decided that to stay relevant and to engage a contemporary adult audience, the museum needs to embrace current technologies and social media. In an effort to meet this goal, Andy has asked your firm to develop an iPad application that will enable patrons to use technology to explore and engage with the artifacts and exhibits in a different way. He hopes this will forge new frontiers in the area of inquiry-based learning. You are leading the team that will design the interface for the application. You will follow the specs provided by the programming team, and you'll manage the interface design project from start to finish. Before you get started, look at a sample interface in Figure 9-50.

Figure 9-50   iPad interface for Montana Museum of Science and History

Complete the following steps:

1. Start Photoshop while pressing the Ctrl+Alt+Shift keys. When you are prompted to delete the Adobe Photoshop Settings File, click Yes. On the Application bar, right-click Essentials, and then click Reset Essentials to reset the default workspace layout. Reset all tools.

2. Open **Specs.rtf** from the Photoshop9\Case4 folder, and read Andy's vision statement and the programming team's specifications and requirements for the interface project.

3. Open WordPad, create a new document, and save the document in the Photoshop9\Case4 folder as **PadPlan.rtf**.

4. Create a list of potential goals for the project, prioritize the list, and combine goals when possible. Narrow the list to five goals, and then write a statement of purpose for the project.

5. Based on what you have been told, identify the target audience and create a viewer profile.

6. Use a search engine to research audience interests and find out what competitors are doing. Provide three insights about your audience and three insights about the competition. Include URLs that support your findings.

7. In Photoshop, open the **Logos.psd** document to view two versions of the museum's logo to gain insight into the museum's current branding and identity.

8. Based on your research and insights, create a concept and metaphor for the project and add them to your PadPlan document.

9. Use Photoshop to create a wireframe for the composition, and save the file in the Phtoshop9\Case4 folder as **Wireframe.psd**. (Use the information in the Specs document to determine the document size, color model, and resolution and to see a list of the components that the interface must include, as well as applicable dimensions.)

10. In the PadPlan document, write a short paragraph explaining how your layout supports your metaphor and project goals. Also, explain how your layout is balanced and how you use white space in the composition.

11. Use the Kuler panel to create a color theme for the project. Save your theme as **Museum iPad**, and add the theme to the Swatches panel. Answer the questions from the "Creating a Graphic Style" section of the tutorial. Select a graphic style, and then write a short paragraph in your PadPlan document explaining your style choice. Save the PadPlan document, and close the file.

12. Create a new Photoshop document using the information in the Specs document regarding size, resolution, and so forth. Save the document as **IPadInterface.psd** in the Photoshop9\Case4 folder.

13. Create each of the following graphic elements on its own layer, and name the layer with the element name. Or, if your style dictates that you use multiple layers for an element, create a layer group with the element name and place all of the layers for the element in the file group. Elements should include the following:
    - Background and border (You can create the border as one object, or you can create each side of the border on its own layer.)
    - Help button
    - Tool button
    - Art button
    - Home button
    - Screen – Right
    - Screen – Left

Remember that each element should have the style that you selected and explained above.

14. Add the museum's logo to the composition. You can use one of the versions included in the Logos.psd file, or you can create a new version of the logo that will work with your design.

15. Using the font, color, and size that you will use for the general body text in the project, add the following text on the left screen: **The interactive tools will be displayed on this screen.** On the right screen, add the following text: **Text and information driven dynamically by the user's interaction with the tool will be displayed on this screen.** (Adding text will help the client identify the various components, and it will provide an example of what text will look like in the project.)

16. Examine what you have created and adjust elements as needed to create a cohesive, harmonious composition that reinforces goals, metaphor, organization branding, and identity and that will appeal to the target audience.

17. Save the file, and exit Photoshop.

18. Submit the results of the preceding steps to your instructor either in printed or electronic form, as requested.

ENDING DATA FILES

Photoshop9 →

Tutorial

AltGraphics.rtf
Color.rtf
Concept.rtf
CurrentBrand.rtf
FFBanners.psd
FishAdjust.jpg
FishAdjust.psd
Goals.rtf
Research.rtf
Target.rtf
Wireframe.psd

Review

FFBanners2.psd
Penguins.psd

Case1

CatPlan.rtf

Case2

ElMailer1.psd

Case3

Plan.rtf

Case4

IPadInterface.psd
PadPlan.rtf
Wireframe.psd

Decision Making

Making Design Decisions

Decision making is the process of choosing the best option among possible alternative courses of action. Decision making is a crucial skill because business people at all organizational levels must make decisions. Understanding the decision-making process will enable you to make better decisions and will give you greater confidence in implementing your decisions.

Typically, when you make a decision, you should complete the following steps:

1. Gather relevant information.
2. Make predictions about factors outside of your control.
3. Select the best alternative.
4. Prepare an action plan to implement your decision.
5. Take action and monitor results.
6. Evaluate the consequences of your decision, and take corrective action, if needed.

Complex decisions—especially those that affect other people and those that could have a significant monetary impact—should be made in a systematic way, following the above steps. This will increase the chances that the decision you make will be the right one. Less complex decisions may require only some of the steps.

Gather Relevant Information and Make Predictions

In order to effectively evaluate a potential course of action, you need to gather information and data. The relevant information may include quantitative factors, such as the required resolution for a Web banner ad, and qualitative factors, such as the concept and metaphor upon which a design decision must be based. You should also make predictions about relevant factors outside of your immediate control, such as how the target audience might respond to a particular color scheme or layout.

Select the Best Alternative

After gathering information and making predictions about outside factors, selecting the best alternative may require asking additional questions, such as:

- Do you have the time and resources to implement each alternative?
- Will each alternative be acceptable even if the outcome is not perfect or if some unconsidered factors emerge after implementation?
- How comfortable are you (and/or your client) with the decision?

If none of the alternatives you have considered appear to be the correct choice, continue to develop and analyze alternatives until one emerges as the best option.

Prepare an Action Plan

Once you have made a decision, prepare an action plan that accounts for all the steps and resources required to implement the decision. Make a list of the specific tasks that must be completed. Develop a schedule that takes into consideration how long it will take to complete each task, as well as what tasks must be completed before others can be started. Determine the key milestones in your action plan, and decide who is accountable for those milestones.

ProSkills

Take Action and Monitor Results

After you develop an action plan, you are ready to take action. Monitor the results of your action plan as you move forward. As progress is made, check off completed tasks and compare your progress to your schedule. Occasionally, the best-laid plans do veer off course. In this case, determine why, when, and where the tasks fell behind schedule to help get back on course.

Evaluate Your Decision and Take Corrective Action

Once you have completed your action plan, evaluate your decision to determine if it was the correct course of action. If necessary, take corrective action to improve the results. To wrap up, document your experiences in case a similar decision needs to be made in the future. By reflecting on the decision-making process and its implementation, you can learn from the experience and make better decisions down the road.

PROSKILLS

Design a Logo and a Brochure

Photoshop is the industry-standard tool for professional graphic design and photo manipulation, and it has a wide array of uses within the industry. In this exercise, you will use Photoshop to design a logo and a brochure for a fictional company. The brochure should include at least three photographic images that you will crop, correct, and retouch.

1. Decide on a business that you will use for this project. Select a name for the business, and determine what products and/or services the business provides.

2. Based on the business you have selected, determine an appropriate vision for the branding and identity of the company. Decide on goals, a statement of purpose, and a target audience for the brochure project. (Develop a viewer profile to help you determine the characteristics of the target audience.)

3. Use the Internet and a search engine to do research into the target audience and the competition. Develop specifications for output, including size, resolution, color space, color profile, and file type. Call a local printer, if necessary, to get the information you need to develop the specifications.

4. Create a concept and metaphor for the project, and decide how you will integrate both to create a unified theme.

5. In Photoshop, create a wireframe of the layout for the brochure (including a spot for the logo), using the specifications you finalized above. Review the wireframe, and decide if any additional changes need to be made.

6. Calibrate your monitor using Windows Color Calibration tool, if necessary. Then, in Photoshop, double check your color settings, create a new document, and set up a soft proof using your specifications.

7. Using the information you gathered about the target audience, and keeping in mind the project's goals and statement of purpose, use the Kuler panel to decide on a color palette. Your color selections should also reflect the decisions you made about the project's concept and metaphor.

ProSkills

8. Select fonts, design a graphic style, and create graphics—including a logo for the business. Then, add colors, text, and the graphics to the composition using layers, shapes, masks, tools, and adjustments.

9. Select at least three photographic images for the brochure; the original images should be in a camera raw format, if possible. Decide on a photographic style, and crop, adjust, and retouch the photos, as necessary. Convert the photographs to the correct color profile, if necessary, and add them to the composition as Smart Objects. Finally, use Free Transform to make any small adjustments to the images in the composition, and add layer styles, as needed.

10. Review the composition as a whole and make any small changes that are necessary to ensure that the composition has a harmonious balance and flow. Create a layer comp that you could use to present your final composition.

11. Using WordPad, create a document in which you provide details on the business you chose. Discuss your vision for the branding and identity of the company, as well as the project goals, statement of purpose, target audience, and project concept and metaphor. Explain how your design choices reinforce the company's identity and the project goals, purpose, concept, and metaphor.

12. Submit your completed files to your instructor, as requested.

GLOSSARY/INDEX

TASK REFERENCE

TASK	PAGE #	RECOMMENDED METHOD
Adjustment layer preset, use	PS 94	On the Layers panel, select a layer to adjust, click ▷ next to the desired preset category on the Adjustments panel, click the desired preset
Adjustment layer, add	PS 91	On the Layers panel, select a layer to adjust, click the desired adjustment on the Adjustments panel, change the settings as desired
Adjustment layer, delete	PS 93	On the Layers panel, drag the adjustment layer to the lower right corner of the Layers panel to 🗑
Background color, change	PS 175	On the Color panel or on the Tools panel, click ▪, click ▫ again to open the Color Picker dialog box to select a color or click 🖉 to sample a new background color
Baseline shift, specify	PS 315	Select the text, type a baseline shift value in the [Aᵃ 0pt] box on the Character panel, click ✔
Blending mode, apply	PS 149	On the Layers panel, select the layer, click the blending modes arrow, click the desired blending mode
Blur Tool, use	PS 375	*See* Reference box: Blurring an Area of an Image
Brush preset library, load	PS 211	On the Brush Presets panel, click ▤, click a preset library
Brush preset picker, open	PS 45	On the Tools panel, click 🖌, click 🖌▾ on the options bar
Brush preset, create	PS 214	On the Brush panel, select a brush and specify the settings, click ▤ on the Brush Presets panel, click New Brush Preset; in the Brush Name dialog box, type a name for the preset in the Name box, click the Capture Brush Size in Preset check box to select it, if necessary, click OK
Brush Tool, activate	PS 207	Press the B key
Brush Tool, use	PS 207	On the Tools panel, click 🖌, set the options on the options bar or click 🖌 to set the brush size and hardness, drag on the canvas to create a brushstroke
Brush tool, use to draw straight line	PS 209	On the Tools panel, click 🖌, set the options on the options bar or click 🖌 to set the brush size and hardness; click on the canvas at the starting point for the line, press and hold the Shift key, click at the end point for the line
Burn Tool, use	PS 372	On the Tools panel, click 🖐, on the options bar select brush type, set brush diameter, select Range, adjust Exposure, click Protect Tones, paint the area in the image to be adjusted
Camera Raw preferences, adjust	PS 393	On the Application bar, click Edit, point to Preferences, click Camera Raw, adjust settings, click OK
Camera Raw, adjust saturation in an image	PS 415	On the Basic tab of the Adjustments panel in Camera Raw, drag the Clarity, Vibrance, and Saturation sliders
Camera Raw, adjust zoom level in	PS 395	On the toolbar located above the Document window in the Camera Raw dialog box, click 🔍, click in the Document window to increase zoom in preset increments
Camera Raw, crop image in	PS 396	On the toolbar located above the Document window in the Camera Raw dialog box, click 🔲, click in the Document window, drag to draw a rectangle that covers the area of the image you want to crop to

TASK	PAGE #	RECOMMENDED METHOD
Camera Raw, display clipped pixels	PS 407	In the Camera Raw dialog box, click ▲ or ▲
Camera Raw, make tonal adjustments	PS 410	On the Basic tab of the Adjustments panel in Camera Raw, adjust the sliders for Exposure, Recovery, Fill Light, Blacks, Brightness, and Contrast
Camera Raw, open a file in	PS 395	*See* Reference box: Opening a File in Camera Raw
Camera Raw, reposition image in	PS 396	On the toolbar located above the Document window in the Camera Raw dialog box, click 🖐, drag the image in the Document window to reposition
Camera Raw, save adjustments and close file	PS 400	In the Camera Raw dialog box, click Done to save adjustments, close the file
Camera Raw, save adjustments and open image as a Smart Object in Photoshop	PS 401	In the Camera Raw dialog box, click Open Object to save adjustments and open a copy of the Camera Raw file as a Smart Object in Photoshop
Camera Raw, set workflow options	PS 399	*See* Reference box: Setting Workflow Options in Camera Raw
Camera Raw, white balance an image	PS 408	*See* Reference box: White Balancing an Image
Canvas, extend	PS 96	*See* Reference box: Extending the Canvas
Canvas, trim	PS 98	*See* Reference box: Trimming the Canvas
Clipped pixels, display in Camera Raw	PS 407	In the Camera Raw dialog box, click ▲ or ▲
Clipping Mask, create	PS 323	On the Layers panel, select a layer to serve as the clipping mask, click Layer on the Application bar, click Create Clipping Mask
Color Balance adjustment, apply to a selection	PS 233	Make a selection in an image, click ⚖ on the Adjustments panel, drag the color sliders to achieve the desired color balance
Color mode, change	PS 80	On the Application bar, click Image, point to Mode, click the desired mode
Color picker, open	PS 47	On the options bar, click the Color box
Color profile, convert	PS 433	On the Application bar, click Edit, click Convert to Profile, select the desired settings in the Convert to Profile dialog box, click OK
Color range, select localized	PS 239	On the Application bar, click Select, click Color Range; in the Color Range dialog box, select Sampled Colors, if necessary, click the Localized Color Clusters check box, click part of the image that includes the desired color range, click OK
Color settings, adjust	PS 431	On the Application bar, click Edit, click Color Settings, select the desired settings in the Color Settings dialog box, click OK
Color, adjust using Auto Color	PS 349	On the Application bar, click Image, click Auto Color
Color, sample using the Eyedropper Tool	PS 168	*See* Reference box: Using the Eyedropper Tool
Color, specify using the Color Panel	PS 171	*See* Reference box: Specifying a Color on the Color Panel
Color, specify using the Color Picker dialog box	PS 173	On the Color panel or the Tools panel, click ■ or ▢, click a color on the color ramp, click a shade of that color in the color field, click OK
Color, specify Web-safe colors using the Color Picker dialog box	PS 173	In the Color Picker dialog box, click the Only Web Colors check box to select it
Complex selection, create	PS 236	*See* Reference box: Adding to a Selection to Create a Complex Selection

TASK	PAGE #	RECOMMENDED METHOD
Content-Aware Fill, use	PS 254	Make a selection in an image, click Edit on the Application bar, click Fill; in the Fill dialog box, select Content-Aware from the Use drop-down menu, set the Blending Mode and the Opacity, click OK
Contrast and tone, adjust using the Curves adjustment	PS 358	On the Adjustment panel, click [icon], click on line in the Curves grid, drag to adjust contrast and tone
Contrast, adjust using Auto Contrast	PS 349	On the Application bar, click Image, click Auto Contrast
Crop Guide Overlay, use to crop an image	PS 344	*See* Reference box: Cropping an Image
Crop Tool, activate	PS 344	Press the Shift+C keys
Curves adjustment, apply	PS 358	On the Adjustment panel, click [icon], click on line in the Curves grid, drag to adjust contrast and tone
Custom document preset, delete	PS 86	*See* Reference box: Deleting a Custom Document Preset
Custom document preset, save	PS 85	*See* Reference box: Saving a Custom Document Preset
Custom Shape picker, open	PS 46	On the Tools panel, click [icon], click [icon] on the options bar
Darkest point in an image, mark using the Threshold adjustment	PS 353	*See* Reference box: Marking Lightest and Darkest Pixels with the Threshold Adjustment
Document preset, delete a custom	PS 86	*See* Reference box: Deleting a Custom Document Preset
Document preset, save a custom	PS 85	*See* Reference box: Saving a Custom Document Preset
Document window, float	PS 19	Point to a Document window tab, press and hold the mouse button, drag the tab to the middle of the workspace, release the mouse button
Document, navigate to an open	PS 17	Click the Document window tab of the desired document
Documents, arrange in Document window	PS 20	On the Application bar, click [icon], click the desired arrangement option
Dodge Tool, use	PS 369	*See* Reference box: Brightening an Image with the Dodge Tool
Eyedropper Tool, use	PS 168	*See* Reference box: Using the Eyedropper Tool
File, close	PS 22	On the Application bar, click File, click Close
File, create using a preset	PS 82	*See* Reference box: Creating a New File Using a Preset
File, navigate to an open	PS 17	Click the Document window tab of the desired file
File, open	PS 9	On the Application bar, click File, click Open, navigate to the folder containing the file, click the file, click Open
File, open recent	PS 17	On the Application bar, click File, point to Open Recent, click the filename
File, save as	PS 16	On the Application bar, click File, click Save As, select a file type in the Save As dialog box, type the new filename in the File name box, click Save
Files, close all	PS 23	On the Application bar, click File, click Close All
Files, display a list of open	PS 18	In the Document window, click [icon]
Filter Gallery, use	PS 271	On the Application bar, click Filter, click Filter Gallery, click a folder, click a filter, adjust the settings as desired, click OK
Font size, set	PS 299	Select the text, type a new font size in the [icon] box on the Character panel
Foreground and background colors, switch	PS 175	Press the X key

TASK	PAGE #	RECOMMENDED METHOD
Foreground color, change	PS 171	On the Color panel or on the Tools panel, click ⬛ to open the Color Picker dialog box to select a color or click 🖊 to sample a new foreground color
Freeze Mask Tool, use	PS 266	*See* Reference box: Using the Liquify Filter
Gradient fill layer, create	PS 195	At the bottom of the Layers panel, click ⬤, click Gradient, click the Gradient arrow in the Gradient Fill dialog box, click a gradient, click OK; on the Layers panel, adjust the Opacity setting as needed
Grid, show or hide	PS 41	On the Application bar, click View, point to Show, click Grid
Guides, add	PS 42	On the Application bar, click View, click New Guide, click the Vertical or Horizontal option button, type a value in the Position box, click OK
Guides, add by dragging	PS 42	Drag down from the horizontal ruler to place a horizontal guide; drag over from the vertical ruler to place a vertical guide
Hand Tool, activate	PS 44	Press the H key
Healing Brush Tool, use	PS 367	On the Tools panel, click 🖊, Alt-click to select source pixels for repair, place pointer at edge of problem area, paint
Help, access	PS 12	On the Application bar, click Help, click Photoshop Help, click the plus sign (+) next to the topic or subtopic, click the subtopic hyperlink
Help, access	PS 12	Press the F1 key
Help, search	PS 13	In left pane of the Help window, type a search term in the Search Help box, press Enter, in the left pane, click the topic
History Brush Tool, activate	PS 249	Press the Y key
History Brush Tool, use to return part of an image to a previous state	PS 248	*See* Reference box: Using the History Brush Tool to Return Part of an Image to a Previous History State
History panel, use to revert to a previous state	PS 244	*See* Reference box: Reverting to a Previous History State Using the History Panel
History state, delete	PS 246	On the History panel, click the history state, click 🗑
Horizontal point type, add to an image	PS 286	*See* Reference box: Adding Point Type to an Image
Horizontal type, rotate	PS 294	Select text with the Move Tool, click the Show Transform Controls check box on the options bar, place the mouse pointer at the corner of the bounding box, drag clockwise or counterclockwise to achieve the desired rotation, click ✔
Image resolution, change using resampling	PS 67	*See* Reference box: Changing Image Resolution Using Resampling
Image, adjust using Lab color mode	PS 378	On the Application bar, click Image, point to Mode, click Lab Color, click Don't Flatten, apply adjustment
Image, brighten shadows, highlights, or midtones using the Dodge Tool	PS 369	*See* Reference box: Brightening an Image with the Dodge Tool
Image, correct using Auto Color	PS 349	On the Application bar, click Image, click Auto Color
Image, correct using Auto Contrast	PS 349	On the Application bar, click Image, click Auto Contrast
Image, correct using Auto Tone	PS 348	On the Application bar, click Image, click Auto Tone
Image, crop	PS 344	*See* Reference box: Cropping an Image

TASK	PAGE #	RECOMMENDED METHOD
Image, crop in Camera Raw	PS 396	On the toolbar located above the Document window in the Camera Raw dialog box, click 🔳, click in the Document window, drag to draw a rectangle that covers the area of the image you want to crop to
Image, crop using the Rule of Thirds	PS 344	*See* Reference box: Cropping an Image
Image, darken shadows, highlights, or midtones using the Burn Tool	PS 372	On the Tools panel, click 🔳, on the options bar select brush type, set brush diameter, select Range, adjust Exposure, click Protect Tones, paint the area in the image to be adjusted
Image, display and pan in the Navigator	PS 102	On the Application bar, click Window, click Navigator, drag the view box in the Navigator to pan the image
Image, fit on screen	PS 341	Press the Ctrl+0 keys
Image, flatten	PS 154	On the Application bar, click Layer, click Flatten Image
Image, increase or decrease saturation, using the Sponge Tool	PS 373	On the Tools panel click 🔳, on the options bar, select brush type, set brush diameter, select Mode, adjust Flow, paint the area in the image to be adjusted
Image, pan	PS 44	On the Tools panel, click 🔳, click in the image, drag in the desired direction
Image, place	PS 139	On the Application bar, click File, click Place; in the Place dialog box navigate to and select the image you want to place, click Place
Image, remove imperfections using the Spot Healing Brush	PS 364	*See* Reference box: Applying the Spot Healing Brush Tool to an Image
Image, repair using the Healing Brush Tool	PS 367	On the Tools panel, click 🔳, Alt-click to select source pixels for repair, place pointer at edge of problem area, paint
Image, reposition in Camera Raw	PS 396	On the toolbar located above the Document window in the Camera Raw dialog box, click 🔳, drag the image in the Document window
Image, resample	PS 67	*See* Reference box: Changing Image Resolution Using Resampling
Image, rotate by a preset amount	PS 105	On the Application bar, click Image, point to Image Rotation, select a rotation option
Image, rotate by an arbitrary amount	PS 105	On the Application bar, click Image, point to Image Rotation, click Arbitrary, type an angle in the Angle box, select a direction option button, click OK
Image, save adjustments and close file in Camera Raw	PS 400	In the Camera Raw dialog box, click Done to save adjustments and close the file
Image, save adjustments and open image as a Smart Object in Photoshop	PS 401	In the Camera Raw dialog box, click Open Object to save adjustments and open a copy of the Camera Raw file as a Smart Object in Photoshop
Image, sharpen using the Sharpen Tool	PS 377	On the Tools panel, click 🔳, on the options bar select brush type, set brush diameter, select Mode, adjust Strength, check Protect Detail, paint the area in the image to be adjusted
Image, soften using the Blur Tool	PS 375	*See* Reference box: Blurring an Area of an Image
Image, straighten with Ruler Tool	PS 341	*See* Reference box: Straightening an Image
Image, white balance in Camera Raw	PS 408	*See* Reference box: White Balancing an Image

TASK	PAGE #	RECOMMENDED METHOD
Image, zoom	PS 44	On the Tools panel, click 🔍, click the image
Image, zoom to 100%	PS 44	Press the Ctrl+1 keys
Image, zoom to a specified percentage	PS 44	On the status bar, double-click the current zoom percentage, type a new percentage value, press Enter
Image, zoom using a preset	PS 100	On the Tools panel, click 🔍, click a zoom preset on the options bar
JPEG file, open in Camera Raw	PS 416	In Mini Bridge, right-click the image, click Open in Camera Raw
JPEG, save a file as	PS 63	On the Application bar, click File, click Save As, click the Format arrow, click JPEG (*.JPG, *.JPEG, *.JPE), click Save; in the JPEG Options dialog box, click the desired Quality setting, click the desired Format Option, click OK
Kuler panel, add a selected theme to the Swatches panel	PS 484	On the Browse tab of the Kuler panel, select a theme, click 🔳
Kuler panel, create theme	PS 485	*See* Reference box: Creating a Theme on the Kuler Panel
Kuler panel, open	PS 484	*See* Reference box: Using the Kuler Panel
Kuler panel, view and edit themes	PS 484	*See* Reference box: Using the Kuler Panel
Lab color mode, adjust image using	PS 378	On the Application bar, click Image, point to Mode, click Lab Color, click Don't Flatten, apply adjustment
Lasso Tool, use	PS 254	On the Tools panel, click ⟳, drag to make a selection
Layer comp, apply	PS 146	On the Layer comps panel, click ▢ to the left of the layer comp
Layer comp, create	PS 146	On the Application bar, click Window, click Layer Comps, click 🔳 at the bottom of the Layer Comps panel; in the New Layer Comp dialog box, type a layer comp name in the Name box, type a comment in the Comment box, click OK
Layer comp, delete	PS 147	On the Layer Comps panel, click the layer comp, click 🗑
Layer edges, display	PS 131	On the Application bar, click View, point to Show, click Layer Edges
Layer edges, hide	PS 131	On the Application bar, click View, point to Show, click Layer Edges to deselect it
Layer Style dialog box, open	PS 185	On the Layers panel, double-click fx or double-click the layer thumbnail, select the desired settings in the dialog box, click OK
Layer style, apply	PS 183	On the Layers panel, select a layer, click a style on the Styles panel
Layer style, copy and paste	PS 324	On the Layers panel, right-click a layer, click Copy Layer Style, right-click the layer you want to copy the style to, click Paste Layer Style
Layer(s), deselect	PS 121	On the Application bar, click Select, click Deselect Layers
Layer, add empty	PS 124	At the bottom of the Layers panel, click 🔳
Layer, add new by copying and pasting	PS 127	On the layers panel, select a layer, click a selection tool on the Tools panel, drag to make a selection on the canvas; on the Application bar, click Edit, click Copy, click Edit again, click Paste
Layer, change color on the Layers panel	PS 129	On the Layers panel, right-click the layer, click Layer Properties, click the Color arrow in the Layer properties dialog box, click a color, click OK
Layer, change opacity of	PS 151	On the Layers panel, drag the mouse pointer over the word Opacity to the right to increase the opacity and to the left to decrease the opacity

TASK	PAGE #	RECOMMENDED METHOD
Layer, create a gradient fill	PS 195	At the bottom of the Layers panel, click ⬤, click Gradient, click the Gradient arrow in the Gradient Fill dialog box, click a gradient, click OK; on the Layers panel, adjust the Opacity setting as needed
Layer, create a pattern fill	PS 196	At the bottom of the Layers panel, click ⬤, click Pattern, click the pattern thumbnail in the Pattern Fill dialog box, click a pattern, click OK; on the Layers panel, adjust the Opacity setting as needed
Layer, create a solid color fill	PS 192	At the bottom of the Layers panel, click ⬤, click Solid Color, select a color in the Pick a solid color dialog box, click OK; on the Layers panel, adjust the Opacity setting as needed
Layer, delete	PS 136	On the Layers panel, select the layer, press Delete
Layer, hide and redisplay	PS 137	On the Layers panel, click 👁 to the left of the layer
Layer, lock entire	PS 144	On the Layers panel, click 🔒
Layer, lock image pixels	PS 144	On the Layers panel, select the layer, click 🖌
Layer, lock position	PS 144	On the Layers panel, click ✛
Layer, lock transparent pixels	PS 144	On the Layers panel, click ▨
Layer, move to change position on canvas	PS 133	On the Layers panel, select a layer, point to the layer on the canvas, click and drag the layer to a new position
Layer, move to change visibility	PS 132	*See* Reference box: Moving a Layer to Change Its Visibility
Layer, redisplay	PS 137	On the Layers panel, click ▢ to the left of the layer
Layer, rename	PS 129	On the Layers panel, click the layer, double-click the current layer name, type a new name, press Enter
Layer, select	PS 120	Click the layer on the Layers panel
Layers, align	PS 135	*See* Reference box: Aligning Layers in a Composition
Layers, distribute	PS 136	*See* Reference box: Distributing Layers in a Composition
Layers, group on the Layers panel	PS 152	*See* Reference box: Grouping Layers
Layers, hide all but selected layer	PS 137	On the Layers panel, select a layer, press and hold the Alt key, click 👁 on the selected layer
Layers, merge selected	PS 153	Select the layers, click Layer on the Application bar, click Merge Layers
Layers, merge visible	PS 153	On the Application bar, click Layer, click Merge Visible
Layers, select multiple	PS 121	*See* Reference box: Selecting Multiple Layers
Layers, select similar	PS 122	On the Layers panel, select a layer, click Select on the Application bar, click Similar Layers
Layers, stamp selected	PS 153	Select the layers, press the Ctrl+Alt+E keys
Layers, ungroup on the Layers panel	PS 152	On the Layers panel, select the group, click Layer on the Application bar, click Ungroup Layers
Lightest point in an image, mark using the Threshold adjustment	PS 353	*See* Reference box: Marking Lightest and Darkest Pixels with the Threshold Adjustment
Liquify Filter, use	PS 266	*See* Reference box: Using the Liquify Filter

TASK	PAGE #	RECOMMENDED METHOD
Magic Wand Tool, use to add pixels to a selection	PS 232	On the Tools panel, click [icon]; on the options bar, specify a Tolerance setting, and select or deselect Anti-alias and Contiguous as desired, click [icon], click the pixels to be added to the selection
Magnetic Lasso Tool, use	PS 257	*See* Reference box: Using the Magnetic Lasso Tool
Mini Bridge, browse files in	PS 71	Click the Browse Files button, click a folder or file in the Navigation pod, and repeat until the desired file appears in the Content pod
Mini Bridge, launch	PS 71	On the Application bar, click [Mb]
Monitor, calibrate	PS 423	*See* Reference box: Calibrating a Monitor
Move Tool, activate	PS 129	Press the V key
Multiple files, open at once	PS 15	*See* Reference box: Opening Multiple Files at Once
Navigator, display and use to pan an image	PS 102	On the Application bar, click Window, click Navigator, drag the view box in the Navigator to pan the image
New file, create using a preset	PS 82	*See* Reference box: Creating a New File Using a Preset
Opacity, change for a layer	PS 151	On the Layers panel, drag the mouse pointer over the word Opacity to the right to increase the opacity and to the left to decrease the opacity
Panel dock, expand	PS 34	Click [icon]
Panel dock, minimize	PS 33	On the right side of the title bar for the docked panels, click [icon]
Panel tab, select	PS 30	Click the desired panel tab in a panel group
Panel, close	PS 32	On the title bar for the panel, click [icon], click Close
Panel, close from Window menu	PS 33	On the Application bar, click Window, click the panel name to remove the check mark
Panel, display	PS 31	On the Application bar, click Window, click the desired panel
Panel group, move	PS 35	Point to the panel bar to the right of the panel tab, press and hold the mouse button, drag the panel group to the desired location, release the mouse button
Panels, hide all	PS 34	Press the Tab key
Panels, redisplay all previously opened	PS 34	Press the Tab key
Panels, stack	PS 35	Point to a panel bar to the right of the last panel tab, press and hold the mouse button, drag the panel group under another panel group until a blue bar appears, release the mouse button
Paragraph text, add	PS 300	*See* Reference box: Adding Paragraph Text
Pattern fill layer, create	PS 196	At the bottom of the Layers panel, click [icon], click Pattern, click the pattern thumbnail in the Pattern Fill dialog box, click a pattern, click OK; on the Layers panel, adjust the Opacity setting as needed
Photoshop preferences, set	PS 26	*See* Reference box: Setting Photoshop Preferences
Photoshop settings file, reset	PS 8	Click [icon], click All Programs, click Adobe Photoshop CS5 while pressing and holding the Ctrl+Alt+Shift keys; when prompted to delete the Adobe Photoshop settings, click Yes
Photoshop, exit	PS 23	On the Application bar, click File, click Exit
Photoshop, start	PS 8	Click [icon], click All Programs, click Adobe Photoshop CS5

TASK	PAGE #	RECOMMENDED METHOD
Placed image, reposition using relative positioning	PS 140	On the options bar, click △, right-click the X or Y box, click the desired units on the shortcut menu, highlight the current value in the X box, type a new value, press Enter, repeat for the Y box
Placed image, resize and maintain aspect ratio	PS 140	On the options bar, click 🔒, highlight the current value in the W box, type a new value, press Enter
Placed image, rotate	PS 141	Place the mouse pointer at the corner of the placed image on the canvas, drag clockwise or counterclockwise to achieve the desired rotation
Placed image, rotate in 15-degree increments	PS 141	Place the mouse pointer at the corner of the placed image on the canvas, press and hold the Shift key, drag clockwise or counterclockwise to achieve the desired rotation
Point type, add to an image	PS 286	*See* Reference box: Adding Point Type to an Image
Preferences, set	PS 26	*See* Reference box: Setting Photoshop Preferences
Rule of Thirds, use to crop an image	PS 344	*See* Reference box: Cropping an Image
Ruler Tool, activate	PS 341	Press the Shift+I keys
Rulers, show or hide	PS 39	On the Application bar, click View, click Rulers
Saturation, adjust in Camera Raw	PS 415	On the Basic tab of the Adjustments panel in Camera Raw, drag the Clarity, Vibrance, and Saturation sliders
Save for Web & Devices	PS 436	*See* Reference box: Saving a JPEG Image Using Save for Web & Devices
Selection, complex	PS 236	*See* Reference box: Adding to a Selection to Create a Complex Selection
Selection, copy and paste	PS 234	Make a selection in an image, click Edit on the Application bar, click Copy, click Edit again, click Paste
Selection, create using a color range	PS 239	On the Application bar, click Select, click Color Range; in the Select box of the Color Range dialog box, select Sampled Colors, if necessary, click the Localized Color Clusters check box, click the part of the image that includes the desired color range, click OK
Selection, expand or grow	PS 232	*See* Reference box: Expanding or Growing a Selection
Selection, fixed ratio	PS 229	*See* Reference box: Specifying a Fixed Ratio Selection
Selection, fixed size	PS 231	*See* Reference box: Specifying a Fixed Size Selection
Selection, save and load	PS 260	*See* Reference box: Saving and Loading a Selection
Selection, select inverse of	PS 262	Make a selection in an image, click Select on the Application bar, click Inverse
Selection, stroke	PS 263	Make a selection in an image, click Edit on the Application bar, click Stroke; in the Stroke dialog box, specify a width, color, location, blending mode, and opacity, click OK
Selection, use Magic Wand Tool to add pixels to	PS 232	On the Tools panel, click 🪄; on the options bar, specify a Tolerance setting, and select or deselect Anti-alias and Contiguous as desired, click 🔲, click the pixels to be added to the selection
Shape layer, create	PS 199	On the Tools panel, click a shape tool, ensure that 🔲 is selected on the options bar, draw the shape on the canvas
Shape, add to	PS 203	On the Tools panel, click a shape tool, click 🔲 on the options bar, draw the shape on the canvas over the existing shape you want to add to

TASK	PAGE #	RECOMMENDED METHOD
Shape, draw	PS 199	On the Tools panel, click a shape tool, ensure that ▢ is selected on the options bar, draw the shape on the canvas
Shape, draw a bitmap	PS 204	On the Tools panel, click a shape tool, click ▢ on the options bar, draw the shape
Shape, exclude overlapping	PS 203	On the Tools panel, click a shape tool, click ▣ on the options bar, draw the shape on the canvas
Shape, subtract from	PS 201	On the Tools panel, click a shape tool, click ▢ on the options bar, draw the shape on the canvas over the existing shape you want to subtract from
Sharpen Tool, use	PS 377	On the Tools panel, click △, on the options bar select brush type, set brush diameter, select Mode, adjust Strength, check Protect Detail, paint the area in the image to be adjusted
Soft proof, view	PS 428	On the Application bar, click View, point to Proof Setup, click the desired proof setting, and then on the View menu, check Proof Colors
Solid color fill layer, create	PS 192	At the bottom of the Layers panel, click ◑, click Solid Color, select a color in the Pick a solid color dialog box, click OK; on the Layers panel, adjust the Opacity setting as needed
Spelling, check	PS 306	Click at the beginning of the text, click Edit on the Application bar, click Check Spelling; in the Check Spelling dialog box, select the correct spelling for the first highlighted word, click the Change button, click OK when the spelling check is complete
Sponge Tool, use	PS 373	On the Tools panel click ⬤, on the options bar, select brush type, set brush diameter, select Mode, adjust Flow, paint the area in the image to be adjusted
Spot Healing Brush, use	PS 364	*See* Reference box: Applying the Spot Healing Brush Tool to an Image
Step backward	PS 243	On the Application bar, click Edit, click Step Backward
Step forward	PS 243	On the Application bar, click Edit, click Step Forward
Style, apply	PS 183	On the Layers panel, select a layer, click a style on the Styles panel
Swatches panel, add sampled color to	PS 180	Sample a color in an image, move the mouse pointer to a blank (gray) area at the bottom of the Swatches panel, when the mouse pointer changes to 🖉, click, type a swatch name in the Name box, click OK
Swatches panel, change palette preset	PS 178	On the Swatches panel, click ▤, click a preset
Swatches panel, customize display	PS 178	On the Swatches panel, click ▤, click a display option
Swatches, delete a color from	PS 181	Press the Alt key to change to the ✂ pointer, point to the color swatch and click
Swatches, load	PS 181	On the Swatches panel, click ▤, click Load Swatches, click the desired swatches preset, click Load
Swatches, reset to default	PS 179	On the Swatches panel, click ▤, click Reset Swatches
Swatches, save as a preset	PS 181	On the Swatches panel, click ▤, click Save Swatches, type a name for the swatches, click Save

TASK	PAGE #	RECOMMENDED METHOD
Tab group, close	PS 33	On the title bar for the panel, click ▼☰ , click Close Tab Group
Tab order, change	PS 18	Point to a Document window tab, press and hold the mouse button, drag the tab to the new location, release the mouse button
Text, add along a closed path	PS 320	Select a drawing tool, click 🖉 on the options bar, draw a closed path on the canvas; on the Tools panel, click **T** , specify type settings, click the path, type to add text along the path
Text, apply style to	PS 310	Select the text, click a style on the Styles panel
Text, center	PS 290	With a text tool active, click ☰ on the options bar, click ✔
Text, find and replace	PS 307	Click at the beginning of the text, click Edit on the Application bar, click Find and Replace Text; in the Find And Replace Text dialog box, type a word in the Find What box, type a word in the Change To box, click Find Next, click Change to make the replacement, click Done when finished
Text, format as small caps	PS 291	Select the text, click Tr on the Character panel, click ✔
Text, scale using Character panel	PS 291	*See* Reference box: Scaling Text Using the Character Panel
Text, scale using Move Tool	PS 293	*See* Reference box: Scaling Text Using the Move Tool
Text, warp	PS 316	*See* Reference box: Warping Text
Threshold, adjust	PS 353	*See* Reference box: Marking Lightest and Darkest Pixels with the Threshold Adjustment
TIFF file, open in Camera Raw	PS 416	In Mini Bridge, right-click image, click Open in Camera Raw
Tone, adjust using Auto Tone	PS 348	On the Application bar, click Image, click Auto Tone
Tool options, set	PS 45	On the Tools panel, select a tool, select the settings on the options bar
Tool preset, delete	PS 49	On the options bar, click ▾ , click the preset, click ▶ , click Delete Tool Preset
Tool preset, save	PS 48	On the options bar, click ▾ , click ▣ , type a preset name in the Name box, select any other desired options, click OK
Tool, reset	PS 45	On the options bar, right-click ▾ , click Reset Tool
Tracking, adjust	PS 298	Select the text, click in the ⅣＶ box on the Character panel, select any existing value, type a new value
Vertical point type, add to an image	PS 286	*See* Reference box: Adding Point Type to an Image
Web-safe colors, specify in the Color Picker dialog box	PS 173	In the Color Picker dialog box, click the Only Web Colors check box to select it
White and Black Points, set using the Curves adjustment	PS 356	*See* Reference box: Setting the White and Black Points of an Image
Workflow options, set in Camera Raw	PS 399	*See* Reference box: Setting Workflow Options in Camera Raw
Work path, create and stroke with brush	PS 212	On the Tools panel, select a drawing tool, click 🖉 on the options bar, draw the path, on the canvas, right-click the path, click Stroke Path; in the Stroke Path dialog box, click the Tool arrow, click Brush, click OK
Workspace, choose a preset	PS 37	On the Application bar, click the desired workspace name
Workspace, reset	PS 30	Click », click Reset [*workspace name*]

TASK	PAGE #	RECOMMENDED METHOD
Workspace, switch	PS 10	Click ⟫ , click the desired workspace
Zoom level, adjust in Camera Raw	PS 395	On the toolbar located above the Document window in the Camera Raw dialog box, click 🔍 , click in the Document window to increase zoom in preset increments
Zoom tool, access	PS 10	Press the Z key